DO ORGANIZATIONS HAVE FEELINGS?

Do those who claim the right to manage organizations know what they are doing? Do they feel responsible to the wider society? *Do Organizations Have Feelings?* argues that any adequate organizational narrative for today must transcend the emotion/rationality divide and challenges the manager, the consultant and the business schools to take sociology seriously.

The four parts of this book offer a serious intellectual engagement with profound issues in the sociological analysis of organizations. Part I, 'Objectivity and Reflexivity', offers social science research rather than organizational rationality as the knowledge base for organization studies, but then shows the essential historical limitations of that knowledge. Part II, 'Reassessing Weber for Current Uses', updates the central thesis on rationalization of the founder of the modern study of bureaucracy and then shows how postmodern conditions require a quite different concept of authority from his. Part III, 'Feeling for New Organization', shows how an adequate organizational narrative for today must transcend the emotion/rationality divide. Part IV, 'Organizing Returns from the Social', shows how specifically sociological research on organization illuminates the social nature of organizing practices.

The papers in this important collection by one of the leading world authorities on the sociology of organizations were written over a period of thirty years. Now presented together for the first time with an extended commentary and discussion by the author and followed by two specially written chapters bringing the story right up to date, they chart the development of the study of organizations during a period of epochal change from the Modern to the Global Age. This book will be essential reading for anyone concerned with the way in which the interplay between organizations and society in all its aspects shapes our world today.

Martin Albrow has been Eric Voegelin Guest Professor in the University of Munich and is currently Research Professor of Social Sciences at Roehampton Institute London. His other publications include *Bureaucracy* (1970), *Max Weber's Construction of Social Theory* (1990) and *The Global Age* (1996).

DO ORGANIZATIONS HAVE FEELINGS?

Martin Albrow

London and New York

First published 1997
by Routledge
11 New Fetter Lane, London EC4P 4EE

Simultaneously published in the USA and Canada
by Routledge
29 West 35th Street, New York, NY 10001

Typeset in Garamond by
BC Typesetting, Bristol
Printed and bound in Great Britain by
Mackays of Chatham PLC, Chatham, Kent

British Library Cataloguing in Publication Data
A catalogue record for this book is available from the British Library

Library of Congress Cataloging in Publication Data
Albrow, Martin.
    Do organizations have feelings?/Martin Albrow.
        p.   cm.
    First published 1997 by Routledge, London.
    Includes bibliographical references (p.   ) and index.
    1. Social responsibility of business.   2. Industrial management-
-Social aspects.   I. Title.
    HD60.A386   1997
    658.4′08—dc21   97-7099
                                                                              CIP

ISBN 0—415—11546—9
        0—415—11547—7 (pbk)

To the memory of Allan Mackintosh FRS 1936–1995

CONTENTS

CONTENTS

PREFACE

Theory in the social sciences always engages with a changing social reality. Theory for organization also contributes to a central feature of that reality, the efforts of human beings to shape their co-operative activities.

Theory, co-operation, social reality are reciprocally related and a *sociological* theory of organization has a very special place in these reflexive relations. It seeks to explore and explain the actual interplay of organization and society. Under its scrutiny societies, states, even the corporation appear as passing experiments in human sociality. This provides the field for my enquiries here. I am aiming to explore and clarify the specific contribution sociology can make to understanding organization.

If my ideas in this book have become stronger and clearer over the period of writing which it spans, it is because the passage of time brings to them two advantages. They have the chance to take root and develop, and they can show their worth by surviving in a rapidly transforming world.

Two ideas have stayed with me and developed over this period and it is the course of their development which I share here with my readers. They are the ideas of sociological objectivity, the unending and necessary quest for true accounts of social reality, and historical relativity, the recognition of the ephemeral nature of that reality. Their unfolding complexity is the common thread in the book.

It is not often that an author is allowed to expose a thirty-year chain of thought and I am particularly grateful to Mari Shullaw, Senior Editor in Sociology at Routledge, and her two anonymous referees, who deem it to be warranted in this case. I am grateful too for the support of Desk Editor Kate Chenevix Trench and copy-editor Susan Dunsmore.

At Roehampton Institute London, thanks are due to the Research Committee, to the Media and Reprographics Unit for scanning published materials, to Neil Washbourne for many stimulating discussions, reflected especially in Chapter 7, and to Willemijn Dicke of the University of Nijmegen, for helpful comments on Chapters 7 and 8.

Other people's experience of organizations has provided a constant source of information and fascination. My greatest debt is to Susan Owen who, having moved from university teaching to senior civil service administration, makes sure that her strategic responsibilities include the opening of organization to ideas and is always generous in sharing her own. The dedication to Allan Mackintosh, former Professor of Physics at Copenhagen University, is to someone who was a close friend for nearly forty years. A member of the Nobel Prize Committee for Physics, he was always fascinated by the history and organization of science and was ever ready with acute observations.

As well as the benefits of the time span there are also disadvantages. There are too many people who have influenced and helped me to make it possible to express my gratitude to each and every one. Some, including those who have had a profound influence on me, are no longer with us to be acknowledged. It is to the profession of sociology generally that I owe most, singling out for particular appreciation those sociologists who have kept the flag flying in business schools while others like myself have enjoyed a wider freedom.

ACKNOWLEDGEMENTS

To the Open University and Open University Press for permission to republish 'The Dialectic of Science and Values in the Study of Organizations', Chapter 13 in G. Salaman and K. Thompson (eds) (1980) *Control and Ideology in Organizations*, Milton Keynes: The Open University Press, pp. 278–96, which was an adapted version of 'Is a science of organizations possible?', Unit 16 in The Open University (1974) *People and Organizations* DT 352, pp. 25–47, Milton Keynes: The Open University Press.

To Walter de Gruyter & Co. for permission to republish '*Sine Ira et Studio* – or Do Organizations Have Feelings?' (*Organization Studies*, 13: 313–29, 1992).

To the *British Journal of Sociology* for permission to republish from 'Weber on legitimate norms and authority: a comment on Martin E. Spencer's account' (*British Journal of Sociology*, 23: 483–7, 1972).

INTRODUCTION
The necessity for the sociology of organizing

BIG IDEAS; SMALL SCIENCES

Building a business, winning an election, reforming social security, changing schools, saving the environment: all are organizing activities, and in each a swarm of experts promotes the claims of specialized disciplines to supply indispensable secrets of success.

The history of organizations is also a story of repeated efforts by intellectuals to demonstrate the necessity for their own specialism. From work study to linear programming, from industrial psychology to econometrics, from industrial relations to business schools, the teachers have sought to merchandise ideas as tools for organizing practice.

This book is also for organizers of all kinds. The discipline it represents, sociology, seeks a deeper understanding of organizing practices. But unlike the academic pantheon of the business schools it lays no claims to solve technical problems. It has much more modest aims. It merely interrogates the very reality of organizing activity.

This is not a technical problem. How we construe the pursuit of human ends in and through our relations with other people is a task of imagination, of representation and construction. It is intellectual in the broadest sense. It is equally practical and embedded in practice. But the use which practitioners make of sociological understanding is down to them.

Sociology regards organization as the outcome of ongoing social activity. Businesses, schools, parties and prisons and the boundaries between them are human creations. Contributing to them has become a rewarding pursuit for technical experts. But sociology studies the manner of their becoming and continued existence which can never be taken for granted. Sociology begins at a point where the purpose of expertise itself comes into question.

In the manner of the media mogul, 'we are proud to present' sociology as the reflexive representation and reconstruction of organization. The subject is social reality. The general questions of how that is created and what variations are possible underpin all possible special techniques. As social reality changes, the big questions may be posed differently. An array of different

1

questions come to the fore at different times. But the core issues are few and fundamental.

In this century the most prominent organizational issues have included (in rough chronological order):

- Can organizational structure respond to human need?
- Is there a unique set of principles for organization?
- Does organization defeat its own ends?
- Does organization simply serve the interests of the powerful?
- What environment best promotes organizational efficiency?
- Are there inherent limits on organizational variety?

Of course, these are very big and general questions, but it is their imponderable, yet insistent, quality which explains the recurring demand for the 'big idea'. These questions have an abiding relevance and demand a response from each generation. Very often we can see that it is the business sciences that have succeeded in determining that response, effectively by treating them as technical problems. We have even reached the point where visions of future society, presented as scenarios, are deemed important as a basis for the strategic planning of business. Sociologists, by contrast, believe they are important for people generally.

If we review the big ideas since 1945 we find that they are effectively proposing answers to all-embracing organizational issues: equality of opportunity, the social market, the enterprise culture, communitarianism, the stakeholder society, globalization promote images of society with specific linkages between different forms of organization, the business, the state, the community and the individual. Each of these images assumes that if business gets on with its job aided by the right experts, it can incidentally fashion the right kind of society.

In totalitarian versions the big idea is an explicit imposition of a crude organization on society as a whole. But democratic order is equally dependent on resolving organizational dilemmas and suffers to the extent that these are often misrepresented as technical issues. The endemic weakness of the democracy of high modernity was the widespread assumption that there was an easy way to confer power on the people and that matters of allocation and control had technical solutions. Totalitarianism was merely the reflex of these assumptions. The weakness of democracy in the new Global Age is reflected in the assumption that it is an easy by-product of business efficiency or free markets.

Sociology is neither for nor against business. It simply seeks a greater understanding of its social reality. It therefore has a vital role to play in bringing people, rulers and ruled, managers and managed, into contact with each other. It has contributed to the big ideas of democracy but it has had an equally important place in bringing them down to earth. It has also been the home for a huge variety of more specific enquiries where researchers have

devoted months to observing behaviour in a tax office or in hospital consulting rooms. If the business corporation is now interested in the future of
society, sociology is equally interested in the way business shapes society.

Other social sciences have been servants of power in the context of organizational studies. Whether they have promoted profit maximization, or incentive schemes, quality circles or global marketing, they have sought to address
those who in some senses set purposes for others, control staff and direct
investment. Sociology has from time to time played its part in this but it
is and always has been as much for those who are controlled as for the
controllers.

It is not that sociology is unworldly; it is altogether more mundane than its
prestigious academic colleagues, for it takes the world as people experience it
as the basis for its investigations. The reality of organization is neither boardroom nor balance sheet but people's practices and encounters, capacities and
aspirations inscribed in social patterns.

The relentless rise of the business schools was a feature of the 1970s and
1980s. For many, including those sociologists who went to work in them,
even to run them, this marked the end of sociology's false dawn. In the 1960s
sociology appeared to offer the young the promise of a new society. When the
flower power students became the power dresser graduates, sociology looked
to be the faded and shabby Carnaby Street of academe.

The mask of fashion can slip. There are moments which reveal the abiding
character of some issues across time and culture. Sociology was no more
born in the 1960s than socialism was buried in the 1980s. In the mid-1990s a
time has been reached when neither the large corporation nor the welfare
state appear as the indefinitely guaranteed dominant forms of social organization ('End of the Welfare State' screamed *The Guardian* headline on 6 May
1996).

This is a time of flux which brings questions of social transformation to the
fore in a more pronounced form than at any time since the first decade of the
twentieth century. That was the time when professional sociology emerged.
From this historical perspective a comprehensive reappraisal of social organization is under way which think-tanks, business schools and policy institutes
cannot ignore. As their scenarios illustrate, the pursuit of their technical
interests depends on it. But it has always been sociology's ongoing task to
provide the audit of social reality which this reappraisal of social organization
requires, and in this respect business organization itself is not exempt from
reassessment.

Sociology's task as a professional activity has endured for a century. What
has changed over the years has been its public reception and, in part, its own
response to fashion. But I believe the persistent quality of the discipline has
always been to question the taken-for-granted, and therefore the ephemeral
features of the social life of the time. It pursues an objectivity which seeks
to serve no particular interest group. It derives this from an accumulated

experience in studying social life across cultures and generations. It belongs, then, to no particular time even if it cannot ever claim a final universality.

PASSING FASHIONS, ENDURING PROBLEMS

As a sociologist I have observed and from time to time participated in the changing course of organizational studies over thirty years. These papers are time samples of one sociologist's response to organizational change. I hope that they show that a hold on enduring issues is the best way to meet the challenge of ever renewed change.

Some changes are merely fashions in terminology. In the 1960s the 'sociology of organizations' was the preferred label for the studies this book includes. It was always a bit of a pleonasm, rather like 'psychology of the psyche' or the 'geography of the earth'. The study of social organization is intrinsic to sociology, not something to which sociology is applied like a template.

In fact the sociology of organizations was the seedbed for many of the special sociologies, of the military, of industry, of education, or religion. Here the central concern for the sociologist is precisely how social relations shape and are shaped in the context of the pursuit of the values and objectives inherent in these special fields of human activity. So they properly bear the name 'sociology of . . .'. Equally they could be called 'sociology for . . .' since sociological enquiries serve clear thinking as much as they illuminate social reality.

In either case the emergence of organizations in a wider context of social relations has always been a prime focus: the school within education, the corporation within the economy, the church within religion. In effect, then, the sociology of organizations, rather than being a special field of sociology, has been the study of those general factors which result in the crystallization of boundaries, the stabilization of power relations and the formation of social entities within different spheres of activity.

Thus the sociology of organizations has had a very powerful and directing influence on sociology as a whole. One of the major thrusts in sociology in the twentieth century has been to identify general structuring principles which underpin the proliferation of organizations of all kinds. In particular it has brought these together under the overarching principle of 'modernity'.

Max Weber is the most notable advocate of this version of the specific features of modern society. The principles of organization taking shape as bureaucracy, pervading the modern state and capitalist organization, for him determined the trajectory of the rationalization of society as a whole. Similarly, we can interpret the work of some of the most prominent figures in the development of sociology like Talcott Parsons, Daniel Bell, Jürgen Habermas, Niklas Luhmann, Alain Touraine and Anthony Giddens as tracing the trajectory of organization structure in their own time. The principles which generate organizations are effectively the generative principles of the organization of contemporary society, hence such popular tags as the 'organizational society'.

It is now time to call these stakes in, not because organization is any less a central theme in sociology but, rather, because it is becoming widely apparent that many of the features associated with modern organization have undergone a rapid transformation. When we drop the 'modern' from the 'modern organization' we strip away features which characterized a passing period of history and face rather more profound organizational issues.

The example which encapsulates most of these issues, and is the most obvious, is the decay of bureaucracy. At the beginning of the twentieth century Max Weber sanitized what had been the prime target for good democrats and old aristocrats alike by stressing the inevitable development of bureaucracy. The large organization with full-time salaried career officials appeared to be the necessary accompaniment of modern life and we had better put up with it. It meant rigidity, true, but with it came predictability; it meant tedious routine, but it gave security. The black suit and the white collar effectively conveyed the funereal atmosphere of both analysis and the reality of Weber's time – not much room in the iron cage for excitement. No wonder that suppressed passion was the problem of the day for him and others.

In the last two decades big bureaucracy has receded as issue and reality. The career has increasingly become a personalized life course rather than a prescribed route through the organization. Social entities which had acquired an apparently permanent place in society have fallen apart. Mergers have proved that boundaries are not permanent. Hierarchies have been dismantled and practices reformed. 'Post-Fordism' has been one way of expressing this but it conveys an impression of change led by and exclusively concerned with industrial organization rather than pervading every aspect of society.

The bureaucratic dilemmas have, then, receded in the public imagination and have been replaced by newer but equally disturbing contrasts. Excitement has replaced boredom, but insecurity is the other side of the coin. Opportunities are more diverse than ever but unemployment has become the scourge of Western countries. Authority has lost its imperative tone, yet the extremes of wealth and power grow further and further apart.

If bureaucracy recedes in reality then, equally, the account of modern organization enshrined in the Weberian or Fordist models appears dated, of historical interest only. But this is the point where acute problems for a science of organizations arise. For accounts of modern organization contained a set of claims not only about the world but about an appropriate scientific method. This is the profound form in which the problem of relativity surfaces in social sciences and which underlies the unending debate about postmodernity and modernity.

FOR A PRAGMATIC UNIVERSALISM

Modern science was never wholly committed to the idea that it was the 'mirror of nature'. Naïve inductivism certainly had its attractions and even its proponents, but equally there were always advocates of science in the mode of model building and of identifying underlying reality. Either way, however, modern science conveyed its sense of powerful method, beyond common sense, with its technical terminology, enhanced precision, immense calculative capacity, in sum, a superior rationality.

This conception of science was congruent with modern forms of organization. Indeed, human organization appeared to run a parallel course with technology, science instantiated in practice, social science as social practice; big science, big organization. This congruence and parallelism between science and human organization were just one, but a very vital one of the features of modernity. If now we recognize the decay of old modern forms of organization, then the questions which arise extend far beyond simply rendering an account of the change; they implicate the very practice and possibility of social science as we have known it. This is the inference which Bruno Latour has drawn recently in declaring that 'we have never been modern' (1993). I, like him, applaud the non-modern, but, unlike him, will speak of a Modern Age which has passed.

A double set of indeterminacies arises from its passage. For simplicity let us refer to 'old' and 'new' organization; 'old' and 'new' science. Our benchmark is the old science (Max Weber, F.W. Taylor) for the old organization (bureaucracy, Fordism), both of course 'modern'. We have to get used to thinking of 'old modern', if we are going to be able to talk of the contemporary world of today as distinct from the early twentieth century.

If the claims of the old narrative, a rational science, are still warranted, then it must be possible to generate an old narrative for new conditions, a Weberian account of the present. But if the new conditions are held to be paralleled by the rise of new science we are left with a double uncertainty. For the new science either makes equivalent claims to the old, that is supplants it with a superior rationality, and then retrospectively rewrites the past, undermining the self-image of previous modernity; or it makes no claims to superiority in the old terms at all, leaving open the possibility that we cannot render definitive accounts of organization, either new or old.

It is this double uncertainty or indeterminacy which makes it so difficult today to provide a coherent account either of organizational change or of organizational science. We cannot depict a smooth passage from one period to another, because the sheer transition shakes all the assumptions of congruence between science and organization. We experience both the intangibility and the ephemerality of contemporary organizational forms at the same time as having to reckon with a huge variety of perspectives on organization, asserting very different and competing views of science.

In other words, we no longer have the comfort of being able to write about organizations with the assumption of a common epochal narrative. We can't background organization with 'modernity', 'modern society', 'Modern Age' and assume the congruence between our scientific analysis and the temper of the time. How, then, do we make sense of this situation?

The question could be posed equally to scientists and practitioners, the latter being anyone engaged these days in organizing activities, which means just about everyone. But it might suggest that scientists are seeking and providing the answers which practitioners fail to find. Quite the contrary. My own attitude here is that scientists are much more in the position of seeking to understand how people are succeeding in making sense of the contemporary situation, rather than being able to supply answers to their problems. The problems in this book are generated within science itself and arise out of its relations with history and its self-understanding. They are not irrelevant to organizational practice for they concern the construction of coherent theory, but theory is always having to catch up with ingenuity of everyday problem-solvers.

Good theory for organization, like all social theory, never claims too much. One of its main contributions is to the medium of discourse between practitioners. As such, in providing a common vocabulary, conceptual frames, paradigmatic cases or known empirical relations, it can have a vital part to play in mutual orientation and productive collaboration. 'Knowing the same things', sharing cognitive maps, assists collective action. But this must be secondary to trust as it is built through the experience of co-operation, art as developed through close acquaintance with the concrete situation, and skill as evinced in practice. And while we can have theory relating to trust, art and skill, they are not learnt through it.

If we concentrate on what theory can do, on its capacity to generate and transform common frames of meaning, this is important enough without expecting it to regulate trust, art and skill, indeed, to rule the world. Even with this relatively limited brief, theory can make a difference and it matters that it should be coherent, precise, predictive, lucid, informative and relevant to human needs and values. Who would wish to defend incoherent, vague and irrelevant intellectual work telling us nothing?

This already may suggest my answer to the conundrum of double indeterminacy. There is actually a position which lies outside either old or new science. We are not forced to choose between the oppositions which the postmodern condition assumes, for the criteria I have just suggested for good theory are neither modern, nor postmodern: they are simply not specific to modernity at all, or indeed to any epoch or culture. Any complex civilization which has developed a narrative of itself has in some degree generated theory to which these criteria have applied.

To this extent we can distance ourselves from some of the more frantic versions of relativism and perspectivism. The reason we are not caught on the dilemmas which arise from the breakdown of the old modern view of the congruence of organization and science is that we do not have to accept the false dichotomy of modern/postmodern. We may be outside either, and, if we are, we can accept that we may live in a postmodern age which has its own characteristics and is not simply the collapse of the modern or some postmodern chaos. If we simply accept that we live in a new age, say, the Global Age (Albrow 1996), then we can recognize the sense which people do make today of their lives, of the particular rationality which informs contemporary organization.

We need an epochal narrative which detaches science, and particularly theory, from modernity, indeed, from any particular epoch. We have to recognize the specifics of the time in which we live while simultaneously cognizing its contribution to understanding problems which transcend times and cultures. It is a kind of universalism, but not to be equated with the universalisms of modern versions of science or older theologies which claimed the acquisition of eternal truths. For we can never be sure of that and we are continually exploring alternative answers as our conditions of life change. I would call it pragmatic universalism to distinguish it from these other universalisms.

For me it is a position which saves theory both from arrogant claims to have found the truth, which invariably are undermined, and from a self-destructive relativism which prevents the possibility of asserting anything about the world. We can both narrate the transformation of contemporary organization and remain phlegmatic about the elapse of modernity. That, indeed, means breaking the assumption of the inherent parallelism between epoch and science, or, indeed, between theory and practice.

However much we recognize that theory contributes to the way people do things, in particular to organizational form, we must avoid the trap of assuming that there is some perfect congruence between them, or that such a congruence would, indeed, represent organizational perfection. We have already mentioned the inherent incongruence between theory, trust, art and skill. For this reason we cannot assume the identity of theory and epoch, for the life of our times is much more than the transient ways in which theory is expressed.

PERSISTING SOCIOLOGY

It is one of the major tasks of sociology to render an account of the relations between theory and practice. It has to stand back from the maxims and theorems of the time, to recognize their contextual limitations. It has to show how contemporary solutions to abiding problems are fitted only to the time. It recognizes that much of what passes as theory is the rationalization of responses to problems of the moment and at the same time acknowledges the everyday ingenuity of people in organizational practices which transcend theory. Sociology is therefore always learning from the people it studies. In this sense it is the learning discipline, reflecting on practice, revising its ways of thinking as a result.

Sociology achieves its detachment from technical theories of organization because it relativizes them against the experience of people as they engage in organizing, on the one hand, and because it relates them to persisting, universal problem settings, on the other. Its distinctive contribution to organizational studies will therefore never be assimilated to business, ergonomics, psychology, law, strategic analysis or any of the varied technical contributions to what is considered to be the current appropriate education for the aspiring business leader.

Sociology is in the business of narrating and accounting for social reality. It cannot determine whether that is on the agenda of business or management education, but it will draw inferences about the place of business in society if social reality is not a reference point for business people. When it is not, it can't be sociology's fault if others draw on it for critique and alternative forms of organization. Sociology is not inherently anti-business, anti-social order, or anti-revolutionary for that matter, but its concern to understand the nature of society and social experience of people in general makes it an obvious resort for all who sense they are excluded from power over their own lives.

In fact, under contemporary conditions it is my belief that the sheer rapidity of the changes overtaking established organizations today must mean that business itself will look to sociology to repair glaring gaps in the contemporary business curriculum. Business is virtually the only profession with extended technical training today which chooses to ignore society and sociology as an integral part of its educational programme. Physicians, lawyers, architects, by contrast, pay due regard to the contribution of sociology to their understanding.

Even as business people bow to the forces of globalization they have to admit their failure to control the world and to acknowledge the strength of those forces they confront as a complex social transformation extending far beyond the next new product. Without a wider orientation to society neither strategic nor human resource management has the resilience or breadth of perspective to cope with the new unpredictability and loss of control.

None of this is to say that sociology itself is in a perfect state. Many of its debates revolve around the double indeterminacy conundrum set out above, and it too has immense difficulty in handling the passing of the Modern Age. I happen to believe, however, that these debates are productive and clarify a relatively settled set of beliefs and practices which constitute the discipline.

Briefly characterizing the constellation of topic, theory, method, practice known as sociology, I would say that it is constituted by a combination of concern for the social, for understanding others and facticity. Those three elements combine in the idea of social reality. Put another way, our collective social units exist in an uncontested way when we relate to other people on the basis of common perceptions. Where those elements coincide we get by without sociology. Very often, as at the turn of the century, in the 1960s and again now, there is a severe disjunction between those elements. There may arise a widespread recognition that governments no longer know their people and sociology receives an extra boost as a result (Newby 1993; Albrow 1994b). Under conditions where we cannot assume common understanding, we feel impelled both to establish facts and to reference them against entities which constitute 'society'.

Where sociologists disagree on this programme it seems to me they do so on good grounds, i.e. hotly contested ones, about just what degree and kind of research is necessary to establish the existence of understanding or of an adequate basis for social interaction, and how far social entities can be inferred from and imputed to influence people's lives.

These debates implicate the very existence of anything called an 'organization'. Sociologists refuse to take organization for granted, which is why their work raises key questions of the balance between researching environment and history and developing analytic models. The importance of institutional approaches to organizations, represented especially in W. Richard Scott's work, is that it finds this balance by providing for autonomous sociological accounts of organization and organizing without prior commitment to organizational boundaries. He rightly refuses to infer that the instability of organizational forms means that we can only have 'theoretical perspectives' on organizations (Scott 1995: xii). Rapid change means we must be even more attentive to our means of registering it. Radical relativism is not the answer.

This is also David Silverman's (1994: 23) expressed view when, from a vantage point in the phenomenological tradition, he deplores the disservice performed by the clustering of sociology into 'schools'. Scott and Silverman converge from very different quarters on a sociology where the major intellectual challenge is to explain the mutual determination of the micro-social and everyday behaviour, on the one hand, and the broader course of social change, on the other. I would add that for the sociologist of organization today this challenge has taken on a global dimension.

We have become accustomed in modernity to thinking about individuals in families, or in communities, organizations or nations and have spent enormous amounts of intellectual energy in exploring how it was possible for these social entities to exist in and through individuals. Under contemporary conditions we have to do the same thing for globality. We need to trace the ways in which emerging global levels of social organization are equally constitutive for people's daily lives and for the working of the organizations in which they are involved. This is the most important challenge facing contemporary sociology.

These chapters illustrate two things: first, that the sociological approach to organization has enduring qualities which mean that it does not have to change its direction or concerns with every change in political context, educational setting or public audience. Second, that organization and organizations are inherently linked to a broader social context which changes over time and across cultures so that sociology is particularly suited to register their historical contingency.

This is not to say that my ideas have not changed and developed over time. It would not be worth offering them in this volume had they not, but it seems to me that the development is in the manner of amplifying the insights available to me from the discipline and in responding to the stimulus of changing social reality, and not in shifting perspectives or outlook. It survives even the transformation from Modern to Global Age which this generation has experienced and which demonstrates that sociology's concerns did not arise simply out of the social problems of old modern class society.

The case this book makes is that the sociology of organization provides an enduring contribution to organizational studies, not reducible to, or replaceable by any other discipline. My business school colleagues would call that a market niche — I am quite happy to let others determine how big that niche might be.

Part I

OBJECTIVITY AND REFLEXIVITY

The intellectual commitments in the first two chapters are to a view of sociology, and therefore of the sociology of organization, which distinguishes it from any other science. It necessarily strives unceasingly to attain objectivity in accounts of social reality. Its efforts inevitably fail ever to achieve that goal but simultaneously help to constitute that very reality.

We may easily recognize that objectivity about ourselves, however hard to obtain, is a vital element in the constitution of our persons. This reflexive knowledge is a spur to further development. It therefore needs to be constantly updated. This reciprocal relationship between objectivity and reflexivity holds also for any science which is concerned to keep a fix on the reality of society.

The relativity of sociological knowledge therefore stems neither from bias, a distorting intrusion of value commitment, nor from relativism, the view that anyone's judgement is as good as anyone else's. These common misconceptions are as misguided an interpretation of sociological relativity as they would be of relativity in physics. In both cases, it is a question of the relative movement of observer and observed and, in the case of sociology, observer and observed are constantly exchanging places.

Critics of sociology are right when they see it as irremediably involved in value commitments, not only to knowledge but to other values too. They are wrong if they think this allows them to substitute prejudice for informed, rigorous research.

Objectivity is constituted by true accounts of reality and we continually adjust our accounts to come closer to that truth. Its reference is not, of course, in the first instance to society, but to all reality, beyond, as well as including, human beings.

But in its broadest sense objectivity depends on the social. For we *regulate* our accounts of reality by checking with and asserting them against other people. This applies to all sciences and provides the basis for sociological work on them. But the additional problem for the social sciences is that the reality of society is always changing.

13

The possibility of getting near to objectivity is also central to the achievement of mutual understanding with other people. As such, it plays a vital role in the construction of social life. Sharing a view of the world which is open to correction from facts is an intrinsic feature of social interaction. The social, then, depends on objectivity, but not in the way mentioned above that objectivity depends on the social. There we spoke of regulation; here we speak of constitution also. For objectivity is in part *constitutive* of social reality. If we cannot generate reliable accounts of our relations with each other, then those relations break down.

The result is that the very concept of objectivity for social life is fraught in a way it is not for natural reality. The practising natural scientist can engage in theoretical debate and pursue empirical research while remaining assured that there is an underlying abiding reality. This is not the case for the social scientist whose very activity is an extension of the everyday activity of shaping social relations. Human beings construct social life, even as they constitute its objectivity. The result is that whatever degree of objectivity is obtained is always of a changing object.

Objectivity is not a problem we solve so that we can get on with the real work. We cannot produce a simple and final formula to guarantee objectivity. But neither can we find any final formula for achieving quality in the arts. This does not mean we refrain from pursuing quality, and tirelessly. The error of methodology is to assume that there are such formulae to be achieved in the social sciences, but avoiding that error does not free us from the obligation to pursue objectivity ceaselessly. It remains as a transcendental requirement for our work and for society generally.

When we come to organizations, these features of sociology appear in sharp relief as compared with many other disciplinary approaches. Its interest is neither technical nor ideological. It is not concerned to develop technical tools which will aid job performance, either by managers or by any other professional group, nor is it campaigning for pure democracy or sacred authority.

But sociological work is essential for any such special aims, since it explores precisely their contribution to a changing and common social reality, which no interest group owns. Sociology is not parasitical on professional expertise nor is it a residue left over from other social sciences; rather, it is concerned with issues which are preconditions for their very existence.

The first two chapters introduce corollaries of this position. Chapter 1 states unequivocally that the sociologist's concern for social reality is not the guarantee of objectivity, but is distinguished by an incessant striving for a goal which is never achieved. It stresses that its approach to organizations is to see them as societies, and therefore not the property of particular sectional groups.

Three points then become paramount and recur throughout the book: first, that rationality is one and only one element within the shaping of organization; second, that a sociological approach is inevitably historical since the social means transactions over time; third, sociology becomes a part of the world it seeks to describe and explain and thus part of its history.

Chapter 1 became the cue for Graeme Salaman and Kenneth Thompson in developing the Open University course People and Organizations. It was included in the set book (Salaman and Thompson 1973) while another paper (Albrow 1971) was reprinted as Supplementary Material for the course. They declared they would 'view organizations in terms of the way they are problematic with reference to sociological theory and discussion' (ibid.: 2) and concurred with me that they did not accept the conceptual limits of organization theory as setting the limits to the sociologist's research interests (ibid.: 374).

Chapter 2 was therefore written for a course which for a long time was the most powerful statement of the intrinsic contribution an independent self-critical sociology could make to organizations. It considers past organizational studies in the light of their historical interplay with organizations. It withdraws the older idea of the dialectic from its temporary home in Marxist grammar and presents that interplay as the continuing story of a century's exchange between theoretical ideas and the construction of organizations; in other words, the reflexive relation of theory and practice.

The chapter's main concern is to put down markers for sociology even while threatened with dissolution into a variety of competing 'perspectives'. In particular it seeks to ensure the preservation of agency and ideas within a macro-sociological framework; in other words, to suggest that sociology is not a branch of 'materialism'. Equally, it is concerned to defend sociology from an opposite individualistic idealism already implied in the use of the idea of reflexivity in some versions of phenomenology.

Since this chapter was written Anthony Giddens (1986) has couched the theme of the interplay of lay and academic ideas of society in terms of a 'double hermeneutic' and, with others (Beck et al. 1994), has raised the idea of reflexivity into a central principle of late modernity. The reader can view Chapter 2 as a historical illustration in both theory and practice of those ideas. But Part IV of the book will suggest that a sociological approach to organization will need to move beyond the idea of modernity if it is to maintain its reflexive relation with the social reality of our time.

The texts of the two chapters are as originally published with very minor presentational changes. These do not extend to changing the sexist use of the male pronoun. That would be just one virtue too many to pretend to have had at the time. I mend my ways later.

1

THE STUDY OF ORGANIZATIONS
Objectivity or bias?[1]

One of the most stimulating recent developments in sociology has been the growing attention given to organizations. Power, authority, the division of labour, rules of behaviour, social control, all difficult to isolate for study in society, present themselves universally in organizations and with much greater clarity and definition. The problems of organization recur in such varied social units as firms, civil services, armies, hospitals, universities, and trade unions, and therefore involve issues which transcend the concerns of the experts on any one of these organizations. They involve an awareness of the distinctive contribution sociologists may make to the understanding of social life. The 'sociological standpoint' insists that human beings must be studied in respect of how they actually act rather than how they might ideally act. This standpoint when applied to problems of organization produces a literature which is distinctive to sociology and which in my view stands at the traditional core of that discipline.

Yet however fervently the sociologist may stress the distinctiveness and the virtues of his approach to the study of organizations, he has to face the fact that any organization he begins to analyse will almost certainly already possess a literature of its own. Manuals of rules, instructional handbooks, descriptive treatises, eulogistic histories, even advertising material are sources of information the sociologist ignores at his peril. Even where this literature is patently concerned with giving instructions and advice to members of an organization, it is by no means irrelevant to the sociologist's task of discovering the facts and accounting for them. For such advice is rarely arbitrary; its force will depend upon an intimate acquaintance with the facts of the organization and a clear idea of what kind of counsel would be necessary and welcome.

Here the problem of objectivity becomes pressing. How can a social scientist, committed to the belief that to be objective is to be free from moralizing and to avoid recommending courses of action, avail himself of a literature which is so plainly involved in a particular set of values? That sociology should be value-free is taken by most sociologists to be axiomatic. This is certainly a worthwhile aim but how elusive it is is not always or fully recognized.

17

Too often people take the profession of faith in value—freedom as a sufficient safeguard against partiality and preaching. And if such faith is regarded as sufficient, it is because the founders of sociology, in particular Max Weber, are held to have dispelled the taint of value so that their successors can work absolved from this original sin of social research. My argument is that such optimism is excessive. The problem of objectivity is endemic in social science. Crude and obvious forms of bias and wishful thinking are expunged only to be replaced by more subtle ones. The sociologist, far from asserting that he has 'attained' objectivity, must be prepared to struggle towards it with every development in his field. The 'recentness' of research, its technical and conceptual sophistication, do not guarantee immunity to bias. A good instance of this point is David Martin's (1965) attack on the neutral-sounding notion of secularization.

Is this too pessimistic an account? Let us look at the standard answer to this problem. In a tradition which goes back to Weber it is commonly held that there are certain conditions under which 'prescriptions' may be incorporated into a value-free sociology. Injunctions which involve stating what means are necessary for the attainment of specific, given goals may be considered as comprising straightforward generalizations about the relations of two or more variables. If prescriptions are capable of being translated into the form 'given this goal, the following actions are necessary for its achievement', the sociologist may be exempted from the charge of preaching. All 'ought' statements must, on this view, be converted into 'if and then' statements. For example, the sociologist may wish to consider the proposition 'the executive ought to ensure maximum communication with employees'. If this advice is directed at executives he can assume that it involves a hidden premise, 'if the executive wishes to maximize productivity'; and he can then go on to assume that behind this lies an empirical generalization, i.e. 'productivity and communication are related in such a way that increases in the latter result in increases in the former'.

However, this procedure is deceptively easy and has severe limitations. Let us examine the case of the Human Relations Movement in industrial management. Under the aegis of Elton Mayo, who became the leading spokesman for the Movement, a long series of investigations at the Western Electric Company's works near Chicago in the 1920s and 1930s were interpreted as providing the empirical foundation for certain recommendations to management, i.e. that improved communications between workers and managers, more co-operation between them in making decisions, and a greater concern for satisfying the social needs of the workers would improve production more than would the use of financial incentives. The Human Relations Movement has frequently been criticized (see Friedmann 1955; Bendix and Fisher 1949; Krupp 1961). What follows is simply a schematic account of these criticisms which focuses on the problems of value—freedom.

18

In the first place, no science for management can assume that production, or indeed any other managerial objective, exists in a vacuum. It is a characteristic of social action that no objective is 'given' in isolation from other objectives. The limits on the attainment of an objective are set not only by the availability of means but also by criteria which determine what means are acceptable. These criteria frequently stem from goals which are independent of the objective from which the analysis began. Thus managers may well have goals other than high production, e.g. profit, industrial peace, the preservation of power and privilege. Explicit recommendations to management may either ignore these while tacitly taking them into account, or else neglect them completely in which case the proffered advice may well have consequences which managers would deplore. In neither case is the advice what it seems to be; in the former it amounts to whitewashing, in the latter to imposing a policy on management. Second, a general assumption behind the advice is that if the interest of managers and workers can be made to coincide, production will be increased. Such a coincidence may well be rare. Managers and workers may have such deep divisions of interests that no amount of communication and schemes for participation will secure harmony. The recommendations are then open to two further charges: that the conditions which would make them applicable are very limited rather than universal, and that where those conditions do not exist, the advice within the industrial situation will not function as a boost to productivity but rather as a programme of propaganda for management to demonstrate to the world its good intentions.

From this example it is clear that information which stems from a concern to develop maxims of conduct cannot easily be incorporated into a neutral and objective social science by the mere affirmation of value–freedom and the routine translation of 'ought' statements into 'if and then' statements. For criticisms levelled at the Human Relations Movement do not amount simply to the charge of covert involvement in managerial values. They relate also to the substantive results of the research programme. The prescriptions for the attainment of a specific goal necessarily involve the prescriber in a much wider complex of value judgements. Furthermore, the generalizations upon which the policy suggestions are based, epitomized in Mayo's claim that they possess 'significance equally for a factory on the Volga or for another on the banks of the River Charles' (Friedman 1955: 325), are shown to be far more limited in their scope than their authors assume.

The story of the Human Relations Movement may be regarded as a cautionary tale for those who are too sanguine about the chances of objective social science. It can equally be seen as encouraging those who wish to rid sociology of evaluative elements, since the criticism to which the Movement has been subjected might itself seem to indicate an advance towards objectivity. Indeed, a heightened consciousness of the biases stemming from the intrusion of practical concerns into empirical research would appear to be a welcome by-product, providing the sociologist with additional safeguards when analysing material concerned to instruct and advise managers and administrators. But this would be to underestimate the changes which have taken place in the instructional literature itself. For over and above the treatises concerned with particular types of organization there has developed a discipline known as 'organization theory' which aims to systematize, supplement and advance the knowledge contained in such work in order to help managers and administrators to make better decisions. In its concern to analyse the logic of organizational decisions, organization theory aims to bring advice to the *administrator* to the level of an applied science; and in its generalizing approach to the study of organizations it appears simultaneously to take on the mantle of sociology. It seems both to cast doubt on the separation of fact and value in social science and to deprive the sociologist of any distinctive contribution to the analysis of organizations.

At this point, to clarify the relation of fact and value in organization theory, I turn to the classic statement of the scope of organization theory by its most distinguished exponent. In *Administrative Behavior* (1957) Herbert Simon lays great stress on two points. First, he argues that it is impossible to assess organizational problems adequately within the context of one type of organization. Organized behaviour is a feature of many different organizations and the findings of research must be interpreted in the widest possible frame of reference. Second, he launches a sustained attack on the traditional maxims of administrative conduct, the principles of specialization, unity of command, span of control, and departmentalization. He contends that the conditions under which these principles are to be applied are never adequately specified. They purport to have a timeless validity when in fact, even in the narrow confines of the industrial firm, to which they most clearly relate, their application is ambiguous. Simon's criticism of earlier theories of administration points to the same kind of flaws as were found in the Human Relations Movement, i.e. that the so-called general principles of action recommended were derived from the experience of a very restricted number of organizations – and a very restricted type as well. He proposes to reverse this situation by developing a science of organizations in general and to offer advice which would be appropriate to a particular situation only.

At this point, however, a crucial qualification must be made. Simon's emphasis on the difficulty of making prescriptions brings him to a position where the role of prescription in organization theory almost vanishes. He contends that the principles of administration amount only to the directing of the administrator's attention to fundamental aspects of organization which he might otherwise have neglected. No general injunction such as 'unity of command must be ensured' is valid, but it is always of relevance to direct the administrator's attention to the problem of unity of command and the information that has been collected on this issue. Organization theory is thus formulated as the study of the categories that are relevant to the making of *administrative* decisions. This makes the relation of the organization theorist to the organization far more complex than hitherto. He is no longer the purveyor of ready-made solutions to unambiguous problems set for him by the administrator. His task is one of illumination.

His position may be likened to that of the psychotherapist helping the patient come to terms with problems which he only dimly perceives without professional help. Like the therapist, the organization theorist eschews injunctions to act and hopes to lead the administrator to the position where he is able to decide for himself on an analysis of the situation in which he himself has participated.

As Simon develops it, organization theory aims to assist men in the running of organizations by building up a set of empirical propositions of wide validity and at the same time refining the terminology used to analyse organizations. From organization theory, managers and administrators can expect both a widening of knowledge about how organizations work and a clarification of the concepts which guide their actions. They are not handed ready-made solutions but rather the means to discover them.

But for the sociologist the development of organization theory poses a problem. Here is a literature which stems from the needs of practical men and which quite openly aims to assist them to achieve their objectives. Yet in the pursuit of this task it goes far beyond the level of a recipe book for managers. It has reached a more sophisticated understanding about the relations of prescription and social research than the Human Relations Movement did, and in its comparative and generalizing approach bids fair to pre-empt anything the sociologist might have to offer in the way of a distinctive contribution to the understanding of organizations.

Organization theory appears to take over the sociologist's programme of research and for good measure to link it with practical needs. It is perhaps small wonder that the attractiveness of such a prospectus should have led sociologists to avoid tiresome demarcation disputes between disciplines, to overlook the question of practical involvement, and to identify their research objectives with those of organization theory. My argument in what follows aims to show that this identification of the sociological approach with organization theory is invalid. The perspective of a theory designed to assist the administrator cannot be merged into an approach which has no concern with the application of its results. The two spheres of interest may frequently overlap, they each have their value, but to confuse them is to allow a persistent bias to intrude.

One of the best illustrations of this identification of the two perspectives is provided by a definition of the organization which has become orthodox among sociologists and organization theorists alike. It is defined as a social unit explicitly established for the achievement of specific goals. To achieve these goals an extensive division of labour is needed – one in which each member of the organization has a prescribed task. This complex division of labour is governed by a formal authority structure and a set of rules and regulations which are normally written down. The social units which this definition has been made to cover are as varied as firms, hospitals, universities, prisons, political parties, governmental departments, trade unions, armies, and voluntary associations.

In sociology this viewpoint has received most authoritative support from Talcott Parsons (1960: 17):

> As a formal analytical point of reference, primacy of orientation to the attainment of a specific goal is used as the defining characteristic of an organization which distinguishes it from other types of social systems. This criterion has implications for both the external relations and the internal structure of the system referred to here as an organization.

The implicit qualification, 'As a formal analytical point of reference', is omitted in later writers who offer the goal-attainment definition of an organization in even more extreme form, for instance by Blau and Scott (1963: 1): 'An organization has been established for the explicit purpose of achieving certain goals' and Etzioni (1964: 3): 'Organizations are social units (or human groupings) deliberately constructed and reconstructed to seek specific goals.'

These seem relatively innocuous and uncontroversial formulations. But I want to show here that the central position of the organizational goal in these conceptions reflects the necessary interest of the theorist concerned to improve administrative decisions, and that a valid sociological definition applicable to the organizations I have mentioned would differ considerably by emphasizing at least four major points: namely, that organizational goals are not normally specific, that formal procedures are more than simply expressions of organizational goals and those goals are regularly implemented in ways other than through formal procedures, that the behaviour of groups within the organization is not simply a function of organizational position, and that the notion of the specific goal as the origin and cause of the organization is an unhistorical myth. In other words, the argument will be that this is not a definition of real organizations but of a hypothetical or idealized situation to which a theorist concerned with improvements and future states might wish them to tend. Such ideal formulations are invaluable in the context of organization theory but a bias results if sociologists employ them uncritically as defining existing situations. The four points are:

1 The requirement of the orthodox definition that the goal of an organization should be specific leads to a host of problems, for it is commonly very difficult to get an agreed statement from members of an organization as to its goal. This is particularly evident in such organizations as hospitals, prisons, or universities. Fundamental dilemmas as to whether the organization exists to promote cure or medical advance, punishment, reform, or restraint, teaching or research, are apparent to all involved (see Stanton

and Schwartz 1954; Galtung 1961). Such dilemmas may be resolved by different people in different ways within the same organization, and each will have considerable latitude to interpret the organizational purpose in his own way. Even within the industrial firm, which is often thought of as having a single and exceptionally clear-cut purpose, there may be multiple and competing objectives. Thus, one investigator analysed company policy statements and found that profit was supplemented or even replaced as an objective by commitments to consumers, the personnel of the firm, corporate growth, technological progress, and society in general (Shubik 1964).

Now the goal-oriented conception of the organization set out above makes the organization's structure dependent on its relation to the specific goal. A clear-cut programme devoted to the achievement of an end is seen as possible only if the end is conceived with clarity and precision. Confusion on objectives entails confusion on means. But the orthodox view of organizations regards their structure as a means for the achievement of the organizational goal. If, in the words of Mason Haire (1962a), the goals of organizations are multiple, vague, and unweighted in relation to each other, then organizations should continually be faced with confusion and disruption. In fact, organizations persist with relatively stable structures in spite of recurrent conflict as to the nature of their goals. Organizational structure must therefore be dependent on factors other than its relation to goals.

What are these factors? Behaviour which is bound by formal rules may originate otherwise than in agreement on a common goal. Co-operation may result from a situation where actors have divergent goals but recognize that each can only obtain his own objective on the basis of an exchange of contributions to the requirements of others. This may be governed by explicitly formulated rules. (The law of contract is an example.) On this basis it would therefore be quite possible to view organizations as collections of such coalitions as much as collectivities orientated to a specific goal. This fact seems to have led at least one writer to drop the orthodox definition of the organization and to substitute 'If several persons agree to follow a certain set of rules we shall say . . . that they are members of an organization.' He recognizes that the concept of goals presents great difficulty ('if psychologically even a single man may lack consistency of goals, what to say of a group of several?') and regards the choice of any particular goal to gauge organizational efficiency as basically arbitrary. One can measure the profits of a business corporation 'without postulating this to be the goal of any of the executives or stockholders' (Marschak 1959: 307, 311). But this solution can scarcely be accepted. Rules are a universal feature of social life. A definition of this kind fails to identify the distinctive characteristics of organizations. None the less, this does at least underline the fact that it is possible to think of organizational structure without reference to goals as the major determinant.

In a situation where the members of an organization themselves disagree as to what constitutes the organizational goal, the requirements of the orthodox definition can seriously prejudice an objective account. At its worst, the student's determination to impute clear-cut goals can lead him to the point where he is actually siding with one party or the other in saying what the objective ought to be. This is obvious if we consider the case of a political party. The statement 'the Labour Party's objective is the increase of equality' is simply a masquerade of an empirical statement. Even if it were accepted by all members of the party, its very generality would make it the topic of fervent political debate. Certainly it will be treated by the members of the organization in the way it deserves to be, as a contribution to the argument about what the policy of the party ought to be.

An extreme example of the knots into which the analyst can tie himself on this issue is contained in Lloyd (1962: 29): 'the comprehensive objective of an organization is to maximise the synergistic effect'. This is difficult to interpret. One of the requirements for the imputation of objectives to an individual or organization is that someone is prepared to avow them. It is hard to imagine Lloyd persuading many members of an organization to concur with this statement of objectives. Indeed, later he indicates that he also does not believe this to be a true statement of the objectives of organizations. He argues, 'Any organization which established objectives not in harmony with this fundamental comprehensive objective and which pursues these dissonant objectives is headed for trouble' (ibid.). If his earlier statement were true then this possibility would not need to be discussed. It looks very much like an interesting variant on the self-fulfilling prophecy, truth by menaces. If an organization dares to deviate from the author's conception it must beware. At the very least we are certainly far from the empirical determination of the objectives of an organization.

2 As mentioned in the last section, the instrumental conception of organizational structure leads to a misinterpretation of the place of formal procedures. Indeed, the fact that rules and regulations are very frequently not the expression of organizational purpose but result from the intervention of outside bodies is scarcely considered. Take the case of safety regulations, contractual agreements, compulsory insurance and all the rules which stem from the activity of trade unions. These rules are obviously *not* the expression of organizational purpose: rather, they may appear to the members as limits on the implementation of that purpose. Not even the extreme proponent of *laissez-faire* would claim that they stem from enlightened self-interest on the part of the organization rather than from outside interference. An odd feature about this neglect of the extra-organizational determination of rules is that it was sharply emphasized by one of the founding fathers of organization theory, Chester Barnard (1938). For him, the

churches and the state were dominant organizations and he described all subordinate organizations as incomplete and dependent. As will be seen later, in other respects also a return to Barnard would be advantageous.

Just as formal procedures which originate from outside the organization tend to be regarded as being determined by the organization, so also those formal procedures which are, strictly, internally determined tend to be regarded as the only way in which organizational purpose is expressed. In both cases formal procedures and organizational structure are regarded as coterminous. This is not the place to review the abundant and often illuminating literature on informal patterns within organizations. But its overriding concern is to establish that informal patterns of behaviour may work to the benefit or detriment of the formal structure. The implication is that formal structure potentially contains within itself its own capacity to implement organizational purpose. The informal elements are extrinsic helps or hindrances. In two respects this is an inadequate formulation of the relations of formal and informal elements.

Normally the formal structure of an organization is held to comprise two elements, the authority system determining who gives orders to whom, and rules and regulations governing work procedures. In respect of the authority structure, it has been pointed out by Parsons (1960) that the orders transmitted may well demand on the part of the recipient a competence which will be outside the experience of the person giving the order. For example, instructions from a headmaster with a degree in history to a teacher whose qualifications are in mathematics must necessarily be ill defined in content, and the teacher receiving the instructions may well be the best person to determine whether they have been implemented. The authority structure of an organization can well be regarded as internal to the organization, although, as will be seen later, this must be severely qualified. But the experience and competence of an individual can never entirely be 'internal' in this sense. For, quite obviously, he can bring it to and take it away from the organization. This kind of competence cannot be conferred by fiat. It is not a mere help or hindrance to the authority system – it is intrinsic to its operation. The formal transmission of orders demands informal implementation.

This intimate relation between 'formal' and 'informal' elements operates also in respect of work governed by rules rather than orders. It is a matter of logic and not experience that it is impossible for a rule to determine the conditions under which it is implemented. It is the agent's perception and interpretation of a situation which decide whether or not the application of a rule is justified. Compliance with a rule therefore is not removed from the area of disputable judgement. Formal organization is not facilitated or distorted by individual judgement and discretion; these are necessary preconditions for its operation. This is why 'pure' administration – if conceived of as the execution of completely rule-determined activity – cannot exist. Many of the complaints against bureaucracy stem from this misconception, the belief that the execution of policy can and ought to be completely routinized. Reinhard Bendix (1949: 12), in a study of American civil servants, argues strongly against this belief:

> Too great a compliance with statutory rules is popularly denounced as bureaucratic. Too great a reliance on initiative in order to realise the spirit, if not the letter, of the law is popularly denounced as an abuse of power, as interfering with legislative prerogative.

Administrative judgement and discretion are an essential part of administration and, as Bendix shows, a product of so-called informal elements – professional ethics, group solidarity, relations with the public, social status, and many other factors.

3 My argument so far has been that the goals of organizations are not necessarily single, precise or specific. Rules in an organization may have other functions than the implementation of a 'goal'. However, this still leaves the question of how we are to account for formal structures which do not depend on the intervention of outside bodies and which persist in spite of conflict on goals. Certainly there is no need to view formal rules and authority as determined by their relation to a specific goal. After all, formalized rules and authority may develop in a society and there is no need to refer to an over-riding purpose to explain them. Feudal society, for example, had such a pattern of authority and Thomism attempted an interpretation in terms of such a purpose. Usually sociologists attempt to explain such structures by reference to the demands of competing groups. There is no reason to think that organizational structure may not be interpreted in the same way.

Certainly one of the earliest complaints against the theories of the Human Relations Movement was that it was unable to conceive of the interests of the members of the organization as being determined by any other social unit. In Friedmann's (1955: 322–3) words:

> The firm is suspended in a void, in a social vacuum ... but the complexity of the firm derives chiefly from the fact that at the same time as each worker belongs to various collectivities within the works, he also belongs to larger external connectivities such as trade union, social class, and nation.

This has clear consequences for the goal-oriented conception of the organization. The individual's commitment to his organizational role will depend partly on how that role is 'evaluated' in his society and on how his other group affiliations put him in a position to make demands on the organization, to negotiate on his commitment, and to take an independent view of the organizational purpose. Thus members of the organization may put job security at the very centre of the organizational goal structure, and commitment to any other goal may be regarded as a price to be paid. Alternatively, it may be the case that an organizational goal is treated by the various social groupings in the organization as purely instrumental in obtaining their own purposes.

These points are best exemplified by the outstanding recent study by Michel Crozier (1964) of two governmental agencies. He shows that the formal authority system of these bodies is determined by the organizational structure of the whole sphere of public services in France and by the hierarchic demands and expectations of French society rather than by the necessities imposed by the implementation of the agencies' goals. Production workers, administrative officers and maintenance workers are all members of strata that are protected from each other by rules which express their relative power positions. In this situation the scope for managerial decision is limited. Does the manager appear as the powerful maximizer of productivity envisaged in the goal-attainment model of the organization? No. His task is to arbitrate and mediate between groups jockeying for position. The rules develop not so much from managerial purpose as from the need of human groups to protect themselves from that purpose.

4 Finally, we must examine a myth about the origins of organizations. The organizational goal is presented as an objective common to a large number of individuals moved to organize themselves to secure its attainment. Take one such account:

> if the accomplishment of a task requires more than a handful of men to work together they cannot simply proceed by having each do whatever he thinks needs to be done: rather they must first get themselves organized. They establish a club or a firm, they organize a union or a political party, or they set up a police force or a hospital.
>
> (Blau and Scott 1963: 1)

Another version relates how 'an organization comes into being whenever a group of people recognize that a synergistic effect will result from the proposed co-operative group action', and 'every religion, every great movement, every company, every organization at its very genesis began in the mind of one man' (Lloyd 1962: 29, 34). Now it is true though trivial that individuals must always be involved in some institution, but whether this primordial conception of a purpose is an adequate account of the origins of an organization seems doubtful.

These accounts are altogether too like the social contract theory of the origins of the state and society. At some point of time, never specified, individuals conceive an objective with uncommon unanimity and clarity to live an organized social life. But just as the social contract theory has been rejected on account of its rationalism, its individualism, and its lack of his-toricity, so must this account of the origins of organizations be rejected. Their formulation of rules and goals is in fact a long and tortuous progress. It is rarely possible to indicate a point of time at which they begin. If organizations have founders, and nearly always the 'foundation' amounts to the reorganizing of existing organizational elements, it is rare for them to have the slightest conception of how the organization is to develop. Of course some organizations may have a relatively clear-cut and abrupt beginning. The founders of a residents' association may have a simple, single purpose in common, e.g. the exclusion of coloured residents; but this kind of single, specific, 'common' purpose is not to be found in the dominating organiz-ations of government and industry.

If we consider the state or the great industrial corporation it is remark-ably difficult to trace their origins back to a common purpose. Their pre-sent highly complex structures are related to a multiplicity of purposes which arise in the course of the organization's development.

Furthermore, to emphasize a common originating purpose blinds us to another important fact. This is that organization may originate in the imposition of one group's purpose on another. The parallel with social contract theory is again quite close, i.e. it minimizes the importance of con-straint. Workers in early factories scarcely 'got themselves organized'. The goal-attainment perspective persistently tends to minimize conflict. With regard to March and Simon (1958), one critic has said, 'they have ignored centuries of highly documented instances of economic, social and political conditions: of conflict taken from the concrete records of government and industry. If their analysis is correct there should never be a union' (Krupp 1961: 164).

It is ironic that a discipline so recent, and in many respects highly devel-oped, should fall victim to an antiquated philosophy of man in society. Rationalism involves an over-emphasis on the differentiating character-istics of the human animal, in particular the possession of reason, to the extent that it is seen as the explanation and essence of all that is truly human and destined to triumph over the animal elements in man. We only have to substitute, 'the rational attainment of the organizational goal' for 'reason', and 'organization' for 'human being' to see this as an account of rationalism in the study of organizations. The lesson of modern histori-ography and psychology is that while rationality may be the distinguishing mark of human beings, it is not an unmoved mover but depends on a variety of social conditions. Far from being in necessary conflict with the animal elements in man, it is an organizing factor in their expression. As far as organizations are concerned, a similar advance in insight will come if we jettison the myth of the original goal and recognize that organizations possess all the social characteristics of collectivities over and above their special features of goal achievement.

What conception of the organization should replace the orthodox model? One possible source of misunderstanding should be dispelled at once. While common conceptions of the functioning of goals within organizations have been criticized, at no point has the argument denied that such goals may indeed exist. It is fundamental to the analysis of organizations that a distinction can be made between action of an individual in a private capacity and his action in an organizational role. (For a philosophical argument on this issue, see Haworth 1959: 59–63.) Members of any organization refer to purposes to legitimate their action – they impute their action not to themselves but to the organization. For that reason a distinction can be drawn between official and unofficial action. What has been criticized is the notion that official action can be interpreted as flowing exclusively and unambiguously from a predetermined specific goal.

In formulating a more objective concept of the organization, three elements in Barnard's classic *The Functions of the Executive* (1938) should be noted. He defines a formal organization as 'a system of consciously co-ordinated activities of two or more persons' (ibid.: 81). This has the advantage of being wider in scope than definitions which emphasize the specific goal – although it may be that its scope is too wide for it to be accepted without modification. In addition, he stresses the multiple nature of organizational goals, and emphasizes that authority is a relationship depending on the beliefs of those who accept it. To bring these elements together and to add another we may refer to an important contribution by E. Wight Bakke. He takes Malinowski's notion of the Charter and applies it to organizations. For him, the 'Organizational Charter' is 'basically a set of ideas shared by the participants which may or may not be embodied in written documents' (Bakke 1959: 38). These ideas include goals, values, symbolic elements, beliefs in what the organization stands for, which facilitate and legitimize interpersonal activities in the organization. I would add the important qualification that there is no reason why members of the organization should have equal shares in the Charter.

The following definition of an organization may be suggested: *organizations are social units where individuals are conscious of their membership and legitimize their co-operative activities primarily by reference to the attainment of impersonal goals rather than to moral standards.* In a subject congested with definitions, a strong argument has to be made for suggesting a new one. It is hoped that in the light of what has gone before, its rationale is clear. In brief, this formulation has three major advantages over the conception of organizations as created for the attainment of specific goals. In the first place, while it still emphasizes the importance of goal attainment as the distinctive characteristic of organizations, it does not assume unity, specificity, or *causal* efficacy as attributes of organizational goals. Second, by stressing the legitimizing functions of goals in an organization it avoids regarding goals as the property of any one stratum. All members contribute to conceptions of legitimacy. For example, if in an organization service to the community has hitherto been regarded as the legitimizing principle *par excellence,* managerial efforts to set up profitability as the prime objective may well be regarded by most members as illegitimate. In this situation a sociologist is not in a position to take sides. A science which instructs managers to treat organizational structure as contingent only on their own conception of its purpose is not only misguided in its empirical analysis of organizations but also taking sides in a struggle for power. Third, the relevance of conventional sociological analysis to organizations is more obvious. Societies also have legitimizing principles. For sociologists they are to be accounted for by such variables as power, conflict, class, status, the division of labour, and culture. However, in contrast to organizations the legitimizing principles of action in society are usually moral standards.

Thus, in relations as varied as those between friends, relatives, politicians and the public, the judiciary and accused persons, individuals regularly justify their actions by reference to notions of right, justice, propriety, equality, or fairness. In the wider society such reference may well be regarded as sufficient justification; in an organization actions need justification primarily by claims to success in achieving an objective. Of course this distinction allows for intermediate cases. In a society at war, goal attainment is so highly emphasized that it does no violence to language to call such a society an organization, and moral standards may frequently be invoked in organizations. To argue that organizations must be studied as societies is scarcely paradoxical when a score of companies have power and income surpassing those of independent states and activities transcending national boundaries, and when nations may be more dependent on one product, be it tobacco, sugar, or oil, than many an organization.

It may well be thought surprising that a plea should need to be made for sociologists to study organizations as societies. Regular definitions of sociology as the scientific study of society would lead one to expect that sociologists would in any case be vocationally inclined in that direction. Their proneness to the biases outlined here is therefore plainly in some need of explanation. The most likely reason is not that organization theory has been uncritically admired. It is rather that sociologists have adhered to an inadequate general theory. This 'theory' identifies research into society with analysis of the concept of a social system and accounts for the integration of that system by attributing to it a set of central values.

It has been all too easy for sociologists to adapt this way of thinking to organizations simply by substituting organization for society and organizational goal for central values. This may be illustrated briefly by reference to two essays on organizational analysis which cover similar ground. Both Alvin Gouldner (1959b) and Amitai Etzioni (1970) have criticized what, respectively, they call 'the rational model' and 'the goal model' of organizations. At first sight they are making the same kind of objections to an over-emphasis on organizational goals as have been set out in this chapter. But as an alternative all they suggest is what they term 'the natural system' or 'the system model'. For Etzioni this means that analysis of the organization in terms of its success in achieving its stated goal (which he argues is unrealistic, since organizations never achieve their goals completely) gives way to comparison of organizations in terms of their relative success in goal achievement and an assessment of their optimum distribution of resources in the light of the general requirements of systems for survival. Etzioni believes this excludes the normative orientations of the goal model. But it is difficult to see how this tallies with an insistence on assessing an optimum distribution of resources. Goal attainment remains as the central measure in organizational analysis even though it may be viewed in a more realistic light.

Similarly, Gouldner argues that the system model emphasizes an equilibrium of parts within which the goal is but one factor, but simultaneously concedes that this formulation exaggerates the integration of the organization around the goal. He takes issue with Parsons on this very point and asserts, 'the statement that an organization is oriented toward certain goals often means no more than that these are the goals of its top administrators or that they represent its societal function, which is another matter altogether' (Gouldner 1959b: 420). Yet, oddly enough, after pinpointing the deficiencies of both the rational and natural system models, all Gouldner calls for is an attempt to bring the two together rather than a break from them. Neither author draws the conclusion that if the system concept fails to do justice to the sociological facts of multiplicity and vagueness of goals, the extra-organizational determination of authority, the societal locus and independent power of the organization's members, their constant redefinition of organizational structure – then so much the worse for the system concept.

Of course, if this argument is valid, it supports the criticism that the system concept is used too hastily and with misleading consequences in sociology (see Lockwood 1956). If organizations cannot simply be conceived of as integrated by means of the specific goal, how much more unlikely it is that societies can be conceived of as integrated solely by means of basic values. If goal determination, formal rules, and authority structure must first be considered as independent factors before being considered as elements of a whole, known as 'the organization', then *a fortiori* the relation of social facts to a much vaguer entity termed 'society' must also be regarded at the outset of any research as problematical.

It is somewhat strange that elsewhere both Etzioni and Gouldner develop implicitly this third view of the strategy of organizational analysis. Thus Etzioni (1961) virtually dispenses with the concept of system and proceeds by taking one variable, compliance, and examining its connexions with others, while Gouldner (1959a) argues at a theoretical level for a revival of the factor approach. So we come round to one of the points which I made at the outset,

31

that the study of organizations has direct theoretical consequences for general sociology.

Let me, finally, take up one broader issue. It has been assumed throughout that there are at least two perspectives on the study of organizations, one known as organization theory, concerned basically with the improvement of organizational efficiency, and another, the sociology of organizations, devoted to discovering the causes and consequences of various types and features of organizations. While the whole argument has been designed to show that the two perspectives may not be confused, it has never been suggested that either in itself is invalid. The organization theorist is concerned to help managers and administrators. By contrast, the perspective of the sociologist is 'impractical'. His search is for understanding, untrammelled by the needs of men of affairs. Therefore he cannot accept the conceptual framework of the organization theorist as setting the limits to his research interests in organizations.

But this appeal for a recognition of the distinctiveness of the two perspectives is not a demand that organization theorist and sociologist must set up intellectual apartheid. On the contrary, the subtlety of the relations between the two perspectives shows that each must have a close understanding of the other. The organization theorist is bound to take cognizance of any contribution to knowledge about organizations, regardless of the motives from which it springs. In his search for value–freedom the sociologist must constantly re-examine the relations between practical discourse and his own language of analysis.

2

THE DIALECTIC OF SCIENCE AND VALUES IN THE STUDY OF ORGANIZATIONS[2]

In recent years we have seen the growing acknowledgement of the complexity of the interplay of science and values in the social sciences. The interpretation of social action, the capacity of human beings to follow rules of their own making and the contribution of social science to structuring the very reality it seeks to analyse all raise issues which transcend the limits of traditional views of a science. Such issues have a heightened importance in the study of organizations where the problems of control and authority are central and where, therefore, the question of whom does organizational science service is always pertinent.

In what follows it will be argued that there is ample evidence from its history that organizational study, even where its proponents may have adhered to public claims of value–freedom, has invariably at fundamental levels both implied and contributed to value–commitment and has thereby helped to structure its own subject matter. The argument follows a dialectical route:

Thesis: organizations may be studied as 'objects' in the manner of the natural sciences; *antithesis:* organizations do not possess the qualities of 'objects'; *synthesis:* organizations are human creations, hence in part the creations of theorists of organizations.

2.1 UTILITY: ORGANIZATIONAL SCIENCE AS TECHNOLOGY

2.1.1 The technocratic view of social science

In the two decades before the First World War the allure of forging an applied science extended to the human side of the large organization. The success of engineers on the material side of the production process encouraged an optimism about similar progress in enhancing the efficiency of the human element in production. The American Society of Mechanical Engineers became a forum for the discussion of 'scientific management'. 'Efficiency experts' were commissioned by railroads, steel firms, printers and other organizations to show the best way tasks might be performed and waste eliminated. To some extent in response to the encroachment of the engineers upon the field of human capacities, psychologists turned to the task of applying their concepts and methods to securing fit motormen for the electric railways, or selecting telephone operators, or finding the right psychological type for the ship's bridge.

In his history of the use of social science in American industry, Loren Baritz recounts how it was in this climate that Henry Ford established his 'Sociological Department' at Detroit in 1914. That department reported in 1916 that, for the Ford Motor Company, concern with human behaviour was, 'looked at from the cold-blooded point of view of business investment . . . the very best investment it has ever made' (Baritz 1960: 33).

An early creed for the social scientist serving industry may be found in *Psychology and Industrial Efficiency* (1913) by Hugo Munsterberg, who taught in both Germany and the United States and may be regarded as the founder of industrial psychology:

> Applied psychology is evidently to be classed with the technical sciences. It may be considered as psychotechnics, since we must recognize any science as technical if it teaches us to apply theoretical knowledge for the furtherance of human purposes. Like all technical sciences, applied psychology tells us what we ought to do if we want to reach certain ends; but we ought to realize at the threshold where the limits of such a technical science lie, as they are easily overlooked, with resulting confusion. We must understand that every technical science says only: you must make use of this means, if you wish to reach this or that particular end. But no technical science can decide within its limits whether the end itself is really a desirable one.
>
> (Munsterberg 1913: 17)

This was written in a chapter headed 'Means and Ends', which was followed by a section 'The Best Possible Man' in which Munsterberg showed how the new 'psychotechnic method' was to be used for the 'selection of those personalities which by their mental qualities are especially fit for a particular kind of economic work' (ibid.: 27). It can be no accident that the section 'Means and Ends' recalls the classic discussion of the limits of objectivity in the social sciences by Max Weber, where he argued that the achievement of given goals is susceptible to scientific analysis, but that the selection of goals to pursue will always remain subjective (Weber 1949). Munsterberg had a high opinion of Weber's own work on the psychophysics of industrial work, describing him as a brilliant political economist, and this research had been published only four years later than the essay on objectivity in the same journal, the *Archiv für Sozialwissenschaft und Sozialpolitik*.

Weber was himself well acquainted with 'scientific management', referring to it as the 'Taylor system', after its prime mover, F.W. Taylor. He viewed it as part of the general movement of rationalization in modern industrial society and regarded it as of pioneering importance in developing rational specialization according to physiological states and in devising aptitude tests (Weber 1947: 261).

Such reciprocal influences may surprise us at first. Scientific management is often thought of as a predominantly American phenomenon, while Weber's work on objectivity and the nature of social science is seen as a typical product of German thought. There is some truth in this. But consider what Lenin had to say about scientific management in 1918:

> The Taylor system, the last word of capitalism in this respect, like all capitalist progress, is a combination of subtle brutality of bourgeois exploitation and a number of its greatest scientific achievements in the field of analysing mechanical motions during work, the elimination of superfluous and awkward motions, the working out of correct methods of work, the introduction of the best systems of accounting and control, etc. The Soviet Republic must at all costs adopt all that is valuable in the achievements of science and technology in this field.
>
> (Lenin n.d.: 332–3)

Thinking in terms of means and ends was common to both capitalist and socialist modes of production and crossed the frontiers of industrializing cultures at the beginning of the twentieth century. We are bound, therefore, to acknowledge that we are concerned here with a cross-cultural phenomenon, a theory of applied social science common to industrial societies. It may be seen as an aspect of the ideology of technocracy, which Jean Meynaud (1968) has characterized as a belief in managerial competence to the extent that political decision-making is rendered unnecessary.

2.1.2 Techniques, consensualism and control

The cross-cultural coincidence of views we have just noticed also appears to be consistent with the belief in the universality of social science. Perhaps the ideology of technocracy is so prevalent precisely because it is well founded, we may suspect. After all, vaccines and gas turbine engines work in any society and testify to the soundness of the principles upon which they are founded. May we not regard aptitude tests and time and motion study as the analogous products of universalizable social sciences? Certainly in the history of modern science there has been a regular inclination to assume that universal utility follows from the universality of theories. The fact that applied science can be put to use anywhere leads to the idea that it is also always for the common good. From Francis Bacon (Crowther 1960) onwards, the progress of science and the coming of utopia have been closely associated ideas.

We may exemplify this from a source contemporary with Weber, Taylor and Lenin, and influenced by pragmatism, the philosophical movement of the time which stressed that the criteria of truth could be found in usefulness, an appropriate philosophy for technocracy. The source is George Herbert Mead and what he has to say is especially impressive evidence of the strength of the idea of natural science in the service of the common good because, as one of the most important founders of modern social science, he is normally thought of, along with Weber, as one of the advocates of a non-natural scientific methodology emphasizing meaning and understanding. Mead wrote, in criticizing a highly influential French philosopher:

> What Bergson failed to realize is that there is nothing so rational, so self-consciously reflective, as the application of scientific method to immediate conditions, and that the use of this method is just the means, under these conditions, that the human race is using for advancing. The anti-intellectualist attitude of Bergson represents a failure to grasp the import of the scientific method, especially that it puts the environment under the control of the individual.

> (Mead 1936: 294)

This is a succinct expression of the extreme consensualism which is so often involved in the idea of an applied science. In two sentences Mead slips from talking about the advance of the human race to the control of the environment by the individual. The interests of all are the interests of each. That conflicts of interest may arise in the course of the application of science is something that is all too often forgotten. The universal benefits of telecommunications, plastics or penicillin have appeared so obvious as to preclude such sophistry.

But in organizations the environment of one individual includes other individuals. Advances in the application of the social sciences therefore enhance the control that some individuals exercise over others. In consequence, the unquestioning equation of applicability with common utility is no longer possible. The applied social scientist, working in an organization, demonstrating that his theoretical knowledge has practical application, achieves this at the expense of having to serve the values of the organization either unconditionally by accepting them as his own values, or expedientially to earn an income and other advantages.

The dilemma of the social scientist in the organization is this: to show that his knowledge 'works' and can fashion techniques that can master the world in the manner of the natural scientists he looks up to, because they are based on valid, objective knowledge, he has to commit himself to values which emphasize control. In his objectivity there is a commitment, not to humanity's control of the natural world, as the applied natural scientist may affirm, but to man's control of man, to one side or another in a field of conflict.

The pioneering social scientists we have mentioned were aware of this dilemma, but they answered it in different ways. F.W. Taylor was extremely sensitive to the charge that he was working only in the interests of management. He hankered always after the utopian consensualism we have seen exemplified by Mead. Efficiency, he felt, necessarily worked in the interests of all. Science could only serve both management and men. A follower of his explained how this came about in the course of Taylor's work in the Midvale Steel Company. He was appointed gang boss and sought to increase output through pressure. A serious struggle ensued which Taylor won, but the experience hurt him and he set his mind to the elimination of such conflicts:

> He gave the matter thought and decided that the cause of such conflicts is that management, without knowing what is a proper day's work, tries to secure output by pressure. If management knew what is a proper day's work, it could then get output by demonstration.
>
> (Taylor 1947: x, originally printed in 1911)

Taylor expresses the technocrat's dream, that science will show that conflict does not pay. But the unions were unconvinced. The benefits of management's interest in human behaviour did not seem so apparent to them if time and motion study led to men losing their jobs. The beneficence of Ford's 'Sociological Department' was not unambiguously demonstrated by the employment of a hundred investigators, empowered to enter men's homes to check on their drinking habits, leisure time, sex life, and cleanliness in order to ascertain whether they were worth the newly established wage of five dollars a day (Baritz 1960: 33).

Weber, and later Munsterberg, were much more prepared to admit that the social scientist must choose which values he was going to serve. Perhaps in the spirit of German *realpolitik*, Weber made it clear that this choice involved taking sides in conflict.

2.1.3 Where technique ends: organization theory and the sociology of organizations

In the 1917 essay on value–freedom Weber argued that the social scientist's concern with values extended to a full examination of their meaning, presuppositions, implications and practical consequences. Only the ultimate choice was beyond the scientific competence of the social scientist (Weber 1949: 1–47).

As soon as these issues are raised, the limited scope of the practical problem-solving organizational science of Taylor and Munsterberg is thrown into sharp relief. For all students of modern organizations are now fully aware that organizational goals are frequently the subject of conflict, that they are more often than not vague and that their implications are often not understood even by those who frame them (Thompson and McEwen 1973). These are circumstances which fall outside the range of vision of scientific management, which must anchor technique upon the assumption of clear objectives. The true successors, therefore, of Taylor and Munsterberg are the linear programmers, econometricians, systems experts, as well as all those who refine methods for the manipulation and control of individuals in organizations through T-groups, job-enlargement, and so on. Frequently referred to under the umbrella term 'management scientists', they have enjoyed considerable success in enhancing efficiency and giving more power to managers. (A concise account of many of these techniques can be found in Hanika's *New Thinking in Management*, 1965.)

Organization theorists and sociologists of organization tend to begin their task at the very point where the very quest for improved control is critically analysed and where it has generated opposition within the organization. Both organization theorists and sociologists take organizational goals and the values on which they are founded to be problematical and the subject of scrutiny rather than purposes to be realized by the researcher himself. This, indeed, is the feature that organizational science possesses along with the social sciences in general, which distinguishes them from the natural sciences, that human values are central objects of enquiry. Various modes of undertaking this enquiry may be distinguished, but in the study of organizations we may distinguish two main ones. Where goals are vague and inexplicit, one intellectual response is to clarify and make explicit. This kind of conceptual enquiry is usually labelled 'organization theory'.

David Mechanic (1963) suggests that one part of Weber's essay on value–freedom may be viewed as a sophisticated form of decision theory, for he aims to outline the necessary elements in any complex decision-making process. Such an enterprise may be considered part of social science, but it is conceptual rather than empirical in nature. The task is one of aiding clear thought rather than providing appliances for a job to be done.

The programme of organization theory (or decision theory, or administrative theory, which for some special purposes may be treated as distinct, but have the same general orientation and are often regarded as synonymous) was set out in Herbert Simon's *Administrative Behavior* in 1946. He aimed there to provide:

> a theory of human choice or decision-making that aims to be sufficiently broad and realistic to accommodate both those rational aspects of choice that have been the principal concern of the economist, and those properties and limitations of the human decision-making mechanisms that have attracted the attention of psychologists and practical decision-makers.
>
> (Simon 1965: xi)

The style of organization theory is normally neither exhortatory nor empirically generalizing. It has a more diagnostic, clinical tone, a 'you-ought-to-realize-what's-happening-before-it's-too-late' slightly intimidatory form of address, evidenced in the paper which considers organization theory to be concerned with identifying the real underlying objectives of any organization and then warns that organizations which fail to adhere to these are 'headed for trouble' (Lloyd 1962: 29).

A British example of this genre is to be found in Wilfred Brown's *Exploration in Management*, where he says his lecture audiences often assume he is giving a set of recommendations. He replies:

> No – I am recommending nothing except that you absorb these ideas, and then see if in your actual experience they are not a description of your own practice – I am not recommending new organizational practices or ideas to you, but I am giving you, in general terms, a description of what I believe goes on in your own company.

Brown then goes on to challenge the reader's view of organization:

> Are you quite sure that your notions about your own practices are consistent with the reality of what really takes place in your company? If you are not sure then I ask you to consider whether the apparent inconsistency between your own practice and the general notions I have put forward might not be dispelled once you have obtained a more objective picture of your own organization.
>
> (Brown 1965: 36)

Brown's belief is that his conceptual framework is generally applicable to organizations he has not personally encountered and will provide a more objective guide to decision-making than the participants possess already. The practice of making people see what is 'really there' has much in common with the psycho-therapeutic orientation to personal counselling, and it underpins much of the theory of the counsellors of organizations, the management consultants, who represent the practical side of organization theory. One consultant, writing about the nature of his role, stresses his position as an outsider with its consequent lack of direct responsibility for taking decisions, but at the same time occupied in seeking 'constantly to reorient the men we deal with so that they can grasp our point of view and begin to think about problems along different lines. In fact much of our work can be thought of as educational' (Gardner 1965: 80). He adds later, 'He must constantly be the educator, trying to pass on his knowledge to the people he deals with. Often the growth of understanding within the organization is his most valuable contribution' (ibid.: 83).

In Chapter 1 I distinguished the intellectual orientation of organization theory, with its diagnostic and clinical aspirations, from the second main mode of enquiry into organizational values, the sociology of organizations. The sociologist may have no interest in organizational improvement; where people are unclear about their purposes he records that fact, and he takes it as axiomatic that management's view of the organization is one perspective among many. The major empirical sociological studies of organizations have this in common, that the views of top management are treated as but one contribution to the structuring of the organization. Gouldner's gypsum miners (1955a), Blau's employment agency clerks (1955), Lipset *et al.*'s printing union members (1956) and Crozier's factory maintenance workers (1964) all have an active and creative part to play in the making of organizational structure.

The sociologist seeks a position from which he can view the conflict of values, the struggles between different groups which are represented in any organization. To do this he is forced to adopt a terminology which is distinct from the parlance of the participants in the organization. He tries to make their values his object for description and explanation, and thereby claims a kind of objectivity. In the Lister Lecture to the British Association for the Advancement of Science (Albrow 1971), I sought to show how a sociological interpretation of changes in the place of public administration in contemporary society emerges from a consideration of the different meanings which are attached to the action of public officials through legal definitions, by the public, by the officials, and by professional groups in administration. Each group has a different capacity to impose its definition of the situation on others, and it is changes in those capacities and their sources which capture the sociologist's attention.

But one may well ask whether the sociologist is any more successful than the organization theorist in developing this objective language for organizational analysis. Indeed, it is evident that having passed beyond viewing a science of organizations as a kind of technology and having recognized that the study of values involves quite distinct approaches from those of applied science, we are faced with a range of problems which bear directly upon the distinctive character of the social sciences. Are objective accounts of the values of others possible at all? Do sociologists also import values into their perspectives? Do accounts merely describe, or do they also help to construct?

These are problems of basic methodology, but they underlie organizational studies as they do the social sciences in general. The second phase of our argument will go on to show their salience for the study of organizations.

2.2 RELATIVITY AND REALITY: FUNDAMENTAL ASSUMPTIONS IN THE STUDY OF ORGANIZATIONS

The decline of faith in the provision of technical, experimentally based knowledge and its replacement by descriptive or diagnostic case studies of organizations are described by Donald Schon in *Beyond the Stable State* (1971). (Schon's own career, philosopher turned management consultant, is itself vivid testimony to the growth of heuristic organization theory.) He describes how the rational/experimental model of social policy, where action is seen as a way of generating valid propositions for widespread application, must in conditions of rapid social change be replaced by systems analysis, by which Schon simply means models of interconnected factors, or existential knowledge, where attempts are made to capture the nature of changing phenomena through case histories, models of sequences of events, and typologies generalized from the cases and models (Schon 1971: 201–37).

Such a distinction emphasizes that, in the face of the conditions of ephemerality of the social and human objects that surround us, the very act of describing, and still more of generalizing, is a hazardous and contentious enterprise. Descriptions are always from a point of view which itself is subject to change. It is always open to question whether the qualities we impute to objects are really there or merely projections of our imaginations. In the natural sciences the idea of objectivity connotes agreement between observers upon descriptions and replication of observations giving the same results. The theory of relativity itself has a limited and defined scope within the whole field of natural science. In the social sciences relativity of perspective seems to pervade every enquiry.

But over and above the problem of perspective arises the question of the very reality of the objects of social scientific investigation. The natural scientist is able to conduct his arguments at various levels of concreteness or abstraction, using terms like particle, field or force without his objectivity being impugned. In organizational studies, on the other hand, the abstractness of terms like 'organization', 'structure' or 'goals' occasions the charge that fictitious entities are being constructed and that the investigator may be importing collectivized values.

We shall now consider specific ways in which the problems of relativity and reality arise in the study of organizations.

2.2.1 Assumptions about human nature

It is when one takes the basic and unanalysed terms of description and the facts which are taken for granted about the world that one can identify the characteristic viewpoint of a social scientist. These are what Gouldner (1970: 29–36) calls 'background assumptions'. Finding this taken-for-granted area is a game social scientists engage in with considerable competitive enthusiasm.

Nowhere is this better exemplified or more contentious than when comments are being made on the nature of human beings. As an obvious example, because its mechanistic orientation was so blatant, we may take the view of human nature found in scientific management. F.W. Taylor asserted that there were some men suitable for management, while others could merely carry out instructions. The handling of pig-iron, for instance, was the kind of task that could be carried out by the 'intelligent gorilla'. But the science underlying the act could not be understood by the kind of person best suited to carry it out: 'the pig-iron handler is not an extraordinary man difficult to find, he is merely a man more or less of the type of the ox, heavy both mentally and physically' (Taylor 1947: 41, 137). Here is a frame of reference which considers human beings to fall into two classes, mentally or physically endowed, which very conveniently mirrors a productive system where some give orders and others do the physical labour.

But can't we consider men to be much more than adjuncts to the productive process? This is the kind of question which springs to mind, and we find that a characteristic way for a new school of thought to emerge in organizational studies is by way of substitution of a different viewpoint on human nature. Thus the human relations movement in industry which supplanted scientific management in the 1930s as the fashionable mode of management emphasized the human being as a member of a group, with more intangible motives than the desire for money, such as needs for esteem, security and self-expression.

Herbert Simon's development of administrative science as the theory of decision-making is founded upon a theory of 'administrative man', who is constrained to make decisions on the basis of very simplified models of what the world is like, rather than on the full knowledge that theories of economic man had tended to assume. Simon argues that his model of man is a 'correct description' (1965: xxvi) and suggests that an adequate theory of human behaviour based on the 'decision premise' is far more likely to emerge than one based on the sociological conception of role. He continues: 'the construction of a satisfactory vocabulary for the description of human behavior is probably the most important task now confronting sociology' (ibid.: xxxii). Here we find an explicit linkage of the problems of basic vocabulary and the development of theories of human behaviour.

If his model of man is the basis of his theory, it is perhaps understandable that he should wish to dignify it with the title 'correct description'. After all, it would be less convincing to begin, 'For the sake of argument I am going to view human beings in this way and erect a major theoretical edifice on foundations which I recognize as arbitrary and subjective.' Yet criticism of this view of man is so readily formulable that it is difficult not to feel that this might be a more judicious claim. Mouzelis, for instance (1967: 38), holds that Simon neglects the individual as a group member subject to imposed norms. Even Simon's limitedly rational individual acts through taking decisions rather than by way of impulse or in solidarity with others.

Simon makes his model of man explicit, but it is still fair to say that it takes much for granted and the bases of the choice of characteristics for administrative man are largely unjustified. Not that it is not possible to find plenty of evidence for limited rationality in human conduct, but the warrant for singling this feature out to be the 'correct' description does not seem to be there. It appears as just one of many possible descriptions.

Some organization theorists have been conscious of the arbitrariness of starting-points. Mason Haire (1962a: 10) points out that organizational principles early in the century assumed man to be short-sighted, lazy and selfish. An example of an explicit reformulation comes from a consultant with GEC who lists a very different set of assumptions on which to base designs of organizational structure. They include:

> Most people want more freedom in their work to decide for themselves...
> Most people have both the desire and the capacity to discipline themselves to a greater extent in their own work...
> Most people already have the competence to achieve significantly greater results than they are currently achieving...
> Most people really want to learn how to do their own work better...
> Most people want the door of opportunity to be open equally to all.
>
> (Estes 1962: 16)

In this case the values of the consultant are clearly implicated in the view of man he outlines. But in general we may say that a view of human nature reflects as much how the observer prefers to regard others as it does their 'real' nature. And in that way, if the observers are influential enough, it can be that their view has a chance of becoming a real influence on human nature. If men are viewed and treated as machines, they become machine-like; if they are considered to be free, they can become free. Such persuasive definitions are, by definition, factors in change, and never mere reflections of the world.

2.2.2 Relative viewpoints on organizations

Such selectivity of perspective is not confined to the assumptions we make about human beings in organizations. It applies to every aspect of the vocabulary we use to describe organizations. The student has already been introduced to the wide variety of conceptual schemes which are in use for the analysis of organizations (Grusky and Miller 1970: 1–158; Silverman 1970; Weeks 1973: 375–95). Whether organizations are described as social, sociotechnical, open or open-adaptive systems, or are defined with special reference to formality, goals, tasks, or complexity, from whatever standpoint the same problems arise as with the conceptions of human nature we have been discussing and which underlie such conceptual schemes.

Each scheme is a way of looking which concentrates the attention on some phenomena rather than others. Moreover that viewpoint can normally be shown to correspond more or less closely to the outlooks of different groups within or concerned with organizations. It is fair to say that in general these viewpoints have normally been associated with managerial perspectives. But the social action perspective of Gouldner's *Wildcat Strike* (1965), or the rationalistic approach in Crozier's *The Bureaucratic Phenomenon* (1964) give more weight to contributions other sections make to organizational dynamics. Whether managerial or not, all these perspectives have at one time or another been adopted by sociologists, with the explicit desire to detach themselves from partial viewpoints. All one can find in common is this aspiration and the mutual recriminations which follow from lack of success.

Simply to take one illustration, we may consider Argyris' critique of Blau (Argyris 1973: 76–90). Blau's focus of investigation is directed to the system of interrelated parts that make up the organization as a whole rather than to the separate components. This is repeated in Blau and Schoenherr (1973: 22–3), where they emphasize that structure is 'independent of the personalities and psychological dispositions of individual members', that 'organizations are not people', and it is time we 'push men finally out'.

Argyris considers that this perspective mistakenly equates the formal and intended aspects of the organization with the whole and forces the investigator to rely on the accounts of a few of top management. He goes on to suggest that Blau's work may more properly be viewed as a quality control check on the effectiveness of civil service regulations. The heart of Argyris' criticism is that Blau neglects the qualities of human beings in his stress on the organization as a whole, and that the features of organization he tries to account for are explicable in terms of what he neglects, namely, human properties.

Linked again with the accusation of possessing a restricted and partial perspective is the implicit charge of bias, conscious or unconscious, towards management. But, of course, it is possible to turn the argument back against Argyris. He asks why specialization has been found to be necessary. His answer is, 'According to engineering economics, *given the nature of people,* it is cheaper to specialize work' (Argyris 1973: 78). He goes on to assert that 'the pyramidal structure is based on the properties of human beings' (ibid.: 79). Later he says it is not merely 'based', but 'because of'. If that is so, we may ask why large bureaucracy has not always been a feature of human society. We may also ask why other non-human, large-scale, complex systems of units develop specialization among those units. Is Argyris eager to exculpate those responsible for creating large-scale organizations by arguing that they have no choice in the kind of structure they choose?

2.2.3 Are organizations real?

Argyris' comments on Blau illustrate the other facet of the methodological problems we are considering here. When we utter statements about organizations, to what sort of reality are we referring? Hitherto, we have not questioned the reality of organizations, merely assumed that there are different ways of looking at them, just as Rosemary Stewart begins her book *The Reality of Organizations* (1972) with a chapter, 'Ways of Looking at Organizations'.

Clearly, if we are going to talk about organizations, it is of considerable importance to have criteria for establishing when it is and when it is not legitimate to regard an organization or any element of it as being in existence. I was concerned with this in Chapter 1 to the extent that I accused sociologists of illicitly assuming that the models of the organization theorist were always actualized in organizations, with clear-cut goals generating formal rules and authority, instead of treating them as idealized constructions, with their empirical reference always being open to investigation. Joseph Albini (1971) has demonstrated that it matters whether the American Mafia exists and what its features are. For one thing, the response of the police will vary according to whether they are dealing with a form of business enterprise or a very extended kinship system.

But these demands for operational criteria for the use of terms like 'organization' assume that the existence of a particular organization or organizational feature is an empirical question. More radical attacks have been mounted which question the reality of organizations, organizational purposes or structure. Max Weber (1947: 101–2), in an early statement of what Karl Popper (1957a: 136) was later to call methodological individualism, considered it illegitimate to impute acts to entities such as 'the state' or 'the nation', since only individuals could act and collective terms were developed for legal and certain practical purposes. Gouldner is acknowledging his debt to Weber when he writes in the same vein:

> But an organization as such cannot be said to be oriented toward a goal, except in a merely metaphorical sense, unless it is assumed that its parts possess a much lower degree of functional autonomy than can in fact be observed. The statement that an organization is oriented towards certain goals often means no more than that these are the goals of its top administrators, or that they represent its societal function, which is another matter altogether.
>
> (Gouldner 1959b: 420)

Gouldner, like Weber, is pointing to what has been called the fallacy of misplaced concreteness (Whitehead 1925: 75) or of reification (Cohen 1931: 224–8), that is, imputing to abstract entities the qualities of concrete units. But there are some strange twists to the course of these arguments. Thus behaviourism, which resists the imputation of mind and purposiveness to individuals on the grounds of their unobservability and therefore aims to counter reification, has been the dominant orientation of academic psychology in this century. A fortiori, psychologists have vigorously resisted applying the language of purpose to organizations, regarding it as merely metaphorical. Instead they have advocated systems theory.

Thus in their *Social Psychology of Organizations* (1966: 14–19) Katz and Kahn reject the use of the language of organizational objectives and state, 'We shall refer to organizational functions or objectives not as the conscious purposes of group leaders or group members but as the outcomes which are the energic source for a maintenance of the same type of output.' Miller and Rice (1967) adopt a similar strategy of attempting to infer the 'primary task' of the organization, which may differ from the leaders' formulations. But systems theory itself has many times been charged with importing metaphor and false concreteness, and Weber himself warned of the danger of relocation (1947: 103). Indeed it reaches the point in structural functionalism where society alone appears to have purpose and individuals none. The ideological bias towards conservatism in this position has been pointed out too often to need detailing here.

To deny reality to the foci of a scientist's enquiries must arouse strong feelings on his part, and often vehement counter-charges. Programmatic statements to the effect that only individuals are real, organizations are fictions, ideas cannot influence events, purposes are unreal, structures are metaphors and so on are the background assumptions of the different schools of thought into which so much of the academic world divides itself.

But these assumptions are not merely indicative of divisions in the academic world. They parallel the great political divides also and help to create them. Such a comment is not peculiar to sociologists. The most influential account of the way the axioms of major schools of thought may have political repercussions is contained in Karl Popper's *The Open Society and Its Enemies* (1957b), where the collectivism and determinism he detects in the philosophies of Hegel and Marx are viewed as major contributions to political conflict in the twentieth century, and certainly, as a philosopher, Popper has been critical of sociologists, in their attempt to develop a sociology of knowledge. In respect of organizations, I have made the analogous point to the one Popper was making for politics and society as a whole. The way we view organizations still appears to be within the realm of our choice, rather than a necessity in the nature of things, and in that choice we may help to make, rather than merely reflect, the world, which brings us to the third phase of our argument.

2.3 REFLEXIVITY: ORGANIZATIONS AS THEORETICAL CONSTRUCTS

Social scientific theories have a dialectical relationship with their subject matter, reflecting on society, being created by it and in turn helping to create. In his *Work and Authority in Industry* (1956), Bendix shows how the schools of scientific management and human relations contributed to the managerial ideologies of the United States. Those ideologies were themselves expressions of the interests of the owners and managers of capitalist enterprise which depended on and made the alienated human being possessed of no qualities but his labour power, the man who fitted so well with Taylor's perspective.

Social scientific accounts share with everyday accounts of social activity the quality which I would want to call 'reflexivity'. This is the quality of being both descriptions and component parts of a situation, so that the accounts themselves help to give an objectivity to the practices they refer to. If we accept this idea, the problem of objectivity and scientific nature of any theory of organization takes on an added dimension, for the character as objects of the phenomena under investigation is dependent on the constructive activity of human beings. Social phenomena are no longer the products of impersonal forces. As we act, and give accounts of our action, we are creating our society and ourselves.

2.3.1 Ethnomethodological and sociological approaches to reflexivity

The ethnomethodological school has made fruitful use of the idea of reflexivity to emphasize the original character of the accounts of organizational structure which are given by the members of the organization. Thus Bittner (1973: 266) insists that 'the idea of formal structure is basically a common sense notion' and suggests that 'the sociologist finds himself in the position of having borrowed a concept from those he seeks to study in order to describe what he observes about them' (ibid.: 265). Bittner does not object in principle to this, but stresses that the 'meaning and import of the formal schemes must remain undetermined unless the circumstances and procedures of its actual use by actors are fully investigated' (ibid.: 267). Zimmerman makes a similar point in discussing organizational rules: 'the issue of what such rules mean to, and how they are used by, personnel on actual occasions of bureaucratic work is ignored as an empirical issue' (Zimmerman 1973: 251) by sociologists who make their own assumptions about what the rules mean and take their own competence to apply them for granted. Manning (1971) advocates that particular attention should be paid to the natural language of organizational members, the way they designate roles and activities in everyday contexts.

Yet, in spite of the way reflexivity has been interpreted recently to give priority to everyday accounts, the constructive part that images and concepts may have in the formation of society is an old theme in social thought going back to Hegel and beyond. Merton made use of the idea in writing of the self-fulfilling prophecy (1957: 28–9), while Berger and Luckmann offer an account of 'society as objective reality' in which everyday pre-theoretical knowledge especially, but also the complex theoretical systems, are essential elements in integrating the institutional order (1971: 83). Topitsch has said of the social sciences:

> A group of theories in a state of change (the word theory is used here in a very wide sense) relates to a society in a state of change, and these theories are themselves a part of the social scene they represent, and react on it in many different ways.
>
> (Topitsch 1971: 24)

He remarks that this interactive relationship of theory and society has received very little systematic analysis. One of the rare examples of such analysis is Paul Halmos' examination of the sources of social work ideology in social and psychological theory and its subsequent influence on society, where he argues that by interpreting the world 'social scientists – *have in fact changed it*' (Halmos 1965 and 1970: 77).

Any mention of the activity of professional groups, such as social workers or managers, must draw our attention to the fact that many occupations base their day-to-day activities on theory of some kind. Douglas McGregor has asserted, 'Every managerial act rests on theory' (1960: 6). The assumptions, generalizations and hypotheses of the manager are more often than not built up from his daily experience, and he may believe that his knowledge is in some way 'practical' compared with social science, but in their form they are just as theoretical and, therefore, compete with the formulations of social scientists.

The instance of 'professional knowledge' offers a corrective to the ethno-methodological account which tends to assume the common availability of meanings to groups of undifferentiated actors. It also corrects the complementary tendency on the part of sociologists to assume that theory is the preserve of detached scholars. Precisely because of the range of control that the manager has, he must think in conceptual dimensions which at least attempt to take in the organization as a whole. Thus Bittner may consider 'formal structure' to be a 'common sense notion', but one may suspect that it is employed by the manager far more than by men on the shop floor, and the manager today is probably believing it to be part of his own home-spun theory rather than derived from the social research of the 1930s, which is the most likely source. For an expression of this relationship between theory and everyday practice we may cite Schon:

> When a person enters a social system, he encounters a body of theory which more or less explicitly sets out not only 'the way the world is', but 'who we are', 'what we are doing', and 'what we should be doing'.
>
> The theory of an industrial firm, for example, includes what the business is, how it works, what the market and the competition are like, and what kinds of performance are valued. The theory of an agency for the blind includes notions about what a blind person can learn to do, what is an appropriate service, what professional behaviour consists in, the difference between good and bad clients, what the objectives of providing service are ...
>
> While the broad theory of the social system may be shared by everyone in it, there are likely to be variants held by people in different parts of the structure. The cop on the beat and the police commissioner have different views of the world and of the police force. Workers on the assembly line, foremen and managers of production all have world views different from one another and from the world view of the president of the firm. ... It is in a way misleading to distinguish at all between

social system and theory, for the social system is the embodiment of its theory and the theory is the conceptual dimension of the social system.
(Schon 1971: 34–5)

These reflections help to throw light on the reasons for the frequency with which the charge of adopting the managerial viewpoint has been levelled at theorists of organizations. For they are already in dialogue with the theories of practical men, and it is those who have power who can give new theories widespread social effect. The differentiation of theorists of organization from organizational members and managers is itself an important feature of organizational development. Reflexivity is itself a developing, not a static element in society.

2.3.2 The development of reflexivity in organizations

In *The Genesis of Modern Management* (1968), Pollard shows how in the nineteenth century there were only few and isolated attempts to set down a theory of management in writing. He identifies three major reasons for this: the difficulty at this stage of isolating a separate 'managerial function'; the highly individual position of each manager; and a view of the work force as a body of men, deficient in character and in need of reform. An exception was Robert Owen at the New Lanark Mills, but his was, for the time, a unique appreciation of the administrative processes of a factory.

Elsewhere I have commented on the relatively sophisticated development of theoretical ideas in state administration on the Continent at the beginning of the nineteenth century (Albrow 1970). The Napoleonic period involved the attempt to reconstruct the state on a theoretical basis, and reforms extended throughout the administrative system. In Germany a number of texts were written to outline the new principles of administration. The finance minister of Westphalia wrote a treatise in 1823 in which he contrasted the old collegial system with the new unitary, or bureau, system and outlined the benefits and defects of each. The terms in which he did this are quite familiar to us today, namely, speed of execution of business, dividing responsibility, amount of discretion, tightness of control. He also made the distinction between specialization by place or by function (Albrow 1970: 27).

The early theory of bureaucratic administration was written by bureaucrats and into the twentieth century the leaders of large organizations wrote their own theory. Peter Drucker's account of General Motors includes details of the explicit theory of decentralization which was propagated by Alfred P. Sloan, Jr, its head from 1921 to 1955. This was an elaborate philosophy of management and self-government designed to reduce conflicts of interest between sections and enhance communication generally. Drucker likens it to the American Constitution in the way it consists of a series of yardsticks rather than a set of overall directives: 'General Motors owes its strength precisely to that use of principles and concepts as guides for concrete, unplanned, and unforeseen action of which the "planner" knows nothing' (Drucker 1964: 70).

Drucker found little evidence of conscious use of theories of governmental organization in General Motors, but Sloan himself established a foundation which had the furtherance of management theory as part of its aims. (Douglas McGregor acknowledges its support for the writing of *The Human Side of Enterprise*, 1960.) This is a sign of the functional differentiation that takes place in this century between the theoretician and the practitioner. One of the best examples of the dialectic to which this gives rise can be found in the work of Philip Selznick on the Tennessee Valley Authority (1966).

The TVA was established by the United States Congress in 1933 with authority to deepen the River Tennessee, construct dams, and produce and distribute fertilizer and electricity. It was established by government, but at the same time its three-man board of directors was given considerable independence. David Lilienthal, chairman of the board, took the major role in expounding a doctrine of grass-roots decentralization, which, he argued, would revitalize local initiative and counteract excessively centralized power. This was Lilienthal's answer to the trend to managerial dominance, although ironically James Burnham singled out the TVA as an example of just this in *The Managerial Revolution* (1962). Lilienthal explicitly rejected Burnham's accusations, basing his own doctrine on Alexis de Tocqueville's classic analysis of centralization in *Democracy in America* (1945). The theory was developed within the organization through training conferences and administrative seminars, and Selznick comments that, as basic organization policy, the theory extended far beyond the views of its chairman (Selznick 1966: 22).

Selznick interprets the use of this doctrine as an ideology serving to define the organization and shape the views of its staff. In other words, it has latent functions beyond those that were intended. He makes use of this idea in his later book *Leadership in Administration* (1957), where he argues that the creative leader will propagate 'socially integrating myths' in order to generate unity of purpose. What was latent in the TVA he makes manifest for the use of future leaders in a book which, in its foreword, claims to help 'in broadening the intellectual horizons of businessmen' (Selznick 1957: viii).

De Tocqueville's theory, Lilienthal's application of it in the TVA, Selznick's interpretation of the TVA theory and then the advice he gives to administrative leaders make up an ongoing cycle of experience and interpretation which has no necessary end point. Whether we consider such a cycle as information feedback keeping organization on course, or the emergence of new social forms through the agency of human creativity is a question of some importance, but in this context what matters most is that it illustrates the importance that theoretical formulations have in the process of organizational change.

When Joan Woodward undertook her ten-year study of the structure of one hundred south Essex firms, she found that 'about half had made some conscious attempt to plan organization and to apply the precepts and principles of the systematic body of knowledge of organizational structure and process contained in management theory' (1965: 17). She also commented that the decade 1953–63 saw the evolution of a ideology among managers which was a barrier to their understanding of reality (ibid.: 254). Her hope was that social science would transform this situation.

But from all that has gone before, we can hardly be as sanguine that social science dispels, rather than assists, ideology. Peter Clark has recently examined the nature of action research in organizations, where programmes are initiated to solve practical problems and to generate more widely applicable knowledge. Here manager and researcher are placed in roles of mutual assistance in thought and action. He characterizes the knowledge the social scientist brings to bear in this situation as consisting of the concepts and propositions of his discipline and also data collected in the particular organization, but he will also have a focus, a set of key variables for manipulation to induce change, and these 'will almost certainly incorporate his beliefs about the nature of man's role in society' (Clark 1972: 68). One can only hope that these beliefs are examined with the same care as the organization.

There is only one full-length treatment of the theme of the application of social science in organizations which gives it full historical significance and that is in the fortunately popular *The Organization Man* (1956) by William H. Whyte. This argues that a new type of man has been created through the propagation of a new ideology to replace the Protestant Ethic. This ideology sees the organization as the source of creativity and 'belongingness' as the ultimate individual need. The Social Ethic is propagated through scientism, the belief that the same methods that have been adopted in the natural sciences can be employed in the study of man and simultaneously solve ethical problems. Whyte identifies the origins of these beliefs in the work of the Human Relations movement and shows how they are translated into reality through the training and control of the individual in the organization.

The historical and cultural specifics of Whyte's account have changed since 1956 when his book first appeared, but the basic theme is as relevant now as then. It is the same as the theme of this unit: the creation of a new social reality in the illusion that it is a given and stable reality which is being analysed. Organizational science is part of organizational life and its active dimension cannot be ignored if an adequate understanding of its relevance to organizations is to be gained.

2.4 CONCLUSION

I hope to have shown that the study of organizations, like the study of society generally, has characteristics which distinguish it sharply from the natural sciences. Its results bear directly on major areas of value conflict, its subject matter comprises human values which cannot take on the qualities of the objects the natural scientist treats, and it has a part in the construction and transformation of its subject matter.

John Child has argued recently that there is far more choice involved in organizational design than has usually been recognized and that the values of those who have power are of vital importance (Child 1973: 252–5). This is a corollary of the arguments expressed here that organizations are human constructions, created by those who have power to bring their accounts to bear on them. He points out that new pressures are mounting to induce those with most power in organizations to make wider reference to the costs and benefits of society at large and to enhance the degree of membership participation. The educational sector is singled out as one of the places where such demands begin.

The People and Organizations course is part of the educational sector and yet another element in the ongoing process of reflection and creation. If the arguments I have used have any validity, its perspectives will play their part in shaping the organizational environment of the future, not as techniques for management, but as part of the conceptual and imaginative resources of every one of its students who subsequently comes into contact with organizations, whether as manager, employee, client, or member of the public – and this, to my mind, is its main purpose.

Part II

REASSESSING WEBER FOR CURRENT USES

Max Weber has had an immense influence on the development of the sociology of organization. Very few have escaped his influence, certainly not this writer, but, equally, most have felt the need to enter disagreements with, or marked qualifications to, his account of bureaucracy in particular.

But he would have been very surprised even in his own terms if his analysis had remained as relevant to contemporary conditions as it was to his then. He looked forward indeed to the obsolescence of his own work, and his own thinking about the relation of research to social life was essentially historically informed and dialectical. He quoted Goethe approvingly to refer to the time when the great cultural problems would move on and leave the specialist work of his time behind (Weber 1949: 112).

We are now far enough from his time to be able to interpret his position on the dialectic of social scientific concepts and social reality as one of high modernity. He stressed their technical and rational nature and to this extent he envisaged them contributing to the cumulative historical development which he called rationalization. This intensification (*Steigerung*, also derived from Goethe) of rationality meant that he had difficulty reconciling a perception of an apparently endlessly developing process with that sense of inevitable decay.

Part of his handling of these disparate orientations to the world was to stress from time to time that there was more to history than rationality. We have to acknowledge non-rational and non-modern elements in social change. In practice, then, his account of rationalization gave weight to all kinds of other non-rational moments in its development, most famous of which was of course the Protestant Ethic rooted in a need for salvation.

Hence if we adopt the wider insights in his account of rationalization and project the narrative forward to our own time, we find not simply the intensification of rationalization but also the impact of elementary social forces for which we need both different non-rational analytical tools and a broader appreciation of the embeddedness of rationality in institutions.

53

So it is now Weber's pure type of bureaucracy which looks dated, depending as it did on a historically very specific set of concepts of authority, while his sense of the direction of change in society, depending on his overall grasp of the forces underlying change, has remained important to this day even though he attended rather little to their analysis. Concepts of values, forces, needs, drives, were important for his account even though he never gave them the same attention as he gave to action, motive and meaning.

Weber remains in so many respects an exemplar for contemporary sociology, not because he foretold the future, though he did this better than any other classical sociologist, but because he developed scholarly analytic methods to handle the problems of his own time and combined this with the most comprehensive comparative and historical grasp of its passing nature. Weber's rationalization thesis is imbued with this intuitive grasp of the transitoriness of contemporary phenomena, and its relatively low level of abstraction and keen and concrete sense of contemporary social conditions invite us to update it for our own time. But when we come to his analytical concepts they betray the limitations of his time much more, even though they appear to be so much a matter of logic.

The lesson we can draw is that we need to reappraise our analytic tools all the time and we can never expect those from an earlier period to be adequate for our present conditions. Profound social diagnosis depends not only on skill and judgement in the application of refined analytical tools, but also on adding some to, and even discarding some from, our repertoire. It is significant that the most important revisions of the concept of economic rationality since his time have come from embedding it in institutional considerations.

Herbert Simon's (1965) satisficing rationality and Oliver Williamson's (1985) analysis of transaction costs both highlight the importance of the social conditions of economic calculation and as those conditions change so new concepts take on a central salience. So Williamson's 'asset specificity', the situational advantage the agent has from knowing the ropes or 'being there', is so important now because standardized, nationwide, centralized bureaucracies no longer dominate industry or the state.

In general, Weber's favourite analytical concepts, whether economic, political or social, were characteristically of an old modern time and shared in its limitations. They had a dominant place in its self-image and constitution. He could not foresee the demise of bureaucracy and his forebodings of its inevitable triumph have not been realized. At the same time his diagnoses depended on a profound sense of historical change and an overall grasp of the forces at work which cries out for emulation rather than imitation or replication.

Chapter 3 is an illustration of how each generation effectively revises its rationality concept in practice. Weber spoke of Western rationalism as opposed to other civilizations. The idea of a single Western rationalism looks very frayed today. Indeed, it is more appropriate to think of a cluster of rationalisms disembedded from West or East. The kind of rationalization I discuss is different from Simon's bounded rationality or Williamson's contractual rationality but coexists with them in a postmodern world. It is a system rationality embedded in the institutional life of contemporary society which replaces some of the manifest inadequacies of older bureaucratic control mechanisms. The regulatory procedures developed for electronic data storage and artificial reproduction are examples of new social technology which Weber would have recognized as solutions to problems bureaucracy could not solve. They illustrate the need to build on Weber's insights into rationalization. They are genuine successors to the models of bureaucracy he embedded in his account of rationalization.

The concepts of authority which he used for the analysis of bureaucracy now appear very much the dated products of his time. They deprived his agents of both moral and personal strategic choice. There is no need for us to remain wedded to them and indeed, if we are, there is every reason to think they will not allow us to appreciate the profound changes which affect every sector of life, and which stem, not from ongoing rationalization, but from the impact of changes which were neither willed nor wanted, most of which are summed up under globalization.

We need to develop new concepts of authority because the world is no longer directed by centralized, authoritarian bureaucracies. Chapter 4 contributes to the reworking of the idea of authority for our own decentred time in which even public officials are rational economic agents too. They are also moral agents. This does not necessarily mean we live in a better world, but we may entertain a guarded optimism, as opposed to Weber's pessimism. It means at least that we can move away, as Richard Sennett (1993: 197) proposes, from the sterile negation of authority, to the endless quest for its amelioration.

In so doing we reveal the limitations of Weber's account of the relation between concepts and society. It was interactive, but not sufficiently transformative. He retained a belief in the efficacy of pure rationality and its immunity to popular re-interpretation. Equally he dismissed the idea that there might be more broadly based non-rational concepts, like the notion of the social, which could serve to mediate across time and place.

To this extent the phenomenological critique of Weber, through Schutz (1967), has done much to entrench a much more broadly based notion of the priority of everyday concepts in social life as compared with scientific ones. If there is one reason for suggesting that the present age needs to rework Weber, it is that the rationality of everyday life is as important for constituting the public sphere now as the large bureaucracy was then.

The bureaucratization of everything in Weber's terms became the colonization of the life-world as Habermas (1981) built on him for new conditions. It is the increasingly active participation of the citizen in that process which

Beck *et al.* (1994) seek to capture with the concept of reflexive modernity. This decentring of rationality takes us far outside the old monoliths.

It is for these reasons, changes in the real world, that the institutional framework for organizations has become a focus for sociologists (Zucker 1983; Scott 1995). Equally it accounts for the foregrounding of the social power of the individual economic agent in Williamson's institutional economics. From these two directions, institution and agency, the new institutionalists converge on the issue of how organizational forms emerge and change when they no longer operate as the iron cage.

Chapters 3 and 4 parallel those discussions and illustrate how those directions are represented in Weber's work. Thus they build on him, but in examining the institutionalization of rationality and the moral basis of organizational authority they come to very different conclusions from his. But it is the times in which we live which call on us to develop post-Weberian approaches.

3

THE APPLICATION OF THE WEBERIAN CONCEPT OF RATIONALIZATION TO CONTEMPORARY CONDITIONS[3]

3.1 DEVELOPING THE RATIONALIZATION THESIS

There is no contradiction involved in saying that Weber's theory of rationalization has enormous relevance to contemporary conditions and has even proved prophetic and, at the same time, that it is undeveloped as a theory. It remained in his work at a relatively low level of abstraction, amply illustrated at a concrete level with examples of a comparative and historical kind. In consequence, it is entirely feasible to illustrate it in a modern society such as Britain and produce an indefinite amount of evidence in support, and at the same time to remain unsatisfied at a more fundamental level as to our understanding of the underlying mechanisms. It is as if we were to analyse Britain under Thatcher in the same mode as *The Class Struggles in France* (1972) and be without the theoretical developments that were to be laid in *Capital.* It could of course be done, and convincingly at an intuitive level; and if Marx had died at an early age, we might have had to be content with that. But it would have been necessary for others to develop the theory of labour and capital, the tendency of the rate of profit to fall and the growing concentration of capital. The underlying forces would have remained relatively unclarified at the level of the *Grundrisse.*

But if Weber had lived longer would he have written the equivalent of *Capital* for the rationalization thesis? There are two counter-indications. The first is that Weber shared Nietzsche's hostility to the creation of intellectual systems. Nourished though he was like all German intellectuals in the thought of the greatest of all the system builders, Immanuel Kant, and working with the concept that was generative of systemic thought, namely, rationality, in close contact with colleagues like Rickert and Simmel, who laid the foundations for systematic sociology, Weber none the less sided with the hammer of the philosophers, the greatest iconoclast of the modern period. 'I mistrust all systematizers and avoid them. The will to a system is a lack of integrity', was Nietzsche's view in 'Maxims and Arrows', No. 26 (1968). 'A systematic science of culture, even only in the sense of a definitive, objectively valid, systematic fixation of the problems which it should treat, would be senseless in itself', was the frequently quoted view Weber expressed in his essay on 'Objectivity' (1949: 84). The Nietzschean allusion is clear enough when one takes into account that, immediately before, Weber rejects a 'Chinese ossification of intellectual life'. (For Nietzsche, Kant was 'the Chinaman of Koenigsberg'.) But it was characteristic of the strenuous efforts that Weber made to mediate between Kant and Nietzsche that much of his intellectual work was systematic to a high degree. The basic concepts of sociology are only the most brilliant example of a formidable drive to consistency and comprehensiveness. The other counter-indication to the promise of theoretical development cut short by Weber's early death is hinted at in that citation from the 'Objectivity' essay. Marx's *Capital* offered a logical analysis of economic relations in the spirit of positive science. Weber acknowledged the possibility of a purely rational economic science, in the sense of a model of activity calculatedly chosen to maximize economic ends, and it was one of the inspirations of his thinking about the methods of social science. But he never developed the idea that similar models might be extended to the sciences of human action in general and more particularly to culture. We can only speculate about what he would have made of the development of linguistics, semiotics, conversational analysis, ethnomethodology, structuralism, or systems theory in general as applied to human social relations. He might have taken them on board in the same spirit as he accepted axiomatic sciences such as jurisprudence or ethics, but any elaborated theory of rationalization would have been bound to take on a different quality from a positivistically conceived economic science.

Weber's thesis was very much a historical one, backed up by a theory of motivation that was adequate at the level of meaning to explain how it was that human beings sought salvation through ascetic innerworldly activity. The evidence of rationality in the West was there for any student to see without any need to devote special attention to the concept. Of course there was the difficulty that what was rational from one point of view might not be from another but, looked at in the round, the growth of rationality was as obvious as the growth of industry or the rise of the modern state. It had a philosophical basis in the Enlightenment; through the advance of science it was successful in pushing back the influence of religion; and through the twin disciplines of market rationality and bureaucracy the rational mode of everyday life became all-pervasive. This was the very characteristic quality of the modern world and could be illustrated in whatever sector one chose, in music, or sex, or architecture.

It is the historical specificity of his analysis coupled with the taken-for-granted nature of the concept of rationality that makes it difficult to sum up Weber's rationalization thesis. But recently Weber scholars have been able to benefit from the best analysis yet, contained in Jürgen Habermas's *Theorie des kommunikativen Handelns* (1981). He adopts a three-way division of the rationalization process into the societal, cultural and personality. At the societal level modernization involves the independent development of the capitalist economy and the modern state. At the cultural level rationalization involves the growth and application of science but also the autonomous development, guided by their own principles, of art, law and morality. At the personality level a methodical lifestyle originally founded in the religious beliefs of the Protestants becomes dominant.

But what is the rationality that extends its influence into all these life-spheres? Habermas suggests that there are five stages within Weber's idea of practical rationality. They are:

1 Rational technique: the calculated use of means.
2 Technical progress: the use of more effective means.
3 Rational choice of ends: choice on the basis of knowledge and precise calculation (as in formally rational economic activity).
4 Life-guiding principles: action guided by generalized value principles.
5 Rational–methodical lifestyle: the unification of the previous four rational steps in a fifth in which they are balanced and their joint success is ensured.

These five points taken together make up Weber's view of practical rationality according to Habermas, but they do not exhaust the rationalization concept since Weber does not confine the idea of rationality to action, but applies it also to symbolic systems. There are then two further elements:

6 The formal structuring of symbolic systems: both professional systems of knowledge and the systematization of beliefs about the world.
7 Value–intensification: the increasing elaboration of knowledge and value–spheres such as art, law and morality (1981 Vol. 1: 225–61).

Habermas's account is of course embedded within a major project that is designed to promote a fundamental shift in the focus of social theory from technically rational action towards full and free communication within social relationships. This is undoubtedly a project with long-term importance, and this is not the place to engage in a detailed examination of it. There is every reason to think that the elaboration of the idea of communicative action takes us beyond Weber's conceptualization of action with its renowned four types of purposive–rationality, value–rationality, affectual and traditional action. But Habermas's intentions do lead him to emphasize along with many others that Weber's account 'investigates the rationalization of action systems solely from the aspect of purpose rationality' (1981 Vol. 2: 449). This judgement sits rather uneasily next to Habermas's account, which we have already set out, with its mention of value–principles and the formalization of symbolic systems. If we look a little more closely at how this judgement of Habermas and many others comes about, we will gain a better idea of the inner structure of Weber's idea of rationality. This will aid us with the purpose of this section, namely, advancing the rationalization thesis.

There is no doubt that purposive–rationality had the central place in Weber's thinking about rationality, but it would be wrong to conclude that he accorded it some metaphysical primacy. Weber had his own methodological reasons for emphasizing action in pursuit of specific goals as the most important source of ideal types in the social sciences. Economics provided him with the obvious exemplar for this way of thinking. But the essay in which he could speak of this form of action as 'rational', and equally the way in which Habermas and the rest of us go along with this usage, requires explanation if we are to understand how 'rational purposive action' and all the other elements of rationality could be taken to belong together.

In fact there was a set of assumptions underlying Weber's usage of which he was quite aware, which he did not have to spell out and which has largely been hidden from our view. The idea of rationality that he drew on had been elaborated in the eighteenth century above all by Kant. In the notion of human reason he brought together both scientific knowledge and moral rules, each governed by the idea of law. The most succinct statement of this outlook was possibly contained in *The Foundations of the Metaphysics of Morals* (1785) in Kant (1949). What a profound confidence, a sense of stating the undisputed nature of the way things are, is contained in this assertion:

> Everything in nature works according to laws. Only a rational being has the capacity of acting according to the conception of laws, i.e. according to principles. This capacity is will. Since reason is required for the derivation of actions from laws, will is nothing else than practical reason.
>
> (Kant 1949: 72)

Kant's critiques established reason as the unifying factor between nature and humanity, and made the understanding of both dependent on transcendental ideas such as universal causality and perfect freedom. The reason the tag 'rational' could be applied by Weber so easily to action where means were chosen to achieve purposes was that for Kant reason was exhibited in two related respects. Knowledge of means involves knowledge of laws, 'how nature works', and that knowledge is advanced by science, which is governed by transcendental ideas. It is a faculty of the human mind that permits the discovery of laws in nature. Second, the employment of those laws for an end of whatever kind is an objective principle valid for every rational being. 'Whoever wills the end, so far as reason has decisive influence on his action, wills also the indispensably necessary means to it that lie in his power' (Kant 1949: 76). This is the basic principle of Kant's famous hypothetical imperative.

Now this terminology and way of thinking are entirely familiar to Weber, as to his generation as a whole in so far as they had received a high-school education. It is therefore no coincidence that we find Kant's doctrine of the hypothetical imperative virtually restated in his essay of 1917 on value–

freedom. There he outlined the fundamentally non-evaluative nature of scientific propositions in economics, stating the causal proposition 'in order to attain the end x . . . under conditions b1, b2, and b3, y1, y2, and y3 are the only or the most effective means' is the simple inversion of 'x, under conditions b1, b2, and b3, is produced by y1, y2, and y3. For these say exactly the same thing, and the "man of action" can derive his prescriptions from them quite easily' (Weber 1949: 45). Both Kant and Weber term this a purely 'technical' problem.

As I have acknowledged, there is good reason for saying that Weber gave technical imperatives or what Kant also termed principles of skill a prime place in his ordering of science and his understanding of the world. But it would be altogether wrong to suggest that he ignored or was uninfluenced by the other side of Kant's doctrine of practical reason, the principles of morality summed up in the idea of the categorical imperative. What one misses in Habermas's account is a sense for the generative factors underlying Weber's idea of value–rationality. For the way Weber applied the tag 'rational' to action that adhered to values is fully comprehensible only within the framework of Kantian philosophy. Anglo-Saxon empiricism and utilitarianism always have difficulty with this idea. It is symptomatic that Weber says about value–rational action that it always involves 'commands' or 'demands' (Weber 1968a: 25). Action is being measured against a rule that it is expected to express. Habermas does point to 'direction by principles' (1981 Vol. 1: 244) in this context and recognizes that the combination of *Zweckrationalität* and *Wertrationalität* forms part of the rational–methodical lifestyle of the ascetic Protestant, but he does not go on to accord 'following rules' the key place it has within the Weberian idea of rationality.

For Kant the supreme product of human reason was the idea of the undetermined human subject freely following the rules of duty or moral obligation. The human personality developed through that free choice of adhering to principles. The subject was also the transcendental premise of understanding nature through laws. Reason, borne by the subject, provided the unity of the moral and natural worlds. Weber's two types of action are 'rational' because they are derived directly from this Kantian idea of reason. They are almost direct parallels to the hypothetical and categorical imperatives. There is ample indication in Weber's work that this heritage of Kantian thinking was taken for granted, not so much as a doctrine but as a mode of discourse. Following rules was rational in itself and needed no explanation. 'Bureaucratic authority is specifically rational in the sense of being bound to intellectually analysable rules; while charismatic authority is specifically irrational in the sense of being foreign to all rules' (Weber 1968a: 244), says Weber at one point. As I have pointed out elsewhere (Albrow 1970: 61–6), a neglect of this facet of Weber's understanding of rationality led Anglo-Saxon theorists in particular to believe that he was advancing a theory of organizational efficiency when he set out his ideal type of bureaucracy. It is clear that

Weber adhered firmly to the Kantian theory of personality too with its emphasis on freedom through self-imposed rules. That position was set out firmly in his rejection of Knies's view that human personality introduced unpredictability into history (Weber 1973: 132).

Laws of nature and principles of action are at the heart of the Weberian idea of rationality. Each permit logical inference to be drawn about the relation of particular acts to a rule; and rules themselves, being part of discourse, may be brought into logical relations with each other. But that idea of rationality was not worked out by Weber from first principles. Rather it was a complex notion handed down over generations, an elaborate frame of thought, most fully expounded, although not by any means exclusively, by Kant, on which Weber could draw without embarrassment, without the need to forge systematic relations because he could take it for granted that they were already there. It is not therefore some special frailty of Weber's thought that the ideas of rationality and rationalization present themselves in a wide variety of contexts and formulations. Those were all sides of the multi-faceted idea of rationality as it presented itself to him in the culture of his time. This is not to say that those formulations are unsystematically related, but only that if the system that was there is to be revealed, then some archaeological work has to be done on the idea. Weber was drawing on a cultural resource, not inventing a new theory. He never claimed to be a philosopher, but he was drawing upon the product of philosophy.

If we attend to the roots of Weber's idea of rationality we are able to resolve the puzzlement that sometimes arises when rationality is found to inhere both in practical action and in symbolic systems. The obvious but fundamental and often ignored point is that reason belongs to the world of thought and that action becomes rational in so far as it is governed by that world. To be rational the act must be regulated by values, clearly conceived purposes, oriented to knowledge. Rationality is conferred on the act by its location within the symbolic systems. On the Kantian account, rationality belongs without question to the ideal world, and it is that world which it systematizes first of all.

> Reason is impelled by a tendency of its nature to go out beyond the field of its empirical employment, and to venture in a pure employment, by means of ideas alone, to the utmost limits of all knowledge, and not to be satisfied save through a completion of its course in a self-subsistent systematic whole.
>
> (Kant 1787: A797, B825)

Reason was bound to tend towards systematic unity, which is 'what first raises ordinary knowledge to the rank of science' (ibid.: A832, B860). Reason is the 'higher faculty of knowledge', the rational as opposed to the empirical or historical (ibid.: A835, B863). Only in the most artificial way, therefore, can one talk of the isolated act of purposive—rationality. For to accord rationality to an act is to recognize its place within a framework of knowledge and belief.

While the Kantian foundations of Weber's thinking about rationality have been inadequately exposed, it is some testimony to their strength that what has happened in the subsequent development of Weberian ideas is that the systematic underpinnings have been developed afresh. In particular the examination of *Zweckrationalität* has led to the demand that the systematic relations of that concept with rational systems of action as a whole should be analysed and that rationality as a regulative idea in social systems should be given full recognition. In fact this illustrates very well that inherent drive towards expansion and unity which Kant attributed to rationality. The quests for universality, comprehensive laws, inclusive theories and exhaustive categorizations may all be seen as part of what he called the architechtonic of pure reason, and they have been pursued relentlessly to this day.

Instead therefore of delving into the archaeology of Weber's rationalization thesis as contained in the Kantian and idealist tradition, it is equally possible for us to act as architects on it, to develop and improve it, to construct a theoretical edifice adequate for the vastly increased scope, power and comprehensiveness of the rationalized society of our own time. We can, in other words, engage in what Weber called *Wertsteigerung,* or value–intensification, which is what he understood to happen in the modern world as value standpoints became increasingly explicit, their implications developed and made more rational. The rationalization process in general may indeed be seen as the intensification of rationality, in the generic cognitive value of which all particular value–intensifications shared.

This chapter can only begin to indicate what might be involved in a theoretical statement of rationality–intensification that would be adequate for the world sixty-five years after Weber's death. It is, however, helped by the fact that considerable progress in this direction has been made through the prodigious efforts of Niklas Luhmann. In his work we can discover a highly elaborated argument for locating rationality in social systems rather than in individual purposes. He draws on the Parsonian analysis of the relations between the individual actor and action systems and combines that with the decision-making perspectives of organization theory. The outcome is a general theory of system rationality in which the uncertainties and complexity, which would attach to individual purposive action were the environment and other people to be unpredictable, are replaced by institutionalized expectations of behaviour that are stabilized over time, objects and people. The actions in which people engage then become part of the wider system, and their rationality is attributed on the basis not of hidden motives but of their relation to the durable and consistent set of normative expectations.

Luhmann's examination of trust provides a good example of his treatment of rationality. It would be wrong, he says, to see this ubiquitous social phenomenon as simply 'a means that can be chosen for particular ends, much less an end/means structure capable of being optimized'; he calls for a more widely conceived sociological theory of rationalization, such as yet does not exist where 'the evaluation "rational" could follow from functional analysis' (Luhmann 1979: 88). Trust and its alternative, mistrust, serve to stabilize a system order that is suited to the capacities of human beings for action. It is like learning, symbolizing and controlling in that it structures the processing of experience. 'Systems are rational to the extent that they can encompass and reduce complexity' (ibid.: 93). The point is not that trust is *per se* rational but that it is one of the mechanisms available within systems of action that permit human beings to proceed about their daily lives, fulfilling their purposes and coping with the complexity of the world around. It is the system as a whole that is rational. It is not my intention to offer a detailed application of Luhmann's system rationality concept to modern conditions. He says that the 'prevailing empirical–descriptive orientation of sociological research' does not provide the necessary preparatory work for this more widely conceived theory of rationalization (ibid.: 88). It is unfortunately also the case that his own theory is not in the kind of codified form that makes it easy to apply. He is surely pointing in the direction in which an intensification of rationalization can be more effectively interpreted by moving away from the individual actor to the system. But it is difficult to avoid the impression that he has moved too far and at too fast a pace in two respects at least. The first is that the systemic character of human action is, in any individual instance, as problematic as the rational character of an individual action. The specification of the dimensions of an administrative rationality, for instance, has taken place in the context of innumerable case studies, which show the shifting nature of criteria and boundaries.

Second, Luhmann is so anxious to attach rationality to social, rather than to individual, action systems that he tends to miss a much more obvious reason for stressing the systemic nature of the concept. Reason belongs to the realm of thought. Not only does it belong to that realm, it is the very principle that provides systematic unity to human ideas. I suspect that Kant would have regarded modern definitions of system as 'any set of interrelated units' as fundamentally defective. 'By a system,' he said, 'I understand the unity of the manifold modes of knowledge under one idea. This idea is the concept provided by reason' (Kant 1787: A832, B860).

The philosophical and mathematical knowledge arising out of reason was for Kant the intrinsically rational, and in so far as that rational knowledge was applied to human behaviour, so far could one call it rational. That rational knowledge is, however, fundamentally systemic, binding individuals together, carried through human history, stored in institutions. Mathematics, logic, the natural and social sciences, law, the systems of religion, administration, and the skills and technology of everyday life make up that total accumulation of knowledge which one can call human rationality.

This train of thought must lead to the conclusion that we are able to address the issue of rationalization of the modern world rather more directly than Luhmann would suggest. We ought to be able to examine contemporary forms of life and ask ourselves, how far do they exhibit more advanced forms of rationality? In what sectors do we identify the intensification of rationality? Can we find more powerful calculation in production whether for needs or demands? Are the modes of interrelation between the sectors of society more highly co-ordinated? We are a long way from confining rationality to technical action and we are able to recognize the rationality of social systems when the case arises. But we do need to preserve a greater distance between the idea of rationality and the degree of rationalization that society exhibits, if only to ensure that an advance in our knowledge of the one can enhance our understanding of the other.

3.2 TWO CONTEMPORARY CASES OF RATIONALIZATION

What is being proposed here is a much more open-ended approach to rationality and rationalization than either offering illustrations of Weberian points in 1985 or alternatively developing an updated concept of rationality for the modern world and then applying it. The first can readily be done, as my paper on Britain showed (1982). The second is a major undertaking, as Luhmann's work demonstrates, and runs the danger of going beyond adequate empirical specification. In the following two cases an alternative procedure will be adopted. In the same spirit as Weber I am going to take a sector of social life that manifestly exhibits rationality in the Kantian sense of being guided by ideas of reason, logic, mathematics, regularity, calculability, coherence, systematic interconnectedness and so on. No attempt will be made to provide an inventory, let alone a general theoretical account of those ideas. They are all included within what Kant meant by reason, but they have been developed far beyond his own formulations. Moreover the development of reason in institutional form has gone beyond any general theory of rationality. That, indeed, is the justification for the approach being offered here. It is simultaneously empirical and analytical. It analyses cases to permit the gradual eliciting of a concept of rationality as already embedded in the institutional life of the modern world.

Apart from the rational organization of economic life, bureaucracy was for Weber the most pervasive expression of institutionalized rationality. It operated on the basis of both rules and knowledge, decisions being made by qualified people on the basis of systematically gathered information and legal–rational rules. In Weber's words: 'the only decisive point for us is that in principle a system of rationally debatable "reasons" stands behind every act of bureaucratic administration, namely, either subsumption under norms, or a weighing of ends and means' (1978: 979). There could not be a better expression of the Kantian origins of Weber's thought. One facet of bureaucracy was the accumulation of knowledge, not only technical, but also in the form of a store of documentary information gathered in the course of routine administration. Factors such as the development of modern means of communication and the development of the office and files as the focus for work were also intimately connected with the rise of bureaucracy. We do not have to look far in modern bureaucracy to see the onward march of rationalization. In particular, methods of processing information have developed at an astonishing rate with the development of the computer and the replacement of the filing cabinet by the disk storage of data. The first case of contemporary rationalization I wish to examine relates to data storage.

The modern computer not only makes it possible for state, commercial and other organizations to store enormously increased amounts of information about individuals, but also permits collation of data on a vastly increased scale. There has been a widespread response to this potential in the form of alarm that it could be used to supply information by the collation of data from several sources to damage individuals. Already a convention of countries within the Council of Europe has tried to set standards for the processing of data, and national legislation has been passed. In Britain this has taken the form of the Data Protection Act 1984 (United Kingdom, 1984). This Act sets out data protection principles, establishes a system for the registration and supervision of data users and computer bureaux, accords rights to data subjects and allows for exemptions from all or part of the Act.

By a series of preliminary definitions the Act provides for an enormously extended scope for state interest in computerized information. It defines data as 'information recorded in a form in which it can be processed by equipment operating automatically in response to instructions given for that purpose'. Personal data are defined as 'information which relates to a living individual', the data subject, and the data user 'controls the contents and use of data' that is to be processed automatically. The Act goes on to prohibit the holding of personal data unless the data user has registered with the Data Protection Registrar and has described the data, their sources and proposed use, providing for access to the data to all data subjects.

The Act is designed to enforce the implementation of a set of principles to be observed by data users. In brief these provide

1 for the fair and lawful obtaining and processing of data;
2 that data should be held for specific purposes only;
3 for disclosure of data only in accord with those purposes;
4 that data should be adequate and not excessive to the purposes;
5 that data should be accurate and up to date;
6 that data should not be retained longer than necessary;
7 that data subjects should have access and rights to amend inaccuracies.

Additionally, computer bureaux are obliged to take appropriate security measures against improper access, damage or loss of data.

These principles provide an impressive instance of the development of institutionalized rationality. They enshrine specificity of purpose as a state-imposed principle on data users whether or not the data user is gathering data for the state. It is not a particular purpose or set of purposes for which legislation is being passed, but the general category of specific purposes. Principles 2–6 all provide at the most abstract level for the rationalization of information-gathering and -processing by anyone for any purpose, provided the data relate to individuals and are machine processed. The European Convention, to which the United Kingdom is a signatory, allows for the extension of the principles to data about companies and manually held data. Were these extensions implemented then the framework for a comprehensive information system for the social life of a nation-state would be largely complete. As it is, the state has provided a major impetus to rationalizing the information systems of all collective and individual systems of action by providing a sanctioned set of principles: specificity; relevance; adequacy; accuracy; and temporality. These were not set out explicitly by Weber as principles of rationality, but they are clearly an elaboration on the concept as he understood it. What has happened is that the technical progress represented by the modern computer, when harnessed to considerations of the rights of individuals, generates argument and reflection leading to the elaboration of the idea of rationality. In other words, rationality does not develop in the abstract as some ideal force, but is the ongoing outcome of an interplay between technical progress and reasoned argument. In the institutions of society the outcomes of that interplay are recorded and provide the premises for the next stage of the argument.

The Data Protection Act provides not only for a system of registration for data users, but also a regulating agency in the person of the Data Protection Registrar with the power to appoint staff and a Data Protection Tribunal to hear appeals against the Registrar's decisions. Provision is therefore made for the continuous monitoring and control of an institutionalized set of rational principles. In Britain at present all bodies concerned with computerized information about individuals are engaged, or ought to be engaged, in identifying their own data protection officers, preparing to justify their holdings of data, checking their security and providing new instructions for staff. The impact of the Act is pervasive and can be far-reaching. Yet as one commentator notes, 'the number of cases of reported misuse is very small, and in most of those the misuse could have occurred equally well with manual files' (Elbra 1984: 9). Indeed, the significance of the Act may well be in respect of the established machinery and the consequences this has for constituting practices rather than in respect of reinforcing individual rights. In fact the Act itself establishes a range of exceptions to the non-disclosure principles that makes sense only in terms of interests of state which are enhanced through the new machinery. A law to protect individual rights simultaneously increases state power, and we shall need to look at this in reviewing that other facet of Weber's rationalization thesis, the loss of meaning and freedom for the individual.

The second instance of the intensification of rationality in the modern world that I wish to examine briefly involves a response to the penetration of science into an area that in Weber's time had not yet been subjected to extensive rationalization. Research into the transmission of inherited characteristics was something Weber acknowledged was possible but had as yet produced nothing to substantiate the wild racial hypotheses that were current. He did not consider the possibility of human intervention in the genetic material of the human race. But in our own time this possibility exists and has been put into practice in a small way in the treatment of infertility in married couples. The use of frozen semen either from the husband or from another donor has been practised freely in Britain and elsewhere. In 1982 the Royal College of Obstetricians and Gynaecologists knew of more than 1,000 pregnancies where a donor other than the husband was involved. A more recent development known as *in vitro* fertilization (IVF) permits fertilization to take place outside the womb and for the embryo produced to be transferred back to the womb for further development. This technique can be used so that a woman may bear a child who is the product of another woman's egg and her own husband's semen. Or further, a woman may bear a child who is the product entirely of another couple's genetic material. The capacity to produce human embryos in a test-tube opens up a chain of research possibilities that include genetic engineering, the production of genetically identical human beings (cloning), the use of other species for gestation, the use of embryos for testing drugs and the production of hybrids with other species. Public anxiety about these actual and potential developments led to a recent government report in Britain by the Committee of Inquiry into Human Fertilization and Embryology, chaired by the philosopher Mary Warnock (Warnock 1984).

The recommendations of the Warnock Committee are that a new licensing authority should be established to regulate all infertility services and related research. Principles for the provision of services are set out including anonymity of the donor, limitation on the number of embryos to be produced from any one donor's semen or eggs, limitations on the storage time for embryos and the creation of a donor register. Research should also be regulated by placing limitations on the use of the embryo, prohibiting its sale and purchase and in general ensuring that all research is subject to restrictions imposed by the licensing authority. It was further proposed that legislation should be introduced to, among other things, make legitimate any child born by donor insemination and to make the woman giving birth and her husband the legal parents of the child, to outlaw surrogate motherhood agreements and to allow the storage authority to use or dispose of eggs, semen, or embryos under certain circumstances without donor permission.

However far the subject matter goes beyond what Weber envisaged, he would have had no difficulty in recognizing the character of the argument with which the report was prefaced. In spite of the high feelings associated with the subject the foreword argues that moral reasoning has an important place, although 'matters of ultimate value are not susceptible of proof' (Warnock 1984: 2). That reasoning is held to produce principles that establish the barriers or limits beyond which people may not go. While there might be argument about the precise nature of those limits, it is held that everyone accepts that limits there must be. It is in general an argument for value—rationality, an exposition of basic principles constituting moral life. But that argument is advanced at two levels. One is that the principles enunciated do correspond with the sentiments of at least some people. The other is that it is better for some principles to be advanced rather than none at all and that incorporated in legislation they can provide a broad framework for action. In Weber's terms a general need for 'legitimate order' is being postulated, in Luhmann's it is system—rationality, the provision of clear premisses for individual decision-making. Whether the law corresponds to the individual's moral sentiments or not, at least it provides a calculable answer to the problem of what is allowed.

'Some principles or other', 'some barrier', 'some limits' would indeed appear to be the preferred basis for the committee's proposals. To the question of 'where do you draw the line?' the answer tends to be 'it does not matter where, as long as it is somewhere'. That clearly is the case in respect of the date beyond which experiments may not be conducted on a live human embryo. The time limit proposed is fourteen days, one day before the formation of the primitive streak in the embryonic disc. This is justified as the 'beginning of individual development of the embryo' (Warnock 1984: 66), but different bodies suggested different limits, and it is difficult to detect convincing arguments for one rather than the other. Similarly, limits of five years for the review of egg and semen stores are proposed and ten years for embryo storage, without any convincing arguments for those limits rather than others. Public alarm was caused by reports of the possibility of producing hybrids of human and other animal species, and the report recommends making such production a criminal offence. One may suggest that the barrier proposed here corresponds to a much more primitive barrier in human culture and to an anxiety with roots in the myths of many cultures, which have imagined such combinations as man and goat, man and bull, woman and fish.

The conclusion of the report provides the best warrant for saying that it is system—rationality that is the main concern. The licensing authority is the linchpin of the whole set of proposals. 'None of our other recommendations can have any practical impact until such a body is set up' (Warnock 1984: 79).

The tasks of the new body would essentially be to provide guidance on good practice in the infertility field and to issue licences to provide infertility treatment or to undertake research on human semen, eggs or embryos. The body should consider setting up a central register of children born as a result of the new techniques, and in the case of applicants for research licences it should satisfy itself on their suitability to carry out such research, with the applicant being 'obliged to indicate clearly the objectives of the research' (1984: 78). In other words, we are dealing with both the technical and the ethical rationalization of scientific research at the level of the society as a whole. In part the proposals are couched in the language of the rights of individuals, to be legitimately born, to have children in their own name, but the measures proposed create a social mechanism that vastly increases the potential for state control. As with the case of data protection this needs to be evaluated in the light of Weber's fears for individual freedom.

The two cases I have taken provide interesting leads as to the directions in which Weber's rationalization thesis can be developed. In the first place they provide evidence for the extension of rationality into spheres far beyond the experience of his time. A computerized information system covering all individuals in a nation-state and the regulation of the scientific control of human genetic material extend the frontiers of rationalization considerably beyond anything Weber conceived. At the same time an intensification of rationality is implemented through the establishment of the rational monitoring and control of rationalization. Rationality is not merely a principle constituting legislative enactment, providing grounds for any particular law. It has now become the very topic of legislation. That was envisaged by Weber in the context of the codification of legal rules. But in the cases we have taken, rationality assumes an even more dynamic aspect.

In the case of the Data Protection Act there is provision for establishing the routine reproduction of specificity of purpose through the agency of the Data Protection Registrar. Additionally the Act permits the responsible minister to modify or add to the eight basic principles of data protection. In the case of the Warnock Committee recommendations, the concern is primarily with providing a regulating machinery, which can then develop its own procedures, and ultimately for arguing the case for some regulation of whatever kind. In both cases one can say that at the most basic level the concern is for establishing an agency and rational procedures that will guarantee the rationalization of conduct as a continuing process, whether on a normative or an expediential basis.

In both cases rationality is being worked through on the most general level possible. At that level certain themes such as purposiveness or monitoring recur. These do not appear in codified form, but one may infer from their recurrence that a theory of rationality appropriate for the institutionalized forms of the modern period would put them in a definite relationship with each other. It may be useful to offer the following preliminary listing:

1 Definition of the set of system units: even with data and embryos, ultimately these are brought into relation with a definite set of living individuals.

2 Generation of principles: provision is made for the ongoing generation of normative principles.

3 Production of purposiveness: aimless or alien activity has no place in the system, and purposiveness becomes a requirement.

4 Enforcing specificity: at every level anything that would make precise calculation difficult is eliminated as far as it can be.

5 Regulation of conduct: human conduct is made regular through regulation and sanctions.

6 Monitoring of performance: provision is made for gathering information to evaluate the effectiveness of the regulation.

7 Reproduction of the system: whether for data or for embryos provision is made for producing new material and destroying the old.

I would argue that this set of seven themes represents an intensification of the idea of rationality as it was to be found in both Kant's and later Weber's formulations. In conclusion I will turn briefly to some of the wider issues involved in the rationalization thesis: the question of the loss of meaning, the decline of freedom and the place of irrationality. For these are the questions that finally delimit the theoretical scope of the rationalization thesis.

3.3 THE BOUNDS OF RATIONALITY

In Weber's view bureaucratic organization was the animate machine that corresponded to the inanimate machine of the factory and fabricated the shell of bondage encasing the modern worker. Since his time the animate machine has been harnessed even more tightly to the inanimate through the application of the computer to administrative settings. Both kinds of machine Weber termed 'objectified mind' (*geronnener Geist*). Both were constituted by human rationality and, in that, their eventual convergence was an ever present possibility. His own evaluation of this situation shared the prevailing pessimism of German intellectuals in the latter part of the nineteenth century. For Kant the growth of reason meant the enhancement of human freedom; for Weber rules meant bondage, work for purposes that the individual had not set under conditions not freely chosen. Sometimes this is viewed as Weber taking over Marx's theory of alienation. It is fairer to see them both sharing the intellectual's distrust of the products of an intellectualized society, where rationality had been harnessed to the production of social life.

If the intensification of rationalization in social life corresponds to Weber's anticipation in so many respects, it is none the less the case that we ought to treat the idea of a concomitant loss of meaning in social life with the utmost caution. Purposiveness and normative regulation must on any analysis be prime elements in endowing individual lives with meaning. Both functionalist and phenomenological approaches to this issue will lead to suggesting that individual purposiveness derives its strength from the social production of meaning. One might indeed suggest that so institutionalized is purposiveness in modern social life that if anything there is an over-production of meaning. The Warnock Committee took evidence from organizations interested in human fertilization as diverse as the Royal College of Surgeons, the Mothers' Union, the International Planned Parenthood Federation, Action for Lesbian Parents and the Catholic Marriage Advisory Council. More than 200 organizations and nearly 700 individuals made submissions to the committee. The issues associated with the unborn child are in fact capable of mobilizing mass support in opposing directions and impinge directly on political life in many Western societies. But that is only one issue, and the proliferation of interest groups each with their own causes, large numbers of which adopt rationalized methods of administration, that mass of cross-cutting affiliations for the individual in modern society, has not begun to be documented.

Even if we accept that the employing organization is the most significant association for framing an individual's activities in modern society, it is by no means established that the modern employee is alienated from work. It was William Whyte (1956) who pointed out that the social ethic had replaced the Protestant ethic for the large organization. There is no need to repeat here the numerous ways in which Weberian notions of formal organization or Taylor-type scientific management have been supplanted in both theory and practice. What may be conceded is that employment and the life cycle have been dissociated in the modern world, and Weber placed great emphasis on providing a meaning for death in life. That issue does need far more analysis. There are paradoxes here, for the organization is successful in managing the entry and exit of members and in providing a framework of purposive activity that outlives them. Death may have become irrelevant in the modern organization but only because its purposes outlive people.

Equally problematical is the issue of the loss of freedom. The Data Protection Act provides an example of the contingent way that issue may be related to rationality. The Act provides for a range of exceptions to its provisions. A minister may exempt people from the provisions and safeguards of the Act on the grounds of national security, while the prevention or detection of crime provides exemption from both subject-access and non-disclosure provisions. There are different ways in which these exemptions can be evaluated. From one point of view, if the Act is seen as providing new rights and safeguards then the exemptions do no more than leave the situation of the individual as it was in those respects. But to judge the situation in this way is to neglect the fact that the machinery for the registration of personal data, created to ensure the rights, remains in existence for the exemptions. The capacity has been created for a national personal data system, and the effect of the Act is to allow this new machinery to be used for security and law-and-order purposes. How it will be used will depend on factors outside the definitions of the Act. In a similar way the creating of a licensing and registration authority for infertility research and services with rights in the storage and use of genetic material opens the way for the state control of genetic engineering.

In my paper on rationalization in Britain (1982) I argued that the relations of rationality and freedom in the case of individuals depended upon the organization of control and access to positions of control, in particular through educational provision. Making institutions more rational opens up the possibility of universal understanding, provided there is universal access to the means of obtaining that understanding. It is not reasonable to reject the possibility that rational administration does genuinely provide a predictable environment for individual decision-making and therefore enhances the scope for individual action on the part of the citizen. But access to appropriate education is greatly differentiated, and, linked with that as both condition and result, the material means for making use of the freedom provided by the rationalized state are distributed in unequal fashion. Any attempt to resolve the argument about rationality and freedom that isolates this formal issue from the material facts of the ownership and control of property runs the risk of lapsing into either Enlightenment optimism or Weberian pessimism. The prospects for individual freedom in the light of continuing rationalization and the issue of the relative power enjoyed by different groups and classes in society should not be analysed in artificial isolation from each other.

Of course Weber did not ignore countervailing and contradictory factors in the rationalization process. Conflicts between groups are in part taken up in his account of the conflict of value–spheres. The rationalization of different life–spheres may on his account result in their growing contradictions, as in the classic example of the nation-state and the market economy, which he addressed in his inaugural lecture. However far the rationalization of social systems proceeds there will be material irrationalities. Population trends, resource limitations, health factors, the outcomes of market processes and of other conflicts, the shifts in public moods, all provide either the boundaries or the material for rational action but are outside the prescriptive rules of rationality. Just as at the individual level the capacities and strength that reason can mould provide limits to action, so at the societal level it is not possible for system–rationality to provide a closed and eternally predictable environment. Indeed, as formal rationality grows, there is good reason to think that material irrationalities increase equivalently. Any attempt to develop the theory of rationalization will need equally to theorize the irrationalities of the modern world. It would be a fatal mistake to imagine that the one is an alternative, much less a conclusive negation, of the other. So long as human culture survives, rationality and irrationality are locked in a dialectical embrace.

4

REDEFINING AUTHORITY
FOR POST-WEBERIAN
CONDITIONS[4]

4.1 THE PIVOTAL PLACE OF LEGAL–RATIONAL AUTHORITY IN MODERNITY

We have seen how Weber's account of the rationalization process provides a basis for understanding rationalization since his time. But it can be no part of the sociology of organization to claim that Weber has provided a permanent canon for interpreting the ongoing present. He uniquely, compared with others, gained the measure of his own time and of trends which persisted for decades, because as many have recognized he was in tune with central themes of modernity. But modernity has lost its centrality in the shaping of our time.

We can in retrospect see how right he was to identify rational–legal bureaucracy as the key organizational control structure in modernity. But it is that form of bureaucracy which has lost its prestige and supremacy in recent decades. Weber centred modern bureaucracy on a clear hierarchy of functionally defined offices, occupied by qualified career officials under contracts. He regarded that as being in a reciprocally supportive relationship with the rationalization process.

In 1970 it was still possible to say that 'the argument must be regarded as evenly balanced' as to whether this relationship would hold for the future.

> The growth of sciences of decision-making, of operational research, of schools of management amounts to an intensification of the importance of science in administration – of formal rationality. On the other hand, it is undeniably true that he did not see a possible conflict between the growth of formal rules and the application of scientific knowledge. Indeed modern emphasis on the necessity of giving experts a free hand, on flexibility in administration, on job enlargement, on increasing discretion, runs counter to Weber's predictions of ever-increasing formalization.
>
> (Albrow 1970: 66)

Since then we can say that the argument has been settled. It is not simply that bureaucracy has become more flexible, the principles of hierarchy and career officials have been dethroned by networking, delayering, team work, open recruitment and contracting out. There is now no template for administrative structure. Government is being reinvented.

But the change is even more fundamental. Weber's account of bureaucracy was grounded in a theory of the legitimacy of authority, and in the modern period this meant obedience to the law and its agents. His theory of bureaucracy was of a system of action co-ordinated by commands issued in accord with the law and obeyed without question. Both the adequacy of authority in that sense for the co-ordination of complex organization and the applicability of such a concept of authority for contemporary conditions are now as open to question as his concept of bureaucracy.

Indeed, if 'Weber was one step ahead of his critics in offering a general theory of modern culture' (ibid.: 65), we have to acknowledge now that the transformation in culture since his time means that we have to reassess the overall relevance of his organizational theory. Not just the account of bureaucracy comes into question but also old modern rational organization, old modern political and economic structures in the broadest sense, and old modern culture generally. As Weber said, authority influenced a far wider area of social life than was usually recognized, including language and writing, and, through schools and parents, the shaping of youth and therefore people (Weber 1956: 123–4). In other words, authority was the pivotal concept in his theory of modern society.

Weber's sociology operated with the point/counterpoint of historical narrative for his time and precise analytical concepts for comparative purposes. This chapter seeks to be true to the spirit of that endeavour. But Weber recognized that the time- and culture-bound imagination of the scholar meant that it was bound to be renewed by every generation. He acknowledged in principle that concepts would undergo change even as he was unable to envisage what change was likely. From his perspective rational modernity was intensifying with no apparent limit even while irrational factors became more obvious. His historical narrative developed through use of an array of analytical concepts such as rationality, action, authority and legitimacy which were in tune with his time. But modernity is no longer the central feature of the history of the present and the analytical concepts which went with it have correspondingly less purchase on our time. In no case is this more true than with his idea of authority.

Weber's definitions of authority went through several versions which betray his recognition that the slightest change in nuance had profound consequences for the rest of his theory. His last formulation was as follows:

Authority (*Herrschaft*) shall mean the likelihood of a command with a specific content finding obedience from identifiable persons.

(Weber 1956: 28)

In a slight amplification he wrote, 'the likelihood of specific (or all) commands finding obedience from an identifiable group of people' (Weber 1956: 122). The difference is actually profound. The small change provides for the case of totalitarian rule. In the same place he emphasizes the central place of obedience by defining it thus:

> Where the action of the one who obeys essentially takes a course as if he had made the content of the command into the maxim of his own conduct, simply because of the formal relationship of obedience, without regard for his personal view on the value or lack of value of the command in itself.
>
> (Weber 1956: 123)

What we have here then in essence is the basis of the statement in self-defence of every agent of authority who, when charged with a crime, says 'I was simply obeying orders'. This was quite distinct from his concept of power which involved only the likelihood that one will could assert itself against another in any possible situation by whatever means. Power, said Weber, was 'sociologically amorphous' and authority was a much more precise concept, relating as it did specifically to commands. The existence of authority depended on someone successfully issuing commands. Sometimes Weber even employs the perfectly usable German word '*Autorität*' as a synonym for '*Herrschaft*' but we should note that Weber is not saying authority is necessarily legitimate.

Indeed, the force of his definition derives from his insistence that obedience means not judging the value of the command. He requires authority to operate automatically, as a machine. This applies whether *Herrschaft* is legitimate or not. To do that he has to push questions of value to a higher level, which he does with his account of legitimacy. In modern authority the removal of obedience from personal valuation was secured even more effectively through the impersonal mechanism of the law. Legal–rational legitimacy, the belief that both the one who issued orders and the one who obeyed were working to a kosmos of abstract and intentionally constructed rules, which permitted precise and definitive application to individual cases, meant that obedience was delivered to law and not to the person in modern authority.

Now Weber knew very well that this machine-like concept of authority was an ideal type, and he acknowledged that in the real world people had many motives for obeying commands quite aside from believing them to be legitimate. Nevertheless even as limiting case he treated this ideal type of rational authority as the animating impulse for the development of modern bureaucracy. Moreover he regarded it as empirically demonstrable that such a body of positive law had indeed developed in which decisions were predeterminable outcomes. The point about legal–rational authority was that the world could be constructed that way, and in Weber's view increasingly it was. It was for him the most powerful form of social ordering and group formation, or, in later terminology, of structuration.

But what if the world is different now?

4.2 ON NOT AMENDING WEBER'S CONCEPT OF AUTHORITY

There can be no denying the power of Weber's account. His is without question the most elaborate and impressive formal conceptualization of authority which we possess. Its purpose was to aid precise thinking about democracy, social order and the state. Coupled with his narrative of social change, the development of modernity up to and including his own time, it has been the most influential non-Marxist political sociology.

Weber's achievement, seen as a contribution to a cumulative social science, appears, then, to invite amendment and amplification. We are often asked to build on him, or to rectify omissions. But I am going to suggest that this can't be done adequately under contemporary conditions. The current tasks of writing the history of the present and developing adequate analytical frameworks make it necessary to depart more fundamentally from what was exemplary at the beginning of the century. The world is now too different and tinkering with Weber's types of authority is not sufficient.

There has been only one significant addition to Weber's three types of authority which, on the basis of the criteria he laid down, could be regarded as a genuine amplification of his scheme, and this was the notion of professional authority which Parsons (Weber 1947: 59) identified and Gouldner (1955a: 24, 187ff., 196ff.) developed later into his notion of representative bureaucracy. In Weber's terms unquestioned acceptance of professional instructions would have to depend on a specific kind of legitimacy belief, crediting the person with technical knowledge rather than, say, extraordinary powers as with charisma. Weber for reasons intrinsic to the German system elided the potential conflict between professional and legal–rational authority by conflating them in his account of bureaucracy. But there is nothing inconsistent with the logic of his procedures if one makes this distinction.

What one cannot do is amplify Weber's account to introduce something called democratic authority. This has consistently puzzled commentators who have felt that Weber was either depreciating democracy or simply missing it by oversight. They are particularly provoked by the fact that Weber introduced a category of value–rational action as one of four types of action but left out value–rationality in identifying only three types of legitimate authority. At one level the reason is simple, as Stephen Turner and Regis Factor (1994: 186) have pointed out: for Weber democracy did not in itself provide a form of administration but only a set of values. But we need to pursue this distinction to gain a fuller appreciation of the importance of this conceptual layering.

We may do this by taking as a good example of such democratic deficit commentary a paper by Martin E. Spencer, who proposes that we supplement Weber's typology with a fourth type, 'value–rational authority which derives from a basic principle, such as natural law, or the consent of the governed' (1970: 133). What Spencer does not do is to ask why Weber might have made such an obvious omission. He was the last one to be casual in his approach to concepts. Indeed, there are good reasons for believing that the omission is both calculated, in that he sees this category as a possibility to be rejected, and cogent, in that it fits his analysis of legitimacy in systems of constitutional government. Moreover, the problems of analysing legitimacy in democratic states, which Spencer feels Weber's account cannot solve, are a major focus for his political writing.

Weber gives full consideration to the relationship of the category of *wertrational* action to the types of authority because it is vital to his analysis of authority to distinguish the variety of motives for obeying commands, or types of compliant action, from the reasons an actor gives for attributing legitimacy to those commands. He makes this important distinction clear in his posthumous (though early) essay, 'The Three Types of Legitimate Rule' (1958c: 1); he refers to it in 'Politics as a Vocation' (1948: 77–128, esp. 79); he devotes a paragraph to it in the third chapter of *The Theory of Social and Economic Organization* (1947: 324–5); and it is this distinction, as Parsons rightly points out, which generates the two classifications of 'legitimate normative orders' in that volume (Weber 1947: 126–32). Spencer neglects this distinction and blurs it by writing of 'attitudes to authority', and indeed writes as if the four motivational categories of action are never considered by Weber in conjunction with authority and as if it is necessary to make the connection for him (1970: 126). The typologies of action and authority are considered together by Weber *because* he wishes to contrast them, as this representative passage shows:

> custom and personal advantage, purely affectual or ideal (*wertrational*) motives of solidarity, do not, even taken together, form a sufficiently reliable basis for a system of imperative co-ordination. In addition there is normally a further element, the belief in legitimacy.
>
> (1947: 325)

He then proceeds to classify types of belief in legitimacy in his famous tripartite scheme of rational, traditional and charismatic.

The deliberateness of this procedure is highlighted by the difference in Weber's treatment of 'legitimate normative order' (henceforward referred to, in agreement with Spencer, as 'norms') and authority. With authority we find a fourfold motivational base and a threefold typology of legitimation, but norms have a fourfold classification both on the motivational base and in the legitimacy schema. Spencer finds rightly that it is *Wertrationalität* which has a place in the classification of the legitimacy of norms, but has no counterpart in the typology of authority.

Now the oddity about this apparent asymmetry is that the category of *Wertrationalität* is an innovation only to be found in those last written but first placed three chapters of *Wirtschaft und Gesellschaft*. Weber uses it to amplify an earlier analysis of action which had concentrated on *Zweckrationalität* (1968b: 427–74). But, since he modifies his action schema with this newly forged category, we would expect him to modify the authority schema similarly, unless he has *good reason* not to do so, especially since the typologies of action and authority are closely associated. Because he does use the new category in the classification of beliefs in the legitimacy of norms, we must surely first hypothesize that Weber has reasons for classifying norms and authority differently. Only if we cannot find these reasons should we consider an alternative explanation of unaccountable omission.

The reasons are clearly discernible, contained in the first instance in Weber's definition of authority. As I have pointed out, at the heart of it is the idea of obedience to commands and obedience in turn is subject to a very precise definition which excludes the possibility of the agent reviewing its justification. This definition makes the notion of value–rational authority a contradiction in terms. Unquestioning obedience involves the renunciation of value standpoints *vis à vis* commands.

The Weberian distinction between action in accord with norms and action in an authority relationship can easily be exemplified. Thus to justify the norm 'contracts should be honoured' one may refer to general conditions of human existence which make the keeping of promises necessary for human well-being, i.e. to some form of natural law, for Weber a *wertrational* justification. An alternative justification is to refer to a law of contract passed by a duly constituted assembly, i.e. legitimacy through legality. But if we consider commands, and imagine the command 'Honour this contract' being obeyed without reference to its content, then it is possible to make only one of the above justifications, i.e. that the command emanated from an authorized source. With legal authority the individual has a generalized preparedness to accept a class of orders from specific persons. No category of 'value–rational authority' is possible. For what would it mean to say that an official obeyed a command to keep a contract because of a personal belief that keeping contracts was morally justified? It would mean subjecting the instructions to be obeyed to some other scrutiny than that of legality. Accepting orders on this basis only would amount to acting in accord with personal values. But then the authority relationship has ceased to exist, by definition, and has been replaced by one of alternating consensus and dissensus on values.

It is no accident that the rise of the category of *Wertrationalität* in Weber's final version of the basic concepts of sociology is paralleled by the omission of the term *Einverständnis* (consensus) which has an important place in the older account (see Weber 1968b: 452–65). He was deliberately recasting his theory to gain the maximum distance from accounts which based social order in some kind of diffuse value consensus. For Weber values were as much a source of disagreement as agreement.

Even where there is agreement on values this does not in itself establish authority relations. 'The good of the people', 'the general will', 'natural justice', etc. do not stipulate who gives orders to whom. One person rather than another has to be designated as a rightful source of commands. Of course legitimizing values are important in maintaining a system of authority, but for clear analysis we must distinguish the different levels of legitimacy. A command may be obeyed because it comes from the holder of an office, this office is established by statute, this statute gains its legality by being properly enacted by an assembly, this assembly in turn is established by a constitution, which in turn may be held to express the will of the people.

But it is a long and tortuous route from the command to the 'will of the people' and Weber often emphasizes the importance of these distinctions of level because he wishes to replace the analysis of legitimacy at the most abstract level with a more empirical account of social interaction. 'For the daily use of authority is primarily: Administration' (Weber 1956: 126). We can see his concern for different levels of analysis of legitimacy in this passage:

> the legitimacy of the power holder to give commands rests upon rules that are rationally established by enactment, by agreement, or by imposition. The legitimation for establishing these rules rests, in turn, upon a rationally established or interpreted 'constitution'.
>
> (Weber 1948: 294)

Spencer seems aware of the problems of levels of analysis when he talks of 'value–rationality' as a 'supervening principle' (1970: 131). But he still falls into the trap of erecting the type of authority Weber excluded as a possibility. He introduces into the typology of authority a category which belongs to a different level of analysis. Certainly if officials infringe values which are commonly held to be expressed in a constitution, their authority may well diminish, but in Weber's terms this no more warrants setting up a new type of authority than reference to the fact that officials only obey commands if they receive their salaries warrants setting up a new type of 'pecuniary authority'.

The merits in terms of precision of Weber's approach become apparent when we consider the problem Spencer sets himself, accounting for 'certain curious waxings and wanings of presidential authority' (ibid.: 129). For we are forced to ask the question Spencer avoids, 'What exactly does it mean to say that a minority president has less "authority"?' Do federal officials and the military leadership refuse to carry out instructions on the ground of their illegitimacy? Only then can we talk of a decline in the president's legal authority, in Weber's terms. Or does it mean that the support of Congress cannot be taken for granted? But for Weber the relations of president and Congress are an example of the limitation of authority by the division of powers.

Presidents have to get Congress to agree. Or does it mean that the party faithful respond less eagerly to the president's appeals? In Weberian terms we are dealing then primarily with the loss of charismatic authority. Or does it mean simply that most voters do not agree with him? Here we are not dealing with a Weberian category of authority at all, but simply with communities of interests and agreements on values which affect a president's strategy in so far as he hopes, or has hopes for someone else, to be elected for the next term of office.

We have no need to resort to an idea like the 'will of the people' in order to understand presidential authority. Weber's approach penetrates the fog of phrases like 'talk of a mandate', the 'somehow suspect' authority of a 'minority president', and reveals them to be what they normally are – mere talk. As he dryly puts it when discussing 'so-called democracy': 'The fact that the head of an association and his staff appear as "servants" of the ruled is naturally no evidence at all against the existence of "authority"' (Weber 1956: 124). His service to the study of power and authority is to show how the vague language of ultimate justifications needs to be penetrated by the basic queries of political sociology, 'Who gives commands, who obeys, for what motives, giving which reasons?' Spencer seeks to disinter the approach which Weber was deliberately and meticulously burying.

We cannot, therefore, amend Weber's theory of authority in a democratic direction without introducing confusion in his conceptual framework. His concept of authority is intrinsically authoritarian in that it does not allow for the recipient of an order to subject it to rational consideration. In his own words it equates with '*autoritäre Befehlsgewalt*', 'authoritarian imperative force' (Weber 1956: 544). So formal rationality may mean substantive irrationality, law combined with unreasoning obedience, but it was precisely this kind of contradiction which Weber saw as a strong likelihood in his time and which his analysis was designed to highlight. For we should acknowledge that Weber himself took no pleasure in depicting the forward march of formal legal–rationality; it was a necessity built into the relentless build-up of modernity. It was for him an ever more authoritarian world.

4.3 CHANGING CONCEPTS FOR A CHANGED WORLD

Weber's concept of authority is identical with imperative or authoritarian control and indeed it is better termed as such. We have to ask ourselves just how much of the work of contemporary organizations is conducted on that basis and the answer would be probably occasionally but not predominantly. We have to ask ourselves too whether there are other ordering principles in contemporary organization, even ones which we can call authority, which have a better purchase on contemporary conditions.

For even if Weber's concept of authority is more developed in formal analytical terms than any other, it is not alone. There are concepts with roots far earlier than his as well as ones which have arisen in criticism of him. We can identify at least three versions of the idea of authority in the English language, none of which is wholly reducible to sub-Weberian notions.

In the first of these versions, authority is what a person or agency has which acts on the safe assumption that others will respect and accept both the acts and their outcomes. Here there is implicit some kind of legitimation from below. In the second, a person has authority who acts under the aegis of such a person or agency. We have then here the notion of a chain of authority of which so much has been made in accounting for social order. In the third, authority is what a person (or a text) represents when expressing soundly based knowledge or using specially acquired skill which others take account of in forming their judgements (for similar distinctions see Raz 1990: 2–3). This latter has some affinity with the idea of professional authority we mentioned above.

In none of these is the idea of command uppermost, although that may be the way in which from time to time authority is expressed. In other words the imperative mood on which Weber placed such emphasis is in these versions replaced by the optative, the expression of wish, the suggestion of preference more than command, and a persuasive or exemplary power.

We should note additionally the way these formulations blur the sharp distinctions Weber draws between authority, modes of legitimation and ethical justification. It is essential to Weber's method that one sharply distinguishes between obedience and modes of justifying it. We can see the reason quite clearly and it is not because Weber sided with unquestioning obedience that he wanted to make the distinctions, rather the opposite. Just because people obey the law doesn't automatically mean they think it right in his terms. As Anthony Kronman (1983: 70) has pointed out, the big distinction between traditional and modern legal–rational authority is that in the latter legality may have no ethical significance.

These alternative ideas of authority on the other hand tend to say that it is precisely the association with rightness which makes acts of authority valid and acceptable. For them illegitimate authority would be a contradiction in terms. But for Weber that would leave authority far too unstable, and open to reasoned challenge. We can see the origin here of Spencer's demands on Weber's typology. But in the breadth of his comparative sociology of structures of imperative co-ordination what clearly impressed Weber was their persistence and success in evading challenges to legitimacy. The paradox is that Weber provided so many different motives and forces for the upholding of these structures that he was in danger of making his typological device, the three modes of belief in legitimacy, redundant as a real historical factor.

In fact a close reading of Weber shows that in considering changes in authority he was aware of the problem of loss of belief in legitimacy but he attributed little of this to rational argument. One kind of belief was much the same as another when it came to legal–rational authority. The facticity of law was what guaranteed the persistence of modern authority for him. And in this he is in a long secular tradition. As Montaigne said, 'Now the laws keep up their credit, not because they are just, but because they are laws; that is the mystic foundation of their authority; they have no other of any service' (1842: 497).

To this secular conception we can oppose one associated with the Christian Church which identifies common elements in these three variants of a non-Weberian idea of authority. In each of them there is a notion of rightness, not as extrinsic to authority, but as intrinsic, and in each case there is an implicit appeal to a source: popular consent, law, or wisdom. Authority is derived, has an origin. Those three origins can easily conflict in practice but each variant shares the idea of a source. And in each case it is always possible to look for a higher or remoter origin.

We can pursue it to an ultimate origin, as in Aquinas:

> For this reason the duty of obedience is, for the Christian, a consequence of this derivation of authority from God, and ceases when that ceases.
>
> (1954: 183)

Deprived of its Christian dogmatic basis, this idea became the basis of every enlightened challenge to the established powers. But every such challenge depended ultimately on a faith in an ultimate source of reason beyond reasoning. Hence Montaigne's reference to 'mystic foundation'.

Here we begin to see deeper intellectual reasons for Weber's analytical strategy. He distinguished traditional from legal–rational authority to ensure that ethical considerations could be separated out, corresponding with the fact/value distinction which for him was integral to modern rationality. His identification of charismatic authority in turn was a means of separating both from any mystical foundation, corresponding with the demystification of the modern world. For in doing so he was producing a concept of authority beyond reason, an aspect of the facticity of the social world. So the belief in legitimacy was itself for him treated in sociological terms as just another factual state of affairs.

We should be aware of the way Weber's typology is dictated by the 'privileged position' (Kronman 1983: 38) of legal–rational authority. It has its stark and authoritarian character because he has separated it out not only from traditional and charismatic elements but also from any idea of rational debate and clarification aside from the technical considerations of lawyers. We can see just how entrenched it is.

First we have unquestioning obedience to commands, which even in a modern state will have the backing of interests of all kinds. Then we have the additional stabilizing device of legality. His sociology of law was designed to show that its positivity and technical nature in modern society made it just another calculable social fact. If on receipt of an instruction the official questions its basis, the authority is contaminated.

There is then no room for lengthy discussions of the legal basis of a decision, for consultation and conferences (elements of the collegialism which Weber considered doomed in the modern world), for securing the respect of one's staff through care and concern for them and routine competence at one's job. It is difficult to imagine Weber's bureaucrat requesting an opinion from a subordinate. As Carl Friedrich pointed out, his 'words vibrate with something of the Prussian enthusiasm for the military type of organization' (1952: 31).

For there is no doubt that Weber's concepts were forged in a real setting and were indeed a rationalization of the practice of the time. Legal positivism and a specifically bourgeois materialism come together (Albrow 1975a). Only when we come to the belief in the grounds of legality, which can itself be purely instrumental (*zweckrational*), do values have a chance to come into play. But even here Weber is not prepared to allow for reasoned debate. Values depend on irrational roots, 'natural law' is indeterminate, and in the end it is the power to impose one's values which matters. If we push back our enquiry into the value basis of legal–rational legitimacy in Weberian terms, we are close to the irrational roots which provide no solid or reliable foundation.

Weber achieves the facticity, the impersonality, determinacy and durability of his legal–rational authority by a series of conceptual decisions which make charismatic authority a necessary repository for all those factors which depend on personal influence, attraction, emotional bonds, faith, commitment, initiative and excitement. What is normal in society becomes in his terms exceptional. Hence in his category of charismatic legitimation his formulations oscillate between a belief in and devotion (*Hingabe*) to a person. Here we can hardly distinguish a legitimation belief from simple surrender of judgement to another's will, an entirely unpredictable basis for the administration required in the modern world. Indeed, for Weber charisma was the last revolutionary force left to resist the relentless rise of modernity.

We have to acknowledge that even if Weber bundled together a whole range of intangible qualities under the label of charisma, it corresponded to much of the inner logic of modernity. He directed attention to the interpersonal quality of the authority relationship because he was emphatic that it was an imputed quality of the person (or office) rather than an objectively possessed characteristic which was the basis of the obedience a follower accorded to the instructions of the charismatic leader. The impressionability of the disciples rather than the capacity of the leader was the first requirement.

His determination to avoid taking sides and to keep to the recorded facts meant he could report devotion, even if, as the sociologist in a disenchanted world, he was unable to accept miracles. His well-known disdain for popular democracy, with its credulous masses and disreputable leaders, fitted with a managerial ideology of responsibility, including training in leadership and techniques for awakening devotion in followers.

Moreover it was clear that not just anyone would gain the charismatic accolade. Personalities could attract. The combination of tricks of the trade and personality characteristics has long made the selection and training of organizational leaders a suitable subject for psychological and psychoanalytical treatment. In each case clearly emotions and their control have been considered in depth. It was therefore no accident that in the 1980s the explosion of interest in organizational culture should also bring with it the widespread popular use of the term charisma.

A double ellipsis is involved here. The managerial interpretation plays down the relational aspect of charisma and draws attention away from the members of the organization to the leader. But that in itself is possibly less important than the drastic separation and curtailment of affectivity involved in Weber's concept and typology of authority. By making unquestioning obedience the key test of authority, with a belief in legitimacy its main support, the charismatic type of authority is easily displaced onto structures rather than people.

We can now see the importance of the alternative versions of authority we set out above. They recombine features which Weber is determined to hold apart. They express themselves in wish rather than command, justification or legitimation is intrinsic to them, they are always open to further question, and the qualities of persons are not irrelevant to determining whether they possess authority. Taken together they amount to a comprehensive alternative to Weber's concept.

4.4 A CONCEPT OF AUTHORITY FOR POSTMODERN ORGANIZING

The Anglo-Saxon world particularly has never been entirely comfortable with the austere and militaristic concept of authority as derived from Weber's work although it undoubtedly represented some kinds of reality well enough. Belief in the rightness of unquestioning obedience is not an unheard-of phenomenon. It has surfaced often enough in defence of the indefensible commission of crimes against humanity. It fitted very well with mechanistic models of organization in which the premises of action were all held to be contained within the organization and not in the individual's judgement. Moreover, as Stanley Milgram's (1974) dramatic experiments on the roots of authoritarianism showed, it can surface in routine acceptance of whatever a scientist demands.

In general it is of credit to sociology and testimony to the fulfilment of its purposes that it steadily advanced beyond the Weberian position and kept pace with a changing world. There is no need at this point to rehearse the pathbreaking work of Merton's students, Peter Blau (1955) and Alvin Gouldner (1955a), whose research can truly be said to be the foundation of the modern sociology of organization. If we add the further development of the ethnomethodological treatment of rules (and regard Weber's treatment of authority as a special instance of the rule 'always do what I am told by X'), we can say that there is no justification whatsoever for regarding the reality of organizational behaviour as grounded in legal definitions of imperative control, however important these may be in some contexts.

However, the most far-reaching break with the authoritarian interpretation of authority comes not from within the sociology of organization, where there is always a premium on greater control, but when modern organizational forms are seen as historically relative and authority as transcultural. In this way the elements we pointed to of a non-authoritarian, non-modern concept of authority can be given full scope. In comparative sociological terms this was represented pre-eminently in Reinhard Bendix's (1956) study of the ideology of work.

In analytical terms the most ambitious attempt among contemporary authors to produce a coherent concept of authority which contains these features is that of Richard Sennett (1993). For although he begins with the premise that authority is a fact of life, it is not authority as Weber defines it. Sennett rejects both authoritarian definitions of authority and that attitude which negates authority of any kind. For him 'The bond of authority is built of images of strength and weakness; it is the emotional expression of power' (1993: 4). It is equally a basic need, for children to have authorities and for adults to be them.

Recollecting his observations of the French conductor, Pierre Monteux, at work, Sennett elaborates what for him is the most vivid image of the qualities of authority: 'assurance, superior judgment, the ability to impose discipline, the capacity to impose fear' (ibid.: 17–18). Authority is then based in strength and in this sense transcends epochs. Sennett easily draws on a non-modern source, like Caxton, and talks of monuments of authority defying time (ibid.: 19). When he draws attention to more recent ideas, it is to the fear of and negation of authority.

In a sense Sennett's attention to the phenomenon of the negation of authority is to those counter-currents in modernity which reinforce Weber's image of a dominant authoritarianism. For the logic of the negation of authority is the inability to see it as potentially benign, an impotence which is itself a product of situations where authority is authoritarian. We have then to see the situational relevance of Weber's account. He made his contemporaries and us see his time more clearly. But the times have changed and Sennett's account is an excellent reflection of those changes. Moreover he effectively generates a critique of modernity which resists relativization by extending his considerations across epochs and coming correspondingly closer to many of the issues in contemporary management. It is implicitly a message for postmodern organizing.

There is for Sennett a kind of authority which is based in respect for differences of strength, does not pretend to autonomy, respects the needs of others and involves an open discourse. It is an ideal or in his terms an imaginative demand made on the world. But it is the corollary of expecting doctors to be caring, teachers to respect individual differences, and managers to be sensitive to personal requirements as well as to tasks. Authority then inheres in the quality of relationships and not in obedience to commands.

The normative emphasis in Sennett's idea of authority contrasts vividly with the facticity of Weber's. To the routine automaticity of executed commands we can contrast the striving for quality performance. Morever this corresponds to much that has changed in the West since the early twentieth century. The sports team, not the military regiment, is the exemplary organization for our time. In this respect Weber's main alternative to modern legal–rational authority, the charismatic, can have only limited purchase on the shift which has taken place.

Let us then conclude by suggesting a new definition of authority, in the style of Weber, which may, like Sennett, be more in tune with the spirit of the times in which the writer lives (Western democratic late twentieth century):

> We can call authority the regard an actor accords to a person or position when the decisions and associated actions issuing from that source are accepted by the actor as a regular and legitimate element in the actor's definition of the situation. The more actors accord this regard to a person or position the greater is the authority.

This avoids mention of orders or instructions. Although they may be involved, they are not intrinsic to the idea of authority in our times which owes much more to the notion of professional judgement serving as the basis of a client's decisions than to the notion of military command. Nor is there any suggestion that authority relations flow in one direction. Again paradoxically in Weber's account, while the subordinate was the source of authority, it depended on the duty to obey instructions coming from above. My definition allows for the regular situation of the subordinate's decisions prompting the superior to act, the subordinate's authority, the sphere of competence in the broadest sense, being recognized by the superior.

Undoubtedly the ramifications of this kind of definition are far more extensive than could be explored fully in this context. It opens up the question of how superiority and subordination are defined, and leaves unresolved just how far imperatives of one kind or another are involved in authority. But these are precisely the questions which have been opened up in the modern organization and which any contemporary conceptualization has to face.

For the 'modern organization' is giving way to postmodern organizing where individuals negotiate their respective relations on the basis of their cultural capital and acquired portfolio of skills. Organizational structure as imperative co-ordination becomes ephemeral, an instrumentality for all involved in it and not invested with an aura of superior rationality. Negotiable authority becomes the medium for the new organizing work. The intellectual challenge this poses for the sociology of organization is only exceeded by the new demands it places on the participants.

Part III

FEELING FOR NEW ORGANIZATION

The chapters in this Part follow up the conclusion of the last, that it is necessary to take organizational analysis beyond Weber, but also to appreciate the profounder thrusts of his work. This means bringing his more general sociological theory to bear on his account of bureaucracy.

In so doing I combine current sociological theory of emotion with research on emotions in organization. This is the kind of work pioneered by Arlie Hochschild (1979, 1983) and richly represented recently in Stephen Fineman's (1993) edited volume. But the linkage has been long in coming and is still difficult to make because organization studies have for so long regarded Weber's account of rational bureaucracy as the main sociological contribution to understanding organization. There is another Weber, the exponent of interpretative sociology exploring motive and meaning in social action.

We can reconcile the two Webers by bringing the repressed topic of organizational emotion to the surface. We then can develop the kind of interpretative organizational sociology he might have produced himself were he living today and had he escaped the spell of modernity.

These are demanding and unfulfillable conditions but are the corollary of a positive evaluation of his work, namely that, though limited by his own times, his work portrayed his period in such a way as to be able to speak to us about issues which transcend it. This is the quality of a contribution to world understanding, an authenticity for its own time which reaches out beyond it to others. We find it in an Aristotle, an Ibn Khaldun, or a Montaigne. It is why Weber's work still finds worldwide resonance (Albrow 1993).

So when we consider Weber on emotion we recognize first of all that he was tied to an old modern polarization of rationality versus emotion, for that was the climate of his time, but equally the breadth of his intellectual commitments permits us to take up suggestions in his work which transcend that polarity and effectively lead us to a postmodern period.

There is ample testimony to Weber's intellectual interest in emotion (Sica 1988; Albrow 1990) and also sufficient biographical evidence (Mitzman 1970) to warrant saying that his own approach to emotions was almost a representative illustration of the cultural configuration of modernity, including both emotional repression on the one hand and a quasi-religious devotion to rationality on the other. In his own life and theory he displayed the disabilities characteristic of inhabitants of the iron cage of the modern organization.

Yet we can escape what confined him. Chapter 5 is dedicated to his and our emancipation from the constraints he imposed on himself and draws the consequences from his own broader theoretical and intuitive grasp of the importance of feelings in social life. We draw on the much wider potential of his interpretative sociology than was contained within his austere and authoritarian account of bureaucracy. In other words we are benefiting from the emotional climate of our own less constrained time to utilize Weber's own insights in a way he could not himself do. It is his own category of emotional action which allows us in the end to argue that, just as it is intelligible in his terms to attribute purpose to organizations, so we may impute emotions to such structures of meaning.

However, in the course of doing this we go a long way towards removing the very polarity of emotion and rationality. Weber advocated an empirical science which could interpret and explain social reality. Following the line developed from there by Alfred Schutz and others we have to treat the organizing polarities of modernity, such as emotion versus rationality, as a social construction. It is not a question of the one side of the coin, rational organization, having the emotional on the other side. Rather, the quality of feeling suffuses all organizational activity. The opposition of the rational versus the emotional is revealed as a polarity specific to modernity.

Chapter 6 takes the argument further and shows that once one has taken this step of acknowledging organizational emotion as a conceptual possibility a great deal else falls into place. A range of phenomena which traditionally were excluded from organization theory and from a rationalistic sociology of organization become integral to accounts of organizing activity.

The chapter uses documents, biographical and documentary materials to reinforce this theoretical reorientation of Weberian perspectives on organization. It draws equally on what is now a flourishing and diverse tradition of empirical work on emotions in organizations. Particularly notable contributions have been Berg's (1979) study of the emotional structure of a Swedish company, Hochschild's (1983) seminal study of the emotional labour of women flight attendants, Hearn and Parkin's (1987) study of sex at work, and Rafaeli and Sutton's (1989, 1990, 1991) series of studies of emotional display in interactions at work. They lead us towards a sociology which no longer makes the rational/emotional opposition the key structural device for organizational narratives.

Moving beyond this opposition also means escaping from the specifically old modern conceptual framework which Weber's typology of action imposed on sociological analysis. This was actually at odds with his sensitivity to historical movement, and it was this historical sense which we required of the sociology of organization in Chapter 1.

We have, then, moved away from a long-standing mechanical application of Weber's action typology and the rational–ideal type of bureaucracy. We need to be as sensitive to our own time as he was to his. This requires new accounts of organization but they will be as dependent as his were on analytical skill and the ability to capture the qualities of a changing social reality. The world has changed, our gaze has shifted and the sociology of organization has changed with them.

5

SINE IRA ET STUDIO – OR DO ORGANIZATIONS HAVE FEELINGS?[5]

5.1 INTRODUCTION

The peculiarity of modern culture, and specifically of its technical and economic basis, demands this very 'calculability' of results. When fully developed, bureaucracy also stands, in a specific sense, under the principle of *sine ira ac studio*. Bureaucracy develops the more perfectly, the more it is 'dehumanized', the more completely it succeeds in eliminating from official business love, hatred, and all purely personal, irrational and emotional elements which escape calculation.

(Max Weber 1978: 975)

In general bureaucratic domination has the following social consequences:

1 The tendency to 'levelling' in the interest of the broadest possible recruitment in terms of technical competence.
2 The tendency to plutocracy growing out of the interest in the greatest possible length of technical training. Today this often lasts up to the age of thirty.
3 The dominance of a spirit of formalistic impersonality: '*Sine ira et studio*', without hatred or passion, and hence without affection or enthusiasm. The dominant norms are concepts of straightforward duty without regard to personal considerations. Everyone is subject to formal equality of treatment; that is everyone in the same empirical situation. This is the spirit in which the ideal official conducts his office.

(Max Weber 1978: 225)

I want to bring the excitement back into management.
(Alan Jackson, new Chief Executive of BTR Industries Ltd, interviewed on the Radio 4 programme *In Business* on 31.3.91)

Social scientists who were writing in the 1960s can derive a certain amount of wry satisfaction from the way the idea of culture has swept through business

93

theory and practice in the 1980s. We were there twenty years ago, they can say at least Elliot Jacques (1951), Michel Crozier (1964), and Barry Turner (1971) can say so. It is an often repeated story how the theory of one generation becomes the practice of the next. The interesting thing about the issue this chapter raises is that it is not another version of that story. Although its concerns are not entirely remote from the interest in mitigating mechanistic views of organization which inspired the culturalist interpretations, it is stimulated as much by the experience of management and administration as it is by social scientific theory. If anything, the theory lags behind.

The issue in question is affectivity – feelings or emotions in other words. Already in the 'experience of management' literature there is an unashamed resort to the irrational as the newly discovered renewable resource (see Tom Peters and Nancy Austin 1986). Work in the sociology of emotions (Hochschild 1979; Kemper 1978; Harré 1988) has, however, barely filtered through to organizational studies. Flam's work (1990a and b) will be singled out later as a notable exception.

In fact, it is probably the very reception of the idea of culture in organizational studies which has created obstacles to the recognition of affectivity as a central theme. At the time of its reception in the organizational literature the idea of culture was employed, above all by Parsons, as a solution to the problem of social order, very different from now, of course, when culture is often treated as the source of disorder. But in the 1950s it was different. Affectivity was carried off by culture in its bag of solutions. Either feelings could be expressed in culturally permissible ways, or they were renounced in favour of affective neutrality (Parsons 1951: 60). Either way, in the normal state, they were under social and cultural control.

Applications of psychoanalytic viewpoints to organizations led to similar results. Jacques' general theory of bureaucracy posited 'an intensely human situation, founded upon a psychologically and emotionally subtle relationship'. This had to be managed properly otherwise there would be an accumulation of stress, unstable power, 'and a potential source of energy for social violence' (Jacques 1976: 66–8). It was a formula which tallied all too well with the most famous sociological intervention in the field of organizations, Weber's ideal type of bureaucracy. There feelings became invisible when the ideal type was lifted out of context and incorporated into rationalistic management theory. Sociology's contribution to understanding organizations appeared to amount to tracing the institutionalization of affective neutrality.

In this chapter the silence on feelings in organizations will be presented as a twentieth-century aberration, indeed an expression of its rationalism, but at odds with earlier understanding of organization on the one hand, and also against the general thrust of Max Weber's sociology on the other. The purpose is to add to those contributions to the recovery of the irrational which mark out much of recent sociology. It suggests too that we are on the brink of relocating feelings as a focal point for organizational studies.

5.2 ORGANIZATION BEFORE BUREAUCRACY

We have become so used to living in a society with a bewildering number of organizations that we tend to forget that there was a time when free organization was either not possible or at least highly suspect. It has always been well recognized that the association of people for common purposes carries with it the potentiality for change. It represents a concentration of power and hence a potential threat to existing authorities.

This of course was nowhere more plain than in the formation of political groups and working men's associations and the attempts to regulate them through Combination Acts and Trade Union legislation. But these forms of association were only special instances of the general laws of co-operation to which Marx alluded when remarking on the forces generated by co-operation in industry:

> Apart from the new power that arises from the fusion of many forces into one single force, mere social contact begets in most industries an emulation and a stimulation of the animal spirits that heighten the efficiency of each individual workman.
>
> (Marx 1970: 326)

The reason Marx could offer was no more nor less profound than simply that it was in human nature, specifically as Aristotle had averred, that people were basically social animals.

This was a well-worn theme. It invoked a long tradition of exploring what Adam Ferguson, for instance, had called 'the principles of Union among Mankind' (1782: 26). He referred to the social disposition of men which was reinforced in society.

> That condition is surely favourable to the nature of any being, in which his force is increased; and if courage be the gift of society to man, we have reason to consider his union with his species as the noblest part of his fortune. From this source are derived, not only the force, but the existence of his happiest emotions; not only the better part, but almost the whole of his rational characteristics.
>
> (Ferguson 1782: 30)

Now, of course, these principles of union, where from our point of view the intensification of feeling is the most interesting, were seen to have their obvious exemplification in family, friendship or nation. But, and this is the point, they were clearly utilizable in other contexts, often to the concern of onlookers.

We have a nineteenth-century example of worry about free association which is particularly intriguing because its author, William Channing, was the pioneer American Unitarian minister, whose writing was popular in liberal Christian circles in the nineteenth century and formed the topic of correspondence between Weber and his mother. Channing wrote a paper in 1829 entitled 'Remarks on Associations' in which he singled out 'the disposition which now prevails to form associations, and to accomplish all objects by organized masses'.

He also called this disposition variously, 'the principle of combination', 'the principle of action by joint numbers', the 'principle of association' or the 'principle of co-operation' and he went on to elaborate the wonderful variety of purposes for which people thought it was worth while forming a society, the social preconditions for this modern development and its consequences. It is a remarkable early anticipation of both Simmel and the sociology of organizations. It contains too reference to the 'principal arguments in its favour' which are basically two in number:

Men grow efficient by concentrating their powers;

and

Men not only accumulate power by union, but gain warmth and earnestness. The heart is kindled. An electric communication is established between those who are brought nigh, and bound to each other in common.

(Channing 1829: 115–16)

This, for Channing, was just the problem. It was all very well people being excited by the associations which God had grounded in human nature, among which were numbered the family, neighbourhood, country and humanity. But Missionary societies, Peace societies or Charitable societies were quite another thing. Some did some good, but often people neglected their family to send something to pagan lands. Worse still, associations set up to give freedom can become tyrannical. Anticipating Michels, Channing writes:

Associations often injure free action by a very plain and obvious operation. They accumulate power in a few hands, and this takes place just in proportion to the surface over which they are spread. In a large institution, a few men rule, a few do everything; and, if the institution happens to be directed to objects about which conflict and controversy exist, a few are able to excite in the mass strong and bitter passions, and by these to obtain an immense ascendancy.

(ibid.: 122)

We should note here that unlike Michels' and Weber's versions of the iron law of oligarchy, the concentration of power in a few hands does not depend on knowledge or secrecy but on emotional manipulation. It is not an implausible hypothesis and it is interesting that it has been forgotten.

5.3 THE WEBER PUZZLE

The idea of organizational affectivity was therefore a commonplace in pre-Weberian literature, but we ought to add, distinct from the idea of bureaucracy, the origins of which are contained within the theory and practice of the state. (For the origins of the idea of bureaucracy in the eighteenth century theory of government see Albrow (1970).) It was Weber's decisive contribution to set the theory of bureaucracy within the framework of a comprehensive architectonic of social order and to generalize the idea of bureaucracy to be the rational apparatus for any large organization. Nevertheless it was precisely the origins of Weber's bureaucracy problematic in the theory of rational–legal administration of the modern state rather than in a theory of human co-operation which meant that organizational affectivity was treated either as a problem of charismatic leadership or as a resource. It was lodged in the organizational environment of bureaucracy, but never actually part of it.

It was not that Weber was uninterested in organizational structures. On the contrary. His dissertation had been written on the social forms of commercial organization (Weber 1889). His theory of legitimacy was intended as a contribution to the understanding of the structure of collectivities. His elaboration of the idea of social relationship up to and including his account of corporate groups may be interpreted as a conceptual framework for organizational studies (Peters 1988; Albrow 1990).

Weber was far from being uninterested in affectivity. It was not one of his four types of social action for nothing and his idea of charisma played a critical part in his understanding of the mobilization of action in the modern mass organization as well as in the formation of religious movements.

Alan Sica (1988) has sought to draw our attention to the way Weber accounted for irrationality but he still regards that as an unduly subordinate aspect of his work. For such has been the resonance of his account of bureaucracy with the rationalism of subsequent writers on organizations that these other aspects of Weber's work which are essential for understanding not only him but also organizations in general have been neglected. His writing on bureaucracy has had to do service as an organizational theory in general which it was never intended to do.

Notwithstanding these provisos the two passages at the head of this chapter appear to put the matter beyond doubt. The cog in the machine, the automaton, the faceless official seem to receive unconditional recognition here and these passages have been cited ever since to underwrite either a view of modern organizational culture as rational and impersonal or a view of Weber as rationalistic and neglectful of other aspects of social reality. They clearly require some heavy interpretative work if one is to sustain the claim being made here that the thrust of Weber's sociology as a whole is towards a full appreciation of the place of feelings in social life, and that a Weberian theory of organization is not inherently rationalistic.

Let us acknowledge at the start that Weber's ideal type of bureaucracy is intentionally rational and that the development of bureaucracy was identified by him as a facet of the overall social process of rationalization. For some, of course, that is sufficient grounds for complaint, but then that is because they neglect the counterpoint to this whole process which, as I have argued elsewhere, amounts to nothing less than the core of his concerns as a man and a scholar, namely the relations between rationality and irrationality (Albrow 1990: 68–71, 129–31). The forces of unreason, power, charisma, faith, emotions, Nietzschean moments are emphatically acknowledged by Weber. The issue, then, cannot possibly be one of omission but rather of demarcation. This is where the puzzle arises.

The first and earlier of those two passages sees bureaucracy as corresponding to a general requirement of calculability in modern culture. This is equated with the elimination of emotional elements. It is not a formula to which Weber always subscribed, or rather, it is probably fairer to say, one which he would elaborate in other contexts to give much greater weight to affectivity. In particular it is necessary to take account of a factor which he regarded as a universal precondition for the exercise of authority, even for a charismatic leader, namely discipline.

His interests in discipline were particularly lively in the cases of armies and factories. Indeed, he likens the two spheres in so far as they are dependent on similar kinds of relationships between givers and receivers of orders. Significantly it is in the discussion of the transformation of charisma that he is very explicit about discipline and makes critical distinctions between calculability, personal and impersonal emotionality. Discipline is a tool for any purpose, providing for uniform action by a plurality of actors, substituting a trained mechanical preparedness for personally acquired skills. But, he goes on, we must not think that this excludes enthusiasm or unreserved dedication. Armies depend on inspiration and empathy, just as much as the Jesuits. Leaders calculate on these things.

Weber then underscores this point by offering a general sociological proposition:

> The sociologically decisive points, however, are, first, that everything is rationally calculated, especially those seemingly imponderable and irrational, emotional factors – in principle, at least, calculable in the same manner as the yields of coal and iron deposits. Secondly, devotion is normally impersonal, oriented towards a purpose, a common cause, a rationally intended goal, not a person as such, however personally

tinged devotion may be in the case of a fascinating leader.

(Weber 1978: 1150)

Here we have a clarification which has not been accorded the attention it deserves, partly, as so often, because of language problems. The German word translated as impersonal in this context is *'sachlich'* which means 'attending to the matter in hand' or 'businesslike'. (In the second passage at the beginning we do, however, see *'Unpersönlichkeit'*.) A good doctor in a consultation will be *'sachlich'* but not 'impersonal'.

The vital point is that not only does Weber allow for emotions within bureaucracy, but their rational calculation becomes an intrinsic part of their working, which is going to be the cue for our later conceptual location of affectivity. Even so we have to admit some surprise that he does not repeat this qualification in the second passage, especially since there is a feature about its structure which makes it different from the first, namely the posing of contradiction. Social levelling is set against plutocratization, formalistic impersonality is set against, in a continuation of the passage, the preference of bureaucrats for material–utilitarian policy projects.

This last point had its justification in the development of the Bismarckian welfare state, but is arguably much more connected with Hegelian notions of class duty and thus German culture than with bureaucratic structure. Why could not Weber have counterposed to his impersonal formalism the passionate commitment of the dutiful bureaucrat, especially since that notion was not strange to him? Indeed, in 'Science as a Vocation' he drew attention to the processes of frenzy, inspiration and passionate devotion which characterized a scientist's work, and in which there was no difference from the artist (Weber 1948: 136–7). Since his bureaucrat received a professional training, as opposed to having mere obedience instilled, there ought to have been even more room for such an idea.

Even more puzzling is the fact that of all the social types for which Weber argued that the Protestant Ethic had a formative influence – entrepreneurs, intellectuals, politicians – bureaucrats, to the best of my knowledge, are never mentioned. 'The Protestant Ethic and the Spirit of Bureaucracy' was never written even though, as with the entrepreneur, it was received wisdom that German officialdom was pervaded with a sense of Kantian, and hence Protestant, duty. If it had been, then of course its centrepiece would have had to be the struggle in the soul of the bureaucrat.

As it was, it was left to Robert Merton to point out that, given Weber's ideal type, the unfortunate official will in fact develop all kinds of personality characteristics which will be disabling. Moreover he does this precisely by using an argument from the nature of discipline which as we have just seen is essentially Weberian:

Discipline can be effective only if the ideal patterns are buttressed by strong sentiments which entail devotion to one's duties, a keen sense of

the limitation of one's authority and competence, and methodical performance of routine activities. The efficacy of social structure depends
ultimately on infusing group participants with appropriate attitudes
and sentiments.

(Merton 1940: 365)

Merton then goes on to develop an image of bureaucracy which is anything
but emotionally neutral, where timidity, defensiveness, harshness and resentment are part of the daily round. Those may indeed have been the qualities of
the German bureaucrat in Weber's time and there is sufficient indication in
his comments on it in political contexts to suggest Weber would not have
necessarily disagreed with Merton. But his concentration on the rationality
of his ideal type deflected him from according such features their due consideration.

It cannot be denied that Weber's account of bureaucracy does 1. push affectivity into the wider organizational context and 2. treat it as a question of
leadership and control. For those reasons it relates uneasily to those aspects
of his work where motivational structures are examined more from the standpoint of individual needs, as in his work on religion. At the same time the fact
that he does indeed tackle organizational affectivity through his ideas of
charisma, motives for obedience, discipline and through the total project of
his interpretative sociology ought to suggest that it is quite mistaken to take
Weber as the authority for a rationalistic sociology of organization. Reference here to the 'total project of his interpretative sociology' is shorthand for
the position maintained in Albrow (1990: 199–226) that the overall thrust of
Weber's work was to explain why people act as they do within the structures
of meaning in which they find themselves. Motivation is of the essence. It is far
more appropriate to suggest that we need to amplify his account of bureaucracy to be more in accord with his general project. We are so dominated by
Weber's image of the passionless bureaucracy that we really need to obtain
distance from it through a-theoretical participant accounts. Biographies,
interview material and memoirs exist in plenty to aid us in approaching
organizational affectivity. Let us, as a start, try to balance real-life data against
the ideal type.

5.4 PASSIONATE BUREAUCRATS AND LOVING ENTREPRENEURS

Anyone working on modern bureaucracy has the benefit of Peter Hennessy's
monumental *Whitehall* (1989) in which it is possible to pursue so many lines
of enquiry. He has collected a wealth of material on the personality of the
modern bureaucrat. One example is that of the maker of the modern British
civil service, Charles Trevelyan. At first glance it bears out the Weberian

traits, especially since he admired German ways: meticulous concern for records, obsession with work, holidays regarded as sinful.

How far, we have to ask, is this emotionless? Admiration, concern, guilt, obsession are feelings expressed in a vocabulary of moral appraisal. This was recognized fully by Trevelyan and all those who deemed the moral qualities of recruits to be decisive for the future of a reformed civil service.

It is also fair to say that Trevelyan was a reformer and that his zeal may have had more to do with that than any requirements of his job. But that is to underestimate the pressures in organizations of all kinds for leaders to innovate and it seems to have been a characteristic repeated in Trevelyan's successor, Sir Warren Fisher, who as the 'quintessential new broom . . . sustained this zest for years' (Roseveare 1969: 252). One of their successors as Head of the Civil Service, Lord Bridges, writing about the profession, suggested that this zeal extended further than was evident to the outsider.

> A civil servant's life makes him above all a realist. He is less easily elated, less easily discouraged than most men by everyday happenings. . . . Once the crust of apparent disillusion is pierced, you will find a man who feels with the fiercest intensity for those things which he has learnt to cherish – those things, that is to say, which a lifetime of experience has impressed upon him as matters which are of vital concern for the well-being of the community.
>
> (Bridges 1950: 31)

One reminiscence of Bridges at work is by Sir Harold Kent, whom he appointed to be Treasury Solicitor in 1953. Kent recalls a summons to see the great man and the apprehension he felt which was dispelled by 'the air of joyful expectation' and Bridges' beaming face. The appointment duly made in a brief exchange, Kent reports Bridges in this way: '"Good man, that's settled then. And don't forget, Harold" – he used the Christian name of the Permanent Secretaries' club – "I'm always here if you're worried about anything. That's what I'm for."' They talked further and Bridges concluded, '"You'll have a lot of fun"' (Kent 1979: 231). Scarcely a Weberian remark for a bureaucrat but one which we are told he used a great deal (Hennessy 1989: 139). It is an exchange which illustrates the manipulation of feelings, but also an emotional climate in which such manipulation can take place. Hennessy's interpretation of the wealth of evidence he has for the importance of zest and enthusiasm in the civil service is particularly shaped by his impression of the recruits to it during the 1939–45 years. He proposes that they brought an unusual degree of zest to their work and this ran counter to dominant norms as expressed in terms like 'Conviction politicians, certainly: conviction civil servants, no' and 'energy but not enthusiasm' (ibid.: 162). Hennessy cites an impassioned speech to First Division civil servants at their 1969 conference by Derek Morrell, 'inspirational maker of progressive social policy at the Department of Education and Science and the Home Office'. Morrell uttered what Hennessy calls a *cri de cœur* against the constraints of Whitehall neutrality:

> we cling to the myth which science has now abandoned. We still do not accept the reality of our individual humanity. . . . Speaking personally, I find it yearly more difficult to reconcile personal integrity with a view of my role which requires the deliberate suppression of part of what I am.
>
> (Hennessy 1989: 163)

Hennessy writes of the great missed opportunity to reform the civil service after the Second World War but from our point of view what is of greatest interest is the way his discussion of zeal and enthusiasm for work appears to be equated with a rejection of Whitehall neutrality. 'Passion for policy is not supposed to be part of their genetic code' (ibid.: 162). That does indeed tally with Weber whom Hennessy cites with approval on occasion. But it is precisely that equation which this chapter has questioned and which, indeed, the material in Hennessy's book goes some way to undermine. The instrumentality of bureaucracy, the necessity to subordinate personal values may cloak the personal expression of feeling in public. It is not inconsistent with work-related expression and utilization of feeling inside a bureaucracy. In fact Hennessy's 'passion' may be a code for the deliberate intrusion into the modern civil service of an entrepreneurial ethos in recent years which required the preservation of an image of bureaucracy as a lifeless machine to justify radical intervention. It is a complex story but vitally important for understanding ideological conflict in the 1980s.

The Thatcher government made a determined effort to disturb what it saw as the entrenched ethos of the civil service by inviting Sir Derek Rayner of Marks and Spencer to head a special unit to place every department of the service under an efficiency scrutiny. Hennessy interviewed Rayner and was struck with his 'passion', his enthusiasm, determination (ibid.: 595). One of Rayner's civil service assistants spoke of the 'exhilaration' of working with him (ibid.: 597). Rayner himself indicated his awareness of the current management theory when he spoke of

> changing the culture in part of the organization. And cultural changes are not brought about even by good desires. They're brought about by acquiring new habits and being able to observe that those new habits are effective and enjoyable to perform.
>
> (ibid.: 605)

Hennessy's admiration for Rayner is tempered by a recognition that the changes he wrought were partial and fell far short of the full institutional reform which he would wish to see. It also reflects a view that passionate leadership is the property of politicians or entrepreneurs. This misbegotten progeny of Weber's theory of charisma has become a codeword for a style of management which aims to undermine established forms of state bureau-cracy. At the same time to legitimate the intervention it cultivates a Weberian image of bureaucracy as passionless impersonality.

Yet it should not be forgotten that it equally functions to subvert ration-alistic theories of management. That subversion has of course already gone very far under the mantle of the idea of corporate culture. No matter how far culture is made object for managerial manipulation, the elements of belief, imagination and interpretation which are intrinsic to that vast idea mean that, unwittingly, management has entered the field of mystery. Correspond-ingly on all accounts magicians in the boardroom are having a wonderful time.

John Harvey-Jones has given us his own sense of the boundless horizons of the top job: 'in reality there are practically no limitations to the ambitions and objectives which you can set yourself as top man' (Harvey-Jones 1989: 234). On his account he determines for better or worse the style of the board, which will have a 'cascade effect' throughout the company. Given this percep-tion of the portentous nature of the task and the amount of power it implies, one can't help feeling that Harvey-Jones should not have felt surprised by the interest his work force took in his mood:

> One of the unexpected problems I have found in being chairman, first of a division and then of a company, is the fact that many people judge the position of the company by one's own apparent mood, even to whether one smiles or not.

> (ibid.: 129)

Indeed his 'reflections on leadership' are pervaded by the vocabulary of feel-ing and moral appraisal to the point where, not unexpectedly, he asserts, 'A congruence between your own values and feelings and those followed by your company in its approach to business is absolutely essential' (ibid.: 239).

This is entirely consistent with the message which Tom Peters and Nancy Austin convey in their book *A Passion for Excellence* (1986). There are values, visions but no formulae. The vision starts with the single individual. 'It must come from the market and the soul simultaneously. It must be felt passion-ately before it is published' (Peters and Austin 1986: 287). Moreover this magi-cal source of success is not confined on their account to the top echelons; it can be found at any lower levels, provided of course a leader is to be found.

The de-rationalization of the organization does not stop there. After values and vision, follow love and empathy. Love is equated with loyalty and team-work and respect for the individual, and what are celebrated in the individual are 'commitment, passion, zest, energy, care, love and enthusiasm' (ibid.: 292).

It is right to see this as an authentic expression of the spirit of the 1980s, embracing explicitly debureaucratization, getting rid of bureaucratic junk as a strategic necessity, only balking at the ultimate acknowledgement that we are dealing in mystery. This is achieved by the imaginative use of the idea of 'ownership' which is the name Peters and Austin give to 'the creative contribution of each person in the organization' (ibid.: 312).

In effect the years have been rolled back; radical reaction is not an inappropriate description. Bureaucracy is the target, as much as it was in Weber's time, and the theory of organization as a system of creative contagion, takes us right back to Channing. But there is also a fundamental change as compared with his time, no doubt because organization itself is now integral to, rather than subversive of, the power structure of the wider society. The organization as the expression of human passion is now legitimate.

5.5 A THEORETICAL SITE FOR FEELINGS

Can anyone doubt that organizations are emotional cauldrons? Only perhaps those who have been schooled in a particular analytical approach. A genuine sociology of organizations, a study which appreciates their facticity, must surely recognize this as much as do the reminiscences of participants.

It appears patently obvious to Jeff Hearn and Wendy Parkin who broke new territory with their 'Sex' at 'Work' (1987): 'Enter most organisations and you enter a world of sexuality.' But, they say, from the literature, 'you would imagine these organisations, so finely analysed, are inhabited by a breed of strange, asexual eunuch figures' (Hearn and Parkin 1987: 3–4). They attribute this to sexist ideology and the interplay between the sexism of managers and the theory of management. Such a feminist interpretation has much on its side but may simply not go far enough. The analytical underpinnings are to be found in the implicit equivalence between male/female and rationality/emotionality which expresses the Western form of patriarchy. The silence on sex in organizations is a special case of the suppression of emotion generally.

This is why we have to put Weber at the centre of the drama. His influence has been so pervasive precisely because he seeks to define Western civilization on the rationality/emotionality axis and it is not unreasonable to see his construction of the relations on that axis as having so much importance for the course of subsequent theory. It is understandable then that the downplaying of emotion in sociology is so often attributed to him and his interest in rational action, as does Jeff Coulter (1988), for instance, in a paper which stresses the contextual dependency of emotional states.

This is, nevertheless, to misconstrue Weber whose counterposing of rationality and affectivity was designed to explore their dialectic. His work is full of references to needs and feelings and the programme of interpretative sociology was precisely one of examining structures of motivation (Albrow 1991a: 213–18). Weber has been regarded as the arch-exponent of rationalistic sociology because his ideal type of bureaucracy is inconsistent with his wider project and has been mistakenly treated by others as a paradigm for organizational analysis, and even sociological analysis in general.

If we return to the spirit of his programme, we will seek to use the new-found recognition of emotions in organizations. We will employ the wider interest in the sociology of the emotions to go far beyond the charismatization of leadership which would appear at the moment to be the extent of the acknowledgment of his interest in affectivity. At the same time we have to address the hypostatization of rational action in so much of the organizational literature which confuses rational models with empirical reality.

To do this, however, we have to overcome a further hurdle in the appreciation of Weber and something which has always presented a real barrier to understanding his sociological contributions generally, namely his resolution of the agency/structure problem. His methodological individualism has been interpreted as a denial of the reality of social structures and a justification for treating organizations or indeed any social collectivity as units only for the sake of analysis. Since the analytic method for determining what is properly part of the organization has been held to be rationality by practitioners and analysts alike, feelings have been attributed to the sphere of concrete reality, i.e. inhabiting individuals and outside the boundaries of what is the organization.

There is no denying that Weber's analysis of bureaucracy has contributed to this blind alley, but it is the rationalism of twentieth-century management and its theory which has given rise to emptinesses like accounts of motivation where feelings are scarcely mentioned. For instance James March and Herbert Simon (1958), proposing their model of the decision-making organism (human being), list 206 variables in which feelings are registered in at most nine, three times as simply 'satisfaction' or 'job satisfaction', and then in forms like 'felt need to participate', 'motivation to produce' or 'level of interpersonal tension'. The relation between cognitive performance and emotions is essentially unexplored.

At best, feelings have been dealt with in cooling-out sessions, in encounter groups or T-groups, designed to defuse threatening build-ups of tension which would interfere with the smooth-running machine. Analytically in Weberian terms there is no warrant for this. It results from the conflation of the organizational level with the personal level of meaning because it is wrongly assumed that the injunction to regard all actions within organizations as being actions of individuals means that organizational rationality must be equivalent to individual rationality. In other words it equates organizational action with one of the analytic types of individual action.

This error, it may be argued, is exemplified to a degree by his discussion of bureaucracy with its association between the passionless official and impersonal rules. But everywhere else the whole burden of his account is to keep the levels of meaning associated with collectivities and individuals distinct from each other – most obviously illustrated by his discussion of the variability of motives for adhering to a legitimate order – it might be out of self-interest, fear or belief in its value and that order might be traditional, based in faith or legality. The meaning of the system of legitimacy and the motives for belonging were distinct in their logics, even though borne by individuals in their actions (Weber 1978: 31–8).

Further, what is obvious from Weber's discussion of legitimacy is that affectivity belongs both at the level of the system and at the personal level, but not necessarily to both simultaneously. The cool logic of Calvinist theology might be propagated with passionate ardour. The ecstatic ceremonies of a Jim Bakker can be coolly calculated for specific effect. There is absolutely no reason in Weber's sociological analysis why organizational action should not be emotional.

It follows that there can be as little objection to speaking of organizations having feelings as there is to speaking of them acting. For the Weberian the feelings will always be borne by people, but it will make every sense to distinguish feelings in their organizational capacity from personal feelings. 'This will hurt me my boy more than it hurts you,' says the traditional headmaster of the boy's public school 'administering' (note the bureaucratic nuance!) a beating. It is precisely the play on the differing levels of personal and organizational meaning with the accompanying ambiguity which makes this a stock item of humour. It is not then just a verbal inexactitude when Harvey-Jones speaks of values and *feelings* followed by your company. We can identify dominant emotions which characterize the organization as a whole, emotions which are appropriate to specific occasions within it, or which belong to the performance of particular roles. None of these emotions should be confused with personal feelings. Sociology, which has long absorbed the dramaturgical perspective, has no difficulty in accepting the authenticity of a public role performance. Anger is no less anger for being expected and displayed in appropriate settings. The place of emotions in social life is clarified still further if we adopt the constructionist position and see them as called forth, formed and labelled and taught in social situations (Harré 1988).

Undoubtedly this causes major awkwardness for all who have been schooled in rationalistic organization theory. They can accept that organizations might act, even have ideas since they are more or less intelligent systems. But the real difficulty is that they have no bodies, and feelings in this perspective are intrinsically associated with corporeal existence. At best the body and its feelings will be a resource or a tool, finely tuned by the human engineers.

This is where the conceptualization of feelings in society has progressed since Weber's time. Any reading of his account of needs and emotions will discover certainly a multi-layered and complex account but none the less one which is too close both to the emerging behavioural psychology and the Freudian problematic to avoid seeing the question of repression of bodily requirements as the central issue (Albrow 1991a: 125). That location of feelings in bodily perturbations was the very stuff of the Puritan construction of emotion and the frame of Weber's own thought and experience through which he struggled towards sociology. Sociology has escaped this fateful inheritance in so far as it has followed his lead and annexed the facts of living to its intellectual purpose. In this respect the emotional construction of social life must be fully acknowledged.

The texture of affectivity is more multi-layered and convoluted than that of rationality and we have scarcely begun the naturalistic tasks of documentation and classification which preoccupied our seventeenth- and eighteenth-century predecessors. Bodily events, changes and states, drives and needs merge into sensations, feelings and moods which in turn inhabit emotions, attitudes, vices and virtues. As with rationality the descriptive and evaluative are hardly to be disentangled except as phases in a process. We hardly advance knowledge by calling greed negatively sanctioned hunger or lust disallowed sexual desire. Rather, for sociologists the task is to account for the construction (and deconstruction) of greed and lust in organizations and in people and society in general. Relabelling must be a very minor aspect of that task.

Future organizational studies will be transformed by the recognition of affectivity as a key aspect of organizational performance. Socio-technical systems will be seen as channels for the flow of emotions which will be understood as being quite as important for output as they are for individual creative achievement. This can be asserted so confidently because the recasting of theory is already under way. Helena Flam has recently provided a fine example of the new theory of organizational feeling with her papers on 'Emotional Man', in which she sets up a model to complement rational and normative man models. Her conceptualization of constrained emotional action fits the constructivist view of emotion and her three-dimensional model of action is extended to provide for corporate actors as, in her words, 'emotion-motivated emotion managers'. One sharply observed comment in her account relates to the 'feeling rule' for British government.

> This rule states that the ridicule which 'the Parliamentary Opposition tries to heap upon the government at every opportunity' (Heclo and Wildavsky 1974: 10–11) is to be incessantly avoided. And, indeed, the constant fear of embarrassment accounts for most of the workload of the British ministers, their staff and the Treasury staff, cooperation between ministers and staff, conflict between the Cabinet ministers, and, finally, the type of information released up or across the government hierarchy and to the media.
>
> (Flam 1990b: 228)

Empirically there is a wealth of evidence to back this up. How many theories of organization can accommodate embarrassment?

Stated as strongly as this, it forces recognition that we are retrieving the old tripartite philosophical distinctions between cognition, conation and emotion and occasions a certain sense of astonishment that the twentieth century could have divorced humanity of its feelings for so long.

5.6 CONCLUSION

We have been aided along the road to recover the emotional dimension of organizational life by a re-reading of Weber. In turn that recovery illuminates the silences and limitations in his work and indicates the points where he has been misunderstood. For the sake of future work in this field they can be summarized as follows:

1 The impersonality of bureaucracy as Weber depicted it in his ideal type is determined by the cultural definition of bureaucratic work in his time, rather than by his sociological analysis.
2 The use by subsequent commentators of his idea of bureaucracy to do service as a rational model of organization neglects the location of that idea for Weber within his wider theory of social relationships and order, with their special emphasis on charisma and discipline.
3 His wider theory and his programme of interpretative sociology allow for a more comprehensive articulation of rationality and emotion than he in fact achieved because the prevalent conceptualizations of emotion in both Freudian and behavioural versions in his time heavily emphasized their pre-social, biological nature.

It took the rationalism of his successors, against whom Weber warned us, to make virtues of these limitations and to laud him as their predecessor. It is they who have suppressed the emotional dimension in his work in the interests of rationalistic organization. The recovery of emotion in Weber is the counterpart of the recognition that organizations have feelings.

6

REVISING ACCOUNTS OF ORGANIZATIONAL FEELING[6]

6.1 RESEARCHING EMOTIONALITY IN ORGANIZATIONS

The 1980s was a period when British organization studies developed a fuller appreciation of the amplitude of Max Weber's work. Michael Reed (1985: 17–18) pointed out that treating Weber as interested in little else other than organizational rationality was a lazy reading, fitting Weber into a particular kind of functionalist interpretation which highlighted problems of technical control. His edited volume (with Larry Ray 1994) provides other possible points of entry into an alternative Weberian theory of organizations. For instance Clegg (1994) begins with culture and Eldridge with authority. Elsewhere, from the Netherlands Gangolf Peters (1988) advocates building a Weberian organizational sociology on the basis of his theory of the social relationship.

This non-rationalistic development of Weber's sociology of organization may be traced in Britain through Salaman and Thompson's Open University course, back to Silverman (1970) and Albrow (1970). In the United States by contrast Weber retains an emblematic position as exponent of organizational efficiency and organization studies there have yet to utilize the fuller interpretation of Weber available in such work as Sica (1988) and Scaff (1989). So Marshall Meyer and Lynne Zucker, even as they call for a departure from 'the traditional sociological perspective' of treating the existence of organization as a matter of superior efficiency, attribute this to a mistake by Weber in confusing the aspiration to efficiency with its achievement (1989: 48, 59). This was not Weber's mistake, and it is rather an American sociological perspective which makes it correspondingly harder for Meyer and Zucker to promote their more truly Weberian sociological perspective on failing organization.

In the last chapter I argued that Weber's interest in irrationality, and in particular affectivity, had been submerged by twentieth-century rationalistic models of organization. But I conceded too that Weber had given the rationalists some good excuses for a one-sided interpretation of his work since his writing on bureaucracy was not the best example of his general approach. It reproduced, in an unacknowledged manner, the peculiarities of German bureaucracy, and played down the place of emotions, to which his interpretative method elsewhere (as in his sociology of religion) gave greater weight. The 'other Weber' was, then, set against the received version and consequently against the tradition of rationalistic technocratic theories of organization for which that received version had so long served as the classic text.

In brief, the case was made for elaborating the place of the emotions within the framework of organizational analysis, not as byproducts, interferences or even repressed potentialities and resources, but as integral and essential modalities of organizational performance. Stated at its strongest it was asserted that, just as organizations act, so they equally have feelings. This chapter is a sequel, backing the earlier claims by elaborating the consequences for organizational analysis if one takes affectivity seriously.

This cannot be a routine exercise, if only because the obstacles which rationalistic models have erected to such analysis are formidable. They extend even to the equation of analysis with rationality itself which leads to emotions being seen as alien objects passing across the analyst's gaze. That rationalism is evident at the deepest level in the form of analysis which has most directly been concerned with emotion, psychoanalysis. By concentrating on repressed feeling and emphasizing the cognition of unconscious processes, psychoanalysis may effectively devalue the emotional content of everyday experience by subordinating it to a discursive rationality shared between analyst and patient. In the context of organizations this outlook presumes a shared rationality of organization and analyst, which locates organizational failure in the individual manager's neurosis (for an example see Kets de Vries and Miller 1985). Older approaches to organization, which did address emotional aspects of human behaviour, such as the socio-technical systems theory of the Tavistock school (e.g. Trist *et al.* 1963) or the self-actualizing theory of McGregor (1966), shared this rationalistic bias of psychoanalysis in treating as both normal and ideal a state in which individual feelings are gathered up in, and absorbed by, rational organizational performance. Radical critiques of this position simply offered a transvaluation of the same ontology, individual feeling viewed as constrained and trapped, as opposed to being enabled or realized, in organizational structure, e.g. as in Morgan's (1986) image of the organization as psychic prison.

The contrasting position offered here is quite different. Purpose, cognition and emotion are seen as intertwined modalities of action *both for individuals and for organizations*. The opposition 'individual feeling':'organizational rationality' as a guiding principle for organizational analysis is replaced by 'personal action':'organizational action'. This need not be at odds with psychoanalytic approaches provided those also discard what Ian Mitroff (1983: 1) has called the 'inside/outside' image of organization. If, like him, we treat the boundaries of organization as constructs and organization as the outcome of the total interplay of a wide variety of stakeholders (see also Mason and Mitroff 1981), whether 'inside' or 'outside', we can view organizational, just like individual, action as a constructed level of meaning. This accords entirely with Weber's own refusal to reify 'the organization'.

The approach here then is broadly Weberian in several respects: organizations will be treated as realities, but existing only in and through people's behaviour; they will be seen as facticities, but constructed out of motives and systems of meaning; they will be seen as systems of action, enduring and cohering only in so far as people sustain them. These conditions make organizations contingent in a double sense, namely they depend on people doing things, but also upon their ability to demonstrate that things have been done. The empirical study of organization has, therefore, a constitutive relationship to organization. The possibility of demonstrating the facts of organizations is a requirement for their functioning. Getting the facts wrong about them means they won't work as expected. If we leave out the facts of people's emotions in our accounts of organizational behaviour, the accounts will be distorted to the detriment of both organizations and people (Albrow 1980).

My account of Weber gives pride of place to the empirical thrust of his work, to the establishment of facts as constitutive of social reality, and hence to the strictly subordinate position of the ideal type. His was an antifoundationalist faith in empirical science, which trusted intellectual constructions only as far as they helped to illuminate the facts (Albrow 1991b). From that point of view the constructs of organization theory over the years have been one-sided distortions of reality, as inappropriately reified as Weber's own ideal type of bureaucracy.

The history of twentieth-century theorizing about organizations is very largely one of accounts born of interests and ideology, leaving large areas of organizational reality out of the frame (Albrow 1980). Actors' own biographical accounts have kept closer to reality and empirical sociology of organization has an honourable place in keeping a firm relation to those accounts. It can recognize the complex interweaving of reason and feeling which makes up the course of daily work. It registers the daily behaviour which constitutes organization, recording the feelings which are as much integral to it as timetables and work schedules.

But then it follows that accounts of organization which pay due regard to emotion will be at their most effective if they record the course of organizational change. An empirical study which exemplifies the way in which the study of change and emotion in organization are intimately connected is Per-Olof Berg's (1979) account of sixty years of organizational drama in the Emmabode Glasverk, an important contribution to what effectively is a Scandinavian culture of organizational studies which has resolutely refused to accept the rationalistic model (see also Brunsson 1985; Flam 1990a and b).

This chapter then advocates an empirical sociology which explores how organizations are constituted over time by people and includes their feelings as elementary facts of the situation as much as their plans, knowledge and resources. Early acknowledgements of emotion in organizations, e.g. in

111

accounts of morale, work satisfaction or leadership (where charisma has recently become an important focus of discussion, Pauchant 1991), were primarily adjuncts to rationalistic models which betrayed their origins in large-scale industrial manufacturing by regarding human feeling as potentially disruptive.

The decline of the old industrial sector correspondingly makes the task of taking emotions as a serious side of organizational analysis much easier for two main reasons. The first is that the ever growing weighting of the advanced economies towards the service sector has led to increasing departures from the classic hierarchical pyramidal shape of organization. Innovative potential is sought in different forms of social relations. As Burns and Stalker (1961: 234) pointed out, emphasis on organizational change may reduce subordination but at the same time it increases incorporation, placing greater demands on the whole personality, including emotions.

The other reason for the new prominence of the emotions in organizations is that the service sector intrinsically orients to a market of expressed non-material needs. Treating the customer as a person means focusing on interaction and may result, as Hochschild has vividly portrayed (1983: 10), in such practices as training employees to smile, paying them for emotional labour. True, this rationalization of feelings is like the rationalization of any other kind of human capacity in Taylorized manufacturing. But emotions have been brought back into the frame of reference and the alienation which results from lack of authenticity means that they force themselves upon the attention of analysts in a more pressing way than was the case with Fordist manufacturing or Prussian bureaucracy. They were never absent in the factory or the government office, but they could be left unthematized. Now even the authentic display of emotion in work can be posed as an imaginable possibility.

Recovering emotion will mean a return to older verities where the language of action weaves purposes, moods, plans and sentiment into complex descriptions of situations which take account of the circumstances of time and place. Rationalism has distorted the language of social description in general and the place of emotion in particular. Contemporary organizational structure must make it impossible any longer simply to elaborate the language of rationality while consigning emotion to an unanalysed motivational reservoir. Not only do we have to accept that there is an emotional structure (Berg 1979: 256), but any account of organizational affectivity is also in effect bound to adopt the full range of appraisal terms for human action which are available in the wider society and employed in everyday life. This is the point of Nils Brunsson's (1989: 234) demand that we must equally use terms like 'sin', 'hypocrisy' and 'responsibility' if we accept the place of irrationality in organization. Language with a far more direct moral and political content must dispel the pretence of a uniquely privileged rational way of describing organizational action.

Undoubtedly the gain in intelligibility achieved by approaching more closely to everyday language will for many analysts be more than outweighed by the loss of systematic rigour and the sense that the lines of organizational structure are blurred or even fractured. But this is a necessary loss, for the relations between emotions are more empirical than they are rational, and it is in fact the case that organizational structure is becoming less categorical and more ambiguous. It is a changed social reality which gives rise to notions of postmodern organization and makes postmodernist analysis relevant (Cooper and Burrell 1988; Burrell 1988; Cooper 1989; Parker 1992), but that reality will only be grasped with a revitalized empirical sociology which seeks to describe and account for this new open texture of organization. Here the concerns of postmodernists converge with the call by Meyer and Zucker (1989: 145) for the sociology of organization to go beyond environmental determination and utility maximization in asking how patterns of interaction sustain organization.

One obvious way to test this approach to organizational affectivity is through the case study based on observation. Examples already exist in Hochschild (1983) and Fine (1988). Another is to confront the concepts of rationalistic organizational analysis with dissonant empirical material and to rework them by dislocating them from their pre-established frame. This is the method which I choose to adopt here.

The chapter proceeds by taking three classic areas of organizational analysis: goals; work performance; communication; and reworks each by recovering the emotional aspect. The choice of these three spheres is of course dictated by the rational model. But we cannot expunge rationality from organizations; it is intrinsic to them. There is every reason for saying that it has developed as organizations have developed and will continue to do so (see Chapter 3). The new recovery of emotionality may indeed prove only to be the next phase of the rationalization process. But it will not leave things as they were. The outcome of reworking the classic themes is the final section of the chapter, 'Emotions and organizational structure', which finds more extensive grounds for reasserting the conclusion of the previous chapter, namely that emotions have to be seen as a property of organizations. They are integral to them and the accomplishment of their tasks. Organizations, viewed as webs of action and interaction, are emotional entities as much as they are rational units.

6.2 ORGANIZATIONAL GOALS

Statements about organizational objectives are notoriously slippery as focal points for organizational analysis and yet traditionally have had a privileged place (Katz and Kahn 1966: 15; Albrow 1968 [Chapter 1]). Rational models of ends/means behaviour appear to require behaviourally defined, unambiguous targets to permit mutual orientation to a common goal by a multiplicity of actors and the possibility of subsequent performance measurement.

But the terminal position of goals in ends/means chains in itself does not make them rational. On the contrary classical economists, and Weber too, shared the presumption of the Latin tag *'de gustibus non est disputandum'*, 'there is no accounting for tastes'. The unbridgeable gulf between facts and valuations led Lionel Robbins, professor of economics at the London School of Economics, to say, 'I confess I am quite unable to understand how it can be conceived to be possible to call this part of Max Weber's methodology in question' (1935: 148).

So we have to explain how organizational goals acquired the epithet 'rational' before we can go on to explain why it is undeserved. There are probably two main reasons. The first is that the commonality of organizational purpose, breaking as it does with the liberal individualism which underpinned so much of classical economics, could be considered in some way to reduce the non-rationality of individual behaviour. The second is that organizational objectives, notwithstanding that their origins may be deemed irretrievably irrational, may, much more than individual goals, be publicly 'rationalized', that is, made rational and open to inspection through specification, formalization, operationalization, measurement.

Taking the commonality of purpose first, we are bound to recognize that for many analysts it is the acceptance of the common objective which creates an organization and on which its rationality hinges. There is a paradox here since the purest common goal organization, if by that is meant one where all members take that goal equally to be their personal objective, resembles much more the religious organization than the capitalistic enterprise which depends on more limited inputs and allegiances. The current frequent use of the idea of a 'mission statement' with its religious overtones is indication enough that the language of common goals is some way from economic rationality, and that something more than self-interest is needed to motivate members.

The roots of many of the themes of modern organizational thinking are to be found in Christianity (alienation, responsibility, vocation, hierarchy, recently given a new boost with subsidiarity) which should be sufficient to alert us at least to the possibility of an emotional dimension to all aspects of organization theory. In this context we simply have to recognize that religious goals are in themselves non-rational, and this regularly applies to common goal organizations of all kinds.

The favourite recourse to shared goals and values as a remedy for worker alienation should be seen as a secular restatement of religious salvation needs rather than a contribution to organizational rationality. The sharing of objectives as such is dependent on so many aspects of trust, commitment and mutual understanding that a verdant field of sentiment opens up before us. As I pointed out in the previous chapter, the emotionality of co-operative work organization was regarded in the earlier periods as its essential feature.

The other way in which rationality has infused organizational purpose has been through rationalization. The Hobbesian problem of order where individuals pursue their discrete ends can be solved by appealing to the hidden hand of the market or to force. Neither appealed to theorists of modern organization. For them the organizational goal arose out of a different social process, collective social choice. But we have to ask how rationality becomes so firmly entrenched there.

Actually even in Hobbes we can find an intimation of how rationality finds a foothold in the individual setting of objectives. For him the will as opposed to desire was simply 'the last appetite in deliberation' (1651: 40). So a reflective process is involved even if the ultimate decision is beyond reason. This notion was developed by Ferdinand Tönnies (who had worked on Hobbes) within his seminal account of *Gemeinschaft* and *Gesellschaft* (1887) by shifting discussion of the will from the individual to the social group. It was the degree of explicitness and calculation which distinguished the social organization of *Gesellschaft* from that of the *Gemeinschaft*. It was the will of deliberation as opposed to the basic will of the natural community.

Tönnies ushered in the age when rationalization became a watchword for the modernization of both industry and personal behaviour. The rationalization of objectives in industry and organizations generally became a movement in the early part of the twentieth century at the same time as the idea of rationalization of individual behaviour became a key term within psychoanalysis. In each case reflection transforms the objective, but in the case of organizations the result was much more likely to be incorporated into manuals, rule books and codes of practice. It was an easy step left to Weber to generalize the process to all aspects of social life.

Organizational objectives, then, have had a privileged place in the rationalization process and individuals orientating to an organization have been deemed to have a special interest in assisting the process. Quite apart from employers and employees, third parties, stakeholders, who treat organizations as within their own field of action benefit from organizational fixity of purpose. As I have stressed before, in Weber's view it was this formal calculability and reliability that made bureaucracy indispensable, rather than its technical efficiency, about which he was far more ambivalent (Albrow 1970: 61–6). Objectives are rationalizable, even if in their origin they are non-rational. It is then a question of increasing the sphere of rationality in the interests of reducing uncertainty, the principle which Luhmann (1985) has made constitutive for the development of law.

The radical separation of organizational purpose from individuals' objectives as effected by the public choice theorists indeed makes a virtue of this alienation effect. It assumes that each person is indeed only interested in organizational participation for his or her own benefit. The organizational objective is then elevated into an entirely instrumental position for each member of the organization rather than a terminal value. Provided it is un-ambiguous, precise and measurable it appears as a rational focus. But this is a recent intellectual development which has kicked away any ladder of mean-ing upon which organizational purpose may have climbed to this elevated position.

For whence this purpose? And if no one believes in its intrinsic worth, how does it survive when it is, as Meyer and Zucker (1989) declare, a measure of permanent failure? They indeed seek to assert the non-rationality of organiz-ation by stressing the disparity between performance and objectives. But that does not yet go far enough. For efficiency models have never claimed that per-fect efficiency is achieved in reality. It is always a limiting case. We need to re-examine the imputation of rationality to the objectives themselves.

We have to ask how far the reduction of uncertainty can in principle go. Every analysis of publicly defined objectives for organizations suggests that they run ultimately into fundamental, rationally unresolvable antinomies, as indeed Weber stressed. Even if we take the simple case of the single over-riding goal of the profit-maximizing organization we have to recognize that non-rationality has an irreducible hold. Let us imagine it hiring and firing at will, manufacturing a single product with the most advanced technology but requiring only the most modest skills on the part of the operatives, where labour is plentifully available and demand for the product buoyant. In this free enterprise utopia there is no need to inspire the workers with common purpose, or anything other than a piece rate payment. Nor would there be any need for management consultants.

So it would have to be a sociologist who would put this question. Do we have here the purest possible case of rational objectives, conceding of course that in its origin, the pursuit of profit is not in itself rational? Do we have clear-cut specified objectives which do not require or allow emotion to intrude? An affirmative answer would presumably require a demonstration that there were no dilemmas arising which required non-rational solutions. That is not easy. Take profit maximizing. Is it this year or next year? What time preference is involved? If it is twenty years, what determination and endurance does this require on the part of the decision-makers? If it is this year how much impatience and recklessness does this imply? Determination and impatience are already terms of behaviour appraisal, with moral over-tones and suggestions of character analysis. We may more readily see impatience as emotive, tallying with the explosive image of emotion. But emo-tion controlled is emotion employed and determination is as much part of the vocabulary of Western emotionality as is excitement.

Any account of the rise of self-discipline necessarily involves reference to the control of anger and fear, or any other emotion which calls for satis-faction. That is the basis of the psychoanalytic tradition, Freud's account of civilization and its discontents, but also equally of Weber's Protestant Ethic thesis and Elias' civilizing process. They each rely on the conversion of a disruptive primal energy into a controlled supply of motivation to behave in a socially acceptable manner. But Weber was also profoundly aware of the psychic economy of discipline: 'Enthusiasm and unreserved devotion may, of course, have a place in discipline; every modern conduct of war weighs, frequently above everything else, precisely the morale factor in troop effectiveness' (Weber 1968a: 1150).

In fact the way we can reduce emotionality in goal setting is to resort to standardized traditional expectations of profit. But then we only move from the irrational to the non-rational. Moreover it is not only time preference uncertainty which has to be resolved arbitrarily. Equally there are questions of expansion and contraction, alternative routes to profit maximization where preferences cannot be resolved without resort to other criteria located ultimately within emotional structures (personalities, boardroom meetings, situational practices and pressures).

Under these circumstances it can scarcely be surprising that the personal qualities of the entrepreneur often become central features in estimates of the direction and future prospects of any organization which remotely approaches our ideal type. The counterpart of the mission statement is the vision, the imagined future state beckoning our hero towards higher things, sometimes even the dream, out of which arises the conviction pursued with iron resolution. Endowed with such characteristics it is small wonder that the entrepreneur will not rest with a strictly impersonal relationship with the wage labourers. Converts, followers, disciples provide more reassurance and replenish the store of confidence more effectively than the payment of wages to casual workers.

All of this disregards the changing environment, suppliers, competitors and customers, with whom relations will vary, in accord with markets but also with the climate of the times. Here the language of appraisal can convey excitement, energy, threat and attack. Hostile bids, dawn raids, frenzied dealing are the clichés of market relations which ruin lives and leave personal visions in fragments.

In such a context the emotions of self and competitors become signs and clues to each of the others' state of mind, of confidence in the future, willingness to take risks, ability to enter into commitments. Objectives themselves become subordinated to a frame of relationships and a status order which generate the guiding principles of entrepreneurial behaviour. The enterprise culture conquers the culture of the enterprise.

Where the sole entrepreneur is replaced by the board of directors and professional management, the objectives of the organization are both detached from personal control and at the same time the necessary focus for interpersonal rivalry, contradictory interpretation, ritual incantation. As a result the personal qualities of the business leaders are called to account in target setting at least as much as they are with the sole entrepreneur. The vision has to be negotiated and communicated as well as generated, while traces of past visions interfere with clarity of purpose.

Objectives, then, far from being fixed points for enduring reference, are constantly revised and renewed in the hands of professional leaders. The task may well be conceived as one of corporate transformation. The 'can-do' team player provides strategic planning and direction in a new model mix for an emerging global market. Purposiveness, rather than a specific purpose, is the animating spirit of the modern organization, and leaders are not the ones who adhere to a pre-given charter but rather those who take over the task of purpose setting. The organization becomes autopoietic, an open-ended resource for the discovery of new objectives rather than a means to achieving old ones. Where purposiveness itself is the product, it is scarcely surprising that those who can claim to create it acquire rewards beyond the dreams of older entrepreneurs.

The appraisal language for the new leadership emphasizes imagination and inspiration, endurance and flexibility, sensitivity and self-motivation, above all vision and creativity. All of these qualities may be seen as necessary accompaniments to the search for the means of organizational survival in a turbulent environment. As such, they are intimately bound up with a more profound organizational rationality. But that is not to deny their emotionality. The relations of rationality and emotionality in the organizational setting parallel their relations in individuals. The modern business leader is required to have the attributes of scientist, artist and politician. We should recall here that Weber's portraits (1947) of the vocations of scientist and politician highlighted emotional requirements. In each case creativity arises from both cognitive abilities and emotional resources. The excitement of discovery is common to each, simultaneously reward for past effort and spur to new achievement.

We have come full circle to the opening theme of this section. For the emotional climate in which these qualities of leadership for the renewal of purpose is going to be promoted is not one of sovereign individuals, or lone entrepreneurs. We will see when we address authority that the co-operative group is again valued as the setting in which the sparks of imagination can fly. The main difference from the early nineteenth century is that the extra impetus gained from the group is no longer feared for its subversiveness.

6.3 TASK PERFORMANCE

Goal setting is itself a variety of work and the descriptions employed above for goal-setting behaviour are simply special cases of work performance vocabulary. No description of work in real time which avoids reference to the state of feelings of the worker can provide an account which will satisfy a third party. Manual labour may be performed alertly, enthusiastically, vigorously, resentfully, steadily, carelessly, heedlessly, effortlessly, painfully, lackadaisically. Mental labour may be performed imaginatively, with concentration, with dour determination, haphazardly, painstakingly, with excitement, passionately.

Actually the lists are interchangeable although the incidence of some descriptions will be greater for the one sphere than the other. But manual labour can be imaginative, as anyone who has seen a good gardener at work will know, and no academic needs reminding that mental labour can be painful.

The demands on descriptive action vocabulary are enormously enhanced as soon as the social dimension of work is taken into the account. The scientist at work with others can be generous, defensive, disturbing, stimulating, self-satisfied; the bricklayer perfectionist, demanding, arrogant, imperious. Here we are drawn easily into the spheres of authority and communication, about which more later. For the moment let us stay with the object environment, remembering always that those objects may sometimes be human beings whether on the operating table, on a passenger flight, or on a payroll, all impersonal elements in someone's work schedule, all personally affected by the performance of that work without ever encountering the worker.

The atmosphere of the working situation of those who work collectively on impersonal tasks can easily affect the product or output. The alienation and resentment of the British car-worker in the 1960s were hardly unconnected with the reputation of British cars for poor workmanship. In the provision of services where there is a division of labour between production and delivery, there has to be particular stress upon the responses of those who move between emotional setting of the producers and provide for the immediate requirements of the customers. The air stewardess, to whose work Hochschild (1983) has given such close consideration, has to cope with the fallout of the air crew's feelings, protect the customer from them, and absorb the emotional demands of the passengers.

In the restaurant trade, the atmosphere in the kitchen can easily be conveyed to the customer in two ways, directly in the quality of the food, and indirectly through the serving staff who have to move between the two settings, in much the same way as the air stewardess. Gary Fine has provided an account based on ethnographic study of the work environment of a kitchen in which he argues that expressive behaviour is integral to the work situation. It is not merely, in his terms, 'letting off steam (in a psychological, hydraulic model)'. He says it contributes to the actual work, so that the boundaries of work and play are erased. He quotes a comment from one cook, 'I just love the activity . . . I concentrate totally, so I don't know how I feel . . . it's like another sense takes over' (Fine 1988: 125).

Such an account is wholly within the frame of analysis which this chapter is proposing. It is illuminating at many levels, structurally and ecologically. The kitchen as an emotional work cauldron, potentially requiring total absorption, has to be physically separated from the area in which food is consumed if the work is to be done to standard. At the same time the serving staff will be subjected to a dual pressure from cooks and customers. Conversely where the work of food preparation is conducted in the presence of its consumption, in a British home, or a fast food restaurant, conflict between the contradictory moods associated with each is an ever present danger. The temperamental cook is a popular stereotype. But it is the work and its milieu which carry the emotional charge.

Work definitions which seek to minimize the emotional aspects of performance are either inadequate and misleading, or more usually in effect making tacit acknowledgment of their existence. The military and bureaucratic sectors have the reputation of requiring soulless automata. Each in its way is seeking to construct a factitious objectivity to force and administration, something which will convert the labile into the fixed immovable object. In each case the effort required to turn people into robots involves a harnessing of energy and determination, sometimes of deliberately frightening intensity. The parade ground sergeant bellows terror into the new recruit. Fear can equally prompt freezing to the spot as it can flight. Rigid, inflexible, cold behaviour is just as emotional as warm and loving responses. But for some sectors it is easier to call upon the rejection of emotions in the name of rationality, than it is to acknowledge that the real requirement is the training of anger, disdain, and contempt.

The requirement as an aspect of role performance that a person should be prepared to use violence or even kill under some circumstances means inculcating a general preparedness for violence. There should therefore be nothing surprising about the regularity with which cases of police violence are reported and even less confidence that there is any simple remedy.

Without doubt the emotional requirements of work performance are now more widely acknowledged than ever in organizations, possibly because the military model has less and less influence on civilian life. The decline in what Andreski called the military participation ratio (MPR) of the citizenry in the modern nation-state (Andrzejewski 1954) means a decline in the general acceptability of military values of discipline. We can see this in contemporary job advertisements. No longer are descriptions confined to traditional leadership qualities as implied by military models. They extend into discretion, self-confidence, risk-taking, imagination, determination and a whole range of qualities which are required for working with other people such as tact, empathy, assertiveness, co-operativeness. These involve a recognition that working in co-operation with other people draws upon and requires a set of responses which go far beyond cognitive aspects of job performance. (Paradoxically advertisements for military careers now ape the civilian sector.)

Of course the decline in the MPR is matched by a rise in organizations linked with the defence industry, and in consequence a growth in secrecy and the acceptability of dissimulation, covertness and evasiveness. But it is a shift which allows for emotions to be invoked, even if their authenticity is in doubt. In fact, as we shall see, emotional ambiguity and the dissimulation of feeling are central issues of controversy in the discussion of organizational feeling.

6.4 COMMUNICATION AND SITUATIONAL LOGICS

It was in the direct interpersonal communication of feeling that the nineteenth-century writers identified the special features of organized co-operation. The contagion of spirit enhanced the effectiveness of work and raised people to tasks which separately they could not manage. Twentieth-century management practices in effect did their best to bring such contagion under control and to limit communication to necessary instructions or data transfer. Production processes at the level of the small group were subordi-nated to the logic of large organization and became defined very much as the informal sector, the human undergrowth to patterned rules and procedures.

This concentration on the internal mechanisms of work group formation and process deflected attention away from communication across groups, which is far more central to the working of the organization in which the work groups are located. This was seen as formal structure, inhabiting a rational sphere, and removed from sociological attention. But this meant that large sectors of organizational behaviour went unreported. Where lateral, or horizontal relations were considered, it was often converted into issues of administrators versus professionals, and again seen as a matter of competing forms of knowledge rather than a matter of emotional expression.

The encounters, conversations and meetings of personnel in which busi-ness is transacted across departmental divisions constitute a large part of the work of organizations. These are complex occasions, involving much more than data exchange. Helen Schwartzman's recent study of meetings empha-sizes how much they are a way of life in which one of the most salient aspects is the way they serve as an arena for the expression of emotion (1989: 134). The demeanour, expression, mood of each party are scrutinized for signs of the real factors which determine the working of other parts of the organiz-ation. Even the written memo has a vast range of stylistic cues which serve to convey feelings and for this reason often requires meticulous care both in preparation and in interpretation. Hostility, insecurity, approbation, dismay, agitation, esteem can all be conveyed in subtle variations of greeting, vocabu-lary and style. The memo is in McLuhan's terms a form of 'cool' communica-tion because it invites so many interpretative activities on the part of the recipient (McLuhan 1964: 22–32).

The phenomenology of emotion in organizational communication has scarcely begun to be examined systematically. We have to rely on memoirs and biographies to get the full flavour. For good examples we can turn to Richard Crossman's *Diaries* and his reports of Cabinet meetings during Harold Wilson's first premiership (Crossman 1976): on 2 March 1967 Wilson accused his ministers of being out of touch with back-benchers. 'It was a long gloomy speech'. Callaghan 'weighed in'. Barbara Castle was 'staunch'. 'All the speeches were full of discontent' (ibid.: 259–60); on 4 May 1967 Wilson 'rebuked' the Home Affairs Committee. Crossman 'got more and more irritated'. Wilson's proposals were 'torn to shreds'. There was no one 'who had much sympathy with Barbara'. The 'Cabinet was absolutely solid against her' (ibid.: 342–3).

On 29 May 1967 Crossman wrote 'Finally I must add that reading Cabinet minutes and comparing them with the accounts Roy and Barbara have given me of the meetings has made me realise once again how misleading the official record can be.' He reports how there had been a full discussion with weighty contributions from major Cabinet figures on aid for Israel. 'The discussion was passionate and extremely stirring yet when it had been boiled down and dehydrated by the Cabinet Secretariat very little of it remained' (ibid.: 356).

The disjunction which Crossman notes between the record and the events parallels the official–unofficial, rational–irrational, formal–informal dichotomies. Indeed, what he describes is an episode in their regular construction, day in, day out in any organization. It is a facet of the general process of organizational construction which is a key aspect of bureaucratic work and has been the focus for a tradition of ethnomethodological research on organizations ever since Bittner's seminal paper (1965). But it is the process of construction, rather than the content, which preoccupies these studies. As one commentator writes, ethnomethodology 'yields subjectivist, idiographic descriptions of everyday situations' (Hassard 1990); we can add that the accomplishment of those descriptions is well described, but their content is regarded as subjective, and the forces which dictate it are left in obscurity.

We can indeed acquire a lot of information about the use of written codes describing what can be communicated in writing. We can at other times record the shared understandings which are normally observed. One civil servant has told me how an experienced official gave him advice when he first had to take Cabinet committee minutes. It was 'Rewrite everything, omitting the adverbs; and then rewrite everything again, omitting the adjectives'. Within the British civil service 'Cabinet Committee style' is as impersonal as a record can be, omitting reference to speakers and views, concentrating on capturing decisions only. It is bound not to satisfy Crossman's desire to record what actually happened. Other media will be more inclusive in their scope, depending on the participants and purpose of the work. But we are still some way from explaining why these forms of communication are shaped in the way they are to exclude some kinds of content.

Thus in one government department the normal written output is a typed Note from one official to another, filed in the writer's files, on which, however, a Comment may be handwritten by the recipient, and then passed on. The Comment can express anything from pleasure to outrage. Written messages can be sent on scraps of paper, sometimes stuck to a Note, and they too can convey emotion information. The implicit rules on emotion reporting vary according to their relation to organizational structure. The Note within a Department will be cool in so far as its subject matter is confined to internal departmental matters, but strong feelings may be expressed in the Note on external relations, with other organizations or other Departments. Letters are only ever written to other organizations or outside individuals, with one exception, the handwritten letter of thanks from a Minister to a top official, which is then circulated and is held to boost morale. However, the cool nature of the Note will not be appreciated in relations between officials adjacent to each other in the hierarchy, where a conversation might have sufficed. The same elaborate conventions on emotional expression exist in relation to Meetings, with subtle gradations relative to rank and rank relations, numbers of people involved, intra- or cross-Departmental basis. Add to that discussion papers, telephone conversations, and now computer communication, all of which are governed by their own rules. (Information based on personal interview.)

What is fully evident is that emotional expression is ubiquitous in organizational communication and its processing is a standard part of organizational work. This is to reject one way of interpreting Crossman's account which would be to argue, in ostensible debt to Max Weber, that the officials take the passion out of the political process. But this is where we have to take a wider view of organizational structure. In Cabinet, ministers are part of the government machine. Their passions are replicated in any boardroom or managing committee. Neither do the officials inhabit a passionless sphere. They too can 'let off steam', urge their point of view passionately, in the right setting and through the appropriate medium. Only the official record becomes an anodyne passion-free statement. Only if we confuse that with the reality of organizational process do we imagine that organizations are emotionless. The problem then arises: 'Why are official records written in this way?'

There is no easy answer to this question to my mind, precisely because of the taken-for-granted nature of the practice. It is not something which the newcomer to an organization is supposed to question, and if they were to do so the likely answer would be something like 'because you can't let feelings into it' or 'because we just stick to the facts'. But these answers are themselves highly problematical and call for much more systematic inquiry. Emotions are in practice an acknowledged and essential part of organizational work. Rafaeli and Sutton's (1989, 1990, 1991) studies of management training for emotional display by police officers or debt collectors provide impressive evidence for the prevalence and impact of organizational feeling rules. On the account here a further area for research would be into the relationship between organizational structure and reports of emotional disclosure when emotional display is proscribed. The 'official record' is an account which potentially can become public; emotional disclosure reveals information on the strength and weakness of the reporting unit, information which in a threatening environment may be used by others against you.

Another line of inquiry might be to look again at the notion of organizational objectives and outputs and see official records as part of that output, in so far as decisions are made and communicated through them, while emotions are part of the input, no more reportable than the skills or any other qualities of the members which contribute to their performance but are not being offered on for further consumption. Here again the question of unit interfaces arises, suggesting that it is in relations and not in bodies that we have to see the problematic of organizational emotion.

Specifically in this context our definition of authority (see Chapter 4) provides for the subsequent incorporation of the emotional subtleties of authority relations into the concept. Authority is constantly negotiated in situations where the emotional exchanges of the parties are a key element in the winning of that kind of regard which can prompt reciprocal responses. For instance authority can be won where competence is demonstrated, enthusiasm communicated, pleasure in the work displayed, there is readiness to accept criticism, confidence in outcomes is expressed, co-operation welcomed. Authority can be lost by an over-bearing manner, displays of anger, unpredictable moods, disregard for others' feelings.

But of course the more people who accord authority to someone, the less likely it is that any particular defect or mistake on any one occasion is going to cause a serious diminution of authority, unless of course it should happen to be highly publicized and breach codes for appropriate expression.

A good instance of such code breaching has been provided by the former chief executive of the largest British jewellery firm, Ratners. Gerald Ratner made a much publicized announcement in a speech to the Institute of Directors in April 1991 that he was selling 'crap'. He intended it as a joke. Indeed, he had used it as such in numerous private gatherings previously. On press commentators' accounts, however, it was responsible for collapsing profits, nose-diving share prices and ultimately for the loss of his job in November 1992 (*The Guardian* newspaper, Frank Kane report 26.11.92; *Sunday Times* newspaper, Jeff Randall report 29.11.92). Here again the situational appropriateness of a particular expression is the key determinant of its effects, and not its intrinsic qualities. In the privacy of the boardroom, Ratner presumably got his laughter and admiration for outrageousness. In the context of a prestigious public gathering the result was a loss of authority.

Situational logics provide the frame for emotional expression in organizations. They determine when and where it is appropriate for what kind of emotion to be expressed. This has long been recognized in accounts of ritual forms of tension release, the office party, or the works outing. But much of the impulse for this kind of account comes from an implicit psychoanalytical framework predicated on the repression of emotion in normal work routines. An approach drawing more on constructionist, interactionist and phenomenological sources can allow for the regular, even necessary expression of emotion in appropriate work situations.

In cases of pressure on a workforce to meet a deadline or production target it may be entirely appropriate for a manager to alternate between expressions of encouragement and exasperation. Where customers arrive in the showroom it would be perverse for the salesman to act with disdain and lack of interest. When a safety rule has been wilfully broken, the culprit will expect an angry response, and not just from superiors, but from any colleague who could be threatened. The situated character of emotional display is a prerequisite for organizational functioning.

So necessary and expected is it that the question of the ownership of the emotions arises. Organizations depend on people behaving in ways which make sense in the frame of organizational meaning. They have to fit their actions to organizational structure, make sure that their own motives and interests are at least not contradictory to organizational requirements, at best make the organization's objectives their own. Nothing is done in organizations except by people, but a fair part of their actions belong to the organization. We do not find it incongruous if the manager says his target is to achieve an output of 3,300 production units a month. That output is the collective product of the organization, his goal the organization's goal. Are his feelings of excitement when the target is beaten his only, or his dismay when they fall short purely private and personal? If feelings are appropriate and required by the organization, just as goals and activities are, can they not equally belong to the organization?

The bodily experience of the emotion does not belong purely personally to the individual any more than the visual inspection of a file in an office or the manual tightening of a nut in a workshop are outside the organization because they involve individual sense data. Moreover the visible display of emotional behaviour is so readily replicated for effect under the right circumstances that the question of whether the person 'really' feels that way often arises only as an academic question. Is the anger of the parade ground sergeant pulling up the slack raw recruit authentic or put on for effect? Does it matter? Could *either* of them tell the difference between the real and the simulated? Can we not have authentic performance? The dramaturgical perspective on human behaviour is often thought of as drawing an analogy between drama and life. The fact is that organizations require the acting out of roles not as a metaphor for real life but in order to instantiate the reality of organization. Employees are playing for real.

This approach, which has much in common with the constructionism of Harré (1988), seeks to avoid the Goffman/Hochschild dilemma, where the former's stress on staged performance (1956) leaves the actor's core feelings vacant while the latter's stress on the falsity of emotional labour posits an alienated core. Nor does it assume or look to a normative harmony of organizational and personal feeling after the fashion of McGregor's Theory Y

(1966). Rather it treats the expression of emotion in organizational situations as an authentic aspect of people's behaviour in organizations, part of the ongoing process of constructing the organization. In principle it is neither more nor less alienated than what goes on in families or between friends.

6.5 EMOTIONS AND ORGANIZATIONAL STRUCTURE

The situated quality of emotions, the dramaturgical abilities of actors, and the differentiated structure of organizations constitute a theoretical frame for understanding a phenomenon which otherwise eludes organizational analysis, namely the often noticed fact of 'atmosphere', a feeling which appears to belong to the setting rather than the people, since each individual may be glad to get out of it, or alternatively, since 'atmospheres' may also be good, may be inspired on entering it.

An example of atmosphere may be taken from an insider's account in the British Treasury staff magazine *Chequerboard* which asked a former member of staff to describe how the 'feel' of his new Department of National Heritage differed from that of the Treasury. In a brief space the author, Nicholas Holgate (1992), ranges confidently over many of the main aspects of the problematic of organizations. As a non-technical account it carries an authenticity which rationalistic models of organization fail to capture. It covers the variable of extra-departmental contacts, greater with the public for the DNH, greater with other Departments for the Treasury, differential satisfaction from 'owning' results, and the chance of a new Department developing a different culture. The author talks of the atmosphere of Treasury as 'a particularly studious school' and of the new Department having an 'uneven feel' with 'several mini-atmospheres that mix at the edges' which, however, provides 'a tremendous opportunity of establishing practices which suit the 1990's, not just adapting a common inheritance of procedure accrued over decades' (ibid.: 9).

This illustrates that total 'feel' for an organization which has still eluded pysychological research into 'climate' and which undoubtedly has fuelled the 1980s' enthusiasm for the idea of corporate culture. In fact this insider's account with its emphasis on tradition coupled with the known relative stability of staffing in a British government Department lends itself to a structural–cultural interpretation of organizational emotion. Anticipatory socialization linked with known personnel selection methods, and then in-service training complete the ingredients for a theory of organizations which evokes the structure, culture, personality dimensions of an older mainstream functionalist sociological theory.

As Robert Merton (1992) pointed out to me, he was lecturing on emotions in organizations in Harvard in the 1930s. His concern there, as in his critique of Weber's bureaucrat (Merton 1940), was to ensure that the emotions were integrated into sociological descriptions of institutions. The thrust of this chapter and the one before (Chapter 5) is to develop action and interpretative approaches in a broadly Weberian spirit, but equally to insist that this entails the full acknowledgement of the vital presence of emotions in organizations.

The theoretical frame is different from Merton's, but just as Weber acknowledged the indispensable preliminary problem setting provided by functionalist questions ('It is necessary to know what a "king", an "official", an "entrepreneur", a "procurer" or a "magician" does ... before it is possible to undertake the analysis itself', Weber 1968a, I: 18) so it is right to recognize a similar priority in relation to organizations. As the quotation from Weber makes clear, the major contribution the functionalist perspective made was to raise questions which demanded and got empirical investigation. The thrust of this chapter is to suggest that there is a further range of empirical issues raised by the interpretative approach.

By situating emotions in organizational contexts and seeing emotional responses as part of the repertoire of the organizational actor rather than as personality characteristics, provision is made both for disjunctions and for matches between organizational requirements and individual needs. Equally there is provision for variations over time and space in the incidence of emotionality within the organization. External contingencies and internal differentiation of task units will create very different emotional settings.

This theoretical locus for emotions provides the scope necessary for explaining otherwise neglected phenomena, like interdepartmental variations in atmosphere. Within British government Departments, as opposed to between them, movement of personnel is rapid, and the staff of a division of a dozen people may have changed completely over a four-year period. But the identity of the division may be associated with a 'feel' or an 'atmosphere' irrespective of the personnel occupying it.

It is not a question here of a personality type but of moods, and expressions appropriate for the situation. As so often is the case, the intuitive, everyday manner of speaking, that these departments have 'a feel to them', has a better hold on the reality of the situation than a rationalistic model which excludes emotions from organizational structure. The contention of this and the previous chapter that 'organizations have feelings' is not a rhetorical flourish. It is a formulation required by the texture of work in contemporary organizations. I hope to have demonstrated it working through the emotional reality of three classic dimensions of organizational structure. In other words the case for a particular theoretical contention has been advanced through the accumulation of empirical illustration to show the inadequacy of rationalistic analysis.

This intellectual strategy is only one of many possible routes to reestablishing emotion in organization theory. But no single route alone will provide the necessary redirection, as evidence from earlier attempts shows. Merton's insights in his 'Bureaucratic Structure and Personality' (1940) were only in part exploited in the work of his pupils, Gouldner and Blau, probably because feelings were themselves tied too closely to the concept of personality. So Gouldner noted differences between miners' and surfacemen's personalities, expressed in dress or readiness to open aggression (1955a: 136), but the theme was largely stillborn in the sociological literature on organizations as cognitive decision-making models came to exclude empirically based work.

The same continual pressure towards cognitive definitions of organizational problems probably accounts for another largely unfulfilled approach to emotion in the long-established tradition of writing on organizational climate. Although the concept arose out of the insight that there were relatively enduring qualities of the organizational environment and in early work attempts were made to specify dimensions of feeling in that climate (e.g. Fiedler 1962; Tagiuri and Litwin 1968), over time the literature became heavily weighted towards studies of the methodological problems of measuring perception of that climate, and thence to seeing those perceptions as individual characteristics. A recent discussion (Patterson et al. 1992) concludes that it is necessary to specify clearly the unit of analysis on which individuals are asked to focus – job, team, organization, etc. We can go further: it is necessary for the analyst to focus on the unit before interrogating individuals and to identify situated feelings before asking people about them. Nothing is more likely to convert emotional states into cognitive maps than asking actors to complete formal grids. Good sociological observational studies are indispensable as ways of registering the emotional climate of organization, matched only by participants' memoirs written in the heat of the moment. Katz and Kahn (1966: 66) long ago pointed out that the organizational climate and culture concepts could only be developed effectively on the basis of participant observation followed by depth interviewing, but their plea went largely unheeded. In conclusion, some work which fulfils this demand deserves to be highlighted.

Hochschild (1983) has made the most important contribution to redressing this cognitive bias by basing her account of emotion on observational study and by seeking to develop a model drawing elements from Darwin, James, Freud, Dewey, Gerth and Mills, and Goffman. Her own research led her to emphasize the efforts individuals expend in the management of their emotions in the course of paid employment and the controls which organizations exert on this process. But her choice of organizational setting, the air flight attendant's work, results in an emphasis on inauthenticity. She provides Goffman's otherwise hollow-souled actor with personal feelings which are managed for money. Where emotional display is less to the forefront as the actual product of work, we are less able to set up a conflict between organizational requirements and individual feeling. The excitement in a foreign exchange dealing room is no less authentic for being situationally induced.

Hearn and Parkin's work on organization sexuality (1987) has, at first sight, much in common with Hochschild's, but, by emphasizing the ubiquity of feeling in organizations, has more in common with the perspective of this chapter and seeks to take issue with what they call the firm tradition of organization theory and management as sexless disciplines. Flam (1990a and b) takes as her starting-point the deconstruction of the rational model of the actor and carries her argument through to constructing a model of the corporate body as both emotion-motivated and emotion manager.

Where these contributions and the interpretative perspective of this chapter agree is on a rejection of a rationalism which requires the recasting of the vocabulary of organizational performance into a mechanistic systems vocabulary, or where it is assumed that the only valid description of organizational action is in terms of an imputed systems teleology. The language of organizational practice is a multi-layered one, and its purposiveness does not emanate from a single privileged source. 'Knocking ideas around', 'shaping up a job', 'defending your patch', 'giving someone a dressing down' refer to practices which exist as the negotiated, ever reconstructed, everyday reality of organizational life. All such practices consist of a varying mix of the ingredients of rationality, emotion and tradition. In sum they constitute a complex culture. Analytical approaches which seek to suppress the contribution which any one of these makes to that complexity distort reality and mislead their customers. For too long the recognition of organizational emotions has suffered from the repression exerted by rationalistic models of organization, even after those models have lost the esteem they once had.

The Weber to whom we return for a reanimated organizational analysis is not the exponent of ideal types and rationalistic methodology. He is the historian and empirical social researcher, the sociologist of religion and interpreter of world-views. In this guise his work examined the facticity of rationality, its origins and influence. Elsewhere I have described his approach as anti-foundationalist, determined to take a hold on a commonsensical social reality (Albrow 1991b), and I have argued that his concern for social facts was quite the equal of Durkheim's (Albrow 1990: 277–9). The consequence for the study of organizations is a firm insistence on their empirical embeddedness in society, on their being sociologically determined.

If this is a different Weber from the one who customarily appears in association with bureaucracy, the explanation has to be that his work was many-sided, and that different orientations often co-exist uneasily within it. The case for giving one of them primacy is never easy to make, but my justification for giving pride of place to the empirical thrust is that Weber himself also wrote of bureaucracy in a vein closer to his more general historical and interpretative approach. His extended notes on charisma, party and bureaucrats (Weber 1968a: 1130–2) and on the defects of bureaucratic power in Germany (ibid.: 1393–442) are decisive corrections to the view that he was in thrall to his rational ideal type. The contention here is that the context into which we have to set his work on organizations is as broad as the frame of reference for his work as a whole, namely that identified by Schluchter (1979), Kalberg (1980), Whimster and Lash (1987) and many others, the rise of modern Western rationalism. It is a frame which can give us radical distance and perspective on any number of the fashions in organizational analysis which have come and gone in the seventy years since Weber wrote. It equally must involve as broad and comprehensive a retrieval of the problem of the interplay of rationality and emotion as was involved in Weber's study of Protestantism and of religion in general.

Part IV

ORGANIZING RETURNS
FROM THE SOCIAL

The next two chapters are state-of-the-art reports. They have been written for this volume, reflecting ongoing work. Equally they seek to exemplify the key messages which the preceding chapters have sought to convey over a period of nearly thirty years. In fact the time span is greater, for we were initially exploring the Weberian and modern tradition of organizational sociology with its roots in high modern capitalism. Now we are looking into a present which is marked off from the past by a gulf so great that I can only call it epochal change.

We have lived through the transition from the Modern Age to the Global Age. The change is no less than that. There is only one reason for suggesting that the subjective extent of the change is greater than the reality and that is because for a long time sociologists have clung to a notion of enduring modernity which has diminished our sensitivity to change.

So even the most dramatic changes in organizational structure are labelled as simply postmodern, partnering the modern, or being regarded as a peculiar modernity, instead of being seen as forms which belong to a new configuration of society altogether.

Now we can only register change of this kind if we hold to a programme of sociology as an engagement with social reality. We can only maintain that, if our theory escapes the confines of an earlier age, the modern, and keeps pace with the change. As we have seen, a theory which keeps pace with the times also contributes to them, just as modern theory did.

But this was implied at the very beginning of this book, from the first chapter which argued that objectivity on organizations could only be achieved if we detached ourselves from the self-images of modernity, in particular its rationalism, and held to a notion of the social which was detached from any sectional interest. This detachment was what sociology could achieve and to my mind the sociology of organization has proved its ability to do this throughout the period, retaining an independent intellectual standpoint, irrespective of fashion, ideology, or inducements.

131

It is in its retention and exploration of the idea of the social in all its changing manifestations that the sociology of organization retains its abiding intellectual validity and its relevance for the way we lead our lives. It is an idea which is non-modern, and which every culture and every period fashion in their own way.

What is exciting for us at this time is precisely the growing awareness that the hold which modernity had over organizational forms and society in general has slackened. The nation-state in modernity succeeded largely in equating the social with its own temporary organization of society. This was why the theory of bureaucracy served for both capitalist and state organization. We are now aware that the shape of organizing in the Global Age is unconfined by models of bureaucracy, or indeed by the conceptual inheritance of modernity.

Even something like technological change, the motor of modernity in so many conceptions, on closer inspection turns out to be a movement of the social. Chapter 7, which draws on Neil Washbourne's fieldwork and is written with him, shows that 'the new technology' is an old-fashioned label for organizing practices which reshape co-operative work. What is different are the open negotiability and indeterminacy in a green movement organization which take us outside the notions of a blueprint or clear dividing line between the social structure and technology.

This is then an exploration of the social taking us beyond the micro, macro and structural levels of an older modern analysis. We need to recognize an irreducibly interstitial nature of the social which negotiates changing boundaries. We have further to acknowledge the reconstitution and reaffirmation of social identity which transcends change as another key aspect of sociality. We offer this as a stronger version of a sociological approach to organization than that available in current institutional theory of organization.

In my view we can only do justice to changes in contemporary organization if we recognize that these are intimately connected with the transformation of modernity. This means we have to regain our links with, rather than lose sight of, grand narrative. Chapter 8 exposes that loss as the product of disillusioned modernity. Rather, we have to recognize that the modern narrative was only one passing variant of human accounting for social existence and that we have to replace it with one different in kind.

On the other hand, we do not replace the certainties of lost modernity by inventing new methodologies, another modern response. Rather, we do our best to be sensitive to the changes around us by using all the methods at our disposal. The new organizational sociology is new not because its science is more advanced, but because the world is different.

If we want to sum up that difference it is that we cannot read off contemporary organizational form from an epochal narrative. We used to speak of 'modern organization' and the 'Modern Age' in the same breath, as expressions of a driving force called 'modernity' and generating 'modernization'.

This was the grandest of the grand narratives which Jean-François Lyotard (1984) so trenchantly criticized. Underlying it was the assumption which characterized Max Weber's account of bureaucracy, namely that the world was converging on one type of rational organization.

There is now nothing like 'modern organization' which served as a template for organizing activity under conditions of modernity. The present Global Age is characterized by orientations to globality and they do not supply a blueprint. To that extent we are warranted in speaking of postmodern organizing. For the sociology of organization this means there is an enormous amount of work, just to record and theorize the change. For people who organize, and that means everyone today, there is everything to learn and even more to do.

7

SOCIOLOGY FOR POSTMODERN ORGANIZERS
Working the Net[7]
with Neil Washbourne

7.1 SOCIOLOGY AND THE SOCIAL REALITY OF ORGANIZATION

The main thrust of the sociology of organization is to base organization in a profound understanding of the social. This is an intellectual activity with practical consequences. But it is not, as with organization theory itself, dedicated to improving organizational performance. Rather it poses a challenge to organizers: Ignore sociology at your peril! For knowledge of the social is a resource, and the lack of it a disadvantage in any competitive struggle.

The sociology of organization is open to any who care to use it. It doesn't take sides but, in a society where access to almost anything is shaped by power relations, free access to sociology means in effect that its use contributes to redressing imbalances of power. The sociology of organization has always spoken to and for workers, customers, or citizens as much as to and for owners, business or the state.

Relativizing knowledge claims against the professional interests and background of the claimants has been part of the stock in trade of sociologists from the beginning. For instance it was a key feature of Max Weber's sociology of law to recognize the interest of lawyers in developing a technical body of law (Albrow 1975a). Similarly claims to uphold the technical autonomy of expertise within organizations, and even more to represent the true nature of the organization, are treated by sociologists with an equally critical gaze.

In these respects and others sociology was postmodern before postmodernism. It never did accept, as we saw in Chapter 1, the claims of the modern organization and its technical experts that its shape represented the most rational, efficient and effective form of organization yet known. It noted always the time- and culture-bound nature of those forms and always retained the ever open possibility of their transformation.

But sociology is not postmodern if by that is meant the promotion of a cognitive and ethical relativism which denies the possibility of grasping social reality or that this reality has any relevance to moral choice. Indeed, in relation to the modern, sociology is non-modern in so far as it contextualizes whatever it studies against the continuous and limitless experience of the social.

At the end and the beginning the sociology of organization and of organizations must be a study of social reality. If that may seem crashingly obvious to some it may be because they have *not* immersed themselves in organizational studies of the last twenty years. If they had, they would have become familiar with perspectives on organizations, images of organization, discourse on organization, not as contributions to the study of reality but as endpoint. The reality of organization would have retreated outside the orbit of enquiry altogether.

These intellectual strategies, in which staging posts towards understanding become final resting homes, have developed contemporaneously with the transformation of the reality of organization. Older structures have crumbled. Whole industrial sectors have decayed, taking with them forms of organization which had seemed intrinsic to modern life. The boundaries of organizations have become more permeable and the commitments of individuals to social units and those units to them have become more conditional. The firm does not offer a job for life and the individual does not see the firm as the prime justification of work.

So we can distinguish two movements in our time. There is first the intellectual, driven especially by academics. On the one hand, they display integrity by refusing hasty and superficial characterization of the 'real world'. On the other hand, they have a vested interest in creative play, in counterfactual exercises exploring alternatives to the present. These features produce intellectual excitement in many fields including organization theory.

Those who aspire to run organizations, but especially the consultants and communicators, have learned how to exploit the creative power of this intellectual movement. It therefore contributes to other far-reaching changes in contemporary organizations like the new communications technology and globalization. But the new conditions of global risk, global communication and globalized markets are not simply intellectual products. Encoded as 'globalization' they are often seen as an economic phenomenon. But they are better viewed as aspects of something broader, a transformation of social reality (Albrow 1994b, 1996). Our second movement is social and involves far-reaching disturbance of what once were modern certainties.

The conjunction of these two movements, with their intellectual scepticism and a general sense of uncertainty, is fertile ground for a relativism or nihilism in which anything goes, no viewpoint appears better than any other, nothing has any intrinsic worth. For those whose bread and butter is to represent the age to itself, to articulate the inarticulate feelings of the many, 'chaos' is the watchword or catchword. The gurus of management have made as much out of this as any other mood merchants.

The sociology of organization, if it is to make any abiding contribution, has to offer something other than disillusion or the mirror of the time. Even as it registers the changes in organization it refers them to a long-term audit of possibilities and outcomes. As it utilizes alternative perspectives it judges their worth in relation to the concrete realities it explores. Even as it recognizes the general sense of unease, or, in the classic formulation, of anomie, it is able to distinguish between changes in social relations and shifts in intellectual outlook.

Sociology is a bulwark against identifying the life and times of people as the product of ideas, or alternatively ideas as simply the product of the time. In other words it has remained equally resistant to extreme versions of the theory of ideology or to idealist history. It is both empirical in respect of ideas and critical in respect of reality, by which is meant that it seeks to document the diffusion and intertwining of ideas with social relations without reducing the one to the other. It is, moreover, and consistent with its general stance, self-critical too about its own ideas, never equating its own solutions and accounts with reality itself, even as it rigorously checks the one against the other.

In the practice of sociology this means that we can never declare that we have finally determined the nature of the social. We have to allow for developments of two kinds, the ever-changing human experience of the social and its shifting intellectual appreciation, which, as we saw in Chapter 2, are closely related. It means that every generation, every age at least, is going to rewrite its sociology.

In this chapter we will offer one example of how that rewriting takes place at the present time in an account of organizing in a distinctively contemporary setting, enacted by people with uncertain employment status, connected to a globalist movement, with the environment as focus of concern, exploring the possibilities of the Internet.

As we take the account forward we will find ourselves exploring the two sides of the social, namely ongoing transformation in the world and the development of our own ideas. And since the main point of this chapter, like this book as a whole, is to indicate the scope and limits of a distinctively sociological approach to organization, we will focus much more specifically than is usually the case, on the social in and for itself.

Sociology can never claim to have finally captured the complex reality of the social which it seeks to depict and account for. At the same time its own accounts contribute to that reality, so complexity is not reduced by sociological work, rather it becomes possible to increase the scope of the considerations which enter into organizational activities. In the context of contemporary changes, sociological accounts draw attention to dimensions of social change which would otherwise fall outside the purview of, or otherwise present problems for, those engaged in routine organizational activity. Let us then illustrate these ongoing contributions from contemporary work.

7.2 THREE OLD MODERN BENCHMARKS FOR THE SOCIAL

To provide a benchmark it may help the reader to begin by stating as given some established sociological concepts and problem settings which set the direction for enquiry in an organizational context. Our account as it progresses will then explore these concepts and topics to deepen our understanding of them and therefore the social as it is characteristic of our time.

We will thus at first distinguish three dimensions of organizational reality which are specifically social, and not reducible to technical definition by lawyers, accountants, economists, ergonomists, or even 'organization theorists'. These are micro-social behaviour, the social composition of the organization, and macro-social change.

It is important to note that in each of these cases 'social' has slightly different nuances so that it has in the past been very easy to separate these dimensions, even to detach them from each other altogether. But what our account will show is that the exploration of their intimate and shifting linkages is one of the most vital contributions sociology can make. Initially let us take each and indicate briefly its usual scope.

1 Micro-social behaviour: here 'social' refers to interactional processes which rely on routines or assumptions which are uncritically accepted by the participants and indeed have to be for daily work to continue. We are dealing with shared understandings which Alfred Schutz (1967) emphasized were intrinsic to constituting social reality and with the arts of impressing others which Erving Goffman (1956) examined to such effect in his series of brilliant essays. Even where acknowledged as indispensable to organizational performance these are often treated as boundary conditions, easily dismissed under the *ceteris paribus* clause precisely because we can rely on them not changing. But this is a dangerous assumption, equivalent to assuming that, however human beings behave towards it, the physical environment will remain ever munificent. Everyday social routines are intrinsic, not just indispensable to organizational life, and disturbances to them can have incalculable consequences.

2 Social composition of the organization: here 'social' refers to distinctions between people which define actual or potential relations with each other. These characteristics therefore arise in and out of society and not simply within an organization and go beyond its capacity to train or influence people for its own requirements. This means that organizations have to be sensitive to the fact that their 'own people' have their own independent lives which they bring with them. It is a perception which underlies the idea of 'stakeholders'. Beyond issues of training and recruitment social composition is a key determinant of intangible aspects of organizational performance, often broadly grouped under 'climate' and 'culture'. It was

central to the structural–functional approach of Robert Merton (1957) and later to the notion of structure developed by Peter Blau's (1977) account of inequality and heterogeneity.

3 Macro-social change: organizational structure and culture are dependent on conditions in the wider society which go beyond the fixing of legal relations as by contract, property or company law, or beyond market position in terms of capitalization, sales and profits. These conditions are in part political, part cultural, part technological, part economic; indeed, they go beyond any checklist of functional areas or institutional spheres, since it is precisely in the way they overlap and interact that the change is noticeable. For this reason social comes to take on a parcel label sense and it is easy to dismiss it as a concept. But the point is that the overlap of spheres is only managed in and through human agents. 'Macro-social change' denotes the dissemination of new ways of organizing social relations. This is why the broadest interpretations of changes in the contemporary world end up by postulating a new kind of society, such as Bell's (1973) 'post-industrial society' or Beck's (1992) 'risk society'. Currently cultural changes encoded with 'postmodernism' (Jameson 1991) or economic ones with 'globalization' (Giddens 1990; Albrow 1996) lead us directly to speculating about new forms of society.

These three aspects of sociological analysis are phases rather than alternatives in a general procedure of seeking to account for change in organizational systems and structures by reference to social factors outside the control of the participants. There are of course social factors within their control; personnel or human resource measures, provision of social facilities, social responsibility measures. But even these operate against the background of the three aspects we have distinguished.

Equally organizations have to seek to predict and adapt to non-social factors outside their control such as market conditions, environmental risks, changes in the law. But these too are strongly conditioned by the social. Aggregate effects of organizational activities increase environmental risk, the globalization of tastes changes markets and the law changes in part to meet broad changes in social expectations.

It is the isolation from each other of the three phases of analysis we have distinguished which has occasioned some of the most acute problems in the last thirty years of the sociology of organizations. For it is only in their combination that we can claim to identify anything called society or to claim that sociology has an independent contribution to make to organizational analysis.

Separated from each other, intellectual claims can be made that each aspect represents a pre-eminent perspective against the others, seeking to dictate the terms of future accounts, reliant on persuasion and an ongoing struggle for control. This contributes to the relativization of perspectives which parallels the sense of contemporary confusion.

But a full sociological analysis requires each to relate to the other. Our purpose in weaving these together is to reclaim for the sociology of organization a strategic position in organizational studies and, by implication, for sociology to re-assert its place as the monitor of social change in our time.

We have chosen to illustrate our argument from environmental organization because it is both highly characteristic of organizing in the present time and manifestly different from old modern forms of organization. It therefore helps us to prise apart that conceptual assemblage 'the modern organization' which previously dominated theory and empirical research. It is also well documented with many published accounts of the recent past which interestingly display the tensions between old modern narrative conventions and new realities.

7.3 ENVIRONMENTALISM AS POSTMODERN ORGANIZATION

Accounts of the origin and development of environmental groups often adopt incongruously traditional story-telling devices. They may focus on an original 'sacred' ceremony as with Greenpeace and the activities of the 'Don't make a Wave Committee' in and around Amchitka Island in 1970 (Pearce 1991: 18; Hunter 1980: 11 ff.) and the naming of this movement as Greenpeace (Hunter 1980: 15; Brown and May 1991: 9). Or, as with Friends of the Earth (FoE) on 10 July 1969, there is an act of creation by a charismatic leader, David Brower (Burke 1982: 105–6).

But even as one seeks to locate an origin at a specific point in time, at a particular place, with a definite programme (in itself, as Chapter 1 made clear, a highly contestable procedure), so the subsequent diverse trajectories of environmental organizations make that locus more an originating mystery than an explanation.

Greenpeace grew from a handful of hardy souls (Hunter 1980: 16) to an organization with 8,000 members in 1976 (Brown and May 1991: 49). In 1985 it numbered 27,000 in the UK alone, and grew to 281,000 by 1989 (Dalton 1994: 90). In 1991 it had 23 national chapters across the world (Brown and May 1991: 192).

David Brower travelled throughout Europe in 1970 meeting like-minded people, leading to FoE groups being established in Sweden, France and Britain. FoE UK was formally incorporated on 5 May 1971 as a company rather than a charity so that it could campaign freely (Patterson 1984: 140–1). It had 6 full-time staff, 8 local groups and 1,000 supporters.

According to FoE in the UK in 1992 there were 130 full-time staff, 330 local groups and around 240,000 supporters as well as 60 Earth Action groups. There were now 47 affiliated national organizations around the world (FoE 1992).

A bare recital of these growth figures fits the metaphor of the seminal idea, with Greenpeace and FoE among others (cf. Dalton 1994) germinating in fertile soil, extending roots and branches worldwide. The originating idea remains as the source of inspiration. With FoE, in Burke's words (1982: 105–6), 'good ideas are usually simple and transmutable to meet the needs of changing circumstances and personalities, while holding true to their intent'. For him it is 'the idea that the earth needs friends'. For Greenpeace it is that 'everyone has the right to clean water, fresh air and a safe future' (Brown and May 1991: 5) even though the name 'greenpeace' alone embodies a 'forceful new vision' via a 'dynamic combination of words' (ibid.: 9). Here then is an ideal history of the present, with continuity through change guaranteed by the original quality of the idea (and the name).

This is a characteristically modern narrative device, preserving the eighteenth-century conviction in progressive human enlightenment even in surrounding chaos. We can recognize the need for this device when we con-sider the organizational transformation which environmental organizations have undergone. For the charismatic founder did not envisage a grassroots organization with mass membership (Patterson 1984: 141) and yet the creation of local group networks became a central stratagem (Burke 1982). Greenpeace did not envisage the bombing of the Rainbow Warrior which transformed the organization, making it headline news around the world and increasing its membership very sharply (Brown and May 1991: 5, 113 ff.).

Growth at this rate means changes in social composition as well as the more obvious change in organizational structure which is familiar in the history of organizations. Environmental organizations have not escaped the crises which accompany such change. Ten years after its foundation FoE UK went through one which culminated in a special conference at Birming-ham in which members of its Board, employees from the London office and representatives of local groups nationwide negotiated a completely new struc-ture for the organization. Local groups were to elect members to the Board of the new FoE Ltd which in turn would be responsible to the groups (Patterson 1984: 153–4).

Greenpeace has, under David McTaggart's leadership, become 'The New Model Greenpeace', heir to a 'hardnosed professionalism' which harnessed the 'bravado' of its volunteers (Pearce 1991: 32, 33). A new head, Thilo Bode, in criticizing Greenpeace, seeks to go beyond 'boarding whaling ships' (Jackson 1996: 51) and transform the perception of environmental problems (ibid.: 55).

Now it is the temptation of an analytic organization theory to instance these developments as examples of necessary change through growth. But such an account would be premised on the continuity and sufficiency of the original organizational idea, in other words change would arise out of the internal dynamics of these environmental organizations. Our idea of 'necessary change' can be quite different. Instead of internal generation it might in fact be the succession of encounters and exchanges with the world around which determines change.

Indeed, histories of Greenpeace suggest that its story is not 'a neat and orderly one' (Brown and May 1991: 4) since it is tied up with the interest that people see in its ideas in relation to their lives. FoE is portrayed as unprepared for the avalanche of interest which assailed it soon after its foundation (Patterson 1984: 141). By 1974 as many as seventy local groups got involved in a bottle day. Tom Burke moved from Merseyside FoE to become the first full-time co-ordinator of local groups. The method of decentralized networked campaigning was beginning to span national boundaries. Patterson suggests this method began in the UK, but in its nature it is unlikely to have such a specific origin, for it partakes of a general potential of the social, which needs no national invention (ibid.: 148). It is a method which exposes organization specifically to the maximum degree of influence from outside, for every person involved can see themselves as an autonomous receptor and judge of environmental imperatives, and as a responsible bearer of the message to others.

This receptiveness is marked by the diverse nature and origins of campaigning issues. For Greenpeace this might include nuclear testing (Mururoa Atoll 1972–95), toxic wastes (Mississippi River 1988, Brent Spar 1995), whaling (Iceland 1986–8) and dolphin slaughter (Pacific 1982–3) (Jackson 1996: 52–3). They arise out of more general protests, or are mobilized very quickly to maximize media attention. They connect to the interests and concerns of specific national chapters or more generally across the (now) 23-strong national chapter membership of Greenpeace International.

For FoE, campaigns might have been centrally orchestrated, like that on the Windscale nuclear plant which involved a 12,000-strong march to Trafalgar Square in April 1978 (ibid.: 51). They could also have arisen directly out of the initiative of local groups, like the 'house-warming weekend', when fifty local groups were involved in insulating the homes of pensioners (ibid.: 146–7); or they might have the symbolic universality which could span frontiers and act as the focus of international conferences, like the meeting of representatives of twelve countries which took place in London in March 1975 and addressed global issues such as energy and whaling.

When an account of the history of environmental organizations depicts this open texture of activities and variety of individual and group involvement it no longer needs an originating myth to explain their transformation. For we see their trajectories inscribed in the public events of the time, tracking, sometimes provoking, political change, becoming an intrinsic part of public discourse (Windscale, CFCs, Mururoa Atoll, Brent Spar). The narratives of Greenpeace, FoE and other groups are links between the big story and the countless tales of individuals and groups. The founder's idea is not the foundation. The founding groups' activities are not a simple template for the future.

This then is contemporary organization and, in our view, not inappropriately called postmodern rather than modern. For we are able to see through the old modern narrative devices sufficiently to be able to detect a reality which is after the modern. Environmental organization is not bounded by some rational frame, it's a cross between a company and a movement. It relies on the organizing capacities of individuals and not on a blueprint. It is not a necessary development from the original idea. It is open to and responds to a multiplicity of stimuli both from *its* environment and *the* environment.

Finally, sociology can do more than any other discipline to explore and explain its dynamics. The reason is that the transformation from modern to postmodern organization is social and it is in revealing the nature of new sociality for a new age that sociology demonstrates its worth.

The reader should be alert to the assertiveness of this claim. For it rejects one of the frequent claims of postmodern theory, namely that society was a conceptual invention of modernity, since revealed as a figment in the flows of postmodernity. It followed from that argument that sociology, as the study of society, was equally exposed as a dated artefact. Our view is directly contrary, namely that modernity possessed only a limited view of society. Sociology, by revealing the polymorphous potential of the social, makes a more and not less vital contribution to a broader and deeper understanding of the contemporary world. We illustrate this by returning to our three benchmark concepts of the social in the context of environmental organizations.

7.4 ORGANIZING WORK

It would be possible to review each in turn, micro-social behaviour, social composition, macro-social change, produce a checklist for each, and effectively reproduce established sociological procedures for assessing social factors in modern organization. It would not be a negligible contribution. Let us see briefly what it would amount to.

In the case of micro-social behaviour we could document how rules were interpreted, how decisions were made on who belongs and who does not. We could focus on the generation of trust which has always been a key problem area of an organization without strong power and authority resources. We could explore the indexical character of these operations and suggest how they might instantiate 'a prospective mode of ordering' (Law 1994: 110).

With social composition we would contrast the personnel involved in the early days of the organization and their use of established friendship and elite networks with the mass involvement of later years. We would consider the different modes of recruitment of employees over time and how social categorization reflected or promoted organizational involvement.

In the case of macro-social change we would trace the development of public discourse on the environment and the explicit involvement of environmental organizations, even to the extent of Ministers speaking in the House of Commons acknowledging their contributions (Patterson 1984: 152). We would document developments in the wider society and establish their impact on the organization, especially assessing the impact of information technology and new means of communication. As an account it would relate effectively to ideas of post-industrial, postmaterialist, or information society.

None of this is irrelevant to a sociology of organization, but we have to admit that even taken together it amounts to a sidelining of sociology as a 'contextual subject'. The social becomes the residual, the background to what is really happening. In fact the image of organization as specifically modern did precisely that, for it turned organization into a series of specialist discourses on technical matters into which organization was disaggregated. Psychometrics, econometrics, ergonomics, capital accounting, human resource management, strategic marketing made the business organization both archetype and model for organizational analysis. They were technical tools for business leaders responsible for blending their use in an organizational structure specifically designed to meet the objectives they set. Potentially recalcitrant human activities could be parcelled up as 'organizational behaviour' as if people in organizations were excluded from more general social qualities.

To this extent an environmental organization could be seen as a-typical and of marginal theoretical interest simply because the business studies paradigm was less applicable. In fact we would argue that the new reality corresponds more to the environmental organization, and a sociological account appropriate for that new reality has a central part to play in understanding new business organization. But we cannot demonstrate that simply through aggregating our findings on our old three social aspects model. If there has been transformation, it will be revealed in and through changes in those older formulations of the social. So we will look rather more closely at them to see if we can detect such changes by referring to our recent fieldwork in the setting of environmental organization.

We mentioned decisions on who belongs and who does not as a key issue in micro-social behaviour. It is the most general of all those decisions which categorize individuals from an organizational standpoint and normally predates the array of labels which attach to individuals through participants' evaluations of them and their work. But suppose there is no initial decision on who belongs but that belonging depends on attaching labels, or even more, on generating membership legitimating labelling devices. Moreover let us suppose that the generation of such devices is a feature not of the organization itself but of a sector of a wider context which has no name (except perhaps 'society'!). Membership then becomes a continuously negotiated status, not simply the occupancy of a position, but the position itself which qualifies as membership. The management of this indeterminacy becomes a skilled capacity of individuals who are then in a position to shape an organization as the outcome of their own organizing activities.

This is not a speculative scenario for the future virtual organization. It corresponds to much of the discussion which we observed in environmental organizing, not as some extraordinary event but as routine, albeit interesting and creative labour. We can take the example of a volunteer, a status which makes her marginal, both outside and inside the organization. She takes part in a meeting to explore the use of the Internet where the marginality of her status is a prompt for a discussion of the difference between 'official' and 'unofficial' statements on behalf of the organization, a distinction which does not map onto a distinction between contracted and non-contracted members.

Throughout the meeting there is a repeated return to issues of mismatch between pairs of distinctions which are expected to regulate organizational work. The distinction personal/political is made to permit an employee or officers to give personal advice on green issues with the disclaimer that they are not official policies. But then, as knowledgeable observers, we can note that official/non-official does not correspond to political/personal since being political in the sense of party political is precisely what this organization seeks to avoid, and the personal is precisely what it seeks to influence. So perhaps it's a question of verbal versus written: 'on the telephone . . . we're not giving official policies', to which the response is 'perhaps we should brainstorm on the differences . . . different media' and a list is reeled off, phone, letter or fax, TV, radio, press, newsgroup as well as face to face.

This is already a sophisticated list of communication channels and six people in quick-fire discussion rapidly generate new pairs of ordering characteristics: legally binding or not; reproducible or not; secure or not; with or without damage potential; which may vary for each kind of communication channel. This is not a pre-planned discussion; the meeting is held at short notice. The topic is newsgroups on the Internet and their uses for the organization, a live issue because of their recent rapid development and their varied unsystematized use by members. Their novelty stimulates a discussion which is based in and recasts reflections on the wealth of experience in the organization of communication of all kinds.

Now if we consider this exchange in relation to two of our modern aspects of the social, the micro-social and social composition, one thing is immediately apparent. Each is only operable in terms of the other. The questions of whether people are to be counted as members, supporters, volunteers, spokespersons, employees are not answered by reference to a pre-set list of job descriptions or role definitions. The descriptions are indeed created and refined in the course of the work, and the work develops through the assignations. There is a three-way contingency and the ongoing negotiations around it are characteristic of the kind of organizing we can call postmodern.

Indeed, that kind of organizing is a large part of the 'work'. It is not a technical sphere removed from ongoing social process.

This has very direct relevance to the question of technological determinism, or indeed any kind of strongly directional theory of social change which prioritizes economy, technology, ideas, environment, defined in some sense as non-social. All such theories depend on an object language which crystallizes entities obeying laws or principles independent of human will. There is no reason to disavow the object nature of these spheres, but every reason to refrain from rushing to the conclusion that objectness guarantees autonomy. Their objectness arises as much from artefactuality as from original nature and human beings are involved in their construction at every stage. There can then be no prioritizing of any one of these spheres or functional areas in relation to each other, or indeed in relation to human beings. Their relations are in a profound sense historical and ever changing, which means that their very identity and existence as spheres are never guaranteed.

We can illustrate this directly from this fieldwork since it has focused very much on the construction of and responses to 'information technology'. The meeting on the Internet concerned itself particularly with newsgroups, those interactive exchanges on screen of information on any topic under the sun: 'not the Anglian fish magazine,' groans one participant (R1); 'there are 10,000-plus newsgroups,' adds another (R2). 'We need to cut out random mail, noise, messages – money and time are key here,' is the answer from a third (R3). We gain a sense of the fear of information overload and of a managerialist response. But this isn't a future threat, it's happening now. Let us follow a brief transcript of the meeting as it picks up at this point:

R4: Is there an appropriate way? Who? Reception, info, campaign teams?

R5: it will be six months to a year time [before it's sorted out]

R4: fair enough

R2: all press releases already go to GreenNet – newsgroups – uk.doc.transport as well

R1: I haven't seen that yet

R2: we are using newsgroups and Internet now – thus need a policy

R1: [to R2] want to get a copy – e-mail me

R3: I will do. We need a contingency now rather than six months time

R6: automated?

R3: it would take months to set up

R4: set up by campaign teams – way of filtering?

R3: entry level recruits today – Jim (R5) training about newsgroups in the next few weeks

R5: it is hard to produce a list – I'll just work on the issues

R1: anything on the environment

R6: but there are grey areas

R4: where is the onus?

R5: if unsure don't post it – if do the use of a disclaimer – to show we're not representing [official] views.

Do we interpret these exchanges as 'impact of information technology'? If we do it is clearly not a question of excluding human choice. For the whole six-sided intense exchange is about options. The problems which the group is tackling are about extensions of possibilities with which they are currently engaged, not about something which has happened to them. For nothing has happened without their active engagement, and whatever is going to happen they assume will arise out of their work.

'Information technology' has no 'impact' apart from the uses which human beings make of it, although technical inventions may open new possibilities. It enables R6 to think about the possibility of an 'automated' screening method for newsgroup material, but the difficult thing is producing 'the list', the 'issues'. As R3 says at one point, 'Technofixes do not solve the real issue.' What is 'the environment' and how do you handle the 'grey areas' and what are the views of the organization and how do you represent them and who does that?

Now there would have been a time when this kind of meeting with these kinds of open questions could have been represented as a crisis. It would have been for old modern organization: for by contrast control is endemically problematical here, and the stimulus for change is as much from outside the organization as inside, i.e from the newsgroups. In fact even outside/inside itself is problematical. But there is no panic, even if there is apprehension, even if the work is intense. This is the organization at work or, more precisely, organizing work.

Let us return to our volunteer who is in the meeting but does not take part in this particular exchange. She has said how she is involved in newsgroups and the whole meeting revolves around the issue of how far involvement in newsgroups is or is not proper organizational activity, and who has responsibility for participating in them. She feels the employees to whom she answers have no time for surfing net/eco which is her interest and will not attend the training groups they are going to set up. 'It's a whole new culture – causes you to be frightened – impressive-looking,' she says. Effectively the newsgroups dynamize the relations between volunteers and others, and bring the status of 'volunteer' into question. It goes as far as the boundaries of the organization.

The salience of the newsgroups to the organization is obvious; the volunteers may even have more interest in accessing them than employees, but they have no job contract which enables responsibilities to be defined and it is not clear that they can be. So are newsgroups part of the organization? Does an employee contributing to a newsgroup on offroad bikes need to use a disclaimer? Is a volunteer asking for information a 'spokesperson'? Or are the exchanges of a newsgroup just 'overheard conversations' or more like 'the media', or just information sources for 'browsing'?

The newsgroups are no more 'technology' than road users are highways, and highways are only such because people use them. So the metaphor of the information highway is far more appropriate to this account than information technology. But the highway is a route open to users in the shaping of their own ends and relations with each other. The information highway is both inside and outside the organization and as such constitutes an uncodified social sphere. It is the setting where formal organization, systems and procedures for controlling people and technology intersect. It is the area where an undetermined sociality is at work.

7.5 SOCIAL CHANGE NARRATIVE

The importance of the last point is only fully appreciated if we turn to the third of our old modern aspects of the social. We have called it 'macro-social change' and suggested this covers all those narratives which point to a direction for society, to axial principles and transformation, such as the account of post-industrialism, or information society, or late capitalism.

Our own account of the newsgroups meeting makes it clear that the construction of the organization is an ongoing enterprise in which micro-social ordering and its social composition mutually condition each other. But the organizing work which goes on is in terms of something we have not registered as being either micro-social or social composition. We have deconstructed a social aspect of technology without finding a place for it in our old modern schema. But equally we have not yet considered the third aspect of that schema.

The reason is that 'technology' is precisely that abstract generality which belongs to the grand narrative of macro-social change. After all, the newsgroups are not the products of the environmental organization, even though it is impossible to account for that meeting except in their terms. They belong to another discourse which no one controls, which spans the globe and is characteristic of change in our time. The informatization of society, post-industrial society, are concepts which seek to grasp the nature of a change which, because it is so widely disseminated, appears far removed from the local concerns of a meeting in a small office in London. But our meeting makes sense only in terms of the engagement of the participants with 'technology', with the transformation of the time in which they work. Indeed, they are working at that transformation.

It is sometimes assumed that a constructionist approach to technology, an emphasis on ongoing social inventiveness, is equivalent to denying the importance of grand narrative, that it makes it easier to decontextualize organization and concentrate on the intrinsic nature of the here and now. In our view a close analysis of organizers at work demonstrates the opposite, namely the necessity to view their interactions and ongoing working exchanges as component aspects of the great transformation.

Which of these meant anything a hundred years ago: TV, radio, fax, Internet, e-mail, newsgroups, keyword, biofuels, uk.doc.transport, technofix? Which current meanings attaching to 'surfing', 'menu', 'surgeries', 'green cooking', 'spokesperson', 'noise', 'default' would have been intelligible? We are dealing with a discourse out of which the technological change or the information society grand narrative is constructed and through which we try to understand our own time. But it is not happening over the heads of our meeting. It is its substance.

7.6 THE NET AND RECOVERIES OF THE SOCIAL

There was a time when we would have read 'surfing the Net' as an information-seeking organizational activity. That was when our organization had something like a traditional modern structure and technology was a set of tools available for use, to be picked up and set down at will. The Net, however, is no more an organizational resource than money is an item of personal consumption. It is a different way of performing organizing activity. The Net is equally no more just technology than money is the economy, for we all know that money is a political artefact.

The transformation which has taken place inscribes individual activities within a field, the Net, which is not *habitus*, a deep ground, but an atmosphere, a sphere of constituted social forms which have their own reality. We are not interpreting hidden presuppositions, rules outside the purview of participants, and the ground for practice is not in their inner understandings, but in their quite overt imputations and positing which constitute their contribution to the Net. It is a new social reality, constraining and enabling like any other.

So the Net is not technology. It is a newly created, specific historical phenomenon, and already inscribed in it are economic and political traces of our time. Of course it depends on knowledge, on technical advances, and on acquired skills. It requires materials, hardware, too. But it is social, not because people have created it (they make bombs too), nor because they have used it (they use cows when it suits them), but because it is a constellation of interdependent human activities borne by a multiplicity of individuals and groups.

The emergence of the Net contributes to that rethinking of our ideas both of the social and of organization which marks the end of the Modern Age. For when we consider the old modern analysis of the social what was missing precisely was what in Chapter 1 was called for, namely the account of the organization as society. Micro-social order, social composition, macro-social change each fail to focus on the generation of new social entities. For the modernist account of social science assumed that these, whatever they were, nation-states, firms, families, were under control, outcome of a founding social contract.

We are now in a much better position, as the Modern Project is dissipated, to recover older ideas of the social and to recognize their importance for understanding the emergence of new social forms. We will mention two which clearly become prominent. The first is the interstitial nature of the social between institutions as a medium for production of all kind. The social appears where politics merges with technology, or economics overlaps with the media, where any activity is problematic in system terms and is being redefined as something else; as in television in parliament, or the law on the sports field, or medicine and personal relations. For what enables us to convert the one discourse into the other is the reliance on a sense of the non-codified social. We do not resort to it as some firm foundation or original text, rather to a source of new insights, for where such functional spheres clash or overlap, it is the social, the free interaction of human beings, which generates new solutions. Old modern organization sought to confine the social in a single rational frame and effectively deprive it and itself of the most potent source of innovation. The Net is the most obvious contemporary example of the limits of those older ideas and the insufficiency of fixed notions of technology, power, information or communication.

If we recognize the innovative features of the social through the case of the Net, in the way it crosses functional boundaries, we can also see a complementary aspect, namely the conservative. Even in the flux of the meeting we could observe respect for ideas of social order which transcended time and place. The meeting even as it was called at short notice was delayed at its start to ensure a proper representation of persons. It took on the character of the 'Meeting', a ritual repeated worldwide in different forms, every one an affirmation of the abiding sense in human interaction. As a medium for any functional sphere of social life, it has a sense beyond any particular constellation of them. Ritual reaffirms the identity of a social entity through time, not because the world is unchanging, but precisely because it does change.

We offer this conception of the interstitial nature of the social as a contribution to resolving a difficulty in institutional approaches to organizations. They still reveal a gap between the cultural definition of institutions exemplified in W. Richard Scott's work (1995) and the rational exchange approach in Oliver Williamson's (1985). The medium in which this antinomy is resolved is the social, the uncodified response to others, where the collective is both inscribed in and rewritten by individual actions.

Let us finally revert to our opening comments on sociology for organizers. The overriding message of the account here for those who would seek to manage organizations under current conditions of rapid social change is that people are only likely to treat a particular organizational form as binding on them so long as it conforms or fits with their broader social experience. They are just as likely to turn it to their ends as have it use them for its. Organizing is no longer the prerogative of managers and insecurity is no longer confined to individuals. Organizations are disposable too.

8

SOCIOLOGY FOR
ORGANIZATION IN THE
GLOBAL AGE

8.1 THE NON-MODERNITY OF THE SOCIOLOGY OF ORGANIZATION

The fascination of the last thirty years of organization theory is in the spectacle of repeated transmutation of theory into history. Each attempt to set out the principles of organization as a coherent rational theory rapidly becomes no more than a relic of the changing times. We can't find a writer who has been able with success to speak across the whole period to every generation of managers and students.

Times change, theories change even faster, and the result has been to emphasize the potentially infinitely variable possibilities of theory construction against the background of changing reality. Postmodern theorizing then ceases to hold the same relation to organizational reality which modern organization theory once had to modern organization, neither foundation, nor mirror.

Indeed, from the later vantage point we can recognize that the aspiration to ground or reflect a distinctive reality was at the basis of the relations of modern theory and modern organization and that it was a function of something else, namely modernity. We understand now that a certain kind of narrative coherence underpinned both theory and empirical studies of modern organizations and this was effectively modernity's self-image.

Postmodernity both undermines modernity and brings the very possibility of such a narrative into question. This also is the premise of much contemporary research on organization. Postmodernity as such appears not to provide the same kind of narrative as modernity. There is no historical direction and its history ceases to be the subtext.

We can now see more clearly how the narrative of the Modern Age served as the integrating background for the relation of theory and organizational reality. But there is no such narrative for postmodernity. The wide array of features we may call postmodern, for instance fragmentation, decentredness or relativism, have no clear-cut social, spatial or temporal location. In other words there is no 'postmodern age'. We can't read off the features of the time in postmodern organization. It is this well-known disjunction between the period and theory which has led to the 'end of history' thematic. So if we want to speak of an age after the modern, it has to be something other than 'postmodern'.

Postmodernity, as a force, leads effectively also to the decay of organizational sociology once there is no linkage between theory and a sense of social reality. It should be very clear to the reader by now that I do not share this relativist view. From the beginning this book has asserted a viewpoint which claims detachment from modernity and postmodernity equally. The historical perspective on organization allows us to appreciate its ever open possibilities across epochs and cultures, before and after modernity. The theory which emerges is then grounded in historical phenomena, in ideas which stand the test of time, not in rational first principles.

The task in this final chapter is to reassert the possibility of the sociology of organization. We do so once we recognize that the peculiar combination: modern theory, modern organization, Modern Age was not actually a necessary linkage.

Indeed, the contention in this book has been that the relations of history, theory and organizational reality were misconstrued in the first place. I never subscribed to that peculiar linkage, and my distance from it provides a common basis for the chapters in this book.

From the outset I have treated rationality as historically grounded theory; not as the application of eternal rational principles, but as the attempt to grasp a meaning which could speak across time. Moreover in so far as an idea of the social bonded a narrative together, it was not peculiar to the modern period, nor to Western society. Far from the latest period of history taking us out of history, it makes us aware that the Modern Age was a transitory one, not especially privileged.

The new age does not impose its narrative on the present in the way modernity did. There is an openness about organizational form, but, at the same time, the multifarious conditions of our time can be read in the diversity of organizational contexts. We have a choice intellectually of seeing the perspectivism of current theory on organizations as the breakdown of objectivity, or alternatively as an expression of the multiplicity and variety of organizational reality. I choose the latter unequivocally.

The paradoxes of postmodernity arise because of the expectations built into old modern narratives. The present age does not impose a logic on organizational form; it does not work from principles, rather, its premises are like impressions from past impacts or fossilized remains in sedimented rock. The conjunctions of the moment are accidental, but no less compelling for that. The impacts of the oil price rise, or the discovery of semi-conductors do not arise from logic, but from a changing social reality.

There is a new awareness abroad that accounting for organization is more present-day history than rational model-building. Richard Colignon (1997) has just illustrated this vividly by reworking Philip Selznick's (1966) influential account of the organizational dynamics of the Tennessee Valley Authority. He finds no original goals or clear-cut structure, only outcomes of political struggles. In so doing he draws heavily on British organizational theory with its emphasis on the historical contingency of institutions.

Without registering those impacts, processes and events specific to historical times, we cannot understand the course which organizations, or any one organization, have traced. Moreover that history is being made in the continuing present. We have to trace the history of the present in our organizational analysis. Which is why 'analysis' now, the work of business, therapeutic, political analysts, all depends on the sensitive appreciation of the rise of contingencies, and why the analyst spends so much time on the minutiae of events as well as on deeper currents. Analysts are all in the business of interpreting ongoing history, the *course* of reality rather than its *nature*.

This final chapter seeks then to restate the place of the sociology of organization as a type of analysis which is true to the time in which it is set and speaks across times and cultures. Far from lapsing into postmodern chaos it finds a narrative which provides comparative reference points and depicts enduring ideas and the transmission of organizational forms across time. It can do this by relativizing both the modern and the postmodern, by setting both in a historical narrative. We do this by recognizing the epochal character of the time in which we live, the age which I call the Global Age (Albrow 1996).

The argument will develop over three sections, through modernity, postmodernity and then to globality. This is not a historical sequence in itself. This must be absolutely clear at the outset. There never was a 'postmodern age'; moreover globality does not provide the same logic for a Global Age as modernity did for the Modern Age. However, the full relativization of modernity, the historical sense of its ephemeral nature, may be best achieved by following the sequence of the sections. This will be apparent as we proceed.

8.2 DECONSTRUCTING THE THEORY OF THE MODERN ORGANIZATION

We have to get used to thinking of 'old modern organization', for we are talking of that time when organization was held to depend on rational principles, when the size and scale of the organization reflected the power of rationality, and when a single organizational form was expected to dominate the world. The usual expression of this expectation was in the prediction of the dominance of monopoly capital, of universal modernization or of bureaucratization. It was also expressed in convergence theory, the idea that socialist,

154

capitalist and fascist forms of organization were all approximating each other.

Undoubtedly Max Weber's was both the most sophisticated and the pivotal representation of this line of thinking, rationality being the source both of principles for organization and for his own social scientific method, with their concomitant growth being aspects of the grand narrative of the West as the rationalization process. It was not so much a philosophy of history as philosophy become history, having once and for all taken hold of the course and direction of development in the Modern Age. Once human beings had discovered the principles of rationality it was as if they had their feet on the rungs of a ladder which would carry them ever onwards and upwards.

In writing about organizations the historical narrative drew its paradigmatic events from advances in rationality, the establishment of the assembly line, the inventions of the telephone, the transatlantic flight. The catastrophes of the capitalist system appeared as checks rather than impending cataclysms, especially as after each collapse new giants arose, with ever greater capital at their disposal. Even the organizations of the proletariat became larger according to the same rational principles to which all democratic values were subordinated. The iron law of oligarchy was only the rationalization thesis as applied to social democracy.

Good sociology never succumbed completely to this dominant view. Even in Weber there is a suppressed thematic about the limits of Western rationality, a pessimism about the 'iron cage', and an acknowledgement of non-rational forces. And the sociology of the 1950s entered qualifications enough about the real workings of bureaucratic organization. Robert Merton's pupils (Blau 1955; Gouldner 1955a) brilliantly demonstrated the reality behind bureaucratic theory. They were the sociological counterparts of Herbert Simon's (1965) insistence on how limited the kind of rationality was which could be implemented in organizations. To this extent sociology was a preparation for the later débâcle of organization theory, but that could not have happened without transformations in social reality which shook the assumption of a conjunction of historical narrative and rational principle.

The collapse of old modern organization theory was precipitated by the developments in real organizations which manifestly began to follow quite different trajectories from those predicted by the theory. It became very obvious that ever larger industrial organizations and equally an ever expanding welfare state were not the only directions in which Western society was developing. The crisis of the welfare state and the decline of old industries came simultaneously.

Decline and crisis were of course linked. Rising unemployment put more pressure on the welfare state. At the same time the increased efficiency of industry meant cost savings relative to the service sector. Therefore relatively the costs of welfare rose at the same time as the demand for welfare became greater.

What was obvious was that efficiency could not be associated with one kind of organizational structure or even one type of socio-political system. Rather, relative efficiency at any one time, the way one form ousted another, was determined by the linkage of the total set of circumstances, capital, labour, state of technology, population structure, institutional arrangements, a configuration which could differ from country to country.

The seminal work of Michel Crozier (1964) illustrated how cultural factors were of prime importance in determining how organization worked; later, translated to the civilizational level, cross-cultural comparison even threw long-cherished assumptions about the Protestant Ethic and the unique contribution of Western work motivation into question.

Even as it appeared that capitalism was becoming a dominant and potentially exclusive world system, the inner logic of that system came to appear much more open and contingent on a range of non-economic circumstances. Indeed, it began to lose its systemic features, becoming in Offe's (1985) and Lash and Urry's (1987) terms 'disorganized capitalism'. Rather than operating in the guise of a juggernaut, an awful machine traversing the world and subduing everything in its path, capitalism lost the kind of coherence which made it an agency in its own right. Having acquired the dominance which the Marxists had long predicted, it lost the capacity to direct events. The triumph of capitalism involved its loss of identity as the collective subject of history. The collapse of capitalism turns out to be not violent revolution but its removal from the subject index of the library. Its end is the scatttering of its elements to cover the world, to recombine in innumerable ways.

But these are the paradoxes of epochal transformation, when both the concepts and the themes of the previous period are transvalued and we can no longer think in the same way. In the new historical period in which we write now, capitalism is decentred to the extent that it no longer has its 'ism', its claim to coherence and unity. We can give 'capital' no more formative, axial position than we give 'property', 'rights', 'value', 'power', 'culture', 'technology' or any other key element in the construction of contemporary society. We are not inclined to speak of 'propertyism' or 'valueism' and we should resist attempts to erect 'technologism' into a capitalism surrogate if only because the narrative of our times requires a different syntax.

Capital itself is defined in so many ways according to different accounting conventions and only through the measure of money does it make sense to equate labour, machines, ideas, images or risks. While money measures are a fundamental feature of our lives, not even the most sectarian and blinkered economist would assert that it is the dynamics of the money markets which determine the course of history or indeed that those markets are not exposed to real, extraneous forces, from politics, the environment, or culture. As capitalism ceases to hold historians of the present in awe, so economists also look outside their encampment to a wider world.

The same decentring has taken place for organizations. We can now see that the centralized industrial organization, with clear managerial hierarchy, departmentalized, with a large manufacturing workforce, turning out a single complex product, in the classic case the automobile, characterized a particular historical period. Factories and manufacturing plants still exist of course but no longer as concentrations of manual labour, nor as the showpieces of industrial empires. The largest corporations are now highly diversified, often very loosely associated chains of enterprises, which have come together sometimes out of the personal, idiosyncratic interests of entrepreneurs. Their normal state is a continual flux of restructuring.

Similarly blurred are the dividing lines between public and private ownership and the idea that there was a single appropriate form of organization for the public sector. With the disaggregation of capital goes the disaggregation of the state. Public sector agencies are expected to operate according to market principles while many functions hitherto thought of as state preserves have been entrusted to profit-making private enterprises. If the last two decades have seen privatization of nationally owned industries, at the same time the state has had to develop increasingly sophisticated monitoring and regulatory systems where the public interest is involved. Privatization has then involved the hybridization of organizational types rather than simply the transfer of ownership.

There is no longer a standard large organizational form, just as there is no longer a standard small business, a standard family, or standard career. The consequences of this for everyday life are of course profound and are registering in the recurrent theme of insecurity, in both political and psychological terms. By comparison the plight of organizational theory must be a minor issue. But relative to its own small concerns the consequences are equally profound. The 'postmodern' turn in organization theory is one response.

8.3 POSTMODERN ORGANIZING OR THE SOCIOLOGY OF POSTMODERNITY

The fluidity and diversification of organizational forms are the main reason for the shift from theorizing organizational structure towards the theory of organizing practices. It has taken place only a little after the same kind of shift has occurred in sociology generally away from accounts of bounded structures and self-sustaining systems towards the recursive reconstitution of social relations through human practices, although as yet there is no statement which has the authority and penetrative power of Giddens' (1986) theory of structuration or Bourdieu's (1977) account of practice.

At the same time Foucault's (1974) radical relativization of passing historical structures in his account of discursive practice has had a pervasive influence, particularly through achieving the recognition that theory and analysis at any point of time are forms of reproduction of power struggles which create social reality even as they seek to represent it. There is now little alternative in sight to the widespread acceptance of organization as the ongoing outcome of organizing practices.

In part, this consensus within the sociology of organization continues a tradition going back to the other Weber; the theorist of social action and forms of social relationship rather than the ideal type of bureaucracy. As others have suggested, it contains a theory of organization open to people's creative potential in determining the terms of their participation. It was the starting-point for David Silverman (1970) from which, after an appreciation of the Schutzean critiques of Weber, he has developed a long series of empirical studies on everyday practical rationality and the local organization of social practices. Ethnography and phenomenology are combined to generate thick descriptions of everyday organizing.

We should note that Silverman (1994: 10) is insistent that his micro-studies of interaction reference broader structures and that wider power relations in society are found inscribed in interaction. It therefore clearly resists a postmodern turn in the sociology of organization. This only comes when these higher ordering factors are neutralized and descriptive frames of reference give way to an emphasis on the free narration of participants, on the open-ended sourcing of ordering principles.

If we seek a fully postmodernist approach we will find it in John Law's *Organizing Modernity* (1994) which strives 'to avoid reproducing the games of classical modernism and put the experience of hideous purity behind us' (ibid.: 16). His is a sociology without nouns (ibid.: 15), agnostic about the entities around which modern narrative centres, and ultra-sensitive to the practices of the observer as much as to the observed. This is postmodernist sociology in the sense that it advances a narrative which deconstructs the modern. It is not a sociology of postmodernity. Ultimately it belongs to the later discourse of a reflexive modernity. Even when Law refers to sources of ordering narrative outside himself, the reference is not the wider transformations of our time, but to a decade of reordering in his own university of Keele. His modes of ordering are Lyotard's 'petits récits' (ibid.: 92).

Yet we have to ask how far Law's own practice of a certain kind of organizational sociology is in point of fact dependent on the transformation of the organizational world. The very seriousness with which he can research organization without privileging managerial standpoints, without documenting anything other than the ordering strategies of participants at any level seeking to keep their heads above water, or, in his terms, keeping all the balls in the air at the same time (ibid.: 188), is not so much a typical, more an outstanding, representation of a genre of sociology which could not have found public expression in an era when organizations were viewed as concretely as the modern architecture which housed them.

It is the widespread sense of the conditional and mutable nature of organization which means that organizing as an ordering practice becomes the central topic for sociologists. But that contingent nature is a change in social reality. There is, in other words, a changed social reality for which the term postmodernity can be appropriate, if only to draw attention to the fact that most of the key features of modern organization have been questioned and at one time or other supplanted at least in some organizational settings.

The issues on which Law is silent are the main focus for Robert Goffee and Richard Scase in their *Corporate Realities* (1995). The emphasis on realities combines with a stress on unprecedented levels of change in the 1980s and 1990s, and while they are sceptical about the demise of bureaucracy they allow full scope for the spread of networks, for the rise of small dynamic organizations and the development of the matrix 'adhocracy'. From the point of view of traditional organization theory probably the most incongruous development is the dynamic network, where the original firm downsizes and outsources. In this context the small entrepreneurial firm becomes part of the large network. The 'organization' is no longer the dominant organizational entity.

Following Clegg (1990) and Bergquist (1993) we may have no difficulty in calling what Goffee and Scase depict 'postmodern'. Postmodern organizing relativizes all organizational structures. It is the social counterpart to the operation of market principles, not just for products, but for modes of organizing too. There is relentless innovation and questioning of the basis for organization equivalent to the quest for new products or marketing methods.

This is a changed social reality, not simply a new perspective on reality, but a reality which generates new perspectives (Morgan 1986). The challenge to sociology under these conditions is to render an account of this changed reality which records flux without losing the discipline's own sense and direction. Goffee and Scase themselves deliver an admirable survey of the changing social reality of organizations. But it is an indicator of the obstacles in the path of sociology that they scarcely acknowledge its place in this account. They make passing reference only to sociologically inspired organization theory. Their ostensible allegiance is to 'organizational behaviour', neutralizing any potential threat from sociology to practical business requirements.

On the one hand, then, we have a postmodern sociology which no longer claims to have a hold on a wider social reality, which questions the basis of its own procedures even as it depicts the muddle of everyday organizational practices. On the other hand, we have a depiction of a wider social reality, in which continual change is accommodated in that reassuringly permanent home 'modern economies' (Goffee and Scase 1995: 20).

It is a disjunction which we fairly attribute to the condition of postmodernity, where the big organizational picture, however complex and diverse, is normalized by reference to the onward march of modernity while at the everyday level that very modernity has no secure foundation. On the one hand, there is a sociology which dare not speak its name, on the other, a postmodern sociology which finds the social infinitely elusive.

Let me be entirely forthright on this disjunction. It concerns me greatly as a reflection on the self-confidence of sociology today. The central task of the discipline is to make more than ordinary sense of the social and make it freely available to anybody. It can and does bring that added sense to every aspect of contemporary life, politics, medicine, sport, sex, the economy. Organization is intimately bound up with the social and yet sociology has so often either vacated or been excluded from the field.

It is still symptomatic that sociologists working on organization so often shelter behind the ambiguities of 'organization theory' (for examples see the collection of papers in Hassard and Parker 1994). I see no reason to modify the position in Chapter 1. If we want to serve organizational goals we have to adopt the full interdisciplinary apparatus of the business schools. There is nothing wrong with this intellectually and we have to acknowledge its practical necessity. We can even call it 'organization theory'. Sociology offers something else, a deeper understanding for all the people.

I have no quarrel with the purely intellectual qualities of the very different endeavours represented by Law and Goffee and Scase. Both books have exceptional merit. Law brings the excitement of an intellectual Odyssey where every page conveys recognition of a fateful strategic intellectual decision. Goffee and Scase display synthetic imagination of a high order in linking business strategies with organizational forms. In their own terms they are entirely successful.

My concern is with the postmodern condition which they effectively register and whether a sociological stance towards it is any longer possible. For one might be forgiven for thinking on the basis of their accounts that sociology has little left to say on organization and that it is now exposed as the product of a passing era.

8.4 THE POSTMODERN CONDITION OF ORGANIZATION

The postmodern condition of organization is not a specific type of organization. In contrast the modern condition of organization meant that there was something called 'the modern organization' or 'modern organization'. There was considerable debate as to whether 'modern organization' was best attached to an ideal type, or a modal example, or a dominant mode. But in every case the argument about the features of either 'the modern organization' or 'modern organization' was confined to a very restricted set of questions, as to the necessity of their linkage, their relative priority and their actual empirical distribution. For it was never denied that pre-modern organization persisted even under the most highly modernized conditions. Modernization sought precisely to root these out, to eliminate what was not progressive or existed as traditional obstacles to modern practice.

The condition of organizational modernity was one where the practice of organizers, the structure of organization and the principles of organizing cohered into a single set of features. In common with the social reality of modernity in general and closely associated with it, organizational reality was represented as the structuring of social life according to known principles by rational agents. Since the rational comprised logic, science, efficiency and effectiveness (at least), it was also the most powerful force in the world and carried all before it. Modernity had limitless horizons and an infinite future.

This 'metaphysical pathos' as Alvin Gouldner (1955b) so aptly dubbed it was never far below the surface of the modernizers' programmes for organizational change. It was shared indeed in both capitalist and socialist versions of modernization. By comparison, the postmodern condition has lost all such illusions with the exception of the illusion that modernity was indeed the period in which the world made sense. Then postmodernity is a condition of senselessness, where there are no foundations, unless arbitrary, no fixed reference points, no shared rational principles.

In these respects the postmodern condition is still under the thrall of modernity, for it is by reference to modernity that it is identified. Those working under its spell have not shaken off modernity. Law for instance appeals to 'reflexive modernity' as the basis for the continuation of the modern project, which leaves him with the inherent problem in all reflexivity, namely, how does one find a basis for the termination of reflection in the face of everyday requirements?

Goffee and Scase hold on to the persistence of modernity so that organizational forms which contradict the old modern model sit easily side by side with it. So while they retain the advantage of reading from a grand narrative, it loses any explanatory purchase. Unchanging modernity hardly accounts for contemporary transformation. They are then victims of the postmodern condition, seeing no way out of an endless modernity, which, however, confers no coherence on their work, even as they appeal to it.

So we need a different kind of grand narrative, one which treats the postmodern condition as a symptom not of the Modern Age, but of a new age. The reason is precisely that the configuration of principles, practice and structure which characterized both modernity in general and the modern organization has broken down. It results in sociologists of organization like Law and Goffee and Scase seeming to work on different planets. This is just one small symptom of the wider dissolution of the linkages which held the modern project together. That far-reaching dissolution of old assumptions is part of an epochal shift.

Before making the nature of that epochal shift more specific let us review the postmodern condition of organizations in more detail. We have already summed it up as the disruption of the linkages between structure, principles and practices. We asserted that rationality was the linking factor. It was that which gave modernity its driving force. We should, however, avoid the tendency to see the postmodern as the incursion of the irrational. The polarity rational/irrational characterized modernity throughout its dominance and to that extent emphasis on the irrational, on the emotional, on forces outside rational control is part of the inner dynamic of modernity.

The delinkage of principles, practices and structure is something else. It is not the negation of rationality but the recognition of non-rational factors which contextualize it and shape it. 'Culture' is the most obvious way this has been expressed in organizational literature. For there is no rational basis to culture, it simply extends over time, is absorbed and promoted by people, crosses boundaries and is equally at times evanescent. Chapters 5 and 6 illustrated the far-reaching consequences of taking emotion into organizational analysis. 'Contingency' is another such theme. It expresses the juxtaposition of circumstances beyond any logic, situations without precedents, requiring non-conditioned responses, intelligent but not from a restricted code of principles.

So what is this delinkage? Let us take each of the three links in turn: first structure and practice. Organizational structure no longer corresponds to boundaries between different practices. There is no longer a set model for the organization of medical, artistic, educational or legal practice. Any one organization can comprise any of them, and any of them may adopt any organizational form. Of course we still recognize the hospital, the theatre, the university and the law firm just as we can identify healing, acting, scholarship and litigation but we are not surprised that any of those practices can take place outside their ostensible home, and that any one of those organizations may house hugely diverse practices.

If we consider practice and principles we no longer expect it to be possible to provide for best possible practice simply through the inculcation of basic principles. The emphasis throughout education and training on transferable skills suggests there are generic capabilities which may be put to good use but these are developed in and through practice, not from learning a set of propositions. Even in narrower professional settings the emphasis in acquiring professional qualifications is increasingly on the experience necessary for handling the indeterminacies of the actual work setting, taking us beyond book learning. Whether we see this as prompted by the move in philosophy away from idealism to anti-foundationalism, from Kant to Wittgenstein, or by the instrumentalism of the business world, practice has acquired its independence from principle.

Structure too has freed itself from principle. There is little attempt now to justify structures on any other ground than their temporary suitedness for the immediate problems. Structures are expedient dispositions of resources for someone's purposes, and for whose purposes depends on the prevailing constellation of power. They are therefore subject to the strategic considerations of whoever happens to be in a position to generate structural change. There is an open repertoire of possibilities available at any time, merging, delayering, downsizing, outsourcing, none of which will be 'principled' decisions.

From this account it seems that 'principles' have suffered most, 'structure' has lost its firmness, while 'practices' have become sovereign as an outcome of their delinkage. That would be true from a modern standpoint. But suppose we find a standpoint outside the modern and seek to render our own times in terms which appeal to any time. Where have 'principles' gone? Their locus has shifted outside organizations in the old sense and they now inhabit the social movements of our time. They belong to people making value choices in elective lifestyles and commitments to collective goals outside employment. Alternatively they condition their own commitments to organizations which employ them, representing alternative foci for the contributions they make to them, thwarting or renewing organizational purpose.

In this respect what happens in organizations is no longer to be read off from organizational goals or structure or rational organizing principles. Perhaps indeed nothing happens 'in' organizations any more, since they no longer throw a canopy over people, either protective or suffocating. It may be more a matter of what happens to organizations. We can gain that impression from Law's account but he studiously refrains from attributing this to any secular change in organizational culture. Yet are we not reading the character of our times at the same time as we explore organizational reality? The Daresbury Laboratory surely is not so unique as to make wider inference implausible; equally it can hardly be so universal as to lead us to assume that it represents the world as it has always been.

At this point we are reminded of Silverman's emphasis on the need to take account of wider institutional factors when researching organizations. In examining communication in doctor–patient situations he points to institutional factors on which they depend and by which they are shaped: health promotion campaigns, the mass media, the rivalries of health care professionals, the politics of health (Silverman 1994: 8–10).

So the postmodern condition of organizations need not be detached from a broader narrative of social change, indeed, should not be if we are to make sense of it. But we are at a loss how to introduce it, for the postmodern condition involves a further delinkage in the configuration of modernity, in this case the separation of grand narrative from the other elements. For the point about the nexus of structure/principles/practices was that an inner momentum was generated and carried forward over time to give us the story of modernity, the history of ever increasing scope, scale, rationality and freedom. If the principles were rational and the practices realized them through structures which became ever more comprehensive, then nothing could compete with modernity and the Modern Age separated us off from the rest of history in perpetuity.

The Modern Age was then the story of the triumph of modernity. May we not therefore infer that there is a Postmodern Age representing the triumph of postmodernity? My answer is no, because the nature of the epochal shift we describe does not permit the inferences which were intrinsic to modernity. Postmodernity is a condition, not, as modernity was, the realization of a project. Hence it has no narrative peculiar to it. Moreover postmodern thinking has difficulty in appreciating grand narrative as such — at best it seeks to accommodate itself to the modern. But my contention is that the postmodern condition reflects a shift profound enough to mark the end of the Modern Age. In the broadest sense a new epoch provides the grand narrative of the present day, conditioning organizational transformation without in any way directing it. The new age is comprehensive without being integrative, it influences all human affairs and dictates none of them.

8.5 EPOCHAL CHANGE AND ORGANIZATIONAL NARRATIVES

Bureaucracy was simultaneously a type of organization and a historically specific form of administration with universal aspirations. Rationally grounded, historically emergent, it was the organizational weapon of the modern project. There is no sign that our own times are producing anything as powerful and potentially dominating. There is no single model of the network to oust all others, no paradigm for movements. The state has been decentred, while the business corporation can operate in virtual space as much as on the factory floor or in the boardroom.

Yet it is those realities of social transformation which have made organizational structures so conditional, have brought social practices to the fore, and sent principles into open competition, which demand a narrative for our times. We do not expect, nor look for, an equivalent structure to bureaucracy but we feel the need for a narrative which makes sense of the social transformation we have experienced. That 'making sense' involves two main aspects, explanatory and evaluative. We want to know how and why the postmodern condition has emerged and we want to explore its significance for the values we hold. In both respects sociologists have a great deal to offer since their concern for the social reveals how the human exploration of value only happens in and through the medium of society. Values extend much further but they are inextricably tied up with society.

The transformation of our time is then bound to be in major respects social, even if the sources of that change are non-social. Considering the social only in relation to the social is effectively to cut society off from history, from all non-social impacts. One of the main differences between the present age and the Modern is that we no longer assume that the course which society takes can be exclusively a matter of human direction. But that in no way derogates from the significance of the social in relation to the course of events. It still occupies a central place in any account of the age in which we live; but our account simply may not centre the time upon human agency as was standard in modern historiography.

The very use of the term 'condition' as in 'postmodern condition' indicates the decentring of historical narrative from collective agency which characterizes our time. It is that which makes it difficult to conceive of the new narrative, so accustomed were we in modernity to putting particular collectivities at the centre. But if there is one collective actor now for contemporary history, it is humanity, and if there has to be any way to identify the condition of postmodernity, it is 'globality'. The decentring which has taken place is because humanity is exposed to globality, to global conditions, in a way that modern man was never exposed to his environment. (I use the gendered subject for modernity precisely to reinforce the point that modernity was essentially male conquest.) No longer does human agency appear to control events. And humanity has at best a fragmented, at worst a completely self-contradictory will.

The public discourse of the Global Age will most probably provide the grand narrative for the sociology of organization for the foreseeable future. Elsewhere I have summarized the features which combine to make globality the defining configuration of our time: global environmental risks; nuclear weaponry; global communication systems; a globalized world economy; social movements which espouse globalist values (Albrow 1996: 4).

It is a configuration of circumstances which does not arise as the willed outcome of the modern project, rather, from its exhaustion and unwilled consequences. For this reason alone it cannot be seen as the extension of the Modern Age, nor as a product of modernity. There has been a rupture, even if it has taken half a century to complete (covering the period 1945–1989).

We can trace the organizational consequences for each one of the five features. Environmental risks now enormously condition the operations of organizations, in terms of legislative limits on autonomy, in requiring new agencies and practices. Nuclear weaponry created the conditions for global security structures which effectively denationalized both weapons and the military, standardizing practices and enhancing professionalization as opposed to popular mobilization. Global communication systems, for purposes of travel, conversation at a distance, remote access to information and a global mass culture have transformed organizations in terms of outputs, control and speed of operations. The global economy involves simultaneously a single world capital market, localized production for world markets and the standardization of products wherever they might be produced. Globalist values legitimate resistance and focus collective responses anywhere to structures which individuals perceive as damaging to human futures.

This is just one very abridged way in which we can sum up major changes in the context of organizational behaviour in the Global Age. Taken together they amount to an epochal transformation which shapes what is possible for organization to achieve and profoundly influences the trajectory and durability of any particular organizational structure. Moreover that influence is multivalent, dependent on place, product, market when each of those changes incessantly. So under new global conditions we find equally global conglomerates centred on one person, or alternatively loosely structured corporate alliances with franchising and leasing agreements crossing continents. We find a commodity produced worldwide adapted for local requirements, or we can purchase something produced in one place only anywhere in the world.

It is therefore no wonder that emphasis has shifted away from organizations as such towards organizing. At the same time the task of identifying and documenting precisely how organized social entities emerge and have a continued existence, however brief, has become even more challenging intellectually. The ephemerality of objects is a challenge to analysis, not its defeat. That applies as much to sociology as it does to physics with its indefinitely renewed quest for ever smaller subatomic particles. It is no coincidence that it is sociologists of science who are refocusing work on the constitution of social objects, organizations included (Latour 1993).

There has been a strong tendency in the literature which has dealt with globalization to see it as the extension of modernization and rationalization. It has been part of the general tendency in modernity to assimilate everything new to itself. The result has been considerable confusion since those impacts I have listed above have contradictory effects and cannot in conjunction generate any determinate direction for future development. Modernization was conceived as inherently unidirectional. That in itself should be enough to caution those who would wish to see globalization as a uniform process. In fact globality sets conditions for organizations which have largely released them from the iron cage of modernity. The diversification of organizational structure is the result.

We can see now why the grand narrative of our times bears a different relation to organization than did the narrative of the Modern Age to the modern organization. We cannot infer from the Global Age a dominant organization called the 'global organization'. Though by inference from those old modern relationships many organizations have sought precisely to do that and go global, with 'global leadership' programmes and global marketing campaigns. It is not the logic of the Global Age which requires this strategy, though there is some reason to think that the acquisition of power and prestige by individuals in a global society will depend in part on participating in such ventures. 'Global leadership' then is more a recruitment sales pitch than a business strategy and human resource specialists probably recognize it as such.

But then this is but an example of the way the grand narrative shapes the frame of reference of individuals in their organizing practices while leaving the structure of the organization quite under-determined. We can't make sense of what individuals do in an organization without reference to the bigger picture, but at the same time we cannot infer organizational structure from what they do, because what they do is far more than simply acting out organizational requirements, nor can we simply derive organizational structure from global realities. It is this which can render ethnographic work on organizing practices simultaneously minutely informative and removed from social reality.

Let me sum up briefly where I think we have reached in the sociology of organization in the mid-1990s. The idea of postmodernity has now entrenched itself but we need to recognize that the current state of organizations generally no longer permits us to identify a single, dominant, or modal type of organization as was common in the past with modern organizations. Postmodernity is a condition in which the assumptions of modernity have been undermined; at the same time it does not generate a sociology of organization which reflects the social realities of the time.

We appear to be faced with two alternatives. We can resort to an older modern narrative, but that perpetuates the myth of everlasting modernity. We can turn to a postmodern sociology, but that cannot supply the missing narrative. There is a third possibility, namely to continue with a sociology of organizing and organizations which is detached from both modernity and postmodernity as I would maintain the best sociology always has been. For although sociology as an academic discipline was born of the social problem of class society, its basis is in intellectual engagement with the conditions for society anywhere, including society under conditions of postmodernity. A sociology for organization in the Global Age has to aspire to be non-modern. In that way it will continue to be the essential counterweight to every attempt to subordinate human organization to merely technical ends.

NOTES

CHAPTER 1 THE STUDY OF ORGANIZATIONS – OBJECTIVITY OR BIAS?

1 First published in Julius Gould (ed.) (1968) *Penguin Social Sciences Survey 1968*, Harmondsworth: Penguin, pp. 146–67.

CHAPTER 2 THE DIALECTIC OF SCIENCE AND VALUES IN THE STUDY OF ORGANIZATIONS

2 Originally published as 'Is a science of organizations possible?', in 'Perspectives on Organizations', Open University third level social sciences course People and Organizations DT 352, Unit 16, pp. 25–47, Milton Keynes: Open University Press, 1974. Subsequently reprinted in slightly abridged form under current title in G. Salaman and K. Thompson (eds) (1980) *Control and Ideology in Organizations*, Milton Keynes: Open University Press.

CHAPTER 3 THE APPLICATION OF THE WEBERIAN CONCEPT OF RATIONALIZATION TO CONTEMPORARY CONDITIONS

3 First published in Sam Whimster and Scott Lash (eds) (1987) *Max Weber, Rationality and Modernity*, London: Allen & Unwin, pp. 164–82.

CHAPTER 4 REDEFINING AUTHORITY FOR POST-WEBERIAN CONDITIONS

4 This chapter incorporates two sections which have been published before: a slightly modified version of my 1972 paper 'Weber on legitimate norms and authority: a comment on Martin E. Spencer's account', *British Journal of Sociology*, 23: 483–7; and a section on authority which was originally included in Chapter 8 when it was published in Larry Ray's and Michael Reed's (eds) (1994) *Organizing Modernity*, pp. 111–15.

CHAPTER 5 *SINE IRA ET STUDIO* – OR DO ORGANIZATIONS HAVE FEELINGS?

5 First presented as a paper to the British Sociological Association Weber Study Group Conference on 'Weber, Work, Organizations and Bureaucracy' at Lancaster University, 17–18 April 1991.

CHAPTER 6 REVISING ACCOUNTS OF ORGANIZATIONAL FEELING

6 This chapter is a revision of a paper 'Accounting for Organizational Feeling' origin-ally written at the invitation of Larry Ray and Michael Reed for their edited volume *Organizing Modernity* (1994) as a sequel to the previous chapter. Their useful com-ments and also the help of Steven Groarke, Roehampton Institute, are gratefully acknowledged. Especial thanks are due to Robert Merton who sent generous and detailed comments on the earlier paper and thus assisted greatly in the writing of this one.

CHAPTER 7 SOCIOLOGY FOR POSTMODERN ORGANIZERS – WORKING THE NET

7 The fieldwork reported here was carried out by Neil Washbourne.

BIBLIOGRAPHY

Albini, J.L. (1971) *The American Mafia: Genesis of a Legend*, New York: Appleton Century Crofts.

Albrow, M. (1968) 'The Study of Organizations – Objectivity or Bias?', in J. Gould (ed.) *Penguin Social Science Survey*, Harmondsworth: Penguin, pp. 146–67 [Chapter 1 in this volume].

—— (1970) *Bureaucracy*, London: Macmillan.

—— (1971) 'Public Administration and Sociological Theory', *The Advancement of Science* 27: 347–56.

—— (1972) 'Weber on Legitimate Norms and Authority: A Comment on Martin E. Spencer's Account', *British Journal of Sociology* 23: 483–7 [part incorporated into Chapter 4 in this volume].

—— (1973) (abridged reprint of Albrow 1968) 'The Study of Organizations – Objectivity or Bias?', in G. Salaman and K. Thompson (eds) *People and Organizations*, London: Longmans, pp. 396–413.

—— (1974) 'Is a Science of Organizations Possible?', in People and Organizations, Open University Course DT 352, Unit 16, Milton Keynes: Open University Press, pp. 25–47, reprinted as Albrow 1980.

—— (1975a) 'Legal Positivism and Bourgeois Materialism: Max Weber's View of the Sociology of Law', *British Journal of Law and Society* 2: 14–31.

—— (1975b) 'Introduction to and translation of Max Weber, "R. Stammler's 'Surmounting' of the Materialist Conception of History"', Part One, *British Journal of Law and Society* 2: 129–52.

—— (1976) 'Introduction to and translation of Max Weber, "R. Stammler's 'Surmounting' of the Materialist Conception of History"', Part Two, *British Journal of Law and Society* 3: 17–43.

—— (1980) 'The Dialectic of Science and Values in the Study of Organizations', in G. Salaman and K. Thompson (eds) *Control and Ideology in Organizations*, Milton Keynes: Open University Press, pp. 278–96 [Chapter 2 in this volume].

—— (1982) 'Max Weber and the Rationalization Thesis: The Case of Modern Britain', paper presented (*in absentia*) to the Tenth World Congress of Sociology, Mexico City.

—— (1987) 'The Application of the Weberian Concept of Rationalization to Contemporary Conditions', in S. Whimster and S. Lash (eds) *Max Weber, Rationality and Modernity*, London: Allen & Unwin, pp. 164–82 [Chapter 3 in this volume].

—— (1990) *Max Weber's Construction of Social Theory*, London: Macmillan.

—— (1991a) 'Irrationality and Personality: Max Weber's Theory of Needs and Emotions', in H.J. Helle (ed.) *Verstehen and Pragmatism*, Frankfurt: Lang, pp. 25–32.

—— (1991b) 'Societies as Constructed Facts: The Weberian Approach to Social Reality', paper delivered to the Twelfth World Congress of Sociology, 1990, Madrid, translated as 'Las sociedads como hechos construidos: el enfoque de Weber de la realidad social', *Estudios Sociológicos de el Colegio de México* 9: 339–56. Separately translated and published in *Sociología: Unidad y Diversidad*, edited by Teresa González de la Fe, Madrid: Consejo Superior de Investigaciones Científicas, pp. 75–92.

—— (1992) 'Sine Ira et Studio' – or Do Organizations have Feelings?', *Organization Studies* 13: 313–29 [Chapter 5 in this volume].

—— (1993) 'Reflections on the World Reception of Max Weber', in H. Martins (ed.) *Knowledge and Passion: Essays in Honour of John Rex*, London: I.B. Tauris, pp. 79–98.

—— (1994a) 'Accounting for organizational feeling', in L.J. Ray and M. Reed (eds) *Organizing Modernity: New Weberian Perspectives on Work, Organization and Modernity*, London: Routledge, pp. 98–121. [Chapter 6 (revised) in this volume]

—— (1994b) 'Globalization: Myths and Realities', Inaugural Lecture, Roehampton Institute, London.

—— (1996) *The Global Age: State and Society beyond Modernity*, Cambridge: Polity.

Andrzejewski, S.L. (1954) *Military Organization and Society*, London: Routledge.

Aquinas, St Thomas (1954) *Selected Political Writings*, edited by A.P. D'Entreves. Oxford: Blackwell.

Argyris, C. (1973) 'Peter Blau', in G. Salaman and K. Thompson (eds) *People and Organizations*, London: Longmans, pp. 76–90.

Bakke, E. W. (1959) 'Concept of the Social Organization', in M. Haire (ed.) *Modern Organization Theory*, New York: Wiley, pp. 16–75.

Baritz, L. (1960) *The Servants of Power*, Middletown: Wesleyan University Press.

Barnard, C. (1938) *The Functions of the Executive*, Cambridge, MA: Harvard University Press.

Beck, U. (1992) *Risk Society: Towards a New Modernity*, London: Sage.

Beck, U., Giddens, A. and Lash, S. (1994) *Reflexive Modernization*, Cambridge: Polity.

Bell, D. (1973) *The Coming of Post-Industrial Society: A Venture in Social Forecasting*, New York: Basic Books.

Bendix, R. (1949) *Higher Civil Servants in American Society*, Boulder, CO: University of Colorado.

—— (1956) *Work and Authority in Industry*, New York: John Wiley.

Bendix, R. and Fisher, L.H. (1949) 'The Perspectives of Elton Mayo', *Review of Economics and Statistics*, 31: 312–19, reprinted in A. Etzioni (ed.) (1964) *Complex Organizations* New York: Holt, Rinehart & Winston.

Berg, P.-O. (1979) *Emotional Structure in Organization: A Study of the Process of Change in a Swedish Company*, Lund: Studenttliteratur.

Berger, P.L. and Luckmann, T. (1971) *The Social Construction of Reality*, Harmondsworth: Penguin.

Bergquist, W. (1993) *The Postmodern Organization*, San Francisco: Jossey Bass.

Bittner, E. (1965) 'The Concept of Organization', *Social Research* 32: 239–55, reprinted in G. Salaman and K. Thompson (eds) (1973) *People and Organizations*, London: Longmans, pp. 264–76.

Blau, P.M. (1955) *The Dynamics of Bureaucracy*, Chicago: University of Chicago Press.

—— (1977) *Inequality and Heterogeneity*, New York: The Free Press.

Blau, P.M. and Schoenherr, R.A. (1973) 'New Forms of Power', in G. Salaman and K. Thompson (eds) *People and Organizations*, London: Longmans, pp. 13–24.

Blau, P.M. and Scott, W.R. (1963) *Formal Organizations*, London: Routledge.

Bourdieu, P. (1977) *Outline of a Theory of Practice*, Cambridge: Cambridge University Press.

Bridges, Lord Edward (1950) *Portrait of a Profession*, Cambridge: Cambridge University Press.

Brown, M. and May, J. (1991) (2nd edn) *The Greenpeace Story*, London: Dorling Kindersley.

Brown, W. (1965) *Exploration in Management*, Harmondsworth: Penguin.

Brunsson, N. (1985) *The Irrational Organization*, New York: John Wiley.

—— (1989) *The Organization of Hypocrisy*, New York: John Wiley.

Burke, T. (1982) 'Friends of the Earth and the Conservation of Resources', in P. Willetts (ed.) *Pressure Groups in the Global System*, London: Pinter.

Burnham, J. (1962) *The Managerial Revolution*, Harmondsworth: Penguin.

Burns, T. and Stalker, G.M. (1961) (1966 edition) *The Management of Innovation*, London: Tavistock.

Burrell, G. (1988) 'Modernism, Post-Modernism and Organizational Analysis 2: The Contribution of Michel Foucault', *Organization Studies* 9: 221–35.

Channing, W.E. (1829) 'Remarks on Associations', in *The Complete Works of W.E. Channing*, London: Routledge, pp. 115–31.

Child, J. (1973) 'Organization: A Choice for Man', in J. Child (ed.) *Man and Organization*, London: Allen and Unwin, pp. 234–57.

Clark, P.A. (1972) *Action Research and Organizational Change*, London: Harper and Row.

Clegg, S.R. (1990) *Modern Organizations*, London: Sage.

—— (1994) 'Max Weber and Contemporary Sociology of Organizations', in L.J. Ray and M. Reed (eds) *Organizing Modernity*, London: Routledge, pp. 46–80.

Cohen, M.R. (1931) *Reason and Nature*, New York: Harcourt Brace.

Colignon, R.A. (1997) *Power Plays: Critical Events in the Institutionalization of the Tennessee Valley Authority*, Albany: State University of New York.

Cooper, R. (1989) 'Modernism, Post-Modernism and Organizational Analysis 3: The Contribution of Jacques Derrida', *Organization Studies* 10: 479–502.

Cooper, R. and Burrell, G. (1988) 'Modernism, Post-Modernism and Organizational Analysis 1: An Introduction', *Organization Studies* 9: 91–112.

Coulter, J. (1988) 'Affect and Social Context: Emotion Definition as a Social Task', in R. Harré (ed.) *The Social Construction of Emotions*, Oxford: Blackwell, pp. 120–34.

Crossman, R. (1976) *The Diaries of a Cabinet Minister*, Volume 2, London: Hamish Hamilton and Jonathan Cape.

Crowther, J.G. (1960) *Francis Bacon: The First Statesman of Science*, London: The Cresset Press.

Crozier, M. (1961) 'De la Bureaucratie comme système d'organisation', *Archives Européennes de Sociologie* II: 18–53.

—— (1964) *The Bureaucratic Phenomenon*, London: Tavistock.

Dalton, R.J. (1994) *The Green Rainbow: Environmental Groups in Western Europe*, New Haven and London: Yale University Press.

Drucker, P.F. (1964) *The Concept of the Corporation*, New York: Mentor.

Elbra, R.A. (1984) *Guide to Data Protection*, Manchester: National Computing Centre.

Eldridge, J. (1994) 'Work and Authority: Some Weberian Perspectives', in L.J. Ray and M. Reed M (eds) *Organizing Modernity*, London: Routledge.

Estes, H. (1962) 'Some Considerations in Designing an Organization Structure', in M. Haire (ed.) *Organization Theory in Industrial Practice*, New York: John Wiley, pp. 13–27.

Etzioni, A. (1961) *A Comparative Analysis of Complex Organizations*, New York: The Free Press of Glencoe.

—— (1964) *Modern Organizations*, New Jersey: Prentice-Hall.

—— (1970) 'Two Approaches to Organizational Analysis: A Critique and a Suggestion', in O. Grusky and G.A. Miller (eds) *The Sociology of Organization: Basic Studies*, London: Collier-Macmillan, pp. 215–25.

Ferguson, A. (1782) (5th edn) *An Essay on the History of Civil Society*, London: Cadell.

Fiedler, F.E. (1962) 'Leader Attitude, Group Climate and Group Creativity', *Journal of Abnormal and Social Psychology* 65: 308–18.

Fine, G.A. (1988) 'Letting off Steam? Redefining a Restaurant's Work Environment', in M.O. Jones, M.D. Moore and R.C. Snyder (eds) *Inside Organizations*, London: Sage, pp. 119–27.

Fineman, S. (ed.) (1993) *Emotion in Organizations*, London: Sage.

Flam, H. (1990a) 'Emotional "Man": I. The Emotional "Man" and the Problem of Collective Action', *International Sociology* 5: 39–56.

—— (1990b) 'Emotional "Man": II. Corporate Actors as Emotion-Motivated Emotion Managers', *International Sociology* 5: 225–34.

FoE (1992) *21 Years of Friends of the Earth*, London: FoE.

Foucault, M. (1974) *The Archaeology of Knowledge*, London: Tavistock.

Friedmann, G. (1955) *Industrial Society*, Glencoe, Ill.: The Free Press.

Friedrich, C.J. (1952) 'Some Observations on Weber's Analysis of Bureaucracy', in R.K. Merton *et al.* (eds) *Reader in Bureaucracy*, Glencoe, Ill.: The Free Press, pp. 27–33.

Friedrich, C.J. and Mason, E.S. (eds) (1940) *Public Policy*, Cambridge, MA: Harvard University Press.

Galtung, J. (1961) 'Prison: The Organization of a Dilemma', in D.R. Cressey (ed.) *The Prison*, New York, Holt, Rinehart and Winston.

Gardner, B.B. (1965) 'The Consultant to Business: His Role and his Problems', in A.W. Gouldner and S.M. Miller (eds) *Applied Sociology*, New York: The Free Press, pp. 79–95.

Giddens, A. (1986) *The Constitution of Society*, Cambridge: Polity.

—— (1990) *The Consequences of Modernity*, Cambridge: Polity.

Goffee, R. and Scase, R. (1995) *Corporate Realities*, London: Routledge.

Goffman, E. (1956) (1971 edition) *The Presentation of Self in Everyday Life*, Harmondsworth: Penguin.

Gould, J. (1968) *Penguin Social Sciences Survey 1968*, Harmondsworth: Penguin.

Gouldner, A. (1955a) *Patterns of Industrial Bureaucracy*, London: Routledge.

—— (1955b) 'Metaphysical Pathos and the Theory of Bureaucracy', *American Political Science Review* 49: 496–507.

—— (1959a) 'Reciprocity and Autonomy in Functional Theory', in L. Gross (ed.) *Symposium on Sociological Theory*, Evanston, Ill.: Row, Peterson & Co.

—— (1959b) 'Organizational Analysis', in R.K. Merton *et al.* (eds) *Sociology Today*, New York: Basic Books, pp. 400–28.

—— (1965) *Wildcat Strike*, New York: Harper.

—— (1970) *The Coming Crisis in Western Sociology*, London: Heinemann.

Grusky, O. and Miller, G.A. (eds) (1970) *The Sociology of Organizations: Basic Studies*, London: Collier-Macmillan.

The Guardian, Frank Kane report, 26 November 1992.

Habermas, J. (1981) *Theorie des kommunikativen Handelns*, Frankfurt: Suhrkamp.

Haire, M. (1959) (ed.) *Modern Organization Theory*, New York: Wiley.

—— (1962a) 'What is Organized in an Organization?', in M. Haire (ed.) *Organization Theory in Industrial Practice*, New York: John Wiley, pp. 1–12.

—— (ed.) (1962b) *Organization Theory in Industrial Practice*, New York: John Wiley.

Halmos, P. (1965) *The Faith of the Counsellors*, London: Constable.

—— (1970) *The Personal Service Society*, London: Constable.

Hanika, F. de P. (1965) *New Thinking in Management*, London: Hutchinson.

Harré, R. (ed.) (1988) *The Social Construction of Emotions*, Oxford: Blackwell.

Harvey-Jones, J. (1989) *Making it Happen*, London: Collins.

Hassard, J. (1990) 'Ethnomethodology and Organizational Research: An Introduction', in J. Hassard and D. Pym (eds) *The Theory and Philosophy of Organizations*, London: Routledge, pp. 97–108.

Hassard, J. and Parker, M. (eds) (1994) *Towards a New Theory of Organizations*, London: Routledge.

Haworth, L. (1959) 'Do Organizations Act?', *Ethics* 70: 59–63.

Hearn, J. and Parkin, W. (1987) *'Sex' at 'Work'*, Brighton: Wheatsheaf.

Heclo, J. and Wildavsky, A. (1974) *The Private Government of Public Money*, London: Macmillan.

Hennessy, P. (1989) *Whitehall*, London: Secker and Warburg.

Hobbes, T. (1651) *Leviathan*, 1955, edited by Michael Oakeshott, Oxford: Blackwell.

Hochschild, A.R. (1979) 'Emotion Work, Feeling Rules and Social Structure', *American Journal of Sociology* 85: 551–75.

—— (1983) *The Managed Heart: Commercialization of Human Feeling*, Berkeley, CA: University of California Press.

Holgate, N. (1992) 'Same Building, Different Department', *Chequerboard: The Treasury Staff Magazine* 4: 7, 9.

Hunter, R. (1980) *The Greenpeace Chronicle*, London: Pan.

Jackson, J.O. (1996) 'Greenpeace Gets Real', *Time*, 147, 24: 51–6.

Jacques, E. (1951) *The Changing Culture of the Factory*, London: Tavistock.

—— (1976) *A General Theory of Bureaucracy*, London: Heinemann.

Jameson, F. (1991) *Postmodernism: The Cultural Logic of Late Capitalism*, London: Verso.

Kalberg, S. (1980) 'Max Weber's Types of Rationality: Cornerstones for the Analysis of the Rationalization Process', *American Journal of Sociology* 85: 1145–79.

Kant, I. (1787) *Kritik der reinen Vernunft*, Riga: Hartknoch.

—— (1949) *Critique of Practical Reason*, translated by L. Beck, Chicago: University of Chicago Press.

Katz, D. and Kahn, R.L. (1966) *The Social Psychology of Organizations*, New York: John Wiley.

Kemper, T. (1978) *A Social Interactional Theory of Emotions*, New York: Wiley.

Kent, H.S. (1979) *In on the Act: Memoirs of a Lawmaker*, London: Macmillan.

Kets de Vries, M.F.R. and Miller, D. (1985) *The Neurotic Organization*, San Francisco: Jossey Bass.

Kronman, A.T. (1983) *Max Weber*, London: Edward Arnold.

Krupp, S. (1961) *Pattern in Organization Analysis*, New York: Chilton.

Lash, S. and Urry, J. (1987) *The End of Organized Capitalism*, Cambridge: Polity.

Latour, B. (1993) *We Have Never Been Modern*, Hemel Hempstead: Harvester Wheatsheaf.

Law, J. (1994) *Organizing Modernity*, Oxford: Blackwell.

Lenin, V.I. (n.d.) *Selected Works*, Vol. VII, New York: International Publishers.

Lipset, S.M., Trow, M.A. and Coleman, J.S. (1956) *Union Democracy*, New York: The Free Press.

Lloyd, L.E. (1962) 'Origins and Objectives of Organizations', in M. Haire (ed.) *Organizational Theory in Industrial Practice*, New York: John Wiley, pp. 28–47.

Lockwood, D. (1956) 'Some Remarks on the Social System', *British Journal of Sociology* 5: 134–45.

Luhmann, N. (1979) *Trust and Power*, edited by T. Burns and G. Poggi, Chichester: Wiley.

—— (1985) *A Sociological Theory of Law*, London: Routledge.

Lyotard, J.-F. (1984) *The Postmodern Condition: A Report on Knowledge*, Manchester: Manchester University Press.

McGregor, D. (1960) *The Human Side of Enterprise*, New York: McGraw-Hill.

—— (1966) *Leadership and Motivation*, Cambridge, MA: MIT Press.

McLuhan, M. (1964) *Understanding Media*, London: Routledge.

Manning, P.K. (1971) 'Talking and Becoming: A View of Organizational Socialization', in J.D. Douglas (ed.) *Understanding Everyday Life*, London: Routledge and Kegan Paul, pp. 239–56.

March, J.G. and Simon, H.A. (1958) *Organizations*, New York: Wiley.

Marschak, J. (1959) 'Efficient and Viable Organizational Forms', in M. Haire (ed.) *Modern Organization Theory*, New York: Wiley, pp. 307–20.

Martin, D. (1965) 'Towards Eliminating the Concept of Secularization', in *The Penguin Survey of the Social Sciences 1965*, Harmondsworth: Penguin, pp. 169–82.

Marx, K. (1970) *Capital*, Vol. 1. London: Lawrence and Wishart.

—— (1972) [1850] *The Class Struggles in France*, Moscow: Progress.

Mason, R.O. and Mitroff, I.I. (1981) *Challenging Strategic Planning Assumptions*, New York: Wiley.

Mead, G.H. (1936) *Movements of Thought in the Nineteenth Century*, Chicago: Univeresity of Chicago Press.

Mechanic, D. (1963) 'Some Considerations in the Methodology of Organizational Studies', in H.J. Leavitt (ed.) *The Social Science of Organizations*, Englewood Cliffs, NJ: Prentice-Hall, pp. 139–82.

Merton, R.K. (1940) 'Bureaucratic Structure and Personality', *Social Forces* 17: 560–8, reprinted in R.K. Merton *et al.* (eds) (1952) *Reader in Bureaucracy*, Glencoe, Ill.: The Free Press, pp. 361–71.

—— (1957) *Social Theory and Social Structure*, Glencoe, Ill.: The Free Press.

—— (1992) personal communication.

Merton, R.K. *et al.* (eds) (1952) *Reader in Bureaucracy*, Glencoe, Ill.: The Free Press.

Meyer, M.W. and Zucker, L.G. (1989) *Permanently Failing Organizations*, Newbury Park: Sage.

Meynaud, J. (1968) *Technocracy*, London: Faber and Faber.

Milgram, S. (1974) *Obedience to Authority*, New York: Harper and Row.

Miller, E.J. and Rice, A.K. (1967) *Systems of Organization: The Control of Task and Sentient Boundaries*, London: Tavistock.

Mitroff, I.I. (1983) *Stakeholders of the Organizational Mind*, San Francisco: Jossey Bass.

Mitzman, A. (1970) *The Iron Cage*, New York: Knopf.

Montaigne, M. de (1842) *The Works of Montaigne*, edited by William Hazlitt, London: Templeman.

Morgan, G. (1986) *Images of Organization*, London: Sage.

Mouzelis, N. (1967) *Organization and Bureaucracy*, London: Routledge and Kegan Paul.

Munsterberg, H. (1913) *Psychology and Industrial Efficiency*, London: Constable.

Newby, H. (1993) 'Social Science and Public Policy', *Royal Society of Arts Journal* May, 365–77.

Nietzsche, F. (1968) *Twilight of the Idols*, Harmondsworth: Penguin.

Offe, C. (1985) *Disorganized Capitalism*, Cambridge: Polity.

Parker, M. (1992) 'Post-Modern Organizations or Postmodern Organization Theory', *Organization Studies* 13: 1–17.

Parsons, T. (1947) 'Introduction to Max Weber', *The Theory of Social and Economic Organization*, Glencoe, Ill.: The Free Press.

—— (1951) *The Social System*, Glencoe, Ill.: The Free Press.

Parsons, T. (1960) 'A Sociological Approach to the Theory of Organizations', in *Structure and Process in Modern Societies*, Glencoe, Ill.: The Free Press, pp. 16–58.

Patterson, M., West, M. and Payne, R. (1992) 'Collective Climates: A Test of their Socio-psychological Significance', Centre for Economic Performance Discussion Paper No. 94, London: London School of Economics.

Patterson, W. (1984) 'A Decade of Friendship: The First Ten Years', in D. Wilson (ed.) *The Environmental Crisis: A Handbook for All Friends of the Earth*, London: Heinemann, pp. 140–54.

Pauchant, T.C. (1991) 'Transferential Leadership: Towards a More Complex Understanding of Charisma in Organizations', *Organization Studies* 12: 507–27.

Pearce, F. (1991) *Green Warriors: The People and Politics behind the Environmental Revolution*, London: The Bodley Head.

Peters, G. (1988) 'Organisation as Social Relationship, Formalisation and Standardisation: A Weberian Approach to Concept Formation', *International Sociology* 3: 267–82.

Peters, T. and Austin, N. (1986) *A Passion for Excellence*, London: Collins.

Pollard, S. (1968) *The Genesis of Modern Management*, Harmondsworth: Penguin.

Popper, K. (1957a) *The Poverty of Historicism*, London: Routledge and Kegan Paul.

—— (1957b) *The Open Society and Its Enemies*, London: Routledge and Kegan Paul.

Rafaeli, A. and Sutton, R.I. (1989) 'The Expression of Emotion in Organizational Life', *Research in Organizational Behavior* 11: 1–42.

—— (1990) 'Busy Stores and Demanding Customers: How Do They Affect the Display of Positive Emotion?', *Academy of Management Journal* 33: 623–37.

—— (1991) 'Emotional Contrast Strategies as a Means of Social Influence: Lessons from Criminal Interrogators and Bill Collectors', *Academy of Management Journal* 34: 749–75.

Raz, J. (ed.) (1990) *Authority*, Oxford: Blackwell.

Ray, L. and Reed, M. (eds) (1994) *Organizing Modernity*, London: Routledge.

Reed, M. (1985) *Redirections in Organizational Analysis*, London: Tavistock.

Robbins, L. (1935) *An Essay on the Nature and Significance of Economic Science*, London: Macmillan.

Roseveare, H. (1969) *The Treasury: the Evolution of a British Institution*, London: Allen Lane.

Rourke, F.E. (ed.) (1965) *Bureaucratic Power in National Politics*, Boston: Little, Brown & Co.

Salaman, G. and Thompson, K. (eds) (1973) *People and Organizations*, London: Longmans.

—— (1980) *Control and Ideology in Organizations*, Milton Keynes, Open University Press.

Scaff, L.A. (1989) *Fleeing the Iron Cage*, Berkeley, CA: University of California Press.

Schluchter, W. (1979) (1985 edition) *The Rise of Western Rationalism: Max Weber's Developmental History*, Berkeley, CA: University of California Press.

Schon, D. (1971) *Beyond the Stable State*, London: Temple Smith.

Schutz, A. (1967) *The Phenomenology of the Social World*, Evanston, Ill.: Northwestern University Press.

Schwartzman, H. (1989) *The Meeting: Gatherings in Organizations and Communities*, New York: Plenum Press.

Scott, W.R. (1995) 'Institutional Theory and Organization', in W.R. Scott and S. Christensen (eds) *The Institutional Construction of Organization: International and Longitudinal Studies*, Thousand Oaks: Sage, pp. viii–xxv.

Selznick, P. (1957) *Leadership in Administration*, London: Harper.

—— (1966) [1949] *TVA and the Grass Roots*, New York: Harper.

Sennett, R. (1993) *Authority*, London: Faber.

Shubik, M. (1964) 'Approaches to the Study of Decision-Making Relevant to the Firm', in W.J. Gore and J.W. Dyson (eds) *The Making of Decisions*, Glencoe, Ill.: The Free Press, pp. 31–50.

Sica, A. (1988) *Weber, Irrationality and Social Order*, Berkeley, CA: University of California Press.

Silverman, D. (1970) *The Theory of Organizations*, London: Heinemann.

—— (1994) 'On Throwing Away Ladders: Rewriting the Theory of Organizations', in J. Hassard and M. Parker (eds) *Towards a New Theory of Organizations*, London: Routledge, pp. 1–23.

Simon, H.A. (1965) *Administrative Behavior*, Glencoe, Ill.: The Free Press.

Spencer, M.E. (1970) 'Weber on Legitimate Norms and Authority', *British Journal of Sociology* 21: 123–34.

Stanton, A.H. and Schwartz, M.S. (1954) *The Mental Hospital*, New York: Basic Books.

Stewart, R. (1972) *The Reality of Organizations*, London: Pan Books.

Sunday Times Jeff Randall report, 29 November 1992.

Tagiuri, R. and Litwin, G.H. (1968) *Organizational Climate: Exploration of a Concept*, Cambridge, MA: Harvard Business School.

Taylor, F.W. (1947) *Scientific Management*, New York: Harper.

Thompson, J.D. and McEwen, W.J. (1973) 'Organizational Goals and Environment: Goal-Setting as an Interaction Process', in G. Salaman and K. Thompson (eds) *People and Organizations*, London: Longmans, pp. 155–67.

Tocqueville, A. de (1945) *Democracy in America*, New York: Knopf.

Tönnies, F. (1887) (1974 edition) *Community and Association*, London: Routledge.

Topitsch, E. (1971) 'Max Weber and Sociology Today', in O. Stammer (ed.) *Max Weber and Sociology Today*, Oxford, Blackwell, pp. 8–25.

Trist, E.L., Higgin, G., Murray, H., and Pollok, A. (1963) *Organisational Choice*, London: Tavistock.

Turner, B. (1971) *Exploring the Industrial Sub-Culture*, London: Macmillan.

Turner, S. and Factor, R.A. (1994) *Max Weber: The Lawyer as Social Thinker*, London: Routledge.

United Kingdom (1984) *Data Protection Act*, London: HMSO.

Warnock, M. (1984) *Report of the Committee of Inquiry into Human Fertilization and Embryology*, Cmnd 9314, London: HMSO.

Weber, M. (1889) *Zur Geschichte der Handelsgesellschaften im Mittelalter*, Stuttgart: Enke.

—— (1947) *The Theory of Social and Economic Organization*, translated by A.M. Henderson and T. Parsons, New York: The Free Press.

—— (1948) *From Max Weber*, edited by H.H. Gerth and C.W. Mills, London: Routledge, 'Politics as a Vocation', pp. 77–128, 'Science as a Vocation', pp. 129–58, 'Bureaucracy', pp. 196–244.

—— (1949) *The Methodology of the Social Sciences*, Glencoe, Ill.: The Free Press.

—— (1956) *Wirtschaft und Gesellschaft*, 4th edn, Tübingen: J.C.B. Mohr.

—— (1958a) 'Der Nationalstaat und die Volkswirtschaftspolitik', in *Gesammelte Politische Schriften*, Tübingen: J.C.B. Mohr, pp. 1–25.

—— (1958b) *Gesammelte Politische Schriften*, Tübingen: J.C.B. Mohr.

—— (1958c) 'The Three Types of Legitimate Rule', *Berkeley Publications in Society and Institutions*, 4: 1–11.

—— (1968a) *Economy and Society*, translated by G. Roth and C. Wittich, 2 vols, New York: Bedminster.

—— (1968b) 'Über einige Kategorien der verstehenden Soziologie', in *Gesammelte Aufsätze zur Wissenschaftslehre*, 3rd edn, Tübingen: J.C.B. Mohr, pp, 427–74.

—— (1973) *Gesammelte Aufsätze zur Wissenschaftslehre*, ed. J. Winckelmann, Tübingen: J.C.B. Mohr [Paul Siebeck].

—— (1978) *Economy and Society*, translated by G. Roth and C. Wittich, Berkeley, CA: University of California Press.

Weeks, D. (1973) 'Organization Theory – Some Themes and Distinctions', in G. Salaman and K. Thompson (eds) *People and Organizations*, London: Longmans, pp. 375–95.

Whimster, S. and Lash, S. (eds) (1987) *Max Weber, Rationality and Modernity*, London: Allen and Unwin.

Whitehead, A.N. (1925) *Science and the Modern World*, New York: Macmillan.

Whyte, W.H. Jr. (1956) *The Organization Man*, New York: Simon and Schuster.

Williamson, O. (1985) *The Economic Institutions of Capitalism*, New York: The Free Press.

Woodward, J. (1965) *Industrial Organization: Theory and Practice*, London: Oxford University Press.

Zimmerman, D. (1973) 'The Practicalities of Rule Use', in G. Salaman and K. Thompson (eds) *People and Organizations*, London: Longmans, pp. 221–38.

Zucker, L.G. (1983) 'Organizations as Institutions', *Research in the Sociology of Organization* 2: 1–47.

INDEX

action 105, 110–11; authority and 78, 79;
  rationality and 62, 64; value–rational
  61, 77; Weber and 59, 60, 61, 62
affectivity 94; in organizations 104,
  105–8, 114–15, 116–30; researching
  109–13; Weber and 89–90, 97–100,
  104–6, 108
Albini, J. 45
Albrow, Martin 8, 10, 15, 40, 49, 61, 74,
  84, 89, 97, 98, 100, 104, 106, 109, 111,
  113, 115, 129, 135, 139, 154, 165
American Society of Mechanical
  Engineers 33
anti-foundationalism 162
applied science 35–6
appraisal 117, 118
Argyris, C. 44
Aristotle 89, 95
asset specificity 54
association 95–6
assumptions, background 41
atmosphere 126
Austin, Nancy 103, 104
authority 82–5, 124; legal–rational 74–7,
  82–4, 86; postmodernism and 86–8;
  structure of 25–6; Weber and 55, 61,
  76–81
axial principles 148, 156

Bacon, Francis 35
Bakke, E.W. 29
Baritz, L. 34
Barnard, Chester 24–5, 29
Beck, Ulrich 15, 56, 139
Bell, Daniel 4, 139
behaviour 3, 10, 23, 25, 48, 63, 111,
  113–17, 119–20, 125; everyday 10, 111;
  group 22; human 34, 37, 42, 64, 110,

125; micro-social 138, 143–4;
  organizational 20, 86, 111, 121, 126,
  144, 159, 165
behaviourism 45, 106, 108
Bendix, R. 26, 46
Berg, P.-O., 111
Berger, P.L. 47
bias 18, 44
Bittner, E. 47, 48
Blau, P.M. 22, 27, 40, 44, 86, 127, 139, 155
Bourdieu, P. 157
Bridges, Lord Edward 101
Brower, David 140
Brown, Wilfred 39
Brunsson, Nils 122
bureaucracy 4, 5, 6, 26, 44, 53, 54, 55, 58,
  61, 66, 74, 75, 76, 77, 89, 90, 93, 94, 95,
  97, 98, 99, 100, 102, 103, 105, 108, 109,
  110, 112, 115, 129, 132, 133, 159, 164;
  emotions in 98, 99, 100, 102; ideal
  type 61, 91, 94, 98, 104, 111, 158;
  organization before 95–7; Weber and
  5, 54, 65–6, 74–5, 93, 100, 105, 108, 109
Burke, T. 141
Burnham, J. 50
Burns, T. 112
business 1–3, 9, 23, 34, 45, 48, 50, 93, 99,
  103, 117, 118, 135, 144, 154, 157, 159,
  160, 162, 164, 166; school(s) 1, 3, 9, 11,
  144, 160

Cabinet records 122, 123
calculability 98, 115
capital 57, 139, 144, 154, 155, 156, 157,
  165
capitalism/ist 4, 35, 46, 59, 114, 131, 132,
  148, 155, 156, 161; disorganized 156
Capital 57, 58

Astrology

Astrology Louis MacNeice

Doubleday & Company Inc.,
Garden City, New York

First published in 1964 by Aldus Books Limited,
Aldus House, Conway Street, Fitzroy Square, London W1
Distributed in the United Kingdom
and the Commonwealth by
W. H. Allen & Company,
43 Essex Street, London WC2
Printed in Jugoslavia

Contents

1 The art of the stars

In June 1941 the Nazis locked up all the astrologers in Germany, partly because their activities were considered unsuitable (if not subversive) in the National Socialist state. This remains one of the more famous, if backhanded, tributes to one of the most diehard of the arts. A similar tribute occurred in the British House of Commons in June 1942. A Conservative M.P. asked the Minister of Information, Mr. Brendan Bracken, "whether his attention has been drawn to the fact that astrologers are predicting that Germany is on the brink of collapse; and whether he will stop astrological predictions about the war in order to counteract the risk that addicts of astrology will relax their efforts?" The minister replied: "Astrologers seem to have the misfortune to be perpetually in conflict. And, as no sensible person takes their predictions seriously, I cannot ask our overworked censors to meddle in their mysteries."

Mr. Bracken showed himself more lenient than the Nazis, or than certain ancient Roman emperors who used to deport their astrologers. But perhaps the astrological profession is not as powerful in modern Britain as it was in Nazi Germany or ancient Rome. Nevertheless, Mr. Bracken was wrong. Many sensible people *do* take the subject seriously. Astrological almanacs and newspaper horoscopes are eagerly read by millions all over the world, many of whom believe or would like to believe at least part of it. And astrology has many addicts in Western countries today among the educated and the sophisticated.

The Dumb-Bell Nebula in the Vulpecula galaxy photographed by a 200-inch telescope at an American observatory. Astronomers are constantly revising their ideas about the universe in the light of fresh discoveries; yet modern scientific advances have never affected the world-wide popularity of astrology today.

In France the astrological author André Barbault has expounded the Zodiac with great elegance and relish (he will tell you that Louis Armstrong is a typical *Aries* character—*"ardeur et improvisation forcenée"*). In Germany the heavier guns of scholarship and of psychological and statistical analysis are trained upon such targets as "astro-biology." In the U.S.A., as in Germany, there has been a serious attempt to correlate modern astrology with the findings of modern psychology.

One of the veterans of American astrology, Dane Rudhyar, describes his art as a "system of symbolical life interpretation." He also calls it "the algebra of life" and, unlike some other of his colleagues (astrologers have always disagreed), flatly denies that it has any empirical basis. In England astrology is on the whole treated more frivolously, or at least on a lower intellectual plane, but it is easy to find British intellectuals who believe there is "something in it." In evidence, however, they usually either refer you to German, French, or American publications, or quote what some mysterious Hindu once said to them in India.

In other countries today astrology retains her old position as queen of the "sciences." In India it may not be true that (as some Indians allege) most of the more conservative members of the cabinet regularly consult astrologers; but it is certain that below cabinet level astrology permeates every sphere of life. Indian astrologers tend to work with collections of allegedly ancient *ready-made* horoscopes (known as *nadi granthams*) written on palm leaves. To the Western way of thinking this may smack of common fortune telling, but many Europeans have returned from India much impressed by what these palm leaves have told them about themselves. And Santha Rama Rau, a westernized Indian writer married to an American, has confessed that a return visit to India converted her from her American-style skepticism. She mentions a friend of hers, a Bombay businessman, who never makes an important decision "without first consulting his astrologer." For that matter, this has been said of J. P. Morgan. According to one authority, the most famous modern American astrologer Evangeline Adams was one of Morgan's advisers.

Professor Morris Carstairs, a social psychologist in Edinburgh University, has made a detailed study of an Indian community and has concluded that Hindus consult astrologers in order to discover their own real wishes: "With the initial premise of this self-centered view of the world, the Hindus' unshakeable belief in astrology became more comprehensible." But there are some Indians who find the whole practice a nuisance. One of them writes of the ubiquitous astrologers: "They draw a red herring across every practical problem—choice of profession, marriage, journeys, treatment in illness—and in truth disturb and upset every practical arrangement."

Many countries in the Western world, at various stages of history, have similarly come under the influence of this very peculiar body of beliefs that has been building up through the ages. That influence, and the reasons for it, is the subject of this book. But, first of all, what *is* astrology?

Even in our skeptical age, astrology numbers many well-known intellectuals and artists among its followers. Right, the Irish poet W. B. Yeats (1865-1939), who was fascinated by the irrational; far right, a pencil sketch of his uncle George Pollexfen, who taught Yeats to cast horoscopes. Below left, the British composer Gustav Holst at his piano, and, right, the cover of a recording of his suite *The Planets* (composed in 1919). Holst's interest in astrology inspired this composition—a musical interpretation of each planet's traditional astrological character.

Left, the American writer Henry Miller (born 1890), whose enthusiasm for astrology has lasted throughout a long literary career. Though he does not claim to "live" by it, Miller admits to finding "disturbing accuracies in everything that concerns astrology."

11

All persons who give any credence whatsoever to any form of astrology must hold one belief in common: that there is some kind of relationship between the stars and human beings. It may not be a relationship of cause and effect (i.e., the stars may not directly influence human beings). But relationship there must be. To put it colloquially, the stars are part of our set-up.

But for many people today, at least in Europe and America, astrology is mainly a matter of horoscopes and predictions; the ordinary man, being selfish, wants to hear about himself and his prospects. The widest appeal, therefore, is much the same as that of fortune telling with crystal balls, cards, etc. (Astrologers have themselves sometimes gone in for such sidelines, though this is usually much frowned upon by the more serious theorists and practitioners.) Some hardheaded students of the subject believe that a good astrologer *can* make

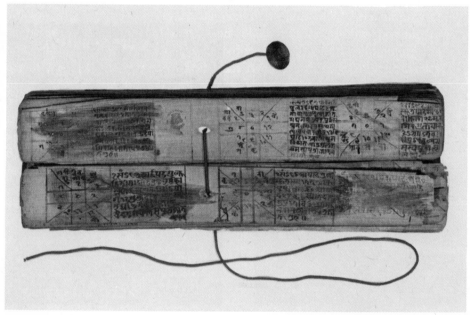

successful predictions, but that he does this without really knowing (consciously, that is) what he is doing. The stars are just as much props to him as the Tarot cards are to a fortune teller, or the lines on the hand to a palmist. The real active agent is his own intuition.

But other believers in astrology regard the prediction of events as its weakest side, and would prefer the art to be restricted to the diagnosis of character, and, at most, the assessment of an individual's *potentialities*. At this they think that it can be of the greatest use socially. The modern English astrological writer Rupert Gleadow maintains that "the comparison of horoscopes is the only certain way of making marriage not a lottery but a partnership." Many astrologers today claim that they can act not only as marriage counselors but as advisers on health, education, and careers.

Above, a scene from the film *Nine Hours to Rama*, recently made in India. The police believe that killers will try to assassinate Gandhi at an astrologically auspicious moment; here two detectives consult an astrologer to find out when that moment might be. Reliance on astrological prediction is widespread in India today, and has been for centuries: Above left, a Nepalese palm leaf horoscope containing prognostications for the years 1362-66. Left, a more recent example of the Indian astrologer's art: a decorative motif of bulls (symbolizing the sign of Taurus) from the horoscope of a 19th-century prince of Lahore.

The subject indeed has many forms and applications, whose order of importance varies according to time and country. Astrological medicine, which in the first century A.D. brought a fortune to a doctor in Marseilles, no longer enjoys a vogue in Western Europe, yet doctors can be found who believe in it. (The American astrological magazine *In Search* has featured articles by Dr. W. M. Davidson and Dr. William Gutman, both practicing medical men.) Similarly, while run-of-the-mill practitioners rest their claims on the hoary antiquity of what skeptics have called this "fossilized science," the intellectuals among modern astrologers are anxious to liberate their subject from the dead hand of tradition. A leading Swiss astrologer, Karl Ernst Krafft (who figures in an extraordinary story to be recounted in Chapter 7), once went so far as to write: "The tradition is like a rotting corpse, and should not be brought to life again." A similar line is taken by several of the leading Americans.

Even within traditional astrology, if we look back through the centuries, we find a great range of beliefs—from the ancient (and medieval) conception of the stars as gods or divine animals (typical question: What food do they eat? typical answer: Purer food than we do) to the 15th-century Italian humanists' comparison of the star-man relationship to a struck harp that sets the strings vibrating in some other harp that no one has touched. And astrology has usually attracted a wide range of adherents. In early 16th-century France, the distinguished court physician Cornelius Agrippa accepted astrology (though he renounced it later) at about the same time that the famous obscurantist prophet Nostradamus was writing his scrambled verse quatrains that have since given much pleasure to lovers of puzzles and prediction.

Many of Nostradamus's prophecies are not overtly astrological, but this is true also of many predictions in astrological almanacs; anyway, it was as an astrologer that people thought of Nostradamus in his own day. And his mystificatory technique in his writing is typical of a certain kind of astrologer through

the ages. The French of his verses is not only the (to us) difficult French of its period; Nostradamus often deliberately misspelled words, and used anagrams, portmanteau words, and telegraphese. So his statements about the future are open to widely differing interpretations, though many commentators have agreed as to the meaning of some quatrains (such as several that apparently foretold the French Revolution).

In the same period astrology numbered among its famous supporters men like Paracelsus, the Swiss physician and alchemist; Melanchthon, the German theologian and friend of Luther's; and Cardan, the Italian physician and mathematician. In 16th-century England, Queen Elizabeth's astrologer, John Dee, could assert that "Astrology is an art mathematical . . ." while his greater contemporary Francis Bacon was writing: "As for Astrology, it is so full of superstition, that scarce anything sound can be discovered in it." (Yet even Bacon could later add: "I would rather have it purified than altogether rejected"— a feeling that has been echoed by the present-day attitude of astrologers like Krafft, quoted above.)

Some astrologers consider their craft an "occult" one; others think it is as much a matter of fact as any empirical science. In 1899 an American astrologer using the pseudonym "Gabriel" (such pseudonyms having long been fashionable) wrote in a book called *The Gospel of the Stars*: "Unlike religion, astrology is based not on faith but on facts. The religious man believes; the astrologer knows. Experiment and observation are his guides." But some of his colleagues at the time were combining their "science" with theosophy, which claims to be in direct touch with the "divine essence," transcending both observation and reason. (The Theosophical Society was founded in the U.S.A. in 1875.) Some years ago a very successful English editor of astrological magazines, who used the alias of "Alan Leo," wrote: "I believe every human being belongs to a Father Star in Heaven or Star Angel . . . ."

Left, a scene from the American film *Love is a Many Splendored Thing* (1960). Two lovers consult a Chinese fortune teller to find out whether they will have a long and happy life together. All the world seems to love a fortune teller—which (since most people equate astrology with prediction) explains much of astrology's popularity.

Right, some prophetic verse written by the 16th-century French astrologer and seer Nostradamus. The stanza printed in green has been translated thus:
By night shall come through the forest of Reines,
Two parts Voltorte Herne, the white stone,
The black monk in grey within Varennes,
Elected captain, causeth Tempest, fire,
blood running.
It has been interpreted as a prediction of the capture of France's Louis XVI in 1791, while fleeing to Varennes (disguised as a monk) to escape the revolutionaries.

CENTURIE IX.   143
XX.
De nuict viendra par la foreſt de Reines,
Deux pars vaultorte Hene la pierre blanche,
Le moyne noir en gris dedans Varennes,
Eſleu cap cauſe tempeſte, feu, ſang tranche.
XXI.
Au temple haut de Bloys ſacre Salonne,
Nuict pont de Loyre Prelat Roy pernicant,
Curſeur victoire aux mareſts de la lone,
D'ou prelature de blancs abormeant.
XXII.
Roy & ſa cour au lieu de langue halbe,
Dedans le temple vis à vis dupalais,
Dans le jardin Duc de Mantor & d'Albe,
Albe & Mantor poignard langue & palais.
XXIII.
Puiſnay joüant au freſch deſſoubs la tonne,
Le haut du toict du milieu ſur la teſte,
Le Pere Roy au temple ſaint Salone,

The more serious modern astrological writers often tend toward caution. Louis de Wohl, for instance, who after a long residence in Germany went to live in England, was not unduly modest: According to himself, he conducted a one-man astrological war with the Nazis. Yet even though de Wohl can write: "A man who plunges blindfold through the London streets is distinctly safer than a man without a horoscope," he can also write of astrology in general: "Let us get this straight from the start: it is not prophecy. It is dealing not with certainties, but with tendencies. It has a fairly wide margin for error—but it works."

But prophecy, of course, is just what the ordinary man wants (hence the popularity of *all* kinds of fortune telling). And in practice de Wohl went in for something very like it. For example: "It was clear to me, as to every student of astrology who knew Hitler's horoscope, that he would launch his great attack against the West when Jupiter was in conjunction with his Sun, in May 1940."

Curiosity about the future is a primary reason for the continuing popularity of astrology. Another reason for many people (though astrologers have often been at pains to deny this) is the almost cosy appeal of fatalism: In times of either stress or failure you can always pass the buck to the stars. But perhaps equally important is the delight most people take in *classification,* especially in the classification of themselves and their friends: "Are you Virgo?" "Oh no, I'm Leo." The bulk of any popular book of astrology is given up to the human characteristics attributed to the influence of the heavenly bodies, whether they are the planets or the signs of the Zodiac. Even animals, plants, precious stones, etc., come under this influence. These will be discussed again, but some samples may be given here from an early 19th-century English astrologer, the first "Raphael" (another celestial pseudonym—real name R. C. Smith):

"Saturn," writes Raphael, "is by universal experience acknowledged to be the most powerful, evil, and malignant of all the planets." Among persons he represents (among others) grandfathers, paupers, monks, and gravediggers; among animals cats and dogs "and all creatures delighting in filth and breeding from putrefaction"; among plants hemlock, hellebore, poppy, mandrake, nightshade, and moss; among trees willow, pine, yew, and cypress; among birds the crow, owl, and cuckoo; among places deserts, churchyards, and all "muddy dirty stinking places, wells, and nuisances of every description." His wind is the east wind and his favorite mineral is lead.

This grouping of interrelated creatures and objects has the same appeal as certain card games with their sequences, flushes, and so on. It all goes back to the basic concept of *sympathy,* which we shall find stressed over and over again when we come to look at astrology's history. There is sympathy between the parts of the universe, between things celestial and things terrestrial. From this stems a whole system of *correspondences,* the most famous perhaps being those between the signs of the Zodiac and the parts of the human body, constituting the so-called "Zodiacal Man."

The city of Jerusalem, usually assigned to the sign of Virgo. Most kinds of terrestrial objects—from cities to blades of grass—have been classified by astrologers in terms of the influence of planets or Zodiac signs:

There is something in this concept of natural correspondences that attracts the mystic in us. And there is an equally strong attraction for the poet in us, or at any rate for the patternmaker. The same Raphael becomes uncommonly eloquent on this principle of sympathy: He speaks (the following quotation is much boiled down) of the "simple and easy but beautiful theory, which presumes that the same sympathetic power which causes the iron and magnet to attract each other, . . . the same occult influence which drives the frantic herd about the pastures; which provokes the gadfly to vex the steed; . . . which seizes with fits of temporary madness the owl and raven; which affects the brains of the maniac *or which circulates through all living nature, pervading all, disquieting all*; . . . this universal sympathy or instinct (for all instinct *is* sympathy) is neither more nor less than the secret but powerful influences of the heavenly bodies."

The pigeon-holing technique of astrology is also extended to the hours of the day, historical periods, and towns and countries. Algiers is assigned to Scorpio, New York to Cancer, London to Gemini, both Jerusalem and Paris to Virgo, Hamburg to Aquarius, and Oxford to Capricorn. Scotland, according to the modern astrologer Maurice Wemyss, "is particularly influenced by Capricorn 26

[each Zodiacal sign consists of 30 degrees], a degree of 'caution,' and its ruling planet Saturn." The U.S.A. is under Gemini and Portugal under Pisces. The seven-day week is apportioned among the planets: Saturday is Saturn's day, Sunday the Sun's day (*Sonntag* in German); in French, *mardi* (Tuesday) is Mars's day, and *mercredi* (Wednesday) is Mercury's day (*mercoledì* in Italian).

These conceptions also survive in the very vocabulary of most modern languages. In English the word "saturnine" is connected, just as much as Saturday, with the planet (which in turn got its name from a god). Similar words are "jovial" and "mercurial," while the English "disaster" and French "désastre" derive from the old Greek word for star. For many people these associations may be as unfamiliar as the ancient doctrine of the four humors, which also survives in modern languages in words like the English "sanguine" and the French "mélancholie." This doctrine, like that of the four elements, was very much involved with astrology; indeed, some modern astrologers still make use of it, as they also make use of the ancient parallel of microcosm and macrocosm. The figure of the so-called Zodiacal or astrological man is just one illustration of this doctrine. And medieval astrologers often combined their craft with that of alchemy, which also presupposes mysterious correspondences in things.

Forms and varieties

Traditionally, astrology was divided into *natural* astrology, foretelling the motions of the heavenly bodies (now absorbed into astronomy), and *judicial* astrology, which interprets these motions in terms of terrestrial life. This latter has many subdivisions, the most important today being undisputedly *genethliacal* astrology, or the art of erecting and interpreting individuals' horoscopes.

Four types of "judicial" astrology, which interprets the heavens in terms of life on earth. Left, some of the people that gathered on Mont Blanc in Switzerland in anticipation of the end of the world (forecast by an Italian astrologer for July 14, 1956). This kind of prediction is "mundane" astrology, which foretells events of national or international importance like earthquakes or revolutions. A more popular form today is "genethliacal" astrology—casting and interpreting the horoscopes or "natal charts" of individuals. Right, an American astrologer with some of his clients' charts.

Casting horoscopes to answer questions is called "horary" astrology; below right, an Italian fortune teller outside a Naples law court undertakes to answer litigants' questions by this method. "Meteorological" astrology is weather forecasting. Below left, a page from an Austrian calendar for 1962 showing the first nine days of January; below them at the bottom of the page are Zodiac signs, and above them symbols for different kinds of weather.

But this was a late comer; it was preceded by *mundane* astrology, the chief interest of the Babylonians (the inventors of the science) who were concerned only with the fortunes of the state or of the king as head of the state. They naturally paid particular attention to such conspicuous phenomena as eclipses of the Sun or Moon. In some circles, these (and comets) are still assumed to portend grand-scale happenings. For Raphael, in his *Manual of Astrology* (1828), an eclipse of the Moon on November 3, 1827, boded no good to the British nation (which was at the time brewing up for the first parliamentary Reform Bill). Raphael's illustrator made a great deal of the occasion: Britannia sits downstage on the left covering her eyes, a bull is being strangled by a snake, upstage right is a gesturing skeleton. Not only national but world-wide disasters are foretold in mundane astrology—disasters like the threatened deluges in 1186 and 1524, neither of which came off. One of the most recent examples of such mundane miscalculation was on February 5, 1962; from the Indian point of view (but not the European) there was a conjunction of all the main planets in Capricorn, which many Hindu astrologers said would mean the end of the world. Crowds of Hindu holy men sat up all night for it in Delhi.

There is also *horary* astrology, extremely popular in the 17th century but now disapproved of by some astrologers. It consists of answering questions by making horoscopic calculations for the moment at which they crop up. Ingrid Lind, author of *Astrology and Commonsense*, writes: "To me this savours of the bead

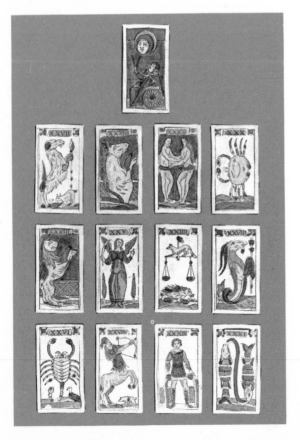

Left, 13 cards from the earliest existing pack of Tarot cards (made in Florence in the 15th century) depicting an astrologer (top) and the 12 signs of the Zodiac. Tarot packs (though not all containing astrological cards) are still used today for fortune telling. Another form of divination sometimes linked with astrology is palmistry—reading the future from a hand. Above, a palm marked with planetary hieroglyphs from a book by the 17th-century English occultist Robert Fludd.

curtain and fortune-telling booth and I will have nothing to do with it." On the other hand, Rupert Gleadow, in his book *Astrology in Everyday Life,* appears to find it both useful and amusing: "If a letter or telegram arrives to announce, for example, an unwelcome visitor whose journey may possibly be postponed, a horoscope set up for the moment when the telegram was read will set all doubts at rest by announcing quite simply whether the visit will take place, and if not why not."

Gleadow, who seems to get great fun out of his astrology (and even the most hardboiled rationalist would find that it affords amusing parlor games), is also prepared to accept *medical* astrology. He says we should watch the 12 "biochemic cell salts," which are essential constituents of the body and which can be related to the 12 signs of the Zodiac. Thus the Libra salt holds the balance (Libra of course *means* balance) between the acids and the alkalis. "It is a good rule," Gleadow writes, "that if any sign contains an afflicted planet [i.e., one that is badly "aspected"; see later], the body will need the salt corresponding to that sign." The 12 cell salts are usually accepted by astrologers in the U.S.A.; but some (in spite of the tempting parallel with the Zodiac) have decided that this was oversimplification, and have added a few more to the tally. On medical astrology generally, a veteran American physician has written: "The doctor needs astro-diagnosis worse than he can ever realize until he has used it for some years."

As for *electional* astrology (the art of horoscopically choosing exactly the right moment for an enterprise), Gleadow warns us to watch the date for laying a foundation stone, or the moment the champagne bottle sends the new craft down the launching slip.

Aside from these general divisions, there are many related sidelines, such as the use of astrological "images" or amulets, or *physiognomical* astrology, concerned with the facial characteristics connected with the stars' influence. As an illustration of the astonishing lengths (or minutiae) to which astrologers can go, consider the "Sabian Symbols" of the American astrologer Marc Edmund Jones, which are presented by Dane Rudhyar in his book *The Astrology of Personality.* Jones devised a separate symbolic image for each of the 360 degrees in the Zodiac. He also halved each sign (containing 30°) to make 24 "spans" (15° each) with different qualities or characteristics assigned to them.

Jones's image for the eighth degree of Aries (under the "Span of Realization") is: "A woman's hat, with streamers blown by the east wind." Jones's explanation: "First real attempt at self-exteriorization and embodiment in consciousness. Individualizing Eastern forces are suggested." For Aries 30° (the Span of Examination) the symbol is: "Young ducklings disport themselves merrily upon a pond." Explanation: "Essential social co-operativeness and appreciation of selfhood." For Cancer 4° (the Span of Expansion): "A hungry cat argues with a mouse before eating her." Explanation: "The urge to self-justification through intellectual sophistry or social-ethical considerations. Sense of self-righteousness."

For Cancer 8°: "Rabbits in faultless human attire parade with dignity." Explanation: "Reaching out to participation in a higher order through imitative behavior." For Sagittarius 29° (the Span of Detachment): "Perspiring fat boy, eager to reduce, is mowing lawn." Explanation: "Desire for fitness inherent in all human beings."

The whole subject seems as involved as a vast Hindu temple (and just as capable of decadence). We will try to avoid as many of the more obscure astrological byways as possible, in order to maintain a view of the forest as well as the trees. And, as a further help, here is a short glossary of some of the basic horoscopic terms that will crop up in later chapters:

Ecliptic: The apparent path of the Sun through the sky. From the earth it appears to describe a great circle.

Zodiac: A band of sky extending about 8° on each side of the ecliptic. This band is the racetrack of the planets; with the exception of Pluto (which we cannot see) we never see them outside it. In orthodox, traditional European astrology this band is divided into 12 segments, each of 30°, known as the

Signs: Though these have the same name as the Zodiacal constellations—Aries, Taurus, and the rest—they are not to be confused with them. The difference will be explained later.

Houses: There are 12 of these too, but they are not the same as the signs (or as the constellations). Astrologers use several different systems of houses,

Some astrological terms explained in diagrams: Right, the signs of the Zodiac and their traditional symbols. Below left, the ecliptic, the Sun's apparent path around the earth. Below right, the distribution around the ecliptic of the 12 signs of the Zodiac—which are also assumed to move around the earth—in relation to the 12 houses (separated by "cusps"), which are fixed.

Aries ♈		Libra ♎
Taurus ♉		Scorpio ♏
Gemini ♊		Sagittarius ♐
Cancer ♋		Capricorn ♑
Leo ♌		Aquarius ♒
Virgo ♍		Pisces ♓

but whatever the system the houses (unlike the signs) stay put. Think of the ecliptic as a clock face: The signs keep moving around it like the hands, while the houses keep their places like the figures.

Cusps: The dividing lines between one house and another. Owing to the disagreement about house division, one man's cusp can be another man's blank.

Medium Coeli (or M.C.): Latin for mid-heaven. This is the point above the observer where the Sun "culminates" at noon. Its opposite number is the *Imum Coeli (I.C.)*. A vertical line drawn between these two points crosses at right angles a horizontal line connecting the ascendant in the east with the descendant in the west.

Ascendant: Technically, this is the degree of the ecliptic that is rising above the eastern horizon at any moment. But more generally the term is used to designate the rising *sign* (which is of the utmost importance in horoscopes).

Angles: The cross formed by the ascendant-descendant horizontal line and the M.C.-I.C. vertical line (or meridian). The angles add importance to any planet found on or near any of the four arms of the cross.

Transit: When a planet passes over a sensitive spot in your natal chart it is said to be "transiting" it. Say your ascendant degree at birth was 23° Taurus. It is known (from astronomically compiled tables) when a certain planet is going to transit that point, so it is easy for the astrologer to tell you to expect certain effects at the time of transit.

Right, the 11 planets with their symbols. Below left, the positions on the ecliptic of the medium coeli (noon), the imum coeli (midnight), ascendant, and descendant. The lines joining these points (which produce the "angles") form the basis of any horoscope chart. Below right, examples of planetary "aspects": Mercury (colored red) is shown in "opposition" to Neptune; in "conjunction" with Venus; in "sextile" with Saturn; in "square" with Uranus; in "trine" with Mars.

Sun	☉	Jupiter	♃
Earth	●	Saturn	♄
Moon	☾	Uranus	♅
Mercury	☿	Neptune	♆
Venus	♀	Pluto	♇
Mars	♂		

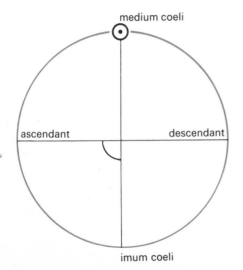

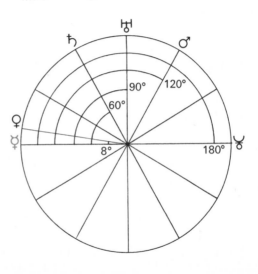

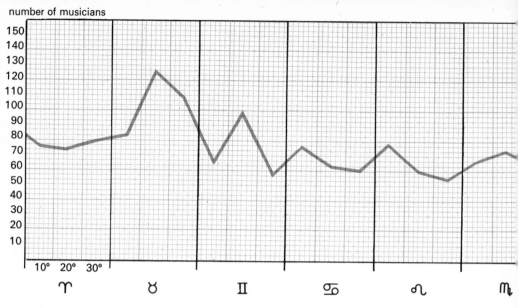

A graph based on the results of
a statistical investigation of traditional
astrology made in 1939 by the great
Swiss astrologer Karl Ernst Krafft.
For this experiment, Krafft took the birth
dates of 2817 musicians, which he allotted
to their correct signs of the Zodiac.
The resulting curve shows that the number
of births varies little from one sign to
another. The highest peak is found under
Taurus—but, traditionally, this sign has
no association with musical talent.

Aspects: These are established geocentrically, like most of astrology. You draw a line from the center of the Earth to one planet and another line to another planet and measure the angle between them. (Don't confuse this with the "angles" just mentioned.) As the whole Zodiacal circle in which the planets travel is 360°, a planet rising is 180° away from a planet setting. Two such planets are said to be in

Opposition: Traditionally a bad aspect, though some modern astrologers dispute this. The opposite of opposition is

Conjunction: Where two planets are very close together (say, within 8° or 10° of each other). This aspect can be either good or bad; it depends on the planets concerned. There are other aspects, but here are the major ones:

Sextile: Two planets 60° apart. Good.

Square: Planets 90° apart. Bad.

Trine: Planets 120° apart. Very good. Unlike a conjunction, it does not matter here if one of the planets concerned is a traditional "malefic." The English poet Dryden, in an epitaph for an admired young lady, writes:

> *For sure the milder planets did combine*
> *On thy auspicious horoscope to shine,*
> *And even the most malicious were in trine.*

The minor aspects have names like *quintile* (72°), *sesquadrate* (135°), and

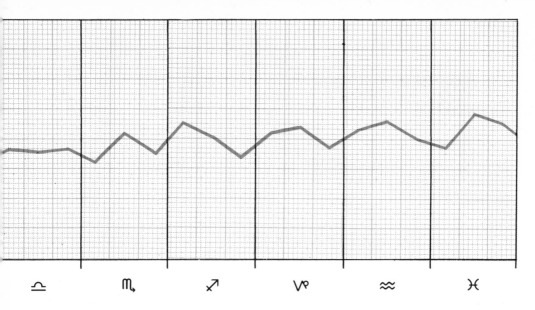

♎︎   ♏︎   ♐︎   ♑︎   ♒︎   ♓︎

quincunx (150°), but we need not bother with them here. There is, however, something called an

Orb : If aspects were limited to the *exact* degrees of the definition, they would not crop up nearly so often as they do. Astrologers allow a margin of about 7° for sextile and about 12° for conjunction or opposition of Sun and Moon. This margin is the orb.

The presence of all this apparently scientific procedure (in a subject so often connected in modern minds with quackery, magic, and occultism) can be ascribed to the fact that, whether astrology now is a "fossilized science" or was never any more than a pseudo-science, it originated in the wish that is at the heart of science—the wish to make sense of the universe. When astrology began, in ancient Babylonia, it was inseparable from *astronomy*. And the two, as we shall see, were not divorced until the time of Sir Isaac Newton.

Attacks and defenses

During its very long history many attacks have been made on astrology, sometimes on rationalist grounds, more often on religious or moral grounds. The astrologers have naturally defended themselves, and the arguments on both sides have been endlessly repeated through the centuries. It should be noted that such opponents of astrology as the Christian Fathers attacked it not because it was a false science but because they thought it was a *science*. Also, some of the attacks on astrology (like Francis Bacon's, quoted above) assume there is something in it, or could be something if only its exponents were more knowledgeable or more scrupulous.

Bacon's demand for a sane astrology is echoed in our own time by some deeply inquiring minds in Germany. Great efforts have been made in that country to vindicate astrology as a science (i.e., statistically ; the French seem to have started this). Various experiments have been made from this angle, the object always being to prove that the diagnoses of astrologers are correct more often than pure chance (as indicated by the laws of probability) would allow. Sometimes the experimenters compare the horoscopes of a large number of people belonging to an easily defined group, such as lunatics or musicians. If a certain pattern in the natal charts recurs too often for the "laws of chance," this is taken as proof of the relationship between human beings and the stars. About 1900 a French artillery officer and amateur astrologer named Paul Choisnard made this sort of investigation into the horoscopes of people of outstanding ability; but he dealt with them only by the hundred. Later, in Switzerland, K. E. Krafft claimed to have made 60,000 observations of the charts of musicians and painters, and to have achieved positive results.

More recently various tests have been made by psychologists, the most famous of these by Carl G. Jung (as will be recounted later). In America in 1960 an Illinois psychologist, Vernon Clark, ran a test using a group of 20 astrologers and a control group (for comparison) of 20 psychologists and social workers. Each of the 40 persons was given 10 horoscopes (of persons unknown) and 10 case histories and was asked to pair them off. According to Mr. Clark, the results of the control group came out "almost exactly at chance"; those of the astrologers were higher. Similar results were obtained from a second and more complicated test on the same lines.

Some modern defenders of astrology, abandoning statistics and empirical criteria in general, have tried to prove that it was in the same category either

Above, a Babylonian boundary stone from about 1200 B.C. showing a king and his daughter at the feet of a goddess; above them are Venus, the Moon, and the Sun. Left, a 16th-century portrait of John Dee, court astrologer to Queen Elizabeth I. Astrology's prestige—gained from long association with royalty—declined in the Renaissance, when printed books gave its mysteries to a wider public. Right, pages from one of the earliest printed books on astrology (1485).

as mathematics (which is assumed to be non-empirical) or as mystical religion or the arts. Some astrologers have insisted that the aesthetic mode must now supersede the ethical; others, especially in America, are trying to make astrology either a substitute for or a culmination of religion.

Some of these controversies on the validity of astrology will appear in the historical chapters of this book. A distinction between "signs" and "causes" was repeatedly and forcibly drawn in past debates; some said the stars were one and some the other. This inevitably involved a discussion of free will, which proved as much of a red herring as it does with philosophers proper. Though the arguments repeat themselves through the centuries, the tone of voice usually varies according to the period and country and also according to the intellectual level or social class of the debaters.

As regards class, astrology for long was considered a *royal* science or art; astrologers (who themselves formed an elite) were accepted attendants upon the kings of Babylon and Assyria, the emperors of Rome, popes in the Middle Ages, and the great ducal families in Renaissance Italy. But by the 16th century, in spite of the fact that John Dee was patronized by Queen Elizabeth and Nostradamus by the queen of France, the social decline of the art was apparently concurrent with the appearance of annual astrological almanacs, which are still popular today. And the almanac makers were rapidly followed by the parodists. For example, in 1544 there appeared in England a satirical pamphlet

entitled *A Merry Prognostication* containing the following stanza :

But I say if the ninth day of November
Had fallen upon the tenth day of December
It had been a marvellous hot year for bees
For then had the Moon been like a green cheese.

Some classical examples of almanacs from an intermediate period can be found in the writings of an English astrologer who called himself "Zadkiel the Seer." In his *Herald of Astrology* (later renamed *Zadkiel's Almanac*) published in 1832, he made predictions for 1833. In his 1834 publication he reprinted some of these predictions together with notes on their fulfillments. Sample prediction : "About the 12th [of February 1833] a vexatious event happens in London." Fulfillment : "A baronet's lady sent to the House of Correction on this day." For 1836 Zadkiel predicted : "About the 9th February lamentable events occur in Ireland; accidents by water will there be frequent." Fulfillment : "On Sunday the 14th inst., a sailboat from Limerick was upset in a squall and went down, when of 15 persons on board only three were saved."

These specimens are typical of almanac predictions from the Renaissance down to our own day. Almanac makers also of course make frequent predictions about international events; but here they tend to play safe or hedge and are rarely overspecific. For example : In April the British government brings out its budget. In *Old Moore's Almanac* (a long-established and popular specimen of its kind) for 1963, the first prediction for April states : "This year the political situation demands a soft budget, but the economic circumstances require a tough one."

For the decline of the royal art there were several probable causes, most of which overlapped each other. Chief of these perhaps were the Reformation, which cast doubt upon all forms of traditional authority or superstition; the increasing use of the vernacular where previously Latin had sufficed; the invention of the printing press and the rapid increase of printed books; and of course the Renaissance spirit of scientific inquiry. To take just one of these : The traditional astrology that was derived from Ptolemy (second century A.D.), so long as it was confined to manuscripts, remained the property and mystery of a few. Once it got into print, it gained in popularity but lost in prestige. Besides all this the telescope was now on its way.

By the 17th century the "scientific revolution" was really gathering force. But at the same time England produced her most popular astrologer, William Lilly, whose name is still honored in most modern astrological textbooks. Yet Lilly's milieu was very different from that of his predecessors in, say, 15th-century Italy; he descended or was forced to descend to repeated undignified mud throwing and squabbling, not only with the enemies of his art but with various rival practitioners who would have liked to take over his following. After Lilly's time astrology lost even more respectability, but made a comeback toward the end of the 19th century that has continued in our own time.

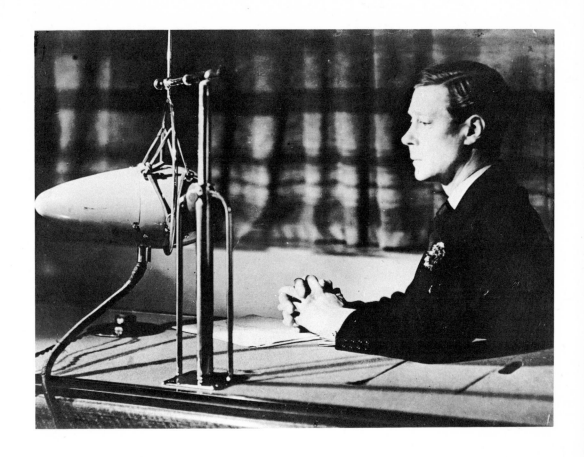

Above, Britain's King Edward VIII (later Duke of Windsor) broadcasting his abdication speech in December 1936. This event was foreshadowed by a newspaper horoscope (right) cast for his niece Princess Margaret at the time of her birth in 1930, which predicted events of great importance affecting the fortunes of the princess in her seventh year. This kind of general and often vague prediction has been (since the 16th century) a feature of most popular almanacs and astrological periodicals.

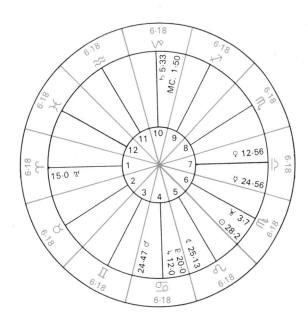

While most of our historical retrospect will naturally be devoted to Europe, it should be remembered that from very early times until today astrology has flourished—and with less fluctuation—in most Eastern countries. The prevalence of the art in 20th-century India has already been mentioned. Indeed, Indian astrologers claim that it was the West (as far back as Ptolemy or earlier) that learned from them. But there are very important differences between Hindu and Western astrology. For one thing, the former presupposes a belief in reincarnation. And the Hindus also have a different conception of the Zodiac.

In China, where astrologers had ranked very high from long before the time of Christ, the great Venetian traveler Marco Polo found them still very powerful in the 13th century. He recounts that in the great city of Kanbalu there were about 5000 astrologers and soothsayers provided for by the emperor. They used astrolabes and made weather forecasts (*meteorological* astrology) but also foretold such things as epidemics, wars, and conspiracies. Moreover, they were great exponents of electional astrology. No one would undertake a long journey without first consulting an astrologer; and no astrologer would give such advice until he knew the year, month, and hour of the would-be traveler's birth.

In a quite different part of the same huge empire, subject at that time to the Mongol Kublai Khan, Marco Polo explains how astrologers there could hold up funerals. No upper-class family would allow any one of its members to be cremated until the astrologers had examined his natal chart and fixed a day for cremation according to the planets or signs. Such a day might be six months off, which meant ordering an extra thick coffin and a large amount of preservatives and deodorants. And sometimes, for good measure, the astrologers would insist on the body being removed from the house along some particular line— which often entailed making a hole in the wall.

Astrology had a long run in China. As long as the old empire lasted, astrologers were as important at court as they had been in ancient Babylon. Thus even the tough old Dowager Empress Tzu Hsi, who ruled China at the time of the Boxer Rising, owed her occasional vacillations in policy to the intervention of astrologers. And when she was buried at 5 A.M. on November 27, 1909, it was the astrologers who had chosen the hour for the funeral. The site of her tomb had been chosen about 35 years earlier when, again thanks to the astrologers, the remains of a former empress had to be shifted to make room.

Mao Tse-tung presumably cares for none of these things. But in most other parts of the Far East astrology appears to be still flourishing. In what used to be Indochina astrological flags feature in the public processions, while there is a 200,000-strong federation in Japan to which professional astrologers belong, as well as palmists, graphologists, etc.

In most countries there are differences in the systems employed by astrologers and in the emphasis given to different aspects of astrology; at the same time there has been a good deal of interplay between most countries in Europe and Asia. In the old civilizations of Mexico and South America, centuries before

The Crown Prince of Sikkim (a province in northern India) and his American bride at their wedding in March 1963. In accordance with Eastern custom, astrologers were asked to select a favorable wedding date; their choice postponed the ceremony for a year.

they had any contact with Europe, some form of astrology was apparently practiced that was almost certainly different from European or Asian forms.

The literature on astrology is vast, and to read much of it at a time leaves one punch-drunk. Most of it is repetitious and much of it is tendentious and ill-written. Also, since the time of the Roman poet Manilius (first century A.D.), and the Greek astronomer-cum-astrologer Ptolemy, whose books are the first two extant that deal with the subject in detail, expositions of astrology have by their nature been cluttered up with technicalities, many of which seem arbitrary to many people (including some astrologers). By now there are so many things to consider in a horoscope that, while it may mean extra work for a scrupulous astrologer, to others it affords a ready let-out. For instance, people who read newspaper astrologers usually assume that your dominant Zodiacal sign is decided by what day of what month you were born on. But Rupert Gleadow writes: "It cannot be often enough repeated that one can be born under any sign of the Zodiac on any day of the year." The confusion will be cleared up in the next chapters.

The literature on astrology is not, of course, confined to sheer textbooks or to those "ephemerides," tables of "houses," etc., which are your necessary tools if you want to cast horoscopes. There is also a mass of casebook material, including *retrospective* horoscopes of famous people or of other things such as the city of Rome or the German Republic. There are the stories of notable predictions, correct or incorrect, and the stories of notable astrologers who made a fortune at court or got themselves burned at the stake. There are great rivers of polemic, for and against, and there are lyrical or mystical effusions by people for whom astrology was primarily neither a science nor an art but a religion. There are allegories and plays and parodies, and, lastly, the descriptions of astrologers or their practices in non-astrological writings such as Chaucer's *Canterbury Tales*. The literature ranges from the cuneiform clay tablets of Ashurbanipal's library in ancient Assyria to the latest almanac, from St. Thomas Aquinas to newspaper columnists like Britain's Gipsy Petulengro, from the adverse philosophical analyses of Cicero in ancient Rome and Pico della Mirandola in Renaissance Italy to a knockabout parody entitled: *Shinkin ap Shone her Prognostication for the ensuing year, 1654 . . . Printed for the Author, and are to be sold at his shop at the Sign of the Cows Bobby behind the Welsh Mountains.*

A sampling of the enormous assortment of astrological literature : top left, a description of the qualities of Libra from a 15th-century English manuscript ; top right, two pages from a 19th-century Indian astrological text, depicting the Zodiac signs used in Eastern astrology. Bottom, a selection of modern astrological journals published in Europe.

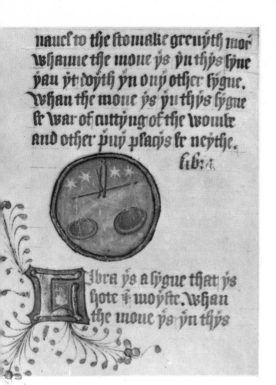

Authors from different times and countries will be quoted in the course of this book, often on particular aspects of astrology. At this point it may be appetizing, as a sort of hors d'oeuvres, to provide a few typical remarks made by writers on astrology in general:

(a) Astrology is the science and art of describing persons and events of the past, present, and future by correctly interpreting maps of the sky drawn up for the appropriate moments and places.

(b) The heavens don't affect our will . . . but they do affect our bodies.

(c) . . . the foolish little daughter of the respectable reasonable mother astronomy.

(d) Astrology is essentially conservative (in the strict sense of the word), sedative, private, unsocial.

(e) I am convinced that the problem of the inequalities of the human race can only be successfully solved by a knowledge of astrology.

(f) At length I learned that wholly and altogether it was based upon no other foundation but upon mere trifles, and feignings of imaginations.

(g) If we listen within ourselves for a moment, then we can hear the breathing of planetary forms.

(h) There is some physical sympathy that makes earthly things depend upon celestial.

(i) . . . *cette chimère d'Astrologie.*

(j) There's not even a blade of grass, however infinitesimal, that is not ruled by some star.

(k) I believe God rules all by his divine providence and that the stars by his permission are instruments.

(l) Astrology stands first among those superstitions of which she is both mother and foster-child.

(m) From the scientific point of view, there is little hope of proving that astrological correspondence is something that conforms to law.

(n) Some astrologers say or write things *after* the event and pretend they had predicted them beforehand.

(o) If astrology is true, why bother with anything else?

These quotations, in the above order, come from the following array of authors:

(a) Rupert Gleadow, already mentioned, who seems (though he is very readable) to have stopped writing books about astrology.

(b) Marsilio Ficino, the founder of the Platonic Academy in 15th-century Florence.

(c) The pre-eminent 16th-century astronomer Johannes Kepler, who cast horoscopes as part of his job and made many confusing pronouncements on the subject.

(d) Tom Harrisson, founder of Mass Observation (a British sociological research organization), who wrote an article called "Mass Astrology" in the British weekly paper *New Statesman* in 1941.

(e) Alan Leo, already mentioned.

(f) Henry Cornelius Agrippa, already mentioned, 16th-century France.

(g) Louis de Wohl, already mentioned.

(h) The Jewish philosopher Philo, who lived in Alexandria in the time of Christ and made allegorical interpretations of the Old Testament.

(i) Voltaire, 18th-century France.

(j) One Rabbi Eleazar, quoted in the 13th-century *Zohar*, a mystical work compiled by Spanish Jews.

(k) William Lilly, already mentioned, 17th-century England.

(l) Pico della Mirandola, late 15th-century Italian humanist.

(m) The psychologist Carl G. Jung.

(n) The 14th-century French mathematician and ecclesiastic Nicole Oresme.

(o) An ancient Roman, about whom little is known, named Arellius Fuscus.

The variety of the names of these authors is nothing to the names that stud the average astrological textbook, some of which we too shall have to use more than once. Names like Mardukshakinshum and Adadshumusur, Adam, Abraham, Enoch and Solomon, Nechepso, Petosiris and Berosus, Nigidius Figulus and Hermes Trismegistus, Alexander of Tralles and Isidore of Seville, Alkindi and Albumasar, William of Auvergne and Moses Maimonides, Marbod and Gerbert, Adelard and Abelard, Albertus Magnus and Guido Bonatti, Madame Blavatsky and Baron Sobottendorff. Also Raphael, Zadkiel, Sepharial, and Gabriel, whose real names were Smith, Morrison, Old, and Hingston. If this looks as forbidding as the New York telephone directory, it does at least (just like that directory) bear witness to the cosmopolitan character of the subscribers.

Such is the cosmopolitan and venerable background to all the goings-on of astrologers both big and little; to the Archbishop of York whose sudden death in his garden was attributed by his enemies to the book of astrology he had hidden under his pillow; to the egg, hatched in Rome in 1680 with markings suggesting a comet, that touched off dozens of sermons and solemn theses in Germany; to such pronouncements as "All moles are the result of the influence of the planets" or "A doctor without astrology is like an eye that cannot see" or "The Sun, Moon, and stars were created on Wednesday, April 22nd, 6 P.M., about 4002 years before Christ"; to, in our own day, an astrological columnist in a Sunday newspaper who answers personally 100,000 letters per year; and also to certain German astrologers working out horoscopes with the aid of eight hypothetical trans-Neptunian planets that hardly anyone elsewhere has heard of. (In the U.S.A. some astrologers have gone even further by postulating at least 18 unknown planets.)

But through all this great range from the sublime to the ridiculous and underlying all the variations, mystical or whimsical, ingenious or plain silly, two things can always be found: a certain sense of mystery, and a certain hankering for harmony. Later chapters may indicate how traditional astrology originated with the first and attempted to satisfy the second.

2 Planets and personality

In a modern city we tend not to notice the stars. But even today, if we are alone in the country, they almost force themselves upon us, and they still excite wonder and a kind of distant affection. To the ancient civilizations, especially those that enjoyed clear skies, the stars were extremely familiar but also extremely puzzling. They were always there (or at least always returning), but with the exception of the two "luminaries"—the Sun and Moon—they never had any immediate effect that one could feel in the way one feels a change in the weather. You cannot grasp the rays of the stars in the way you can grasp any terrestrial object, animal, vegetable, or mineral.

There was another worrying thing about the stars. Most of them—the "fixed" stars—appeared vastly more stable and predictable than other natural phenomena. But a small minority seemed disturbingly wayward. These were the planets (the word comes from a Greek word meaning "wanderer"), which the Babylonians had called the "stray sheep." Sometimes they appeared to go forward, sometimes to go back, sometimes to stand still. It was probably in Mesopotamia that men first pondered the relations between the fixed stars and the straying ones, and first thought that they affected human life.

So began astrology. Very early it had been noticed (especially by shepherds and navigators) that however the Sun, Moon, and other planets may seem to wander, they do not just wander anywhere in the heavens. They keep within a

An 18th-century British "orrery" (named after the Earl of Orrery)—a clockwork mechanism that demonstrates the positions and motions around the Sun of the six planets known at that time, with their accompanying moons. Men have known since the 18th century (some guessed earlier) that the planets, including the earth, revolve around the Sun. But, in spite of astronomers' findings, astrologers still work from an earth-centered conception of the universe and treat the Sun and Moon as planets.

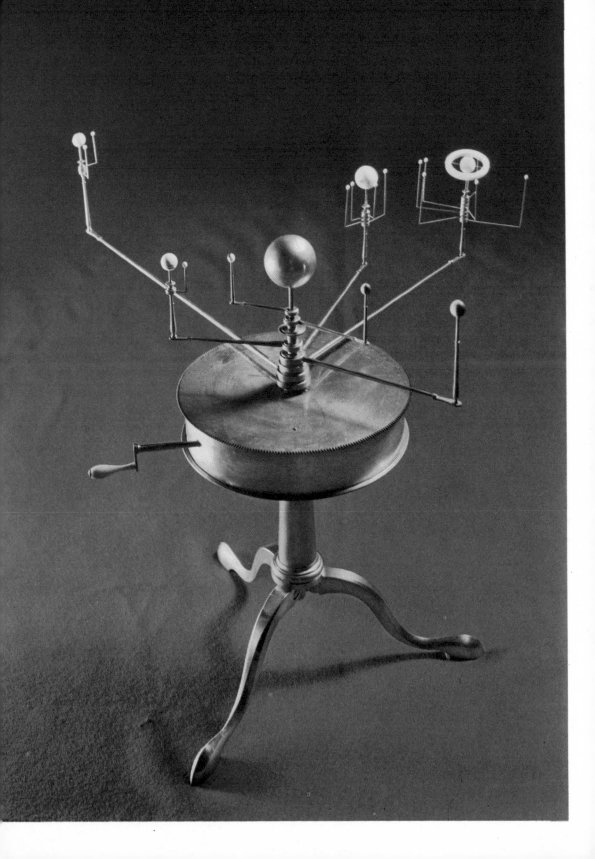

definite track, which eventually was called the Zodiac and divided into 12 parts bearing the same names as 12 of the constellations. The ancients decided that the position of the planets within the Zodiac at any one time must be what affected human beings. By the time of the Christian era the Roman poet Manilius could take as an established fact this significant interrelationship of planet and Zodiacal constellation (or "sign"):

> *No sign nor planet serves itself alone,*
> *Each blends the other's virtues with its own,*
> *Mixing their force, and interchanged they reign,*
> *Signs planets bound, and planets signs again.*

It was some time before the 12 signs of the Zodiac were identified and named. But the planets—Mercury, Venus, Mars, Jupiter, and Saturn—were known to everyone almost from the start. As, of course, were the Sun and Moon, which for millennia were also to count as planets. So before we consider the signs (which have been of great importance in astrology for at least 2000 years), it seems proper to look at the traditional pictures of the planets.

These pictures are highly anthropomorphic: Though some of the more sophisticated modern astrologers would like to explain this away as a convenient means of summarizing the planets' effects on human beings, even they sometimes find themselves talking as if the planets were human neighbors to be liked or admired or feared. The leading British astrologer Ingrid Lind writes: "I find that I come more and more to regard some of the planets at least as having distinct personalities." She adds (on the assumption that each of us contains *all* the planets, rather in the way that each of us contains the same set of organs) that the relationship between man and the planets resembles that between an actor and the various roles he must play: "If our Jupiter is weak he must be rehearsed until he no longer spoils the part with illtimed buffoonery."

(Incidentally, because astrological books and authors are so numerous, and repeat each other so much, I shall be quoting in this chapter and the next from only a few of them, selected on the sampling principle. One of them will be a 15th-century French work called *The Kalendar and Compost of Shepherds,* which not only is a valuable source of traditional astrological thinking but manages to make the most ancient commonplace fresh. Ptolemy has proved useful, as have the 19th-century authorities, mentioned in Chapter 1, "Raphael" and "Zadkiel." Aside from these, my principal sources have been modern books by such astrological writers as Ingrid Lind, Margaret E. Hone, A. J. Pearce, Furze Morrish, Rupert Gleadow, and W. J. Tucker—many of whom were mentioned in Chapter 1.)

The names we use today for the planets are Latin god-name equivalents of the earlier Greek god-names, which the Greeks themselves had matched to the god-names of those pioneering stargazers the Babylonians. Thus Mercury is a translation of Hermes (the Babylonian Nebo), Venus of Aphrodite (Ishtar), Mars of Ares (the red Nergal), Jupiter of Zeus (Marduk), and Saturn of Kronos

(Ninib). One would naturally assume that Babylonians, Greeks, and Romans (and for that matter Egyptians too) all called their planets *after* their gods. But a few astrologers maintain that it happened the other way around; i.e., that a certain planet was found to affect people's love-lives and that a goddess was then invented to represent this planet and was called Ishtar or Venus.

Nevertheless, before the Greeks gave their planets the names of gods (whom they had *already* invented), they seem to have given them names derived from their visible characteristics: Venus was the Dawn-bringer and Mars, because of his red color, the Fiery One. It seems possible that they changed to the god-names when they met with the astronomy-cum-astrology of Babylon. But perhaps after all we are not up against the old hen-and-egg dilemma (did god or planet come first?), because in early cultures these distinctions were often irrelevant. In Babylon some of the heavenly bodies *were* gods—or should we say some of the gods were heavenly bodies? Or should we say certain gods controlled certain heavenly bodies? Anyway, the great triad in that country was Sin the Moon-god (who was masculine and the most powerful), Shamash the Sun-god (feminine), and Ishtar, the goddess of love. Symbols of all three appear in stone carvings from the 14th century B.C.

This historical background will be considered further in later chapters. The immediate business here is to introduce the cast, the broad lines of whose behavior have hardly altered for over 2000 years. And a very strong cast it is. As an English astrologer put it in the 17th century, "you must know that the seven planets are the seven rulers of the world, by their different natures, and are God's instruments." Among the ancients the normal order of the planets, based

A diagram of astrology's spherical universe. The celestial equator is an extension of the earth's equator; the ecliptic is the apparent path of the Sun through the sky within the band of the Zodiac. The other planets also appear to travel more or less within the limits of the Zodiac.

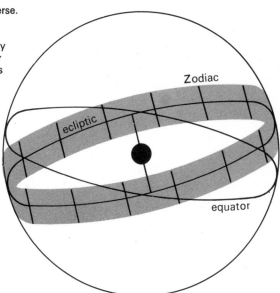

Zodiac

ecliptic

equator

The seven planets of traditional astrology as depicted in the 15th-century French astrological work *The Kalendar and Compost of Shepherds*. Below the planets are the 12 signs of the Zodiac as they appear in a 15th-century edition of a ninth-century Arabian textbook. Each planet is said to "rule" two Zodiac signs (except the Sun and Moon, each of which rules one) ; here the signs are shown in the same colors as their ruling planets.

on their supposed distance from the earth, was : the Moon, Mercury, Venus, the Sun, Mars, Jupiter, and Saturn. (There are inscriptions at Nineveh, however, with the peculiar order : Moon, Sun, Jupiter, Venus, Saturn, Mercury, Mars.)

When astrologers say that someone is a typical Jupiterian or Martian or other type, they mean that he displays some or all of the qualities associated with the planet, and they assume that this planet was in some way dominant at the moment of his birth. There are various ways in which a planet achieves dominance : For one thing, each planet is the "ruler" of one or two of the Zodiacal signs. Thus Mars is the ruler of both Aries and Scorpio ; if he is found in either of these at the moment of your birth, he will tend to make you not only more of an Aries (or Scorpio) type but more of a Mars type. (This applies whatever the position of the sign.) As will be seen in Chapter 3, the Aries man has much in common with the Mars man, just as the Leo man has with the Sun man, and so on. A planet has a similar (though lesser) effect if it is in a sign that is sympathetic to it. Technically, this is known as "exaltation" ; Mars has his exaltation in Capricorn.

Some other factors that enhance the power of a planet are the following : If a planet is found at any of the four highly sensitive points in the heavens—the

ascendant, its opposite the descendant, the mid-heaven (M.C. or medium coeli), and its opposite the imum coeli or I.C.—it will have something extra to say to you. So will a planet that is the ruler of the sign rising at your birth: If you have Taurus rising, Venus (the ruler of Taurus) will have more strength in your horoscope. The same is true of a planet that is the ruler of your Sun-sign: Venus will again be strengthened in your horoscope if you are "born under Taurus" by being born between April 21 and May 21. (Serious astrologers, by the way, would not admit that this necessarily merits the label "born under Taurus.") Lastly, a planet can become prominent or dominant in your natal chart if it is strongly "aspected" by other planets. But aspects are a complicated subject that will be dealt with later.

All this should be enough to indicate that there is more than one way of becoming a "planet type" or of being "born under" any planet. The same is only too true of being "born under" any Zodiacal sign. And of course all the possible combinations and permutations that these factors supply not only give the astrologer a chance to show his skill but can also provide him with a let-out if his predictions go wrong.

Now let us turn to the characteristics of the individual planets, taking the Sun first, since he is pre-eminent in modern astrology. (Though modern astrology is not anthropomorphic, I prefer to call the Sun "him," the Moon "her," etc., in accordance with mythological tradition and also because, like Ingrid Lind, I am tempted to think of the planets as having "distinct personalities"—which would obviously not be neuter.) For people who read only the newspaper "prediction" columns, the Sun-sign (i.e., the Sun's position in the Zodiac on the day of one's birth) is the only thing in astrology that matters. Even through the long geocentric ages (and astrology still carries on as if the Sun went around the earth) the Sun was always unique. Some of the ancient Romans called him "the chorus-master of the planets." The point does not need laboring; after all, the Sun is something that hits you. The centuries-old Hermetic writings on astrology, alchemy, magic, and so on describe the stars as visible gods of whom the Sun is far the greatest. The Sun's astrological symbol, or hieroglyph, is a dot within a circle: The circle is said to symbolize eternity or primal power; the dot pinpoints the emergence of that power.

Sun ☉

According to the British astrologer Margaret E. Hone, the "keywords" of the Sun (i.e., words that express the aspects of human personality connected with the Sun) are *power, vitality,* and *self-expression.* In contrast with the Moon, who represents the female principle and the unconscious, the Sun stands for the male principle and consciousness. Traditionally, he was neither a good planet like Jupiter and Venus nor a bad planet like Mars and Saturn. He had something of both, like Mercury. On the other hand, Indian astrologers tend to consider him powerful but on the whole malefic. For them the Sun controls the heart and the Moon the mind; but the latter, luckily, is generally considered to be the more powerful.

The Kalendar and Compost of Shepherds describes the Sun as "a planet of great renown and king of all the planets . . . he is hot and dry of nature, and the planet Saturn is to him full contrary." As for his effects on human beings, "all men and women that be born under the Sun be very fair, amiable of face, and their skin shall be white and tender, and well colored in the visage with a little redness. . . . They shall be clean and good of faith and shall be governors of other people. . . . The children that are born under the Sun shall desire honor and science, and shall sing very pleasantly. And they shall be of courage good and diligent, and shall desire lordship above other people. . . . And of all the members in man's body, the Sun keeps the heart as most mighty planet above all others."

Ptolemy states that of the seven ages of man the Sun controls the fourth, from about 20 to 40 (though other authorities apportion the ages differently). The Sun naturally rules Sunday; but, as the *hours* of the day were also shared out among the seven planets, on the Sun's own day his particular hours were the first, eighth, fifteenth, and twenty-second. The child in the womb was thought to be ruled by the Sun during the fourth month when the heart was formed. On the hand he rules the third finger. And Ptolemy (who attributed diseases to the planets as well as to the signs of the Zodiac) makes the Sun responsible for afflictions of the sight, brain, heart, sinews, and right-hand parts.

Toward the end of the ancient world, mystical thinkers made much of the strange behavior of the heliotrope, the plant that, like the sunflower, turns its flowers to the Sun. The fifth-century Neoplatonist Proclus writes: "Thus the heliotrope moves itself in so far as it is easy for it to move, and if one could only hear how it beats the air as it turns on its stalk, one would understand from this sound that it is offering up a sort of hymn to its King, of such kind of singing

Right, an engraving of the Emperor
Napoleon (based on a painting by the
Italian artist Toffanelli). Napoleon's
personal power and energy would be
ascribed by astrologers to the Sun's
prominent position in his horoscope. The
Sun is one "planet" whose traditional
astrological qualities have a factual
basis : It *is* a source of life and power.
Below, its energy is stored in a modern
solar power station in Israel.

as a plant can manage." This is one of the more obvious "correspondences" so much favored in the first Christian centuries and in the Middle Ages. Among the animals, vegetables, and minerals that the Sun rules are such obvious ones as the lion, the marigold, and gold.

But more important than the Sun's patronage of actual lions is his rulership of the Zodiacal sign Leo. The Sun and Leo both pull in the same direction, and the account of the Leo type of man in Chapter 3 will fill out the picture of the Sun type. This means that if in your natal chart you are born between July 23 and August 23 (which makes Leo your Sun-sign) and also born about sunrise (which makes Leo your ascendant, since naturally the Sun's sign rises when the Sun does) your solar and/or Leonine qualities should be doubled or more than doubled. Such a doubling-up is not necessarily an advantage, especially since the Sun is not necessarily a "good" planet. "Too much Sun," writes Ingrid Lind, "tends to make the individual overbearing." She also points out that you can have too much Sun, regardless of your Sun-sign or whether the Sun was rising or not, if there were at your birth too many planets in Leo (which is *always* the Sun's own sign).

It has already been emphasized that no planet can be assessed as if it existed in a vacuum. Its influence varies according to the sign in which it is found. The textbooks say that the Sun in Taurus or Pisces makes you rather short, in Virgo or Sagittarius tall, while in Capricorn he gives a "mean stature." But this material belongs more to the next chapter. Something else that affects the Sun's or any other planet's influence is the whole pattern of the sky—i.e., the aspects— at the moment of birth or any other moment of importance. The American astrologer W. J. Tucker says that the Sun and Venus in conjunction lead to a "finely poised character" (both Chopin and Bernard Shaw were born under this conjunction) while the Sun and Jupiter in opposition or square (both bad aspects) lead to financial entanglements.

From very early times eclipses of the Sun were regarded as portents of great events, usually disasters. The same of course was true of eclipses of the Moon; Ptolemy attaches enormous importance to both. Now that mundane astrology is so much overshadowed by genethlialogy, astrologers tend not to bother so much with eclipses. When they do they prefer to deny, in the words of the late A. J. Pearce, that "the mere eclipse portends anything." What counts again here is the over-all picture, the relative planetary positions. Pearce instances an eclipse of the Sun visible in England on September 7, 1820, at a time when the bad planet Mars was nearly in opposition to the bad planet Saturn in Aries, the ruling sign of England. "Within a few months England was on the verge of revolution." Great stress was traditionally laid on where the eclipse itself takes place; for example, in Libra it might cause ecclesiastical schism, while in Cancer it might make the fruit crops go bad.

Sun-worship—the exaltation of the Sun into the supreme deity (sometimes the only one)—has been common at various periods and in various countries.

Above, sunrise at England's Stonehenge, an ancient circle of stones probably used for Sun worship. In many past societies, the view of the Sun as the most powerful of the planets (a view shared by astrologers) led to worship of the Sun as the supreme god. Elements of this worship still survive today : Right, a participant in the centuries-old Swiss ceremony of goose-cutting (held every year at Lucerne) wears a Sun mask—perhaps a relic of some forgotten Sun ritual.

45

For that matter, in Baghdad about A.D. 900 there was a sect that prayed to the spirits of the planets. The ancient Persians sacrificed to the Sun; in Egypt as far back as the second millennium B.C. King Akhenaton attempted to overthrow the long-established polytheism and substitute a monotheistic Sun-worship; and in the declining days of the Roman Empire the Sun was proclaimed the supreme god on the Capitol. Of course, astrologers do not necessarily regard the Sun (or any other heavenly body) in a spirit of worship. There have been many astrologers who thought of *all* the heavenly bodies as divine beings; there have also been many who denied that they were anything more than inorganic objects. For all that, of the heavenly bodies that have been deified, the Sun (alias Sol, alias Helios, alias Shamash) takes first place. The only possible runner-up to him is the Moon, alias Luna, alias Selene, alias Sin.

Moon ☽

The fast-traveling and ever-changing Moon traditionally and obviously stands for the female principle (in spite of the Babylonians, who curiously made the Moon male). She brings out the lyrical vein in astrologers no less than in other people. The American astrologer Evangeline Adams writes: "She is the lustral water and the mystic bearer of the Holy Grail." In a different style the *Kalendar of Shepherds* says: "Such men and women as be born under the Moon shall be lowly and serviceable, and very gentle . . . and they shall be well favored both man and woman, and their faces shall be full and round. . . . They hate lecherous talkers and speakers of ribaldry. . . . They shall gladly go arrayed in many colored clothes, and they shall soon sweat in the forehead. Also they will have great desire to be masters and mistresses over great streams, rivers, and floods, and shall devise many proper engines to take fish and to deceive them. . . . And the lights and the brains of man are under the governance of Luna." The word lunacy, of course, comes from Luna; in the 16th century, Paracelsus taught that lunacy grows worse at the full and the new Moon because the brain is the moon of the microcosm.

In the Middle Ages, when some astrologers held that different historical periods fell under the sway of different planets, it was suggested that the Moon was in command when Sodom and Gomorrah were destroyed. This seems to fit with the *Kalendar*'s conception of the Moon as a patroness of chastity. But there are other facets of the lunar image. According to Raphael, the Moon is especially responsible for rather low-grade persons and sailors, for amphibious animals, all shellfish, such birds as geese and swans, such plants as seaweed, melon, cucumber, and mushrooms, and, among places, sewers.

The connection with water is obvious: From early times men had noticed the Moon's effect on the tides. Menstruation was also (understandably) referred to the Moon. In more recent times a lunar periodicity has been observed in the behavior of land crabs, palolo worms, and certain sea-urchins. The Moon, like the Sun, rules only one sign—Cancer the Crab (which is a "watery" sign). At one time astrological physicians advised that purges should be taken while the Moon is in a watery sign, the others being Scorpio and Pisces. The Moon has also been held to be involved in nearly all cases of drowning. And Rupert Gleadow writes that a dominant Moon may give you long, thin, damp hands.

Margaret Hone gives as the Moon's keywords *response* and *fluctuation*. The Moon governs babyhood and is concerned with the passions and emotions and also with changes in health. Unlike the Hindus, Western astrologers do not allow her control of the mind; for them the intellectual planet is Mercury. She is, however, of great importance if you want to marry.

W. J. Tucker assumes that the human character is threefold and gives its three components the somewhat arbitrary names of "individuality," "personality," and "temperament." Individuality, he says, is the product of the solar position and is "superconscious" (Evangeline Adams once defined individuality as the thing we feel behind a handshake); personality is of the lunar position and is subconscious; temperament is of the ascendant and is just plain conscious. The American astrologer Zoltan Mason states that the Sun represents your relationship to the divine spirit, the Moon your soul, and the ascendant your physical body. Australia's Furze Morrish holds that the Moon represents the pull of matter (subconscious) and the Sun the pull of spirit ("superconscious" again). Anyhow, whether the Moon is linked with the soul or with matter, the subconscious character seems to be a constant. So it is no wonder, in these days of psychoanalysis, that the Moon's position in the horoscope is considered by many astrologers to be almost equal in importance with the positions of the Sun-sign and the ascendant sign.

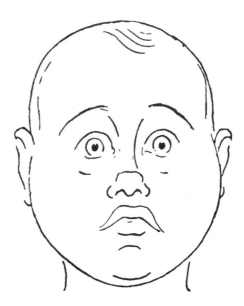

A "lunar" type as depicted in a modern French handbook of astrology. Such a childish "moon" face with its innocent, naïve expression can be (according to "physiognomical" astrologers) the result of the Moon's prominence in a horoscope.

Above, a 17th-century French engraving depicts the Moon's rays affecting the minds of women. Astrologers may not be able to prove the Moon's effect on the mind, but they can show that it (like the Sun) has *some* influence on earthly things—for instance, on the sea. Right, a diagram shows how the Moon's gravitational attraction creates high tides : It draws up the sea at A, leaving low tides at B and B[1]. Astrologers often go a step or two further and say (in effect) : The Sun and Moon affect the nature of the earth, so it is likely that they also affect peoples' natures. And if this can be said of the Sun and Moon, why not of the other planets as well ?

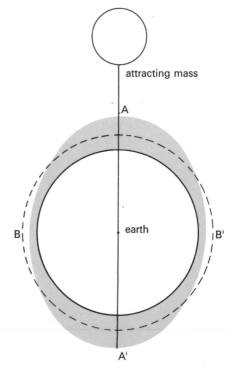

attracting mass

A

earth

B

B'

A'

Once again it is the over-all pattern that has to be considered. Tucker explains that, while the Moon in Gemini gives you the personality of a very successful commercial traveler (which seems to imply that what makes a salesman is the subconscious), the Moon in Capricorn will make you very disagreeable if you don't control yourself. Napoleon, he adds, had the Moon in Capricorn. The Moon in Scorpio is generally considered dangerous or undesirable, while the reason that Shakespeare did not invent his own plots (according to Evangeline Adams) was because he had his Moon in Taurus. As for aspects, the Sun and Moon in sextile or trine (both good aspects) are supposed to help you to get what you want, though perhaps you will get it too early.

The Moon's connection with health has always made her prominent in astrological medicine. The 17th-century English satirist Samuel Butler, in his burlesque poem *Hudibras,* caricatures William Lilly (the most famous astrologer of the day) as one who

> *. . . with the Moon was more familiar*
> *Than e'er was almanack well willer.*
> *Her secrets understood so clear,*
> *That some believed he had been there,*
> *Knew when she was in fittest mood,*
> *For cutting corns or letting blood.*
> *When for anointing scabs and itches,*
> *Or to the bum applying leeches;*
> *When sows and bitches may be spayed,*
> *And in what sign best cider's made. . . .*

It is quite clear that in Butler's and Lilly's time many people did take the Moon into account when going about their household business. But other people flew higher, into more nebulous realms. A treatise in 1652 explains how "to extract a white milkie substance from the raies of the Moone." All you need is a glass and a sponge; but it is not clear what you do with the substance when you have it. In all such practices the *phase* of the Moon was always of utmost importance. In the Hermetic writings the peony is assigned to the Moon as one of her special plants; we are told that it grows as she waxes and wilts as she wanes. If you are going to use this flower for medical or magical purposes you must pluck it while the Moon is waning. On the other hand, the American astrologer Max Heindel held that surgical operations should be performed when the Moon is waxing. And medieval alchemists had found their experiments were more successful when the Moon was both waxing and ascending.

The use of the Moon in astrological medicine or magic had most respectable precedents. In Constantinople in the sixth century A.D. a physician at the court of the Emperor Justinian recommended that gout could be cured by inscribing a verse of Homer on a copper plate when the Moon is in Libra or Leo. In the Renaissance it was thought that dreams come true when the Moon is in any of the four "fixed" signs—Taurus, Leo, Aquarius, and Scorpio. The idea that the

Moon is concerned with diseases of the stomach, the womb, and "all left-hand parts" goes back to Ptolemy. And in relation to the four-temperaments or "humors" or "complexions," she was connected by some with the melancholic (though more usually that humor belonged to Saturn).

So much for this "subconscious" lady. Let us now turn to a planet who, if anything, is almost too conscious. His hieroglyph is equated by some astrologers with the *caduceus*, the wand that was always carried by the god Mercury (or Hermes) in his double role of divine herald and conductor of souls to the underworld.

Mercury ☿

"The fair planet Mercury," says the *Kalendar of Shepherds*, is "very full and dry of nature" and is "lord of speech, as the Sun is lord of light. . . . Who so is born under Mercury shall be subtle of wit . . . [that is, and always has been, Mercury's first characteristic] and shall be very crafty in many sciences. . . . He shall ever follow and resort to them that be of good manners, and shall be fortunate on the sea to use the course of good merchandise." Mercury is the traditional patron not only of intellectuals but of merchants. He is also the patron planet of transport.

But the Mercury man, according to the *Kalendar*, will not have it all his own way. "He shall be very gracious, and he shall have harm by women, and when

he is married, men shall not set so much by him as they did before." All the same, "he will have great love to ladies and gentlewomen, but yet they shall not be masters over him. He will be a very good man of the church or a religious man, and he shall not love to go to a warfare. . . . He shall love well to preach and to speak fair rhetoric language, and to talk of philosophy and geometry."

The *Kalendar* details other intellectual, artistic, and commercial activities and ends: "He shall be servant to some great lord or else a receiver of his money." (The original god Mercury himself had been something of a lackey on Olympus, always running errands for the greater gods.) "He shall have a high forehead, a long visage, black eyes, and a thin beard. He shall be a great pleader in the law, and will meddle with other men's deeds if they do not well and say against it."

There has been general agreement that Mercury stands for the intellect and for most types of communication, whether mental or physical. Not surprisingly, however, he is undependable; astrologers have named him "the chameleon among planets" (compare the adjective "mercurial") and have explained that he is neutral because, in the aspects, he takes color from other planets but does not give color in return. This idea goes back to Ptolemy, who says that Mercury is "generally speaking in nature like whatever of the planets may be associated with him." By Ptolemy's time he was also firmly established as the ruler of two signs, Gemini and Virgo. Rupert Gleadow, who calls him a "sexless planet," points out that both these signs are "somewhat lacking in emotion."

The Russian writer Leo Tolstoi (1828-1910), right, typifies the great intellect and powers of expression that are among the qualities associated with the planet Mercury—the ruler of Tolstoi's Sun-sign, Virgo.

Left, the Roman god Mercury, in a French bank's advertisement for travelers' checks. In both mythology and astrology, Mercury is considered to be the patron of commerce and transport: Thus the two roles here symbolized by the god are equally typical of the planet.

Mercury can make you a genius; he can also make you a crook. The original god had been both, as is shown by the early Homeric *Hymn to Hermes,* in which he is described (in Shelley's translation) as

A schemer subtle beyond all· belief;

A shepherd of thin dreams, a cow-stealing,

A night-watching and door-waylaying thief

who yet, while still an infant, went on to invent the lyre, killing a tortoise to use its shell for the purpose. An English earl in the reign of Elizabeth I cited this traditional idea of crookedness to bolster up his attack on astrology in general, taking Mercury's influence as an example of unjust determinism: "If by nature no man ought to spoil or rob another, how cometh it to pass that Mercury, disposed thus or thus at the time of our birth, enforceth theft?"

In the field of diseases Mercury has been held responsible for ailments both of speech and of thought and for troubles in the bile and the buttocks (or, as Pearce puts it, "mania, apoplexy, convulsions, impediments of speech, coryza, and dry cough"). His day is Wednesday (French *mercredi,* Italian *mercoledì*) and, according to Ptolemy, in any man's life he rules the period from four to 14 when education is most necessary. Mercury's finger is the little finger, and physiognomical astrologers allot him the bridge of the nose. Three lines on the bridge of the nose denote eloquence and wit; more than three denote loquacity and deceit.

The planet Mercury, like Venus, owing to its *actual* nearness to the Sun, is always seen from the earth as lying in a sign near the Sun. Consequently Mercury and Venus are comparatively often found in conjunction. In spite of the frequency of such conjunctions an 18th-century English astrologer, Ebenezer Sibly, used one of them (retrospectively) to explain the French Revolution: "The active position of Venus and Mercury, conjoined, denotes much restlessness and instability in the councils of France, which seem distracted by the arbitrary will of the Gallic Queen, here represented by Venus, upheld and assisted by light, volatile, time-serving men, pre-noted by Mercury."

Similarly, Raphael says that Mercury is concerned among human beings with philosophers, secretaries, merchants, teachers, ambassadors, "and all ingenious clever persons" (with whom Raphael includes astrologers) but also, when he is in a wrong position, with thieves. Among the beasts of Mercury, Raphael continues, come "all such as are of quick sense, ingenious, inconstant, and swift; also such as are easily taught by man," including the ape, fox, weasel, hare, squirrel, hyena, and spider. Among fishes there are "the mullet and all swift reptiles"; among birds "all those that are naturally witty and inconstant," like the nightingale, blackbird, parrot, swallow, jay, and jackdaw; among places schools, tennis courts, fairs, markets, bowling greens, libraries, and counting-houses. According to modern astrologers, Mercury is also the ruling planet of the telephone system, radio, and other means of communication. Altogether a versatile, volatile planet.

As for aspects, it is generally considered that Saturn, having such a different and therefore complementary nature, is the best influence on Mercury. Saturn also has a steadying effect upon the next planet to be considered.

Venus ♀

Venus, whose hieroglyph is used in zoology to indicate that an animal is female, is a good and beneficent planet but does not always make a character strong. In ancient Babylon, under the name of Ishtar (goddess of love), she was the most powerful heavenly body after the Sun and Moon and her eight-pointed star is often found carved on the Babylonian boundary stones. She was traditionally known as the "lesser fortune" (Jupiter, another beneficent planet, was the "greater fortune"). She governs adolescence and is the giver of harmony, being especially influential in personal relationships and (more surprisingly) in money matters. Evangeline Adams holds Venus liable to produce "the dilettantes of the world"; she can make you graceful or lazy, gentle or indecisive. This is where Saturn is needed. As Pearce puts it: "If Venus be afflicted, there is a tendency to dissipation. A friendly ray of Saturn to Venus is exceedingly useful in steadying the character."

Her signs are Taurus and Libra, and she is very closely connected with the malefic Mars, as she was in mythology with the god of the same name. (Homer

A 15th-century woodcut depicting
the pleasure-loving, sensual Venus type.
On the left, Venus herself.

A third-century B.C. statue of the ancient love goddess Ishtar, who was identified by the Babylonians with the planet that we know today as Venus.

The French actress Brigitte Bardot, whose film roles have made her one of the modern world's "love goddesses"—and whose Sun-sign is Libra, a sign ruled by Venus.

tells a story about them being caught together in a net.) Mars stands for sex where Venus stands for love; if they are in a good aspect to each other, it bodes well for any lovers who are concerned. If they are in a bad aspect, then don't do it!

Raphael assigns to Venus "all such animals as are amorous in nature," such as the swan (which he also gives to the Moon), kingfisher, swallow, turtledove, lobster, salmon, and dolphin. Her flowers include the violet, rose, and lily, and she also rules many fruit trees. Among winds hers is the south wind, and her day is Friday (*vendredi, venerdì,* etc.). Pliny, the Roman author of the *Natural History,* thought that this planet had a *direct* influence on terrestrial beings through scattering some kind of genital dew. According to the textbooks she can (as one would expect) make you very beautiful, but when she appears in some of the signs she does nothing of the sort. Pearce writes that Venus in Capricorn "gives but a mean stature, pale sickly complexion, face thin and lean, hair dark or black." (In Pearce's discussion of hair color, Venus provides a good example of the variations caused when the same planet is found in different signs: The score seems to be three to four real blondes, three real brunettes, the rest in between.)

As usual, Venus and "her properties" are most sympathetically described in the *Kalendar of Shepherds.* She herself is "the gentle planet Venus, and it is a planet feminine, and she is lady over all lovers." As for her properties, the man or woman born under Venus "shall be a very gay lover, pleasant and delicious, and most commonly they shall have black eyes and little brows, red lips and chests [cheeks?], with a smiling cheer. They shall love the voice of trumpets, clarions, and other minstrelsy, and they shall be pleasant singers with sweet voice . . . and shall greatly delight in dancing and gambols with leaping and springing, and will use playing at the chess, and at the cards and tables, and desire oft to commune of lust and love, and covet oft sweetmeats and drinks as wine and be oft drunken, and oft desire lechery and the beholding of fair women, and the women of men in likewise, and use fleshly lust oftentimes."

The Venus types, as here described, seem to be more sensual than in modern astrology, where sensuality comes rather from Mars. But the sensuality of the *Kalendar* Venusians is not of the violent "dark god" type. The passage continues: "They will desire fair clothes of gay color and fine with rings of vanity, and all vain pleasure of the world, with fair and rich clothes, and pelts and precious stones. They shall love flowers with sweet smells. *Yet shall they be of good faith* [italics mine], and they shall love others as well as themselves. They shall be liberal to their friends. They shall have few enemies. If they be brown [of face] they shall be well proportioned of body. If they swear it is true, ye may believe them. And Venus governs the thighs of man." Easy on the eye, as they say, but also nice to know. The *Kalendar* writes very differently of Venus's opposite number, Mars, whose very hieroglyph is the opposite of hers, a symbol of male aggression.

Mars ♂

"This planet Mars is the worst of all others, for he is hot and dry, and stirs a man to be very wilful and hasty at once, and to unhappiness. . . . He causes all wars and battles. . . ." After stressing the old war-god character of the planet (in Homer Ares had been a most disagreeable god), the *Kalendar* comes on to the man born under Mars who "in all unhappiness is expert. He shall be a nourisher of great beasts [this would suggest violent stallions, bulls, and maybe bear-baiting dogs of the mastiff variety]. He is full of malice, and ever doing wrongs. Under Mars are born all thieves and robbers that keep highways and hurt true men, and night workers, quarrel pickers, boasters, and scoffers. And these men of Mars cause war, murder, and battle, and will gladly be smiths or workers on iron, light fingered and liars. . . . [The Mars man] is red and angry with black hair and little eyes. He shall be a great walker, and maker of swords and knives, and shedder of man's blood, a lecher and speaker of ribaldry, red bearded, round visaged, and good to be a barber and letter of blood, and to draw teeth, and is perilous of his hands. And he will be rich of other men's goods." In fact, as we should say now, a very fine specimen of an extravert. (In ancient times the planet seems to have been also identified with that notable performer Hercules.)

This is the traditional Western picture of Mars and the Mars man. But it should be pointed out that in ancient Egypt the planet was called Horus—the

red Horus. This fact is used by the modern scholar Robert Eisler in *The Royal Art of Astrology*, a book that is violently hostile to that art; Eisler makes the point that Horus, in whatever form, was a favorite figure in the Egyptian pantheon, so there could not have been any question of turning him into a "malefic." Modern astrologers do not try to make Mars good but at worst they regard him as a necessary evil. Without him no one would have martial qualities, and no one would be either feared or loved when he wanted to be.

Margaret Hone gives as his keywords *energy, heat, activation.* The two signs ruled by Mars—Aries and Scorpio—both show the same dangerous energy. In Ptolemy's queer scheme of things, in which different countries were governed by different planets and signs, both Gaul and Britain were closely linked with Mars and Aries. "For the most part," writes Ptolemy, "their inhabitants are fiercer, more headstrong and bestial" than other people. Fairly recently a French astrologer who called himself "Papus" explained the English character by the fact that England's ruling planet is Mars and her national sign "the monstrous sign of Aries": The pure English type, the "John Bull," was according to Papus essentially Martian. But he wrote this while that type was still comparatively common. Nelson, who was not a John Bull but who certainly was successful in battle, was born with Mars rising in the second Martian sign of Scorpio. The great German soldier Wallenstein, one of the heroes of the Thirty Years' War and himself a devout believer in astrology, seems to have regarded this planet

Left, the great British military leader Field Marshal Lord Montgomery signs the terms of surrender with Germany in May 1945. Astrologers would attribute his military success to the favorable influence of Mars, which is the ruling planet of England and of Montgomery's Sun-sign, Scorpio. Right, an artist's impression of some quite contrasting Mars attributes: The features express the fierceness and brutality that are said to result from the planet's *adverse* influence in a horoscope.

as his patron; at any rate, this is suggested by a ceiling fresco in Prague entitled "The Triumph of Wallenstein."

Raphael, as usual, outlines the chief spheres of the planet's influence: Mars is concerned not only with military men but with surgeons and barbers and "all such as use implements of a sharp nature, all trades wherein fire is used." The creatures proper to him include the "mastiff, wolf, tiger, panther, and all such beasts as are ravenous and bad," also sharks and "all stinging water serpents and hurtful fish," and, needless to add, all birds of prey. His plants include thistles, brambles, nettles, ginger, pepper, garlic, "and all trees that are thorny or prickly." Among his minerals are bloodstone, asbestos, iron, and brimstone, and he is the patron of such places as furnaces, distilleries, and butchers' shops. His day is Tuesday (*mardi, martedì*, etc.), which in the Middle Ages was considered the best day for blood-letting.

Ptolemy points out that Mars dries up rivers and causes the loss of crops. A maleficent planet, Ptolemy also explains, causes *injuries* when it is rising as distinct from *diseases* when it is setting. As regards diseases, Pearce (who was strongly opposed to vaccination) states that unless Mars afflicts either the ascendant or the luminaries "there is little if any liability to take smallpox." Traditionally, Mars was known as the "lesser infortune" and Saturn as the "greater infortune." (Saturn was always considered the most powerful of the planets.) Of these malefics, Saturn's effects have been compared to a consumption, Mars's to a fever. Inevitably, the relations between them are to be watched. Mussolini had them in conjunction, Hitler in square, and Goering in opposition. It is a relief to turn from these infortunes and attend to the "greater fortune."

Jupiter ♃

Jupiter is the tycoon planet and it is after him, since he is also known as Jove, that people are described as *jovial*. His keywords are *expansion* and *preservation*; Papus describes him as "un mélange de père, de patriarche, et de roi." Mythologically, of course, Jupiter (the Greek Zeus) had been the king of the gods, as had Marduk at one time in ancient Babylon. The great 13th-century Dominican doctor Albertus Magnus argued that the pagan assignment of the thunderbolt to the *god* Jupiter was a mistake due to the influence of the *planet* Jupiter in bringing about thunderstorms. (Dominicans could not accept the pagan pantheon but some of them could accept astrology. And, astrologically, they regarded Jupiter, together with the Sun and Mercury, as one of the planets who patronized the Christian religion.)

In spite of Albertus Magnus and others, the traditional character of this planet continues to remind us of the old Greco-Roman father figure who would have been so at home on any board of directors or in any senate or country club. Of all "lucky stars" he is the most patently lucky. He can see through illnesses and he can help you to survive disasters. He is rather like those good old rich men in Dickens. This "noble planet," says the *Kalendar of Shepherds*, "is very

Pope John XXIII (1881-1963). Jupiter was
a strong influence in the pope's horoscope,
since it rules his Sun-sign, Sagittarius,
and was at the mid-heaven at his coronation
in November 1958. And the pope's career
reflected Jupiter's astrological association
with patriarchs and ecclesiastics.

pure and clear of nature, and not very hot, but he is all virtues. And there are
fixed in Jupiter two noble signs of love; the one is Pisces and the other is
Sagittary, signs of no evil nor unhappiness. This planet may do no evil; he is
best of all the other seven. He keeps the liver of man and maintains it joyously."

Whether he can do evil or not, Ingrid Lind and other astrologers admit that
he *can* cause boredom or embarrassment. The Jupiter man tends to get things
too easy, to talk too big, to deceive himself. The *Kalendar* is unaware of these
dangers and portrays the Jupiter man as a model of physical cleanliness, virtu-
ous living, and good clean fun. It is not suggested that he has much intellect
but "he shall be a fair speaker and say well behind a person. He shall love green
color and grey. He shall be very happy in merchandise, and shall have plenty
of gold and silver, and he shall love to sing and to be honestly merry. And of
the man he governs the stomach and the arms."

On the other hand, Raphael makes Jupiter responsible for quacks, cheats,
and drunkards—but only when he is weak in the chart. When he is strong, he
produces men like judges and archbishops. His beasts include "generous crea-

tures of most descriptions" and his places include palaces, courts of justice, and wardrobes. Pearce assigns to him not the stomach and the arms but "the lungs, the blood, and viscera." Some astrologers say that the typical Jupiter sins are more of omission than commission. Furze Morrish suggests that the proper "sublimations" for Jupiter people are "religious methods and philanthropy, ranging from conviviality to devotion." As to his aspects, Jupiter in square with Mars will exaggerate the Martian effects. And throughout history special importance has been attached to the "great" conjunctions of Jupiter and Saturn, that cold old planet who is our next subject.

Saturn ♄

Until fairly recent times Saturn was the most distant of the known planets. His distance made him seem both slow and cold and these qualities were enhanced by the traditional character of the god Saturn (the Greek Kronos) who got identified with Chronos—i.e., Old Father Time—scythe and all. (In the Middle Ages, Saturn was said to carry a scythe or a sickle because he does more execution when receding than when advancing.) And just as Kronos, before Zeus, had been king of the gods, so Saturn in many times and places was thought of as the most powerful single planet—perhaps because he was a notorious malefic. The Roman historian Tacitus wrote that "of the seven stars that rule human affairs Saturn has the highest sphere and the chief power." Like many of the ancients and their successors, Tacitus would have assumed that the highest sphere (i.e., the greatest distance from the earth in the center of the system) actually conferred the chief power.

Saturn is the governor of old age and his keyword is *limitation*. He is essentially cautious; even the ancient Babylonians called him the "steady one." (He is the ruling planet of Scotland.) As far back as Tacitus, Saturn was considered the planet of Judaism: Tacitus uses this to explain the Jewish observation of the Sabbath, which was also Saturn's day. In the Middle Ages the famous Scottish astrologer Michael Scot, contrasting him with Jupiter (the patron of true believers), points out that Saturn is the patron of pagans and Jews, who are as slow to believe as the planet is slow in getting about the sky.

Raphael's description of Saturn was quoted in Chapter 1. *The Kalendar of Shepherds* is equally eloquent: "When he reigns there is much theft used and little charity, much lying, and much lawing one against another, and great prison-

A 15th-century German allegorical picture of Saturn and some of the types of people associated with this planet. Saturn, depicted as a horseman, rides in the sky above his two Zodiac signs, Capricorn and Aquarius. To astrologers, Saturn's influence is mostly malignant, causing misfortune, disease, and death—indicated here by the criminals in the stocks and on the gallows and the hobbling cripple. Some less unfortunate Saturn types portrayed are the farmer (plowing), the gardener (digging), and the tanner (skinning a horse).

ment, and much debate, and great swearing. . . . And old folk shall be very sickly, and many diseases shall reign among people, and specially in the chief hours of Saturn. And therefore this planet is likened to age, as hard, hungry, suspicious, and covetous, that seldom is content with anything. For Saturn is enemy to all things that grow and bear life of nature, for the cold and stormy bitterness of his time." Where Venus and Jupiter are warm and moist, Saturn is traditionally cold and dry and so is linked with the humor of melancholy. According to the ancient Hermetic books, his plants include the asphodel and the house-leek.

The qualities assigned by the *Kalendar* to Saturnian types seem an odder mixture than with most of the other planets. "He that is born under Saturn shall be false, envious, and full of debate, and full of law. And he shall be cunning in curing of leather, and a great eater of bread and flesh. And he shall have a stinking breath, and he shall be heavy, thoughtful, and malicious; a robber, a fighter, and full of covetousness; and yet he shall keep counsel well and be wise in counseling, and he shall love to sin wilfully." Not all these traits seem in keeping with the planet of old age and caution. No more does what follows: "He shall be a great speaker of tales, jousts, and chronicles. He shall have little eyes, black hair, great lips, broad shoulders, and shall look downward. He shall not love sermons, nor go to church."

The *Kalendar* goes on to recount how vindictive Saturn people are and how "cold in charity." Their favourite color, of course, is black. Much of all this is derived from Ptolemy, who also noted that Saturn makes you hairy-chested, but only when he is rising. In Hindu astrology the planet is given an equally gloomy character: He is personified as lame, clothed in black, with long nails and teeth, and "skilled in all kinds of wickedness." In spite of this bleak picture, Saturn, like Mars, is needed in the heavenly kaleidoscope. Ingrid Lind (who presumably would not accept the more lurid details in the *Kalendar*) writes: "A person with a good Saturn is like a plant with sound roots."

In the Middle Ages Saturn was much connected with magic. Some even thought that for magical purposes he was more use than the Moon. On astrological images (small amulets inscribed with astrological symbols and designed to do the wearer good or his enemies harm), Saturn was represented as a man riding a dragon, holding a sickle, and dressed in black or a panther skin. What powers were attributed to him are shown by the remarks of a 13th-century bishop of Paris who was extremely interested in astrology but would not go so far as to admit "what is so celebrated among the astrologers . . . viz., that a statue will speak like a man if one casts it of bronze in the rising of Saturn."

In Renaissance Florence the scholar Marsilio Ficino (a protégé of the Medici family) worked out his own doctrine of melancholy—the *saturnine* humor—as the one of the four humors that most influenced intellectuals. In fact he tried to turn Saturn into a good planet and was proud that it featured largely in his own horoscope. Kepler also had Saturn prominent in his horoscope; skeptical though he was about the practices of astrologers, he could write quite seriously: "With me Saturn and the Sun operate together: therefore my body is dry and knotty, not tall. The soul is faint-hearted, it hides itself in literary nooks; it is distrustful, frightened, seeks its way through brambles and is entangled in them. Its moral habits are analogous." One more historical example: In the 17th century William Lilly described the hard-drinking Welsh clergyman who had taught him astrology as "the most Saturnine person my eyes ever beheld . . . seldom without a black eye."

Saturn's Zodiacal signs are Capricorn and Aquarius. Pearce, in supplying his usual catalogue of the effects of the planet in all 12 signs, finds few in which Saturn makes for an agreeable temperament. Of his own signs, Saturn in Capricorn is most unfortunate, but in Aquarius, apart from crooked teeth, he gives you a *mens sana in corpore sano*. Of the others, Saturn in Aries makes you "quarrelsome, fretful, and austere," in Taurus "avaricious, secretive, and envious," in Gemini "perverse, selfish, and austere," and so on. A notable exception is Saturn in Sagittarius, which makes you "affable, obliging, generous, honest, and upright, merciful to an enemy, and constant to a friend, profuse in promises through excess of good nature."

Other astrologers are more ready to recognize the helpful side of Saturn. Evangeline Adams writes: "The Saturn position of any man represents his wisdom; that is to say, his innate and accumulated experience." She instances

The Russian leader Joseph Stalin (1879-1953), whose Sun-sign, Capricorn, is ruled by Saturn. Many astrologers have called Stalin typically "saturnine," pointing out that his personality seemed to reflect the planet's astrological nature—somber, melancholy, and suspicious.

Gladstone and Woodrow Wilson as Saturnian types and also notes that self-made persons often come under Saturn. The 19th-century German astrological writer Countess Wydenbruck gives as Saturn characteristics "selfishness, reticence, diplomacy" and "disappointment, delays, constriction in every respect," and then adds "hard work and perseverance."

In the matter of aspects, where Jupiter tends to exaggerate, Saturn tends to limit or devaluate. Venus is the planet of personal relationships, but Saturn in too close conjunction with her will limit your power to make friends. Tucker maintains that while Saturn in sextile or trine (both good aspects) with the Sun will make you philosophize, Saturn in sextile or trine with Jupiter can contribute to genius—as with Bismarck and Dickens. More important still is Saturn in conjunction with Jupiter, which can lead to outstanding genius as with Shakespeare and Newton; but this same conjunction can also cause frequent attacks of gloom. Morrish points out that Saturn, who is especially concerned with the mineral kingdom, is the planet you want in the second house (the house, among other things, of finance) if you're after a mining contract.

For millennia Saturn was the farthest planet known to astrology or, for that matter, to astronomy. Then in 1781 Uranus was discovered. The impact of this most startling event will be discussed later; here we may confine ourselves to his characteristics, which have gradually accrued to him through the observation (or invention) of astrologers.

Uranus ♅

As has been observed by modern astrologers, the hieroglyph for Uranus looks like a television aerial, and they have now agreed that among other things he stands for mechanical inventiveness. Louis de Wohl (who was mentioned in Chapter 1) goes so far as to attribute the inventions of World War II—including radar, penicillin, V-1s and V-2s—to "Uranus running amuck," adding that his worst but perhaps most typical invention was "that dreadful super-Uranian thing made of uranium 235—the atom bomb." (Some astrologers, however, blame the bomb on Pluto.) He is also held responsible for the Industrial Revolution with which, some say, his discovery more or less coincided.

He is also regarded as the planet of rebellion and eccentricity; but, because it takes him seven years to pass through a single sign of the Zodiac, most astrologers agree that his influence falls on generations rather than on individuals. Pearce, however, holds that he can be very powerful in nativities when in aspect to the Sun or Moon, and attributes the mistakes made by earlier astrologers to their ignorance of his existence. He considers Uranus "very inimical to conjugal happiness" but admitted that there was not really as yet enough evidence about him.

Raphael (writing at a time when Uranus was still called "Herschel" after his discoverer) describes his effects as "truly malefic." The first Zadkiel, though also considering him more potent for evil than for good, adds that he might

Some astrologers regard the planet Uranus as the patron of the heavens (relating it to the Greek sky god Uranus) ; others connect it with mechanical invention. Right, a 16th-century German woodcut shows that these two ideas were linked long before the discovery of the planet Uranus : A curious human peers through the vault of the universe and sees the mechanism that moves the stars. Another "heavenly" mechanism is the steam engine (below right), driven by two wheels called "sun and planet wheels." This machine was patented by the British inventor James Watt in 1781—the year that Uranus was discovered. Below left, Russia's Yuri Gagarin, the first astronaut. The date for his flight into space (April 12, 1961) was favorable in astrologers' terms—partly because Uranus and the Sun were in trine (which is regarded as a good aspect).

lead to a "great love of truth." But Zadkiel makes no mention of machinery—nor of democracy, with which some modern astrologers associate Uranus.

But even now astrologers seem in considerable disagreement about this planet. Some make him (like Neptune, the next planet to be discovered) a patron of things occult. An American astrologer at the end of the last century noted that the planet "lorded it in the ascendant at the birth of Mrs. Annie Besant" (who was the second president, after Madame Blavatsky, of the British Theosophical Society). Furze Morrish (who is himself much influenced by theosophy), in calling for a "World Aristocracy of Integrated Minds," wants as his pioneers men like Franklin D. Roosevelt in whose chart Uranus is positively emphasized. But, he adds, this could hardly happen under the "democratic" electoral system.

On the other hand, Rupert Gleadow insists that Uranus is a supporter of democracy. (His anthropomorphic account of the struggle between Uranus and Saturn for the rulership of Aquarius will be summarized in more detail in Chapter 6.) His point is that Aquarius represents the ordinary man and that Uranus by rights should be his ruler since Uranus represents, among other things, international collaboration and the brotherhood of man. On the same assumption, some astrologers have entitled Uranus "the emancipator." Ingrid Lind rather hedges her bets by associating this planet with "change (revolutionary, disruptive, dictated)." Most astrologers would agree that he is concerned with change; the question is what *kind* of change. Gleadow is banking on a change in the right (i.e., truly democratic) direction and therefore opposes Uranus not only to the repressive Saturn, but to the mysterious and sinister Neptune.

Neptune ♅

According to Gleadow, Neptune stands not only for *sensation* but for "the absorption of the self into something great and wonderful"—such as modern dictatorships. Margaret Hone and Ingrid Lind give as his keywords *nebulousness* and *impressionability*, which might possibly have applied to the Nazi masses but do not seem to fit, say, the Soviet Union or Communist China. On the other hand, Gleadow considered Hitler a typical Uranian, which makes it the more confusing when he lines up Neptune with Saturn against Uranus. We can sympathize with Zadkiel who wrote soon after Neptune's discovery: "Nothing has been satisfactorily proved as to the nature of this planet, astrologically, hitherto." He added (rather surprisingly, since Neptune was also the Roman god of the sea): "So far as we know, he seems to be dry, warm, and genial, or of fortunate 'influence'." But later astrologers, agreeing that nothing has been proved about the planet's nature, have not endorsed this individual view.

Countess Wydenbruck includes among Neptunian characteristics emotional genius and mysticism and, "if badly aspected, drunkenness, drugs, fraud." Ingrid Lind, who suggests that with slow-running planets the *transits* are the things to look for, notes that Neptune's transits lead to muddle, and adds: "It really takes a strong and sane man to control the Neptune in him." It must be remembered that it takes this planet 15 years to pass through one sign, and that neither he nor Pluto can get around the Zodiac in an individual's lifetime. As Evangeline Adams put it, he has more to do with the *Zeitgeist* than with individuals. She suggests that, historically, Neptune in Leo may have been responsible for national revolutions, in Virgo for great lawgivers, and in Sagittarius for artistic revivals or new ideas in religion. Furze Morrish, who assigns the five senses to the five "older" planets, connects both Uranus and Neptune with extrasensory perception (E.S.P.).

Margaret Hone, thinking of Neptune's nebulous character, points out that he was discovered in 1846, the same year in which ether was first used in surgery. She also connects his discovery with the introduction of gas lighting. As with

Gleadow's remarks about Uranus, many people may fail to see why the *discovery* of a planet should be responsible for anything. One possible answer available to modern astrologers lies in the suggestion that the time was ripe for *both* the discovery of Neptune and the first use of ether and gaslight.

Some astrologers (rather obviously connecting the planet with the god) would like to transfer to Neptune the rulership of Pisces, which traditionally belongs to Jupiter. Some, apparently also working by association of ideas, attribute to him occupations to do with the sea (which Raphael had given to the Moon). In the same way Pearce, not having had long acquaintance with Neptune, is cautious about him, suggesting that he might give one a bent for foreign travel. As for the qualities of sensationalism and nebulousness and mysticism and mediumism and so on, these too may well have been suggested to astrologers by the enormous distance from us of this planet and by the mere chance of his name. (On this second point, however, some astrologers are capable of replying that the planet himself—or perhaps the whole starry set-up—imposed the inevitable name upon the people who thought they were inventing it.)

Russian revolutionaries in 1917 firing on their tsarist enemies. Although astrologers disagree as to the spheres of Neptune's influence, some have suggested that this planet in Leo causes revolutions. The slow-moving Neptune was last in this sign at the time of the Russian Revolution.

Whether Neptune himself is as eccentric or not as they say he is, he certainly seems to make some human beings so. Max Heindel, wanting to equate the planets with "the seven spirits before the throne of God" (excluding the Sun and Moon, which the ancients had counted as planets, but including the earth and Uranus), disposed of Neptune by stating flatly that he "does not really belong to our solar system." What *is* Neptune then? Answer: "The embodiment of a Great Spirit from the Creative Hierarchies which normally influence us from the Zodiac." This was written in 1919. Today Furze Morrish, whose bugbear is jazz, assumes that Neptune of all planets is the one to remedy this: With his entrance into Libra (which of course represents balance) we may find, he hopes, "a change from the abominable, destructive, and maniacal type of music." He even adds optimistically: "Ugly music could be banned."

That leaves us with little far-flung Pluto, compared with whom (in terms of being known about) Uranus and Neptune are veterans. He has not as yet even acquired a proper hieroglyph.

Pluto ♇

Pluto was not discovered till 1930 and many astrologers are still naturally reluctant to diagnose his significance. Presumably Max Heindel, if he were alive, would explain that he had just dropped in from the Zodiac. Pluto is as far away again as Uranus and his apparent motion is only one and a half degrees a year, so it would seem safe to say that he is even less concerned with the human individual than Uranus and Neptune. Ingrid Lind, however, ventures the opinion that he may be "associated with divorce and re-marriage"—but then such things these days are practically a mass movement. On the other hand, Gleadow considers Pluto very important just because he is so slow-moving: In contrast with the Moon, who is transiting all the time, Pluto barely makes a dozen transits in a lifetime.

Unlike other astrologers, who connect this planet with Scorpio or Pisces, Gleadow says that Pluto appears to rule Aries (what would Mars say?) and that, when he was in Gemini, he produced the airplane. He adds: "Of course it must not be thought that Pluto had no influence before he was discovered." Furze Morrish says that Pluto's entrance into Cancer led to a wave of sensationalism and World War I and his entrance into the next sign, Leo, to World War II and dictatorship. Margaret Hone gives as his keywords *elimination, renewal, regeneration.* She connects him with the blackout in World War II (association with the kingdom of Hades?) and with the eighth house, which is the house of death.

The discovery of Uranus fluttered the astrologers for some time but they eventually adjusted; however, they are still having trouble adjusting themselves to Neptune and Pluto. Some astrologers now, at least in Germany and the U.S.A., follow the principle that attack is the best form of defense and are casting and interpreting horoscopes with the aid of a whole set of hypothetical planets lying on the *far* side of Pluto. These planets are properly equipped with names as well as with orbits, but, because there is no astronomical evidence of their existence (though some *astronomers* are, in fact, looking for a trans-Plutonian planet), they will be ignored in this chapter.

As far as the "old" planets are concerned, the traditionalists among modern astrologers (which means the vast majority of them) still use them in interpreting horoscopes very much as they were used by Ptolemy. It must be repeated that the planets are regarded as having influence *only* in relation to each other and to the signs of the Zodiac. And with the signs, just as with the planets, it must always be remembered that there are a great many factors and relationships to be considered before it can be established that so-and-so is such-and-such a "type." With that word of warning we can turn now to the signs of the Zodiac themselves, without which the planets would be not just wandering but lost.

St. Paul's Cathedral above the smoke of the London Blitz in 1940. Many astrologers assign explosive and destructive qualities to Pluto, and regard the planet's discovery in 1930 as the starting point of a period of darkness and violence that culminated in world war.

3 The signs of the zodiac

For the sake of convenience (but quite incorrectly) the planets were considered in Chapter 2 more or less on their own. In this chapter the signs of the Zodiac will be treated in the same way, though always with the reservation that, in Ingrid Lind's words, each sign, planet, or other element of a horoscope "has its own characteristics, and like the ingredients of a cake before mixing can be seen and described separately. But, as any cook knows, separate ingredients when treated and mixed produce totally different results." In fact, the Zodiac considered apart from the planets is like an empty stage or empty race track.

The more confusing technicalities, such as the vexed question of "houses," need not concern us at this stage, though I should repeat the warning that the 12 houses, to which astrologers have attached such importance for centuries, do not coincide with the 12 signs of the Zodiac. But we will come to these questions later. Now we are going to concentrate on the signs.

The name "Zodiac" comes from the Greek word *zodiakos,* meaning "to do with animals." This in turn is derived from the Greek *zodion* (strictly *zoïdion*), meaning "a little (painted or carved) animal." The plural *zodia* was used by Aristotle for the Zodiacal constellations, presumably because the ancients pictured many (though not all) of them in animal form. The Zodiac itself, which contains these little animals, is a circular band of sky spreading some eight degrees either side of the ecliptic (the path of the Sun), and it is only within

An illustration from a 15th-century
French text depicting the relationships of
the seven planets to the 12 signs of the
Zodiac. Within a conventional portrayal
of the Zodiac band (with the earth at the
center), a personification of each planet
is shown linked to the signs it rules:
For example, Mars (an armored knight)
is joined to Aries and Scorpio.

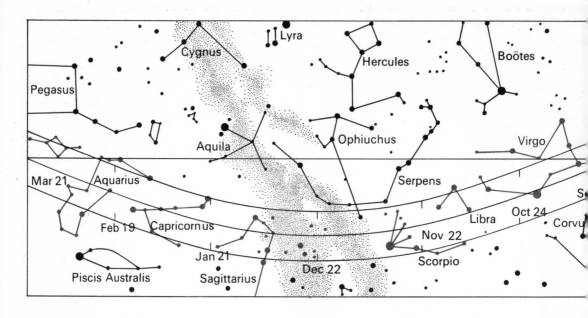

Pegasus · Cygnus · Lyra · Hercules · Boötes · Aquila · Ophiuchus · Virgo · Mar 21 · Aquarius · Serpens · Feb 19 · Capricornus · Libra · Oct 24 · Corvu · Nov 22 · Jan 21 · Scorpio · Dec 22 · Piscis Australis · Sagittarius

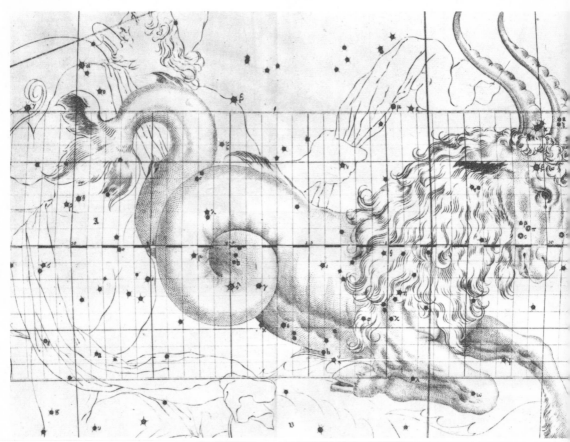

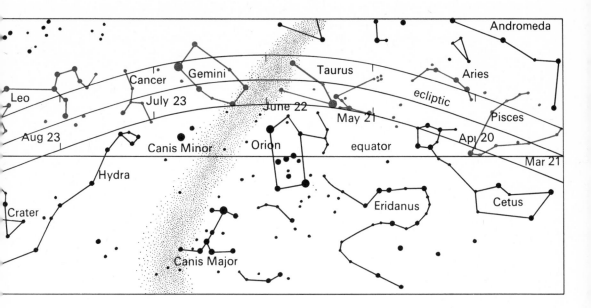

Left, Capricorn the Goat (with the figure of Aquarius visible in the background), as personified in *The Celestial Atlas* of John Bevis, printed in England in 1789. The drawing is superimposed on a map of the constellation; but (as with most Zodiac signs) the shape of the figure has little in common with the pattern of the stars.

Above, a star map relating the actual Zodiac constellations to the imaginary Zodiac band. Due to a "shift" in the stars' positions over many centuries, the dates of the Sun's entry into each constellation no longer correspond to the dates still used by astrologers. For example, the Sun now "enters" Taurus in May, not in April.

this band that the planets are seen from the earth. Astrology always has been, is, and always will be geocentric; but the *astronomical* reason that the planets appear to confine themselves to the Zodiac is that their real orbits around the Sun are all more or less in the same plane. The Zodiac does not lie flush with the "celestial equator" (an imaginary extension of the earth's equator) but is hitched at an angle to it, rather in the manner of a cowboy's belt.

When the Zodiac was divided into the 12 signs is not known for certain, but it was certainly long after men had identified the planets and endowed them with astrological significance. Here another distinction must be made. Within the Zodiac there are 12 constellations (though once, it seems, there were only 10). These bear the same names as the 12 signs used by astrologers; but astrologically they have nothing to do with the case. If you are told that your Sun-sign is Aries—which means that the Sun was in that particular sign when you were born between March 21 and April 20—this does not mean that you were born under the actual group of *stars* known as Aries. Once upon a time the Sun *was* (or appeared to be) among that group at that time of year; but he is not there now, thanks to what is known as the "precession of the equinoxes" (a very slow shift in the sky pattern, as observed from the earth, that takes 25,800 years to come full circle). The signs that most modern astrologers deal with are 12 exactly equal sections of the total circle of the Zodiac. Each section measures 30° and it makes no difference what fixed stars are contained in it.

This disconcerting fact provides ready ammunition for opponents of astrology. Robert Eisler (whose polemic book *The Royal Art of Astrology* was mentioned earlier) pounced with joy on this divorce of the two Zodiacs. "If it is conceivable," he wrote, "that the sector in which Taurus stood two thousand years ago can still impart 'Taurine' qualities to children born or conceived when this sector was just rising above the horizon, why is this 'Taurine' influence of a constellation which is no more there—i.e., of a pure memory-image—not overwhelmed by the quite different influence of the stars of Aries, which *are* actually there now, for everyone to see?" Eisler would certainly have an almost unanswerable point if modern astrologers (like many of their predecessors who were only too ready to talk about "radiation," etc.) really believed that the stars exercised a direct *influence* upon human beings. But most of them do not believe this. They consider, as did some astrologers in the Middle Ages and the Renaissance, that the stars are merely "signs," not "causes."

In a passage much quoted by modern astrologers, Carl G. Jung wrote that all of us, being born at a given moment and a given place, are invested for life with the qualities of the time of our birth. According to himself, Jung was not presupposing a *causal* relationship but rather relying on that presumed "unity of things" which has so often been a cornerstone of astrology. Anyhow, many astrologers find it logical to attach such importance to the moment of birth; some

even claim that there is a mass of empirical evidence (like the statistics referred to in Chapter 1) proving that, other things being more or less equal, people born at the same time (i.e., under the same stars and planets) tend to have certain characteristics in common.

But some more sophisticated modern astrologers, who stress the psychological side of their art, are usually embarrassed by the mass of astrological lumber in their attics. They feel vulnerable to charges like the one made in *Chambers's Encyclopaedia* (1959) that "the fundamental flaw in the whole system of astrology is the arbitrary character of the presuppositions made." In an attempt to get rid of these arbitrary elements, there is accordingly a modern movement away from traditional astrology.

For all that, the pictures of Zodiacal human types given by such a cultured and amusing astrological writer as André Barbault still remain pretty traditional and, if only from an aesthetic point of view, it would be a pity to scrap some of the more "arbitrary" detail. In fact, since ours is a period when people have a passion for classifying each other (compare Jung's "psychological types"), Barbault has watched his detail and provides a set of self-consistent pictures. He also is very well aware of the poetic or symbolic appeal of his subject matter. But with most of the moderns, psychology is what they go for. Rupert Gleadow writes : "The chief advantage of studying astrology is that it gives the power to understand the feelings and temperaments of others." Which, as he says, can be very useful when asking people to dinner or contemplating marriage.

How or why the signs got the names that they share with the constellations we do not really know. Of the constellations, Leo is the only one who looks

Many of the Zodiac signs we use today can be traced back 3000 years, though their exact date of origin is uncertain. Three of the earliest known representations are from Babylonian *kuddurus* (boundary stones) of the 10th century B.C.: Sagittarius (with two heads, a man's and a lion's), Capricorn, and (right) Scorpio.

anything like his name. Some people have tried to derive the Zodiac names from seasonal activities—Virgo from young girls harvesting and Pisces from the fishing season—but this often seems conjectural and forced. Gleadow denies "that the signs were named after the constellations with which they once coincided." He thinks it was the other way round : that the signs—the mechanically baconsliced 30° strips of Zodiac—"were named symbolically after the effects they were found to have, and that these names later became attached to the constellations." This seems very odd, especially if one thinks of the effects ascribed to some of the signs. Why should the quality of tenderness, for instance, make people think of the name Crab? Or fixity of purpose suggest the name Water-carrier?

Traditionally, the 12 signs fell into groups of three in accordance with the four elements—so that there are fiery, earthy, airy, and watery signs—and into groups of four in accordance with the three "qualities"—so that there are "cardinal" (i.e., predominant), "fixed," and "mutable" signs. The ancients stressed some other groupings : male and female signs, human and brute signs, single and double signs, land and water signs, and also mixed signs such as Capricorn, the goat-fish. Ptolemy gives four categories : "solstitial" (Cancer and Capricorn), "equinoctial" (Aries and Libra), "solid" (Taurus, Leo, Scorpio, and Aquarius), and "bicorporeal" (Gemini, Virgo, Sagittarius, and Pisces). The first and second of these groupings make good sense but some of that arbitrariness already mentioned seems to have crept into the third and fourth.

The groupings by elements and qualities seem to be of primary importance to most astrologers. In 17th-century England, the famous William Lilly pointed out that the great conjunction of Saturn and Jupiter in 1603 was "their entrance into the fiery Triplicity." By "triplicity," which he also called "trygon," Lilly meant the triangle made by the three *fiery* signs—Aries, Leo, and Sagittarius. "This Trygon is called by Ptolemy the first of the Zodiac ; and by the Arabians, the fiery Trygon." Lilly also remarked that this "trygon" was always connected with "memorable and notable changes in the Church and Commonwealth : . . . great actions and alterations have happened under it." He added, by way of proof, the fact that James VI of Scotland became king of England in 1603. (Incidentally, this dissertation on the great conjunction was published about 40 years after the event.)

Most astrologers hold that it makes a great difference whether you are fiery, earthy, airy, or watery. In early 19th-century Britain, John Varley, author of *A Treatise on Zodiacal Physiognomy,* wrote : "The fiery trigon . . . contains the spirited, generous, magnanimous, and princely natures. The earthy trigon, Taurus, Virgo, and Capricorn, contains the careful, sordid, and penurious qualities ; the aerial trigon, Gemini, Libra, and Aquarius, contains the humane, harmonious, and courteous principles ; and the watery trigon, Cancer, Scorpio, and Pisces, the cold, prolific, cautious, and severe qualities." (Not all of this attribution of qualities would be endorsed by modern astrologers.) Varley added, but without giving statistical evidence, that vastly more people are born under "the earthy, melancholic Saturnine, and the watery, phlegmatic signs" than under the other two groups.

In the 20th century America's W. J. Tucker (drawing on another American, Max Heindel) explains the psychological differences between the cardinal, fixed, and mutable signs: A cardinal sign (i.e., Aries, Cancer, Libra, or Capricorn) has a dynamic influence, though lacking directive power, and affects your conscious mind; a fixed sign (Taurus, Leo, Scorpio, or Aquarius) awakens your desire-nature, makes you stubborn but dependable, and affects your subconscious mind; a mutable (Gemini, Virgo, Sagittarius, or Pisces) deals with your superconscious. Heindel had also asserted, specifically in regard to the treatment of invalids, that with the cardinal signs you can expect co-operation from the patient, whereas the fixed signs (such as bovine Taurus and arrogant Leo) are so fixed in their ways that they are difficult to handle.

Louis de Wohl distinguishes between signs that encourage the man of action (such as Aries, Scorpio, and Sagittarius) and signs like Gemini and Virgo that encourage the man of system. If you are born under the latter you might well make a Chief-of-Staff, but don't go near the front! Of the relationships between signs, all astrologers hold that some signs are mutually congenial and some are not; for example, many astrologers would advise a Pisces type to marry a Cancer but not a Virgo. Gleadow maintains very plausibly that the greatest contrasts are between adjoining signs, as between Taurus and Gemini. And he differentiates between the behavior of the "trigonal" or elemental groups: "The fiery signs, for example, eat a great deal, not from greed, but because their internal combustion proceeds very rapidly."

The traditional order of the signs—Aries, Taurus, Gemini, Cancer, Leo, Virgo, Libra, Scorpio, Sagittarius, Capricorn, Aquarius, Pisces—represents, according to Ingrid Lind, "a progress from primitive unity and simplicity to complexity." This notion of Zodiacal evolution has been elaborated by much less orthodox astrologers, such as Furze Morrish. For Morrish the circle of the Zodiac is a pilgrimage. The first six signs, beginning with Aries ("nescience" or ignorance), represent the achievement of full objective consciousness (culminating in Virgo) and the latter (or homeward?) six represent "evolution into the subjective states, or yoga." The 12th sign, Pisces, corresponds to the ascension into heaven (which should comfort those Pisceans who have been told by popular books of astrology that they are just a lot of woolgatherers).

Aside from these groupings—the relationships of the signs with one another— the signs also form other relationships. As already mentioned, from the time of the Greeks and Romans the signs were distinguished according to their planetary rulers: Many, say, of the Sun's qualities would be found to characterize the sign Leo; many of the qualities of Venus would be associated with her signs Taurus and Libra; and so on. There are also relationships between signs and houses, between signs and "aspected" planets. And, as another kind of relationship, the apportioning of parts of the human body to the signs was considered gospel even in ancient Rome, where the first-century A.D. poet Manilius wrote (in a 17th-century translation):

> *The Ram defends the Head, the Neck the Bull,*
> *The Arms, bright Twins, are subject to your Rule:*
> *I' th' Shoulders Leo, and the Crab's obeyed*
> *I' th' Breast, and in the Guts the modest Maid:*
> *I' th' Buttocks Libra, Scorpio warms Desires*
> *In Secret Parts, and spreads unruly Fires:*
> *The Thighs the Centaur, and the Goat commands*
> *The Knees, and binds them up with double bands.*
> *The parted Legs in moist Aquarius meet,*
> *And Pisces gives Protection to the Feet.*

These relationships (or correspondences) are just a few of the "ingredients" referred to earlier. One can easily agree with Rupert Gleadow that "with so much material to go on one is never long at a loss to analyse anyone in terms of the Zodiac."

But before we enter this gallery of 12 archetypes, one very popular fallacy must be ruled out. To be, say, an "Aries type" you do not need Aries as your Sun-sign; i.e., you need *not* have been born between March 21 and April 20.

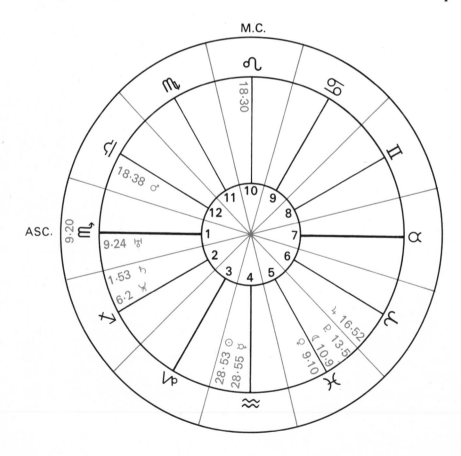

One should know one's Sun-sign—as practically everyone does—but there are two other things, as suggested in the last chapter, of at least as great importance in and to a horoscope. These are, first, the position of the Moon in regard to the planets in the Zodiac, and, secondly, the ascendant, the sign that was rising above the eastern horizon at the moment of birth. If you were born at sunrise— i.e., if your Sun-sign and ascendant coincide—the effect of the sign, as one would expect, is taken to be greatly enhanced. The same is true if the planet that "rules" the sign is present in it at the time of birth. And the story does not end here; there are yet other things in the whole pattern of the heavens (as we saw in Chapter 2) that can make you an Aries type: For instance, Aries may be neither your Sun-sign nor rising when you are born, but if there are enough planets in conjunction in Aries (no matter where Aries is in your horoscope) this may be enough to make you an Aries type.

It should be added that very few people are "pure" Zodiacal types. The great majority are noticeably influenced by more than one sign. This is where the really subtle astrologer (of whom there are not so many) can show his skill in *interpretation*. Even the most naïve astrologer would not claim that there are only 12 types of human being; but we will now look at the 12 *basic* types, giving just a hint here and there of the countless possible variants.

Right, the American poet Edgar Allan Poe (1809-49). Poe's life and writing were haunted by a morbid obsession with violence and death—both associated by astrologers with Scorpio. Poe was "born under" Aquarius; but Scorpio is in the ascendant in his horoscope (left). In many horoscopes, the ascendant sign (or other features) can be more influential than the Sun-sign.

Aries the Ram ♈

March 21 to April 20. The hieroglyph for Aries looks like a ram's horns (though Morrish says it might just as well represent a fountain). A cardinal, fiery sign, ruled by Mars: cardinal in that it serves as the ignition key for the year, fiery in that it symbolizes the explosive suns of spring. This is the sign of the vernal equinox when the ecliptic crosses the equator and day and night are of equal length. To the ancients it seemed natural to begin the astrological year on March 21 with the first degree of Aries (0° Aries), though the people in the southern hemisphere were not consulted about this. That Aries is a "priority" sign in almost every respect is shown by the instructions given in some of the early Hermetic writings as to the use of "Zodiacal plants" for magical purposes: Whatever the plant and whatever other sign is concerned, it should be picked and its juice extracted when the Sun is in Aries.

Aries is in general the adventurous pioneer sign and, like all the other signs, has the vices of its virtues. It had been assigned to Mars and its basic character established by the time of Ptolemy, and the association of Britain with Aries goes back to that time. The traditional qualities of the Aries man were briefly and

Courtesy: Museum of Modern Art, New York

clearly outlined by Raphael in the early 19th century: "Aries, the house of Mars and exaltation of the Sun, . . . is a vernal, dry, fiery, masculine, cardinal, equinoctial, diurnal, moveable, commanding, eastern, choleric, violent, and quadrupedian sign." It will be remembered that, apart from the sign that a planet "rules," there is usually another sign in which he feels particularly at home; this is the sign in which he is said to have his "exaltation." So Aries's fiery furnaces are kept doubly stoked, by Mars who rules it and by the Sun who is exalted in it.

On the other hand, a planet who is not at ease in Aries is Venus, as should be obvious from her character given in the last chapter. André Barbault stresses that the fire of Aries, in contrast with that of the other two fiery signs, Leo and Sagittarius, is the *primal* fire that both creates and destroys. So the Aries type of person tends to be an impetuous juvenile type taking no thought for the morrow. And not only juvenile but primitive: Ingrid Lind says there is something of the cave man about him.

There is a general agreement about the character of the Aries man: He is an enthusiast, tough, rather reckless, impetuous always and irritable sometimes, and he falls in love like a thunderbolt. Aries moves much too fast for the Taurus

Left, *Starry Night,* painted by the Dutch-born artist Vincent Van Gogh (1853-90). The explosive quality of the painting reflects the fire and passion that are usually said to be the dominant qualities of the first sign of the Zodiac, Aries (which was Van Gogh's Sun-sign).

Astrologers in the past considered that Aries may sometimes cause a ram-like appearance. Above, two drawings from a 17th-century Italian book of physiognomy representing Aries and its human counterpart.

type (to be discussed next) and is exasperated by the fussiness and exactitude of Virgo. From early times astrologers have also described his physical characteristics, making him strong, with powerful shoulders, and so on. After a warning about Zodiacal morphology, Barbault suggests that the Aries type does tend to look like a ram (Gleadow writes that "his nose, even when small, has an energetic arch") and notes that he walks rapidly and has a strong, quick hand-grip. He is something of a menace as a driver, and does not like wearing a hat. As for Aries women, in dress they don't wish to follow the fashion but to lead it; on the other hand, they are almost aggressive in their non-use of make-up.

As examples of Aries types, Barbault gives Louis Armstrong (who invented "hot" jazz), Marlon Brando, George Sand ("the first feminist"), Savonarola, and St. Teresa of Avila. To prove the point that two Aries types can be thoroughly Aries and yet, owing to the positions of the planets, in many ways very different, he contrasts two French writers, Baudelaire and Zola. Each of them had a notable conglomeration of planets in Aries but whereas Zola had the Sun, Moon, Mars, and Pluto, and at that in trine (a good relationship) with Saturn, Baudelaire had the Sun, Venus (bad, as just mentioned, in this sign), Jupiter, and Saturn—and at that in the eighth house, the house of death.

Morrish's evolutionary theory has already been mentioned. According to this scheme—in which the whole Zodiac symbolizes the universal "Wheel of Life and Death"—Aries, the first sign, represents ignorance (at whatever level) in contrast

A drawing of the French writer Honoré de Balzac (1799-1850). Balzac's Sun-sign was Taurus; to astrologers, his personality and even his appearance expressed the sign's strong, earthy character.

with the last sign, Pisces, which represents universality (at whatever level). Focusing in, Morrish makes the first three signs stand for "unit germination." Aries here stands for the male creative impulse (to be quickly followed by the traditionally feminine sign, Taurus, which represents *matrix* or matter). Morrish, like many artists, believes in the fertilizing effects of conflict, and stresses the importance of Zodiacal opposites; for example, "in a physical analogy Libra (air) is required to enable Aries (fire) to 'burst into flame.' " As well as making Aries play the male to the female matrix of Taurus, Morrish makes him stand for motion in contrast with the Taurine inertia. This evolutionary scheme of Morrish's, which involves the concept of yoga, is a peculiarly modern outcrop to which we shall return later. But, on the traditional premises, he has not miscast either Aries or Taurus. We can now turn our attention to the latter.

Taurus the Bull ♉

April 21 to May 21. To the layman it may seem comic that Taurus should be feminine, but the horned moonface of its hieroglyph certainly looks less aggressive than Aries' hieroglyph, which is almost all horns and nothing else. Moreover, Taurus is a fixed and earthy sign, and is ruled by the opposite of Mars, the gentle Venus. It is not surprising that Taurus is slow and long-suffering, in fact "bovine"; the hostile Robert Eisler even suggests that he was never a bull, only an ox, and quotes the ancient Roman champion of astrology Firmicus Maternus to the effect that this sign is responsible for the birth of impotent people and perverts. But most astrologers have been less insulting. A slow sign, yes, but a sure sign certainly. Nor is the Taurus type traditionally a sissy: Pearce writes that he is "slow to anger but, when provoked, furious."

Just as Aries was connected with both Mars and the Sun, so Taurus is connected with the Moon as well as with Venus. Barbault describes the Taurus type as essentially a *ruminant*, a creature of a leisurely rhythm who tends to walk slowly looking at the ground, obedient to the law of his sheer weight. The physiognomists, of course, make him *look* like a bull: thickset, thick-necked, and thick-lipped, with a broad forehead, wide nostrils, and a tuft of hair on the forehead. Countess Wydenbruck notes that he is "not very intelligent," but everyone agrees that he can be a tower of strength. Barbault, in discussing Freud (whom he makes a Taurus type) and his Taurine psychological universe, moves from the love of the child for its mother to the conclusion that "we are here at the heart of Taurus, which represents the meat-safe of the Zodiac . . . and, through displacement of the oral tendency, the strong-box of the Zodiac."

Working on the same strong-box lines, Tucker finds in Taurus a symbol of the Golden Calf; but he concedes that the Taurus man worships money not for itself but for the pleasure and ease it will bring him. He adds that, if the Taurus man does have enough money to eat well, he should cut down on the carbohydrates. He is a reliable husband and family man, pays his debts, and enjoys a joke; but too much of the "ruminant" quality can make him slothful.

Cars speeding along the San Francisco
freeway against a background of towering
skyscrapers suggest the speed and material
progress that characterize the American way
of life. Mobility and energy are qualities
of Gemini—the sign that is particularly
associated with the United States.

Right, the British actor Basil Rathbone
as Sherlock Holmes in the film version of
The Hound of the Baskervilles (made in
1939). The great intellect of the fictitious
detective is a typical characteristic of
Gemini—the Sun-sign of Holmes's
creator, Arthur Conan Doyle.

The two points to remember are that Taurus is essentially fixed and essentially earthy. Gleadow instances as Taurine types George Washington and Arnold Bennett. Barbault gives Balzac and Karl Marx as well as Freud. Marx had Taurus as his Sun-sign and it contained at his birth both the Taurine females, the Moon and Venus. Dialectical materialism, Barbault says, falls naturally under this sign. The next, the first of the airy signs, is a very different kettle of flying fish.

Gemini the Twins II

May 22 to June 21. A mutable, airy sign, Gemini is ruled (easy to guess) by Mercury. The word "dialectical" might be applied here too, but more in the original Greek sense where "dialectic" meant conversation—a quick and most argumentative conversation, full of twists and traps and contradictions. All astrologers agree that the Gemini type enjoys argument; after all, this comes naturally to a double man, born under a double sign. Barbault stresses this "bipolarity" and points out that Gemini rules the lungs with their double process of breathing in and breathing out. He adds that if Aries symbolizes the original fire at the source of life, and Taurus the condensation of this life in a material form (as it were, an egg), it is when the process arrives at the stage of Gemini that this egg is polarized and we meet the differentiation into the masculine and feminine principles.

Morrish, in a not altogether dissimilar way, having equated Aries with the male creative impulse and Taurus with the matrix, takes Gemini to stand for that "self-conscious entity which is the result" (being the third and last sign in his phase of unit germination). And in a discussion of "astro-symbolism" in which Aries represents motion and Taurus inertia, he makes Gemini represent "rhythmic balance or oscillation." Also, Morrish finds in the hieroglyph of this sign two pillars, one light and one dark, a "portal through which every human being must pass." Alternatively, he suggests that the two uprights of the hieroglyph, traditionally equated with the "heavenly twins" Castor and Pollux, could as well be equated with two apes—the divine ape of intelligence and the chattering ape of imitation. This last piece of symbolism brings us back to dialectic or, we might as well say, to the good and the bad sides of Mercury.

Being both mutable and airy, Gemini is intellectual but fickle. (Pearce describes the Germini type as having "disposition fickle, understanding good.") Ingrid Lind writes that he goes to "extremes of rationality" and possesses the "ability to live a double life." It has often been claimed by astrologers that many intellectuals are born under this sign. But, as indeed is often the case with intellectuals, the Gemini person is often emotionally cold. His congenial signs are Aquarius and Libra; he would not get on with cosy old Taurus. When we are told by Gleadow that Gemini is "pure intellect" and that no one is more mobile (a word frequently used of this sign), it is surprising to find him quoting Queen Victoria as someone who was born with Gemini rising.

Unfortunately, Gemini is the patron not only of intellectuals but of egocentrics and, in some cases, of lunatics. Thus another British monarch, the notorious George III, is quoted by Raphael as an example of the *bad* influence of Gemini, "the sign remarkable for producing insanity" when the planetary picture goes askew. But in the late 19th century (after Raphael) a study of a number of well-known cases of insanity was made by the British scholar Richard Garnett; while he was struck by the frequent conjunction of Mercury and Saturn, he found Gemini featuring only once in his chosen group of mad monarchs.

As regards the minor characteristics of Gemini people, Tucker notes that, if this is your Sun-sign, you may be inclined to vegetarianism. Barbault observes that Gemini women prefer two-piece suits and checkered materials. The physiognomist John Varley writes: "Gemini, though a beautiful and human sign, yet occasionally gives to persons born when it is rising [note that he is concerned with the ascendant, not the Sun-sign] a strong resemblance in the head and neck to the characteristic forms of goats, kids, and deer."

This sign stands for nervous energy; the United States is said to be very much under its influence. Among people born with Gemini rising many astrologers include Dante, Kepler, Wagner, Bernard Shaw, and Clemenceau. Barbault includes Conan Doyle in his list of Gemini types; he adds that Sherlock Holmes is a "popular Gemini hero." On the debit side, apart from producing madmen, it can (like its ruler Mercury) produce crooks and very selfish people. Once again, in moving from this sign to the next, we find a complete change of atmosphere.

Cancer the Crab ♋

June 22 to July 22. In spite of its name, Cancer is a homey, motherly sign, but also perhaps the most vulnerable. It is the sign of the summer solstice, from which it will be nine months before Aries comes around again; it can therefore be regarded as a symbol of fecundation and conception. As with the other signs, Barbault makes much of its position in the year, forgetting that many other countries have their spring and summer at different times from his. But on the symbolism of this sign and the psychology of Cancer people, he is at his most eloquent and suggestive. Because it is a cardinal sign and the first of the watery signs, he treats it as symbolizing the primal water—*les eaux-mères*—in the same way that Aries symbolizes the primal fire. It therefore stands for our ancestral origins, all organic life being assumed to have begun in the waters. It also stands, like the sea, for both intuition and introversion. It is the one and only sign ruled by the Moon, so Cancerian qualities are very much the same as the lunar qualities described in Chapter 2. The Moon, it will be remembered, is Our Lady of the Waters.

In accordance with this watery character, Barbault says that the Cancer type tends to be *un végétatif*. And the Cancer man (it is easier to be a Cancer woman and work it out in motherhood and the home) is often unduly feminine; as Pearce puts it, "effeminate in constitution and disposition." Cancer people can

Above, the French novelist Marcel Proust
(1871-1922), whose introversion and
sensitivity typify Cancer (his Sun-sign).
Above right, the modern artist Salvador
Dali represented as a fetus in an egg.
This "return to the womb" idea also ties up
with Cancer (linked with fertility and
birth), which was Dali's ascendant sign.

easily become "drowned in their own insecurity": They are over-emotional and
sub-active. But there is another side to the picture. In its earlier pictorial representations, Cancer was drawn as a crayfish, a creature that can give one a terrible
nip. And even crabs, however soft inside, have a very hard shell and are difficult
to dislodge from their chosen crannies. So throughout the centuries this sign
has stood for tenacity. Not only for tenacity of purpose but also for tenacity of
memory—especially memory of childhood. Which brings us round to the home
again. "*Cherchez la mère*," writes Barbault, "*et vous trouverez le Cancer!*"

This sign, however, stands for not only motherly people but mother-fixated
people. Being extremely sensitive, it is in fact a sign of many colors and moods.
Many astrologers consider that it makes excellent teachers (or actresses) and in
it Barbault distinguishes what appear on the surface to be two quite different
types: the stay-at-home, sufficient-unto-the-day type and the explorative, castles-
in-the-air type. (Actually he would not claim that these are more than subtypes.)
The examples that he gives of Cancer people include Byron, Cocteau, Salvador
Dali, Rembrandt, Rousseau, and Schubert. And he refers to the great stress laid
upon *intuition* by the philosopher Bergson, who had his Moon in Cancer.

Earlier astrologers laid less stress on the profundities and sensitivities of this sign and more on its crab nature. According to Varley, Cancer tends to give "a crabbed, short-nosed class of persons, greatly resembling a crab in features, when viewed in front; these persons resemble crabs, also, in the energy and tenacity with which they attack any object." And in spite of his shy and retiring nature a Cancer friend can be a social asset. Gleadow advises anyone about to give a dinner party: "If you want to know about food or wine ask Cancer." (He adds unkindly: "And if you want someone who will not object whatever you do choose Pisces.")

Morrish, in his ladder of Being (or, more strictly speaking, of Becoming), makes Cancer the first of three rungs representing gestation and birth. (He suggests that the hieroglyph could stand not only for crab-claws but for breasts.) The Zodiacal opposite to Cancer is of course Capricorn, an earthy no-nonsense sign that does not suffer from hypersensitivity. The signs that Cancer gets on with are Pisces and Taurus; but in *mundane* astrology Cancer and Capricorn are bracketed together, not only because they are both solstitial signs (one summer, one winter) but because they are the traditional fields for world-wide disasters. A third-century B.C. astrological missionary from ancient Babylon to Greece named Berosus taught that, when all the planets are in conjunction in Cancer, there will be a universal conflagration (a summery type of disaster); when they get together in Capricorn, there will be a universal deluge.

So there is Cancer, the only sign ruled by the Moon. Water, water, every-where—but also tenacity and patience, maternal love, understanding of others, extreme sensitivity, and introversion. And next door to it, with the usual dramatic juxtaposition, what should we find but the only sign ruled by the Sun?

Leo the Lion ♌

July 23 to August 23. A fixed and fiery sign. With Leo, Ingrid Lind begins by picking on the apparent paradox "or contradiction . . . in the thought of fixed fire." The answer, she says, lies in "molten gold," but she could also perhaps have used her cookery ingredients analogy. She goes on to contrast Leo with the first fiery sign, Aries, who is anything but fixed. Aries is impulsive and restless; Leo, like the Sun, stays put on his throne. People born with Leo rising include Bismarck, Garibaldi, Huey Long, and Picasso. Among those who had Leo as their Sun-sign were Lorenzo de Medici, Louis XIV ("le Roi Soleil"), Napoleon, and Rubens.

This, then, is obviously an extravert sign; it has produced far more than its share of presidents both in the U.S.A. and in France. As to the physical char-acteristics of Leo men, Pearce attributes to them "a large, fair stature, broad shoulders; prominent and large eyes; hair generally light and often yellowish; oval, ruddy countenance; of a high, resolute, haughty, and ambitious temper." Varley less flatteringly describes the Leo physiognomy as "most resembling a lion, especially in the nose and retreating chin; such as the profile of King

The Italian fascist leader Benito Mussolini (1883-1945) was born with the Sun in Leo. The planet and the sign have a similar astrological character; when combined (as in Mussolini's horoscope) they are said to lead to aggressive ambition and power seeking.

George III." Barbault distinguishes two physical types of Leo—the Herculean and the Apollonian—but they are both athletic and fine figures of men. He instances Dumas *père* as an almost pure specimen of the Herculean type. As for Leo ladies, Barbault notes that they go in for *la grande toilette*.

The Sun in Leo is at his greatest strength, and it is this strength that is the essence of this sign—the strength of a fire that has now been brought under control and is harnessed to useful ends. Morrish (in his psycho-evolutionary scheme) brackets Leo with Cancer as the "fundamental positive and negative polarities underlying everything." Barbault contrasts Leo with Cancer: In Cancer the umbilical cord has not yet been cut; it is Leo who breaks out into independence. But though independent and very full of himself, the Leo man is far from anti-social: "His ego disappears in his vocation" and he is a great worker. However passionate and ambitious he may be (with him "*vouloir c'est déjà pouvoir*"), Barbault says, his ruler the Sun acts as a sort of internal gendarme. Not that he always obeys this gendarme. As with any other sign, the types can go wrong. One should specially beware of Saturn in Leo, a sign in which he is "in exile": This can produce people like Cesare Borgia.

There seems no need to stress the animal symbolism of Leo—the king of beasts, etc. His 30° of the Zodiac are filled with roaring. But when we step over the border between this sign and the next we perhaps hear a typewriter, or a

A Swiss craftsman assembling a watch
exhibits the precision and attention to
minute detail that astrology connects with
the sign of Virgo—which, appropriately,
is the patron sign of Switzerland.

vacuum cleaner, a secretarial voice drily reading the minutes, a whispered aside of criticism. We have entered territory where everything must be "just so"— floors must be swept, files must be kept, *i*'s must be dotted and *t*'s crossed, beds (in all senses) must be properly made.

Virgo the Virgin ♍

August 24 to September 23. A mutable, earthy sign, ruled by Mercury. Ingrid Lind once again asks straight away: How can earth be mutable and mercurial? And the answer yet again is in the other ingredients (though, as she says, this internal conflict does tend to make a Virgo type a worrier). Gleadow calls Virgo "perhaps the most earthbound" of the 12 signs, but her earthiness is very unlike the earthiness of Taurus: Mercury could never rule Taurus. In fact the earth gives Virgo common sense and Mercury supplies an unusually keen intelligence. The two together make for disciplined thinking and acting. Cardan (Girolamo Cardano), the famous 16th-century Italian physician, mathematician, and astrologer, was grateful to the Mercury in his horoscope; Mars, he said, was casting an evil influence on both the luminaries, so "I could easily have been a monster, except for the fact that the preceding conjunction had been 29° in Virgo, over which Mercury is the ruler." N.B.: Virgo is a *human* sign.

Virgo is thought of as the patroness of critics and craftsmen, but not of creators or commanders. Louis XIV, though he had his Sun in Virgo, is regarded as a Leo type owing to the position of the planets in his horoscope. But Virgo is a great deal more than a sharp-tongued and keen-eyed housewife. It is the patron sign of Switzerland (which was to be expected), but also of Paris and of cats (no doubt because cats are so neat). Morrish connects it with diet and also with psychology. And Tolstoi is accepted by astrologers as a Virgo man, having had not only the Sun and Mercury in the sign but the Moon as well. Which would suggest that Virgo *can* be creative sometimes, though perhaps what is most obviously Virgonian about Tolstoi is the exact and conscientious way in which he tried to lead a new life in his old age.

Virgo is traditionally represented holding a sheaf of corn and, in western Europe at least, its time of year is the time of harvest, which means both fulfillment and desiccation. The idea of granaries may connect with Virgo's place in the picture of Zodiacal Man; it is assigned (in the phrase of the *Kalendar of Shepherds*) "the belly and the entrails"—i.e., it rules the digestive system. Barbault typically pounces on this to prove that the ancients anticipated modern Freudian psychoanalysis: What we find in the Virgo types is the "anal complex," hence their tendency to hoard things. But he admits that there is a small subspecies of Virgo in which the anus is equally important but plays an opposite role—"*anal relâché*" instead of "*anal contrôlé*." Ivan the Terrible was one of these; such people are really more like Scorpio. There is also, says Barbault, a somewhat larger subspecies of "ambivalents," who are holding back one moment and letting go the next.

A painting by the Italian artist Canaletto
(1697-1768) of the Grand Canal in Venice.
Libra (which was Canaletto's Sun-sign) is
the sign of harmony and balance—qualities
that are suggested by the symmetry of the
painting's composition and the detailed
representation of the architecture.

Anyway, the traditional Virgo type is somewhat dry and cold, a fusser over
detail, a discriminator, a rationalist, a perfectionist, yet prepared to sacrifice
himself. Barbault suggests that if the Pisces man is like an astronomer brooding
on the infinite spaces, the Virgo man is like a biologist with a microscope. For
Morrish, Virgo is the third of his second group of three signs, the triad that
denotes gestation and birth. So here Virgo, in spite of the name (but compare
the harvest symbol), represents "conscious birth into the outer world, and
objective powers of observation and selection." The sign is a halfway house:

You can go no further in the way of *objective* consciousness. But at the same time it is the beginning of "the cycle of evolution from the material back to the spiritual."

As already mentioned, the remaining six signs represent for Morrish "evolution into the subjective states, or yoga." The next sign, Libra, the first of the third triad, represents *collective* germination. But whereas Virgo (as halfway house) stands for the *first* stage of discrimination, with Libra there begins a second stage, which means the control of emotion.

Libra the Scales ♎

September 24 to October 23. A cardinal, airy sign, ruled by Venus. One would not expect to find Venus as Libra's ruler (it has little in common with the other Venusian sign, Taurus) but Venus, as we saw in the last chapter, stands for harmony and so can promote a proper balance not only between persons but also within an individual. So the Libra type is easy to get on with, being diplomatic, gentle, and tolerant. Tucker comments that this type has "many of the traits common to the Chinese race." (This was before China went Red.) Being the other equinoctial sign, Libra is the opposite number to Aries, and we could well imagine that it might do Aries some good. But this is contrary to the opinion of most astrologers who think that any two signs 180° apart *must* be opposed to each other in every sense, just as planets are when in "opposition." There are, however, a minority who think that such opposed signs would naturally *complement* each other, and certainly the signs of the spring and autumn equinoxes would seem to be a case in point.

Note that Libra is the only one of the signs that is inorganic; thus it seems quite fitting that Varley summarizes its "elementary notions" as follows: "Libra, independently of its appearing in the world's horoscope, to mediate the Zodiac horizontally, and to balance, as it were, the sign Aries, has been found to signify straight lines and regular buildings, and the sublime uninterrupted horizon line of the sea; it represents also the blue color of the sky and the distances." We might add, thinking of this blue seascape, that the Venus who rules Libra is more the Venus Anadyomene of Botticelli than the sensual goddess who prompted the Wife of Bath.

The picture that emerges of the Libra person is a sociable, cultured, and courteous person, perhaps only too pleased to sparkle in embassies. He seems to be humanist, empiricist, and eclectic, and almost entirely lacking in aggression. He would do most things for peace and finds it very difficult to say no. Perhaps his chief virtue is that he can see both sides of a question; his chief failing that he is too easily influenced. As for the Libra woman, she is extremely *soignée*. Barbault includes among Libra types Erasmus, Katherine Mansfield, Gandhi the apostle of non-violence, and, as its typical painters, Boucher and Watteau. Libra could hardly frighten anyone. We now move on to a sign that has long had a sinister reputation.

The Dutch-born spy and *femme fatale* Mata
Hari (1876-1917). Astrologers relate
Scorpio to both eroticism and death ; and
they would detect its sinister influence on
Mata Hari (Scorpio was her Sun-sign),
whose career of amorous and political
intrigue ended with her execution.

Scorpio the Scorpion ♏

October 24 to November 22. A fixed, watery sign, ruled by Mars. Traditionally, people were frightened of Scorpio, since it is the eighth of the signs, and was thus often related to the eighth house, the house of death. Varley gives it rather alarming physical characteristics: "Scorpio has been occasionally found to afford to one class of human form when it is rising, a near approach to serpents, in the expression of the countenance, especially in the eyes and mouth; and when doing or saying cruel and bitter things, they are apt to be assimilated to the nature of snakes, scorpions, etc." This animal symbolism has been made much of by most astrologers, but it is surprising to find a scorpion, usually encountered in hot, dry countries, established as a watery sign. (All the same, we are told that some modern Scorpio types excel at skin diving.)

The watery significance of Scorpio has been explained in different ways. Ingrid Lind says it is "the tidal wave of the thundering weight of Niagara." On the other hand, Barbault contrasts it with the water of Cancer (the source) and the water of Pisces (the ocean) and makes it essentially stagnant, the kind of water that is found in marshes. This does not seem to fit with the energy and passion attributed to Scorpio characters, but Barbault no doubt is basing this diagnosis on the fact that Scorpio is a *fixed* sign; after all, Cancer is cardinal and Pisces is mutable.

Stagnant or tidal, Scorpio is very peculiar. Barbault points out that the scorpion is the only animal that can kill itself (whether deliberately or not) by stinging itself with its tail. And he describes the sign as "the cemetery of the Zodiac." But readers who think themselves Scorpio types need not be alarmed: Scorpio has enormous stamina and can make a comeback like a phoenix. Having Mars as its ruler, it shows two main Martial qualities: aggressiveness and eroticism. Barbault writes that "the most murderous sign is also the most fecund." And to explain the apparent contradictions in Scorpio he once again, as with the preceding sign Virgo, calls in the anal complex. The Scorpio infant gets its first taste of power on the pot—and it will never look back.

Some modern astrologers prefer to think that it is the newcomer Pluto, rather than Mars, who is the ruler of Scorpio. This would only emphasize the dark side of the sign, Pluto being the lord of the underworld. To look on the bright side of the sign, we are told that though the Scorpio man doesn't set out to please and doesn't like taking advice, he can be very good company just because he enjoys things so much. We are also informed that he often excels as a physician or a practical engineer and that Scorpio women make excellent cooks —and tend to have sexy voices like Edith Piaf. Born with Scorpio rising (which, according to some, endows a man with Spartan qualities) were Nelson, Kemal Ataturk, Goering, Mussolini, Franco, Nietzsche, Goethe, Victor Hugo, and Edgar Allan Poe. Goethe's great hero Faust has been taken as a Scorpio type. Dostoevski, Goebbels, and Madame Curie had it as their Sun-sign. Scorpio, being simultaneously fixed and watery, is like the two preceding signs, Libra and Virgo—complex if not self-contradictory. The next sign, Sagittarius, being mutable and fiery (which seems to make more obvious sense), is comparatively straightforward.

Sagittarius the Archer ♐

November 23 to December 21. Ruled by Jupiter, Sagittarius is accordingly an expansive sign. From ancient times it has been represented by a centaur drawing a bow, which is why Ptolemy classed it as a "bicorporeal" sign, and many astrologers nowadays lay stress on this double nature. So after all it is not 100 per cent straightforward. With its animal half and its human half, it provides a good theme for a sermon or, as Barbault puts it, gives the "best image of sublimation." It has its four feet (or hooves) firmly on the ground and yet is shooting at the highest targets. On its centaur make-up Varley comments that, whereas its human half signifies "the deliberation or temperate resolves of humanity," its latter half "often exhibits more of the excessive impulses and nature of a race-horse, an animal most specifically described by Sagittarius." It is this latter half that may affect you if you were born roughly between December 6 and 20; it can lead to nasty accidents.

As one would expect with a ruler like Jupiter (see Chapter 2), it is a *success* sign. Abraham Lincoln and Cecil Rhodes were born with Sagittarius rising, and Winston Churchill had it as his Sun-sign with Venus also present. (Countess Wydenbruck, however, did point out that Churchill's horoscope shows him "likely to be subordinate to others in his profession.")

As to the *fire* of Sagittarius, Barbault describes it as a purifying fire, very different from that of either Aries or Leo, and suitable to later middle age when the desires of the flesh are waning but the spirit can still have a burning desire for social, political, intellectual, or spiritual objects. Morrish writes: "Whereas Aries represents the red, smouldering fires of creation, and Leo the yellow-golden fire of organized mentality, Sagittarius represents the blue fire at the heart of the flame. This is the hottest part of the flame." Sagittarius always wants to go further: He is a born explorer and adventurer and loves the wide open spaces. Everything he does is done in a big way. In music the Sagittarian type is Beethoven.

In the Zodiacal Man, Sagittarius is connected with the thighs, which brings us back to the power of horse and horseman. Many astrologers use this horse motif literally as well as symbolically. We are told that many Sagittarians are very horsey (and for that matter doggy) people: The eccentric and dynamic Queen Christina of Sweden, who dressed like a man, was mad about horses and also had something of a "horse face." (So had Milton, who was born with Sagittarius rising.) We are also told that the typical Sagittarian is "as strong as a horse." He has a very healthy appetite and in middle age has a tendency to *embonpoint*.

America's James Thurber (1894-1961)
often illustrated his humorous essays with
cartoons of which the best-known are
probably "Thurber's dogs." An affinity
with animals is a key characteristic of
Sagittarius (Thurber's Sun-sign)—an
association that perhaps originated from the
idea of the sign as half-man, half-beast.

He is a very strong individual but, like Jupiter his ruler, is a good mixer and, indeed, finds himself only in communal concerns. Barbault does suggest that there is an introverted subspecies (where Saturn dominates) whose member is concerned with the "beyond" within himself, but the typical Sagittarian throws himself into things outside himself, sometimes even achieving a "global vision." He has a hearty handshake, slaps his cards on the table, and tends to be euphoric. It is a little hard to recognize him in Morrish's system, where he stands for the "abstract, higher consciousness." But then Sagittarius has to conclude the second of Morrish's four stages, the stage of "control of emotion" : In this sign human emotions have to emerge from animal desires (the centaur again) and these emotions, in turn, must be directed into lofty aspirations—the arrow must leave the bow. Morrish squeezes his next and third stage, the "control of wind," into the confines of one sign only, which is naturally our next sign.

Capricorn the Goat ♑

December 22 to January 20. A cardinal, earthy sign; also an equinoctial sign, the equinox of course being the winter one. So Capricorn's ruler, predictably, is frosty old Saturn. "One does not invite to dinner the same evening Leo and Capricorn"; so writes Gleadow and, if you look back in this chapter to the account of Leo and in the previous chapter to the account of Saturn, you will have a notion of what Capricorn is like. With this sign one is (in western Europe) at the midnight of the year, so no wonder Morrish makes this the stage for "control of the mind." Tucker says that if Capricorn is your Sun-sign you should avoid alcohol in any form, if it is rising you will be inclined to be very pessimistic, and if you have the Moon in Capricorn you will be very disagreeable if you don't exercise control—witness Napoleon.

In the mid-19th century, when astrology was getting more mixed up with Biblical symbolism, Frances Rolleston (author of an odd book called *Mazzaroth*, the Hebrew name for the Zodiac) equated Capricorn with the kid of sacrifice. But then she had already equated Aries (of all the signs!) with the lamb of innocence and meekness. From more orthodox angles A. J. Pearce ascribed to this sign a "disposition subtle, collected, calm, witty, and yet melancholy" and Ingrid Lind speaks of "action allied with caution and commonsense." Through the ages Capricorn has been more often than not represented as a goat *with a fish tail* : Varley comments that while some Capricorn people look like goats, others look like fish. Symbolically, however, we can go deeper—or higher—than that : This is a fish with ambition that would like to clamber up the mountains.

Barbault stresses the opposition—and complementary relationship—of Capricorn and Cancer : Cancer is to Capricorn what the mother is to the father, the base to the summit, etc. In Capricorn we are getting away from matter (compare Morrish). Collectivization is coming in and the state or religious conscience may take over. Saturn is casting a chill or a shadow and yet he may be a liberator. If Saturn the ruler is actually in this sign, then everything is cut to the bone:

You get people like Kant and Mallarmé. Among other Capricorn types Barbault instances Queen Elizabeth II (Capricorn rising and in sextile to Saturn, so strongly Saturnian), the stolid Marshal Joffre (both Sun-sign and ascendant), Kepler (of whom more later), Pasteur, Woodrow Wilson, and, above all, Stalin. The last named had his Sun in Capricorn, in aspect with all the slow-moving planets, Mars, Jupiter, Saturn, Uranus, and Neptune. Get the idea?

Capricorn people are thought to be born traditionalists, yet they are not so much disciplinarians as diplomats. They like traditional ceremonies, religious or

The yearly spectacle of the state opening of Britain's parliament is an example of the pomp and ceremony that surround the British monarch. Such a concern with tradition and ritual is usually associated with Capricorn—the ascendant of Queen Elizabeth II.

civil, and are upset if they are dressed wrongly for the occasion. It is also conceded that many of them are religious in a deeper sense; this might provide a bridge from traditional astrology to Morrish's astro-psychology. For Morrish, Capricorn is the gate to the spiritual life just as Cancer was the gate to "form-life." We are now getting into yoga (under Capricorn, like a yogi, one practices control) and are on the brink of spiritual rebirth, which for Morrish is represented by the next sign, the last but one in the Zodiac.

Aquarius the Water-Carrier ≈

January 21 to February 19. A fixed, airy sign. Aquarius's ruler is traditionally Saturn, though some astrologers (such as Varley) prefer to promote Uranus or at least make him co-ruler. This sign provides some of the most graceful illustrations to medieval textbooks and has long been thought of as a particularly *human* sign; Gleadow calls it "the only completely human sign in the Zodiac." But there seems to be a divergence of opinion as to whether he represents the ordinary man or an especially gifted man. On the former premise he is linked with democracy, on the latter with science and the capacity for abstract thought. This was the Sun-sign of Galileo, Francis Bacon, and Darwin.

Some years ago the French amateur astrologer Paul Choisnard investigated the horoscopes of 119 outstanding intellectuals and claimed to have found that under only three signs was the incidence more than average—Gemini, Libra, and Aquarius. These, of course, are the three *airy* signs and the symbolism of air here is obvious. Traditionally Aquarius rules the circulation of the blood, and this has been correlated with the circulation of ideas. If Uranus is brought in, one would expect to find Aquarians showing the characteristics of that planet (like mechanical inventiveness) and also what Ingrid Lind calls the "Uranian urge to disrupt." Miss Lind, on the assumption of co-rulership, would like to distinguish Saturnian Aquarians from Uranian Aquarians. Rupert Gleadow, writing of the so-called "Aquarian Age" (see below), foresees the spread in the immediate future not only of such Uranian effects as machinery and inventions, but of "world-wide organizations, . . . international collaboration, and the Brotherhood of Man."

The Aquarian, unlike his predecessor the Capricornian, is no respecter of tradition or convention (otherwise he would not be so well equipped for scientific research). But he *is*, in the best sense of the phrase, a respecter of persons because, once again, he is human. He pours out the water freely: "Your need is greater than mine." He can be tactless, though, and other faults ascribed to him are obstinacy (after all, this is a fixed sign), fanaticism, and (more surprisingly) inefficiency. Countess Wydenbruck describes him as "popular yet solitary, often abnormal." It has been observed that Aquarius men often have beautiful profiles but tend to look unduly feminine. But this is not mentioned by that old traditionalist Pearce, who merely says that the Aquarian is "of prepossessing appearance and good disposition," and has a "long and fleshy face." Here we have a minor inconsistency, since in another passage describing the influence of Aquarius as a Sun-sign, Pearce speaks of "a round full face," and again goes on to mention "good disposition, though tinctured with, pride and ambition; artistic or scientific."

Apart from the scientific thinkers already mentioned, other people who had Aquarius as their Sun-sign were Abraham Lincoln, Franklin D. Roosevelt, and James Dean. Edward VIII (the Duke of Windsor) was born with Aquarius as his ascendant sign.

To return to the "Aquarian Age" : Many astrologers block out history in periods of roughly 2000 years, each such period falling under the tutelage of a particular sign. This is dictated by the movement of the vernal equinoctial point (i.e., 0° Aries), which goes very slowly backward through the signs (because of the "precession of the equinoxes," mentioned earlier). So in the last 2000 years B.C., 0° Aries was in Aries the constellation. Then it moved into Pisces— very suitably, since the Piscean Age coincided with the Christian era, and the fish was an early symbol of Christ. As to whether the Aquarian Age has yet begun, astrologers disagree. Ingrid Lind thinks that it has, and ascribes to it much the same characteristics as Gleadow : "All the modern trend of thought and invention." For Morrish also, but in a different way (since what he is

The American film actor James Dean
(1931-55). Astrologers would label his
sensitive good looks as typically Aquarian
—and Aquarius was Dean's Sun-sign.
Equally typical of this sign was the youthful
spirit of rebellion against convention
that James Dean stood for during his career
and, especially, after his death.

concerned with is *subjective* development) Aquarius is "the awakener." For him it is the sign not of the scientist but of the yogi—"the development of spiritual consciousness through contemplation." This development will be completed in the next sign, which he takes as representing the "cosmic ocean."

Pisces the Fishes ♓

February 20 to March 20. A mutable, watery sign. To be both mutable and watery might be thought to be overdoing the fluid element; traditionally Pisces types are liable to lack both stability and precision. But the ruler of this sign is Jupiter (though some would substitute Neptune), which tends to correct the balance. The water symbolism is made much of by astrologers (Pisceans are said to be wonderfully adaptable and to make good actors) but the actual fish reference has mostly been dropped. Varley provides an example of the latter: "Pisces was found to signify persons who were employed in fishing, and in other watery concerns. . . . It is a sign under which many fishmongers are born . . . and some of the persons born when it is rising approximate to fishes in their eyes, which are somewhat conspicuous and phlegmatic."

Modern astrologers do not mention fishmongers but they stress the fact that Pisceans at their best are idealists and, at their worst, drifters. They are not individualists and in fact seem hardly conscious of their own individuality. And they certainly are not go-getters: They are gentle, shy, sensitive (often hypersensitive), vague, and prone to melancholy. Some retire from ordinary life by drifting (astrological textbooks always warn them against drink); others retire into lives of dedication, in cloisters or hospitals. They are extremely malleable, often hesitant, and keep changing course; Barbault says that the Piscean voluntarily loses himself in a labyrinth. When they lie it is not usually intentional but just part of their general confusion. The Moon in Pisces is dangerous for she encourages fantasies and hallucinations. At one extreme the Piscean can lapse into schizophrenia.

All this being so, it is not surprising that some of the artists born under this sign (it could be said to be a natural sign for artists) should have had tragic careers. It was the Sun-sign of the unfortunate German poet Hölderlin, who went mad. Nijinsky was born with Pisces rising, and also went mad. And the pessimistic German philosopher Schopenhauer was born under Pisces with Saturn very prominent in his horoscope. A tragi-comic example from fiction is Dickens's Mr. Micawber in *David Copperfield*, a person who (according to Gleadow) "is notoriously Piscean."

The Polish-born pianist and composer
Frédéric Chopin (1810-49). Chopin's career,
devoted to romantic music and romantic love
affairs, ended in early death. Elements
of love, art, and tragedy are all attributes
of Pisces, which was Chopin's Sun-sign.

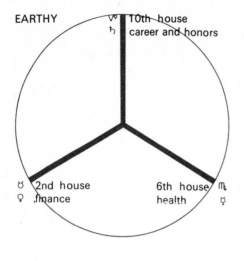

EARTHY

10th house
career and honors
♑ ♄

2nd house
finance
♉ ♀

6th house
health
♍ ☿

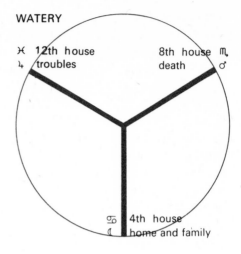

WATERY

12th house
troubles
♓ ♃

8th house
death
♏ ♂

4th house
home and family
♋ ☾

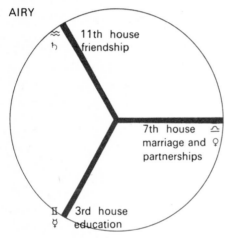

AIRY

11th house
friendship
♒ ♄

7th house
marriage and
partnerships
♎ ♀

3rd house
education
♊ ☿

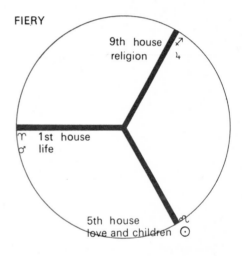

FIERY

9th house
religion
♐ ♃

1st house
life
♈ ♂

5th house
love and children
♌ ☉

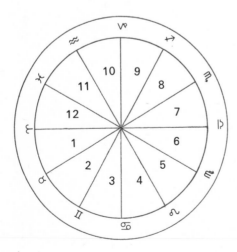

Above, four diagrams setting out the usual
astrological meanings of the 12 houses, which
are classified (like the signs) as either
earthy, watery, airy, or fiery. Each house is
also traditionally associated with a particular
Zodiac sign and its ruling planet (here
indicated by their symbols). For example, the
second house (finance) is linked with the
"earthy" sign Taurus and its ruler, Venus.

Left, the positions of the 12 houses on a
horoscope chart. Each house is shown in its
traditional relationship to a particular
sign—for example, Aries is associated with
the first house (life). But the relationships
shown here do not always apply: Although
the positions of the houses never change, the
positions of the signs vary in each chart.

On the brighter side of the picture, Pisceans are very lovable people because they are very loving. Not only is Pisces ruled by Jupiter (which tends to redress the shyness, neurosis, etc.) but it is in this sign that Venus is exalted. And, true to the oceanic nature of the sign, the Piscean tends to "lose himself" in love. In Morrish's scheme there is a similar merging or fusion but here it is a "liberation" in the symbolic ocean of the cosmos: We have reached the highest point of yoga or spiritual consciousness, the top of the Zodiacal ladder. As usual, this is Morrish's own formulation, but he also accepts the traditional idea of the Piscean Age and, unlike Gleadow and others, deplores the fact that it is passing: Everywhere he sees a "characteristic destruction of Piscean values."

With this sign we have come the full circle of the Zodiac. It is hoped that the rather sketchy summary of the signs in this chapter will at least throw some light on the historical chapters to follow. There has not been space here to say much about "mixed" Zodiacal types; but some very important matters, such as the effect of the aspects, will be discussed again in Chapter 8, which will also give a glance at such things as "transits" and "revolutions." In that chapter we shall also see how astrologers disagree as to "house arrangement."

What the 12 houses mean, however, has been fairly well established since ancient times, so, as the houses will be referred to here and there in the historical chapters, it is worthwhile ending this chapter by giving very approximately their traditional significations. (Remember that, though they may have affinity with the respectively numbered signs, they do *not* coincide with them. The seventh house, say, is always in the same position; the seventh sign is not.)

First house: The life of the individual, the self, his general potentialities.

Second house: His possessions (compare old strong-box Taurus), finance, etc.

Third house: Education; relationships with what Americans call one's "peer-group."

Fourth house: Family origins, parents, home.

Fifth house: Loves, recreations, children.

Sixth house: Hard work, health, domestic chores. (Compare poor Virgo.)

Seventh house: Marriage, partnerships, enmities, etc.

Eighth house: Death. Also inheritances.

Ninth house: Higher life of the intellect and spirit. (Compare Sagittarius.)

Tenth house: Social life, profession, reputation, honors, etc.

Eleventh house: Friendships, objectives.

Twelfth house: Troubles of various kinds, illnesses, betrayals, disgrace.

There is a Latin mnemonic distich that puts these in a nutshell:

> *Vita, lucrum, fratres, genitor, nati, valetudo,*
>
> *Uxor, mors, pietas, regnum, benefactaque, carcer*

and that can be translated: Life, lucre, brothers, father, children, health, wife, death, duty, career, benefits, prison.

And now, having assembled our cast of both planets and signs, let us go back into history and see how the first directors or stage managers managed them.

4 The ancient world

According to one modern astrologer, echoing historians from the early Christian era, "Adam was instructed in astrology by heavenly inspiration." Without bringing Adam into it, the fact remains that astrology *is* of great antiquity. The brand practiced in Europe today derives originally from ancient Mesopotamia. The Greeks and Romans tended to call all astrologers "Chaldeans" (i.e., Babylonians), while their name for a horoscope was "Babylonian numbers."

In these beginnings astrology was still intertwined with astronomy, which had come into being when people began to ask for an accurate time reckoning. Such a time reckoning was required for agricultural purposes, but most of all by religion. Religious ceremonies had to take place at fixed dates, so the astronomers were the priests. A Babylonian priest in the early days must have been something of a commissar: The land belonged to the gods, and the priests were the gods' stewards. (In other countries farther east, such priestly astrologers retained their powers till fairly recent times—for instance, the Brahmin *purohitas* who published the Hindu almanac, and at a word from whom parents abandoned their babies.)

The dry, cloudless Mesopotamian climate is naturally favorable to astronomy; in Babylonia the priests were observing the heavens from the third millennium B.C., and many of the fixed stars and constellations (such as the Pleiades and Orion) were known and named by them. The 12 signs of the Zodiac probably

Part of a second-century A.D. Roman relief showing the casting of a child's horoscope. A nurse presents the child to its mother, while two women (probably two of the three Fates) read the child's future in the "celestial globe." By Roman times astrology had become for most people an accepted part of everyday life.

Left, a 20th-century B.C. copy of an older Babylonian clay tablet recording the movements of the planet Venus and omens indicated by her risings. Such records were compiled by Babylon's priests (represented, right, by a statue of 2700 B.C.), who were both astronomers and astrologers, and who predicted (and guided) the future of the state and its rulers. Priests in modern India (like the Hindu holy man, below right) are also partly astrologers: They use astrology to choose the best dates for religious festivals, weddings, and other ceremonies.

came later. But what we think of today as the astrological approach seems to have been there from the start.

The idea that the stars condition human behavior and fortunes rests on the notion that the world is *one*—a whole of interdependent parts. This world is full of correspondences between things above and things below—in the way that the ziggurat (the holy mound) in any Sumerian temple was a meeting place between heaven and earth, where the gods could converse with men. In other words, the ancient world seems to have automatically correlated human experience with natural phenomena.

The determinism (or fatalism) that this correlation implies can have been no more discouraging, before the development of science, than the concept of the world as an unintelligible plurality ruled by blind chance. So, though astrology today may look to many people like sheer superstition, we should not forget that it made very good sense at a time when man was at the mercy of a great many uncontrollable forces—the elements, warlike neighbors, the gods. Perhaps one reason why men of the old civilizations turned to the stars was to find an antidote to the precariousness of life.

The first Babylonian Empire lasted into the first millennium B.C., when the Assyrian came down like a wolf on the stars and made Babylon's lore his own. The Assyrians were modified and humanized by the people they conquered. Their capital was Nineveh, but they preserved and respected the civilized city of

Babylon and the cuneiform texts in its temples. Among such texts were many dealing with those Siamese twins, astronomy and astrology. The Assyrian king Ashurbanipal compiled a library of clay tablets from the earliest days of Babylonia down to his own time. In these latter texts the astronomical records become surprisingly detailed; the stargazers had been working overtime.

This wealth of detail was needed for fortune telling. But in Babylon and Nineveh the fortune to be told was that of the state, not of individuals—except the king, who himself personified the state. It was partly for this reason that astrology never had the wide popularity in Mesopotamia that it was to achieve in Greece or Rome.

In Ashurbanipal's library many letters from priests to their sovereigns illustrate this narrow application of astrology. The tone is appropriately dry, the objects utilitarian. One priest writes to Ashurbanipal: "This eclipse of the Moon that took place has destroyed the lands . . . . It has cast down the land of Amurru and the land of the Hittites and again the land of the Chaldeans. It is favorable for the king my lord . . . ." Eclipses, being such a sensational phenomenon, naturally concerned the priests a good deal, but their predictions were often inaccurate: "As for the eclipse of the Sun, it did not take place. It is over. The planet Venus is approaching the constellation Virgo. The appearance of the planet Mercury is approaching. Great wrath will come."

A ceiling from the Egyptian tomb of Sethos I (1300 B.C.), decorated with constellations, including the lion, the bull, and (unique to Egypt) the crocodile. These figures are not Zodiac signs : Astrology did not develop in Egypt until the sixth century B.C., over 2000 years after it started in Babylon.

During the sixth century B.C., astrology caught on in Egypt. (Later, in Roman times, Egypt was to claim that she had been the pioneer in this field; but in fact she did not turn to it until long after the great days of the pharaohs.) At the same time, scientific inquiry was bursting out in the Greek cities of Asia Minor—first of all in Miletus with the famous Thales (the first European who could properly be called a scientist). Not that the Babylonians were finished; their greatest achievements in astronomy proper were to come. So far as time reckoning went, the Greeks could still learn from the Babylonians. And the Greeks were also to become the pupils of the "Chaldeans" in astrology, though not for a few hundred years. It should be noted that, whereas in Mesopotamia astronomy proper was developed later than astrology, in Greece it was the other way around.

Astronomically, then, the Babylonians made great strides—though one would not guess this from, say, the Book of Daniel, where Nebuchadnezzar's wise men ("the magicians, and the astrologers, and the sorcerers, and the Chaldeans") were invariably defeated by Daniel. (But then all the Hebrew prophets were good at propaganda. The "Second Isaiah," pronouncing God's judgment on Babylon, cries out with relish: "Let now the astrologers, the stargazers, the monthly prognosticators, stand up and save thee from these things that shall come upon thee. Behold, they shall be as stubble; the fire shall burn them . . . ." etc.)

Ruins of a Greek amphitheatre at Miletus in southwest Turkey. The city was the birth-place of Thales, founder of the "Ionian" school of philosophy. Thales was concerned with scientific observation rather than metaphysics; because of his influence, astrology suffered a temporary setback.

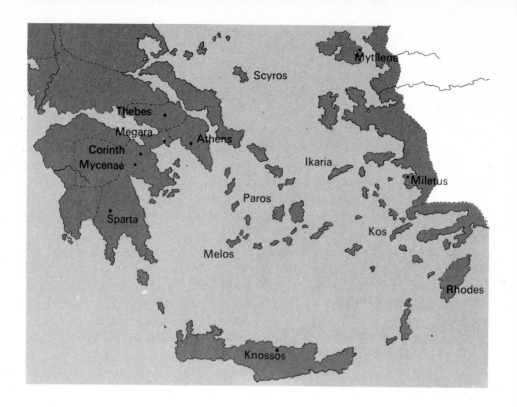

It was astrology, not astronomy, that seems to have declined during the sixth century B.C. Possibly, when Babylon lost her imperial power, the skies were observed more for their own sake or for the old time-reckoning reasons than in order to bolster up the government. Anyhow, it looks as if astrology entered a slump period (except in Egypt). In view of the "Enlightenment" that swept the Greek world during the next centuries, one might have expected it never to emerge from this slump. But history does not work like that.

The inquiring mind of the Greek Enlightenment did not arise in a vacuum; it was conditioned by politics that were conditioned by economics that were conditioned by geography. Mesopotamia had to be politically centralized, largely because the water supply desperately needed strong government control. So the pattern was one water supply, one ruler, one religion—and hence one hierarchy of priests, who also monopolized what science there was. Greece was entirely different: a congeries of city states in remote mountain valleys and islands where centralization, whether political or religious, was not possible. So whereas science in Babylon never got out of the temple, in Greece it never got into it.

Thales and the sixth-century "Ionian Physicists" certainly had no time for astrology—though this does not prevent some modern astrologers from including them in the fold. It is easier to lay claim to Pythagoras later in the century—as, of course, astrologers do—because, unlike Thales, he had a religious bent. It has been said that Pythagoras put the "supernatural" back into astronomy. In particular, his mystique of numbers and his famous "Harmony of the Spheres" would make him irresistible to name-collecting modern astrologers.

dome -

heavens - - - - - - - - - - - - - - - - -

wall -

earth - - - - - - - - - - - - - - - - - - -

oceans - - - - - - - - - - - - - - - - - -

chamber of water - - - - - - - - - - -

In the separate city-states of ancient Greece (left), science (including astrology) flourished independently of religion—unlike centralized Babylon, where science was the monopoly of the priests.

Above, the Babylonian idea of the universe: The earth lies enclosed beneath the dome of the heavens, surrounded by oceans and resting on a chamber of water. Below, the universe as conceived by Philolaus of Tarentum, a fifth-century B.C. Pythagorean. Pythagoras had believed that the earth was at the center, but Philolaus substituted a "central fire" around which the earth, a "counter-earth," the seven planets (including the Sun and Moon), and the fixed stars revolve, all attached to spheres.

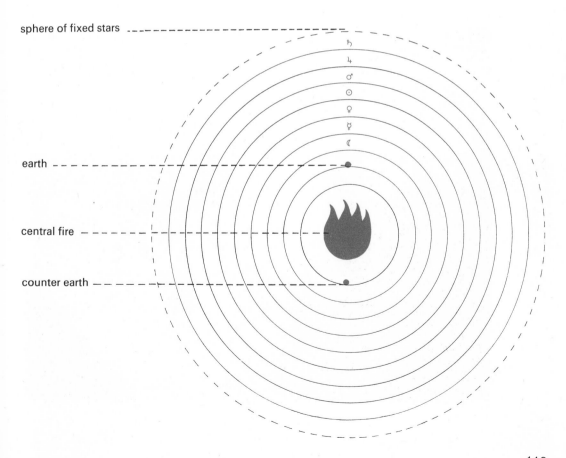

sphere of fixed stars -

earth -

central fire - - - - - - - - - - - - - - - -

counter earth - - - - - - - - - - - - - -

Like the Babylonians, Pythagoras and his followers saw the universe as a system of correspondences, a unified whole made up of interlocking component parts. This is especially clear in Pythagorean astronomy. The universe, as the Master himself conceived it, was still geocentric (as it had been for the Babylonians). But the Babylonian earth-disk had now become a sphere; Pythagoras was probably the first to maintain that the earth is round. The planets (which still included the Sun and Moon) and the fixed stars were fastened to spheres or wheels that revolved round the earth in concentric circles, each humming on a different pitch, the whole constituting the "Pythagorean Scale."

This sort of geometrical perfectionism (which was extended by Pythagoras's followers, and by others, like Plato) imposed a sort of deep freeze on the universe and encouraged others to give up careful observation. Nevertheless, later centuries did see further original work in Greek astronomy. In the third century B.C., a very careful observer called Aristarchus developed the concept of the heliocentric universe, and so anticipated Copernicus by 17 centuries. But no one believed him, and the universe remained geocentric and rigid. As the astrologer's universe is also geocentric and rigid, this retrogression of astronomy can be considered one of the probable causes of the coming triumph of astrology in Greek life.

But it was not, of course, the only cause. All the ancient Greeks were by no means well-balanced, clear-eyed rationalists. There was in the Greek character and culture what Nietzsche calls a "Dionysiac" or irrational strain. After the fifth century, and largely owing to the internecine wars of the tiny Greek city states, a great gulf seems to have developed between the few—the intellectuals— and the many; the former were no longer at home in society. Among the intellectuals the result was the appeal of new individualist cults like Stoicism and Epicureanism; and among the masses, a falling back into superstition and a renewed interest in magic. Various new and very un-Greek orgiastic cults were being imported from countries like Phrygia and Thrace. And Alexander's conquests had an effect on Greece like that of Renaissance sea voyages upon Western Europe.

Particular results were an increase of interest in the ancient East and better communications between Greeks and "barbarians." Some of the latter started visiting Greece not only to acquire culture, but to spread it. All this prepared the ground for the astrologer.

In 280 B.C. the Babylonian astrologer Berosus set up a school in the Greek island of Cos. And in the second century B.C., a number of popular manuals— especially one supposedly composed by an imaginary pharaoh, the *Revelations*

Left, the Greek fertility god (and god of wine) Dionysus, depicted with two followers on a sixth-century B.C. vase. The orgiastic cults associated with the worship of Dionysus were one expression of the "irrationalism" of ancient Greece, which made way for astrology's comeback around 200 B.C. Such cults were not confined to Greece: Right, a second-century A.D. Roman statue of Cybele, a fertility goddess of Phrygian origin.

of Nechepso and Petosiris—began to circulate widely. Practicing astrologers appeared as far afield as Rome. Chaldean astrology became the vogue.

One more reason might be suggested for the Greeks' embracing astrology. For some centuries these rationalist people had been intellectually free, their own masters. Perhaps the responsibility became too heavy—and so they preferred to give up their self-rule and place themselves in the hands of an astrological Fate.

But astrology among the Greeks (as, later, among the Romans) turned into something different from what it had been in Babylon. These younger and more individualistic peoples asked the stars not only about the nation or its rulers, but about each man's personal destiny. Astrology became primarily *genethliacal*—which, of course, is a Greek word. The long queue for horoscopes had started.

Rome and the stars

The Romans, though in many ways a practical and hard-headed race, were superstitious from the start, always fussing over omens of thunder or intestines or the flight of birds. This tendency, plus the influence of Greek culture and thought, opened the floodgates to astrology. For the more cultured Romans of the Republic, the new form of divination made more sense (and implied a wider view of the universe) than their own traditional forms.

But astrology appealed to the masses as well. One of the first Roman mentions of the subject was an objection (by the third-century B.C. poet Ennius) to various vulgar quacks, including *"de circo astrologos"*—which means not astrologers who perform in the circus but those who hang around the circus grounds. Ennius's remark, of course, shows that astrology didn't appeal to everyone. Many of the great men of the Roman Republic opposed it. In the second century B.C., the Elder Cato warned farmers not to go consulting "Chaldeans." And in the first century B.C. a sustained attack on astrology was launched by that versatile character Marcus Tullius Cicero.

In this last chaotic period of the Republic the Romans were taking to horoscopes as if they were drugs. They seemed only too willing to swap their uneasy (if not illusory) political freedom for a tyranny that offered peace and quiet. Cicero, however, fought to forestall the break-up of his traditional world. His efforts included writing the *De Divinatione,* an attack on all forms of divination including astrology. "Superstition," he wrote, " . . . has usurped nearly everyone's wits and scored over human silliness."

But Cicero's opposition was in vain against the prevailing mood of the early Empire, reflected by the poet Manilius's statement : "The world is ruled by Fate ; there are fixed laws for everything." These words are appropriate to the reign of Augustus. Whatever was the case before, the stars were now running on time.

By the second century A.D., the horoscopic "science" was fully developed. Most of the astrological lore of preceding centuries was gathered together in Claudius Ptolemy's *Tetrabiblos,* which has been described as "the world's greatest astrological textbook." Ptolemy was concerned with the "celestial bodies" not

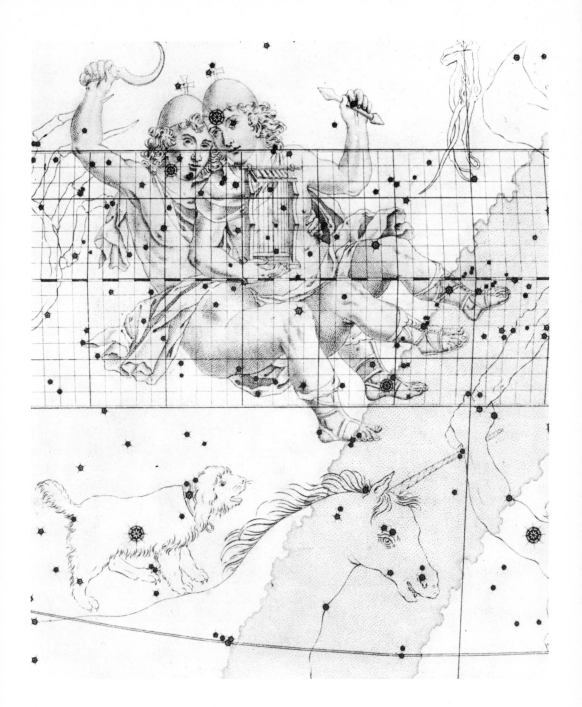

The ancient Greek personification of Gemini
(from an 18th-century star map). The Greeks
took their mythology into the skies by
identifying constellations with gods and
heroes. Gemini was seen as the twin
gods Castor and Pollux.

ETVS.OPINIO.EST.IAM VSQVEAB.HE
rotes ducla temporibus eaq; & p. r. & omnium
gentium firmata confensu uersari quandam in
ter homines diuinationem quam graeci inanti
cen appellant. id est presensionem & scientiam
rerum futurarum. magnifica quaedam res & salu
taris si modo est ulla . quaeq; proxima ad deorú
uim natura mortali possit accedere . Itaq; ut alia nos melius multa
q̃ graeci sic huic prestantissime rei nomen nostri a diuis graeci ut
plato interpretatur a furore duxerunt. Gentem quidem nullam ui
deo neq; tam humanam atq; doctam neq; tam imanem tamq; bar
barám quae non significari futura & a quibusdam intelligi predicíq;
posse censeat. Frincipio assiri ut ab ultimis auctoritatem repetam
propter planiciem magnitudinemq; regionum quas incolebant cü
caelum ex omni parte patens atq; apertum intuerentur traiecho
nes motusq; stellarum observauerunt . quibus notatis quid cuiq;
significaretur memoriae prodiderunt . qua in natione chaldei nõ
ex arte sed ex genus uocabulo nominati diuturna obseruatione si
derum scientiam putarentur effecisse . ut predici posse . quid cuiq; cõ
turum & quo quisq; fato natus esset. Eandem artem etiam egyptii lõ
ginquitate temporum innumerabilibus pene seculis consecuti pu

Left, a page from a 15th-century manuscript of Cicero's *De Divinatione* (which was written about 44 B.C.). Astrology was only one of the forms of divination that the Romans used (and that Cicero attacked). Below, a second-century A.D. bas relief of another popular form—seeking auguries from the entrails of a bull. Other societies before Rome practiced entrail divination : Right, a head imitating intestines, used for fortune telling in seventh-century B.C. Babylon. Far right, a fourth-century B.C. Etruscan mirror case depicting entrail divining. And oracles as well as entrails gave views of the future : Below right, a fifth-century B.C. Greek bowl showing King Aegeus of Athens consulting the oracle at Delphi.

only as astrologer but as astronomer. It was Ptolemy who invented what Arthur Koestler has called "the ferris-wheel universe," a cumbrous affair that, though accepted by everyone down to the time of Copernicus, was laughed at by Milton in *Paradise Lost*:

> *With centric and eccentric scribbled o'er,*
> *Cycle and epicycle, orb in orb.*

Ptolemy's assertion of the value of astrology (or, more precisely, of the value of knowing your future) is double: On the one hand, foreknowledge can reconcile you to your fate; on the other, once you know the dangers to which you are predisposed, the better equipped you are to avoid them. You can take precautions against your own temperament just as against bad weather.

The Greeks seem to have been the first to combine astrology with the doctrine of the four elements (fire, air, earth, and water) or the four basic qualities (hot, cold, dry, and moist). Ptolemy writes: "The ancients accepted two of the planets, Jupiter and Venus, together with the Moon, as beneficent because . . . they abound in the hot and the moist, and Saturn and Mars as producing effects of the opposite nature, one because of his excessive cold and the other for his excessive dryness . · . . ." He applies the same treatment to the signs of the Zodiac: Leo and Cancer are warmest; Capricorn and Aquarius, which are opposite to them, are "cold and wintry" signs.

Ptolemy, in his discussion of genethliacal astrology, is not a little shifty on the subject of "starting points." In general astrology, "we have to take many starting points, since we have no single one for the universe"; but with individuals "we have both one and many starting points." Having rashly conceded that the best would be the moment of conception, he hurries on (since hardly anyone knows his father all that well) to claim that the moment of birth is good enough. (This conception-birth dilemma still worries modern astrologers. But we might add that, long before Ptolemy's time, the authors of the *Revelations of Nechepso and Petosiris* had got around it by assuming that the sign the Moon was in at your conception will be in the ascendant at your nativity.)

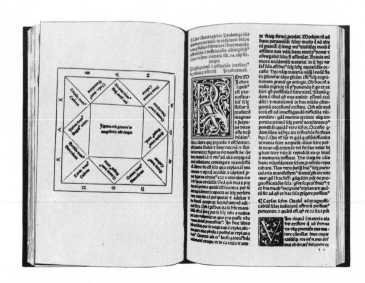

Left, a horoscope from the earliest printed edition (produced in Venice in 1482) of the *Tetrabiblos*, Ptolemy's vast compilation of astrological information. Above, an illustration (from an atlas printed in Amsterdam in 1661) of the Ptolemaic universe—the rigid geocentric system that remained unchallenged for over 1000 years. Around the earth rotate the seven planets (*septem orbes planetarum*), each depicted as a god driving a chariot. Each planet's hieroglyph is indicated on its orbit. Beyond the planets is the sphere of the fixed stars, marked with the signs of the Zodiac and their symbols.

By Ptolemy's time, astrology had triumphed throughout the Roman Empire, the emperors themselves often leading the way. The early emperors may have kept their tame astrologers for the same reason that many too powerful men have done since—simply because their high position gave them little sense of security. The young Augustus, though a hardheaded and calculating person, was so impressed by the glorious future foretold to him (by an astrologer named Theagenes) that he published his horoscope and struck a silver coin stamped with Capricorn, the sign under which he was born. Tiberius had a favorite astrologer called Thrasyllus (another Greek name; under the Empire the Greeks in Italy made corners in whatever needed wits). The crazy Caligula was said to have been warned of his impending death by a *mathematicus*—i.e., astrologer—called Sulla.

In A.D. 52, under the next emperor, Claudius, the astrologers were expelled from Rome. (The historian Tacitus called the decree "ruthless but ineffectual," adding that nearly everyone at the time believed that each individual's future is predetermined from birth.) But Nero returned to the old ways and consulted astrologers. He was told by some of them that if he had to leave Rome, he would find another throne in the East; one or two even specified the throne of Jerusalem.

Not only the emperors turned to the stars. Even in a thesis on architecture, there is a passage that implies that astrology was common knowledge—and practice. When drawing the ground-plan of a theatre, the thesis says, the best procedure is to inscribe four equilateral triangles in a circle "as the astrologers do, in a figure of the 12 signs of the Zodiac, when they are making computations of the musical harmony of the stars."

Right, the ruins of a Roman theatre (about A.D. 30) near Arles in France. Above, a plan of the theatre, based on the astrological method of drawing four equilateral triangles to form the circular figure of the 12 signs of the Zodiac.

Left, a coin minted about 19 B.C. in Spain (then part of the Roman Empire) during the reign of Augustus. The coin shows the emperor's birth sign, Capricorn, operating a rudder attached to the world globe (symbolizing Rome's rule over the world).

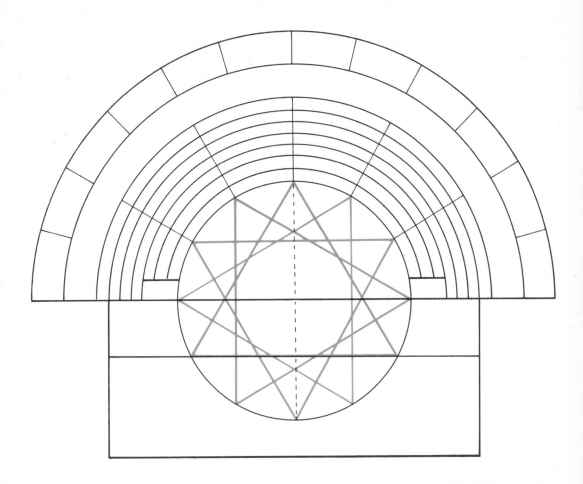

An engraving of Trimalchio's feast, from
an 18th-century Dutch edition of Petronius's
Satyricon. According to Petronius, the food
merely symbolized the Zodiac (beef for the
Bull, etc.). Here the artist has depicted
each dish in the *shape* of a Zodiac sign.

The establishment of astrology in Rome comes in for its share of mockery in the *Satyricon,* a picaresque novel by Petronius, part of which describes a vulgar and fantastic banquet given by a vulgar and fantastic "self-made man" named Trimalchio. This provincial freedman (freedmen, or emancipated slaves, had become very prominent at this time from court circles downward) displays his "culture" by serving a plate of titbits representing the signs of the Zodiac—beef for the Bull, kidneys for the Twins, a barren sow's paunch for Virgo.

Later, Trimalchio expounds the Zodiac as follows: The heaven in which the 12 gods live turns into an equal number of figures—the Ram and the rest. So anyone born under the Ram has plenty of flocks and wool and a hard head into the bargain. And so on. He himself was born under the Crab: "So I have many legs to stand on." Trimalchio also assigns butchers and perfumers to Libra, poisoners to Scorpio, cross-eyed men to Sagittarius, innkeepers and men with water on the brain to Aquarius, and to Pisces chefs and rhetoricians. "And so," he concludes, "the world turns like a mill, always bringing some misfortune, so that men are either born or die."

In A.D. 77 (nine years after Nero's death) there appeared a massive work that was to have a great influence on the Middle Ages: the *Natural History* of Pliny the Elder. This book begins with the stars. Pliny says in his first sentence that it is right to believe that there is something divine in the world and in the sky. There is no one, he says, who does not want to know his own future and who does not think this is shown most clearly by the heavens. This remark clearly indicates the mental climate of the day.

But a generation later this climate apparently didn't suit the gloomy satirical poet Juvenal. In his longest satire, an attack upon the female sex, Juvenal finds one of the gravest faults of women to be their susceptibility to oriental cults—and to astrology.

> *And Mankind, ignorant of future Fate,*
> *Believes what fond Astrologers relate.*

A woman, says Juvenal (as translated by John Dryden), will consult an astrologer for the most abominable reasons:

> *From him your Wife enquires the Planets' Will,*
> *When the black Jaundice shall her Mother kill:*
> *Her Sister's and her Uncle's end would know;*
> *But, first, consults his Art, when* you *shall go.*

Juvenal's attack on oriental cults stemmed from his general hatred of all things foreign. By his time, of course, Rome was thoroughly cosmopolitan. The Roman Empire, an astonishing conglomeration of countries and races, was geographically more unified and socially more standardized than the British Empire ever was. In literature and the arts, Greece had taken her captor captive long before the Roman Republic came to an end. And by the time of the emperors, the Asian provinces of the Empire were also exerting a powerful influence over their mistress.

From Egypt (which had been annexed in 30 B.C.) came that peculiar bundle of mystery, the cult of "Hermes Trismegistus" (Thrice Greatest Hermes), with which astrology was closely linked. The name "Hermes" is Greek of the brightest water; but the voice is a dark voice, linking primitive and medieval man, the witch doctor's medicine and the old wives' tale. Hermes was not, of course, a real person. Like Nechepso and Petosiris, he was literally a name to conjure with.

The Hermetic literary corpus consists of 17 or 18 fragments (it was once believed that Hermes wrote more than 20,000 books); but this is quite enough to show the appeal of these esoteric doctrines. According to Hermes, there are seven human types, corresponding to the seven planets, and the 12 signs of the Zodiac govern different parts of the human body. This is the notion of the Zodiacal Man, mentioned earlier and still current today. It is based on that ever-recurring concept of *correspondences*. Hermes writes:

"The macrocosm has animals, terrestrial and aquatic; in the same way, man has fleas, lice, and tapeworms. The macrocosm has rivers, springs, and seas; man has intestines. The macrocosm contains breaths (the winds) springing from its bosom; man has flatulence. The macrocosm has Sun and Moon; man has two eyes, the right related to the Sun, the left to the Moon. . . . The macrocosm has the 12 signs of the Zodiac; man contains them too, from his head, namely from the Ram, to his feet, which correspond to the Fish."

This general principle of correspondence, which may well go back to the days of the pharaohs, became greatly elaborated in the Hermetic scriptures. In particular, the authors of these works went in for medical astrology. Different ailments were assigned to the various signs of the Zodiac or their subdivisions, the decanates. (A sign can be divided into three decanates of 10° each.) Stomach troubles belong to the first decanate of Virgo, lung troubles to Cancer's second, while gout falls under both Aquarius and Pisces. As in most forms of astrology, these Zodiacal influences have to be correlated with those of the planets. The ears, for example, are ruled by Saturn, the brain by Jupiter.

The correspondences were extended to include, among other things, stones (certain stones are in "sympathy" with certain decanates, and help to effect a cure if the image of the decan is engraved on the stone and worn as a ring). Plants and herbs play an important role: The peony, for instance, is medically useful for anointing, for plasters, and for fumigation, and is otherwise helpful in business affairs. The directions for the peony's use are detailed: You must look for it when the Moon is waning, you can start operations when the Sun has

An illustration of the "Zodiac man" from a 14th-century German astrological manuscript. The figure shows the correlation of the signs of the Zodiac with parts of the human body. Man is ruled by the stars from his head (by the Ram) to his feet (by the Fish)—one example of the constantly recurring idea of "sympathy."

entered Virgo, you must be in an open place, and you must come equipped with a properly consecrated piece of seal skin. On this skin you must draw certain magic signs, then fix it around the root of the peony with genuine raw silk, uttering at the same time a long repetitive prayer, followed by incantatory words in Chaldean, Syriac, and Persian.

A further system of correspondences includes the individual fixed stars. The theme is the quadruple relationship of star, stone, plant, and talisman (or magic image). The talisman is to be engraved on the proper stone, under which the plant is inserted. Some examples of these correspondences are the following (the names in the text being usually the Arabian ones):

Aldebaran—ruby—spurge—a god or man fighting; Alhaioth (Rigel)—sapphire—horehound—a man about to amuse himself with chamber music; Alhabor (Sirius)—beryl—a kind of juniper—a hare, or a pretty young girl; Regulus—garnet—celandine—a cat or a lion, or a seated dignitary; Alchimech Abrameth (Arcturus)—jasper—plantain—a man dancing or playing, or a horse, or a wolf.

Many of the Hermetic prescriptions are primarily medical; but many more are obviously magical. Magic (in the form of incantations, talismans, etc.) had been in use medically and otherwise long before the Hermetic writings got to Rome. What is new here is the adulteration of astrology with such practices. But perhaps this was inevitable once astrologers, instead of confining themselves to foretelling things, set themselves up as healers.

Enter certain Christians

Certain facts about the second century A.D. clearly differentiate it from the pre-ceding century. Where there had been a series of bad emperors, there came a series of good emperors, culminating in the philosopher-ruler Marcus Aurelius (A.D. 161-80). Yet in this same period Rome for the first time had seriously to contend with two of the chief disruptive forces that were to undermine her—the barbarians outside and the Christians inside.

Marcus Aurelius fought the former and persecuted the latter, and managed to stave off both of them temporarily. But neither the Danube in the one case nor traditional Roman culture in the other proved a strong enough bulwark. And where the traditional culture failed, so also did the modern eclectic culture that included the oriental cults and astrology.

At the same time that Ptolemy was summarizing the astrological knowledge that had been accumulating for centuries, counter-attacks on these beliefs were being prepared in various quarters, both pagan and Christian. The most im-portant (because most passionate) of these attacks came from the Christian "apologists" who were then finding their voices. And powerful voices they were. Most of their apologies for Christianity were just as much attacks on pagan doctrines, or else were angry replies to people who denounced Christ as a magician. Usually, the Christians simply turned the tables on their attackers, rejecting necromancy, oracles, liver divination, augury, and astrology, *all* as being inventions of demons.

With most of these Christian writers, their indignant replies to the charge of practicing magic fail to show a return to the rational tone and the clear light of the older Greek tradition. Instead, they anticipate the sin-ridden and fear-ridden world of the Middle Ages. The Christians were not opposed to astrology because it was unscientific, but because it was immoral. They tended to think that science was immoral too.

Not all the Christians as yet were completely opposed to astrology. Many of them, for instance, seem to have accepted the Star of the Nativity as evidence of astrological truth. And the strange apocryphal work known as the *Clementine Recognitions* describes astrology as "the science of mathesis" (the Greek word has the general meaning of the acquisition of knowledge). Abraham, according to the *Recognitions,* "being an astrologer, was able from the rational

Both a first-century A.D. Roman statue of the god Pan (right, teaching a youth to play the pipes) and a 16th-century Swiss drawing of a devil (above) have cloven hoofs and horns. To many early Christians, pagan gods were "demons," and pagan thought (including astrology) the product of demons.

system of the stars to recognize the Creator, while all other men were in error . . . ."

The astrological arguments (and the broader philosophical and theological ones) continued to rage, and gradually the Christians appeared to be winning the day. But paganism did not give up so easily. In the third century, many of the emperors were mystics and Asianizers. Heliogabalus (who became emperor in A.D. 218) took his name from the Syrian Sun-god, who was worshiped in Syria in the form of a conical black stone. This stone was transported to Rome (as Gibbon describes it) "in a solemn procession through the streets of Rome, the way . . . strewed with gold dust; the black stone, set in precious gems, was placed on a chariot drawn by six milk-white horses richly caparisoned . . . ."

Sun worship is not of course to be identified with astrology, but it satisfied some of the same needs. And there is no doubt that some astrologers were Sun worshipers; after all, as astrology developed, the Sun had become increasingly dominant in the heavens. (In early Christian art, Christ is often depicted with some of the attributes of a Sun-god; even as the good shepherd, while he has the lamb on his shoulder, he wears the seven planets around his head.) The later emperor Aurelian (A.D. 270-275) followed Heliogabalus in one respect: He imported an image of the Sun from the East and made Sol Invictus the supreme god in his capital.

The old Roman gods had long ceased to satisfy anyone except the uneducated or simpleminded; the Sun-god from the East fulfilled a spiritual need, and at least was a magnificent symbol. But there was another new god who could beat him on his own ground—or should we say in his own sky?—and fulfill yet more of people's needs.

The last serious persecution of the Christians took place under the emperor Diocletian in A.D. 303. Ten years later, the Edict of Milan assured freedom of worship to men of every religion. Ten years later again, Constantine became sole emperor. Christianity had triumphed; the old pagan gods of Greece and Rome and the comparatively new gods from the East were to fall alike under a shadow, and so were astrology and other "demonic" practices. At the end of the fourth century, the militant Christian fathers came in for the kill: St. Gregory of Nyssa; St. John Chrysostom; St. Ambrose; St. Basil; and especially St. Augustine.

Augustine had an enormous influence on the development of Christianity— which means that he was one of the main founders of the world we live in. It is well known that this scourge of sinners had once cried out: "Lord, make me chaste, but not yet!" It is almost equally striking that this scourge of astrologers (his arguments against them were the best known in the Middle Ages) had as a young man consulted them himself—thereby, as he later put it, sacrificing himself to demons. In his *Confessions* he explains that he was weaned from astrology not by argument but by hearing that a certain wealthy landowner had been born at precisely the same moment as a wretched slave on his estate.

The earliest known portrait of St. Augustine
from a sixth-century Roman fresco. Greatest
of the Fathers of the Western Church, he
attacked astrology on several counts, but
mainly on the ground that its claim to
influence human destiny challenged the
supremacy of God. His arguments dis-
credited astrology for four centuries.

In one of his letters Augustine writes that it is better to reject the errors of the astrologers "than to be forced to condemn and repudiate the divine laws or even the supervision of our own households." An astrologer who sells his silly horoscopes (*fatua fata*) to well-off persons will nevertheless "reprove his wife and even beat her—I won't say if he catches her being improperly playful, but even if she stares too long through the window." But supposing the wife were to say: "Why are you beating *me?* Beat Venus if you can; it's *she* who makes me behave like this." In other words, Augustine is saying, if you throw responsibility for your own actions on Fate, you must be consistent when dealing with other people.

Rome fell in A.D. 410. Augustine's main attack on astrology comes in his last and longest work, *The City of God,* which he wrote after that event and which indeed was inspired by it. Book Five of this work begins, once more, with an attack on the concept of Fate: "Those who hold that stars manage our actions or our passions, good or ill, without God's appointment, are to be silenced and not to be heard . . . for what doth this opinion but flatly exclude all deity?"

Augustine grants that astrological predictions sometimes prove correct. But he ascribes their correctness to "evil spirits (whose care it is to infect . . . and confirm men's minds in this false dangerous opinion of Fate in the stars) and not by any art of discerning of the Horoscope, for such is there none."

For such is there none! Augustine was a doctor of the Church and his words were all but law. What had not been accomplished by arguments was now at last achieved by a gesture of authority. The astrologers were put in their place—outside the pale.

For all that, even in the period of Augustine, astrology had its apologists. The famous Synesius of Cyrene, who began as a country gentleman and ended as a bishop in Alexandria, maintained that astrology can prepare one for the nobler science of theology. He stressed, like so many before him, that the universe is a whole in which the parts are bound together by *sympathy.* (Synesius is also said to have written on alchemy, which again of course is ruled by the principle of sympathy.) One of the reasons he gives for accepting astrology is that history repeats itself because the stars return to their former positions. It is surprising that an early Christian could accept this cyclic view of history; but then the concept has appealed to a certain kind of intellectual (W. B. Yeats for one) down to our own times.

Earlier in the fourth century, there was an aristocratic Roman intellectual— and Christian—who wrote a massive defense of astrology that is still today regarded as an astrological classic. This writer, Julius Firmicus Maternus, held that because the astrologer mediates between human souls and celestial beings, he must lead a pure and austere life. The human soul itself is a spark of that divine mind that exerts its influence through the stars. Therefore astrology is a useful and elevated pursuit; its truth, Firmicus believes (as do its latter-day champions), can be tested experimentally.

Aside from Firmicus, there were some less well known (and less intellectual) writers who appear to be looking backward, but who in fact would have been very much at home in Europe a thousand years later. Solinus (date uncertain but possibly fourth century), wrote a hotchpotch geography that was much used in the Middle Ages and was interested in occult medicine. He sometimes refers to the "discipline of the stars," and repeats from earlier writers a description of the horoscope of the city of Rome itself. This retrospective horoscope apparently revealed that Rome's first foundation stone was laid by Romulus on the 11th day of the Kalends of May between the second and third hours when Jupiter was in Pisces, the Sun in Taurus, the Moon in Libra, and the other four planets in Scorpio.

Horapollo, another diehard (fourth or fifth century), wrote a book called *Hieroglyphics*, to explain the hieroglyphics or written symbols of the ancient Egyptian priests. It is largely concerned with the marvelous behavior of animals (or the behavior of marvelous animals); but what is relevant to our subject is its astrological allusions.

According to Horapollo, the scarab or sacred beetle, so often represented in Egyptian art, rolls its ball of dung from east to west to simulate the Sun and imposes on it the perfect (i.e., spherical) shape of the world. Also, it buries the dung ball for 28 days conformably to the course of the Moon but, to square this with the number of days in the month, is equipped with 30 toes. Another rightly sacred animal is the baboon, who is born circumcised and neither sees nor eats during lunar eclipses. He is understandably kept in the temple, since at the equinoxes he makes water 12 times by day and 12 times by night exactly on the hour; this is why the Egyptians engraved him on practically all of their water clocks.

Pliny, in his *Natural History,* three to four centuries earlier, had been not at all averse to marvels, yet Horapollo belongs to a different world. Though both his astrology and frivolous garrulity would have been frowned upon by the Christian Fathers, his complete lack both of sophistication and of a scientific spirit parallels the Christian mentality that accepted both miracles and demons —a mentality that, combined with the overrunning of Western Europe by the barbarians, among other factors, allowed the so-called Dark Ages to slide over most of Europe.

What happened to astrology in this obscure era? Perhaps to all intents and purposes it vanished. But it is more likely that it continued to flourish (though driven underground) in spite of the Church's disapproval. When we remember how long witches enjoyed a vogue against all the odds, we may guess that astrologers could still get their fees, at least from the less sophisticated or less devout persons. What is an established fact is that astrology eventually made a comeback and was welcomed by the Church herself. But that was some centuries after the fall of Rome, and ahead of our story. Let us go on from where the ancient world left off.

5 The stars on top

In sixth-century Western Europe, most thinkers rejected pagan philosophy, except for its most mystical or anti-scientific branches. So far as the natural sciences were bothered with at all, the attempt to squeeze them into a Christian framework outweighed both observation and reason. Long obsolete cosmologies were revived: A monk named Cosmas attacked the belief that the universe is spherical and claimed instead that it is shaped like the Holy Tabernacle as described in the Book of Exodus. But a spherical heaven is required by astrology; so here a Christian writer shows himself less scientific than the people he condemns for superstition or magical practices.

We have now arrived at the "Dark Ages," or early Middle Ages. A hundred years ago, historians could assume that there were clearly definable borders between one "age" and another. But today, most people tend to think of these "ages" as shading or cross-fading into each other. Old concepts refuse to drop out, while new ones often jump the gun. All the same, after the sixth century, astrological writings in Western Europe were extremely scarce for 400 years. Meanwhile, of course, Byzantium remained civilized, while, far to the west, there was a high degree of culture in Ireland. But for astronomy-astrology we have to wait till the ninth century and then look east to Baghdad.

In that city of Arabian Nights, astronomy and astrology (still playing Siamese twins) regained some of their ancient glory under the patronage of caliphs

Two extracts from a 15th-century fresco illustrating the months of the year, painted by the Italian artist Francesco del Cossa for the Duke of Ferrara. Above, March is represented by the figure of a girl (a personification of spring) over Aries the Ram; below, April is depicted as a man holding the key of spring, seated above Taurus the Bull. The fresco was designed by the duke's court astrologer—a reminder that astrology was in its heyday during the Middle Ages and Renaissance.

like the famous Harun al-Rashid. An observatory (sure proof that these studies were serious) was built in Baghdad, and was used by astrologers like Albumasar, whose book on astrology was one of the first to see print after the invention of the printing press. These protégés of the caliphate, like their predecessors long before in the same part of the world, were also great observers and measurers, as well as makers of astronomical instruments.

In the 10th century the caliphate declined, and by the year 1000 Islamic culture had had its day in Baghdad. It was, however, to flourish for two more centuries in Spain (where an Arabian astronomer published a famous astronomical calendar known as the Toledo Tables), from which country the heritage of paganism was to flow into the rest of Western Europe. By the year 1000 the West was beginning to stir, in astrology as in other things. The 10th century ended with the all-round scholar Gerbert enthroned in Rome as Pope Sylvester.

Though the legend quickly grew that this pope was a magician, in fact he was an intellectual pioneer. At the turn of the millenium, under the aegis of Gerbert, Cosmas's conception of the universe as a tabernacle went out and the spherical universe came in again. The Earth once more sat in the center of things, surrounded by nine concentric spheres—the seven spheres of the planets, that of the fixed stars, and Aristotle's Primum Mobile. This was to become the orthodox medieval picture of the universe. It was wrong, but it was a great advance—or recovery.

In the 11th century, astrology and its peripheral practices were in the air again. There were "Moon books" in circulation and "spheres of life and death" and spheres of "Petosiris" or "Apuleius" and lists of "Egyptian [i.e., unlucky]

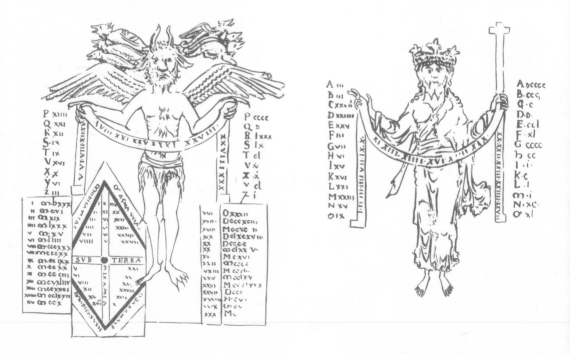

days" (about 40 or 50 of them in the year). And by the 12th century, astrology had become thoroughly re-established as a subject of serious study.

The views about astrology of the clerical intelligentsia varied, but they all were concerned with it, and with relating it to other branches of learning. An anonymous 12th-century manuscript, for instance, connects different religions with different planets. Judaism is allotted to Saturn, as it had been by the Roman historian Tacitus. Islam, being a religion both sensual and warlike, falls under both Venus and Mars; its holy day is Friday because that is Venus's day. Christianity under the Roman Empire was related both to the Sun (which stands for honesty, liberality, and victory) and to Jupiter (which stands for peace, equity, and humanity). It is noted by the 12th-century writer that neither Mars nor Saturn is ever in a friendly relationship with Jupiter. Later, the Christian religion became assigned to Mercury; according to Roger Bacon in the 13th century, Mercury's difficult orbit corresponds to the Christian mysteries. Also, Mercury is dominant only when in Virgo, which in this context could be equated with the Virgin Mary.

Astrology by this time covered all fields, from the sublime to the ridiculous: "William of England," who apparently was a citizen of Marseilles, wrote a treatise called *De Urina non Visa* (Of Urine Unseen), explaining "how by astrology to diagnose a case and tell the color and substance of the urine without seeing it."

At this time some astrologers divided their subject into eight branches: the science of judgments (i.e., judicial astrology); medicine; "nigromancy"; agriculture; illusions, or magic; alchemy; the science of images; and the science of

Left, the "sphere of Apuleius" (from an English prayer book written about 970), probably used to predict whether a sick man would live or die. The two figures symbolize life and death. The fate of the sufferer was determined by adding the numbers corresponding to the day of the week and the month to the numbers set against the letters of the sick man's name, and dividing the total by 30. If the result fell below the line marked *sub terra* (underground) the man would die; if above, he would live.

Taking dips into the future still fascinates people today, whatever the method. For instance, in *The Ladies' Oracle* (right), published in Britain in 1962, the reader chooses one of 100 questions about the future, picks a symbol from a chart with her eyes shut, and relates the two to get her answer. Sample question: Shall I be loved long? Answer: As long as you deserve.

THE LADIES' ORACLE by Cornelius Agrippa

mirrors. The inclusion of nigromancy (necromancy) and "illusions" was the cause of astrology's bad name in certain quarters, while it is interesting that alchemy should be treated as a branch of astrology instead of as a parallel science. The mysterious "science of mirrors" was divination by means of polished or reflecting surfaces rubbed with oil, usually in accordance with the astrological hours. Though to a modern reader this practice might seem nearer to optics than to astrology, it provides further proof of some kind of association in the Middle Ages of the natural sciences with the "sciences" of astrology, magic, and fortune telling in general.

In an attempt to find a rational basis for astrology, various spurious works were attributed to Aristotle (who was acquiring an authority almost equal to Holy Writ). Thus we have "the book of Aristotle from 255 volumes of the Indians, containing a digest of all problems, whether pertaining to the sphere or genethlialogy." Aristotle's name (this would have puzzled him) was being linked with that of Hermes. Also attributed to him was a work called *The Secret of Secrets*, which was very popular in the Middle Ages and contained plenty of astrological lore, correlated (in the manner described in Chapter 4) with the virtues of herbs and stones.

Before leaving this century of revivals, we may note that in 1186 the much trusted Toledo Tables foretold a conjunction of the seven planets in Libra, which was bound to cause terrible disasters including hurricanes. The conjunction occurred—but not the hurricanes (unless they took place in some unknown part of the world, like Florida).

In the 13th century the astrological pace became even hotter. In England the center of learning was the new university of Oxford. Learning, of course, included astronomy, and astronomy included astrology. The first recorded chancellor of the university, Robert Grosseteste, accepted astronomy-astrology as the supreme science and held that hardly any human activity, whether it were the planting of vegetables or the practicing of alchemy, could dispense with the astrologer's advice.

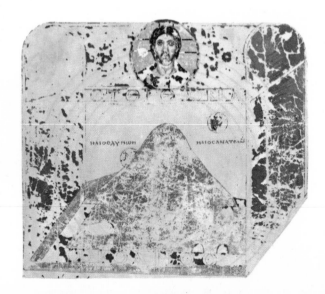

Above, an early 18th-century engraving of Catherine de Médicis (queen of France 1547-89) consulting a magician—possibly the prophet-astrologer Nostradamus. The magician (standing in a magic circle of astrological signs) reveals to the queen in a mirror the faces of future rulers of France—an example of prediction by the "science of mirrors."

Left, a ninth-century copy of a sixth-century world map by the Alexandrian monk Cosmas. The Creator presides over the world within a universe shaped like the Holy Tabernacle in the Book of Exodus. This concept of the universe was widespread in the Dark Ages, though the spherical universe came back into favor about 1000.

His pupil, Roger Bacon (who was suspected in his own time of practicing magic, which in fact he condemned), distinguished two kinds of "mathematics," one being magic and the other legitimate judicial astrology. Bacon believed in "elections" (i.e., using astrology to choose the right hour to do something) and also in astrological images and astrological medicine. This last, for Bacon, explained the remarkable case of "the woman of Norwich," who ate nothing for 20 years but retained her health. Also, as a good Franciscan friar, he welcomed the astrological prediction that Islam would endure, from its beginning, for only 693 years. This figure, he says, agrees with the famous "Number of the Beast" in the Apocalypse, which in fact (astrological license?) is 666. Whether the Moslem Era is dated from A.D. 610 or 622, this prediction meant that Islam should have ended near the beginning of the 14th century. Bacon himself died in 1296.

A great academic name on the continent was that of the Dominican Albertus Magnus, the master of Thomas Aquinas. Albertus was a typically medieval figure in that he combined very high intellectual powers with what (to us) seems a naïve credulity. He believed in the magical use of herbs; and he was probably the author of a popular work entitled *The Secrets of Women,* which included the astrological doctrine that a child receives its various qualities from the different heavenly spheres. Also, according to this work, each planet has control for one month over the child in the womb. And it is the constellations that account for monstrous births.

It was Albertus's pupil St. Thomas Aquinas who imposed *system* upon the body of existing knowledge in the Middle Ages, and thereby imposed a "Thomist" world-view upon Western Christendom. Even he allows that the stars have some influence: They serve as media between "the separate intelligences" (such as angels) and our material world. God rules inferior creatures through superior creatures, and so rules our earthly *bodies* through the stars. But Aquinas leaves room for free will, as did the poet Dante, whose whole *Divine Comedy* presupposes a Thomist universe. There are several passages in the *Divine Comedy,* and elsewhere, acknowledging or implying the influence of the stars. In the "Paradiso," referring to the fact that he was born under Gemini, Dante writes (in the Temple Classics translation): "O stars of glory, O light impregnated with mighty power, from which I recognize all, whatso'er it be, my genius . . . ." A striking passage, which looks back to Augustine, is to be found in the "Purgatorio," Canto XVI, where Dante asks one of the suffering spirits about the causes of vice. The spirit replies: "The heavens set your impulses in motion; . . . but . . . a light is given you to know good and evil, and free will [*e libero voler*], which, if it endure the strain in its first battlings with the heavens, at length gains the whole victory. . . . Ye lie subject, in your freedom, to a greater power and to a better nature; and that creates in you mind [*la mente*], which the heavens have not in their charge. Therefore, if the world today goeth astray, in you is the cause, in you be it sought. . . ."

Above, two pages from the *Naturalia* (printed in Germany in 1548) by Albertus Magnus, one of the great 13th-century Dominican teachers. Albertus related the magical and medicinal properties of herbs to planetary and Zodiacal influences—another example of the idea of correspondences. Of the two plants shown here, the Martagon lily (left) is "in sympathy" with Saturn, who rules Capricorn and Aquarius, and chicory (right) is "in sympathy" with the Sun, who rules Leo.

Right, a 13th-century seal (probably made for Robert Grosseteste) depicting a chancellor of Oxford surrounded by scholars. Grosseteste was an ardent advocate of astrology, which was studied at Oxford as at most other medieval universities.

per del vecter Dinanti tra los torto.
Forse p forza gia Di parlasia.
si travolse cossi alchun del tutto.
ma io nol vidi ne credo che sia.
Se vio ti lasa lector prender frutto.
Di tua lectione or pensa p te stesso.
chomio potea tener il viso asciutto.
Quando la nostra vmagine Da presso.
vidi si torta chel pianto De gliocchi.
le natiche passava per lo fesso.

Above, an illustration from a 15th-century
Italian manuscript of Dante's "Inferno":
Dante (center, in blue) is led by his
guide Vergil to see the fortune tellers
in hell, whose heads are twisted so they
can only look backward. This is their
punishment for looking into the future
(which is the prerogative of God). Right,
a 15th-century portrayal of Guido Bonatti,
one of the most famous astrologers of the
13th century, who was among the sorcerers
consigned to hell by Dante. In spite of
the Church's opposition to his unorthodox
views, Bonatti escaped the long arm of
the Inquisition.

Thus man's "nature" (subject to the stars) is in opposition to a "better nature" (which must be referred to God). The fact that free will has to *battle* with the stars imputes a very great power to them; neither Dante nor Aquinas would have dreamed of denying this. Repeatedly quoted during this period was a Latin tag: *sapiens dominabitur astris*—the wise man will rule the stars. It was still being quoted in the 17th century, and no doubt was so popular just because people were so frightened. It was both a piece of "wishful thinking" and a gesture, though a cautious one, of defiance.

Among Dante's contemporaries and immediate successors, the huge wings of astrology gave shelter to all types of men, from truth-seeking philosophers to profit-seeking quacks, and to all types of opinion from the profound to the cranky. A 13th-century monk, Ristoro of Arezzo, believed that the northern part of the sky was the nobler and that *therefore* only the northern hemisphere was inhabited; he also was much interested in the horoscopes of horses. One Thomas of Cantimpré held that the brains of wolves and the livers of mice vary in size with the waxing and waning of the Moon. The *Franciscan Chronicles* (by a Franciscan friar named Salimbene) provide an engaging 13th-century example of an astrological quack (translated by G. G. Coulton):

"The Inner Party of Modena [in Northern Italy] had a man of Brescia who called himself an astrologer and diviner, to whom they gave daily ten great pennies of silver, and nightly three great Genoese candles of the purest wax, and he promised them that if they fought a third time they should have the victory. And they answered him: 'We will not fight on a Monday or a Tuesday, for we have been conquered on those two days. Choose us therefore another day; and know that if we gain not this time the promised victory, we will tear out thy remaining evil eye'; for he was one-eyed. So, fearing to be found out in his falsehood, he carried off all that he had gained, and went his way without saluting his hosts."

Italy seems during the Middle Ages to have been the leading country in astrology, which infiltrated not only into the Church but into the new universities. Thus in the school of medicine in Bologna in the 13th century the dictum quoted earlier ran: "A doctor without astrology is like an eye that cannot see." A century later Bologna had a chair of astrology.

Astrology was popular not only among men of learning in the Middle Ages. By the 13th century it had become firmly embedded in the everyday life of the people. The 19th-century Swiss historian Jacob Burckhardt writes: "In all the better families the horoscopes of the children were drawn as a matter of course, and it sometimes happened that for half a lifetime men were haunted by the idle expectation of events that never occurred." There were many instances of astrologers intervening in public affairs, such as the journeys of princes, the laying of foundation stones, or the management of military campaigns. One of the most famous astrologers of the 13th century, Guido Bonatti, assisted the Ghibelline leader Guido da Montefeltro to win a series of battles.

When the constellations were right for victory, Bonatti used to ascend a high church tower with his book and astrolabe and at the exact moment give the signal. The great bell was then rung and there was (presumably) victory.

In Bonatti's influential Latin book the *Liber Astronomicus* (he used the words astronomy and astrology interchangeably), he ranks the astronomer-astrologer above the physician, because human bodies are merely composed of the four elements with the four qualities, whereas the bodies studied by astrologers are composed of a fifth and incorruptible essence. The opposition that Bonatti's teachings met among the clergy was not surprising, seeing that he held that astrologers know more about the stars than theologians do about God. At the same time he reveals that many of the clergy in the 13th century consulted astrologers about their prospects of promotion (which is a good example of an "interrogation").

Bonatti himself claimed to believe that, if you are hesitating to accept an invitation to dinner, the astrologer can help you by predicting the menu. As regards "elections," he held that there was a favorable moment for almost every possible activity, including trimming one's nails. In the field of "revolutions," he thought astrologers could foretell which would be a good year for bishops, monarchs, or cucumbers.

Many other astrologers of the time got into serious difficulties with the Church—like the physician Arnald of Villanova, who wrote a treatise on *Judgments of Infirmities by the Movements of the Planets*. Though Arnald moved in high ecclesiastical circles, the Inquisition (whose attitude to astrology often appears ambiguous) declared some of his writings heretical. Another suspected heretic was Peter of Abano, also called Peter of Padua. Peter was a champion of astrological medicine and of images : He believed that a figure of a scorpion made when the Moon is leaving Scorpio will cure the bite of a scorpion. He also held that the revolution of the eighth sphere (that of the fixed stars), which, he reckoned moved one degree in 70 years, could even turn land into sea ; hence the disappearance of Atlantis.

Peter distributed history among the seven planets, each being in charge of 354 years plus four lunar months. Thus Sodom and Gomorrah were destroyed when the Moon was supreme. (Some modern astrologers carve history into much larger slices—of roughly 2000 years each—determined by the *constellations*.) The seven planets, according to Peter, are also associated with seven angels; Mercury is paired with Raphael, the Moon with Gabriel, and so on. What may have involved him with the Church authorities was his discussion of Christ's nativity : It was said that Christ was born when there was a great conjunction of Jupiter and Saturn in the beginning of the first degree of the sign of the Ram (which of course was the very beginning of the Zodiacal system).

The retrospective casting of the nativity of Christ was at this time commonly linked with the prospective casting of that of Antichrist, presumed to depend on a conjunction of Jupiter and the Moon. This also shocked the authorities. But

The original Royal Observatory at
Greenwich, which was built for the first
English Astronomer Royal John Flamsteed
Flamsteed is said to have chosen the date
for laying the foundation stone by means
of an astrological "election" (erecting a
horoscope to find a favorable time for a
particular project). The date selected
was August 10, 1675.

Peter weathered whatever storm there was. There is a statue to him in Padua, on which he is described as "in astrology indeed so skilled that he incurred suspicion of magic, and, falsely accused of heresy, was acquitted." Less fortunate was Cecco d'Ascoli, who had taught astrology at Bologna and had been court astrologer to the Duke of Florence. He was condemned by the Inquisition and burned at the stake in Florence in 1327; orders were also given to burn his Latin astrological book. One of Cecco's heresies seems to have been that he taught that Christ came to earth in accordance with the will of God *and* with the principles of astrology.

In spite of Cecco's fate (which was most untypical), astrology continued to flourish in the Middle Ages. Italian artists glorified it in frescoes like those in Padua and Ferrara, and in the 15th century those ruthless adventurers the Condottieri each had his own pet astrologer. And Lorenzo de' Medici allowed Marsilio Ficino of Florence to cast all the little Medicis' horoscopes.

Astrology also played a part in the literature of the period—as in the poetry of Geoffrey Chaucer, who was born about 20 years after Dante died and who died himself in 1400. Chaucer is a typical medieval figure. Although most of the astrological references in his *Canterbury Tales* would have been commonplace to his readers, his own astronomical-astrological knowledge was better than commonplace. He pretends modestly in one passage that he knows "no termes of astrology," but he found time and was interested enough to write a treatise on the astrolabe. In the Prologue to the *Canterbury Tales*, he has hardly begun describing his Doctor of Physic before he mentions, high in the list of credentials, the Doctor's astrological knowledge, which includes the use of images. Similarly, that earthy lady the Wife of Bath brings in the stars to explain her own distinctive temperament :

> *Venus me yaf my lust, my likerousnesse [lecherousness],*
> *And Mars yaf me my sturdy hardynesse;*
> *Myn ascendant was Taur and Mars therinne . . . .*

According to Britain's Ingrid Lind, writing today, "Taurus women are good-looking and have solid, well-made bodies [the Wife of Bath had a bold red face and large hips] with a good notion of what such bodies can produce in the way of agreeable sensation."

On the whole, Chaucer seems to have taken his astrology with a grain of salt. (He took plenty of salt, of course, in other spheres, being a typical English empiricist and good-humored iconoclast.) In his longest and most technical astrological passage, in "The Franklin's Tale," he speaks of an astrologer who is setting out "to maken his japes" (i.e., tricks) with his "supersticious cursednesse." Chaucer is obviously no admirer of this astrologer (or "magician"). A lovesick young Englishman has come to consult him, and the magician is about to calculate by astrology the right hour for contriving a monstrous illusion for his client's benefit. Here is some of the description of this operation (from Nevill Coghill's modernized version, for easier reading) :

Above, an engraving from an 18th-century
edition of Chaucer's *Canterbury Tales*,
showing the Wife of Bath as the center
of attraction. Though Chaucer was no
admirer of astrology, he often referred
to it : For example, the Wife of Bath
attributes her boldness and earthy vigor
to her ascendant sign, Taurus.
Right, a 19th-century astrologer's idea
of a Taurus woman, showing the heavy
features traditionally ascribed to people
influenced by this sign.

His calculating tables were brought out
Newly corrected, he made sure about
The years in series and the single years
To fix the points the planets in their spheres
Were due to reach . . . .
And finding the first mansion of the Moon,
He calculated all the rest in tune
With that. He worked proportionally, knowing
How she would rise and whither she was going
Relative to which planets and their place,
Equal or not, upon the Zodiac face.

Not long after this, in 15th-century France, we find an attack on astrology in the form of an allegory, *The Dream of the Old Pilgrim*, by Philippe de Mézières. The scene is a debate in Paris presided over by Queen Verity. An aged hag enters, wearing a robe embroidered with geometrical figures. She holds a book in one hand and an astrolabe in the other, and wears spectacles because she is nearly blind from stargazing. In her time, we learn, she has been in the employ of King Ptolemy of Egypt, Albumasar, and Neptanebus. Her name is Old Superstition.

Opposing her is a lady delegate from the university of Paris. She is only 18 years old, and wears a close-fitting green dress (which gets greener every moment) and a beautiful green hat with 12 flowers of a ravishing scent around the brim. In one hand she holds a flaming cross, in the other a compendium of theology. Her name is Bonne Foy; and, needless to say, she wins the debate.

Her argument rests on a basic distinction between the two kinds of astronomy (or, as we should now say, between astronomy and astrology). Old Superstition, though discomfited, sweeps off saying she will still find followers among both laity and clergy, not to mention royalty. Bonne Foy returns to the university.

Astrology did find followers elsewhere. Nearly two hundred years later, the Elizabethans still readily accepted the astrological mode. Even a man with such a reputation for free thinking as Sir Walter Raleigh was prepared to concede that there was something in astrology, although (like so many before him) he was careful to leave room for free will. And Raleigh, for all his inherited medieval concepts, was standing on the threshold of the world we know.

The planet Jupiter, with its Zodiac signs Pisces and Sagittarius, from a 15th-century Italian manuscript. The scenes depict three medieval occupations thought to be under Jupiter: An apothecary serves a customer; an alchemist sieves precious metals from sand; a mathematician is consulted by a client. Many astrological texts of the time were illustrated with traditional ideas of the planets and planetary "types."

The Renaissance

Newton's *Principia* was published in 1687. The two preceding centuries had been a period of constant, almost unprecedented intellectual ferment and discovery; yet through at least most of the period there are plentiful examples of diehard traditionalism and, even among the innovators, of an ingrained reluctance to go the whole way with themselves. The pioneers of modern astronomy were still hampered by medieval modes of thought. It was only with Newton that men's minds appear to have been finally freed from the medieval shackles (or, depending on your viewpoint, the medieval supports and underpinning).

This is where astrology comes in—or rather stayed in. In 1488 the prominent astrologer Johannes Lichtenberger wrote: "Attention must be paid to the weighty planets Jupiter and Saturn, whose conjunction and coincidence threaten terrible things and announce future calamities . . . and to this terrible conjunction the horrible house of the ill-fated Scorpion has been assigned." And a preface to another of Lichtenberger's books states: "The signs in heaven and in earth are surely not lacking; they are God's and the angels' work, and they warn and threaten the godless lands and countries and have significance." The author of this preface was Martin Luther.

Even while Luther was underwriting the astrologers, the Italian humanist Pico della Mirandola was preparing a massive assault on astrology. Over and over again, Pico makes one basic (and radical) distinction: between astrology and astronomy. This distinction was not observed by 15th-century astronomers like Regiomontanus—or, for that matter, by their more famous successors, such as Kepler. In the mid-15th century, Regiomontanus was an outstanding astronomical observer and inventor of instruments; but he also introduced the particular division of the sky into 12 houses that is used by many astrologers

An illustration from a work by the 15th-century German astrologer Johannes Lichtenberger, showing the "terrible conjunction" that, to Lichtenberger, meant calamity. The sign of Scorpio hovers over personifications of Saturn (right) and Jupiter (with Taurus).

today. To Pico, however, the astronomer (or the true philosopher) does not believe or affirm anything that cannot be demonstrated by evidence or by reason.

Pico also attacked astrology on the evidence of his own experience, this evidence consisting largely of disasters in his family. Astrologers had promised his brother-in-law a year completely free from danger or misfortune; he died in the course of it. The same thing happened to Pico's nephew-in-law and sister-in-law. The sister-in-law, in fact, while she clasped her husband's hand on her deathbed, had exclaimed: "Look! So much for the predictions of astrologers!" Her husband, on the other hand, had been promised every sort of misfortune and had survived the year unscathed.

At about the same time that Pico was preparing his attack (and when the young Copernicus was studying at Cracow University), an astrologer called Luc Gauric erected the horoscope of the young Giovanni de' Medici and predicted (correctly) that he would become pope. The Italian nobility were by then making a regular practice of employing astrologers. But this does not mean that the "royal" art was not also exceedingly popular among the common people. In the same year (1493) that Gauric made his prediction, a work was published in Paris that has been extensively quoted from in earlier chapters —*The Kalendar and Compost of Shepherds*. The art of printing was barely half a century old, and this was one of the very first books to be printed for the amusement and instruction of the ordinary literate man. It was widely popular and was reprinted in many cities of Europe.

Whoever was the author of this book put his lore into the mouths of shepherds (in accordance with an ancient literary tradition that made shepherds the repositories of wisdom). A good part of the wisdom in this "Compost" is, as we have seen, familiar astrological material. The author accepts the division of the sky into 12 houses (the House of Life, the House of Substance and Riches, and so on) and also the doctrine that each hour is ruled by one of the planets. He slips from prose into verse when he comes to the planets' qualities. To quote from a translation of about 1518:

> *For to know their natures all*
> *In sooth it is a great conning,*
> *And shows what may befall*
> *When every planet is reigning . . . .*
> *Saturn is highest and coldest, being full bad,*
> *And Mars with his bloody sword ever ready to kill;*
> *Jupiter very good, and Venus maketh lovers glad,*
> *Sol and Luna is half good and half ill . . . .*

Immediately preceding the astrological section of the book there is a section entitled "Of Physic and Governance of Health." The first part of this section is captioned: "How shepherds by calculation and speculating knoweth the twelve signs in their course reigning and dominating on the twelve parts of a man's body; and which be good for letting blood, and which be indifferent or

Alter Bauernkalender

evil for the same." There follows a chapter entitled "A picture of the physiognomy of man's body that showeth in what parts the seven planets hath domination in man." The chapter in fact *consists* of a picture. This was the kind of teaching that was most readily acceptable to people in general in the lifetime of Copernicus, the Polish cleric who destroyed the Ptolemaic universe.

Whether Copernicus himself believed in astrology or not, the Austrian professor known as Rheticus (who became his self-appointed impresario) made use of astrology to sell the Copernican revolution. In the middle of a correct account of the new heliocentric system, the *Narratio prima*, Rheticus introduced a digression in which among other things the Second Coming was made dependent on changes in the eccentricity of the Earth's orbit.

Many of the best minds of the age certainly could reconcile astrology with a more "scientific" approach to their own subjects. From the Christian Fathers down, there had always been objections to astrology on *religious* grounds. *Scientific* considerations in the 16th century were just as likely to predispose scientists, or at any rate astronomers, in its favor. A notable example is Tycho Brahe (1546-1601), one of the first great observational astronomers, who spent much of his time casting horoscopes. While he may have done this with his tongue in his cheek (he considered all other astrologers charlatans) or mainly to oblige his friends, he did believe that the stars influenced a man's character and life. He backed up his belief with history. "In 1593," he wrote, "when a

Left, a woodcut from a 1527 edition of *The Kalendar of Shepherds* shows sheep shearing in June attended by the month's Zodiac signs —Gemini (top right) and Cancer (bottom right). Astrological calendars still appear today: Below left, the cover of a 1962 Austrian farmers' calendar, which provides details of weather and Zodiac influences.

Below, a diagram of the heliocentric universe from Copernicus' *De Revolutionibus* (1543). The Sun, at the center, is surrounded by the orbits of the seven planets (in their true order) and the sphere of the fixed stars. This revolutionary concept finally displaced the Ptolemaic, or geocentric, idea of the universe.

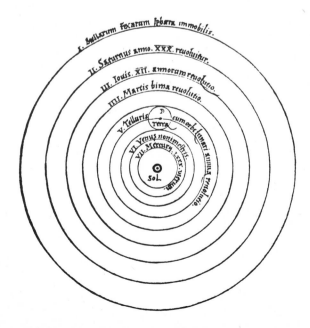

great conjunction of Jupiter and Saturn took place in the first part of the Lion, near to the nebulous stars in Cancer, which Ptolemy calls the smoky and pestilent ones, did not the pestilence which swept over the whole of Europe in the years that followed, and caused innumerable people to perish, confirm the influence of the stars by a very certain fact?"

And Tycho did make one famous prediction. Writing in 1572 on the astrological significance of a comet that had appeared in that year, he predicted that the comet's influence would be greatest in 1592, when a man would be born in Finland "ordained for a great enterprise" in a religious cause. The comet's effect would also be strong in 1632, which, Tycho added, would be the date of the man's death. The career of Gustavus Adolphus of Sweden fitted the prediction almost perfectly. He was born in 1594 (not 1592) in Stockholm (not precisely Finland, though Finland *was* at the time a province of Sweden). But these were the only inconsistencies. Gustavus was one of the greatest champions of Protestantism of the century and led his armies to great victories in the Thirty Years' War (primarily a religious war). And he was killed on the field of his most glorious victory, the battle of Lützen in 1632—a victory over the German imperial forces commanded by Wallenstein.

The irony is that it was Tycho who dealt a serious blow both to Aristotelian cosmology *and* to astrology by proving with his instruments that the famous new star of 1572—the short-lived "nova" that appeared near Cassiopeia—was

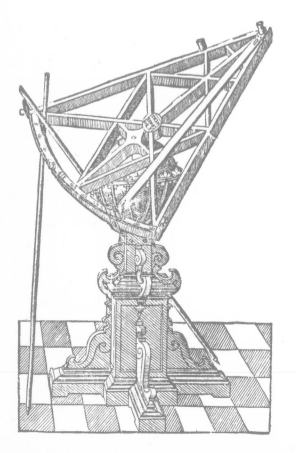

Left, an illustration of a sextant from Tycho Brahe's book on astronomical instruments. With the sextant he proved that the new "comet" of 1572 was actually a fixed star, thus shattering the traditional idea of the immutability of the fixed stars. But, though a pioneer of modern astronomy, Brahe remained an astrologer—as did the astronomer Johannes Kepler. In 1624 Kepler cast the horoscope of the famous German general Wallenstein and predicted from it that March 1634 would bring "dreadful disorders over the land." Wallenstein was killed on February 25, 1634 (depicted in a 17th-century print, right).

a genuine "fixed" star belonging to the eighth sphere (which traditionally was assumed to be free from mutability). This astounding phenomenon (at its brightest it could be seen at midday) had, to start with, given astrologers a field day. They treated it as a sinister omen; one theory was that, though lacking a tail, it was a comet, condensed out of human sins and touched off by the wrath of God. Some also thought that it foretold the Second Coming. But to consider it a *fixed* star was astrological and Aristotelian blasphemy. In proving its true status, Tycho unintentionally gave support to the Copernican system (which he did not accept), and also to his young collaborator Kepler (1571-1630), who was one of the great architects of the astronomical revolution.

There is no doubt that Kepler was a genius who, in his own words, "cleansed the Augean stables" of traditional cosmology. At the same time he was a confused and confusing character; his references to astrology often seem ambivalent. Einstein wrote that Kepler's remarks on astrology "show that the inner enemy, conquered and rendered innocuous, was not yet completely dead." In fact this "inner enemy" was probably more alive than Einstein assumed. Like Tycho, Kepler had to practice astrology whether he liked it or not. Also like Tycho, he thought or wanted to think there was something in it somewhere. As a young man he published annual astrological calendars, which no doubt he had to do in order to further his career. Thus for the year 1595 he predicted unrest among the peasants of upper Austria and the flight of the Austrians

before a Turkish invasion. Both these predictions came true, though they were probably just shrewd guesses.

In a letter in 1598 to his old tutor Mästlin, Kepler writes of his most recent calendar: "As to all the prognoses, I intend to present to my above-mentioned readers a pleasant enjoyment of the grandeur of nature along with the statements which appear true to me, thus hoping that the readers may be tempted to approve a raise in my salary . . . . If you agree with this you will, I hope, not be angry with me if, as a defender of astrology in word and action, at the same time I try to implant the opinion in the masses that I am not an astrological buffoon." In 1611, writing to a confidant of his patron the Emperor Rudolph (at the time involved in a crisis), he makes a distinction not between astrology and astronomy but between two *kinds* of the former: "Ordinary astrology . . . can easily be used to please both parties. I believe that in such weighty reflections one should not only exclude ordinary astrology but also the one which I have recognized as being *in accordance with nature*" (italics mine).

Kepler knew what was not good for emperors or for the masses; and, whatever truth he may have found in astrology, he obviously loathed the way in which it pandered to human credulity and wishful thinking. Twenty years later, he scoffed at what obviously was one of the sensations of the day: "A girl of eleven living in Kottbus prophesies the end of the world. Her age, her infantile ignorance, and the number of her listeners have provided her with a faithful following."

Some peculiarities of Kepler's views of astrology are discussed (in terms of Jungian psychology) by the physicist W. Pauli, in an essay entitled "The Influence of Archetypal Ideas on the Scientific Theories of Kepler" (translated from the German by Priscilla Silz). Here Kepler appears to be what orthodox astrologers might call a mystical deviationist: Pauli comments that his "peculiar conception of astrology met with no recognition." This conception hinges on the stellar *rays*; Kepler believed that the rays strike the earth at different angles and form harmonious patterns comparable to those of music. The soul, he says, recognizes these patterns *instinctively* and without conscious reflection "because the soul, by virtue of its circular form, is an image of God in Whom these proportions and the geometric truths following thereupon exist from all eternity." And he adds: "If I should express my *own* opinion, it would be that there is no evil star in the heavens . . . chiefly for the following reasons: It is the nature of man as such . . . that *lends to the planetary radiations their effect on itself* [italics mine]; just as the sense of hearing, endowed with the faculty of discerning chords, lends to music such power that it incites him who hears it to dance."

This was a revolutionary idea in astrology: Kepler was, so to speak, transferring the initiative from the stars to man. He goes so far as to say that "the soul bears within itself the idea of the Zodiac." This apparent transposition of the astral and human roles, combined with Kepler's insistence on instinct (which would, for example, invalidate the traditional use of books of ephemerides), makes it not at all surprising that his theories met with no recognition. Neither the astrologers nor the public wanted their astrology blown up into mysticism.

In 1608, when Kepler was in his prime, the telescope was invented. Within two years Galileo had used it to show things contrary to Aristotle; he published his findings in 1610 in a booklet entitled *The Star Messenger*. The messages here delivered were sensational, and not everyone welcomed them. The Moon, for instance, traditionally thought of as a perfect crystalline sphere, was now declared to have a highly irregular surface. And there were vastly more fixed stars than anyone had ever thought. Worse than that, Galileo had discovered four new "planets." (These were, in fact, the satellites of Jupiter, but their discovery was nearly as disturbing to traditional attitudes as the later discoveries of the three planets proper—Uranus, Neptune, and Pluto.) All this hit the astrologers at least as hard as anyone else. Not that this would have worried Galileo. In Kepler the skeptic and the mystic were interlocked, but Galileo was a consistent debunker—though even he (like Kepler) found himself sometimes forced to make astrological predictions. (In 1609 he drew up a horoscope for his patron, the Grand Duke of Tuscany, promising him long life. The Grand Duke died a few weeks later.)

Two pages from Galileo's *The Star Messenger* (1610). Galileo's discoveries of new stars— made with the newly invented telescope— helped to discredit the old cosmology of the astrologers.

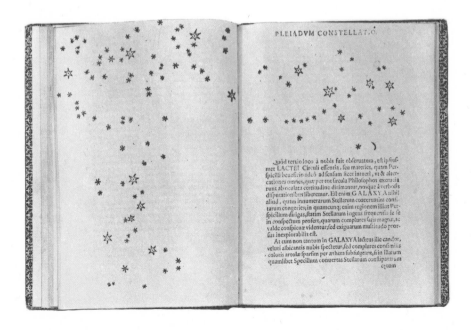

After Kepler and Galileo, and largely because of their own discoveries (which were suspect to the forces of the Counter Reformation), the scene of scientific inquiry shifted to northern Europe and particularly to France, the country of Montaigne and Descartes, and to England, the country of Francis Bacon and Newton. Francis Bacon is generally regarded as the herald of the new era; unlike Galileo, he was not himself a scientific observer and experimenter, but he passionately believed in observation and experiment and made eloquent propaganda on behalf of them. Nevertheless, the mass of works produced by the English astrologers proves that they enjoyed a large public. Early in the 16th century, the famous Dr. John Dee (who also practiced alchemy and crystal gazing) was casting horoscopes for the Tudor royal family. He was later patronized by Queen Elizabeth, but it looks as if his successors made their living on the whole from much humbler clients, who not only believed in astrology but found that it gratified the prevailing taste for the marvelous. On their maps it said "Here be dragons." In the stars it said "Here be your own dragons."

Elizabethan literature makes it obvious that people's forms of expression were conditioned by such long-accepted concepts as those of astrology and of the four humors. We have only to skim through the poets and playwrights to see that it was second nature to them to use astrological terms (though for technical knowledge of the subject they could not have competed with Chaucer). In Christopher Marlowe's *Doctor Faustus*, one of Faustus's friends asserts:

He that is grounded in Astrology,
Enriched with tongues, well seen in minerals,
Hath all the principles Magic doth require.

(Here we have the old linking of astrology and alchemy and the familiar subsumption of both under magic.) In Edmund Spenser's *Faerie Queene*, when the months parade in the so-called "Mutability Cantos," each month either rides upon or is equipped with a Zodiacal emblem. (In fact, of course, the emblems should change about the middle of each month.) Some of their mounts are rather awkward: "Joly June" is carried by a crab "With crooked crawling steps an uncouth pace." And as for February:

And lastly, came cold February, sitting
In an old wagon, for he could not ride;
Drawn of two fishes for the season fitting . . . .

Pisces being traditionally represented by a *pair* of fishes. All this, of course, is mere visual illustration, but it should be remembered that the Crab or the Fishes, even though clichés, meant as much to Spenser's readers as Freudian clichés mean to the average reader in the 20th century.

Shakespeare is full of astrological allusions, which come in very handy when a character wants to comment on the unfairness of it all, as when in *King Lear* the contrast is pointed between the two wicked sisters and Cordelia:

It is the stars,
The stars above us govern our conditions.

Above, a 17th-century English cartoon of an astrologer weighing bags of money taken from clients. In spite of the scientific advances of the period, astrology stayed popular with the majority of people, and continued to be reflected in the literature of the period— for example, in Christopher Marlowe's *Dr. Faustus* (1601), one of many versions of this legendary magician's career. Right, a 17th-century English woodcut showing Faust conjuring up the devil with the aid of a magic Zodiacal circle.

But in the same play the bastard Edmund produces the cynical view of astrology: "This is the excellent foppery of the world, that when we are sick in fortune—often the surfeit of our own behavior—we make guilty of our disasters the Sun, the Moon, and stars. . . ."

Of other Shakespearean characters who draw on this pool of imagery and excuses, Antony complains that he is deserted by his "good stars," while Cassius, in a famous passage in *Julius Caesar*, makes the same point as Edmund but with more dignity:

Men at some time are masters of their fates.
The fault, dear Brutus, is not in our stars,
But in ourselves, that we are underlings.

In Shakespeare's romantic comedies there is Beatrice's remark about herself in *Much Ado about Nothing*: "There was a star danced, and under that was I born"; toward the end of the play her sparring partner, Benedict, says wryly: "I was not born under a rhyming planet, nor can I woo in festival terms." A more brittle example comes from *All's Well that Ends Well*, where the bombastic Parolles is baited by Helena with a play upon words typical of the period and of Shakespeare:

HELENA: Monsieur Parolles, you were born under a charitable star.
PAROLLES: Under Mars, I.
HELENA: I especially think, under Mars.
PAROLLES: Why under Mars?
HELENA: The wars have so kept you under that you must needs be born under Mars.
PAROLLES: When he was predominant.
HELENA: When he was retrograde, I think rather.
PAROLLES: Why think you so?
HELENA: You go so much backward when you fight.

And there is a similar (and perhaps better-known) passage in *Twelfth Night*, involving Sir Toby Belch and Sir Andrew Aguecheek, two titled parasites whose spiritual heirs today would have another drink on the ground that all the bad weather we have been having is due to the nuclear tests:

SIR TOBY: . . . I did think by the excellent constitution of thy leg it was formed under the star of a galliard [an Elizabethan dance].
SIR ANDREW: Aye, 'tis strong, and it does indifferent well in a flame-colored stock. Shall we set about some revels?
SIR TOBY: What shall we do else? Were we not born under Taurus?
SIR ANDREW: Taurus? that's sides and heart.
SIR TOBY: No, sir, it is legs and thighs.

Of many other passages in the Elizabethan playwrights one of the most striking comes toward the end of Webster's grim tragedy *The Duchess of Malfi*. The Machiavellian villain Bosola, who has successfully organized the strangling of the duchess, her children, and her maidservant, overhears the wicked cardinal,

In Shakespeare's *King Lear*, Edmund (here
played by James Booth in the 1963 London
production of the play) ridicules belief
in the influence of the stars. (The
"astrological" instrument he is toying
with bears no resemblance to anything
used by astrologers in real life.)
Unlike Edmund, many of Shakespeare's
characters accept astrology, often
alluding to it in general comments on
the vagaries of fate.

Four human types as seen by the 18th-century Swiss physiognomist Johann Lavater. In the Middle Ages it was believed that individual temperament and physique were determined by the "four humors" (or body liquids)— blood, phlegm, yellow bile, and black bile. For instance, a melancholic nature was thought to result from an excess of black bile.

his employer, planning to have him killed in turn. Bosola, like a good Elizabethan villain, attacks first but stabs the wrong man in the dark :

> *Antonio!*
> *The man I would have saved 'bove mine own life!*
> *We are merely the stars' tennis-balls, struck and bandied*
> *Which way please them.*

Such a view of astral influence is in tune with the stock Elizabethan concept of "blind Fortune" with her wheel.

Typical of the earlier part of the 17th century (in England the Civil War and Protectorate made a great strange gulf in the middle of it) are such peculiar figures as Sir Thomas Browne and Robert Burton. The former, who has one foot in the old world and the other in the new, speaks of astrology without clearly committing himself. Burton (in his *Anatomy of Melancholy*) is also cautious. He uses the famous Latin tag *sapiens dominabitur astris* to make the point that the stars "do incline, but not compel . . . ; and so gently incline, that a wise man may resist them; *sapiens dominabitur astris*: they rule us but God rules them." Yet Burton mainly uses astrology to reinforce his theory of "humors," in particular of melancholy : "The most generous melancholy . . . comes from the conjunction of Saturn and Jupiter in Libra : the bad . . . from the meeting of Saturn and the Moon in Scorpio." Elsewhere he discusses, with a typical massive display of latinity, the astrological causes of love-melancholy.

In the diagram below, each humor (indicated by a color, as in the key, right) is related to its appropriate planetary and Zodiacal symbols : For example, the melancholic (blue) is connected with Mercury (who rules Gemini and Virgo) ; Venus (Taurus and Libra) ; and Saturn (Aquarius and Capricorn).

- sanguine
- phlegmatic
- choleric
- melancholic

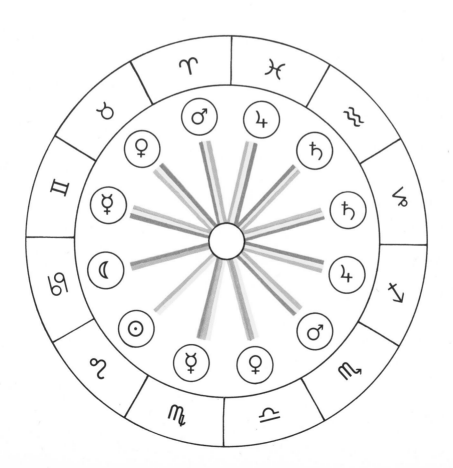

Burton seems to have been less aware of the new horizons than Browne, but Browne for his part remained a religious man. The Anglican bishop Jeremy Taylor expressed about this time what was probably the orthodox position of the young Church of England: "Let no man let his hopes wander toward future and far-distant events and accidental contingencies"; and quoted St. James on the folly of men who consult "astrologers and witches, oracles and devils."

Astrologers of the people

Taylor was 17 years younger than the French philosopher Descartes, who in this period was, like Galileo in Italy or Thomas Hobbes in England, exploding long-established preconceptions. But this kind of free thinking would have had little appeal to ordinary people, who still found it possible to reconcile both their common sense and their faith with a belief in astrology. This is proved by the great popularity of such astrologers as the Englishman William Lilly (1602-81), who died shortly before Newton published his *Principia*. Lilly's own autobiography is revealing in several respects. He was 30 before he was converted to astrology or saw the prospect of a career in it; when he came to practice, he seems to have been suspect to most groups, even to those to whom he politically adhered. When Cromwell became Protector, one of Lilly's books of predictions "was for a whole week every day in the Parliament House, peeped into by the

Left, a portrait of the astrologer William Lilly. In 1651 Lilly foretold disasters for England, symbolized by his drawing (above) of Gemini falling into flames. Gemini is the sign of the city of London, which suffered the Great Fire of 1666 (shown in an engraving of the time, right).

Presbyterians, one disliking this sentence, another finds another fault, others misliked the whole." In the same year, 1653, a violent attack was published by Thomas Gataker, B.D., "Against the Scurrilous Aspersion of that grand Imposter Mr. William Lillie," of whom he writes: "There needs not much skill in his pretended Art, to discover the vanity of it."

Two years later Lilly was in trouble again; he writes that he was "indicted . . . by a half-witted young woman . . . for that I had given judgment upon stolen goods, and received 2s. 6d. And this was said to be contrary unto an Act in King James's Time made." For good measure the young woman added "that she had been several times with me, and that afterwards she could not rest a Nights, but was troubled with bears, lions, and tygers etc." There were many other attacks on Lilly; and, though eight years later (in 1663) he was appointed churchwarden of Walton upon Thames, this respectable position did not save him in October 1666 from being summoned before a committee investigating the causes of the Great Fire of London. But this turned out to be an advertisement for his art: "Having found, Sir, that the City of London should be sadly afflicted with a great plague, and not long after with an exorbitant fire, I framed these two hieroglyphics . . . which in effect have proved very true." He records that he was dismissed by the committee with "great civility."

ISAACUS NEWTON EQ. AUR. ÆT. 83.

PHILOSOPHIÆ
NATURALIS
PRINCIPIA
MATHEMATICA.

AUCTORE
ISAACO NEWTONO, Eq. Aur.

Editio tertia aucta & emendata.

LONDINI:
Apud Guil. & Joh. Innys, Regiæ Societatis typographos.
MDCCXXVI.

Above, two pages from an edition printed in 1726 of Isaac Newton's *Principia* (first published in 1687) showing a portrait of the author and the title page. Newton proved that all physical phenomena, stars and planets included, are subject to natural—and rational—laws. In the "Age of Reason," satirists as well as scientists contributed to astrology's disrepute : right, a detail from an 18th-century woodcut of Jonathan Swift (holding a satirical pamphlet) who, under the pseudonym of Isaac Bickerstaff, made a laughing stock of the astrologer John Partridge.

As a *public* astrologer, Lilly had anticipated many astrological journalists of our own day. In 1644 Lilly wrote: "Saturn in the fifth house causeth more abortives than usually have been, the destructions of many men's sons or children, much tergiversation with Ambassadors and foreign Agents, and that they perform not what may be expected from them." It should be noted that the Civil War had *already* broken out.

Of course, Lilly had his rivals. In 1662 one John Gadbury published a *Collectio Geniturarum*, which he describes as "being of Practical Concernment unto Philosophers Physicians Astronomers Astrologers and others that are friends unto Urania" (the muse of astronomy). In his introduction he appears on the defensive, specifying three sorts of people that "seem most of all to oppugn this Noble Art, viz. the *Seeming Religious,* the *Politique,* and the *Ignorant.*" His nativities include Nero, Henry VIII, Queen Elizabeth, James I, Charles I, Luther, Richelieu, Regiomontanus, and Pico della Mirandola. And of Louis XIV (who, unlike the others, was still alive) Gadbury predicted that, if he survives this year (1662) which involves "dangerous Surfeiting, the Stone, and Treachery," then he may enjoy very good health till his 41st year. In fact Louis survived till 1715 and died at the age of 77.

And so it went on through the 17th century—a whole pack of astrologers boasting and backbiting, and most of them, clearly, doing quite well for themselves. Practitioners of related "sciences" were also thriving, like the famous herbalist Nicholas Culpeper, who ascribed the virtues of his herbs to the influence of the planets. But what with Copernicus and Kepler and Galileo's telescope, the writing, so to speak, was on the sky. Just as the ancient Greeks when they stopped asking "How?" declined in astronomy and turned to astrology, so the 17th-century French and English when they stopped asking "Why?" and concentrated on "How?" were inevitably bound to turn their backs on astrology.

It was Newton, of course, who completed the revolution; from then on (at least till recently) the universe has been thought of as *a machine that works.* God could be smuggled in by compromise or presupposed in the wings of the theatre, but this was only because God could neither be seen nor measured. The heavenly bodies, on the other hand, could now be seen and measured better than ever before. Recent astronomy had made sense of the solar system and, both literally and figuratively, put the Earth in its place; this undermined the astrologers' premises, which presupposed the Ptolemaic system.

Recent astronomy had also proved that change and irregularity were not confined to the sublunary sphere. There was Tycho's nova that had flared up, then vanished again; the Moon's surface was full of ups and downs; there were even spots upon the Sun itself. Moreover, instead of a compact and symmetrical universe (as Ptolemaic astronomy and all astrology had presupposed), there was now the dangerous idea of infinite space. In Catholic Italy, Giordano Bruno had been burned for suggesting just this in 1600. Lastly, when Newton explained all the motions of the heavenly bodies by four comparatively simple laws, he explained away the mystery that from the days of ancient Babylon had supplied an incentive, a rationale, and an excuse for astrology.

Newton, by the way, has repeatedly been called by modern astrologers as a witness in their own defense. This rests entirely on the story that the astronomer Edmund Halley, who gave his name to the famous comet, criticized Newton for accepting astrology and that Newton tartly replied to him: "I have studied the subject, Sir, you have not." But there seems to be no historical evidence for this story. The authoritative Ingrid Lind admits: "I do not know if this conversation did in fact take place." And the modern opponent of astrology Robert Eisler takes a very definite stand: "It remains an incontrovertible fact that after the discovery of Kepler's laws and Newton's principles—in other words, ever since the regular movements of the earth and the planets around the sun have been satisfactorily understood and explained—no professional or amateur astronomer of any repute has ever said another word in defense of astrology."

But the astrologers have gone down fighting, even if this fight has largely consisted in ignoring the overwhelming enemy. At the very end of this eye-opening century, well after Newton had worked out his theory of gravity, a typical rearguard action occurred in a book called *The Angelical Guide,* published in 1697. The author, John Case, makes some fascinating assertions, including the statement (quoted in Chapter 1) that the creation of the heavenly bodies took place "on Wednesday, April 22, 18 h.p.m. [6 P.M.] *about* 4002 years before Christ" (italics mine). And Adam (whom Case regards as the first astrologer) "was created in that pleasant place Paradise, *about* [italics mine] the year before Christ 4002, viz. on April 23, at 12 a clock or Midnight."

Later in the same book Case comes down to the practical uses of astrology— ". . . to know by this Angelical Lot or Guide what is to come, Good or Bad." Questions a man (or an unborn child?) may put to an astrologer are answered by consulting different signs of the Zodiac. Examples follow of the kind of questions asked of each sign:

What shape of body shall I have? (Aries)

Whether the thing lost was stolen? (Taurus)

How to know our Brother's Sisters' kindred or relations? (Gemini)

To know when my Grandfather, or my Great-grandfather, or that Old Rogue my Father, will die? (Cancer)

Whether I shall get a good Mistress? (Leo)

To know whether I shall ever keep a pack of Good Hounds, or a parcel of good Hogs or Sheep, or ever to be plagued with Rats or Mice? (Virgo)

Will my Wife be a Whore, or Honest? (Libra)

If I lend my Money, shall I gain? (Scorpio)

Shall I have the Bishopric or Abbey I desire? (Sagittarius)

To know whether I shall ever come to Honour, or be a Justice of the Peace? (Capricorn)

Will Fruits of the Earth be cheap or dear? (Aquarius)

Will any Old Woman chatter against me like a Devil? (Pisces)

Some of these questions might suggest that Case had his tongue in his cheek, but the fact remains that he had a successful practice.

Most of these astrologers must have been as difficult to caricature as, say, advertising men are today. But the wits of the Age of Prose and Reason attempted it. One of the most famous of these satires was directed at an astrologer named John Partridge, who used his almanacs to plug his own prejudices (such as anti-popery), to advance his own political interests, and to become very rich. In the reign of Queen Anne, Partridge was immortalized in print by a hoax that amounted to a practical joke. The joker was Jonathan Swift (writing under the name of Isaac Bickerstaff), who published certain "Predictions for the Year 1708." This was Swift's usual satirical technique: to pretend to believe in the ideas he was attacking, and then to carry them (with a straight face) to absurd extremes. So, as "Bickerstaff," he first states his belief in the art of astrology, while he deplores "those gross impostors who set up to be the artists." He is therefore setting out to provide his own reliable predictions to put imposters like Partridge to shame.

Swift goes straight to his target: "My first prediction is but a trifle; yet I will mention it, to show how ignorant those sottish pretenders to astrology are in their own concerns: It relates to Partridge the almanack-maker. I have consulted the star of his nativity by my own rules; and find he will infallibly die upon the 29th of March next, about eleven at night, of a raging fever: Therefore I advise him to consider of it, and settle his affairs in time."

People bought "Bickerstaff's" predictions and took him seriously. But they may have taken him less seriously when he changed his ground, assumed the name of Partridge himself, and wrote a farcical attack on "Bickerstaff's" predictions. This essay relates what happened on "the 28th of March, anno Dom. 1708, being the night this sham prophet had so impudently fixed for my last." "Partridge" complains of a bell being tolled for him, of the undertaker and then the sexton calling, and many other inconveniences: "I could not stir out of doors for the space of three months after this, but presently one comes up to me in the street, Mr. Partridge, that coffin you was last buried in, I have not yet been paid for . . ."

That Partridge really did suffer from this hoax is obvious. We do not know whether he ever lived it down (the phrase in this context carries more meaning than usual); he died in 1715. It seems that he actually tried to advertise in the papers that he was "not only now alive, but was also alive on the 29th of March in question." As for "Bickerstaff," he suffered too. His "Predictions" was burned by the Inquisition in Portugal, presumably because, besides predicting the death of Partridge, it had also pretended to predict many unfortunate events on the continent, including the death of Louis XIV. So ends a whole era of astrological theory and practice, not with a bang but with a coffee-house giggle.

6 The loss of respectability

In the 16th century a papal astrologer made a mistake in the date when casting Luther's horoscope retrospectively. In the 18th century (the "Age of Enlightenment") this incident was seized upon with delight by the English humorist Laurence Sterne in his novel *The Life and Opinions of Tristram Shandy*. Sterne envisaged a scene in Strasbourg where the two universities, "the Lutheran and the Popish," were "employing the whole depth of their knowledge . . . in determining the point of Martin Luther's damnation."

"The Popish doctors had undertaken to demonstrate, *a priori,* that from the necessary influence of the planets on the twenty-second day of October, 1483,—when the Moon was in the twelfth house, Jupiter, Mars, and Venus in the third; the Sun, Saturn, and Mercury, all got together in the fourth;—that he must in course, and unavoidably, be a damned man; and that his doctrines, by a direct corollary, must be damn'd doctrines too.

"By inspection into his horoscope, where five planets were in coition all at once with Scorpio . . . in the ninth house, which the Arabians allotted to religion,—it appeared that Martin Luther did not care one stiver about the matter;—and that, from the horoscope directed to the conjunction of Mars,—they made it plain likewise he must die cursing and blaspheming; with the blast of which his soul (being steep'd in guilt) sailed before the wind in the lake of Hell-fire." The above horoscope looks pretty odd (one cannot see how there were five

The frontispiece to *Raphael's Witch* or *Oracle of the Future* (published in England in 1831) depicting the mystical wheel of Pythagoras, which is used in a method of numerical divination. The decorative figures include a witch (center) and an astrologer (bottom left)—a typical 19th-century linking of astrology and occultism.

planets to spare for the ninth house) but presumably was meant to be. Sterne was enjoying himself at the expense of a subject that was gradually reaching a stage where it was no longer taken seriously. The late 17th-century English poet John Dryden was probably the last important English writer (at least till nearly our own day) to regard astrology as a serious subject.

Yet Dryden himself also exploited it as a source of rather crude comedy. In a play of his entitled *An Evening's Love* or *The Mock Astrologer* (the plot and title were borrowed from the French dramatist Corneille) a young Englishman in Madrid pretends to be an astrologer because he has designs on a senorita. Unfortunately the heroine's father has studied astrology in his youth and proceeds to test the hero's knowledge by asking him "the best way of rectification for a nativity." The Englishman answers: "Mars rules over the Martial, Jupiter over the Jovial . . . ." "This," says the father indignantly, "every school-boy could have told me." The hero's friend then advises him to be better prepared in future: "If at any time thou ventur'st at particulars, have an evasion ready like Lilly."

Lilly's name is honored again today (and not only by astrologers), but Dryden's successors in the forefront of the Enlightenment had very little respect for him or his kind. A very lean period was beginning for the once proud "queen of the sciences." The modern astrologer Louis de Wohl dates the beginning of the rot from the 16th century with its wars of religion from which "revolution was born and with it that terrible time of gross rationalism" (which, he apparently hopes, is now drawing near its end). But it was in the 18th century that this rationalism became truly free—or gross. Throughout the 16th and much of the 17th century (as we saw in Chapter 5) it was still hampered and complicated by old modes of thought and a residue of superstition.

In England the Royal Society (which was the spearhead of what has been called the "scientific revolution") had been founded in 1662; and yet, on the appearance of the great comet of 1680, we find an educated man like the diarist John Evelyn writing of comets: "They *may* be warnings from God." In Germany, on the same occasion, we find professors and Lutheran ministers stressing the length of the comet's tail and regarding it as a rod of chastisement that God has put in his window—"and all the children fear, but he has in mind only the mischievous." Erhard Weigel, a professor of mathematics whose astrological views admittedly were eccentric, interpreted the vanishing of this comet when about to enter the Milky Way as a warning to parents to feed their children on the milk of true piety. And on the same occasion great attention was paid by serious Germans to the report that a hen in Rome had laid a comet-marked egg; engravings of this hen and her egg were circulated through the country. Many German pamphlets and theses were published about this comet; very few of them were skeptical.

In America the puritanical preacher Increase Mather grabbed at the 1680 comet as the excuse for a hell-fire sermon on "Heaven's Alarm to the World."

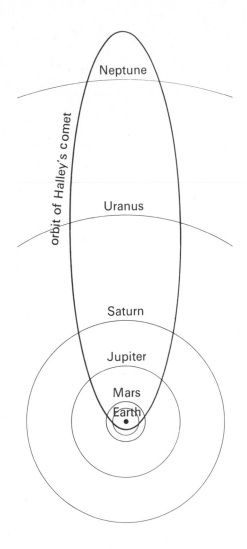

orbit of Halley's comet

Neptune

Uranus

Saturn

Jupiter

Mars

Earth

ISTIMIRANT STELLA

HAROLD

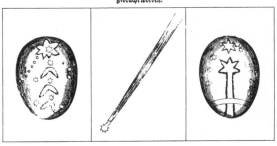

Wunder-Ey.

Welches den ,¹. Decembris dieſes mit B.Oẛ zu Endlauffenden 1680.
Heil-Jahrs zu Rom / von einer Henne mit groſſen Geſchrey iſt geleget / und von
hoher glaubwürdiger Hand ſolcher Geſtalt in den Entwurff und Abriß
gebracht worden.

Above, a diagram based on the calculations made in 1682 by the English astronomer Edmund Halley, who proved that comets revolve in long elliptical orbits around the Sun (the dot at the center of the planetary orbits). Comets had always been regarded as omens of disaster: Top right, a detail from the 11th-century Bayeux Tapestry records King Harold's dismay when a comet appeared in 1066; center right, a German pamphlet of 1680 depicts a comet-marked egg that was allegedly laid when the comet reappeared that year. This irrational attitude to comets lasted after Halley: It was mocked by an American cartoon of 1910 (right) showing people digging holes in New York's Central Park to escape a comet's "fallout."

Revolution of America

In Holland and France the reactions were less old-fashioned. In the former, the simpler flocks of Calvinists were generally as susceptible as that of Increase Mather, though most of the Dutch elite were contemptuous of the comet as a portent (and of astrology in general). In France the *philosophes* went into action, encouraged by Louis XIV. The famous letter-writer Madame de Sévigné was lightheartedly skeptical. The Protestant professor of philosophy Pierre Bayle delivered a violent attack on the "science" in his *Pensées diverses*—an attack inspired by the comet and by the fact, as he admitted, that France was overrun by astrologers. He seems to have suspected, like many astronomers of the time, that comets might be *periodic;* this hypothesis, which would knock the bottom out of cometary superstition, was proved correct when Halley's comet returned at the end of 1758, as predicted by the followers of Newton. Bayle's book was widely circulated. His equally famous colleague Fontenelle chose the favorite French weapon of mockery. He had a comedy staged in Paris, entitled simply *Le Comète* (see Chapter 9). And in the next generation Voltaire dismissed astrology with contempt in his *Dictionnaire Philosophique*.

As the 18th century's emphasis on reason took firmer hold, European astrology began to lose the ground that it had gained and held during Lilly's time and before. England offers a few isolated examples of astrological writing: For instance, an unorthodox book called *Astro-Theology* by William Derham (who was both a clergyman and a Fellow of the Royal Society) ran through nine editions between 1715 and 1750; but this was really more a work of imaginative astronomy than astrology. And a qualified surgeon, Ebenezer Sibly, who described himself as an "astro-philosopher," wrote a vast book entitled *The Celestial Science of Astrology*. It contained many nativities, including those of Christ and George III, and was illustrated with curious copperplates including a symbolic representation of the American Revolution.

One of the few astrological works that appeared during the 18th-century "Age of Reason" was *The Celestial Science of Astrology* (published in England in 1790) by the self-styled "astro-philosopher" Ebenezer Sibly. Left, one of the book's illustrations symbolizes the American Revolution: The angel in the clouds holds a horoscope cast for the Declaration of Independence in 1776. Right, also from the book, a portrait of the author (within his own horoscope).

Sibly began his book by admitting that he was aware "of the rotted prejudices of the times against the venerable science of Astrology." These prejudices were probably still intact in 1828 when John Varley published his *Treatise on Zodiacal Physiognomy,* which has often been quoted from in earlier chapters. In France, at the end of the century, it was claimed that the revolution had been foretold by Nostradamus in 1555; but the trend of post-revolution France itself was right away from such a "conservative" activity as astrology. In the next hundred years there is far less record of its practice in France and the rest of continental Europe than in England.

In Germany, Goethe is sometimes claimed as an adherent by modern astrologers, but the evidence is not strong. It is true that he starts his autobiography (translation by John Oxenford): "On the 28th of August, 1749, at mid-day, as the clock struck twelve, I came into the world, at Frankfort-on-the-Maine. My horoscope was propitious . . . ." He then gives the details. That he should have bothered to do this does not necessarily prove that he believed in horoscopes; he was a man of vast curiosity who was interested in the sciences of the past as well as those of the present—and future. He did not believe in either magic or Christianity, though both are essential to his story of Faust.

Of course, astrology did not entirely die out in this period. But to find it being practiced and respected with anything like the style it enjoyed in its European heyday, one has to look outside Europe. The Abbé Dubois, a missionary in India toward the end of the 18th century, wrote disapprovingly of the Brahmin *purohitas*: "There is no one in high position who has not one or more official purohitas living in the palace; and these men act, so to speak, like rulers of the universe. They go every morning and with ludicrous gravity announce to the prince, to his state elephant, and to his idols, each in their turn, all that is written in the almanac relating to that particular day."

In 1800 a traveler in Persia, James Morier, was not allowed to leave Basra before the hour decided upon by the astrologers and was also warned to time his arrival at the next place as exactly as possible. The Moslem governor of Basra told Morier that once, when he was about to embark for Calcutta, he "was ordered by these astrologers (as the only means of counteracting the influence of a certain evil star) to go out of his house in a particular aspect; as unfortunately there happened to be no door in that direction, he caused a hole to be made in the wall, and thus made his exit." People often used to say that the East was unchanging: It was mentioned in Chapter 1 that Marco Polo had described central Asian funerals (five centuries before Morier) in which a hole would be broken in the wall so that the corpse might be carried out in the direction ordered by the astrologers.

A British Egyptologist, E. W. Lane, who went to live in Egypt in 1825, wrote: "It was a custom very common in Egypt, as in other Muslim countries, to consult an astrologer previously to giving a name to a child, and to be guided by his choice; but," he adds rather surprisingly, "very few persons now conform

Geomancy is a complicated form of divination (closely connected with astrology) from rows of marks in the sand, which were sometimes interpreted mechanically. This medieval Arab geomancy machine was operated by knobs, some representing astrology's 12 houses.

with this old usage." He does stress, however, that astrology was more studied there than astronomy: "To say that the earth revolves round the Sun, they consider absolute heresy." Also, though his Egyptians may have become careless about giving a child a name, whatever name it received remained numerologically—and therefore astrologically—important. Lane explains that their astrology was "chiefly employed in casting nativities, and in determining fortunate periods, etc.; and very commonly, to divine by what sign of the Zodiac a person is influenced; which is usually done by a calculation founded upon the numerical value of the letters composing his or her name, and that of the mother . . . ." He adds that the Egyptian brand of geomancy (divination by marks made in the sand, which is still performed for tourists) is "mainly founded on astrology."

For most of the 19th century, thanks largely to the success of the "scientific revolution," astrology's disrepute in Europe continued, at least among educated people. Thus Sir Walter Scott had originally intended his second Waverley novel, *Guy Mannering*, to have an astrological motivation and framework. He had got the idea from a story told by an old servant of his father's: A child is due to be born in a great house when a stranger drops in, who happens to be an astrologer. He studies the heavens and begs his host "to retard the birth if practicable, were it but for five minutes"; but, alas, it is not practicable, so the astrologer warns the father that a terrible crisis will come to his newly born son about his 21st birthday. When the birthday approaches, the father sends the son to the astrologer, in whose house, as it befalls, he has to face the Devil and fight for his soul and his life.

The more Scott pondered this plot the more he began to suspect that what was good enough for his father's servant was not good enough for the readers of *Waverley*. As he explained himself: "It appeared, on mature consideration, that Astrology, though its influence was once received and admitted by Bacon himself [he means Francis Bacon, not Roger], does not now retain influence over the general mind sufficient even to constitute the mainspring of a romance."

Scott wrote this in 1829. Five years earlier in England the Vagrancy Act had backed up the Witchcraft Act of 1736 in outlawing the astrologers. Astrology's reputation had now reached one of the lowest points in its history, and it was becoming more and more diluted by association with the occult and those other irrational practices that always seem to flourish (as a kind of underground counterpoint) in societies that lay heavy stress on the rational side of human nature. This process was especially obvious on the continent of Europe: For instance, in France about the middle of the century, a man calling himself Eliphas Lévi (real name: Alphonse Louis Constant) gained a measure of fame by pepping up astrology with the occult. In fact, Lévi (who believed in a universal medium called the "Astral Light") seems to have been an occultist first and an astrologer second (a combination that was to become more common as the century progressed). In his *History of Magic* Lévi quotes from an older authority (whom he refers to only as Ballanche): "Astrology is a synthesis because the Tree of Life is a single tree and because its branches—spread through heaven and bearing flowers of stars—are in correspondence with its roots, which are hidden in earth."

Lévi and his successors in France worked hard to introduce the cabalistic science of numbers into astrology, and the resulting mixture soon made its way from the continent to Britain, where later astrologers were to apply it to horse racing and the stock exchange. The first Zadkiel himself, in his *Handbook of Astrology* (1861), provided fodder for gamblers when he wrote self-righteously of horse racing: "I would not encourage anyone in the pursuit of this pernicious, foolish, and discreditable practice, for the sake of mammon; but if anyone be already engaged therein, and be really anxious about the result"—why, then Zadkiel's book can help him a lot. "If the ninth [the house of honor for the horse] be strong, and the lord of the twelfth be there and not afflicted, then the horse will gain honour by the race and be well placed therein."

Zadkiel (Richard James Morrison) was a typically English figure. Born in 1795, he resigned from the Royal Navy in 1829 and devoted the rest of his life to astrologizing and inventing. His inventions included a bell buoy and a plan for "propelling ships of war in a calm." In 1831 he published *The Herald of Astrology* and followed it with numerous publications including, in particular, the famous annual almanac.

The almanac sold about 60,000 copies annually. The first Zadkiel (the almanac was later continued by others, who also used the pseudonym "Zadkiel") claimed that he had been making correct and unchallenged predictions for over three decades. According to himself this was not only a trade but a crusade: He was devoted to the task of "re-establishing the doctrines of Astrology in the public mind, after being obscured for a season by the spread of *infidelity in religion*" (italics mine). And in *Zadkiel's Legacy* (1842) he brings a high, prophetic tone of voice to his preface: "Many generations shall pass by, many centuries roll away, and this book shall still remain a memento of the sublime powers of astral influence." Like some other modern astrologers, the first Zadkiel also went in for crystal gazing; in 1863 he was described by an indignant rationalist admiral in a letter to the press as "the crystal globe seer who gulled many of our nobility." Zadkiel brought an action against the admiral and was awarded 20 shillings damages and no costs.

Zadkiel did not go out of his way to gloss things over for his public. He was more ruthless than many of his successors in detailing the characteristics of certain signs. He writes of Cancer, for instance: "if a female, prolific, dull, and timid." And of Scorpio: "ill-made feet or bow-legged . . . generally deceitful."

An illustration from *The History of Magic* (1855) by the French occultist Eliphas Lévi. The branches of the "tree of life" contain the seven wonders of the world, which are linked with the seven planets of traditional astrology (indicated by their symbols) and seven metals. For example, the Moon is related to the Temple of Diana (the Roman Moon goddess) at Ephesus, and to silver.

Possibly those of his Victorian public who were dull, deceitful, etc., preferred to be told that the fault was in their stars.

But in spite of Zadkiel's fame, his pronouncements did not go unchallenged. *A Complete Refutation of Astrology* by T. H. Moody, a professor of mathematics, was published in Britain in 1838 by subscription; the subscribers included clergymen, generals, and schoolmistresses. "During the last twenty years," complains Moody, "several new astrological works have appeared, and the high tone of confidence adopted in some of them is truly remarkable." Moody quotes an interesting historical argument from Zadkiel: "We are quite certain that the prejudice against astrology owes its origin chiefly to the cant and hypocrisy of the Puritans in the time of Cromwell." "This is a fine specimen of astrological certainty," says Moody. (But he omits one possible answer: Why, then, did not Charles II, at the Restoration, restore astrology too?) He also sets out to pick holes in some of Zadkiel's horoscopes and in some of the details of his almanacs. When Zadkiel writes of a certain Sunday: "This day is evil till after one o'clock, when you may write letters, commence short journeys, and ask favours," his mathematical opponent makes a sabbatarian choice of weapon: "But God has blessed every Sabbath in the year, and commanded us to rest from all mere worldly occupations."

Moody complained of the "high tone of confidence" employed by the new astrologers. Just as confident as the first Zadkiel was the first "Raphael" (R. C. Smith). While Lieutenant Morrison was still in the Navy, Raphael had published his *Manual of Astrology*. And in the year that Zadkiel published his *Herald*, Raphael came out with his *Witch*, with its strange illustrations like "The Mystical Wheel of Pythagoras" or "The Cabalistical Tablet of the Stars." Typically of its period, this book aspires to be simultaneously awesome and genteel,

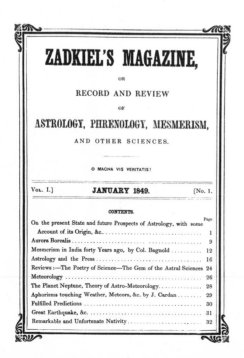

Aside from handbooks of the occult, 19th-century astrologers produced a spate of almanacs. Typical examples were the two founded by Britain's Zadkiel and Raphael. Left, the title page of one of Zadkiel's many astrological publications. Right, from *Raphael's Almanac* of 1824, a hieroglyph (a skeleton on the French throne) that was later claimed as a prediction of the death of Louis XVIII. Far right, a drawing from the 1963 edition of the same almanac, which correctly foretold a high proportion of Irish winners in English horse races that year.

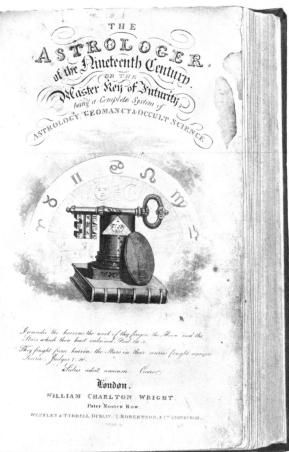

Above, the title page and frontispiece from a "complete system of occult philosophy" published in 1825. The book includes information on summoning the dead, magic talismans, prophecy—and astrology.

and is described by its author as "adapted to lay about in *drawing rooms*—to be read in *gardens* and *groves*—to ornament a *boudoir*." (All the italics are his.)

These were the sort of people Moody was up against. But it is to be doubted if he converted many of those who had *Raphael's Witch* lying about in their drawing rooms, or any less genteel readers who were ready to lap up the astrological almanacs. Moody uses both scientific and mathematical arguments (he makes play with the precession of the equinoxes as Robert Eisler did; see page 74) and the common-sense appeal to experience (against mundane astrology he gives historical instances of predictions of floods and storms that never happened). But his voice is not the voice of the Enlightenment. One doubts if he would have felt at home with Voltaire or Swift or Hume. In England at least, a new era was beginning; Queen Victoria had ascended the throne a year before Moody's *Refutation* was published. Moody's main approach both reminds us of the early Christian Fathers and anticipates orthodox Victorian Christianity: "Astronomy," he writes, "connects the mind with heaven; but astrology associates it with the daemons of darkness."

One instance of astrological quackery quoted by Moody takes us into the streets and the minds of ordinary people. A certain Charles Paddon had put up the following advertisement (no doubt it was one of hundreds): "The Astrologer of the Nineteenth Century, 32, Grafton Street, Tottenham Court Road. By knowing the time of birth, we are enabled to read in the heavens the story of our whole lives. N.B.—All letters must be post paid. Please to ring the first floor bell." In January 1836, a woman who was a policeman's wife rang the first floor bell and was introduced to Paddon, an impressive gentleman "in a large dressing gown, seated in an immense arm chair," who promptly predicted that her husband, the policeman, would die in the near future. For this she paid him a fee of two shillings and sixpence. As she left the house her husband was waiting outside; he entered and arrested Paddon, presumably on a charge of obtaining money by false pretenses. Moody says that Paddon "appeared almost planet struck and exclaimed 'I am ruined!'" (In Britain, astrologers and fortune tellers had been classed among "rogues and vagabonds" by the two Acts mentioned before. Their legal position remains unaltered today.)

The new planets

Meanwhile, the usurping astronomers continued their ruthless discoveries. The telescope had long since opened up those infinite spaces that horrified Pascal and put paid to the old tidy Aristotelian (or Ptolemaic) universe. From then on the world was to see bigger and bigger telescopes and many more startling advances in the science, the most upsetting for the astrologers being the discovery of the new planets Uranus and Neptune. Some astrologers, admittedly, made these an excuse for the inaccuracies of their predecessors; but others, who wanted to keep the old *septizonium* (the elegant, time-honored, and mystical set-up of seven planetary spheres), argued that these new planets could *not* influence human beings because they could not be seen with the naked eye (an argument that presumed a very narrow and dubious interpretation of the nature of planetary influence).

Uranus, which lies vastly farther out in the solar system than Saturn, was discovered in 1781 by William Herschel. As a gesture to his patron, George III of England, Herschel attempted to call the new planet "Georgium Sidus" (the Georgian Star), while his friends wanted to call it "Herschel." Foreign astronomers prevailed over both and the new planet eventually fell into line with the old ones under the classical name of Uranus. Some 40 years later Uranus was noticed to be behaving strangely (the French astronomer Pierre de Laplace spoke of "some extraneous and unknown influence that has acted upon the planet") and for the next 20 years astronomers in several countries investigated the possibility that there might be yet another unknown planet pulling Uranus out of course.

Finally, in 1846, J. G. Galle, an astronomer in Berlin, prompted by a French colleague, Urbain Leverrier, managed to put his finger (in fact his telescope's refractor) on the very distant planet that was given the name of Neptune. It should be noted that, though these planets were named in an arbitrary manner (see Chapter 2), astrologers ascribed to them influences that seem derived from these names. The same process was repeated when Pluto was discovered in 1930.

"Three new forces to consider should make a great deal of difference," wrote Rupert Gleadow in *Astrology in Everyday Life* (published 1940). "They do," he went on, carrying the war to the enemy, "but it is worth observing that they correspond chiefly to things that have been invented since they were discovered; Uranus, for example, is connected with machinery, and the industrial revolution happened shortly after he was found." In a chapter on the "Aquarian Age" (see Chapter 3) Gleadow attempted to explain contemporary history by picturing it as a conflict between "the old ruler of Aquarius"—Saturn, who represents control, restriction, and slavery—and its new ruler Uranus, who represents "culture, civilization, intelligence," etc. Incidentally, though Gleadow saw Uranus primarily as a good planet, the first Raphael had predicted that "the influence to be expected from this newly discovered star would be eminently evil," its effects being "truly malefic."

Gleadow's description of this conflict, though he may have been merely speaking symbolically, sounds startlingly anthropomorphic: "Saturn does not want to give up his rulership over Aquarius. Uranus began the work of overthrowing him at the end of the eighteenth century. But then in 1846 Neptune was discovered, and Neptune was an ally for Saturn, since his sign *Pisces* [the influence of the name again?] is in sextile [a good aspect] to Saturn's sign Capricorn . . . ." Neptune, he explains, "stands for the absorption of the self into something great and wonderful" and so can be held responsible for the growth of modern dictatorships. But we need not despair since Pluto was discovered in 1930 and "Pluto appears to rule Aries [though Ingrid Lind connects it with Scorpio], which

The new planets

William Herschel **1738-1822**

Urbain Leverrier 1811-77

Percival Lowell 1855-1916

Astrology's traditional seven-planet system was badly shaken when Uranus was discovered in 1781 by the English astronomer William Herschel (far left). Left, the reflector telescope with which he is said to have made the discovery. Gear wheels (right) illustrate astrology's view of Uranus as the patron of machinery. This planet was also declared to be the ruler of Aquarius, here shown with Uranus's symbol.

Astrologers were again disconcerted when calculations made by the French astronomer Urbain Leverrier (far left) led to the discovery of Neptune in 1846. Left, a cartoon by France's Honoré Daumier shows a couple gazing awestruck at the new planet. The "watery" associations with the ocean god Neptune led astrologers to connect the planet with the sea (a connection represented by a submarine, right), and with the sign of Pisces.

America's Percival Lowell (far left) was the first to suspect the existence of the newest planet, Pluto, which was detected in 1930. Left, two photographs taken at a three-day interval show how the changing position of a pinpoint of light (arrowed) confirmed it as a planet. Astrologers still disagree over Pluto's astrological role (though many relate it to Aries). Britain's Margaret Hone connects Pluto's influence with darkness and death, and specifically with the atom bomb (right).

is in sextile to Aquarius and in square [bad relationship] to Capricorn; Pluto is therefore an ally for Uranus and an enemy of Saturn."

This sort of astral battle is complicated by the fact that the opponents can sometimes borrow from each other's armory. Thus, though Uranus is the patron of machines, Gleadow tells us that Pluto in Gemini (which is an airy sign and the sign of transport) produced the airplane. But on the whole modern astrologers employ a certain caution when dealing with the three outer planets. Ingrid Lind explains that, because they take so long to pass through any particular sign of the Zodiac, they are not so relevant to individual horoscopes (this is a let-out for previous horoscopists) but rather must be regarded as "affecting a generation, or as providing background conditions for a period."

Similarly, the American astrologer Grant Lewi (who writes under the name of "Scorpio") attaches historical importance to Uranus being in square (bad relationship) with Neptune: "This position, because of the slow motion of the two planets involved, lasts for many years at a time and consequently influences many people. It is the aspect of the so-called 'younger generation' that ran rampant right after the [first] World War, overturning law, and order, and especially personal morality."

Turning from these debatable planets back to the late 19th century in general: About this time astrological writers began to make very free with tradition, mixing in (to taste) every kind of symbolical significance, especially if it could be drawn from the Bible. This tendency was to develop further toward the end of the century. In 1862 Frances Rolleston published her book *Mazzaroth* (which was mentioned in Chapter 3) in which she not only makes the claim that the astral names and emblems "express the promises and prophecies revealed to Adam, Seth, and Enoch" but commits herself to many fairly exact equations between the Scriptures and the stars. For the Book of Revelation, she finds that its chief revelations are Zodiacal: Thus the 12 precious stones of the Holy City inevitably correspond to the 12 Zodiacal constellations.

A quarter of a century later another lady, Rosa Baughan (women from now on were to take much more part in this once almost entirely masculine mystery), combined astrology with chiromancy. She apportions each finger to a planet and does the same with the lines on the face. Apart from assigning the nose to Mercury, she assigns six lines between the hair and the eyes to the six other planets; in each case, if the line is broken, it indicates something unfortunate. And she explains that Saturn gives you black moles, whether on face or body, and Jupiter purple-brown ones. The appeal of all this detail presumably lay in that age-old principle of correspondences or "sympathy." She herself describes her writings as "Old World lore": "Macrocosm and microcosm must be no longer divorced." She also retains the ancient doctrine of the four humors.

In the U.S.A. about the same time (1892) a curious book was published in Boston called *Astrology of the Old Testament*. Its author, Karl Anderson (who belongs to the same category as Frances Rolleston), described himself as Professor

The 19th-century astrologer Rosa Baughan's version of the wheel of Pythagoras—a method of prediction by numbers that answers questions with "yes" or "no." Here is how it works : A questioner named, say, Tom shuts his eyes and picks a number—say, 9—from the table (right). To this he adds the number that, on the wheel, is opposite his initial T, which is 6, making 15. Next he takes two numbers from the list (right) : One for the day of the week—say, Thursday, which is 31 —and one for Thursday's ruling planet, Jupiter, which is 78. He adds 31 and 78 to 15 making 124, which he then must divide by 30, leaving the remainder 4. If the remainder is among the numbers written in the *lower* half of the inner wheel, the answer is "no." If it is one of the numbers in the *upper* half, the answer is "yes." The answer can be further qualified by the position of the number either on the left side or the right side, which indicate a "long time" and a "short time" respectively. Since Tom's number, 4, is on the upper left side, the answer to his question is "yes, in a long time."

1	11	22	28	29
6	2	12	23	30
15	7	3	13	24
19	16	8	4	14
25	20	17	**9**	5
27	26	21	18	10

Saturday 45   Saturn 55
Sunday 106   Sun 34
Monday 52   Moon 45
Tuesday 52   Mars 39
Wednesday 102   Mercury 114
Thursday 31   Jupiter 78
Friday 68   Venus 45

of Chaldean, Arabian, and Egyptian Astrology. He also likes a rich, complicated recipe and flavors the soup with the Free Masons, the Great Pyramid, and some odd etymology: The word "angel," he says, is a corruption of the astrological term "angle." This book, like *Mazzaroth*, presupposes a fundamentalist cosmology. But this time the signs of the Zodiac are linked with the 12 tribes of Israel; for example, Taurus with Ephraim and Leo with the Old Testament's "Lion of Judah." And, though Anderson much prefers the Old Testament to the New, he can also explain whatever is valid in the latter: Thus he asserts that when Christ "stooped and wrote upon the ground" he was casting a horoscope or horary question.

These 19th-century writers have been quoted not for their intrinsic merit but because their oddity is a historical phenomenon. As the century wore on, there was in certain circles (in Britain and America especially) a swing away from the rationalist concept of a mechanical universe and a renewed hunger for the irrational. In 1875 the Theosophical Society (with an American, Colonel Olcott, as its president) was founded in the United States by that supercharged eccentric, Madame Blavatsky. This extraordinary woman, whose "lamasery" (i.e., sitting room) was crowded with stuffed snakes and monkeys, specialized in producing psychic phenomena. She always attributed her powers not to herself but to her invisible Himalayan "Masters" (the "White Brotherhood"), chief among whom was "Koot Hoomi." *"Someone who knows all,"* she said, "dictates to me."

Repeated attempts were made to discredit her as a charlatan, but at the time of her death in 1891 she numbered over 100,000 followers.

Soon after Theosophy was founded, it recruited a new leader in the equally dynamic but more socially conscious and more intellectual Mrs. Annie Besant. The movement had by this time become linked with India and therefore could not remain untouched by astrology: Indian astrology contained elements that, though suspect to the more intelligent astrologers whether of the Renaissance or the 20th century, had a natural appeal to many theosophists (who preferred their universe to be mystically sensational). Their obsession with a mystical "divine nature" would encourage the acceptance of the early more hermetic view of the stars as divine creatures—and perish the thought that they might be mere "signs," not "causes."

In 1885 there was published in Madras an English translation by N. Chidambaram Aiyar of an alleged astrological classic, the *Brihat Jataka*. The translator explains in his introduction: "The difficulty in conceiving active agency as possessed by the planets when viewed in the light of huge inert balls, will be removed when we suppose that each planet possesses a soul." Not only do they possess souls: They are "rewarding and chastising officers." And that is where we come in, or rather where we never got out. For, according to this Hindu textbook, "the science [of horoscopy] treats of the effects of the good and bad deeds (karma) of men in their previous birth."

Left, Madame Blavatsky, founder of the Theosophical Society in 1875, with two of her disciples. Since the society derived many of its theories from Indian mystical thought, it was inevitably colored by Indian astrology. Below, a monument dedicated to Theosophy at Adyar, India, where Madame Blavatsky established her headquarters in 1879.

THERE IS NO RELIGION HIGHER THAN TRUTH

This involvement of astrology with the doctrine of reincarnation, which would *ipso facto* be unacceptable to any Christian astrologer, would have caused no difficulty to most of the theosophists, who were only too conscious of their "karma." In her often reprinted book *The Secret Doctrine*, Madame Blavatsky, who looked like a gypsy, indulges in what appears to be gypsy-like mystification. Most of her doctrine is highly esoteric and some of the astrological portions would be repugnant to orthodox astrologers. For instance, she has an original view of the Moon, whom she seems to consider primarily evil: "Constantly vampirised by her child [i.e., the earth], she revenges herself on it by soaking it through and through with the nefarious, invisible, and poisoned influence which emanates from the occult side of her nature."

As a double-dyed or multiple-dyed universalizer, Madame Blavatsky will have none of the fixed and specific notations of orthodox Western astrology: "Why see in the Pisces a direct reference to Christ—one of the several world-reformers, a Saviour but for his direct followers, but only a great and glorious Initiate for all the rest—when that constellation shines as a symbol of all the past, present, and future Spiritual Saviours who dispense light and dispel mental darkness?"

Annie Besant was much less extravagant. Though she once wrote of "this ancient and much maligned science," she admitted that she had little knowledge of astrology and in her *Autobiography* makes only moderate, and comparatively conventional, claims for it: "Keeping in view the way in which sun, moon, and planets influence the physical condition of the earth, there is nothing incongruous with the orderly view of nature in the view that they also influence the physical bodies of men. . . . At the most, astrology, as it is now practised, can only calculate the interaction between these physical conditions at any given moment, and the conditions brought to them by a given person whose general constitution and natal conditions are known. *It cannot say what the person will do, nor what will happen to him . . . .*" (italics mine).

Note that in her first sentence Mrs. Besant omits the fixed stars (including the Zodiacal signs), which no one, she says, has ever proved can "influence the physical condition of the earth." And in her second sentence (like a few 20th-century astrologers but unlike the vast majority of their predecessors, who said all they needed was the natal chart) she states that an advance knowledge is required of the "general constitution" of the "given person."

Some popular astrologers

So much for the two great theosophical Amazons. As an example of a theosophist of the time who was also a professional (and highly successful) astrologer, we may take Alan Leo, the son of a soldier in a Scottish regiment. Leo believed he had lived before and also believed, as we saw in Chapter 1, that "every human being belongs to a Father Star in Heaven or Star Angel as did Jesus Christ according to our Scripture." (Most earlier astrologers had denied that

Christ was *influenced* by the Star of Bethlehem.) Leo added: "And I am convinced that every man derives his will power from a Planetary Sphere of Influences which he uses, or abuses, by which we can overcome evil tendencies, and control his animal nature, hence Astrology teaches that Character is Destiny, also [the old cliché] that the Wise man rules his Stars while the fool obeys them."

Leo began his astrological work in the 1880s and soon made friends, or enemies, of other astrologers who gave themselves names like Aphorel, Charubel, Casael, and Sepharial. Together with Aphorel (F. W. Lacey) he launched *The Astrologer's Magazine.* The first number included three horoscopes: those of Jesus Christ, of the then Prince of Wales (Edward VII), and of Stanley, the explorer of Africa.

Leo and Aphorel encountered some antagonism from the editor of *Zadkiel's Almanac,* whose system they did not accept. (The Jacobean situation of quarreling within the fraternity seems to have come around again.) But their paper survived and in 1895 was renamed *Modern Astrology.* They were thus pioneers of the present era of astrological journalism. Leo, who specialized in Uranus (which was very strong in his own horoscope), was an odd person, as was his wife Bessie, who could not agree to any marriage that was not platonic. Bessie received her first lessons in astrology from Leo on the sands of Bournemouth, on which he drew the signs and the planets for her. Later, finding that his Moon and her Sun were in the same degree of Aries, they decided to get married—platonically. Leo agreed because "I have a work to do for the world for which celibacy is

Mrs. Annie Besant, who succeeded Madame Blavatsky as president of the Theosophical Society. Mrs. Besant's views on astrology were less extreme than those of her predecessor: While ascribing some influence to the planets, she denied that astrology alone could provide a true picture of an individual's future.

Britain's Alan Leo (1860-1917)—astrologer,
theosophist, and co-founder of *Modern
Astrology*—depicted in his own horoscope.

essential." Leo died in 1917, after which people began writing to his widow to tell her that he was still teaching them astrology and theosophy "on the astral plane." It seems likely that these people's receptivity was enhanced by their world-war experiences.

But back in the period when Leo was beginning his crusade, a very different type of Englishman lent his weight to the astrological cause by admitting to a qualified belief in the subject. Richard Garnett (1835-1906), Keeper of Printed Books at the British Museum, came of a distinguished family and was not only a well-known author but also a brilliant linguist. And so he can be said to have been one of the first persons in Europe of high intellectual caliber to have taken a serious interest in astrology since the 17th century. Though he himself claimed that his reasoning on the subject was "wholly empirical," he seems to have had a naturally mystical bent that, in reaction against 19th-century materialism and a purely mechanistic cosmology, led him to plump for astral influences. His empiricism consisted in collecting evidence from the horoscopes, for example, of well-known madmen like George III, on the strength of which he claimed to have established "a *prima facie* case." No astrologer at that time had based his defense upon statistics (though modern statisticians would not allow that Garnett had considered nearly enough instances).

Garnett was wary of astrology's "pretension to foretell the *times* of events." What he did attribute to it was the explanation of certain aspects of human character—and therefore the power to estimate the *likelihood* of an individual's behavior. His physics (he assumes the astral influences are transmitted through an "all-pervading aether") would be suspect to modern physicists and astronomers; but his motivation, of course, was not so much scientific as religious. What seems to have appealed to him in astrology is what had appealed to so many before him—the "marvellous harmony" it implies in the universe.

While Richard Garnett was still Keeper of Books in the Museum, another intellectual of vastly greater originality was probing around the fringes of astrology under the influence of a crank. The great man was Sigmund Freud; his mentor was Dr. Wilhelm Fliess, a nose-and-throat specialist with a passion for numerology. Fliess, who within his own field tried to connect the nose with menstruation, was determined to discover a similar periodicity in all the spheres of human and animal life. He was especially obsessed by the numbers 28 (for a woman) and 23 (for a man). Starting with the Moon, which is traditionally linked with menstruation, Fliess seems (in the words of Freud's biographer Ernest Jones) to have been looking for "a deeper connection between astronomical movements and the creation of living organisms. From the nose to the stars, as with Cyrano de Bergerac!"

Fliess's puzzling influence over Freud ceased about the turn of the century and no recognition of numerology, astrology, or related subjects entered the canon of orthodox Freudian psychoanalysis. (Later, as we shall see in Chapter 7, Freud's pupil and rival, C. G. Jung, who looked for something in everything, made an "astrological experiment" in an attempt to relate astrology to his psychological principles.) But, whether or not any professional psychologist has accepted astrology wholly or in part, modern astrologers have attempted to assimilate modern psychology. The ingenious French astrologer André Barbault studied Freud's own horoscope (in which Scorpio was in the ascendant and the Sun, Mercury, Uranus, and Pluto all in Taurus) and comments: "The psychological universe that Freud discovered is that of Taurus (associated with Scorpio)." In a passage quoted in Chapter 3, Barbault sees Taurus as "the meat-safe of the Zodiac . . . and ultimately, through displacement of the oral tendency, the strong-box of the Zodiac." And he continues: "The discovery of the oral *libido* (Taurus) was completed by that of the anal and general *libido* that one meets precisely in Scorpio, Freud's second dominating sign."

In the intervening half-century, which included two world wars, a new school of psychological astrology was to appear in Germany, and K. E. Krafft from Switzerland (see Chapter 7) was to develop what he called "astro-biology," while in the English-speaking countries *traditional* astrology was to flourish in its more popular, and certainly less trustworthy, forms in the annual almanac and the Sunday newspaper. Just before World War I *Zadkiel's Almanac*, now edited by A. J. Pearce, was selling more than 200,000 copies per year.

A typical figure in England was Walter Gorn Old, who called himself "Sepharial" and who, apart from orthodox astrology, went in for fortune telling with cards, crystal gazing, and numerology. Just before World War I he published a "Guide to Speculators" called *The Silver Key*. This book offers an analysis of planetary influence on the turf, partly by names (which are reduced to numbers and then equated with the planets) and partly by colors. He explains that the horoscope for the last Lincoln Handicap race showed "Uranus in the fifth division of the heavens, which is held to rule speculative concerns. This planet indicates grey, or black and white hoops with stripes." The Lincoln Handicap was won by a horse named "Kaffir Chief," whose jockey wore black and white hoops.

In a handicap race, moreover, according to Sepharial, there are also the weights to be considered: You must find out what the Moon's position corresponds with at the time of the race "for inasmuch as the Moon is a proved weight-lifter, we may naturally expect that gravity will be the more readily overcome in that instance, and that the performance of the animal carrying that weight will be proportionately good."

Such were the preoccupations of popular astrologers and their public in 1913. But Sepharial himself, like most of his colleagues, was able to adjust with no trouble to what happened next. In *The Great Devastation* (the foreword is dated October 1914) he bases his preview of the war on a cyclic view of history: "History repeats itself. Substituting Germany for Persia, and France for Greece, you will find the whole history of the war in the eleventh chapter of Daniel." His prose in this booklet has a purple and sometimes semi-biblical quality and the general tone is optimistic: "We are about to enter upon the Aquarian Age wherein Humanity will be its own Dictator, when the public conscience shall be a law unto itself, and the service of Goodwill shall become the sweet slavery of the Soul." In the same year he predicted "a tremendous social upheaval" in Russia; but if he meant the Revolution, he dated it at least a year too early.

In 1915 Sepharial published another booklet: *Why the War Will End in 1917*. (This was sold for a penny by the same publisher who put out, also for a penny, a booklet entitled *The Angel Warriors of Mons*, in which it was argued that this legendary apparition of angels who fought on the Allied side was supported by good evidence.) Sepharial here stresses the sinister horoscope of Kaiser William, whose Moon was "in direct opposition to Uranus, the planet of disruption," and whose mid-heaven was ominously occupied by the malefic planets Mars and Neptune.

Sepharial foretold a German surrender in August 1917. In a section called "The Readjustment" he foresees an "Aquarian Age of a liberated humanity . . . marked by a beneficent Communism." Still, before the millenium comes (in A.D. 2449) the world will have to face "the great climacteric, which lasts from 1991 to 1997, and which ensanguines the whole of the East." But whatever happens in the East the English can be of good heart (Sepharial is always a patriot): "The Anglo-Saxon race will be the paramount power for good in the world during the next sixteen hundred years."

Throughout history all forms of divination have tended to thrive on major wars. World War I was no exception. Alan Leo, who among popular astrologers was far more successful than Sepharial, gave three lectures in 1915 on "Mars; the War Lord." He too is patriotic and looks for historical precedents. "At the time of the Crimean War, the War Lord Mars was in the sign Leo, and it ended in a victory for the British Lion." This astral pattern was repeated in the Boer War. (Leo is careful to point out that Mars is not necessarily malefic.)

As in the Second World War, astrologers were on the whole optimistic. And precise—when they were retrospective. Many accurate horoscopes were produced retrospectively—for example, one was cast for the *Lusitania* for the time of her launching. It seems also clear that astrology emerged from the war stronger than it had been before it. And this in spite of many exploded predictions like Leo's or Sepharial's.

Examples of this aftermath in the 1920s will be given in the next chapter. The most remarkable developments were in Germany; England produced curiosities, like a book published in 1928 entitled *The Brontës and their Stars,* by Maud Margesson. Its publication implies at least that the sort of people who would read the books of the Brontë sisters, or who would be interested in them as personalities, would also be interested in them astrologically. The author

Sigmund Freud (right) with his friend Wilhelm Fliess, a fellow doctor from Austria who postulated a numerical relationship between human physiology and the stars.

admits that her own book can only be approximately correct astrologically, since with all of the Brontës only their birth *days* are known, never their birth *hours*. Thus there is the problem of deciding the rising signs; but this does not deter Miss Margesson. The "only sure and dependable guide to the ascendant," she says, "where the time of birth is unknown, is an intimate knowledge of character and career." Following this topsy-turvy procedure, she finds with Emily, for example, that "there seems to be only one sign that could possibly represent her, and that is the fixed, intense, reserved sign Scorpio." She also stresses the family resemblance in the four Brontë children's horoscopes, pointing out that in each of them "Mercury, the ruler of the mind, is in aspect to the mystic Neptune and the occult Uranus." Unlike the astrologers quoted above, Miss Margesson has no qualms about making these two planets work for individuals.

In the United States (which, with the exception of the theosophists, had been slow to take to the "royal art") the great pioneer was Evangeline Adams (1865-1932), whose married name was Mrs. George E. Jordan and whose philosophy, according to herself, was "a compound of truths of all truths." She was said to be a descendant of John Quincy Adams, sixth president of the United States, which is easy to believe, in respect at least of her drive, courage, and success. According to Irys Vorel, the author of the American *Astrological Handbook,* Miss Adams's career "was truly meteor-like. . . . 'I have Mars conjunct my natal Sun in the 12th House. I will always triumph over my enemies!' she said." Her first arrival in New York City, to set up as a reader of horoscopes, had indeed been meteoric in more senses than one.

Having checked in at the Windsor Hotel on Fifth Avenue she proceeded to inspect the natal chart of its owner, Warren F. Leland. The chart told her that he was threatened immediately with a terrible disaster. Mr. Leland at once thought of a crash on the stock market but then remembered that the next day was a holiday, which meant that stocks couldn't go down at least till after that interval. But what the stars were threatening was not Wall Street but the Windsor, which was burned to the ground next afternoon. Miss Adams lost many of her belongings but had laid the foundation of her future fame as the most popular reader of horoscopes in America.

For all this, in 1914 she was arrested for fortune telling and, instead of buying herself off with a fine, elected to stand trial. She appeared in court loaded with reference books, explained how she made her forecasts, and then capped theory with practice by reading from a birth date of a person unknown to her, who happened to be the judge's son. The judge concluded that: "The defendant raises astrology to the dignity of an exact science." Contemporary astrologers in New York have reason to bless Evangeline Adams for this showdown: Fortune telling there is still illegal but, as is not the case in England, astrology is no longer deemed to be fortune telling. In Washington, D.C., however, as late as November 1959, an astrologer named Katherine Q. Spencer was brought to court on a fortune-telling charge. Still, she too was acquitted.

	Sun	Mon	Tues	Wed	Thurs	Fri	Sat
I Saturn	4	0	3	0	9	9	9
Jupiter	5	1	4	1	1	1	1
Mars	4	0	3	0	9	9	0
Sun	4	9	3	9	9	9	9
Venus	8	4	7	4	4	4	4
Mercury	7	3	6	3	3	3	3
Moon	2	7	1	7	7	7	7

hours

II

Sunday	Sun
Monday	Moon
Tuesday	Mars
Wednesday	Mercury
Thursday	Jupiter
Friday	Venus
Saturday	Saturn

III Monday

Moon	1	8	15	22
Saturn	2	9	16	23
Jupiter	3	10	17	24
Mars	4	11	18	
Sun	5	12	19	
Venus	6	13	20	
Mercury	7	14	21	

IV

AYIQJ	=	1	BKRC	=	2
GLS Sh	=	3	DMT	=	4
EN	=	5	WVXU	=	6
ZO	=	7	PHF	=	8

V

Alexandra Park	=	5
last winner	=	2
planetary hour	=	0
winning number		7

How to pick the winner in horse racing by a numerological system (evolved by the British astrologer Sepharial) that includes the use of "planetary hours." Take a race run at Alexandra Park at 4 P.M. on Monday, April 22, 1963. First, the name "Alexandra Park" is converted into numbers by relating each letter to the figures in Table IV : A=1, L=3, E=5, and so on. These numbers are added together, and then the figures of the total (41) are added : 4 + 1=**5**. This process is repeated with the name of the winner of the preceding race ; say the result is **2**. Next, the planetary hour is calculated. Each hour in a day is ruled by a planet (Table III). The race was run on Monday, the Moon's day, so the first hour is the Moon's. So are the eighth hour (since only seven planets are used) and the 15th. As Table III shows, the 16th hour (4 P.M.) is Saturn's. Table I shows that Saturn on Monday has a numerical value of **0**. Now, as shown in Table V, the three numbers that have been calculated are added : 5 + 2 + 0=**7**. Finally, all the names of the runners on the race card (right) are transposed into figures ; and the one with the value of 7 will win.

Alex. Park   Mon. 22nd Apr. 1963

5th Race 4.0   M. & C. (Racing) Ltd.

1 ....
2 ....
3 WESTERN QUEEN *7*
4 AYLWIN *8*
5 ANAHITA *3*
6 ESCORT *5*
7 FANCY NANCY *5*
8 PREPOTENT *6*
9 THE TEASE *8*

(An earlier astrologer whose fame equaled Miss Adams's had not been so lucky. In 1917 Alan Leo had been prosecuted in London on a charge of "pretending and professing to tell fortunes." Leo's lawyers brought a good defense. They argued that Leo was not an imposter, because he was practicing a science in which he had a *bona fide* belief. They pointed out that free will was an integral part of the science; that astrology merely told "tendencies"; that if a man chose to go out when bombs were falling and get killed, the fault was his own and not in the stars. Leo himself stated that he did not claim to be able to predict the future or the fortunes of others, and tried to emphasize his legitimacy by adding that his clients were mostly of the rich and intellectual classes. But this judge was unimpressed; he fined Leo £5 and £25 costs.)

Having thus made astrology respectable, Miss Adams began to be consulted by the great. In her studio at Carnegie Hall, New York City, she was visited by King Edward VII, Caruso, and Mary Pickford. As for J. P. Morgan, Evangeline Adams wrote: "He was sceptical at first but I convinced him. During the last years of his life I furnished him a regular service. It explained the general effects of the planets on politics, business and the stock market." In *Your Place among the Stars* Miss Adams explained Morgan's success: Among other things in his chart, Jupiter was "tied down very firmly to the material plane, but on that plane he is made very strong." It is probably due to this dynamic lady more than to any other individual that today, according to the American Federation of Astrologers (who admit these figures are merely estimates), the number of horoscopes cast per year runs into millions. The money spent on them would probably run into millions also.

On April 23, 1930, Evangeline Adams began to broadcast three times weekly on her subject. Three months later she announced that she had received 150,000 requests for horoscopes. A year later the letters and requests were coming in at the rate of 4000 a day. It seems clear that she was a "radio personality" and that listeners regarded her as almost a friend. She died on November 10, 1932. Two days later the *New York Times* published some rather pained paragraphs—pained not by her death but by her life: "Radio and astrology dancing to victory hand in hand make a sufficiently odd couple; but that is not all. This incongruous fellowship has flourished in an age of intellectual emancipation . . . ," etc. For the writer of this piece Miss Adams had obviously been both anachronism and arch-enemy.

On November 13 she lay in state in her studio at Carnegie Hall; the public was admitted from noon till 7 P.M. On November 14 her funeral service was thronged with both personal acquaintances and listeners and there were thousands of telegrams of condolence. The preacher commented on Miss Adams's "love and understanding" of her fellow men. To add a posthumous touch of myth, Irys Vorel declared later that Evangeline Adams had predicted her own death and for that reason had politely declined a 21-night lecture tour which had been offered her for the autumn of 1932.

By this time the once royal art had become almost wholly the property of the people, and the mass-communication media were fully aware of its drawing power. In Britain, one of the principal channels for mass astrology was the more "popular" kind of Sunday newspaper such as the *People* and the *Sunday Express*. In the *People* Edward Lyndoe (who claimed to be "the most consulted astrologian of all time") was by the end of 1934 foretelling the immediate decline of Hitler. Also, like so many successful journalists in other spheres, he exploited the good will of his readers by publishing books. A typical example is *Your Next Ten Years and After* (1935), which professed to help anyone, in accordance of course with his stars (no trouble here about *exact* horoscopes), to better himself and his career.

Lyndoe's recommended method is autosuggestion. Size yourself up according to your stars, then make the appropriate suggestions to yourself over and over: "Then go out and win!" All he asks his reader to go by is the *day* of his birth—i.e., what sign the Sun was in at the time (a very rough-and-ready starting-point but the usual one, inevitably, in astrological journalism). Knowing then what sign you belong to, since you know your own birthday, all you need to do is to repeat to yourself a particular set of slogans supplied by Lyndoe, one for each day of the week. Thus on Tuesday, if you are Leo, you will say over and over to yourself when you are alone, as when in bed: "I am more positive today than ever before." If you are Virgo: "One thing at a time, and that one done efficiently"; if Sagittarius: "As a sportsman I take the rough with the

America's Evangeline Adams helped to make astrology both respectable and popular. Her acquittal in 1914 on a fortune-telling charge improved astrology's status as a profession; later, her regular radio broadcasts attracted a vast audience and a huge fan mail.

smooth"; if Aquarius: "I believe passionately in the brotherhood of man." Lyndoe also advises each group what they should concentrate on in each of the next 10 years.

A similar book, *What Your Birthday Stars Foretell* (1933), was written by Lyndoe's rival, R. H. Naylor of the *Sunday Express*. Lyndoe's book had contained no predictions; Naylor, knowing only too well that hardly any of his readers will know what their birthday stars really are or were, is careful to admit in his introduction that his book is by its nature rough-and-ready or, as he calls it, "generalized." And, he goes on, "it has all the faults of a generalization." For all that, it must contain some truth and therefore be some help to the reader. It deals, he explains, with "basic fundamentals of character and fortune. Superficial differences will result from variation in place of birth (horizon), from year of birth, *and even from heredity and environment*" (italics mine). But for truly professional astrologers, as we have seen, the basic fundamentals of character and fortune could not be established without a knowledge of the moment of birth, which gives one the all-important ascendant.

Apart from this catering for stock-type "individuals" (all humanity being divided into 12 groups), this period saw a boom in *mundane* astrology—the foretelling of public events by people who were as often off the target as the politicians themselves. Thus Louis de Wohl wrote in June 1938: "To an astrologer the world picture is perfectly clear." He saw, for instance, that "the dominion of the Mercury types, that is the purely intellectuals [*sic*] of a people, no matter which it may be, *must* have disastrous consequences at the present stage of culture and civilization." Note here the anti-intellectual bias that modern astrologers tend to share with modern politicians (though, to be fair to de Wohl, he was thinking mainly of Hitler and Mussolini).

As we shall see in Chapter 7, de Wohl was to be involved in the coming war in his capacity as astrologer. In the meantime his predictions were, true to type, optimistic—and unfortunately incorrect. He finds his adopted country a model of stability because Chamberlain had an excellent horoscope and because the British Government is a solar system in miniature; so there would be no war in the near future. And (writing in June 1938) he can see that "Autumn 1938, the first three months of 1939 and summer 1940 bring heavy weather for Germany." He adds: "I do not believe that Mahatma Gandhi will survive the first half of 1939." (Gandhi lived till 1948.)

As World War II approached, the astrological journalists (in Britain at least) were almost unanimous in denying that it would happen. In 1939 a peculiar book appears, by one "Leonardo Blake," called *Hitler's Last Year of Power*. Blake is a much lower grade writer than de Wohl, but his statements demonstrate the sort of thing people read and find consoling. The foreword of his book states flatly: "Be reassured: there will be no war."

Blake explains why: The destiny of German was "fixed unalterably by the horoscope of January 18, 1871, when that country was first unified by Bismarck." Though this horoscope is the really important one, it is confirmed by the horoscope of the German Republic for November 9, 1918. As for Hitler's horoscope, it compares very badly with Mr. Chamberlain's: Hitler's power will "ebb away" in September 1939 and in June and July 1940 his "attempts to extend his activities will not succeed." Blake added the prediction that Goebbels "will not survive the crisis of 1940," and that the summer of the same year would see the defeat and downfall of Hitler.

While harnessing the stars to Chamberlain's chariot, Leonardo Blake naturally played down Churchill, though admitting that his horoscope showed profundity, magnanimity, and breadth. He foresaw that "Mr. Churchill's role in affairs during the decisive years to come will not be played at the head of a British Cabinet. Nor will he become a factor in turning the scales of British policy . . . . But when, in 1941, the progressed Sun transits together with the progressed Saturn, a quiet and even a little less happy period breaks for him. He is going to retire more and more from public life . . . ."

It is unnecessary to multiply instances of such popular astrological predictions made on the very eve of the war. We shall see in the next chapter how these astrologers were in no way deterred from continuing such predictions while the war was being waged. And their public were in no way disenchanted with them. At the same time, this was not the whole wartime story of astrology. The whole story was a good deal odder than that.

7 Coming up to date

Just before the Second World War broke out, people like Leonardo Blake were only too ready to foretell that it would not happen. But as soon as it happened they snatched up their pens and were at it again. Thus Blake followed his *Hitler's Last Year of Power* with *The Last Year of War—and After*. For him the last year of war was to coincide with the first year of war: He seems to have written his book in the autumn of 1939. Anyway, it was all to be over by the middle of 1940. Blake was well pleased with himself: He claimed that 10 of his predictions in *Hitler's Last Year of Power* had been verified. As for this new book, here, said Blake, "we are writing history in advance."

The crux of the new book was that in 1940 the German nation would revolt and overthrow the Nazi party. His more particular predictions were as follows:

(1) On March 7, 1940, there will be "brilliant successes" for Chamberlain.
(2) April 20 will be Hitler's last birthday when his Sun will be in conjunction with Saturn and both square to Pluto.
(3) "About May 5, 1940, the transiting Jupiter has to pass over Saturn: a black day for Nazi Germany."
(4) June 1940 will be crucial.
(5) "The July days of 1940 are dark days indeed for Hitler."

Throughout the book Blake keeps threatening Hitler with "universal law." We all know how that law functioned in 1940.

One of the weekly lectures organized by the Astrological Lodge of the Theosophical Society in London. Countless associations and societies—which include every type of astrological enthusiast and cater for every shade of astrological belief—have sprung up all over the modern world.

The overwhelming German successes in Europe did not discourage the astrologers of Britain—especially not those of the popular papers like Edward Lyndoe. He came out with the hopeful statement: "The big event of 1941 will be the sudden emergence of a World Leader." This would be the beginning of a new era; but as to the nature of "this coming" (a phrase with a religious sound), Lyndoe wrote: "I reserve my statement." Nor would he commit himself as to the length of the interim period before right triumphed over wrong; he merely hinted that in 1943 investment possibilities would be better than they had been in previous years.

It was this incurable optimism on the part of British astrologers that in June 1942 occasioned that question in Parliament mentioned in Chapter 1. The questioner, who wanted a ban on astrological prediction about the war, got little satisfaction from the Minister of Information. The former had quoted the *People* (Lyndoe's paper) to the effect that a German invasion of England was impossible. The Minister merely commented that astrologers in other papers said England *could* be invaded.

Some 10 months before this, when Britain had been at her most defenseless, the anthropologist Tom Harrisson (founder of Mass Observation) had published an article on "Mass Astrology" in the *New Statesman and Nation* of August 16,

Three British newspaper astrologers, whose astrological predictions on the course of the war were a regular feature of the popular press during the 1940s: left to right, Edward Lyndoe, R. H. Naylor, and Adrienne Arden. All three appeared in a survey by a British magazine in 1941, which analyzed the accuracy of their forecasts. Out of a possible total of 30 marks, Lyndoe scored 9, Naylor 12, and Adrienne Arden 4.

1941. In a cautious footnote to this article Harrisson explains that he is not concerned with "astrological theory, accuracy or intention" but "only with the social effects of contemporary mass astrology." Astrology, he points out, had become "an extensive British interest" since Naylor started in the *Sunday Express* in 1930 and the current war had given it a big additional boost. Mass Observation had accordingly been conducting for the past three months a detailed study of the effect of astrology upon ordinary people. (What this means is that, in accordance with Harrisson's own directives, a large number of researchers—"mass observers"—had gone round with notebooks interviewing people.)

The findings of the observers, as summarized by Harrisson, were roughly as follows: Interest and belief in astrology had "tended steadily to increase since the war," the chief channel being the Sunday press and the chief, addicts being women. Astrology had a complex appeal that included a "constant emphasis on the bright side." Harrisson admitted that, especially among housewives, "the immediate effect is favourable to morale . . . . But the long-term effect is to stress fantasy confidences rather than real ones, and to emphasize the personal interest rather than the common interest."

This article sparked off a couple of others in the illustrated British weekly *Picture Post*. These were more journalistic in tone than Harrisson's. The first

IL VOSTRO DESTINO

LEONE
23 LUGLIO
22 AGOSTO

Non siate pessimisti, ma pratici e realisti, specie se doveste decidere un fidanzamento. Telefonate interessanti.

Divertitevi, lavorate, ma non eccedete in fatiche prolungate.

FRANCESCO WALDNER
horoscope

Leon Zitrone, né le 25 novembre 1914, Sagittaire.

SEMAINE DU 23 AU 29 NOVEMBRE

BELIER

(21 mars-20 avril)
Signe de feu.
Planète : Mars.
Action et lutte.

TAUREAU

(21 avril-21 mai)
Signe de terre.
Planète : Vénus.
Charme et douceur.

GEMEAUX

(22 mai-21 juin)
Signe d'air.
Planète : Mercure.
Intelligence et mouvement.

CANCER

(22 juin-22 juillet)
Signe d'eau.
Planète : Lune.
Rêves et sensibilité.

LION

(23 juillet-23 août)
Signe de feu.
Planète : Soleil.
Eclat et domination.

VIERGE

(24 août-23 septembre)
Signe de terre.
Planète : Mercure.
Intelligence, sens pratique.

PUSHING YOUR LUCK

HOROSCOPE BY CELESTE, AUGUST 14 TO 28, 1963

CAPRICORN (Dec. 23 Jan. 20) You can expect to see all your affairs show a marked improvement during the coming fortnight. This is especially true in regard to conditions in the home. Through an investment of some kind which you made in the past, or through the generosity of a woman, the domestic scene will be much happier. Whether this will be a passing thing or of a more permanent nature remains to be seen. Your great attraction to foreign interests or people continues and it will last for some time to come. This will be most

CANCER (June 22 July 23) There are three important dates for you during the coming fortnight. The first is August 16 and 17 which could raise your personal or professional prestige. This may cause a break with an older partnership or allegiance. The second is August 26 which could take you out of your present home and into an entirely new situation in life. The third is August 29 and 30 when you could fall madly in love, or have some unexpected piece of good luck. All of this, whatever form it may take, will leave you gasping for breath.

began: "The war has brought to millions of minds a new kind of faith, a new kind of stimulus, a new kind of drug or habit . . . . About forty per cent of the people, mainly women, have some belief in astrological prediction." The author again drew heavily on the Sunday newspapers and stressed the way so many of these journalists avoided discussion of the events that really called for it. He noted that many astrologers had predicted that Hitler would invade Sweden, one of the few countries near him that he left alone. As for the German invasion of Russia, Lyndoe had successfully predicted it in the *People,* whereas in the *Sunday Express* for June 22, 1941, Naylor stated defiantly of Germany and Russia: "I still hold to my forecast that they won't quarrel yet." It was on June 22, 1941, that Germany invaded Russia.

In November 1941, *Picture Post* published another article entitled "Astrologers Again," occasioned by a lunch given to astrologers by Miss Christina Foyle, London's biggest bookseller. At the lunch Naylor, irritated by his critics, accused them of having "the immovable idea that astrology postulates that the stars influence mankind. The modern astrologer makes no such absurd statement." In the speech that immediately followed, one Gipsy Petulengro (of the *Sunday Chronicle*) said: "I firmly believe that the stars rule the destiny of

Left, extracts from three astrological features published in women's magazines in Italy (top), France (center), and Britain (bottom). Below, a group of women gathered around a market stall buying prefabricated horoscopes based on Sun-signs. As Britain's Mass Observation found, this type of popular astrology makes its greatest appeal to women.

The well-known British newspaper astrologer
Gipsy Petulengro addressing guests at a
London luncheon held in 1941. At the
luncheon, he and other authors of astrological columns in the popular press made
speeches justifying both their astrological
beliefs and their wartime predictions.

mankind and nations." Petulengro also stated that he had foreseen the fall of France but had kept it dark in case he should be thought defeatist.

Several grades up from the Sunday fortune tellers was the area in which Louis de Wohl operated. Though he claimed Hungary as his fatherland, de Wohl had lived till 1935 in Germany, where he was fairly well known (under the name of Ludwig von Wohl) as a novelist, journalist, and film scriptwriter. He had also been an enthusiastic amateur astrologer; when he came to London he began to turn professional.

Unlike most British astrologers he had the entrée to what would now be called "Establishment" circles and the war gave him the chance to exploit these connections. According to himself, de Wohl met the British Foreign Secretary, Lord Halifax, who asked him for information about Hitler's horoscope. Following this, about September 1940, it seems that he entered the Psychological Research Bureau, after which he was commissioned in the British army with the rank of captain. He had in fact become the British government's official astrologer. (He claimed to have been the sole such official on the Allied side as against six working for the enemy.)

His activities were by their nature secret and for his conduct of this astrological war we must rely mainly on his own account. That he was employed at all does not mean that his distinguished employers believed in astrology. Like a great many other people, they believed that Hitler employed astrologers; de Wohl's job was to check what Hitler might be told by *his* astrological advisers.

In fact, there is no evidence (whatever was the case with the other Nazi leaders) that Hitler himself had any belief or even interest in astrology. Indeed, there is evidence to the contrary. But during the war and even up to the present day many people have chosen to believe that Hitler was as superstitious as some of the Roman emperors and that, like them, he employed his own pet astrologer. De Wohl mentioned six antagonists, but he too seems to have thought that there was one in particular who was Hitler's right-hand star man. In fact, it was owing to the existence of one very original astrologer, who was supposed to be filling this role, that de Wohl himself got his curious job with the British. The name of this bogyman (whom we have met before) was Karl Ernst Krafft.

Krafft was an essentially "modern" astrologer who wished to cut out the dead wood from the ancient art. Shortly before the war he had published in Switzerland a *Treatise of Astro-Biology*, in which he employed the modern statistical method. He was an exponent of "astral heredity," coining the phrase *"astro-hérédonomie,"* in an attempt to answer a common objection and to reconcile astrology with the incontestable facts of heredity. He pointed out the coincidences of birth dates within the same family and suggested that members of the same family tend to resemble each other not only in their physical and psychological make-up but also in their natal charts. All this seems rather a far cry from political warfare; but Krafft, who chose to stay in Germany when the war broke out, found himself involved in it—to his cost.

The Swiss astrologer Karl Ernst Krafft. During World War II, Krafft, while a prisoner of the Nazis, was compelled to produce "astrological" propaganda; he finally defied his captors, and died in 1945 on the eve of his transfer to Buchenwald.

(For much of what follows I am indebted to Mr. Felix Nebelmeier of Switzerland, who was himself involved in political warfare—on the Allied side. Since the war Mr. Nebelmeier has made an intensive study of astrology as a social phenomenon and, as part of this, has done some remarkable detective work on the true and sad story of Krafft.)

To appreciate this story we must go back to the days of the Weimar Republic. After Germany's defeat in 1918, astrology had a 15 years' boom in that country: No other country in Europe could show such a large and active astrological movement. This phenomenon was probably occasioned by Germany's economic and social collapse, by the disappearance of the monarchy and the old military caste, by inflation, unemployment, and poverty. As had happened often before in history, people (including very well-educated people) turned in such circumstances to the stars for consolation.

Among the astrologers under the Weimar Republic there was a small but vocal minority of violent nationalists, who published more than their share of books and pamphlets. This minority included four confirmed racialists whose writings were revealingly anti-Semitic. As Mr. Nebelmeier says, "no astrological movement ever produced anything quite like this particular group."

Louis de Wohl refers to one of these nationalist astrologers, whom he (wrongly) calls "Baron Sobottendorf." According to de Wohl, in 1923 the baron warned Hitler against undertaking "anything of importance" in November of that year. "Hitler neglected the warning and undertook his famous beer cellar *Putsch,* which landed him in jail." But de Wohl is wrong on two counts. First, the man's name was not Baron Sobottendorf. He called himself Rudolph Freiherr von S*e*bottendorf, but his real name was Adam Glandeck. Just after the armistice on the Western Front in November 1918 he was a member of the ultra-nationalist Bavarian "Free Corps" movement. He was also a member of the secret *Germanen* order, an anti-Semitic, right-wing, esoteric association.

More important, he bought a small Munich newspaper that later, under the new name of *Völkischer Beobachter,* he sold to the Nazi Party, who made it one of their chief organs of propaganda. As such it survived till 1945. Before he sold this afterward notorious paper, von Sebottendorf was also the editor of the leading German astrological monthly *Astrologische Rundschau.* This paper belonged to a "Dr." Hugo Vollrath, proprietor of the Theosophical Publishing House at Leipzig, who later was to join the Nazi party and try to establish himself as national leader of the German astrological movement.

Furthermore, it was *not* von Sebottendorf (or Baron Sobottendorf or Glandeck) who made the famous prediction in 1923. It was a well-known lady astrologer named Frau Elsbeth Ebertin, who edited a popular annual called *Ein Blick in die Zukunft (A Glimpse into the Future).* In the spring of 1923 someone sent her Hitler's birth date (though not the hour of his birth) and asked for a diagnosis of his character. Some months later she published such a diagnosis together with the warning that it would be unwise for this character to take any precipitate action during the coming November. Hitler is said to have been shown this piece of Frau Ebertin's and to have exclaimed: "What have women and the stars got to do with me?" He made his *Putsch* on November 8; two days later he was arrested and sent to prison, where he wrote the final draft of *Mein Kampf.*

"Sobottendorf" continued to be at least the nominal editor of his astrological paper until about 1930, though it seems that he spent much of his time in Turkey studying old Turkish freemasonry. Having failed to make Frau Ebertin's prediction for her, he now rather disappears from the story. More sinister characters, apart from the Dr. Vollrath mentioned above, were fishing in those troubled waters where the stars were reflected among eddies of racial prejudice.

There was a Munich physician called Dr. Wilhelm Gutberlet who was said to move in Hitler's circle and was credited with "mystic powers." He was an enthusiastic amateur astrologer and also claimed that he could identify people as Jews by the use of a pendulum. Another medical doctor who lived his astrology was Karl Günther Heimsoth, a great friend of Ernst Röhm, the S.A. commander. Dr. Heimsoth, it seems, cast and interpreted Röhm's horoscope in 1929 but was unable to provide a satisfactory reason for Röhm's notorious homosexuality.

It might be expected that these people would have been made welcome when the Nazis got power. But it did not work out like that. When Hitler came to power in 1933 he frowned upon both Gutberlet and Heimsoth, and in the following year they were both liquidated. Dr. Vollrath was still going strong and a Dr. Hugo Korsch (a *legal* doctor this time, who was also President of the Central Astrological Office) joined the Nazi Party just in order to stop Vollrath making a corner in the stars in the name of National Socialism. Yet none of the astrologers who tried could persuade the Nazis to adopt him and grant him a monopoly.

On the contrary, Hitler's assumption of power in 1933 was, to put it mildly, a considerable source of worry to Germany's leading astrologers. Some of them had recently published articles unfavorable to Hitler and his movement, so there was some twisting and covering of tracks. Hitler's official birth hour (and hence his probable ascendant) was well known to astrologers, but juggling attempts were made to provide him with a different birth hour and thereby a different ascendant. (The object was to shift his traditionally disastrous Saturn out of the 10th house, a position associated with an unfortunate end to a public career.) But on the whole, while there had been many references to Hitler's horoscope in the astrological journals during 1931 and 1932, such references began to dwindle. And the fate of Dr. Heimsoth in 1934 showed that Nazi Germany was not altogether safe for astrologers. This moral was to be driven home later.

When Hitler came into power there were half a dozen "serious" astrological periodicals in Germany, including the two conducted respectively by Dr. Korsch and Dr. Vollrath. In five years' time three of these had ceased publication, including those run by Korsch and Vollrath. Vollrath was especially hard hit, since the German branch of the Theosophical Society had also been dissolved. Also, there had been popular astrological weeklies and monthlies crammed with political predictions of the same type as those made by the English Sunday journalists, but after 1933 there were none such in Germany. This particular opium for the masses was under a ban. In the same way every year since 1922 there had been well-attended astrological conferences in Germany; but in 1938 a congress held near Munich was only allowed on condition that no congress report was published. Moreover, the Gestapo was present.

Then came the war and the importance of being Krafft. In 1939 Karl Ernst Krafft was living in a village in the Black Forest not far from the Swiss border. He could easily have returned to Switzerland, but it seems that Germany suited him. He was a great admirer of the Third Reich and was not too worried by the plight of its astrologers; though he was an outstanding authority on astrology, he preferred to call himself a psychological consultant. Also, through a member of Himmler's Head Office for State Security, he was in touch (at least indirectly) with most important people.

His link was a Dr. Fesel. Shortly after the war broke out, Dr. Fesel asked Krafft to write some memoranda for him. These memoranda contained, among other things, economic forecasts based on Krafft's interpretation of planetary cycles and major conjunctions. Fesel presumably intended to circulate them among members of Himmler's organization. (Himmler was apparently one of the Nazi leaders who did have some belief in astrology.) But Krafft did not confine himself to these commissioned memoranda. He had been watching Hitler's horoscope and now issued a prediction that Hitler's life would be in danger during the first 10 days of November 1939. This prediction (just like Frau Ebertin's in 1923) came home to roost in the Munich Beer Cellar. Hitler had

The ruins of the Munich Beer Cellar after
the assassination attempt on Hitler in 1939.
Krafft had earlier predicted a threat to
Hitler's life from his horoscope ; though he
was arrested for questioning, there was
no evidence to implicate him in the plot.

been there celebrating the *Putsch* of 1923 but he left before the bomb that was to assassinate him went off. Krafft promptly sent a telegram to Berlin drawing attention to his prediction and adding that Hitler's life would be in danger for a few days longer. Whereupon Krafft was arrested and questioned, only to be released for want of evidence that he had been in any way connected with the bomb. (It reminds one of William Lilly's being questioned—and also dismissed— by the committee that was set up to investigate the causes of the Great Fire of London in 1666.)

After this Krafft moved, or was moved, to Berlin. He may have made himself suspect, but somebody must also have thought him potentially useful. In 1940, keeping closely in touch with various government departments, he was engaged in political warfare, working on the prophecies of Nostradamus. These cryptic and concentrated pieces of apparent nonsense had always come in very handy for political warriors. Krafft did some lengthy and scholarly research on them, which was taken over by the Propaganda Ministry and angled, inevitably, to point to a German victory.

During 1940, Krafft got involved in a curious way with London (and this in its turn had repercussions on Louis de Wohl). The Romanian Minister to London, M. Virgil Tilea, being on leave in Bucharest, took it into his head to write to Krafft asking him for information about coming events. It was not that Tilea believed in astrology as such; but he had met Krafft once in Zurich and decided he had a flair as a prophet. Krafft was flattered by this letter and, being anxious to reply to it, asked his friend Fesel, Himmler's man, how his reply could be forwarded to London. The security high-ups agreed to arrange it, provided they could dictate the general nature of the reply. Once again political warfare was rearing its dubious head. Krafft would have liked to let the whole thing drop, but not so Dr. Fesel and the heads of his department. The letter was drafted and re-drafted seven times. At last M. Tilea received it in London and Krafft handed back his last month's salary to Fesel and said he was finished with that sort of work.

The letter that Tilea read, being by now a pure piece of political warfare writing, made him think that Krafft must be working directly for the Nazis and possibly for Hitler himself. This suspicion was enhanced by the fact that the letter had been sent from Berlin. Tilea showed the letter to various important people in London and suggested that, if Hitler was employing an astrologer (Krafft), it would be sensible of the British to employ another astrologer to tip them off as to what his opposite number would be up to. At first the British high-ups did not respond to this suggestion very eagerly, but finally (on Tilea's suggestion) accepted Louis de Wohl. De Wohl went through the rest of the war imagining he was countering Krafft in Berlin.

But Krafft did not spend the rest of the war in the way de Wohl assumed. On June 12, 1941, he was arrested. Like many other things this was the fault of Rudolf Hess, another Nazi leader who, like Himmler, was generally thought to be under the influence of astrologers. Hess's unauthorized flight into Scotland precipitated a great deal of face-saving and scapegoat-finding in Germany. Among those who suffered, thanks to Hess's reputation, were the astrologers. After all, Hess had had one on his staff at the Brown House in Munich—a certain Ernst Schulte-Strathaus, who was officially an expert on art. Schulte-Strathaus denied that he had ever given Hess any astrological advice or that he had any idea that Hess was going to leave Germany, but the sheer fact of their association provided another weapon against the astrologers. The Gestapo went into action.

The object of this action was twofold : first, to discover whether any astrologer had been connected with Hess ; secondly, to destroy the whole astrological movement in Germany. It had been decided that the astrological *Weltanschauung* must by its nature be unsympathetic to National Socialism and that the astrologers as a class were socially undesirable and politically unreliable. The *Aktion Hess* began on June 9, 1941, and continued for several weeks. Amateur and professional astrologers were rounded up left, right, and center and their technical libraries and personal papers confiscated. Also seized were all publishers' and booksellers' stocks of astrological literature.

Most of the people arrested at this time were released fairly soon, after signing an undertaking to cease practicing astrology or even discussing it. But there were two or three of the more serious astrologers who were never released. Among these was Krafft (though this was not known to his opposite number de Wohl). After spending a year in solitary confinement in the Alexanderplatz police prison in Berlin, Krafft was transferred during the summer of 1942 to a Propaganda Ministry building in north Berlin. Here, though still a prisoner, he was once more forced or persuaded into harness for political warfare purposes and for three or four months tried to work his passage to freedom via the stars.

It seems that he had been promised his release provided that over a certain period his work met the requirements of his masters. But there was a proviso that he would have to continue to work for them. Whether his work satisfied the Propaganda Ministry or not (if not, it would be to his credit), he obviously began to suspect that the promise would not be kept. Eventually he refused any further collaboration with his jailers. He was then shut up in the Lehrterstrasse prison from which he was transferred to the Oranienberg concentration camp. He was being transferred again (this time to Buchenwald) when he died on January 8, 1945. (More details about Krafft's astrological theory and practice will be given in the next chapter.)

In spite of the official "extermination" of astrology in Germany, a few practitioners did continue to be employed after the Aktion Hess, presumably because (to save their own skins) they were more willing or able than the perhaps over-scrupulous Krafft to divert their art to the needs of political warfare. One such was a well-known Hamburg astrologer called Wulff who specialized in Hindu techniques and who is mentioned in *The Last Days of Hitler* by the British

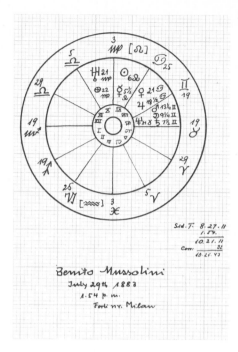

Below, the Hungarian-born astrologer Louis de Wohl. During World War II the British Government employed de Wohl to anticipate predictions by Hitler's alleged astrological advisers. From Mussolini's horoscope (right), cast in 1941, de Wohl correctly predicted "a violent and sudden end" for the Italian dictator.

historian Hugh Trevor-Roper. But it should be noted that Wulff was to all intents and purposes a prisoner on the estate of Himmler's masseur. It seems he was used by the head of the German secret service Schallenberg to influence Himmler, who toward the end of the war was in a vacillating but suggestible state of mind.

Further evidence that astrology had not completely disappeared is implicit in a letter written by Gerda Bormann to her husband (Martin Bormann, Hess's Chief of Staff and later Hitler's third deputy) on October 26, 1944: "Just as at the end of the last war," she observes, "fortune tellers and prophets have a strong following." On which Bormann has scribbled the comment: "I never even get such rubbish! Don't want to see it either!"

But much more striking than this is another episode recounted in *The Last Days of Hitler*. Hitler himself, as already stated, had little use for astrology and since 1941 the art had been officially condemned by his government. All the same, by the second week of April 1945 it was perhaps a case of any star in a storm. Goebbels in that week sent for two horoscopes—those of Hitler and of the German Reich itself; both had been "carefully kept in one of Himmler's research departments." These he discussed with the Führer in the light of an encouraging historical precedent: When Prussia was on the verge of defeat at the end of the Seven Years War, the tsarina of Russia had unexpectedly died and saved the situation for Frederick the Great. Sure enough, the two more recent horoscopes did hold forth the prospect of a similar "reversal of fortune." For both these horoscopes, according to Professor Trevor-Roper's informant, "had unanimously predicted the outbreak of war in 1939, the victories till 1941, and then the series of defeats culminating in the early months of 1945." The point was that these disasters were to be followed by an overwhelming victory in the second half of April 1945, and by peace in August: Germany would be great again by 1948.

Then followed the death of Roosevelt (compare the tsarina in the other war) and Goebbels at once telephoned to Hitler: "My Führer, I congratulate you. Roosevelt is dead. It is written in the stars that the second half of April will be the turning point for us. This is Friday April the Thirteenth. It is the turning point!" A fortnight later both men were dead.

What was Louis de Wohl doing on the allied side while all this was going on? He himself gives us some of the answers in *The Stars of War and Peace* (published 1952). His initial job, to counter Hitler's (presumed) astrological advisers, simply meant "making the same calculations so as to come to the same interpretative results, which enabled us to know what he ought to be told"—after which it remained only to guess how much they would dare to tell Hitler or how much they would cook their findings.

But some of de Wohl's activities were more positive than this. While he wrote that it was "to the honour of American astrologers" that "many of them had warned their country of the imminent Japanese attack" on Pearl Harbor, he himself claims to have foretold the result of the battle of Alamein after comparing the horoscopes of Montgomery and Rommel, which had been submitted to him without his knowing whose they were. And after 1942, when Hitler lost the initiative, de Wohl claims triumphantly: "Now *we* would time our actions against him . . . . Thus, when we attacked Sicily at the beginning of July 1943 when Jupiter was in 'square,' in an angle of 90 degrees, to the Sun position at Hitler's birth, Hitler knew that 'luck' was against him." De Wohl adds that Hitler also knew that astrology was being used against him: "We had seen to it that he knew." And he spares a word of pity for Mussolini who "had a beautiful horoscope" and who should have had sound astrological advice.

Another activity of de Wohl's during the war is mentioned in *Black Boomerang* by Sefton Delmer (published 1962). Delmer was the chief of British "black" political warfare, which specialized in disseminating lies of every sort for the confusion and undermining of the enemy. At one point it was decided that astrology too was worth a fake. There had been published in Germany up till 1938, when it was stopped, a successful astrological periodical called *Zenit.* Delmer revived *Zenit* for a few issues and de Wohl wrote the texts for him. These contained astrological predictions written *after* the events to which they referred—predictions of a kind, say, that might well put off German submariners from going to sea in their U-boats.

When we now read de Wohl's rather pompous accounts of his own astrological war (the gallant captain with a bandolier full of horoscopes) or think of the ups and downs of the German astrologers, the Second World War starts to resemble one of those galleries of distorting mirrors in a funfair. We saw in Chapter 2 how de Wohl himself attributed the technical inventions of the war to "Uranus running amuck." As for the bomb that ended the war with Japan, he naturally could explain that too. He cast Japan's horoscope retrospectively for July 16, 1945, and found that Mars was in conjunction with the fixed star Algol, known as the Head of the Medusa, "the worst fixed star we know of." (Algol had had an evil reputation through the ages, being called by the Arabs "the Demon." This presumably was because of its fluctuations in brightness. We now know that it is an example of a "binary system"; i.e., Algol is really *two* stars that revolve around, and therefore at intervals eclipse, each other.)

The postwar world

So much for World War II. What of astrology since? In defeated Germany, astrology made the same sort of comeback after its suppression under the Nazis as after the Kaiser's war. And for very much the same reasons. In Hamburg in 1947-48 a popular lecture on astrology could attract an audience of 500 or more. This is not so today, perhaps because Germany has become too prosperous.

Mr. Nebelmeier, who supplied me with the sad tale of Krafft, makes the comment that "if any moral at all can be drawn, it is that astrology cannot flourish under either a totalitarian regime or conditions of almost universal prosperity."

In Germany today, astrology flourishes
again in spite of its wartime suppression.
One of the best-known German astrologers
is Elfriede Keiser, who is said to number
leading politicians among her clientele.

But, if popular astrology is on the wane in Germany, it still remains the country
where astrology is treated most seriously, if only by a handful of unusually
imaginative scholars.

Among these scholars, Dr. Walter Koch might be selected as representative
of the highly academic approach to astrology—an approach that is becoming
more and more widespread today. With other German astrological scholars,
Koch has been deeply involved in investigating the controversial question of the
12 houses and the mathematical principles involved; and he has published
versions of the Regiomontanus and Placidus tables of houses. Koch's other
prewar works include numerous articles on Greek and Roman astrology, a book
on *Astrological Teachings Concerning Colors* (which grew out of his interest in
psychology), and another entitled *The Soul of the Gemstone*, which deals with
the occult properties of precious stones.

Koch's career suffered a serious setback during World War II, since he was one of the astrologers imprisoned by the Nazis, and his astrological library was burned by the Gestapo. But after the war, Koch returned to his astrological studies, and was one of the founder members of the Cosmobiological Society in 1946. This society published the first edition of the *Astrological Monthly* in 1949, to which Koch has since been a regular contributor.

In 1959, Koch was appointed scientific adviser to the Association of German Astrologers and that year read a paper on "The Symbolism of Astrological Geometry" to a congress of German astrologers. He has been in the forefront of the modern astrological tendency (which is especially obvious in German astrology) to seek tie-ups between astrology and psychological knowledge. One of the most interesting of this academic scholar's publications, called *Introvert and Extrovert,* is "a study in psychological astrological interpretation."

Introversion and extraversion are, of course, terms given to us by another imaginative scholar who gave astrology the benefit of the doubt—C. G. Jung. Jung also investigated the possibility of links between astrology and psychology; but he was one of a very few who approached the subject from the psychologist's viewpoint, not the astrologer's. He is always being claimed by modern astrologers as a champion of their cause; but, apart from his rather general statement that the moment of a man's birth remains part of his make-up, it would seem that he kept an open mind. He would certainly not have committed himself to the more specific (or arbitrary) assertions so beloved by most astrologers.

In 1950, Jung wrote a treatise called *Synchronicity: an Acausal Connecting Principle.* The word "synchronicity" has since been snapped up by astrologers in their eagerness to find a substitute for the now generally discarded idea (*pace* Gipsy Petulengro and the Hindus) of "astral influence." Thus in 1962 a lady astrologer named Katina Theodossiou declared in a British radio program that cause and effect were out and synchronicity was in: When the planet Mars is active certain things happen on earth (wars, revolutions, etc.) but "the one does not cause the other, they merely coincide."

But what does synchronicity mean? In his treatise Jung starts from the assumption that "the connection of events may in certain circumstances be other than causal." If one could prove, he argues, that "there are genuinely non-causal combinations of events," we should have drastically to revise our view of things, as man has had to before and perhaps is being impelled to now by such

Above right, Reinhold Ebertin, the leading light of the German "cosmobiologists"—a rebel group that has rejected many of astrology's most fundamental theories. Right, the cover of *Kosmobiologie,* which was founded by Ebertin in 1928— today one of Germany's best-selling astrological magazines.

KOSMOBIOLOGIE

Mitteilungsblatt des „Arbeitskreises für kosmobiologische Forschung"
und der „Kosmobiologischen Akademie Aalen, Arbeitsgemeinschaft e. V."

30. Jahrgang   1   Januar 1963

AUS DEM INHALT:

Zum Beginn
des 30. Jahrgangs

Möglichkeiten und
Grenzen kosmischer
Thematik

Die persönlichen
Punkte im
Kosmogramm

Medium coeli =
Ichbewußtsein

Abnormitäten

u. a.

A mandala (or "magic circle") drawn by C. G. Jung in 1928. The mandala form is fundamental to many of the great Eastern religions, such as Taoism or Buddhism. Though it can be seen as a symbol of the soul or psyche, it is also a representation of *totality*—in effect, of the oneness of all things in the universe (whose interrelationships depend more on synchronicity than causality). As Jung points out, this oneness is much the same as the ancient concept of correspondence, or *sympathy*, which was long used to explain and defend astrology.

phenomena as E.S.P. "We should then have to assume that events in general are related to one another on the one hand by causal chains, and on the other hand by a kind of meaningful cross-connection." In other words, events that happen at the same time can be related either because one has *caused* the other or because they each have a similar *meaning* to the mind that perceives them. (Or, of course, they can be chance occurrences, not related at all.)

To give a concrete example of what he means, Jung tells a striking but rather long true story about a recurrent plum pudding. It is easy to invent more brief examples with numbers: A man who had been born at 19.58 hours (7.58 P.M.) might have noticed on his birthday (though not necessarily on his birthday) in A.D. 1958 that his bus ticket was numbered 1958 and then have gone on that evening to score 1958 in some game of chance. That would either be pure chance —a concept that worries Jung as much as the rest of us—or an example of his non-causal principle of meaningful coincidence. There have been many cases where a clock has stopped ("never to go again," as an old song says) at the instant of its owner's death. This, too, would be synchronicity: The clock's stopping would be symbolically (not causally) related to the person's death.

"The primitive mentality," Jung writes, "has always explained synchronicity as magical causality right down to our own day, and on the other hand philosophy assumed a secret correspondence or meaningful connection between natural events until well into the eighteenth century. I prefer the latter hypothesis. . . . ." It will have been noticed that, through the centuries, some astrologers have worked on the former hypothesis and some on the latter. In the concept of synchronicity there are echoes of the idea of "sympathy" (between human life and the universe) that has cropped up so often in our history of astrology.

It was the search for meaningful connections that led Jung to undertake his "astrological experiment." With the usual kinds of check and precaution to avoid foreknowledge or cheating on the part of the investigators, he took as his field of statistical study 483 marriages (i.e., 966 horoscopes). These horoscopes were paired off in different ways, and the object was to establish the differences between the married couples and the non-married. As often happens in such experiments, the first results were the best : In the married couples' horoscopes certain aspects (for example, the woman's Moon in conjunction with the man's Sun) appeared most frequently ; and these aspects were the same ones that, according to the long astrological tradition, most favored marriage. But the experiment as a whole was judged by Jung to be inconclusive.

Jung had defined synchronicity as "a psychically conditioned relativity of space and time." To the modern way of thinking, if there is anything at all in astrology, it must involve a rearrangement of our concept of *time*. The Australian astrologer Furze Morrish writes (in a comment on Jung) : "It seems, indeed, as though time . . . is a concrete continuum which contains qualities of basic conditions manifesting simultaneously in various places in a way not to be explained by causal parellelisms." Synchronicity (or, as Morrish calls it, "synchronism") might "help some scientists to understand how astrology could work without any mechanical apparatus linking star and human." On the other hand, he does allow that there may be "astro-causation" between *planets* and persons, possibly by waves through the ether.

This concession of Morrish's about astro-causation resembles a process of thought not uncommon among many modern astrologers. It seems to be assumed that, if proof is given that the planets (or, for that matter, the Sun and Moon) can affect things on earth, then everything else follows, including the significance of the Zodiacal signs—which are for most astrologers not even groups of fixed stars but merely mechanically divided strips of sky. Geophysicists, radio meteorologists, biologists, and others claim to have correlated various terrestrial phenomena (such as electromagnetic storms) with goings on in the solar system. But, assuming these claims are correct, it still seems rather a long jump to the casting and interpretation of horoscopes.

Before leaving Morrish it is worth noting that, unlike the ancients who automatically thought of astrology as a science (and unlike those modern astrologers who lay such stress on observation, experiment, and statistics), Morrish flatly contrasts "science" (as something "strictly inductive") with astrology (which

	male ☉	☾	♂	♀	Asc.	Desc.
☉	☌☍	☌☍	☌☍	☍☌	☌	☌
☾	☌☍	☌☍	☍☌	☌☍	☌	☌
♂	☍☌	☌☍	☌☍	☌☍	☌	☌
♀	☌☍	☍☌	☌☍	☍☌	☌	☌
Asc.	☌	☌	☌	☌	☌	☌
Desc.	☌	☌	☌	☌		

female (left margin)

conjunction ☌   opposition ☍

First Batch		
180 Married Pairs		
Moon	☌ Sun	10.
Asc.	☌ Venus	9.
Moon	☌ Asc.	7.
Moon	☌ Moon	7.
Moon	☍ Sun	7.
Mars	☌ Moon	7.
Venus	☍ Moon	7.
Mars	☌ Mars	7.
Mars	☌ Asc.	6.
Sun	☌ Mars	6.
Venus	☌ Desc.	6.
Venus	☌ Asc.	6.
Mars	☌ Desc.	6
Sun	☌ Asc.	6.

deals with "universals"). This was to be expected from his theosophical background: In a chapter entitled "Shadows of Changes in World Thought" he likes to think that he can perceive a swing toward religion. He notes with approval that there is a rapid change going on today from the ethical mode to the aesthetic. The high priests of science were wrong, he proclaims, but so were the high priests of religion. So open the door and let the yogi come in—the yogi who is aware of "the Universal Integrative Factor which turns out to be ONESELF." And Morrish's yogi is, of course, just another name for the astrologer. Tell that to Ptolemy or Firmicus Maternus or Albertus Magnus or even William Lilly!

As regards religion, Ingrid Lind has asked "whether it is possible to believe in astrology and still have a religion." (This, as must have emerged in our historical chapters, is not a new question.) Her answer is that she finds "nothing in it, *if taken at a high enough level* [italics mine], that is incompatible with religion." She falls back on the traditional unity of the world and interdependence of parts. "Is it fantastic," she asks, "to conceive of God, or at any rate of the Solar Logos, as embodying His universe, with the Sun at His heart and the Planets, including Earth, as vital organs of His being?" Still one is tempted to ask: What about Pascal's interstellar spaces? And is the rest of our own galaxy Godless? (Not to mention all those other never-to-be-numbered galaxies.)

Still, many modern astrologers would probably agree with Ingrid Lind that their art has not only a moral but a religious justification. American astrology, at least since the beginning of the theosophical movement, certainly seems to have had a bias in favor of the mystical rather than the scientific. There was,

Second Batch			
220 Married Pairs			
Moon	☌	Moon	10.9%
Mars	☍	Venus	7.7%
Venus	☌	Moon	7.2%
Moon	☍	Sun	6.8%
Moon	☍	Mars	6.8%
Desc.	☌	Mars	6.8%
Desc.	☌	Venus	6.3%
Moon	☍	Venus	6.3%
Venus	☌	Venus	6.3%
Sun	☍	Mars	5.9%
Venus	☌	Desc.	5.4%
Venus	☌	Mars	5.4%
Sun	☌	Moon	5.4%
Sun	☌	Sun	5.4%

Both Batches			
400 Married Pairs			
Moon	☌	Moon	9.2%
Moon	☍	Sun	7.0%
Moon	☌	Sun	7.0%
Mars	☌	Mars	6.2%
Desc.	☌	Venus	6.2%
Moon	☍	Mars	6.2%
Mars	☌	Moon	6.0%
Mars	☍	Venus	5.7%
Moon	☌	Asc.	5.7%
Venus	☌	Desc.	5.7%
Venus	☌	Moon	5.5%
Desc.	☌	Mars	5.2%
Asc.	☌	Venus	5.2%
Sun	☍	Mars	5.2%

Above left, a table setting out the various astrological aspects considered by Jung in his analysis of the horoscopes of 400 married couples. The couples were divided into two groups of 180 and 220 : The middle two tables list the results yielded by each batch of horoscopes ; the last table combines the figures of both. Jung points out that the aspect traditionally most connected with marriage—a conjunction between Sun and Moon—occurred most often in Table 1 and next most often in Table 3. As a famous instance of this aspect, Jung cites the horoscopes of Goethe and his mistress Christiane Vulpius (sketched by Goethe, right).

A crowded gathering of delegates to a
convention held in 1950 by the American
Federation of Astrologers. Federation
members (like those of the British Faculty of
Astrological Studies) must pass examinations
and subscribe to a code of ethics.

for instance, Max Heindel, astrologer and founder of the Rosicrucian Fellowship in San Francisco. And today there is the Presbyterian minister Marc Edmund Jones who issues mimeographed lessons on astrology. As long ago as 1922 Jones founded the "Sabian Society," borrowing the name from an ancient mystical brotherhood in Baghdad. (Some of his "Sabian Symbols" were displayed in Chapter 1.) In 1925 he published in Los Angeles his *Key Truths of Occult Philosophy*: The first key truth is that "Time is Illusion" and the second that "Space is Relationship."

Belonging to the same American school as Jones is Dane Rudhyar; both have contributed to the quarterly astrological magazine *In Search*. For Rudhyar the aim of astrology is a high one: "to transform chaotic human nature into a microcosm." Like Krafft in Europe, he would like to be rid of "European 'classical' astrology" as being "a spiritually lifeless rebirth of Greco-Latin intellectualism." In his best-known book, *The Astrology of Personality*, Rudhyar emphasizes that "Wholeness" is all, a target to be achieved not through the analytical mind but through intuition. Intuition leads to "functional coherency." Rudhyar is another modern astrologer who pays attention to modern (particularly Jungian) psychology. Astrology is the male element (that which gives the formula) while psychology is the female element (that which gives the substantial contents).

True to the theosophical tradition, Rudhyar calls for a "creative aristocracy," being influenced here by his American predecessor Alice Bailey, who had proposed a "New Group of World Servers." He is much concerned with "group personalities" and likes to formulate things in triads—for example, "individual," "collective," "creative." Thus he distinguishes three types of astrology: First, the astrology thought of in terms of the axial motion of the earth (which concerns the *individual* and constitutes natal and horary astrology); second, the type thought of in terms of the earth's orbit around the sun (this is *collective* and constitutes natural or mundane astrology); third, there is occult astrology (which is *creative*). Rudhyar, who also flirts with such things as the number symbolism of the Great Pyramid, would appear to hope that astrology will one day take over from religion.

Whether they make any mystical claims or not, whether they welcome or eschew occult studies, all serious modern astrologers regard themselves as useful members of society. There is a constant lament that universities no longer offer degrees in astrology (as they did in the Middle Ages). But it is interesting that not all universities in the world refuse to acknowledge astrology's existence. Recently one of India's best-known astrologers—Prof. B. V. Raman, scholar and editor of an astrological magazine—gave a series of lectures that prompted the Chancellor of Mysore University to advocate (publicly) the founding of "faculties for astronomical and astrological studies" in Indian universities.

And in 1960 one of the most eminent of America's universities—Harvard itself (specifically, Radcliffe College, an offshoot of Harvard)—permitted a woman student to present a thesis on astrology for her B.A. degree. The student, Marcia Moore, called her thesis "Astrology Today—a Socio-Psychological Survey." Part One of this scrupulous and detailed report summarizes the history of astrology and examines it in relation to modern science—particularly psychology. In his foreword, Charles A. Jayne Jr. (editor of *In Search*) emphasizes the vital distinction between what he calls "the gypsy and fortune-telling element, and those whose interest in astrology is to exploit it commercially, on the one hand, and the quite different element, on the other hand, those for whom it is a serious study."

The second part of the thesis comprises the results obtained from a questionnaire (compiled by a panel that included such big astrological names as Margaret Hone and Marc Edmund Jones) that was designed to discover the collective attitudes and ideas of those most concerned with the validity and practice of astrology—a sort of group analysis. This analysis revealed that only about 20 per cent admitted to earning *any* income from astrology. The questionnaire was sent out to 900 subscribers to *In Search*—mostly members of the American Federation of Astrologers, a highly respectable body with its own code of ethics. (Of the probable 100 or so astrological societies that flourish in America, 25 are affiliated to the A.F.A.)

The magazine *In Search* first appeared in New York in the spring of 1958 and was hailed by astrologers overseas, both in Europe and India. In the first number its editor wrote an article entitled "Toward a New Astrology" in which he suggested that the new astrologer has to reckon with "at least eighteen unknown planets." This is beating the German scientific astrologers at their own game; it looks as if American astrologers are now serious contenders for the heavyweight title. Among others there is Carl Payne Tobey, founder and director of the Institute of Abstract Science (its headquarters are in Arizona) where astrology is taught as "a branch of mathematics." (According to Mr. Tobey himself, his interest in astrology started in the 1920s, when he had lost money in the Florida boom but learned from an acquaintance that "only astrology could explain these things.")

Throughout the world, various kinds of astrological institutes, groups, societies, etc., have been formed to advance the serious study of astrology. Many such organizations offer academic facilities (often in the form of correspondence courses) to would-be astrologers. In London the Faculty of Astrological Studies (founded in 1948, and affiliated with the Astrological Lodge) sets its students examinations: After one year of study you can get a Certificate, after two years a Diploma. If you get a Diploma you have the right to put after your name the letters "D.F. Astrol.S."

While on the subject of serious astrology, it ought to be mentioned that, like the American Federation of Astrologers, the London Faculty of Astrological Studies has a printed code of ethics that is largely intended to counteract any hint of charlatanism attaching to its name. Any student attached to the faculty is

Astrology—always a rich source of allegory and symbolism—provided the British choreographer Frederick Ashton with the theme of the ballet *The Horoscope* (composed by Constant Lambert and first produced in 1938). The ballet tells the story of two lovers (right) who are separated by the contrasting personalities of their Sun-signs Leo and Virgo, but who are finally reconciled by the efforts of Gemini and the Moon (above).

bound by this code to abide by the following rules:

"(a) I will undertake no natal work unless the time and place of birth are stated with reasonable accuracy, or if these are not available, I will explain clearly and unequivocally that any work supplied in such circumstances can only be regarded as inadequate and general.

"(b) In all professional work I will charge a fee commensurate with the dignity of astrological science, except in cases wherein the inquirer, being a genuine seeker after help and not impelled by idle curiosity, is unable to make a payment. In such instances I will give information and advice gratuitously.

"(c) I will in every case make an original and individual study of the case before me and will not use any form of reduplication, nor will I use in my work extracts from others' writings without due acknowledgment.

"(d) In work stated to be astrological I will not insert anything that is not founded upon true astrological science. Should I desire to impart advice for [or?] information derived from other sources I will write this upon a separate sheet with an express statement that it is not based upon Astrology.

"(e) I agree to respect in the strictest manner all confidences reposed in me, unless my duty as a loyal and law-abiding citizen of my country compels me to act otherwise.

"(f) I will use discretion in making any public statements regarding political matters or persons prominent in public life, and will avoid all such as are contrary to good taste and the practice of a decent reticence.

"(g) I undertake to make no improper or unethical use of the Diploma and my status as a Holder thereof and a Member of the Faculty; and as far as in me lies I will conduct all professional astrological work, should I be engaged therein, in accordance with high professional standards.

"(h) I will hold for the general good and not for my private use or advantage any discoveries that I may make or conclusions that I may reach, save only such as might, if divulged in public, conduce to results undesirable in the general interest."

On the other side of the astrological coin, there are a great many practitioners of the ancient art whose interests lie elsewhere than serious scholarship. These are the working professionals: The astrologers who cast horoscopes for clients, write or compile columns in newspapers and magazines, and so on. Of course, this does not mean that there are two distinct camps of "serious" and "popular" astrologers. There are merely different levels, ranging from the academic (who may have a few private clients) to the semi-charlatan who may not subscribe to any code of ethics and who may very likely make a lot of money by selling largely prefabricated horoscopes. (In countries like Britain or America, however, where astrological societies keep an eye out for quackery, clients can be fairly sure that a member of such a society is a reliable practitioner.)

It has been estimated that in the U.S.A. there are over 5000 working astrologers, who cater for about 10,000,000 customers. The charge in America for an individual horoscope can often get as high as $100; in Britain the average fee is about £10 ($28) though it can be as low as £2 or as high as £50. Their clients come from all walks of life: from young girls in search of romance to politicians and financiers. Thus there is little doubt that astrology today is very much alive (perhaps more alive than ever before) and on a popular level as well as a serious one—even if to most people it merely means a surreptitious glance at a horoscope column in the newspaper.

Newspaper horoscopes are astrology's most obvious medium in the modern world. Almost every major popular newspaper in America and Britain features an astrological column, as do many big newspapers in Europe. Even in Belgium, where astrology suffered something of an eclipse immediately after the war, half the daily newspapers run a "What the Stars Say" column. And, apart from the large numbers of magazines devoted exclusively to astrology (in the U.S.A. the most popular, *Horoscope*, has a monthly circulation of 170,000), there are innum-

Ingrid Lind, one of Britain's top astrologers and vice-principal of the London Faculty of Astrological Studies, signs diplomas watched by a fellow tutor. Diplomas are awarded by the Faculty to students who successfully complete a two-year course.

erable periodicals that run a regular horoscope feature. These are usually women's magazines, though evidence shows that men read them too.

Perhaps the best known of these newspaper astrologers is Italy's Francesco Waldner, who produces a syndicated horoscope column that appears in Britain, Italy, and France. Indeed, his feature in the French magazine *Elle* proved so popular that the magazine opened a special horoscope bureau for answering personal questions. And *Elle* (which, incidentally, is read by over half the French adult population) lately ran a feature on the kind of clothes that should be worn by those born under the various Zodiac signs.

As a further sign of astrology's prominence in the 1960s, it should be noticed that advertising people—those knowledgeable takers of the public pulse—often use astrological motifs as eye-catching gimmicks for advertisements. On the assumption, apparently, that the average consumer knows his way around the Zodiac, astrology has been used to sell anything from pre-shrunk shirts to alcoholic drinks. A recent example is a mail-order advertisement in a British women's magazine for a Paris perfume that comes complete with your personal horoscope.

Astrology has also been used in political propaganda, as in the case of a leaflet that was dropped by the French into Austria during World War II. This two-page pamphlet contained stock definitions of Zodiac signs and their effects on individuals; the propagandist part, held back till the last, consisted of the following jingle (entitled "Austrian Groan") bewailing the plight of Austria under the oppression of the Third Reich:

> *Under the banner white and red,*
> *We still had plenty of butter and bread,*
> *Under the Social Democrats*
> *We had lots of roast pork for our lads.*
> *But under your government with Goebbels and Goering,*
> *We only have potatoes and herring.*
> *The Chancellor without spouse,*
> *No bread in the baker's house,*
> *No sow in the butcher's shop:*
> *That's the latest command of the Reich.*

Today, it seems, you can hardly get away from astrology. Israel, for instance, has issued stamps bearing the signs of the Zodiac; and there is an astrological

Many of the institutes and colleges that treat astrology as a serious study hold examinations in order to qualify candidates to practice professionally. Far right, the certificate of proficiency granted by the American Federation of Astrologers; above right, a Belgian certificate issued to students of "scientific astrology"; right, the diploma of the London Faculty of Astrological Studies.

INSTITUT CENTRAL BELGE DE RECHERCHES ASTRO-DYNAMIQUES

ASSOCIATION SANS BUT LUCRATIF, FONDÉE EN 1926

Cours public d'Astrologie Scientifique

DEGRÉ

(1ᵉʳ DEGRÉ — ÉTUDES PRÉLIMINAIRES)
(2ᵉ DEGRÉ — ÉTUDES GÉNÉRALES)
(3ᵉ DEGRÉ — ÉTUDES SPÉCIALES)

CERTIFICAT

Nous attestons que M —————————————

demeurant à ——————— *rue* ——————— *nᵒ* ——

a subi avec ———————————

l'examen d'études astrologiques du ——————— *degré.*

Bruxelles, le ———————

LES MEMBRES DU JURY :

VICE-PRÉSIDENT · PRÉSIDENT · PROFESSEUR

FACULTY OF ASTROLOGICAL STUDIES

founded under the auspices of the Astrological Lodge of London

◆

THIS

DIPLOMA

has been awarded by the Faculty of Astrological Studies

to ___JOHN SMITH___

who has satisfied the Examiners in the subjects set forth

in the syllabus for the FINAL EXAMINATION held in

___FEBRUARY 1964___

Principal

Vice-Principal

(TUTOR)

Secretary of Registrars

AMERICAN FEDERATION OF ASTROLOGERS

Hereby certifies that

_____

has been issued this

Certificate of Proficiency

after successfully passing the

Professional

examination in

Natal Astrology

The holder of this Certificate subscribes to the Code of Ethics
of the American Federation of Astrologers.

	President
	Executive Secretary
Issued	*Chairman, Board of Examiners*

booth in a large Paris department store that gives off-the-cuff predictions to customers.

The different levels of astrology today—from very serious to very popular—are usually well represented at the conventions and conferences that astrologers seem fond of holding. The "International Congress of Astro-Science" (which was held in California from August 29 to September 3, 1963, and which was organized by Dr. Adrian M. Zeigler, President of Astrologers International Ltd.) featured just such a range of interests, from the highly academic to the more light-hearted. On the one hand, there were discussions of astrology and hand-writing (or grapho-analysis), of astrology and criminology, and of meteorological astrology; on the other hand, there were talks on subjects like "The Funniest Virgo in Town," and visitors were treated to a "Zodiacal fashion show" and an astrological dance revue.

By way of contrast to this sketch of popular astrology in the Western world today, we can look at its equivalent in Japan: the street-level fortune telling that is carried on from pavement booths in Tokyo. The pavement astrologers,

The familiar figures of the 12 Zodiac signs
reappear in an up-to-date form as decoration
on Israeli postage stamps (above) and on a
British greetings telegram (above left).

FOR ALL THOSE BORN UNDER

Leo *(July 21 - August 22)*
You get a pleasant surprise.
You discover that a new Rolls Rapide
costs only 39 gns cash price because
you buy at straight-from-the-factory cost.

who are known as *Ekisha*, set up their booths at night in shop doorways to attract strollers. Dressed in black kimonos, the Ekisha sit waiting with their books of astrological tables. Forecasts are made from the customer's date and hour of birth, which is then related to the appropriate sign of the Japanese Zodiac. (Incidentally, the Zodiac used by the Japanese has no resemblance to the Western Zodiac. Each of the 12 signs corresponds exactly to one calendar month and all are named after animals: March, for example, falls under the Tiger, and May under the Dragon.) This forecast is tallied with the lines on the customer's palm (read with the aid of a large magnifying glass). The chances of the prediction's being fulfilled are determined by shaking a number of sticks in a shaker, removing a handful, and then counting the remainder. (Different numbers imply different degrees of accuracy.) It is said that most Ekisha are too busy to close their booths much before dawn.

Apparently, in Japan as in the West, demand has created supply. That is, astrology seems to be "what the public wants"; and so they get it. And they get it in a wide variety of forms and, sometimes, from some quite unexpected quarters. Perhaps to end this chapter, we may offer two recent examples—one from India and the other from Britain—that demonstrate how astrology is liable to crop up even today in the most remarkable and unexpected places.

The universal appeal of the Zodiac (as well as its decorative value) has often been exploited as a sales device. Here the signs are featured by two British firms in advertisements for washing machines (left) and non-shrink cottons (right). Below, a display of Zodiac jewelry in a Paris department store.

YOUR HOROSCOPE

TAURUS *The Bull*
April 21 – May 22

Taurus subjects can look forward in complete confidence. A year free from the worries of shrinkage is forecast, under the guiding star of "Sanforized". Familiar faces will be unusually welcome. "Sanforized" will continue to give a strong helping hand with cottons.

"Sanforized" Service
20 St. Ann's Square, Manchester 2. BLA 8489/2916

238

The popular Japanese pavement fortune tellers known as *Ekisha* usually combine astrology with palmistry. Left, an Ekisha examining a client's palm with a magnifying glass; above, he holds the sticks that are used to assess a forecast's chances of fulfillment. Astrologers are regularly consulted in Thailand as well as in Japan: The Thai boxer Pone Kingpetch (left of picture, right) has publicly stated his reluctance to fight on days that are astrologically inauspicious.

INTERNATIONAL CONGRESS OF ASTRO SCIENCE

THE ZODIAC

MIRAMAR HOTEL

PACIFIC OCEAN PARK

MARINELAND

Astrology often makes news, even in the non-specialist press. Above, the British astrologer Edward Whitman, whose comments on the end of the world that was forecast by Indian astrologers for February 5, 1962, were published in a top Sunday newspaper. Left, the cover of a brochure produced for the widely publicized International Congress of Astro-Science held in California in September 1963. Right, a cartoon from a British newspaper that followed a magistrate's suggestion that horoscopes should be cast and interpreted for "juvenile delinquents."

The first was mentioned in Chapter 1 : the end of the world on February 5, 1962, which caused such a stir among the wise men of India. The writer of an article in the British *Sunday Times* for February 4 had taken the trouble to interview a number of people on this prospect. Among others he interviewed Edward Whitman, Secretary of the Federation of British Astrologers. Mr. Whitman was not worried about the morrow : He explained that the Hindus use a fixed Zodiac whereas he, like all good Westerners, uses a moving Zodiac. Moral (apparently) : The world may end for them, but not for us. Over in the U.S.A., however, 22 members of a society called "Understanding Inc." believed the Hindu astrologers and retreated to a small town in the Arizona mountains that they considered, for some reason, to be one place fated to survive the general catastrophe.

Another story reported in the British papers (in December 1962) was that of Charles Legh Shuldham Cornwall-Legh, chairman of the Cheshire Police Authority, and chairman of the Magistrates' Bench at Lymm, Cheshire. This important person came out into the open as saying : "I look forward to the time when it will be standard practice to have available for magistrates an interpreted horoscope of every child charged with a serious offence."

Just how much Mr. Cornwall-Legh was asking will be seen in the next chapter. To *cast* the horoscope of a juvenile delinquent, or anyone else, it would be necessary to know the exact time of his birth (how many people do?). To *interpret* a horoscope, as will be seen, requires a great deal of skill and a good deal of time and trouble.

8 The anatomy of the horoscope

Earlier in this book we looked at some of the basic constituents of a horoscope: the planets, the signs of the Zodiac, and the houses. Some knowledge of these things was necessary before one could move with any sureness through the centuries of astrology's history. Now, having brought that story up to date, we must change our ground and go back to looking at astrological fundamentals —in other words, at the horoscope itself, which is as basic to astrology as, say, the plan of a building is to an architect.

Most of the more technical details in the following pages have been supplied by a very reliable authority on the subject; but, as far as traditional astrology is concerned, there are many textbooks in which the same details are available (though sometimes in an over-simplified or, more often, an over-complicated form). Apart from house division, there is little argument about what the astrologer does when he is casting a horoscope. And in fact anyone can learn to erect a "natal chart" in an hour or two. Just as anyone can learn to draw a building plan. But this doesn't mean he can build the building; or, if he can, that it will stay standing. In the same way, it is the *interpretation* of the horoscope that separates the astrological men from the boys—and that causes the arguments to rage.

But we are first concerned with casting or erecting the chart. To refresh the reader's memory briefly: A horoscope consists of a geocentric map of the solar

A 17th-century Dutch map of astrology's
earth-centered universe encircled by the
Zodiac band—the system that appears in
diagrammatic form on every horoscope
chart. The various lines connecting the 12
Zodiac signs illustrate the planetary aspects:
The red lines link four planets in "square";
the light blue lines, six planets in "sextile";
other lines forming equilateral triangles
join three planets in "trine."

system at a given moment of time. On this map the positions of the Sun, Moon, and the other eight planets are calculated in relation to the signs of the Zodiac. The Zodiac is an imaginary band of sky representing the Sun's annual path through the fixed stars. (The Sun's apparent "movement" along this path is, of course, produced by the earth's own annual orbit around the Sun.) With the exception of Pluto, all the planets also appear to move around the earth within about 8° of the center of this band of sky.

Most modern astrologers are primarily interested in "natal" or "genethliacal" horoscopy—that is, they are interested in the individual horoscope, which is erected for a specific *time* (if possible, to the nearest minute) and takes into account the exact *geographical position* (latitude and longitude) of the individual's birthplace. (The individual for whom a horoscope is cast is usually called the "native.") These, then, are the essential data that the astrologer must have to cast a horoscope: date of birth, accurate time of birth, place of birth. With these, the astrologer sets out to compute the native's *ascendant* and its related *medium coeli* (M.C. or mid-heaven).

He makes his computations with the aid of two reference books (which are not difficult to find in libraries or bookshops). One is called an *ephemeris* (we have inherited the name and the thing from the Greeks), which tells you what was where in the solar system at any particular time. The other book is called a *table of houses* by which the astrologer makes corrections with regard to the position of the individual's birthplace. (Some ephemerides include tables of houses for particular latitudes.)

The astrologer's first step is to find out (from his ephemeris) what the *sidereal time* was at noon on the day of birth in question. Sidereal time is measured by the stars and not (like ordinary clock time) by the Sun. In a sidereal day the stars appear to have made one complete circuit of the sky; but the Sun hasn't quite completed its apparent circuit. So the sidereal day is a few minutes (of clock time) shorter than the ordinary day. This discrepancy, known as the "acceleration on interval," must be allowed for when calculating the sidereal time at birth.

Astrology uses sidereal time (usually written as just S.T.) as a means of indicating the positions of the stars as seen at a given time and place. To put it briefly, the astrologer must translate his information (birth time and birthplace) into S.T. so that he can use his tables—since these give the positions of the stars and planets in terms of S.T. The S.T. is found by simple arithmetic.

The ephemeris obviously cannot give the S.T. that corresponds with every minute of every day; so all it gives is the corresponding S.T. to noon on the day in question. Then the astrologer must work out the S.T. of the moment of birth. He works this out by *adding* the necessary number of hours and minutes for births after noon, and *subtracting* them for births before noon. For example:

Assume that the birth date in question is July 5, 1960, and that the time of birth is 7.20 P.M. (We will also assume, to avoid questions of longitude for the moment, that this is the birth date of someone born near the meridian of Greenwich. Thus that time of birth—7.20 P.M.—will be in Greenwich Mean Time, or G.M.T.) The ephemeris tells us that, on that date, the S.T. at noon was six hours, 53 minutes, and 56 seconds. Now, since the time of the birth in question was *after* noon, to find the S.T. for the precise moment of birth we must add seven hours 20 minutes (known as the "interval") to the S.T. at noon. We must also allow for the "acceleration on interval" by adding 10 seconds for each hour—which works out at one minute 13 seconds. We get the following total:

$$6^h\ 53^m\ 56^s$$
$$+\ 7^h\ 20^m\ \ \ 0^s$$
$$+\ \ \ \ \ \ \ \ \ 1^m\ 13^s$$
$$\overline{14^h\ 15^m\ \ \ 9^s}$$

Most of the commonly used ephemerides use G.M.T. as a standard. So, for natives not born on the Greenwich meridian, the time of birth must be converted into G.M.T. before the above addition can be performed. For instance, Central European Time is one hour fast by comparison with G.M.T. while Eastern Standard Time (U.S.A.) is five hours slow. So for a birth at New York at 9 P.M. the G.M.T. is 4 P.M.; for a birth at Munich at 1 P.M. C.E.T., the equivalent G.M.T. is noon.

Now we have established the S.T. that corresponds to the time of birth in Greenwich time. We must next convert this into *local* S.T. for people born in places other than on the Greenwich meridian. This involves *longitude*: We must

A world map shows the earth divided into 24 different time zones. (The international date line marks the point where one weekday becomes the next.) The figures at the bottom show the time in each zone corresponding to noon in Greenwich Mean Time.

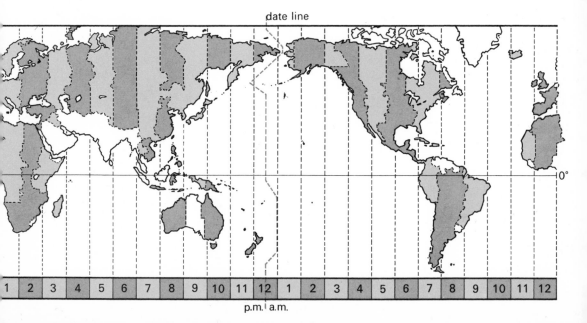

An astrologer casting a horoscope : His equipment consists of a protractor to plot the exact positions of the various elements of the horoscope ; an ephemeris (a book containing the tables necessary for his calculations) ; and a blank horoscope chart on which he writes the specific details of the "native's" horoscope. Here he is writing in the planet Venus (having already filled in the ascendant, Zodiac signs, and M.C.).

convert degrees and minutes of longitude (east or west of the Greenwich meridian) into minutes and seconds of time. This, too, is a simple process. Longitude is transformed into time simply by multiplying by four. For instance :

Vienna is 16° 22′ 54″ east of Greenwich. Multiply this by four, and the result is 65 minutes 32 seconds (of time). Now, because Vienna is east of Greenwich, this 65ᵐ 32ˢ would be added to the s.t. at Greenwich. (Subtract for all points west.)

Here we might pause and review these manipulations of time. The astrologer first takes the moment of birth as it is expressed in *local time* (Central European, Eastern Standard, or whatever) and translates it into Greenwich Mean Time. Then, using the ephemeris, he translates that into sidereal time *for Greenwich*. Finally, using longitude, he arrives at the moment of birth expressed in sidereal time *for the birthplace*.

Next, *latitude* (north or south of the equator) comes in. The astrologer looks into his tables of houses and finds that, at the already-established sidereal time of birth and at the given latitude of the birthplace, a certain degree of the Zodiac was "rising" over the eastern horizon. This is the ascendant. And now the job of calculating the horoscope is nearly done.

(The astrologer must know the exact latitude—for the same sidereal time will give different ascendants for different latitudes. For example, an s.t. of 13ʰ 2ᵐ 40ˢ gives an ascendant of 20° 19′ Sagittarius at the latitude of 46° North, but gives an ascendant of 10° 26′ Sagittarius at 56° North.)

When the ascendant has been calculated, it is marked on the blank circle of the horoscope chart. A line is drawn connecting the degree of the ascendant with a point exactly opposite on the other side of the chart—which is the descendant. The table of houses also gives the related *mid-heaven* or M.C., and so the astrologer draws a line bisecting the ascendant-descendant line connecting the M.C. and the *imum coeli*. And there he has the four angles of the chart and its quadrants.

During any period of 24 hours there are 360 possible ascendants, each with its related mid-heaven. A different (succeeding) degree of the ecliptic (and therefore of the Zodiac) "rises" above the horizon every four minutes. So if Smith was born five minutes after Jones (even if they were both born in the same place), Smith will have a different degree of the Zodiac for his ascendant. And if Jones's ascendant was, say, 30° Scorpio, Smith will also have a different ascendant *sign*—1° Sagittarius.

Unfortunately, with the vast majority of people it is not so easy to establish the ascendant and mid-heaven with the proper accuracy. You are lucky if the ascendant is accurate to within even three or four degrees—i.e., 12 to 16 minutes of time. This might make a very serious difference, since the sign on the ascendant may have changed in that time; and, as we have seen, adjacent signs (like Aries and Taurus) tend to be very unlike each other. Both ancient and modern astrologers have stressed the deplorable results of such vagueness about the time of one's birth. But the same vagueness does, of course, supply the astrologer with a ready-made excuse for an inaccurate prediction.

Assuming that the ascendant and mid-heaven *have* been accurately established, the astrologer then proceeds to fill in the so-called "house" boundaries. (The data for these is obtained from tables of houses for the latitude in question.) Commencing at the ascendant, which is the "cusp" or beginning of the first house, the horoscope is then divided into 12 sectors or houses.

Incidentally, very few astrologers understand the various mathematical theories of house division, since an expert knowledge of spherical trigonometry is required. Most people use Placidus tables (named after Placidus de Tito, the 17th-century Italian astronomer and astrologer), not because they are necessarily the best but because they are most readily available. Regiomontanus and Campanus tables can also be found, as well as the new *Geburtsorthäuser* (birthplace) tables recently calculated by Dr. W. A. Koch of Germany, who is one of the world's greatest experts in this very difficult field. But in all the latter cases the degree values of the intermediate cusps (i.e., for houses 2, 3, 5, 6, 8, 9, 11, and 12) will be different from the Placidean cusps. Thus four different astrologers, each using a different house division system, will produce four different horoscopes as far as the intermediate houses are concerned, although the ascendant and mid-heaven will be the same in each case.

Enemies of astrology like the late Robert Eisler have found in these disagreements about house division some very nice fuel for their polemics. Eisler

I

14 **JULY, 1960** [*RAPHAEL'S EPHEMER*

D M	D W	Sidereal Time.	☉ Long.	☉ Dec.	☽ Long.	☽ Lat.	☽ Dec.	MIDNIGHT ☽Long.	MIDNIGHT ☽Dec.	♆ Long.	♅ Long.	I
		H. M. S.	° ′ ″	° ′	° ′ ″	° ′	° ′	° ′ ″	° ′	° ′	° ′	
1	F	6 38 9	9♋37 48	23 N 6	1♎43 14	1 N13	0 N26	8♎11 7	1 S 38	6♏26	18♌51	1.
2	S	6 42 6	10 35 0	23 1	14 44 55	2 18	3 S 42	21 25 5	5 45	6 ℞26	18 54	1.
3	𝔖	6 46 3	11 32 11	22 56	28 12 1	3 17	7 46	5♏ 5 59	9 43	6 25	18 58	1
4	M	6 49 59	12 29 22	22 51	12♏ 7 7	4 7	11 33	19 15 21	13 15	6 25	19 1	1
5	Tu	6 53 56	13 26 34	22 46	26 30 28	4 43	14 47	3♐52 0	16 6	6 24	19 4	1

How to cast the horoscope of a "native" born in London on July 5, 1960, at 7.20 P.M. The first step is to calculate the sidereal time at birth. The time of birth and the "acceleration on interval" (which is worked out as explained on p. 245) are added to the S.T. for noon on July 5 (found on Table I). The result of this addition (far right) is the S.T. at birth. The next step: The S.T. at birth is related to Table II, which gives 0° 29′ Capricorn as the ascendant and 6° Scorpio as the M.C. These are plotted on the horoscope and the other Zodiac signs written in.

Next, the positions of the faster-moving planets must be found—for example, Venus. Find the *motion* of Venus on Table III (1°14′). Then find on Table IV the log of 1°14′ (12891) and the log of the interval of 7h 20m (5149); add these and convert the total (18040) into degrees (23′) in the way explained on p. 250. Add this figure to the position of Venus at noon, found on Table 1—16°59′ in Cancer—and you have Venus's position at the birth time (17°22′ Cancer). The process is repeated for the other fast-moving planets. The positions of the slower planets (in red on Table I) are transferred straight onto the chart. (The position of Pluto is found on Table V.) The chart is now complete.

II *TABLES OF HOUSES FOR LONDON*

Sidereal Time.	10 ♏	11 ♏	12 ♐	Ascen ♐	2 ♒	3 ♓
H. M. S.	°	°	°	° ′	°	°
13 51 37	0	22	10	25 20	10	27
13 55 27	1	23	11	26 10	11	28
13 59 17	2	24	11	27 2	12	♈
14 3 8	3	25	12	27 53	14	1
14 6 59	4	26	13	28 45	15	2
14 10 51	5	26	14	29 36	16	4
14 14 44	6	27	15	0♑29	18	5
14 18 37	7	28	15	1 23	19	6
14 22 31	8	29	16	2 18	20	8
14 26 25	9	♐	17	3 14	22	9

III

JULY

D	☉	☽	♂	♀	☿	☽ dec.
	° ′ ″	° ′ ″	′	° ′	° ′	° ′
1	0 57 12	13 1 41	42	1 14	0 7	4 8
2	0 57 11	13 27 6	43	1 14	0 3	4 4
3	0 57 11	13 55 6	43	1 13	0 3	3 47
4	0 57 12	14 23 21	43	1 14	0 6	3 14
5	0 57 10	14 48 48	42	1 14	0 12	2 22

IV

PROPORTIONAL LOGARITHMS FOR FINDING THE PLANETS' PLACES

Min.	0	1	2	3	4	5	6	7	8	9	10	11	12	13	14	15	Min.
	DEGREES OR HOURS																
0	3.1584	1.3802	1.0792	9031	7781	6812	6021	5351	4771	4260	3802	3388	3010	2663	2341	2041	0
1	3.1584	1.3730	1.0756	9007	7763	6798	6009	5341	4762	4252	3795	3382	3004	2657	2336	2036	1
2	2,8573	1,3660	1,0720	8983	7745	6784	5997	5330	4753	4244	3788	3375	2998	2652	2330	2032	2
3	2.6812	1.3590	1.0685	8959	7728	6769	5985	5320	4744	4236	3780	3368	2992	2646	2325	2027	3
4	2.5563	1.3522	1.0649	8935	7710	6755	5973	5310	4735	4228	3773	3362	2986	2640	2320	2022	4
5	2.4594	1.3454	1.0614	8912	7692	6741	5961	5300	4726	4220	3766	3355	2980	2635	2315	2017	5
6	2.3802	1.3388	1.0580	8888	7674	6726	5949	5289	4717	4212	3759	3349	2974	2629	2310	2012	6
7	2.3133	1.3323	1.0546	8865	7657	6712	5937	5279	4708	4204	3752	3342	2968	2624	2305	2008	7
8	2.2553	1.3258	1.0511	8842	7639	6698	5925	5269	4699	4196	3745	3336	2962	2618	2300	2003	8
9	2.2041	1.3195	1.0478	8819	7622	6684	5913	5259	4690	4188	3737	3329	2956	2613	2295	1998	9
10	2.1584	1.3133	1.0444	8796	7604	6670	5902	5249	4682	4180	3730	3323	2950	2607	2289	1993	10
11	2.1170	1.3071	1.0411	8773	7587	6656	5890	5239	4673	4172	3723	3316	2944	2602	2284	1988	11
12	2.0792	1.3010	1.0378	8751	7570	6642	5878	5229	4664	4164	3716	3310	2938	2596	2279	1984	12
13	2.0444	1.2950	1.0345	8728	7552	6628	5866	5219	4655	4156	3709	3303	2933	2591	2274	1979	13
14	2.0122	1.2891	1.0313	8706	7535	6614	5855	5209	4646	4148	3702	3297	2927	2585	2269	1974	14
15	1.9823	1.2833	1.0280	8683	7518	6600	5843	5199	4638	4141	3695	3291	2921	2580	2264	1969	15
16	1.9542	1.2775	1.0248	8661	7501	6587	5832	5189	4629	4133	3688	3284	2915	2574	2259	1965	16
17	1.9279	1.2719	1.0216	8639	7484	6573	5820	5179	4620	4125	3681	3278	2909	2569	2254	1960	17
18	1.9031	1.2663	1.0185	8617	7467	6559	5809	5169	4611	4117	3674	3271	2903	2564	2249	1955	18
19	1.8796	1.2607	1.0153	8595	7451	6546	5797	5159	4603	4109	3667	3265	2897	2558	2244	1950	19
20	1.8573	1.2553	1.0122	8573	7434	6532	5786	5149	4594	4102	3660	3258	2891	2553	2239	1946	20
21	1.8361	1.2499	1.0091	8552	7417	6519	5774	5139	4585	4094	3653	3252	2885	2547	2234	1941	21
22	1.8159	1.2445	1.0061	8530	7401	6505	5763	5129	4577	4086	3646	3246	2880	2542	2229	1936	22
23	1.7966	1.2393	1.0030	8509	7384	6492	5752	5120	4568	4079	3639	3239	2874	2536	2223	1932	23

	♂	♀	☿	Lunar Aspects.								
ng.	Long.	Long.	Long.	⊙	♇	Ψ	♅	♄	♃	♂	♀	☿
18	8 ♉ 4	12 ♋ 4	0 ♌ 5	⊻	⊻	∠		□				✳
10	8 46	13 18	0 12	□	∠	✳	□			□		
3	9 29	14 32	0 15	✳			✳		✳		□	
56	10 12	15 45	0 ℞12	△		☌	□	✳	∠	♂	△	
49	10 55	16 59	0 6	□				∠	⊻		□	△

V THE POSITION OF PLUTO (♇) IN 1960.

Date.	Long.	Lat.	Dec.
	° ′	° ′	° ′
May 10	3 ♍ 36	12 N 30	21 N 48
20	3 D 36	12 27	21 45
30	3 39	12 24	21 41
June 9	3 45	12 21	21 36
19	3 54	12 18	21 30
29	4 5	12 16	21 24
July 9		12 14	21 16
19	4 35	12 12	21 9
29	4 53	12 11	21 1
Aug. 8	5 12	12 10	20 53
18	5 31	12 10	20 46

---

date of birth	July 5, 1960		
place	London		
latitude	51° 30′		
time of birth	19hrs. 20mins.		
time of birth	19	20	0
−noon	12	0	0
interval	7	20	0
+sidereal time	6	53	56
	14	13	56
+acceleration on interval		1	13
sidereal time at birth	14	15	9
motion of ♀ on July 5	1°	14′	
log of 1° 14′	1.2891		
+constant log	5149		
	1.8040		
position of ♀ on July 5	16°	59′ in ♋	
+converted result of log=			
movement of ♀ in 7° 20′		23′	
position of ♀ at birth	17°	22′ in ♋	

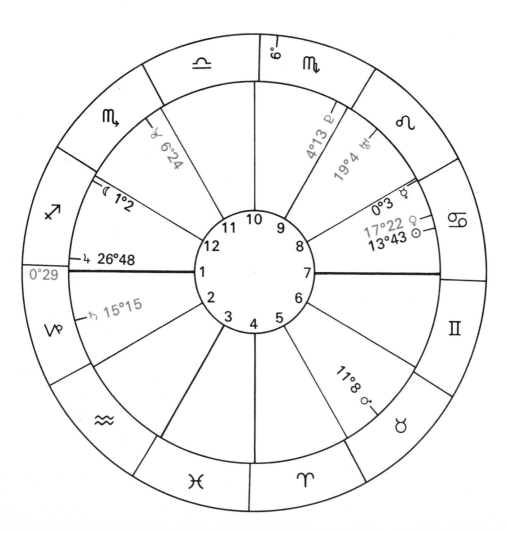

maintains that in the ancient world the original division was into *eight* houses, arrived at simply by halving each quarter of the heaven. The division of 12, he argues, has nothing to do with the divisions of the horizon "but rests originally on the division of the day into twelve hours of *variable* seasonal length" (italics mine).

But to get back to our horoscope: The astrologer now fills in the position of the Sun, Moon, and planets. In the case of the *slower*-moving planets (Saturn, Uranus, Neptune, Jupiter, and Pluto), this is a simple matter of referring to the ephemeris, finding the positions for noon on the day of birth, and transferring these straight onto the chart. But for the *faster*-moving planets (Venus, Mercury, the Sun and Moon), the positions must be adjusted to allow for planetary movement between noon and the time of birth. To clarify the calculations involved, refer to the sample horoscope on p. 249 and find the position of Venus.

First, since we are dealing with time after noon, we look up in the ephemeris the planet's motion at noon on the day of birth. (For before-noon time, look up the planetary motion for the previous day.) We then turn to the log tables at the back of the ephemeris and find the log of this motion; to this we add the log of seven hours 20 minutes (the interval) and convert the total back into degrees. This gives us the difference in Venus's position between noon and 7.20 P.M. We add this figure to the noon position of Venus (given in the ephemeris) and we have the position of Venus at 7.20 P.M. Incidentally, for a planet that is retrograde (marked by R in the tables), the whole process would be reversed; that is, we subtract the movement on interval from the planet's position at noon.

A word of reminder about aspects is necessary here. Obviously, among the slower-moving planets, such important aspects as conjunctions, squares, and oppositions can occur only at rare intervals. During a period of five years Saturn moves only about 60°, Uranus 20°, Neptune 10°, and Pluto 8°. But during the same five-year period the Sun will have circled the Zodiac five times (5 × 360°

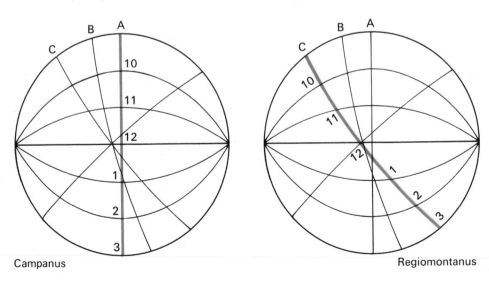

Campanus   Regiomontanus

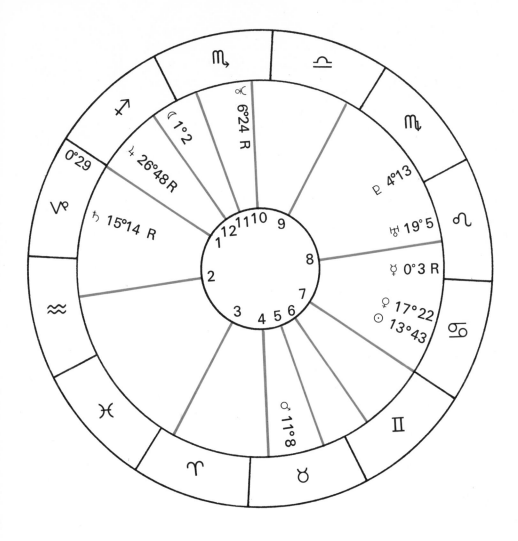

Above, a chart showing "unequal" house division according to the system evolved by Regiomontanus. Left, a diagram of Regiomontanus's "space" system shows six of the 12 circles that represent the houses (like segments of an orange) marked off along the celestial equator (C). The houses' divisions, or cusps (which must be calculated by trigonometry), are the points on the ecliptic (B) cut by the circles. Far left, a diagram of Campanus's method of house division, which also results in their unequal size. In this case, the houses are divided along the "prime vertical"—the line joining the zenith and the nadir (A).

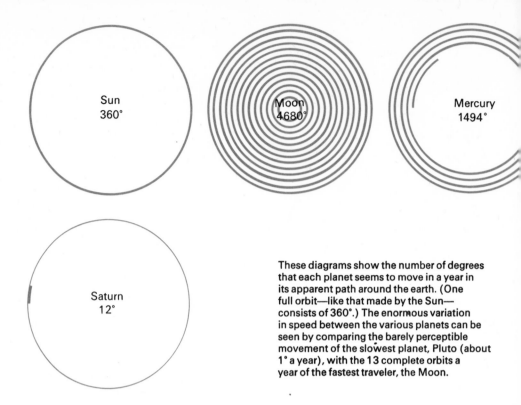

Sun
360°

Moon
4680°

Mercury
1494°

Saturn
12°

These diagrams show the number of degrees that each planet seems to move in a year in its apparent path around the earth. (One full orbit—like that made by the Sun—consists of 360°.) The enormous variation in speed between the various planets can be seen by comparing the barely perceptible movement of the slowest planet, Pluto (about 1° a year), with the 13 complete orbits a year of the fastest traveler, the Moon.

= 1800°) and the Moon will have circled it about 60 times. Thus while a Saturn-Jupiter conjunction, for instance, will occur only once every 19,859 years, Sun-Moon conjunctions occur monthly, and the faster planets (including the Sun and Moon) are constantly forming new aspects with each other and with all the slower planets.

It thus follows that everybody born during a given month of any year will have four of the eight planets in very much the same positions in their horoscope charts. Again, if one ignores the Moon (which moves about 12° during 24 hours and will therefore pass from one Zodiacal sign to another every two or three days), there is no marked change during the course of a week as far as the aspects are concerned, although one or more planets may have passed into a fresh sign of the Zodiac.

Here, finally, is a quick summary of the entire procedure:

1. Find out the native's date of birth, exact time of birth, and place of birth. Also the longitude and latitude of place of birth.

2. Find out from the ephemeris the sidereal time at noon (G.M.T.) for the given day of birth.

3. By simple addition or subtraction, find the equivalent s.t. for the moment of birth (making sure that the moment is expressed in G.M.T.).

4. Convert the longitude of the native's place of birth into hours, minutes, and seconds by multiplying by four.

5. Find the *local* s.t. for the place of birth by adding or subtracting the longitude to or from the Greenwich s.t.

Venus
585°

Mars
191°

Jupiter
30°

Uranus
4°

Neptune
2°

Pluto
1°

6. Look up the local s.t. in a table of houses to find the ascendant and the mid-heaven.

7. Fill in the ascendant, descendant, mid-heaven, and *imum coeli* on the blank horoscope chart.

8. Fill in the positions of the houses, according to the tables.

9. Fill in the positions of the planets, also according to the tables (remembering again to convert Greenwich s.t. into local s.t.).

10. Interpret the completed horoscope.

The problem of interpretation

Anyone can soon memorize and master the first nine steps of the astrologer's procedure. The stumbling block is number 10. How (and from where) can a beginner learn what the chart itself "means"?

For most astrologers, the conventional basis for interpretation is "the tradition"—essentially a literary tradition, based upon a long succession of astrological manuscripts (for the centuries prior to the invention of printing in 1440) and upon the many hundreds of books and manuals published after that date. The tradition is immense, varied, and still growing. To read the entirety would require an incredible effort of scholarship on the part of a would-be astrologer. What actually happens instead is that every new generation of astrologers, in its own manuals, rewrites the fundamental principles of astrology in a contemporary idiom. Even A. J. Pearce's once immensely popular *The Text-Book of Astrology* (two volumes, 1879-89) now seems fairly outdated.

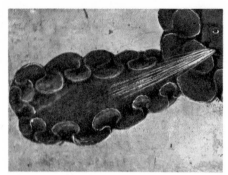

air: Ⅱ ≈ ♎︎   water: ♋︎ ♏︎ ♓︎

The majority of astrologers learn interpretation from such books. Margaret E. Hone, for instance, advises the student of astrology that he "will *never* become fluent and quick in interpretation until he so thoroughly grasps the nature of each *planet, sign, house* and *aspect,* that he can apply them as related in any chart, without constant reference to books." But, she adds, the beginner "needs the help of books in his work, at first."

The heavy weight of the tradition thus prevents the astrologer from bringing very much originality into his interpretative work. The meanings of the various parts of the horoscope were settled long ago; and most astrologers accept them. This acceptance can be seen in practically any set of excerpts, dealing with the same subject, from the astrological textbooks. For example, the following is a set of quotations concerning the first house of the horoscope (which begins at the point of the all-important ascendant). To lead off, here is the meaning of the first house according to John Gadbury's *The Doctrine of Nativities* (1658), which corresponds in most respects with similar examples from 16th- and 17th-century French manuals:

"This House hath proper Signification of the Life of the Native; his Stature, Form and Shape; the Temperature and Accidents of the Body; the Qualities of the Minde; the Visage, its Fashion, Complexion and Colour, and all the Parts thereof . . . Sun in the first [House] makes the native honoured among his brethren . . . he will rule over others; will acquire Authority, Honour, and Dignity from Princes; he will have a great increase of Riches; he will be of long life and powerful."

Sepharial, one of the British astrological writers whom we have met before, closely follows Gadbury in his *A New Manual of Astrology* (1898):

"The first House denotes the body of the native, his physical condition and appearance. . . ." And further: "Sun in First House gives honour and success. A proud disposition; frank, outspoken, generous; despising cliques and coteries; independent and firm. It also gives a love of display and publicity, accompanied by high motives."

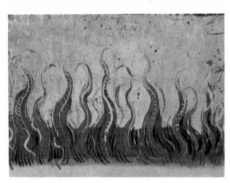

fire : ♈ ♌ ♐

earth : ♉ ♏ ♑

As well as ascribing individual qualities to the signs and houses, astrology also classes them into various groups, whose meanings must also be considered when a horoscope is interpreted. The medieval German paintings (above) illustrate the four "elements" of air, water, fire, and earth. The four "triplicities," each comprising three signs, are as follows : *airy* signs indicating "intellectual and articulate" character ; *watery*, "emotional and unstable" ; *fiery*, "ardent and keen" ; *earthy*, "practical and cautious."

Right, a diagram representing the "quadruplicities"—a division of the signs into three groups of four : The *cardinal* signs are linked by the blue lines ; the *fixed* by the red ; the *mutable* by the black.

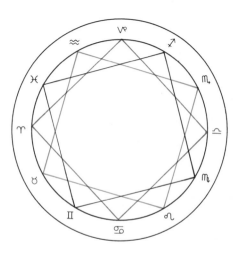

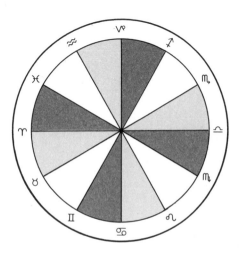

Right, a diagram shows the 12 houses colored to show their classification into *angular* (light blue), implying initiative ; *succedent* (white), steadiness of purpose ; *cadent* (dark blue), widespread activity.

A sample interpretation based on the horoscope on p. 249

1 General view of the chart	No marked tendency for harmony or disharmony, though the influence of Saturn is strong (see below, 11 and 14).
2 The quadruplicities	These are well balanced : three planets in cardinal signs, three in mutable, and four in fixed. The slight edge toward fixed is offset by the fact that neither the ascendant nor the Sun is in the fixed quadruplicity.
3 The elements	There are four planets in fiery signs, three (and the ascendant) in earthy, three (and the M.C.) in watery, but none in airy. The absence of "airiness" might result in a lack of intellect, though the native is strong in common sense ("earthy") and intuition ("watery").
4 Rising and setting planets	Saturn in the first house and Jupiter above the horizon in the 12th (both rising) may produce a conflict between restraint and expansiveness. Sun and Venus setting indicate an orientation toward others.
5 Position of the planets above or below the horizon	More planets are above the horizon, adding to the "outward" orientation of the personality.
6 Planetary occupation of the four quadrants	The accent is on the third quadrant (five planets from the seventh house to the M.C.), emphasizing the importance of the seventh, eighth, and ninth houses.
7 The decanates	Since the ascendant is in the first decanate of Capricorn, the native's personality will be almost entirely Capricornian.
8 The Sun's position in relation to the Zodiac	The Sun is in Cancer, which gives Cancerian qualities to the "deeper self."
9 The Moon's position in relation to the Zodiac	The Moon is in Sagittarius, whose qualities will affect automatic reactions and manner. The strong difference between Sagittarius and Cancer will create some deep-seated conflict.
10 The ascendant's position in relation to the Zodiac	Capricorn as the rising sign or ascendant will affect physical appearance.
11 The ascendant's ruler	Saturn, ruler of Capricorn, is in Capricorn, and in the first house, which gives the planet an immense influence in the horoscope. The native must try to overcome his excess of "Saturnine" coldness, caution, meanness, etc.
12 Planets in relation to the houses	Sun, Mercury, and Venus in the seventh house help to orient the native toward others, offsetting Saturn's selfishness. Mars in the fifth gives physical energy and magnetism. Neptune in the 11th—in conjunction with the M.C., the "career point"—lends ambition and creativity to the personality. Uranus in the eighth gives an interest in mysticism, counteracting Saturn's "heaviness."

Jupiter and Saturn are (as we have seen) in their own signs, increasing the strength of each. Mars in Taurus adds to sensuality.

The Sun is in conjunction with Venus, in good aspect to Mars and Neptune, and in bad aspect to Saturn. Some effects of these aspects we have seen. The Sun's good aspect to Mars adds to the strength of personality, and the Moon's good aspect to Mercury gives emotional stability. Mercury's bad aspect to Neptune might add to the tendency to escapism. Venus's bad aspects to the Moon, Saturn, Pluto, and Uranus indicate difficulties in love and marriage. Mars's good aspect to Saturn balances energy with caution. Mars's bad aspect to Uranus could mean an explosive nature under the surface.

A generation later V. E. Robson, in his *A Beginner's Guide to Practical Astrology* (1931), wrote:

"[The first house indicates] the Native, or subject of the Horoscope himself; his appearance, habits, characteristics, health, temperament and the general way in which he looks on the world. . . . Sun in 1st: generous, dignified, proud, ambitious, confident, boastful, fond of display, independent. Honour and success. Good vitality. Few brothers."

The modern German "cosmobiologer" Reinhold Ebertin is one of the mavericks who prefer to bring in their own interpretative meanings, breaking entirely with the traditional formulations of the Gadbury-Sepharial-Robson school. In his book *The Combination of Stellar Influences* (1950) Ebertin defines the ascendant as "Personality (Environment)," adding that the individual's psychological characteristics would then depend upon the Zodiacal sign in which the ascendant happened to be. He also relates the ascendant to "reactions to the external world, the 'I' in relation to other people, especially those in the native's environment."

But even with all the reference books at his elbow the beginner still will not find interpretation a simple process. The horoscope contains a great many factors, some quite complex, all of which (if the job is to be done properly) must be taken into consideration. To underline some "ingredients":

There are the quadruplicities—i.e., the number of planets respectively in cardinal, fixed, and mutable signs of the Zodiac. (Aries is cardinal, Taurus fixed, and Gemini mutable, and the succession runs cardinal, fixed, mutable throughout the remaining signs. An excess of planets of one "quality" is said to make the native psychologically one-sided.) And there are the triplicities—the number of planets in fiery, earthy, airy, and watery signs. (Aries is fiery, Taurus earthy, Gemini airy, Cancer watery, and so on in the fire-earth-air-water succession throughout the remaining signs. A person with many planets in *fixed* and *earthy* signs, for instance, might be considered potentially phlegmatic.)

Also important are the number of planets in the east and west respectively (it is thought that if the majority of planets are in the western half of the chart, their effects would be especially noticeable in the second half of the native's life); and the number of planets above and below the horizon—the line joining the ascendant and descendant (planets below the horizon are considered less "effective" than those above it).

These are only a few of the separate elements of an individual horoscope—quite a long way from the "if you were born with your Sun in Taurus" kind of astrology popularized by the newspapers. What is required is the ability to grasp and interpret all these combinations and then, from the available "evidence," to arrive at a reasonable synthesis of what it all means or is supposed to mean.

Whatever else they may have invented, the early astrologers were responsible for the first known attempt at a complete system of human typology. Nearly all astrologers classify people by their *Zodiacal* types; but for one "pure" type there are many mixed, where more than one Zodiacal sign has a say in the native's constitution. Oddly enough, we are assured, the pure types are often quite evident and a skilled astrologer will be able to hit upon a person's Sun-sign and/or ascendant with remarkable accuracy without knowing the birth month. This can often be done on the basis of only a casual encounter and a few minutes of conversation, during which the subject will give himself away quite unconsciously.

There are "planetary" types as well: The man with the "sunny" disposition, the "lunatic," the mercurial, martial, jovial (Jupiter), and saturnine characters. The basic meaning of any planet, when it is in a given Zodiacal sign, will of course be modified by the interpretative meaning ascribed to that sign. And the traditional interpretations accorded to the houses (outlined briefly in Chapter 3), especially if occupied by planets, should also assist the astrologer to pinpoint a number of important factors concerning the native's "type."

As for the meanings of the *aspects,* there is sometimes a lack of unanimity among the various authorities, but some general statements can be made. The interpretation of conjunctions will obviously depend upon the planets in question, since Sun conjunction Jupiter will obviously be "better" than Sun conjunction Saturn. Oppositions can be taken to indicate a "stress" of some kind. Sextiles and especially trines are supposed to be "good" or favorable aspects, while the square (90°) is considered "bad." Hans Genuit holds the view that a multiplicity of aspects in a chart indicates a complicated personality, but he is careful to add that it is difficult to decide how the aspects will work out. Ingrid Lind stresses that the strength of the planets, as indicated by the aspects, gives the key to the native's personality—in her words, to his "power to make use of his qualities."

It is just possible, though, that all these complex considerations to be included in the interpretation of a horoscope may serve to blind people by science. No matter how many factors must be considered in determining the meaning of a horoscope, the interpretations offered by the majority of astrologers seem to be simply collections of conventional statements culled from the vast number of astrological cookbooks.

Too often, interpretations are produced by what is called "blind diagnosis," which means that the astrologer does not meet his client but simply provides a written interpretation that has been made with little or no knowledge of the native's social background, education, and psychological temperament. (This is just the kind of interpretation that Margaret Hone dismisses contemptuously as "astrology by post." It is "astrology by interview" that she insists on.) The written statements offered in this way usually fall into the lowest category of astrological interpretation: the "character analysis" that is vague and obscure

A "telefortune" machine at a British holiday resort represents prediction by astrology in its simplest (and most suspect) form. The girl has set the right-hand dial (marked "female") at her Sun-sign, and is listening to a recorded forecast of her future.

enough to allow almost anyone to recognize himself or herself (especially if the vagueness seems complimentary). Statements like these crop up continually in such interpretations:

"This is a strong chart."

"There is a promise of eventual success."

"You are approaching a time of change."

"The horoscope indicates that you dislike being 'trapped in a rut.'"

"You possess many neglected or little-used abilities."

"Romantic feelings are strong."

Some of the more sophisticated astrologers might argue in favor of blind diagnosis, believing that prior knowledge of the native is quite unnecessary to a talented and perceptive interpreter. But most others look down on the popular type of blind diagnosis as a piece of inferior and cut-price magic. K. E. Krafft, for instance, always refused to provide any kind of interpretation without first having a personal interview with the client. Or, in the absence of an interview, he invariably demanded specimens of handwriting executed at different periods of the native's life, and photographs as well. It might seem that Krafft wanted things made easy for him; but we should remember that he called himself a "psychological consultant." Any kind of psychologist must know who he is dealing with; yet in a truly blind diagnosis the subject is completely unspecified. It might be a man or a woman—it might be a white mouse. All the astrologer is given is the time and place of birth.

For all this, and in spite of all the arguments against astrology (and there are many), the fact remains that some accomplished astrologers (and there are a few) have the unexplained ability to analyze accurately a person's character and personality as it is revealed in the horoscope's cosmic symbolism. Later in this book we will look at some examples of interpretative (and predictive) successes, and they will make one thing certain: When such positive results occur, they are not obtained on the basis of mechanical or rule-of-thumb interpretation of the chart's various combinations. Nor can they be explained in terms of coincidence. The odds are usually too heavy against "lucky guesses."

Then how are the successes achieved? There is no ready-made answer, but *intuition* obviously plays an important part. C. G. Jung (who included astrology among what he called the "various intuitive methods of interpreting fate") once drew an interesting analogy that can help to explain what is meant by intuition here. Jung pointed out that "whatever happens in a given moment has inevitably the quality peculiar to that moment." (Paraphrased into less precise terms, this implies that the qualities of the moment of one's birth—the time of year, etc.—leave a lasting mark upon one.) Jung continues:

"There are certain connoisseurs who can tell you merely from the appearance, taste, and behavior of a wine the site of its vineyard and the year of its origin. There are antiquarians who with almost uncanny accuracy will name the time and place of origin and the maker of an *objet d'art* or piece of furniture on merely looking at it. And there are even astrologers who can tell you, without any previous knowledge of your nativity, what the position of the sun and moon was and what zodiacal sign rose above the horizon at the moment of your birth."

Turning the analogy round, we can say that there are the rare few astrologers who can look at a map of the heavens as they supposedly were at the moment of your birth and tell you what kind of person you are, and even what seems to be in store for you in the future. This, then, must be intuition, combined with experience and with a highly developed ability to assess people's characters (these rare astrologers seldom stoop to blind diagnosis). In such cases the horoscope seems to function as merely a kind of "focusing point" for the intuition. A clairvoyant's crystal ball (for an exceptional clairvoyant) serves a similar purpose; and, it might be suggested, so do dreams or various association tests in psychiatry.

But leaving this rarefied atmosphere and getting back to the ordinary astrologer (the majority) whose interpretations derive more from the tradition than intuition: If the recipient of a chart has some astrological knowledge, he can usually disentangle or analyze (and thus compensate for) the reasoning that lies behind the interpretation. But he will find this much more difficult in relation to *predictive* statements. Here we are no longer concerned with a fairly well-defined tradition but with the choice of one of a number of rather speculative procedures. Yet prediction is what most people who go to astrologers want— prediction dealing with their problems (usually rather obvious problems involving things like love or money).

This is asking a lot. The natal horoscope itself is at least an expression of certain astronomical *facts* that have been wedded to a symbolic system. But this is not the case with the so-called "progressed" horoscope, in which the various factors (planets, ascendant, etc.) are advanced or "progressed" in accordance with given keys to give a reading for the native's future.

"A day for a year" is the phrase used to describe one system of progression, which is based on the assumption that one day's movements of the planets after birth corresponds to a year in the native's life. The astrologer decides which day in the ephemeris of the birth year corresponds to the year that he wishes to assess. Thus to cast a progressed horoscope for a person approaching his 50th birthday, the astrologer would erect and interpret a chart corresponding to the 50th *day* following his birth.

The so-called *primary system* is based not on the orbital movements of the planets but on the rotation of the earth. To avoid getting bogged down in this system's mathematical and astronomical complications, it need only be mentioned that this system involves difficult calculations, and at the same time can be wrecked by the smallest error. For instance, an error of only four minutes for the birth time would result in a further error that would be equivalent to 12 months for the "prediction."

There are other complex and symbolic keys for progressing the planetary positions, but the "day for a year" is most widely used. Any of these systems seems arbitrary enough to give ammunition to a dozen enemies of astrology. Even astrology's friends have pointed out their weaknesses. For fun K. E. Krafft once invented a legendary personality to whom he ascribed a birth date, time, and place selected at random. Then, before erecting a natal chart or calculating any progressions, he wrote down a score of imaginary events supposedly experienced by this native during his fictitious lifetime. When he investigated the native's progressions he was amused (but not surprised) to find that he could almost invariably see something in the progressed horoscope that, logically seemed to fit the case.

Much predictive work is done on the basis of the so-called "transits"; and the mechanics of this system are not quite as speculative as they are in the case of directions according to hypothetical keys or rates of progression. A transit is defined as the actual passage of a planet over the position of any planet or point in the birth chart. Thus, if one has an ephemeris for any particular year (past, present, or future), it is easy enough to check the transits. And according to the nature of the transiting planet the transit itself may be interpreted as favorable or unfavorable in nature. For example, a person born on January 23, 1898, would have had his natal Sun in 3° 34' of Aquarius. Saturn exactly transited this position at about midnight on February 2-3, 1962. Transiting Saturn conjunction Sun would not be considered favorable.

Many of the best modern astrologers prefer to avoid any kind of predictive work—perhaps in the light of its associations with cheap fortune telling, but also because predictions can be dangerous. It is very likely that certain kinds of prediction (such as the "beware of accidents during the first three days of February" variety) are often fulfilled because the native is unconsciously impelled —by what is popularly called "the power of suggestion"—to make them come true. K. E. Krafft, for instance, always refused to undertake predictive work for individual clients, partly because of the uncertain techniques (of "progressing" horoscopes) but also because of the moral and psychological dangers.

Science or mystery?

Krafft's own astrological career (before he fell into the Nazis' hands) itself represents the two camps into which many modern astrologers are divided. First of all, many are insistent that astrology itself should be recognized as a *science*. No field of inquiry would appear so unsuitable for serious scientific investigation. Nevertheless, the full strength of modern statistical analysis has been turned on astrology: Krafft himself spent nearly a decade collecting and analyzing statistics to prove astrology's validity.

He began his huge and gallant undertaking while he was still a natural-sciences student at the University of Geneva in 1921. He produced detailed statistical studies (mentioned in Chapter 1) of the planetary factors and angles in the charts of more than 2000 musicians; also, on the basis of data from the official registers at Geneva, he completed studies relating to hereditary factors (of a planetary nature) in the horoscopes of members of several generations in the same family. His preliminary findings were presented at a Statistical Congress at Geneva in 1923, and caused a certain amount of interest in academic circles (the more so because Professor L. Hersch, who had taught Krafft statistical methods, vouched for the scientific nature of his procedures).

But in spite of Professor Hersch's recommendations, the authorities refused to allow Krafft to present a thesis on "Cosmic Influences on Human Life" for a doctorate. Krafft thereupon left Geneva without a diploma of any kind and removed himself to London, where he spent six months of 1924 studying advanced statistical techniques at the University of London before returning to Switzerland in July 1924.

During the next three or four years Krafft combined a successful career in a large Zurich printing and publishing firm with the continuation of the statistical enquiry that he had begun in 1921. By 1929 he had assembled a body of material consisting of more than a million individually numbered observations. He published a preliminary synthesis of his findings in several articles published between 1926-29 in the more respectable German astrological journals; and he himself had no doubt whatever that he had succeeded in providing sound scientific evidence for the existence of "cosmic influences."

Official science (foreseeably) ignored his work. But, surprisingly, even in German astrological circles Krafft's work apparently failed to stimulate more

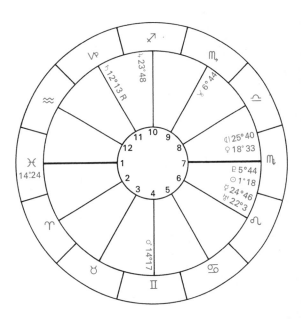

Here the chart interpreted on p. 256 has been "progressed" by 50 years (one day for each year)—which, when related to the natal chart may reveal possible future trends in the native's life. The Sun is now in Virgo, which favors practical work. Saturn, who dominated the natal chart, comes into exact opposition with the Sun when the native is 21—perhaps marking the removal of conflicts and frustrations. The ascendant, now in Pisces and in trine with the natal Sun and in sextile with Saturn, emphasizes the Sun-Saturn opposition, indicating that the native may now reap the reward of his former hard work. Another important aspect is Mercury in trine to the natal Jupiter, implying mental stimulation. All progressed charts, most astrologers agree, must be studied in relation to the birth chart.

than a mild interest. (These circles had also initiated their own statistical project at much the same time but did little or nothing with the material that they assembled.) So Krafft was let down, so to speak, by both the sheep and the goats. In any case, very few people were qualified to follow his mathematical arguments. Poisson's Law (of probabilities) might be all very well in its way, but what most of these people wanted were comprehensible and moderately foolproof methods by which they could demonstrate that astrology "works."

Nor are the requirements any different in astrological circles today. During the past 60 years there have been many isolated attempts other than Krafft's to prove the validity of astrology upon an objectively statistical basis. There were the investigations made early in this century by the French amateur astrologer Paul Choisnard (mentioned in Chapter 1); and the experiments in blind diagnosis made in the last few years by Professor Hans Bender of the Institute of Parapsychology of the University of Freiburg (Breisgau, Germany); and many more. But perhaps one of the most striking of all modern statistical examinations of astrology was made in the early 1950s by Michel Gauquelin, a Parisian academic psychologist who had a first-class knowledge of modern statistical techniques. Gauquelin read Krafft's *Traité* and, although completely uninterested in the astrological tradition as such, decided to try to reconstruct some of Krafft's major experiments. He soon discovered that it would not be possible even to check them on the basis of the material presented in the *Traité*, and also came to the conclusion that even Krafft's statistical methods were in themselves highly suspect. He thereupon resolved to mount a full-scale experiment of his own.

Whereas Krafft had to a very large extent worked without birth-hour data, Gauquelin laboriously collected such material from official registers in France, Italy, Germany, Belgium, and Holland and eventually erected and analyzed about 24,000 horoscopes, which must have contained a total of about a quarter of a million factors. These horoscopes were then filed under "professional" categories—i.e., for scientists, sporting champions, soldiers, politicians, actors, painters, musicians, men of letters, journalists, and industrial magnates.

Much to Gauquelin's surprise (and, it seems, not without a certain embarrassment) he ultimately arrived at the conclusion that certain propositions contained in the astrological tradition *could* be substantiated to some extent. For example, he found that a dominant Jupiter *does* particularly concern ecclesiastics and a dominant Mars does link up with sportsmen. His work met with a mixed reception: The scientific critics were more disapproving than approving and, again, even the astrologers were not as interested as they might have been.

Both before and after the Second World War various groups of astrologers or individual astrologers have attempted fairly ambitious statistical investigations, although never on the same scale as either Krafft's or Gauquelin's. Furthermore, it would appear that the majority of them were initiated without a detailed

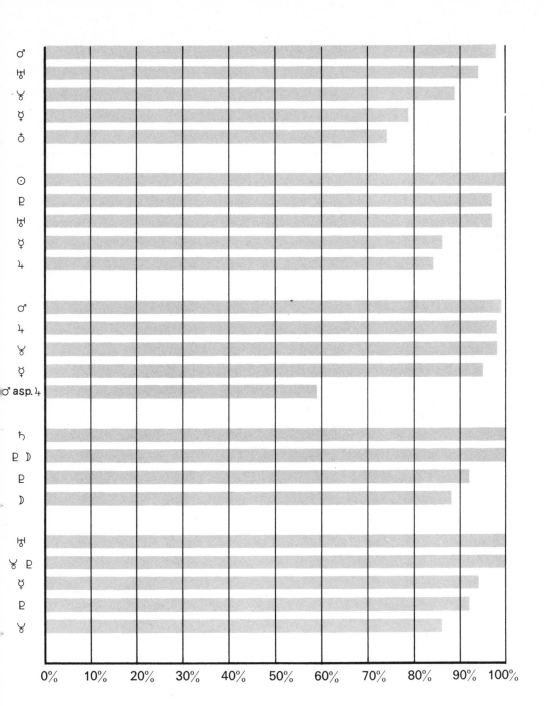

An immense statistical examination of astrology was begun in 1924 by the Church of Light, Los Angeles, U.S.A. Thousands of horoscopes were erected, progressed, and tabulated ; among the findings were statistics that seem to indicate what planet governs a given job or profession. Here, simplified charts show the dominant planets of film stars, politicans, athletes, farmers—and astrologers.

knowledge of what had been attempted in the past by men like Choisnard or Krafft, or even of what was being done by contemporaries. If one characteristic of a science is the free and ready pooling of information, then astrology is not a science. And the astrologers who, like Krafft, have attempted in a scientific manner and for scientific ends to base their beliefs upon statistics have failed to interest more than a tiny minority of their colleagues.

Incidentally, along with all these batteries of statistics, some modern adherents of astrology point to other "evidence" of its rational (i.e. scientific) basis. In fact, such people go much further than most modern astrological writers (who, as we have seen, believe that the stars are merely "signs"); they claim that the heavenly bodies actually have a *causal* effect on people. This hypothesis is presented in objective detail by C. G. Jung (who, like a good scientist, wished to examine every possible view of astrology before presenting his own view in terms of synchronicity). Jung writes:

"In the light of the most recent astrophysical research, astrological correspondence is probably not a matter of synchronicity but, very largely, a causal rela-

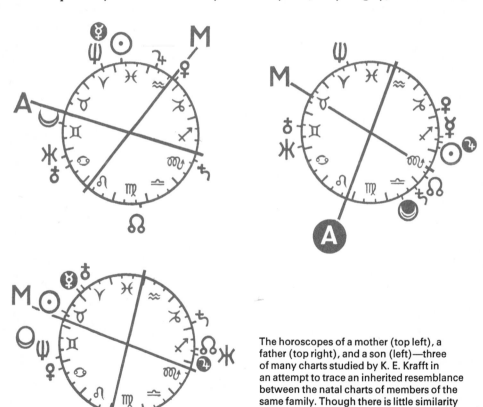

The horoscopes of a mother (top left), a father (top right), and a son (left)—three of many charts studied by K. E. Krafft in an attempt to trace an inherited resemblance between the natal charts of members of the same family. Though there is little similarity between the charts of mother and son, those of father and son have several factors in common: Both have Jupiter in Sagittarius, Moon in Libra, and adjacent ascendants (though these are in different signs).

tionship. As Professor Max Knoll has demonstrated, the solar proton radiation is influenced to such a degree by planetary conjunctions, opposition, and quartile aspects that the appearance of magnetic storms can be predicted with a fair amount of probability."

Therefore, on the basis of new scientific knowledge, Jung suggests that "it is just conceivable that there is a causal connection between the planetary aspects and the psycho-physiological disposition."

But Jung's cautious words "just conceivable" are just a scientist's way of saying that one should not dismiss any possibility before investigating it. And his own investigation (the astrological experiment discussed in Chapter 7) proved to his own satisfaction at least that, if there was anything in astrology, it was due to the operation of the *non*-causal principle of synchronicity. He concludes: "Although I was obliged to express doubt, earlier, about the mantic [i.e., divinatory, irrational] character of astrology, I am now forced as a result of my astrological experiment to recognize it again."

K. E. Krafft also came to recognize the irrational nature of astrology. When at the end of the 1920s he had been disappointed by the reception of his statistics, he tired of the statistics themselves and turned in the opposite direction. He had always had something of a mystical bent; this tendency flowered in the development of his complicated astro-psychological symbolical system, which he called *Typocosmy*.

If in the final analysis we agree with Krafft and Jung (and of course many others) that astrology is an irrational phenomenon, then the door is opened to a great many of these eccentric, "breakaway" systems of horoscopic interpretation. Obviously, the mechanical application of the tradition's stereotyped meanings has in many cases served to reduce modern astrology to the level of a parlor game. In an attempt to counteract this tendency, many modern astrologers are working to replace the tradition with a more up-to-date brand of irrationalism—for example, Furze Morrish's mystical "psycho-evolutionary" system (which was described in Chapter 3), or the German "cosmobiologists" of the Reinhold Ebertin school. Ebertin's astrological rebels completely ignore house division and do not even appear to bother overmuch about the signs of the Zodiac. They work almost solely with "complexes" of planets on a common axis. Faithful traditionalists regard Ebertin and his followers as dangerous heretics; on the other hand, Ebertin believes that the sooner the astrologers throw overboard what he calls astrology's "medieval ballast," the better.

It seems that Germany is the home of a great many modern astrological heresies. There is also the so-called Hamburg School, founded by Alfred Witte some 40 years ago, which uses eight completely hypothetical trans-Neptunian planets and, furthermore, has produced ephemerides showing their movements. This system, it is claimed, can yield excellent interpretations of horoscopes. Even traditionalist astrologers, who look askance at the Hamburg school's interpretative methods, have been known to fall back on them when all else fails.

L'AMOUREUX.

LAROUE DE FORTUNE

The success of any form of divination—whether from palms or horoscopes—may depend on an incalculable element of intuition. A tea-cup fortune teller might see among the tea leaves (left) the shapes of a lion (meaning influence), of Libra the Scales (meaning marriage), of the letter M (the initial of a loved one). But his final interpretation would depend on several factors, including position and clarity of outline. Similarly, in the interpretation of Tarot cards (which are usually set out as in the diagram above right), the stock meaning of a card varies according to its position in relation to the "significator" card (marked 1), which represents the person whose fortune is being told. The Tarot cards depicted here are (from left to right) the Lovers, the one of Cups, the Wheel of Fortune, the one of Clubs, the Knight of Wands, and Death.

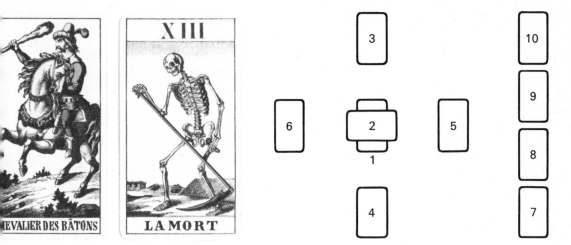

In Vienna, a member of this school (signing himself simply Herr Stuiber) has in the last few years written several short monographs entitled "Some Remarkable Astrological Experiments." These indicate that the Hamburg School astrologers can on occasion give precise and surprising answers to even improbable questions. For instance, one of these astrologers was told the time and place of birth of a woman whose identity was quite unknown to him; and he was asked what happened to the woman on March 4, 1954, at 4 P.M. in Vienna. His answer was correct: The woman had been shot in the back.

Such systems, like the tradition, could presumably be taught; but whether they could then be applied by the students with any success seems more than doubtful. It would be as impossible to create (by whatever system) a new race of astrological *virtuosi* as to create a hundred violinists or painters of genius. The short answer would be that gifted astrologers are "born, not made" with the necessary qualities—though, apart from the general idea of intuition, these qualities are apparently quite inexplicable.

It is perhaps just this irrationalism, this intuitive and mysterious basis of astrology, that is (and has always been) the sole source of its appeal—and one of the main reasons why scientific investigations of astrology seem to lack appeal even for astrologers. Most people who think about it all would *like* there to be some validity in astrology—something, it would seem, that cannot be scientifically proved but has to be taken on trust and perhaps with a catch in the breath. Such people will point to successful interpretations or predictions as indications that "there's something in it." And then they will be shaken by interpretations that failed, predictions that never came true. The next chapter will include a few of each kind of prediction; but what, if anything, will be proved by such occurrences must remain dependent on the individual reader, and which side of the fence he finds himself on.

9 Predictions and pronouncements

This chapter is simply a short anthology, containing examples from the past and present of two kinds of astrological statement. First, there are statements of opinion, setting forth the attitudes to astrology held by various authors (many of whom are well known outside the astrological realm). Some of the authors approve, others disapprove. A few of them more or less reserve their opinion (as Plutarch does); others take astrology's value for granted and merely describe some specific application (as Culpeper does). Also, some of these quotations are taken from works of literature—plays, poems, novels—and, whether for or against, reflect the interest taken by literary men of all ages in astrology as a social phenomenon.

Interspersed throughout the opinions are samples of *predictive* statements. Astrology has always taken upon itself the double function of providing a key to character and personality and of providing glimpses of the future. (More recent astrologers, however, have turned away from divination, and consider astrology to be more a form of psychology than of fortune telling.) Throughout previous chapters we have occasionally looked at examples of prediction; and we have seen that astrology's friends often use successful predictions as proof of the art's validity, while its enemies often use unsuccessful predictions to prove the contrary. The examples that follow are not put forward to prove anything: Included are some predictions that came true and some others that didn't.

A prophetic vision of a bad harvest (from a German woodcut of 1627) based on "celestial signs" that allegedly appeared in the sky at the time.

Planets and shepherds

My son thou shalt understand
That, to avoid all idleness,
This matter oft thou shalt take in hand
To read of shepherd's business;
And special of the planets seven,
Of Mars and Saturn that is full high
Also of Sol, the middle heaven,
And under him Venus, Luna, and Mercury.
For to know their natures all
In sooth it is a great conning,
And show what may befall
When every planet is reigning;
By their working oft we be moved
To look lusty and plays of jollity,
And by some of them as clerks have proved
They steer us to theft, murder, and vility.
Some be good, some be bad verily,
Some be not comfortable to man nor beast;
Some hot, some cold, some wet, some dry,
If three be good, four be worse at the least;
Saturn is highest, and coldest being full bad,
And Mars with his bloody sword, ever ready to kill;
Jupiter very good, and Venus maketh lovers glad,
Sol and Luna is half good and half ill,
Mercury is good, and evil verily.
And hereafter thou shalt know
Which of the seven most worthy be,
And who reigneth high and who a-low;
Of every planet's property—
Which is the best among them all
That causeth wealth, sorrow, or sin.
Tarry and here, son thou shall
Speak soft, for now I begin.
—from *The Kalendar and Compost of Shepherds,*
published in Paris 1493, translated about 1518

A woodcut of an idealized medieval shepherd
from the frontispiece to a French edition of
The Kalendar of Shepherds.

Organs of providence

"And if we cannot deny but that God hath given virtues to springs and fountains, to cold earth, to plants and stones, minerals, and to the excremental parts of the basest living creatures, why should we rob the beautiful stars of their working powers? For, seeing they are many in number and of eminent beauty and magnitude, we may not think that in the treasury of his wisdom who is infinite there can be wanting, even for every star, a peculiar virtue and operation; as every herb, plant, fruit, and flower adorning the face of the earth hath the like. For as these were not created to beautify the earth alone and to cover and shadow her dusty face but otherwise for the use of man and beast to feed them and cure them; so were not those uncountable glorious bodies set in the firmament to no other end than to adorn it but for instruments and organs of his divine providence, so far as it hath pleased his just will to determine."
—Sir Walter Raleigh, *History of the World,* 1614

One of Europe's greatest calamities—the Black Death of 1348—was foreseen by two medieval astrologers. John of Bassigney, an English scholar writing in the 1340s, proclaimed that in the year 1352 (a few years late), a pestilence would cover the whole world that would kill about two thirds of the population. His prediction, he said, rested partly on information that he had obtained from other scholars on his travels, and partly on his study of the stars. (It should be mentioned that almost all of John's predictions concerned disasters, devastations, scourges, wars, and the like.)

Another 14th-century scholar, England's John of Eschenden, is supposed to have predicted the Black Death from an eclipse of the Moon and certain planetary conjunctions that occurred in 1345. He stated that the effects of the eclipse would last for eight years and six months, during which time "men and beasts will suffer long diseases and there will be death and many wars and flight; . . . great corruption in the air, and great scarcity of crops from excessive cold and rains and worms."

The beginnings of Rome

"Likewise in the time of Marcus Varro (as a man learned, and one that had read as much of ancient stories as any Roman) there was a friend of his called Tarrutius, a great philosopher and mathematician, who being given to the calculation of astronomy for the delight of speculation only, wherein he was thought most excellent: it did fall out that Varro gave him this question, to search out what hour and day the nativity of Romulus was, who gathered it out by certain accidents, as they do in the resolutions of certain geometrical questions. For they say, that by the self same science, one may tell before of things to come, and to happen to a man in his life, knowing certainly the hour of his nativity: and how one may tell also the hour of his nativity, when by accidents they know what hath happened to him all his life.

"Tarrutius did the question that Varro gave him. And having thoroughly considered the adventures, deeds, and gests of Romulus, how long he lived, and how he died: all which being gathered and conferred together, he did boldly judge for a certainty, that he was conceived in his mother's womb, in the first year of the second Olympiad, the three and twentieth day of the month which the Egyptians call Choeac, and now is called December, about three of the clock in the morning, in which hour there was a whole eclipse of the sun: and that he was born into the world, in the month Thouth which is the month of September, about the rising of the sun. And that Rome was begun by him on the ninth day of the month which the Egyptians call Pharmuthi, and answereth now to the month of April, between two and three of the clock in the morning. For they will say that a city hath his revolution and his time of continuance appointed, as well as the life of a man: and that they knew by the situation of the stars, the day of her beginning and foundation.

"These things and such other like, peradventure will please the readers better for their strangeness and curiosity, than offend or mislike them for their falsehood."

—Plutarch, *Life of Romulus*, Englished by Sir Thomas North, 1603

Women to avoid
> *Beware the Woman, too, and shun her Sight,*
> *Who, in these Studies, does her self Delight.*
> *By whom a greasie Almanack is born,*
> *With often handling, like chaste Amber, worn:*
> *Not now consulting, but consulted, she*
> *Of the Twelve Houses, and their Lords, is free,*
> *She, if the Scheme a fatal Journey show,*
> *Stays safe at Home, but lets her Husband go.*
> *If but a Mile she Travel out of Town,*
> *The Planetary House must first be known:*
> *And lucky moment; if her Eye but akes*
> *Or itches, its Decumbiture she takes.*
> *No Nourishment receives in her Disease,*
> *But what the Stars, and Ptolemy shall please.*

—Juvenal, from *The Sixth Satire*,
translated by John Dryden (1693)

According to the "English Chronicles" of 1186, all Europe panicked at one time in that century because of a prediction by astrologers of an approaching conjunction of planets in the constellation Libra. The fact that the conjunction was to take place in an "airy" or "windy" sign was interpreted as signifying (in addition to other horrors) a terrific wind-storm. In many parts of Europe people built themselves caves underground and special services were held in many churches. Aside from earthquakes and hurricanes, it was prophesied that cities in sandy regions were to be completely buried and that Egypt and Ethiopia were to become uninhabitable. Storms apparently did occur, but nothing of the magnitude indicated in the predictions.

Aphorisms of Cardan

When the Moon is in Scorpio in square of Saturn in Leo, or in his opposition when he is in Taurus partilely, the Native rarely has either Wife or Children, but if Saturn be in Aquarius, he will be a mere Woman hater.

Mercury, mixing his Beams with Mars, is a great argument of a violent death.

When Venus is with Saturn, and beholds the Lord of the Ascendant, the Native is inclinable to Sodomy, or at least shall love old hard-favoured Women, or poor dirty Wenches.

The Moon, full of Light in Conjunction with Mars, makes the Native be counted a Fool, but if she be void of light and with Saturn, he is so indeed.

A Woman that has Mars with the Moon is *Right,* I'll warrant her.

The Moon in Aquarius or Pisces, makes the Native not at all acceptable amongst Princes or Grandees.

In Purging, 'tis best that both the Moon and Lord of the Ascendant descend and be under the Earth, in vomiting that they Ascend.

In the past women were often seen as the dupes of superstition (and astrology). In this satirical engraving (1792) a corrupt fortune teller exploits an innocent maiden.

Make no new Clothes, nor first put them on when the Moon is in Scorpio, especially if she be full of light and beheld of Mars, for they will be apt to be torn and quickly worn out.

If a Comet appear whilst a Woman goes with Child, if it be either in the fourth, fifth, or eighth month, such Child will prove very prone to anger and quarrels, and if he be of quality, to sedition.

Saturn in fixed signs causes scarcity of Corn, dear years, and the Death of many Men.

When Saturn is in Libra and Jupiter in Cancer, great Changes and Alterations shall happen in the world.

—Jerome Cardan, *Seven Segments,*
1547, translated by William Lilly, 1676

Calvin condemns

"There hath been of long time a foolish curiosity to judge by the stars of all things what should chance unto men: and thence to enquire and take counsel as touching those matters which are to be done. But we will by and by God willing declare that it is nothing but a devilish superstition. Yea, and it hath been rejected by a common consent as pernicious to mankind. And yet at this day it hath got the upper hand in such sort that many which think themselves witty men, yea and have been so judged, are as it were bewitched therewith."

—John Calvin (1509-63)

A page from *The Ravens Almanack*—a parody of the astrological almanacs that were popular in England during the 17th century.

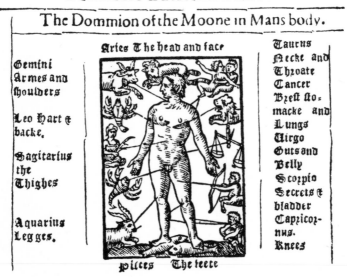

Rauens Almanacke.

The Dommion of the Moone in Mans body.

Aries The head and face

Gemini Armes and shoulders

Leo Hart & backe.

Sagitarius the Thighes

Aquarius Legges.

Taurus Necke and Throate

Cancer Brest stomacke and Lungs

Virgo Guts and Belly

Scorpio Secrets & bladder

Capricornus. Knees

Pisces The feete

Louis XI of France (1423-83) often consulted a famous astrologer named d'Almonsor. Others consulted him as well : According to one story that attached itself to this astrologer's name, he was visited late one night by two knights and their armed retainers. The knights ordered d'Almonsor to read their fates.

D'Almonsor cast their horoscopes and predicted that one knight would die violently—but heroically, and for a good cause. As for the second knight, d'Almonsor also foretold death, adding that this knight was menaced by a power-ful man and that death would probably come through a poisoned drink.

The first knight was the Duke of Burgundy, who was killed in battle shortly after the prediction. The second knight, the Duke of Berry, also died shortly afterward : His death was widely thought to have been due to poison given to him on the orders of Louis XI.

A 17th-century manuscript records a prediction that is supposed to have been made of the death of Henry IV of France in 1610. According to this story, an Italian astrologer named Francisco Corvino was working quietly in Florence when, suddenly, he announced to his companions that "tomorrow, one of the greatest monarchs in Christendom will be slain." And, the manuscript says, the very next day in Paris Henry IV was stabbed to death by an assassin.

A mock almanac

"To the Lyons of the Wood (the young Courtiers), to the wild Buck of the Forrest (the gallants and younger Brothers), to the Harts of the field, and to all the whole Countrie that are brought up wisely, yet prove Gulls and are borne rich yet die beggars : the new English astrologer dedicateth his Ravens Almanack.

"Amongst Gentlemen that have full purses, and those that cry 'tillil, let the world slide,' the week shall run out so quickly and so merrily, that on the Satur-day morning it shall be hard for them to tell whether the day that went before were Friday.

"The same losse of memorie will fall upon many that shall go drunk to bed.

"O you common Fiddlers likewise that scrape out a poor living out of dryed Cats guts : I prophesy that many of you shall this year be troubled with abomin-able noises and singing in your heads, in so much that a great part of you shall dye beggars."

—*The Ravens Almanack,* 1609

In medieval and Renaissance times, astrologers seem to have predicted the end of the world more frequently than anything else. Here are a few examples :

In 1500 an Italian astrologer, Agostino Nifo, asserted that the starry portents of a flood were undeniable, adding that this disaster was due to the sins of man, which cried out for divine punishment. In 1520 Johann Virdung, an Austrian astrologer, declared some meteors seen at Vienna to be warnings of a flood to take place at the time of some important planetary conjunctions in 1524.

The "floods in 1524" cry was taken up by scores of astrologers and almanacs. From Rome in 1521 one Sebastian Constantinus announced that he had seen a solar eclipse in the house of death, a most ominous position. And then a famous German astrologer, Johann Stoeffler, forecast in February 1524 that 20 conjunctions would take place that year, of which 16 would occupy "a watery sign." This signified, he said, floods of such an extent that the world would be destroyed.

These predictions set off a continent-wide panic. People apparently built arks, boats, and rafts to save themselves. Whole communities packed and left home for higher ground. It was said that even Charles V, emperor of Spain and Germany, had men mark out places that would be less exposed to flood waters, in the hope that the floods would be only partial.

To keep the record straight, it should be added that during that year there *were* abnormally heavy rains, and considerable flooding, in many parts of Europe.

Edmund disagrees

"This is the excellent foppery of the world, that, when we are sick in fortune— often the surfeit of our own behavior—we make guilty of our disasters the sun, the moon, and the stars; as if we were villains by necessity, fools by heavenly compulsion, knaves, thieves and treachers by spherical predominance, drunkards, liars and adulterers by an enforced obedience of planetary influence; and all that we are evil in, by a divine thrusting on: an admirable evasion of whoremaster man, to lay his goatish disposition to the charge of a star! My father compounded with my mother under the dragon's tail, and my nativity was under *ursa major*; so that it follows I am rough and lecherous. 'Sfoot! I should have been that I am had the maidenliest star in the firmament twinkled on my bastardizing."

—Shakespeare, *King Lear*, I, ii

When Marie Thérèse of Spain (daughter of Philip IV) was a child, the court astrologer told her that she would some day marry the greatest king in all Europe and that this marriage would avert a war. In June 1660 she married Louis XIV of France and the marriage prevented a war between France and Spain over a territorial disagreement.

Fate of an astrologer

"Nectanebus, King of Egypt, was driven into Macedonia by fourteen nations in rebellion and later he wished to teach astrology to King Alexander who, they say, was his son. Alexander gave him a push and knocked him into a pit where he broke his neck. So it would have served him better to have watched the earth than the heavens."

—Nicole Oresme, from *Livre de Divinacions*, 1361-65

Fate of an anti-astrologer

"[Sir Christopher Heydon] the author of that incomparable *Defence of Judicial Astrology*, written in answer to a book against Astrology, by Mr. John Chambers; in which Defence, this learned Knight was so exact in his Responses, so satisfactory and full in his Arguments, so strenuous in his Proofs thereof, that when once Mr. Chambers (who no question was a great Scholar) had seen and perused it, and found the same unanswerable, and his own Arguments so fully refuted and retorted, he for very grief died."

—John Gadbury, *Collectio Geniturarum*, 1662

A grain of salt

"[The astrologer sat] before a Square Table, covered with a green Carpet, on which lay a huge book in *Folio*, wide open, full of Strange Characters, such as the *Aegyptians* and *Chaldaeans* were never guilty of; not far from that, a silver Wand, a Surplus, a Watering Pot, with all the superstitions or rather fayned Instruments of his cousening Art. And to put a fairer colour on his black and foul Science, on his head he had a four-cornered Cap, on his backe a fair Gown (but made of a strange fashion) in his right hand he held an Astrolabe, in his left a Mathematical Glass. . . .

A fraudulent astrologer (from the title page of *Astrologaster*), equipped with astrolabe and "mathematical glass," receives a client.

"He was as well acquainted with the Twelve Signs in Heaven, as any Trades-man with those in Cheape-side, and run over the Nature of the Seven Planets as nimbly as the French Vaulter over the Ropes. And I myself . . . could discourse to you what a sullen fellow *Saturn* is (on whom the permanent continuation of all things depend), what a jovial fellow *Jupiter* (on whom the fecundity of Agent Causes rely), what a quarrelling Swash-buckler *Mars* (on whom the swift expedition of any thing to the effect doth hang), what a hot fellow *Sol* (whom all Agent Causes follow), what a wanton wench *Venus* (on whom the fecundity of all Material Causes look after), what a merry fellow *Mercury* (in whom a manifold virtue doth flourish), and what a mad Lass *Luna* (on whom the increase and decrease of Human things consist)."

—John Melton, *Astrologaster,* or the *Figure Caster,* 1620

Heaven's alarm to the world

"The Great God, when he made the world, placed the stars in heaven, to be for signs as to events that in the ordinary course of nature should come to pass. (Gen. I : 14.)

"There are also extraordinary stars sometimes appearing in the heavens . . . blazing stars called comets, from the streamlike long hair which attends them. Such a star is prodigious and a fearful sight. . . . As for the sign in heaven now appearing, what calamities may be portended thereby? . . . In general we have cause to fear that sweeping judgments are thereby signified; that the Lord is coming down from Heaven with a long beesom of destruction which shall sweep away a world of sinners before it.

"Judgments, which are God's sharp razors on mankind whereby he doth shear down multitudes of sinful people, draw near. . . . God by the blazing star is speaking to other places, and not to New England only. And it may be He is declaring to that generation of hairy scalps who go on still in their trespasses that the day of the Calamity is at hand.

". . . I am persuaded that the floods of great water are coming. I am persuaded that God is about to open the windows of heaven and to pour down the cataracts of his wrath ere this generation is passed away. Let us then prepare for trouble, for the Lord has fired his beacon in the heavens. Let everyone that is godly pray unto the Lord before the Floods of great waters come nigh unto us."

—The American religious leader Increase Mather, from a sermon
on the comet of 1680

An astrologer recants

"I also being a boy learned this Art of my Father, afterward I lost much time and labour therein; at length I learned that altogether it was built upon no other foundation but upon mere trifles, and feignings of imaginations. . . ."

—Henry Cornelius Agrippa, *Of the Vanitie and Uncertaintie of
Artes and Sciences,* translated by James Sanford, 1569

In 1583 the English astrologer Richard Harvey (along with many other astrologers) predicted a conjunction of Saturn and Jupiter for high noon on April 28 of that year. He pointed out that these two planets had been in conjunction in the watery sign of Cancer just prior to the Biblical deluge in Noah's time. This time they would be together in the fiery sign of Aries: The result, he said, would be burnings, strife, and other fiery calamities (including the appearance of a great comet). "The very frame of the world cannot endure long after," he added, and "the same Jesus Christ shall come again in unspeakable majestie!"

An attack on Lilly

"Mr. Lillie in all these dreadful Eclipses and malignant Aspects, finds much matter of bad, dismal and disastrous concernement, to Princes, Potentates, Priests, Lawyers, Husbandmen, Graziers, etc. but none at all ever to Wizards, Witches, Conjurers, Fortune-tellers, Sorcerers, Stargazers, Astrologers, etc. No malignity of any Aspect belike is able to reach them."

—Thomas Gataker, *Against the Scurrilous Aspersion of that grand Imposter, Mr. William Lillie,* 1653

The astrologer-astronomer William Whiston (who succeeded Isaac Newton at Cambridge in 1703) gave a lecture in 1736 predicting an eclipse of the Moon, accompanied by the appearance of a great comet, for precisely five A.M. on the following Thursday. These portents, Whiston told his audience, would herald the return of the Messiah to earth; the world would end on the next Friday, by fire and earthquake.

In fact, a comet did appear at about the appointed time. The prediction had been fairly widely publicized, and the city of London was briefly thrown into panic. Thousands of people fled the city.

Planets and plants

(The Stars' own Vegetable Garden and Medicine Chest)

Celandine: This is an herb of the Sun, and under the celestial Lion: it is one of the best cures for the eyes; for the eyes are subject to the luminaries: let it then be gathered when the Sun is in Leo, and the Moon in Aries.

Cucumbers: There is no dispute to be made, but that they are under the dominion of the Moon, though they are so much cried out against for their coldness, and if they were but one degree colder they would be poison.

Fennel: One good old fashion is not yet left off, viz. to boil Fennel with fish; for it consumes that phlegmatic humour, which fish most plentifully afford and annoy the body with, though few that use it know wherefore they do it; I suppose the reason of its benefit this way is, because it is an herb of Mercury, and under Virgo, and therefore bears antipathy to Pisces.

Peach-tree: Lady Venus owns this tree, and by it opposes the ill effects of Mars; and indeed for children and young people, nothing is better to purge cholera and the jaundice, than the leaves and flowers of this tree, being made into a syrup or conserve : let such as delight to please their lust, regard the fruit ; but such as have lost their health, and their children's, let them regard what I say, they may safely give two spoonfuls of the syrup at a time ; it is as gentle as Venus herself.

Nettle (*Urtica Vulgaris*) : This is an herb Mars claims dominion over. You know Mars is hot and dry, and you know as well that winter is cold and moist ; then you may know as well the reason why Nettle Tops, eaten in the spring, consume the phlegmatic superfluities in the body of man, that the coldness and moistness of winter has left behind.

Wild carrots : Wild Carrots belong to Mercury, and therefore break wind, and remove stitches in the sides, provoke urine and women's courses, and help to break and expel the stone ; the seed also of the same works the like effect, and is good for the dropsy, and those whose bellies are swollen with wind.

Houseleek : It is an herb of Jupiter ; and it is reported by Mezaldus, to preserve what it grows upon from fire and lightning.

Lettuce (*Common Garden*) : The Moon owns it, and that is the reason it cools and moistens what heat and dryness Mars causes, because Mars has his full in Cancer ; and it cools the heat because the Sun rules it, between whom and the Moon is a reception in the generation of men.

Hellebore : It is an herb of Saturn, and therefore no marvel if it has some sullen conditions with it, and would be far safer, being purified by the art of the alchymist than given raw.

Saffron : It is an herb of the Sun, and under the Lion, and therefore you need not demand a reason why it strengthens the heart so exceedingly.

Lily of the Valley : It is under the dominion of Mercury, and therefore it strengthens the brain, recruiting a weak memory, and makes it strong again.

Artichokes : They are under the dominion of Venus, and therefore it is not wonderful if they excite lust."

—Nicholas Culpeper, *The English Physician Enlarged*, 1653,
(revised and amplified by G. A. Gordon)

Postscript :—In the same work some other plants of interest are assigned as follows :

To the Sun : The olive, peony, vine, and walnut.

To the Moon : Water-cress and water lily, pumpkin and turnip, sea holly, willow, and white rose.

Mercury : Mushrooms, lavender, and parsley.

Venus : Apple and cherry, gooseberry, raspberry and strawberry, primrose, sorrels, wild thyme, and violet.

Mars : Chives, onion, mustard, radish and horse-radish, hops and peppers, tobacco, honeysuckle, wormwood.

Jupiter : The oak and the orange, peas and dandelion.

Saturn : Holly and ivy, hemlock and nightshade, poplar, quince, and yew.

Two 17th-century English doctors who successfully practiced both medicine and astrology: Left, Nicholas Culpeper (depicted within his own horoscope) above his house in London; above, a portrait of John Case from his book *The Angelical Guide.*

The star-doomed infant

No sooner does he peep into
The world, but he has done his do . . . .
Married his punctual dose of wives,
Is cuckolded, and breaks, or thrives, . . .
As if men from the stars did suck
Old-age, diseases, and ill-luck,
Wit, folly, honor, virtue, vice,
Trade, travel, women, claps, and dice;
And draw with the first air they breath,
Battle, and murther, sudden death.
Are not these fine commodities
To be imported from the skies?

—Samuel Butler, *Hudibras,* 1664

An astrologer's advertisement

Within this place
Lives Doctor Case.

He is said to have got more by this distich, than did Mr. Dryden by all his works.

—Joseph Addison in *The Tatler,* October 21, 1710

The star-struck valet

(*Scene: House of an Astrologer*)

The Valet: Lord, save us, Françoise, there's a career for one—Astrology! I'm trying to learn it on the side. I'm carefully collecting notes of everything our master says, and to show you how far I've progressed, you're now going to be completely astonished. Look, I'm working on an almanac for the year Sixteen Eightyone that we're just about to enter. . . . I've already done a good part of it. I've filled in all the days of all the months and I've almost this moment polished off December. But I'm left with one little difficulty, about which I want to consult you. I don't know if at the end of my almanac (for I must fill it out a little) I ought to put in 'Some Lives of Notable Persons' or 'The Methods of Planting Cabbages.'

[*Later in the play the action is affected by the great new comet of 1680; the Astrologer has received a letter from Rome.*]

The Countess: Monsieur, I observe strong signs of astonishment on your features.

The Astrologer: Ah, Madame, what a prodigy!

The Countess: Explain yourself immediately.

The Astrologer: Here's certainly something no one can have seen before.

The Countess: What's happened at Rome that's more terrible than here?

The Astrologer: A comet—

The Countess: Yet *another* comet! You terrify me.

The Astrologer: But you'd never guess what *kind* of comet!

The Countess: What is it this time?

The Astrologer: A comet in an egg.

The Countess: A comet in an egg! I'll never eat eggs again.

The Valet: Nor me either! Suppose I were to turn up a whole omelette of comets?

—Bernard Fontenelle, *La Comète,* 1681

A British astrological writer using the pseudonym "Astrologus" stated in 1793 that, from eclipses (especially of the Sun), astrologers can safely predict "notable events concerning the rise or fall of governments; the foundation or fall of cities, towns or fortifications—the breach of leagues among princes, the captivity, sorrow, or sickness of their miserable subjects; wars, quarrels, and tempests; inundations, duels, and litigations—religious controversies, and irreligious persecutions among mankind—the death or destruction of cattle, the infidelity of servants and the treachery of friends—the decay of navigation and the loss of shipping."

He offered the following instances as proof:

On April 30, A.D. 59, an eclipse of the Sun was followed by the murder of Agrippina by Nero. In A.D. 463, an eclipse was followed by a war in Persia. On March 20, 1140, after a total eclipse of the Sun, King Stephen lost a battle with

William II, the German kaiser, reviewing
troops in 1918. A British almanac forecast
war from the kaiser's horoscope in 1908.

the Earl of Gloucester and was taken prisoner. In 1536 an eclipse was followed
by the separation of England from the Church of Rome and the death of Queen
Catherine. Two eclipses in 1781 (one in April and the other in October), which
were total eclipses as seen from the West Indies, were accompanied by "terrible
storms and tempests that almost desolated the West India Islands, sunk the
Ville de Paris, many other ships . . . and a great number of merchant men."

We can add to this list two examples (from other sources) of events that coincided with eclipses of the Moon: In 1870, three days after a total eclipse of the
Moon, the Emperor Napoleon III declared war on Prussia. And in 1897 the
catastrophic collapse of the Tay Bridge in Scotland while a passenger train was
crossing it took place during a partial eclipse of the Moon.

In 1908 the British periodical *Old Moore's Monthly Messenger* analyzed the
chart of the kaiser of Germany as follows:

"The Kaiser's Ascendant is nearly opposite the Mars of King Edward of
England, while Mercury is on Mars in the latter, a certain indication of disputes
and quarrels, and that natural action of the latter is likely to militate against
the former's colonial policy. We call special attention to the point,
because in view of the coming planetary influences and especially eclipses there
is no doubt that the dogs of war cannot be held in the leash much longer. . . ."

Betting by the stars

"Most of Priscilla's days were spent casting the horoscopes of horses, and she invested her money scientifically, as the Stars dictated. She betted on football too, and had a large notebook in which she registered the horoscopes of all the players in all the teams of the League. The process of balancing the horoscopes of two elevens one against the other was a very delicate and difficult one. A match between the Spurs and the Villa entailed a conflict in the heavens so vast and so complicated that it was not to be wondered at if she sometimes made a mistake about the outcome."

—Aldous Huxley, *Crome Yellow*, 1921

In 1946 a popular British astrological magazine stated: "Because of the astrological portents in his horoscope, rumours of Stalin's ill-health may be taken seriously." The writer went on to say that Stalin's disappearance from the international scene within the next 18 months was almost a certainty, and then there would be an astonishing reorientation in U.S.S.R. internal and foreign policies. (Stalin lived and remained in power until 1953.)

A recent "end-of-the-world" forecast was the catastrophe predicted by Indian astrologers in 1962. In Britain, a mountain-side prayer meeting was held to avert this disaster.

In January, 1910, *Old Moore's Monthly Messenger,* dealing with the chart of King Edward VII, warned against "accidents and indisposition." In April 1910 the magazine considered the new Moon and drew from it an indication of future "illness and death in Royal circles." In the same issue, an article devoted to the king's son, the Prince of Wales, stated: "It is not pleasing to note that Sun is directed to square Saturn, an influence which operates from 1908 to 1910. . . . Saturn rules MC, which denotes the father. It is therefore clear that a family loss is foreshadowed in the near future." (King Edward VII died in May 1910.)

Mr. Nehru writes

(Referring to the birth of his first grandson in 1944): "In my letter to Indu I suggested to her to ask you to get a proper horoscope made by a competent person. Such permanent records of the date and time of birth are desirable. As for the time I suppose the proper solar time should be mentioned and not the artificial time which is being used outside now. War time is at least an hour ahead of the normal time."

—Prime Minister Nehru, *Letters to his Sister,* 1963

A German astrologer, Herr Troinski, wrote in the December 1958 issue of the *Berliner Auskunftsbogen:* "In the year 1963, Pope John XXIII will come under very dangerous tertiary directions, both primary and secondary. . . ." He alluded to certain aspects that would occur—specifically Mars in opposition to Saturn and the Sun in square to Mars, Uranus, and Pluto. And he concluded with the prophecy: "This could mean the death of the Pope."

A superstitious residue

"They [modern defenders of astrology] will not acknowledge honestly the decisive fact that their futile practices have been investigated with the greatest care and impartiality by the foremost scholars of the leading Western nations for now almost three centuries, and that not one of these has failed to condemn them as the stale, superstitious residue of what was once a great, pantheistic religion and a glorious philosophical attempt to understand and rationally to explain the universe, a bold enterprise to which we owe not only the whole of our astronomical knowledge, but the most essential part of all our physical science."

—Robert Eisler, *The Royal Art of Astrology,* 1946

A British astrological publication in 1959 predicted trouble for the year 1962. An eclipse of the Sun would be accompanied with a conjunction of the malefics Mars and Saturn, Neptune in square to Mars and Saturn, and other similarly calamitous portents. Many sudden and violent events would occur, the article said, among which would be a period of great hardship for the British royal family. Also, during this period Britain itself would go through terrible turmoil: The existing form of government would be overthrown with much bloodshed.

A science of relating

"Astrology does not offer an explanation of the laws of the universe, nor why the universe exists. What it does, to put it in simplest terms, is to show us that there is a correspondence between macrocosm and microcosm. In short, that there is a rhythm to the universe, and that man's own life partakes of this rhythm. For centuries men have observed and studied the nature of this correspondence. Whether astrology be a science or a pseudo-science, the fact remains that the oldest and the greatest civilizations we know of had for centuries upon centuries used it as a basis for thought and action. That it degenerated into mere fortune-telling, and why, is another story.

"It is not to discover what is going to 'happen' to us, it is not to forestall the blows of fate, that we should look to our horoscopes. A chart when properly read should enable one to understand the overall pattern of one's life. It should make a man more aware of the fact that his own life obeys the same rhythmical, cyclical laws as do other natural phenomena. It should prepare him to welcome change, constant change, and to understand that there is no good or bad, but always the two together in changing degrees, and that out of what is seemingly bad can come good and vice versa. Astrology might indeed be called a science of relating, whose first fruit is the dictum that fate is character."

—Henry Miller, from the foreword to *Henry Miller: His World of Urania*,
by Sydney Omarr, 1960

As for the future, the famed 16th-century astrologer and seer Nostradamus perhaps deserves the last vaguely ominous and cryptic word. The following quatrains are from the *Complete Prophecies* of Nostradamus, translated in 1951 by Henry Robert:

> *In the year 1999 and seven months*
> *From the skies shall come an alarmingly powerful king,*
> *To raise again the great king of the Jacquerie,*
> *Before and after, Mars shall reign at will.*
>
> · · · ·
>
> *The year seven of the great number being past*
> *There shall be seen the sports of the ghostly sacrifice*
> *Not far from the great age of the millennium,*
> *That the buried shall come out of their graves.*

The translator in his notes on the quatrains states that the first of these apparently means that a tremendous world revolution is predicted for the year 1999, which is to bring about a complete upheaval of existing social orders, and that this revolution is to be preceded by world war. And the second of the quoted quatrains, the translator says, means simply that in the year 7000 judgment day will be pronounced, the dead will rise from their graves, and the world will come to an end.

Appendices

Appendix 1

The 10 planets

Here in capsule form are the planets, signs, and houses with their hieroglyphs, their interrelationships in the horoscope, and some of the qualities assigned to them. This last information has (in the case of the planets and signs) been based on the meanings detailed in the German astrologer Reinhold Ebertin's book *The Combination of Stellar Influences*. The meanings of the houses have been adapted from those suggested by the British astrologer Sepharial.

	Spheres of Influence	Related Signs
	Sun The masculine principle; spirit, mind, the living being; the will to live, vitality, willpower, determination; health and the heart; the man, the father, authority.	Leo
	Moon The feminine principle; the soul, the psyche; the mother, fecundity, adaptation; the wife, the family, the nation; hereditary qualities.	Cancer
	Mercury Intellect, mediation, transmission of knowledge; judgment, critical ability, analysis.	Gemini Virgo
	Venus Love and art; physical attraction; feeling, sense of harmony and beauty; girl or maiden, sweetheart or mistress.	Taurus Libra
	Mars Energy and action; courage and determination; impulsiveness, ruthlessness, brutality; soldiers, sportsmen, technicians, craftsmen, surgeons.	Aries Scorpio

Related Signs	Spheres of Influence

Jupiter

Sagittarius
Pisces

Harmony, law, and religion; expansion and enlargement; ownership; moral and religious aspirations; judges, high ecclesiastics, bankers, wealthy people, fortune hunters.

Saturn

Capricorn
Aquarius

Inhibition and concentration; consolidation, perseverance. seriousness, caution, and economy; melancholy, reserve, and taciturnity; segregation and seclusion; calcification, old age; agriculture, mining, and real estate.

Uranus

(Aquarius)

Suddenness, revolution, transmutation; independence, excitability, and impulsiveness; innovators, reformers, inventors, and technicians; magicians, occultists, and astrologers (the "paranormal").

Neptune

(Pisces)

Impressionability; fantasy and imagination; inclination to mysticism; vagueness, confusion, deception; people of doubtful character, confidence men.

Pluto

(Scorpio)

Higher power or providence; invisible forces or powers; the will to exercise power, to influence the masses; propagandists and politicians, actors and orators.

The 12 signs of the Zodiac

	Spheres of Influence	Related Planets
	Aries Will, the urge to act, the spirit of enterprise, leadership, passion, ambition, impatience, rashness.	Mars
	Taurus Perseverance, consolidation, endurance, sense of form.	Venus
	Gemini Vicariousness, adaptability, mobility, superficiality.	Mercury
	Cancer Wealth of feeling, parenthood, the quality of "attachment."	Moon
	Leo The will to create, self-confidence, self-reliance, action, the sex urge.	Sun
	Virgo Diligence and care, tidiness, correct behavior, the critical faculty.	Mercury

Related Planets	Spheres of Influence	

	Libra	
Venus	Sense of justice, desire for harmony, sociability.	

	Scorpio	
Mars (Pluto)	Tenacity, endurance, perseverance, overestimation of self, passion, the struggle for survival.	

	Sagittarius	
Jupiter	Cultivation of inner or spiritual side of life; planning, striving, action, expansion.	

	Capricorn	
Saturn	Concentration on personal self; conservatism, zeal, and industry; a sense of reality.	

	Aquarius	
Saturn (Uranus)	Expectancy, powers of observation, adaptability, planning, helpfulness.	

	Pisces	
Jupiter (Neptune)	Vagueness, sensitivity, emotionalism, intuition; self-sacrifice.	

The 12 houses

	Spheres of Influence	**Related Signs**
	First	
	The body of the native, his physical condition and appearance.	Aries Mars
	Second	
	Money, possessions of value; trade; gain or loss.	Taurus Venus
	Third	
	Letters, papers, writings; all means of communication and transportation; brothers and sisters, near relations, neighbors.	Gemini Mercury
	Fourth	
	The residence; the place of birth; houses, landed property, grounds, mines, underground places; the mother in a man's chart, the father in a woman's.	Cancer Moon
	Fifth	
	Pleasures, love affairs, non-marital sex ties; children, schools, theatres, education; places of amusement and all sensual enjoyments.	Leo Sun
	Sixth	
	Health, servants, food, clothing, physical comforts; employees, small animals, and domestic creatures; climatic and other conditions affecting health.	Virgo Mercury

Related Signs	Spheres of Influence	

Seventh

Libra
Venus

The husband in a woman's chart, the wife in a man's; partners, contracts, agreements; litigation, open enemies.

Eighth

Scorpio
Mars

Death, dissolution, loss; the wife's or husband's wealth and possessions; the partner's property; legacies, bequests, and wills.

Ninth

Sagittarius
Jupiter

Religion and philosophy; publications; sea voyages, foreign countries; dreams, spiritual occurrences; the clergy and church affairs; relatives by marriage.

Tenth

Capricorn
Saturn

The occupation; credit, honor, and rank; employer, superior, or master; business affairs, government.

Eleventh

Aquarius
Saturn
(Uranus)

Friends, counselors, companions, society; wishes and hopes; financial affairs of employers or others in command of the native.

Twelfth

Pisces
Jupiter
(Neptune)

Confinement, restraint, prison, exile; secret enemies, plots; large animals.

The major aspects

No hard-and-fast meanings can be ascribed to the planetary aspects, which (more than any other horoscopic element) must be judged in relation to the chart as a whole. This list merely explains their general tendencies. Aspects have always been classified as "good" or "bad," though today they are often labeled "easy" or "difficult." (Conjunction falls into neither category, since its influence depends entirely on the qualities of the two planets involved.)

Name	Meaning
☌ **Conjunction**	In a conjunction, the planets' natures must be considered in relation to each other; in some cases they will harmonize and in others, conflict. For example: Saturn (traditionally cold) in conjunction with Venus (naturally loving) will tend to limit or chill the affections. Mars and Venus in conjunction will enforce each other's sensuality and will lead to happy love relationships.
☍ **Opposition**	Traditionally a "difficult" aspect, implying tension that may lead to an aggravation or a conflict of the planets' influences: On the other hand, this "bad" effect may sometimes be modified: For example, Jupiter and the Sun in opposition, which could produce conceit and extravagance, might be offset by the caution of a well-placed Saturn.
△ **Trine**	An "easy" aspect, indicating a harmonious relationship of the planets involved. Some astrologers regard, say, Venus trine Jupiter as a mark of too easy-going a nature; but Mars and Saturn in trine might well imply practical ability and courage.

Meaning	Name	

A "difficult" aspect showing an uneasy struggle between the various planetary principles. Moon square Venus (both planets concerned with the home) might show a lack of domestic harmony. With Mars square Saturn, Mars's fierceness might aggravate the coldness of Saturn to produce brutality.

Square □

Like trine, a favorable aspect (though not so strong), but more usually applied to mental rather than physical characteristics. Mercury (traditionally connected with the intellect) in sextile with Mars would give strength of mind; Mercury in sextile with Jupiter would show a witty and cheerful mentality.

Sextile ✳

Some other less important aspects (to which most astrologers today tend to give little weight in horoscopes) are briefly as follows:

Like square, a difficult aspect.

Semi-square ∟

An "unnatural" aspect, implying strain.

Quincunx ⊼

Traditionally considered, like sextile, to be a favorable aspect. Today both semi-sextile and quincunx are treated by most astrologers as "stressful" relationships.

Semi-sextile ⊻

Appendix 3

National horoscopes

Italy

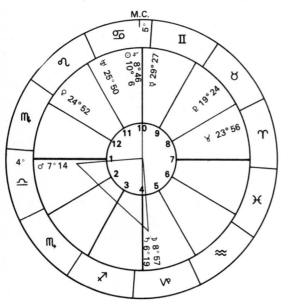

In this chart (cast for July 2, 1871, the date of King Victor Emmanuel's triumphal entry into Rome) heavy "afflictions" are apparent across the "angles" formed by the ascendant-descendant and the M.C.-I.C. These imply that, despite good intentions, the consolidation of the new unified nation could be a long and difficult process. Under Mussolini's regime, Mars's aggressive and ambitious elements (in conjunction with the ascendant, Libra) were in full play. For example, the invasion of Abyssinia on October 3, 1935, took place when the Sun was in conjunction with Mars and in square with Italy's Jupiter, Saturn, and Moon. The failure of Mussolini's later policies is suggested by Saturn square Mars ; and on July 25, 1943, Uranus trine Italy's Mars coincided with the fall of Fascism.

England

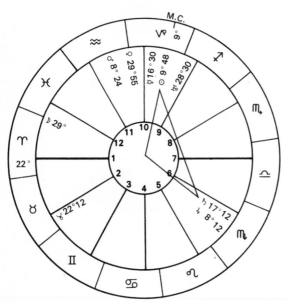

A horoscope cast for the coronation of William I, the first king of England, on Christmas Day, 1066. The emphasis on the ninth house considered together with the nature of the fiery sign Aries (the ascendant) adds up to the conventional picture of England as an adventurous, pioneering, and empire-building nation. At the outbreak of World War II, the Sun was exactly trine the position of the Sun in this horoscope, whereas Saturn was placed exactly over Hitler's Sun. The determined resistance offered by the English during the Battle of Britain is reflected in the protective position of Saturn, in trine to England's Sun.

Israel

Traditionally, the Taurus-Scorpio polarity is associated with the Jews, but in this chart (cast for the proclamation of the State of Israel on May 14, 1948) the Sun in Taurus and the Cancerian mid-heaven can be said to imply the Jewish people's centuries-old longing for a national home. Neptune rising suggests that the high aspirations of Zionism may be achieved only at the expense of strife and bloodshed, since the Sun is in square with Mars and Saturn. So-called "friends" of Israel could provoke conflict, and internal political feuds could hamper the State's development. The opposition of Jupiter (which, due to its position in the third house, could be associated with the Arabs) to Uranus is a warning of sudden and explosive outbreaks whenever major transits "activate" these points on the chart.

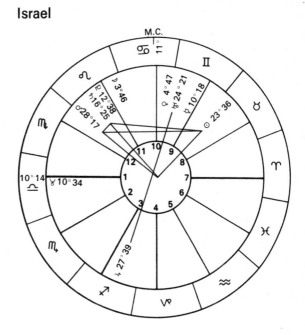

France

A horoscope cast for September 4, 1870, when the Third French Republic was proclaimed. Disrupting and dangerous aspects of Mars and Uranus (here in opposition to the ascendant) and an unsettling tension across the chart have been persistent features of many of the crises in recent French history. For example, when war broke out on August 4, 1914, the Moon was in conjunction with the ascendant and in opposition to Uranus and Mars, which was square Saturn and Jupiter. Similarly, when the cease-fire in Algeria came into force on March 19, 1961, Saturn was in opposition to Mars-Uranus—an aspect that cannot be said to promise peace.

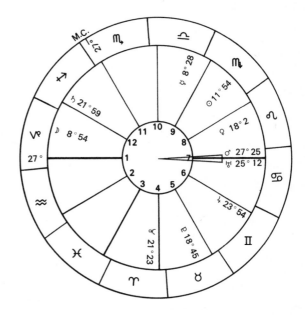

West Germany

A horoscope cast for the formation of the West German Republic on May 23, 1949, reflects the pattern of Germany's prosperity and progress since the war. A capacity for hard work and discipline and a sense of national duty are apparent from the positions of Capricorn in the ascendant, the Moon in Aries, Scorpio at the mid-heaven, and Mars in Taurus. The aspects of Mars square Pluto and the Sun square Saturn might prove ominous, if Germany's interests should ever conflict with the present balance of world power. This unfortunate possibility is further emphasized by the difficult relations of Mars and Pluto to Russia's fateful Saturn-Sun-Mercury-Uranus T-square formation.

U.S.S.R.

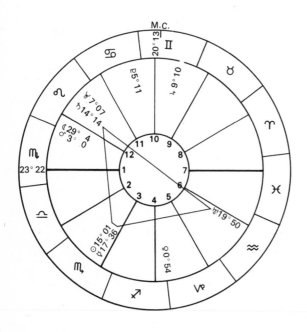

The most significant feature of this chart (cast for November 8, 1917) is the difficult "T-square" pattern formed by the opposition between Saturn and Uranus, both of which are in square to the Sun and Mercury. This configuration of planets suggests the underlying conflict and disagreements between the supreme authority (the Sun), scientists (Uranus), and the state administrators and police (Saturn), which could periodically bring about drastic changes in internal policy. Nazi Germany's preparations for invading Russia (April-May 1941) took place when Germany's Saturn was transiting the U.S.S.R.'s Sun-Saturn-Uranus. When the invasion began on June 22, 1941, Neptune (treachery and fanaticism) and Mars (aggression) were in opposition on Germany's chart and were bisecting the "polarity" formed by Russia's ascendant and descendant.

U.S.A.

The chart has been cast for the Declaration of Independence on July 4, 1776. It shows Gemini (traditionally the sign of America) in the ascendant, the Sun in conjunction with Jupiter, and the Moon at the mid-heaven in Aquarius—all of which reflect the self-confidence, patriotism, and enthusiasm that are often associated with America. The positions of the ascendant, the mid-heaven, and the Moon are always considered to indicate events of national importance. For example, on November 22, 1963, the day of President Kennedy's assassination, Saturn was in conjunction with America's Moon, and Mars was in opposition to its position in the U.S.A.'s original chart.

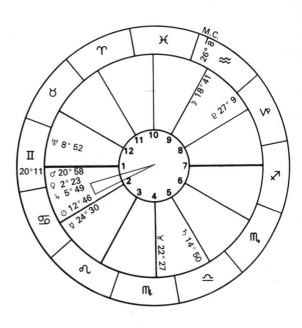

The Atomic Age

The positions of Uranus and Pluto—the planets associated with atomic power—are the most significant factors in this chart cast for the first controlled atomic chain reaction on December 2, 1942. Fortunately, Pluto receives strong beneficial aspects, and is favorably linked with both Uranus and Saturn. The friction between the planets grouped in the first and seventh houses underlines nuclear power's possible threat to world peace, but Saturn's key position gives hope of its eventual limitation to purely peaceful and domestic purposes (Saturn-Uranus trine Moon-Neptune). A world crisis threatens from October 1965 to June 1966, when Uranus and Pluto will be in conjunction in Virgo. But since the planets will be trine to the ascendant, it seems that this crisis will give way to a new era of constructive use of atomic energy.

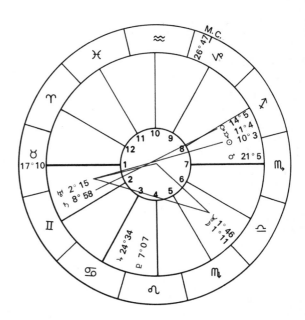

301

Appendix 2

Tables of sidereal time

Everyone knows his Sun-sign—the sign he was "born under"—but few people know their ascendant, which is far more important in deciding one's astrological "type." The following tables list the sidereal time at noon at Greenwich for every day since January 1, 1901 ; and from them anyone born anywhere in the Northen Hemisphere can calculate the S.T. of his birth time. (For the Southern Hemisphere, see p. 326.) Once the S.T. has been worked out, finding the ascendant is a simple matter of reference to the appropriate table.

1901

	Jan.	Feb.	Mar.	April	May	June	July	Aug.	Sept.	Oct.	Nov.	Dec.
1	18 41 46	20 43 59	22 34 23	0 36 36	2 34 53	4 37 6	6 35 22	8 37 36	10 39 49	12 38 5	14 40 19	16 38 35
2	18 45 43	20 47 56	22 38 19	0 40 32	2 38 49	4 41 2	6 39 19	8 41 32	10 43 45	12 42 2	14 44 15	16 42 32
3	18 49 39	20 51 52	22 42 16	0 44 29	2 42 46	4 44 59	6 43 16	8 45 29	10 47 42	12 45 59	14 48 12	16 46 28
4	18 53 36	20 55 49	22 46 12	0 48 26	2 46 42	4 48 55	6 47 12	8 49 25	10 51 39	12 49 55	14 52 8	16 50 25
5	18 57 32	20 59 46	22 50 9	0 52 22	2 50 39	4 52 52	6 51 9	8 53 22	10 55 35	12 53 52	14 56 5	16 54 21
6	19 1 29	21 3 42	22 54 6	0 56 19	2 54 35	4 56 49	6 55 5	8 57 18	10 59 32	12 57 48	15 0 1	16 58 18
7	19 5 25	21 7 39	22 58 2	1 0 15	2 58 32	5 0 45	6 59 2	9 1 15	11 3 28	13 1 45	15 3 58	17 2 15
8	19 9 22	21 11 35	23 1 59	1 4 12	3 2 28	5 4 42	7 2 58	9 5 12	11 7 25	13 5 41	15 7 54	17 6 11
9	19 13 19	21 15 32	23 5 55	1 8 8	3 6 25	5 8 38	7 6 55	9 9 8	11 11 21	13 9 38	15 11 51	17 10 8
10	19 17 15	21 19 28	23 9 52	1 12 5	3 10 22	5 12 35	7 10 51	9 13 5	11 15 18	13 13 34	15 15 48	17 14 4
11	19 21 12	21 23 25	23 13 48	1 16 1	3 14 18	5 16 31	7 14 48	9 17 1	11 19 14	13 17 31	15 19 44	17 18 1
12	19 25 8	21 27 21	23 17 45	1 19 58	3 18 15	5 20 28	7 18 45	9 20 58	11 23 11	13 21 28	15 23 41	17 21 57
13	19 29 5	21 31 18	23 21 41	1 23 55	3 22 11	5 24 24	7 22 41	9 24 54	11 27 8	13 25 24	15 27 37	17 25 54
14	19 33 1	21 35 15	23 25 38	1 27 51	3 26 8	5 28 21	7 26 38	9 28 51	11 31 4	13 29 21	15 31 34	17 29 50
15	19 36 58	21 39 11	23 29 35	1 31 48	3 30 4	5 32 18	7 30 34	9 32 47	11 35 1	13 33 17	15 35 30	17 33 47
16	19 40 54	21 43 8	23 33 31	1 35 44	3 34 1	5 36 14	7 34 31	9 36 44	11 38 57	13 37 14	15 39 27	17 37 44
17	19 44 51	21 47 4	23 37 28	1 39 41	3 37 57	5 40 11	7 38 27	9 40 41	11 42 54	13 41 10	15 43 23	17 41 40
18	19 48 48	21 51 1	23 41 24	1 43 37	3 41 54	5 44 7	7 42 24	9 44 37	11 46 50	13 45 7	15 47 20	17 45 37
19	19 52 44	21 54 57	23 45 21	1 47 34	3 45 51	5 48 4	7 46 20	9 48 34	11 50 47	13 49 3	15 51 17	17 49 33
20	19 56 41	21 58 54	23 49 17	1 51 30	3 49 47	5 52 0	7 50 17	9 52 30	11 54 43	13 53 0	15 55 13	17 53 30
21	20 0 37	22 2 50	23 53 14	1 55 27	3 53 44	5 55 57	7 54 14	9 56 27	11 58 40	13 56 57	15 59 10	17 57 26
22	20 4 34	22 6 47	23 57 10	1 59 24	3 57 40	5 59 53	7 58 10	10 0 23	12 2 36	14 0 53	16 3 6	18 1 23
23	20 8 30	22 10 43	0 1 7	2 3 20	4 1 37	6 3 50	8 2 7	10 4 20	12 6 33	14 4 50	16 7 3	18 5 20
24	20 12 27	22 14 40	0 5 4	2 7 17	4 5 33	6 7 47	8 6 3	10 8 16	12 10 30	14 8 46	16 10 59	18 9 16
25	20 16 23	22 18 37	0 9 0	2 11 13	4 9 30	6 11 43	8 10 0	10 12 13	12 14 26	14 12 43	16 14 56	18 13 13
26	20 20 20	22 22 33	0 12 57	2 15 10	4 13 26	6 15 40	8 13 56	10 16 10	12 18 23	14 16 39	16 18 52	18 17 9
27	20 24 17	22 26 30	0 16 53	2 19 6	4 17 23	6 19 36	8 17 53	10 20 6	12 22 19	14 20 36	16 22 49	18 21 6
28	20 28 13	22 30 26	0 20 50	2 23 3	4 21 20	6 23 33	8 21 49	10 24 3	12 26 16	14 24 32	16 26 46	18 25 2
29	20 32 10		0 24 46	2 26 59	4 25 16	6 27 29	8 25 46	10 27 59	12 30 12	14 28 29	16 30 42	18 28 59
30	20 36 6		0 28 43	2 30 56	4 29 13	6 31 26	8 29 43	10 31 56	12 34 9	14 32 25	16 34 39	18 32 55
31	20 40 3		0 32 39		4 33 9		8 33 39	10 35 52		14 36 22		18 36 52

1902

	Jan.	Feb.	Mar.	April	May	June	July	Aug.	Sept.	Oct.	Nov.	Dec.
1	18 40 49	20 43 2	22 33 25	0 35 38	2 33 55	4 36 8	6 34 25	8 36 38	10 38 51	12 37 8	14 39 21	16 37 38
2	18 44 45	20 46 58	22 37 22	0 39 35	2 37 52	4 40 5	6 38 21	8 40 35	10 42 48	12 41 4	14 43 18	16 41 34
3	18 48 42	20 50 55	22 41 18	0 43 32	2 41 48	4 44 1	6 42 18	8 44 31	10 46 44	12 45 1	14 47 14	16 45 31
4	18 52 38	20 54 51	22 45 15	0 47 28	2 45 45	4 47 58	6 46 15	8 48 28	10 50 41	12 48 58	14 51 11	16 49 27
5	18 56 35	20 58 48	22 49 11	0 51 25	2 49 41	4 51 54	6 50 11	8 52 24	10 54 38	12 52 54	14 55 7	16 53 24
6	19 0 31	21 2 45	22 53 8	0 55 21	2 53 38	4 55 51	6 54 8	8 56 21	10 58 34	12 56 51	14 59 4	16 57 20
7	19 4 28	21 6 41	22 57 5	0 59 18	2 57 34	4 59 48	6 58 4	9 0 17	11 2 31	13 0 47	15 3 0	17 1 17
8	19 8 24	21 10 38	23 1 1	1 3 14	3 1 31	5 3 44	7 2 1	9 4 14	11 6 27	13 4 44	15 6 57	17 5 14
9	19 12 21	21 14 34	23 4 58	1 7 11	3 5 27	5 7 41	7 5 57	9 8 11	11 10 24	13 8 40	15 10 53	17 9 10
10	19 16 18	21 18 31	23 8 54	1 11 7	3 9 24	5 11 37	7 9 54	9 12 7	11 14 20	13 12 37	15 14 50	17 13 7
11	19 20 14	21 22 27	23 12 51	1 15 4	3 13 21	5 15 34	7 13 50	9 16 4	11 18 17	13 16 33	15 18 47	17 17 3
12	19 24 11	21 26 24	23 16 47	1 19 0	3 17 17	5 19 30	7 17 47	9 20 0	11 22 13	13 20 30	15 22 43	17 21 0
13	19 28 7	21 30 20	23 20 44	1 22 57	3 21 14	5 23 27	7 21 44	9 23 57	11 26 10	13 24 26	15 26 40	17 24 56
14	19 32 4	21 34 17	23 24 40	1 26 54	3 25 10	5 27 23	7 25 40	9 27 53	11 30 6	13 28 23	15 30 36	17 28 53
15	19 36 0	21 38 14	23 28 37	1 30 50	3 29 7	5 31 20	7 29 37	9 31 50	11 34 3	13 32 20	15 34 33	17 32 49
16	19 39 57	21 42 10	23 32 33	1 34 47	3 33 3	5 35 17	7 33 33	9 35 46	11 38 0	13 36 16	15 38 29	17 36 46
17	19 43 53	21 46 7	23 36 30	1 38 43	3 37 0	5 39 13	7 37 30	9 39 43	11 41 56	13 40 13	15 42 26	17 40 43
18	19 47 50	21 50 3	23 40 27	1 42 40	3 40 56	5 43 10	7 41 26	9 43 40	11 45 53	13 44 9	15 46 22	17 44 39
19	19 51 47	21 54 0	23 44 23	1 46 36	3 44 53	5 47 6	7 45 23	9 47 36	11 49 49	13 48 6	15 50 19	17 48 36
20	19 55 43	21 57 56	23 48 20	1 50 33	3 48 50	5 51 3	7 49 19	9 51 33	11 53 46	13 52 2	15 54 16	17 52 32
21	19 59 40	22 1 53	23 52 16	1 54 29	3 52 46	5 54 59	7 53 16	9 55 29	11 57 42	13 55 59	15 58 12	17 56 29
22	20 3 36	22 5 49	23 56 13	1 58 26	3 56 43	5 58 56	7 57 13	9 59 26	12 1 39	13 59 55	16 2 9	18 0 25
23	20 7 33	22 9 46	0 0 9	2 2 23	4 0 39	6 2 52	8 1 9	10 3 22	12 5 35	14 3 52	16 6 5	18 4 22
24	20 11 29	22 13 43	0 4 6	2 6 19	4 4 36	6 6 49	8 5 6	10 7 19	12 9 32	14 7 49	16 10 2	18 8 18
25	20 15 26	22 17 39	0 8 3	2 10 16	4 8 32	6 10 46	8 9 2	10 11 15	12 13 29	14 11 45	16 13 58	18 12 15
26	20 19 22	22 21 36	0 11 59	2 14 12	4 12 29	6 14 42	8 12 59	10 15 12	12 17 25	14 15 42	16 17 55	18 16 11
27	20 23 19	22 25 32	0 15 56	2 18 9	4 16 25	6 18 39	8 16 55	10 19 9	12 21 22	14 19 38	16 21 51	18 20 8
28	20 27 16	22 29 29	0 19 52	2 22 5	4 20 22	6 22 35	8 20 52	10 23 5	12 25 18	14 23 35	16 25 48	18 24 4
29	20 31 12		0 23 49	2 26 2	4 24 19	6 26 32	8 24 48	10 27 2	12 29 15	14 27 31	16 29 45	18 28 1
30	20 35 9		0 27 45	2 29 58	4 28 15	6 30 28	8 28 45	10 30 58	12 33 11	14 31 28	16 33 41	18 31 58
31	20 39 5		0 31 42		4 32 12		8 32 42	10 34 55		14 35 24		18 35 54

First, refer to the map of time zones on p. 245 and translate your own time into Greenwich Mean Time. Then find the S.T. at noon on your birthday in the following tables. Add to this figure the number of hours you were born after noon, plus 10 seconds for every hour. (Subtract in both cases if you were born before noon.) Next, if you were not born on the Greenwich meridian, you convert this S.T. into the S.T. for your birthplace. Find in an atlas the longitude of your birthplace; multiply this figure by four to convert the total into minutes and seconds of time. Add this total (if born east of Greenwich) to the S.T. (or subtract if west) and you have your S.T. at birth. Now you can find your ascendant in a table of houses for your specific latitude.

1903

	Jan.	Feb.	Mar.	April	May	June	July	Aug.	Sept.	Oct.	Nov.	Dec.
1	18 39 51	20 42 4	22 32 28	0 34 41	2 32 57	4 35 11	6 33 27	8 35 40	10 37 54	12 36 10	14 38 23	16 36 40
2	18 43 47	20 46 1	22 36 24	0 38 37	2 36 54	4 39 7	6 37 24	8 39 37	10 41 50	12 40 7	14 42 20	16 40 37
3	18 47 44	20 49 57	22 40 21	0 42 34	2 40 50	4 43 4	6 41 20	8 43 34	10 45 47	12 44 3	14 46 16	16 44 33
4	18 51 41	20 53 54	22 44 17	0 46 30	2 44 47	4 47 0	6 45 17	8 47 30	10 49 43	12 48 0	14 50 13	16 48 30
5	18 55 37	20 57 50	22 48 14	0 50 27	2 48 44	4 50 57	6 49 14	8 51 27	10 53 40	12 51 56	14 54 10	16 52 26
6	18 59 34	21 1 47	22 52 10	0 54 24	2 52 40	4 54 53	6 53 10	8 55 23	10 57 36	12 55 53	14 58 6	16 56 23
7	19 3 30	21 5 43	22 56 7	0 58 20	2 56 37	4 58 50	6 57 7	8 59 20	11 1 33	12 59 50	15 2 3	17 0 19
8	19 7 27	21 9 40	23 0 4	1 2 17	3 0 33	5 2 46	7 1 3	9 3 16	11 5 30	13 3 46	15 5 59	17 4 16
9	19 11 23	21 13 37	23 4 0	1 6 13	3 4 30	5 6 43	7 5 0	9 7 13	11 9 26	13 7 43	15 9 56	17 8 12
10	19 15 20	21 17 33	23 7 57	1 10 10	3 8 26	5 10 40	7 8 56	9 11 9	11 13 23	13 11 39	15 13 52	17 12 9
11	19 19 17	21 21 30	23 11 53	1 14 6	3 12 23	5 14 36	7 12 53	9 15 6	11 17 19	13 15 36	15 17 49	17 16 6
12	19 23 13	21 25 26	23 15 50	1 18 3	3 16 19	5 18 33	7 16 49	9 19 3	11 21 16	13 19 32	15 21 45	17 20 2
13	19 27 10	21 29 23	23 19 46	1 21 59	3 20 16	5 22 29	7 20 46	9 22 59	11 25 12	13 23 29	15 25 42	17 23 59
14	19 31 6	21 33 19	23 23 43	1 25 56	3 24 13	5 26 26	7 24 43	9 26 56	11 29 9	13 27 25	15 29 39	17 27 55
15	19 35 3	21 37 16	23 27 39	1 29 53	3 28 9	5 30 22	7 28 39	9 30 52	11 33 5	13 31 22	15 33 35	17 31 52
16	19 38 59	21 41 12	23 31 36	1 33 49	3 32 6	5 34 19	7 32 36	9 34 49	11 37 2	13 35 19	15 37 32	17 35 48
17	19 42 56	21 45 9	23 35 33	1 37 46	3 36 2	5 38 15	7 36 32	9 38 45	11 40 59	13 39 15	15 41 28	17 39 45
18	19 46 53	21 49 6	23 39 29	1 41 42	3 39 59	5 42 12	7 40 29	9 42 42	11 44 55	13 43 12	15 45 25	17 43 41
19	19 50 49	21 53 2	23 43 26	1 45 39	3 43 55	5 46 9	7 44 25	9 46 38	11 48 52	13 47 8	15 49 21	17 47 38
20	19 54 45	21 56 59	23 47 22	1 49 35	3 47 52	5 50 5	7 48 22	9 50 35	11 52 48	13 51 5	15 53 18	17 51 35
21	19 58 42	22 0 55	23 51 19	1 53 32	3 51 48	5 54 2	7 52 18	9 54 32	11 56 45	13 55 1	15 57 14	17 55 31
22	20 2 39	22 4 52	23 55 15	1 57 28	3 55 45	5 57 58	7 56 15	9 58 28	12 0 41	13 58 58	16 1 11	17 59 28
23	20 6 35	22 8 48	23 59 12	2 1 25	3 59 42	6 1 55	8 0 12	10 2 25	12 4 38	14 2 54	16 5 8	18 3 24
24	20 10 32	22 12 45	0 3 8	2 5 21	4 3 38	6 5 51	8 4 8	10 6 21	12 8 34	14 6 51	16 9 4	18 7 21
25	20 14 28	22 16 41	0 7 5	2 9 18	4 7 35	6 9 48	8 8 5	10 10 18	12 12 31	14 10 47	16 13 1	18 11 17
26	20 18 25	22 20 38	0 11 1	2 13 15	4 11 31	6 13 44	8 12 1	10 14 14	12 16 27	14 14 44	16 16 57	18 15 14
27	20 22 21	22 24 35	0 14 58	2 17 11	4 15 28	6 17 41	8 15 58	10 18 11	12 20 24	14 18 41	16 20 54	18 19 10
28	20 26 18	22 28 31	0 18 55	2 21 8	4 19 24	6 21 38	8 19 54	10 22 7	12 24 21	14 22 37	16 24 50	18 23 7
29	20 30 15		0 22 51	2 25 4	4 23 21	6 25 34	8 23 51	10 26 4	12 28 17	14 26 34	16 28 47	18 27 4
30	20 34 11		0 26 48	2 29 1	4 27 17	6 29 31	8 27 47	10 30 1	12 32 14	14 30 30	16 32 43	18 31 0
31	20 38 8		0 30 44		4 31 14		8 31 44	10 33 57		14 34 27		18 34 57

1904

	Jan.	Feb.	Mar.	April	May	June	July	Aug.	Sept.	Oct.	Nov.	Dec.
1	18 38 53	20 41 7	22 35 27	0 37 40	2 35 56	4 38 9	6 36 26	8 38 39	10 40 53	12 39 9	14 41 22	16 39 39
2	18 42 50	20 45 3	22 39 23	0 41 36	2 39 53	4 42 6	6 40 23	8 42 36	10 44 49	12 43 6	14 45 19	16 43 35
3	18 46 46	20 49 0	22 43 20	0 45 33	2 43 49	4 46 3	6 44 19	8 46 33	10 48 46	12 47 2	14 49 15	16 47 32
4	18 50 43	20 52 56	22 47 16	0 49 29	2 47 46	4 49 59	6 48 16	8 50 29	10 52 42	12 50 59	14 53 12	16 51 29
5	18 54 40	20 56 53	22 51 13	0 53 26	2 51 42	4 53 56	6 52 12	8 54 26	10 56 39	12 54 55	14 57 8	16 55 25
6	18 58 36	21 0 49	22 55 9	0 57 22	2 55 39	4 57 52	6 56 9	8 58 22	11 0 35	12 58 52	15 1 5	16 59 22
7	19 2 33	21 4 46	22 59 6	1 1 19	2 59 36	5 1 49	7 0 6	9 2 19	11 4 32	13 2 48	15 5 2	17 3 18
8	19 6 29	21 8 42	23 3 2	1 5 16	3 3 32	5 5 45	7 4 2	9 6 15	11 8 28	13 6 45	15 8 58	17 7 15
9	19 10 26	21 12 39	23 6 59	1 9 12	3 7 29	5 9 42	7 7 59	9 10 12	11 12 25	13 10 42	15 12 55	17 11 11
10	19 14 22	21 16 36	23 10 56	1 13 9	3 11 25	5 13 38	7 11 55	9 14 8	11 16 22	13 14 38	15 16 51	17 15 8
11	19 18 19	21 20 32	23 14 52	1 17 5	3 15 22	5 17 35	7 15 52	9 18 5	11 20 18	13 18 35	15 20 48	17 19 4
12	19 22 15	21 24 29	23 18 49	1 21 2	3 19 18	5 21 32	7 19 48	9 22 1	11 24 15	13 22 31	15 24 44	17 23 1
13	19 26 12	21 28 25	23 22 45	1 24 58	3 23 15	5 25 28	7 23 45	9 25 58	11 28 11	13 26 28	15 28 41	17 26 58
14	19 30 9	21 32 22	23 26 42	1 28 55	3 27 11	5 29 25	7 27 41	9 29 55	11 32 8	13 30 24	15 32 37	17 30 54
15	19 34 5	21 36 18	23 30 38	1 32 51	3 31 8	5 33 21	7 31 38	9 33 51	11 36 4	13 34 21	15 36 34	17 34 51
16	19 38 2	21 40 15	23 34 35	1 36 48	3 35 5	5 37 18	7 35 35	9 37 48	11 40 1	13 38 17	15 40 31	17 38 47
17	19 41 58	21 44 11	23 38 31	1 40 45	3 39 1	5 41 14	7 39 31	9 41 44	11 43 57	13 42 14	15 44 27	17 42 44
18	19 45 55	21 48 8	23 42 28	1 44 41	3 42 58	5 45 11	7 43 28	9 45 41	11 47 54	13 46 11	15 48 24	17 46 40
19	19 49 51	21 52 4	23 46 25	1 48 38	3 46 54	5 49 7	7 47 24	9 49 37	11 51 51	13 50 7	15 52 20	17 50 37
20	19 53 48	21 56 1	23 50 21	1 52 34	3 50 51	5 53 4	7 51 21	9 53 34	11 55 47	13 54 4	15 56 17	17 54 34
21	19 57 44	21 59 57	23 54 18	1 56 31	3 54 47	5 57 1	7 55 17	9 57 30	11 59 44	13 58 0	16 0 13	17 58 30
22	20 1 41	22 3 54	23 58 14	2 0 27	3 58 44	6 0 57	7 59 14	10 1 27	12 3 40	14 1 57	16 4 10	18 2 27
23	20 5 38	22 7 51	0 2 11	2 4 24	4 2 40	6 4 54	8 3 10	10 5 24	12 7 37	14 5 53	16 8 6	18 6 23
24	20 9 34	22 11 47	0 6 7	2 8 20	4 6 37	6 8 50	8 7 7	10 9 20	12 11 33	14 9 50	16 12 3	18 10 20
25	20 13 31	22 15 44	0 10 4	2 12 17	4 10 33	6 12 47	8 11 4	10 13 17	12 15 30	14 13 46	16 16 0	18 14 16
26	20 17 27	22 19 40	0 14 0	2 16 13	4 14 30	6 16 43	8 15 0	10 17 13	12 19 26	14 17 43	16 19 56	18 18 13
27	20 21 24	22 23 37	0 17 57	2 20 10	4 18 27	6 20 40	8 18 57	10 21 10	12 23 23	14 21 39	16 23 53	18 22 9
28	20 25 20	22 27 33	0 21 53	2 24 7	4 22 23	6 24 36	8 22 53	10 25 6	12 27 19	14 25 36	16 27 49	18 26 6
29	20 29 17	22 31 30	0 25 50	2 28 3	4 26 20	6 28 33	8 26 50	10 29 3	12 31 16	14 29 33	16 31 46	18 30 3
30	20 33 13		0 29 47	2 32 0	4 30 16	6 32 30	8 30 46	10 32 59	12 35 13	14 33 29	16 35 42	18 33 59
31	20 37 10		0 33 43		4 34 13		8 34 43	10 36 56		14 37 26		18 37 56

1905

	Jan.	Feb.	Mar.	April	May	June	July	Aug.	Sept.	Oct.	Nov.	Dec.
1	18 41 52	20 44 5	22 34 29	0 36 42	2 34 59	4 37 12	6 35 29	8 37 42	10 39 55	12 38 11	14 40 25	16 38 41
2	18 45 49	20 48 2	22 38 25	0 40 39	2 38 55	4 41 8	6 39 25	8 41 38	10 43 51	12 42 8	14 44 21	16 42 38
3	18 49 45	20 51 59	22 42 22	0 44 35	2 42 52	4 45 5	6 43 22	8 45 35	10 47 48	12 46 5	14 48 18	16 46 34
4	18 53 42	20 55 55	22 46 19	0 48 32	2 46 48	4 49 2	6 47 18	8 49 31	10 51 45	12 50 1	14 52 14	16 50 31
5	18 57 38	20 59 52	22 50 15	0 52 28	2 50 45	4 52 58	6 51 15	8 53 28	10 55 41	12 53 58	14 56 11	16 54 28
6	19 1 35	21 3 48	22 54 12	0 56 25	2 54 41	4 56 55	6 55 11	8 57 25	10 59 38	12 57 54	15 0 7	16 58 24
7	19 5 32	21 7 45	22 58 8	1 0 21	2 58 38	5 0 51	6 59 8	9 1 21	11 3 34	13 1 51	15 4 4	17 2 21
8	19 9 28	21 11 41	23 2 5	1 4 18	3 2 35	5 4 48	7 3 4	9 5 18	11 7 31	13 5 47	15 8 1	17 6 17
9	19 13 25	21 15 38	23 6 1	1 8 14	3 6 31	5 8 44	7 7 1	9 9 14	11 11 27	13 9 44	15 11 57	17 10 14
10	19 17 21	21 19 34	23 9 58	1 12 11	3 10 28	5 12 41	7 10 58	9 13 11	11 15 24	13 13 40	15 15 54	17 14 10
11	19 21 18	21 23 31	23 13 54	1 16 8	3 14 24	5 16 37	7 14 54	9 17 7	11 19 20	13 17 37	15 19 50	17 18 7
12	19 25 14	21 27 28	23 17 51	1 20 4	3 18 21	5 20 34	7 18 51	9 21 4	11 23 17	13 21 34	15 23 47	17 22 3
13	19 29 11	21 31 24	23 21 48	1 24 1	3 22 17	5 24 31	7 22 47	9 25 0	11 27 14	13 25 30	15 27 43	17 26 0
14	19 33 7	21 35 21	23 25 44	1 27 57	3 26 14	5 28 27	7 26 44	9 28 57	11 31 10	13 29 27	15 31 40	17 29 57
15	19 37 4	21 39 17	23 29 41	1 31 54	3 30 10	5 32 24	7 30 40	9 32 54	11 35 7	13 33 23	15 35 36	17 33 53
16	19 41 1	21 43 14	23 33 37	1 35 50	3 34 7	5 36 20	7 34 37	9 36 50	11 39 3	13 37 20	15 39 33	17 37 50
17	19 44 57	21 47 10	23 37 34	1 39 47	3 38 3	5 40 17	7 38 33	9 40 47	11 43 0	13 41 16	15 43 30	17 41 46
18	19 48 54	21 51 7	23 41 30	1 43 43	3 42 0	5 44 13	7 42 30	9 44 43	11 46 56	13 45 13	15 47 26	17 45 43
19	19 52 50	21 55 3	23 45 27	1 47 40	3 45 57	5 48 10	7 46 27	9 48 40	11 50 53	13 49 9	15 51 23	17 49 39
20	19 56 47	21 59 0	23 49 23	1 51 37	3 49 53	5 52 6	7 50 23	9 52 36	11 54 49	13 53 6	15 55 19	17 53 36
21	20 0 43	22 2 56	23 53 20	1 55 33	3 53 50	5 56 3	7 54 20	9 56 33	11 58 46	13 57 3	15 59 16	17 57 32
22	20 4 40	22 6 53	23 57 17	1 59 30	3 57 46	6 0 0	7 58 16	10 0 29	12 2 43	14 0 59	16 3 12	18 1 29
23	20 8 36	22 10 50	0 1 13	2 3 26	4 1 43	6 3 56	8 2 13	10 4 26	12 6 39	14 4 56	16 7 9	18 5 26
24	20 12 33	22 14 46	0 5 10	2 7 23	4 5 39	6 7 53	8 6 9	10 8 23	12 10 36	14 8 52	16 11 5	18 9 22
25	20 16 30	22 18 43	0 9 6	2 11 19	4 9 36	6 11 49	8 10 6	10 12 19	12 14 32	14 12 49	16 15 2	18 13 19
26	20 20 26	22 22 39	0 13 3	2 15 16	4 13 33	6 15 46	8 14 2	10 16 16	12 18 29	14 16 45	16 18 59	18 17 15
27	20 24 23	22 26 36	0 16 59	2 19 12	4 17 29	6 19 42	8 17 59	10 20 12	12 22 25	14 20 42	16 22 55	18 21 12
28	20 28 19	22 30 32	0 20 56	2 23 9	4 21 26	6 23 39	8 21 56	10 24 9	12 26 22	14 24 38	16 26 52	18 25 8
29	20 32 16		0 24 52	2 27 6	4 25 22	6 27 35	8 25 52	10 28 5	12 30 18	14 28 35	16 30 48	18 29 5
30	20 36 12		0 28 49	2 31 2	4 29 19	6 31 32	8 29 49	10 32 2	12 34 15	14 32 32	16 34 45	18 33 1
31	20 40 9		0 32 45		4 33 15		8 33 45	10 35 58		14 36 28		18 36 58

1906

	Jan.	Feb.	Mar.	April	May	June	July	Aug.	Sept.	Oct.	Nov.	Dec.
1	18 40 55	20 43 8	22 33 31	0 35 44	2 34 1	4 36 14	6 34 31	8 36 44	10 38 57	12 37 14	14 39 27	16 37 44
2	18 44 51	20 47 4	22 37 28	0 39 41	2 37 58	4 40 11	6 38 28	8 40 41	10 42 54	12 41 10	14 43 24	16 41 40
3	18 48 48	20 51 1	22 41 24	0 43 38	2 41 54	4 44 7	6 42 24	8 44 37	10 46 50	12 45 7	14 47 20	16 45 37
4	18 52 44	20 54 57	22 45 21	0 47 34	2 45 51	4 48 4	6 46 21	8 48 34	10 50 47	12 49 4	14 51 17	16 49 33
5	18 56 41	20 58 54	22 49 18	0 51 31	2 49 47	4 52 0	6 50 17	8 52 30	10 54 44	12 53 0	14 55 13	16 53 30
6	19 0 37	21 2 51	22 53 14	0 55 27	2 53 44	4 55 57	6 54 14	8 56 27	10 58 40	12 56 57	14 59 10	16 57 27
7	19 4 34	21 6 47	22 57 11	0 59 24	2 57 40	4 59 54	6 58 10	9 0 24	11 2 37	13 0 53	15 3 6	17 1 23
8	19 8 30	21 10 44	23 1 7	1 3 20	3 1 37	5 3 50	7 2 7	9 4 20	11 6 33	13 4 50	15 7 3	17 5 20
9	19 12 27	21 14 40	23 5 4	1 7 17	3 5 33	5 7 47	7 6 3	9 8 17	11 10 30	13 8 46	15 11 0	17 9 16
10	19 16 24	21 18 37	23 9 0	1 11 13	3 9 30	5 11 43	7 10 0	9 12 13	11 14 26	13 12 43	15 14 56	17 13 13
11	19 20 20	21 22 33	23 12 57	1 15 10	3 13 27	5 15 40	7 13 57	9 16 10	11 18 23	13 16 39	15 18 53	17 17 9
12	19 24 17	21 26 30	23 16 53	1 19 7	3 17 23	5 19 36	7 17 53	9 20 6	11 22 19	13 20 36	15 22 49	17 21 6
13	19 28 13	21 30 26	23 20 50	1 23 3	3 21 20	5 23 33	7 21 50	9 24 3	11 26 16	13 24 33	15 26 46	17 25 2
14	19 32 10	21 34 23	23 24 47	1 27 0	3 25 16	5 27 29	7 25 46	9 27 59	11 30 13	13 28 29	15 30 42	17 28 59
15	19 36 6	21 38 20	23 28 43	1 30 56	3 29 13	5 31 26	7 29 43	9 31 56	11 34 9	13 32 26	15 34 39	17 32 56
16	19 40 3	21 42 16	23 32 40	1 34 53	3 33 9	5 35 23	7 33 39	9 35 53	11 38 6	13 36 22	15 38 35	17 36 52
17	19 43 59	21 46 13	23 36 36	1 38 49	3 37 6	5 39 19	7 37 36	9 39 49	11 42 2	13 40 19	15 42 32	17 40 49
18	19 47 56	21 50 9	23 40 33	1 42 46	3 41 2	5 43 16	7 41 32	9 43 46	11 45 59	13 44 15	15 46 29	17 44 45
19	19 51 53	21 54 6	23 44 29	1 46 42	3 44 59	5 47 12	7 45 29	9 47 42	11 49 55	13 48 12	15 50 25	17 48 42
20	19 55 49	21 58 2	23 48 26	1 50 39	3 48 56	5 51 9	7 49 26	9 51 39	11 53 52	13 52 8	15 54 22	17 52 38
21	19 59 46	22 1 59	23 52 22	1 54 35	3 52 52	5 55 5	7 53 22	9 55 35	11 57 48	13 56 5	15 58 18	17 56 35
22	20 3 42	22 5 55	23 56 19	1 58 32	3 56 49	5 59 2	7 57 19	9 59 32	12 1 45	14 0 2	16 2 15	18 0 31
23	20 7 39	22 9 52	0 0 15	2 2 29	4 0 45	6 2 59	8 1 15	10 3 28	12 5 42	14 3 58	16 6 11	18 4 28
24	20 11 35	22 13 49	0 4 12	2 6 25	4 4 42	6 6 55	8 5 12	10 7 25	12 9 38	14 7 55	16 10 8	18 8 25
25	20 15 32	22 17 45	0 8 9	2 10 22	4 8 38	6 10 52	8 9 8	10 11 22	12 13 35	14 11 51	16 14 4	18 12 21
26	20 19 28	22 21 42	0 12 5	2 14 18	4 12 35	6 14 48	8 13 5	10 15 18	12 17 31	14 15 48	16 18 1	18 16 18
27	20 23 25	22 25 38	0 16 2	2 18 15	4 16 31	6 18 45	8 17 1	10 19 15	12 21 28	14 19 44	16 21 58	18 20 14
28	20 27 22	22 29 35	0 19 58	2 22 11	4 20 28	6 22 41	8 20 58	10 23 11	12 25 24	14 23 41	16 25 54	18 24 11
29	20 31 18		0 23 55	2 26 8	4 24 25	6 26 38	8 24 55	10 27 8	12 29 21	14 27 37	16 29 51	18 28 7
30	20 35 15		0 27 51	2 30 4	4 28 21	6 30 34	8 28 51	10 31 4	12 33 17	14 31 34	16 33 47	18 32 4
31	20 39 11		0 31 48		4 32 18		8 32 48	10 35 1		14 35 31		18 36 0

1907

	Jan.	Feb.	Mar.	April	May	June	July	Aug.	Sept.	Oct.	Nov.	Dec.
1	18 39 57	20 42 10	22 32 34	0 34 47	2 33 4	4 35 17	6 33 33	8 35 47	10 38 0	12 36 16	14 38 30	16 36 46
2	18 43 54	20 46 7	22 36 30	0 38 43	2 37 0	4 39 13	6 37 30	8 39 43	10 41 56	12 40 13	14 42 26	16 40 43
3	18 47 50	20 50 3	22 40 27	0 42 40	2 40 57	4 43 10	6 41 27	8 43 40	10 45 53	12 44 10	14 46 23	16 44 39
4	18 51 47	20 54 0	22 44 23	0 46 37	2 44 53	4 47 6	6 45 23	8 47 36	10 49 50	12 48 6	14 50 19	16 48 36
5	18 55 43	20 57 57	22 48 20	0 50 33	2 48 50	4 51 3	6 49 20	8 51 33	10 53 46	12 52 3	14 54 16	16 52 33
6	18 59 40	21 1 53	22 52 17	0 54 30	2 52 46	4 55 0	6 53 16	8 55 29	10 57 43	12 55 59	14 58 12	16 56 29
7	19 3 36	21 5 50	22 56 13	0 58 26	2 56 43	4 58 56	6 57 13	8 59 26	11 1 39	12 59 56	15 2 9	17 0 26
8	19 7 33	21 9 46	23 0 10	1 2 23	3 0 39	5 2 53	7 1 9	9 3 23	11 5 36	13 3 52	15 6 6	17 4 22
9	19 11 29	21 13 43	23 4 6	1 6 19	3 4 36	5 6 49	7 5 6	9 7 19	11 9 32	13 7 49	15 10 2	17 8 19
10	19 15 26	21 17 39	23 8 3	1 10 16	3 8 33	5 10 46	7 9 2	9 11 16	11 13 29	13 11 45	15 13 59	17 12 15
11	19 19 23	21 21 36	23 11 59	1 14 12	3 12 29	5 14 42	7 12 59	9 15 12	11 17 25	13 15 42	15 17 55	17 16 12
12	19 23 19	21 25 32	23 15 56	1 18 9	3 16 26	5 18 39	7 16 56	9 19 9	11 21 22	13 19 39	15 21 52	17 20 8
13	19 27 16	21 29 29	23 19 52	1 22 6	3 20 22	5 22 35	7 20 52	9 23 5	11 25 19	13 23 35	15 25 48	17 24 5
14	19 31 12	21 33 26	23 23 49	1 26 2	3 24 19	5 26 32	7 24 49	9 27 2	11 29 15	13 27 32	15 29 45	17 28 2
15	19 35 9	21 37 22	23 27 46	1 29 59	3 28 15	5 30 29	7 28 45	9 30 58	11 33 12	13 31 28	15 33 41	17 31 58
16	19 39 5	21 41 19	23 31 42	1 33 55	3 32 12	5 34 25	7 32 42	9 34 55	11 37 8	13 35 25	15 37 38	17 35 55
17	19 43 2	21 45 15	23 35 39	1 37 52	3 36 8	5 38 22	7 36 38	9 38 52	11 41 5	13 39 21	15 41 35	17 39 51
18	19 46 59	21 49 12	23 39 35	1 41 48	3 40 5	5 42 18	7 40 35	9 42 48	11 45 1	13 43 18	15 45 31	17 43 48
19	19 50 55	21 53 8	23 43 32	1 45 45	3 44 2	5 46 15	7 44 31	9 46 45	11 48 58	13 47 14	15 49 28	17 47 44
20	19 54 52	21 57 5	23 47 28	1 49 41	3 47 58	5 50 11	7 48 28	9 50 41	11 52 54	13 51 11	15 53 24	17 51 41
21	19 58 48	22 1 1	23 51 25	1 53 38	3 51 55	5 54 8	7 52 25	9 54 38	11 56 51	13 55 8	15 57 21	17 55 37
22	20 2 45	22 4 58	23 55 21	1 57 35	3 55 51	5 58 4	7 56 21	9 58 34	12 0 48	13 59 4	16 1 17	17 59 34
23	20 6 41	22 8 54	23 59 18	2 1 31	3 59 48	6 2 1	8 0 18	10 2 31	12 4 44	14 3 1	16 5 14	18 3 31
24	20 10 38	22 12 51	0 3 15	2 5 28	4 3 44	6 5 58	8 4 14	10 6 27	12 8 41	14 6 57	16 9 10	18 7 27
25	20 14 34	22 16 48	0 7 11	2 9 24	4 7 41	6 9 54	8 8 11	10 10 24	12 12 37	14 10 54	16 13 7	18 11 24
26	20 18 31	22 20 44	0 11 8	2 13 21	4 11 37	6 13 51	8 12 7	10 14 21	12 16 34	14 14 50	16 17 4	18 15 20
27	20 22 28	22 24 41	0 15 4	2 17 17	4 15 34	6 17 47	8 16 4	10 18 17	12 20 30	14 18 47	16 21 0	18 19 17
28	20 26 24	22 28 37	0 19 1	2 21 14	4 19 31	6 21 44	8 20 1	10 22 14	12 24 27	14 22 43	16 24 57	18 23 13
29	20 30 21		0 22 57	2 25 10	4 23 27	6 25 40	8 23 57	10 26 10	12 28 23	14 26 40	16 28 53	18 27 10
30	20 34 17		0 26 54	2 29 7	4 27 24	6 29 37	8 27 54	10 30 7	13 32 20	14 30 37	16 32 50	18 31 6
31	20 38 14		0 30 50		4 31 20		8 31 50	10 34 3		14 34 33		18 35 3

1908

Jan.	Feb.	Mar.	April	May	June	July	Aug.	Sept.	Oct.	Nov.	Dec.	
18 39 0	20 41 13	22 35 33	0 37 46	2 36 3	4 38 16	6 36 33	8 38 46	10 40 59	12 39 16	14 41 29	16 39 46	1
18 42 56	20 45 9	22 39 29	0 41 43	2 39 59	4 42 12	6 40 29	8 42 42	10 44 56	12 43 12	14 45 25	16 43 42	2
18 46 53	20 49 6	22 43 26	0 45 39	2 43 56	4 46 9	6 44 26	8 46 39	10 48 52	12 47 9	14 49 22	16 47 39	3
18 50 49	20 53 3	22 47 23	0 49 36	2 47 52	4 50 6	6 48 22	8 50 36	10 52 49	12 51 5	14 53 19	16 51 35	4
18 54 46	20 56 59	22 51 19	0 53 32	2 51 49	4 54 2	6 52 19	8 54 32	10 56 45	12 55 2	14 57 15	16 55 32	5
18 58 42	21 0 56	22 55 16	0 57 29	2 55 45	4 57 59	6 56 15	8 58 29	11 0 42	12 58 58	15 1 12	16 59 28	6
19 2 39	21 4 52	22 59 12	1 1 25	2 59 42	5 1 55	7 0 12	9 2 25	11 4 38	13 2 55	15 5 8	17 3 25	7
19 6 36	21 8 49	23 3 0	1 5 22	3 3 39	5 5 52	7 4 9	9 6 22	11 8 35	13 6 52	15 9 5	17 7 21	8
19 10 32	21 12 45	23 7 5	1 9 19	3 7 35	5 9 48	7 8 5	9 10 18	11 12 32	13 10 48	15 13 1	17 11 18	9
19 14 29	21 16 42	23 11 2	1 13 15	3 11 32	5 13 45	7 12 2	9 14 15	11 16 28	13 14 45	15 16 58	17 15 15	10
19 18 25	21 20 38	23 14 58	1 17 12	3 15 28	5 17 42	7 15 58	9 18 11	11 20 25	13 18 41	15 20 54	17 19 11	11
19 22 22	21 24 35	23 18 55	1 21 8	3 19 25	5 21 38	7 19 55	9 22 8	11 24 21	13 22 38	15 24 51	17 23 8	12
19 26 18	21 28 32	23 22 52	1 25 5	3 23 21	5 25 35	7 23 51	9 26 5	11 28 18	13 26 34	15 28 48	17 27 4	13
19 30 15	21 32 28	23 26 48	1 29 1	3 27 18	5 29 31	7 27 48	9 30 1	11 32 14	13 30 31	15 32 44	17 31 1	14
19 34 11	21 36 25	23 30 45	1 32 58	3 31 14	5 33 28	7 31 44	9 33 58	11 36 11	13 34 27	15 36 41	17 34 57	15
19 38 8	21 40 21	23 34 41	1 36 54	3 35 11	5 37 24	7 35 41	9 37 54	11 40 7	13 38 23	15 40 37	17 38 54	16
19 42 5	21 44 18	23 38 38	1 40 51	3 39 8	5 41 21	7 39 38	9 41 51	11 44 4	13 42 21	15 44 34	17 42 50	17
19 46 1	21 48 14	23 42 34	1 44 47	3 43 4	5 45 17	7 43 34	9 45 47	11 48 0	13 46 17	15 48 30	17 46 47	18
19 49 58	21 52 11	23 46 31	1 48 44	3 47 1	5 49 14	7 47 31	9 49 44	11 51 57	13 50 14	15 52 27	17 50 44	19
19 53 54	21 56 7	23 50 27	1 52 41	3 50 57	5 53 11	7 51 27	9 53 40	11 55 54	13 54 10	15 56 23	17 54 40	20
19 57 51	22 0 4	23 54 24	1 56 37	3 54 54	5 57 7	7 55 24	9 57 37	11 59 50	13 58 7	16 0 20	17 58 37	21
20 1 47	22 4 1	23 58 21	2 0 34	3 58 50	6 1 4	7 59 20	10 1 34	12 3 47	14 2 3	16 4 17	18 2 33	22
20 5 44	22 7 57	0 2 17	2 4 30	4 2 47	6 5 0	8 3 17	10 5 30	12 7 43	14 6 0	16 8 13	18 6 30	23
20 9 40	22 11 54	0 6 14	2 8 27	4 6 43	6 8 57	8 7 13	10 9 27	12 11 40	14 9 56	16 12 10	18 10 26	24
20 13 37	22 15 50	0 10 10	2 12 23	4 10 40	6 12 53	8 11 10	10 13 23	12 15 36	14 13 53	16 16 6	18 14 23	25
20 17 34	22 19 47	0 14 7	2 16 20	4 14 37	6 16 50	8 15 7	10 17 20	12 19 33	14 17 50	16 20 3	18 18 19	26
20 21 30	22 23 43	0 18 3	2 20 17	4 18 33	6 20 46	8 19 3	10 21 16	12 23 29	14 21 46	16 23 59	18 22 16	27
20 25 27	22 27 40	0 22 0	2 24 13	4 22 30	6 24 43	8 23 0	10 25 13	12 27 26	14 25 43	16 27 56	18 26 13	28
20 29 23	22 31 36	0 25 56	2 28 10	4 26 26	6 28 40	8 26 56	10 29 9	12 31 23	14 29 39	16 31 52	18 30 9	29
20 33 20		0 29 53	2 32 6	4 30 23	6 32 36	8 30 53	10 33 6	12 35 19	14 33 36	16 35 49	18 34 6	30
20 37 16		0 33 50		4 34 19		8 34 49	10 37 3		14 37 32		18 38 2	31

1909

Jan.	Feb.	Mar.	April	May	June	July	Aug.	Sept.	Oct.	Nov.	Dec.	
18 41 59	20 44 12	22 34 36	0 36 49	2 35 5	4 37 19	6 35 35	8 37 49	10 40 2	12 38 18	14 40 32	16 38 48	1
18 45 55	20 48 9	22 38 32	0 40 45	2 39 2	4 41 15	6 39 32	8 41 45	10 43 58	12 42 15	14 44 28	16 42 45	2
18 49 52	20 52 5	22 42 29	0 44 42	2 42 59	4 45 12	6 43 29	8 45 42	10 47 55	12 46 12	14 48 25	16 46 41	3
18 53 49	20 56 2	22 46 25	0 48 38	2 46 55	4 49 8	6 47 25	8 49 38	10 51 52	12 50 8	14 52 21	16 50 38	4
18 57 45	20 59 58	22 50 22	0 52 35	2 50 52	4 53 5	6 51 22	8 53 35	10 55 48	12 54 5	14 56 18	16 54 35	5
19 1 42	21 3 55	22 54 18	0 56 32	2 54 48	4 57 1	6 55 18	8 57 31	10 59 45	12 58 1	15 0 14	16 58 31	6
19 5 38	21 7 51	22 58 15	1 0 28	2 58 45	5 0 58	6 59 15	9 1 28	11 3 41	13 1 58	15 4 11	17 2 28	7
19 9 35	21 11 48	23 2 12	1 4 25	3 2 41	5 4 55	7 3 11	9 5 25	11 7 38	13 5 54	15 8 8	17 6 24	8
19 13 31	21 15 45	23 6 8	1 8 21	3 6 38	5 8 51	7 7 8	9 9 21	11 11 34	13 9 51	15 12 4	17 10 21	9
19 17 28	21 19 41	23 10 5	1 12 18	3 10 34	5 12 48	7 11 4	9 13 18	11 15 31	13 13 47	15 16 1	17 14 17	10
19 21 24	21 23 38	23 14 1	1 16 14	3 14 31	5 16 44	7 15 1	9 17 14	11 19 27	13 17 44	15 19 57	17 18 14	11
19 25 21	21 27 34	23 17 58	1 20 11	3 18 28	5 20 41	7 18 58	9 21 11	11 23 24	13 21 41	15 23 54	17 22 10	12
19 29 18	21 31 31	23 21 54	1 24 7	3 22 24	5 24 37	7 22 54	9 25 7	11 27 21	13 25 37	15 27 50	17 26 7	13
19 33 14	21 35 27	23 25 51	1 28 4	3 26 21	5 28 34	7 26 51	9 29 4	11 31 17	13 29 34	15 31 47	17 30 4	14
19 37 11	21 39 24	23 29 47	1 32 1	3 30 17	5 32 30	7 30 47	9 33 0	11 35 14	13 33 30	15 35 43	17 34 0	15
19 41 7	21 43 20	23 33 44	1 35 57	3 34 14	5 36 27	7 34 44	9 36 57	11 39 10	13 37 27	15 39 40	17 37 57	16
19 45 4	21 47 17	23 37 40	1 39 54	3 38 10	5 40 24	7 38 40	9 40 54	11 43 7	13 41 23	15 43 37	17 41 53	17
19 49 0	21 51 14	23 41 37	1 43 50	3 42 7	5 44 20	7 42 37	9 44 50	11 47 3	13 45 20	15 47 33	17 45 50	18
19 52 57	21 55 10	23 45 34	1 47 47	3 46 3	5 48 17	7 46 33	9 48 47	11 51 0	13 49 16	15 51 30	17 49 46	19
19 56 53	21 59 7	23 49 30	1 51 43	3 50 0	5 52 13	7 50 30	9 52 43	11 54 56	13 53 13	15 55 26	17 53 43	20
20 0 50	22 3 3	23 53 27	1 55 40	3 53 57	5 56 10	7 54 27	9 56 40	11 58 53	13 57 10	15 59 23	17 57 40	21
20 4 47	22 7 0	23 57 23	1 59 36	3 57 53	6 0 6	7 58 23	10 0 36	12 2 49	14 1 6	16 3 19	18 1 36	22
20 8 43	22 10 56	0 1 20	2 3 33	4 1 50	6 4 3	8 2 20	10 4 33	12 6 46	14 5 3	16 7 16	18 5 33	23
20 12 40	22 14 53	0 5 16	2 7 30	4 5 46	6 7 59	8 6 16	10 8 29	12 10 43	14 8 59	16 11 12	18 9 29	24
20 16 36	22 18 49	0 9 13	2 11 26	4 9 43	6 11 56	8 10 13	10 12 26	12 14 39	14 12 56	16 15 9	18 13 26	25
20 20 33	22 22 46	0 13 9	2 15 23	4 13 39	6 15 53	8 14 9	10 16 23	12 18 36	14 16 52	16 19 6	18 17 22	26
20 24 29	22 26 43	0 17 6	2 19 19	4 17 36	6 19 49	8 18 6	10 20 19	12 22 32	14 20 49	16 23 2	18 21 19	27
20 28 26	22 30 39	0 21 3	2 23 16	4 21 32	6 23 46	8 22 2	10 24 16	12 26 29	14 24 45	16 26 59	18 25 15	28
20 32 22		0 24 59	2 27 12	4 25 29	6 27 42	8 25 59	10 28 12	12 30 25	14 28 42	16 30 55	18 29 12	29
20 36 19		0 28 56	2 31 9	4 29 26	6 31 39	8 29 56	10 32 9	12 34 22	14 32 39	16 34 52	18 33 9	30
20 40 16		0 32 52		4 33 22		8 33 52	10 36 5		14 36 35		18 37 5	31

1910

Jan.	Feb.	Mar.	April	May	June	July	Aug.	Sept.	Oct.	Nov.	Dec.	
18 41 2	20 43 15	22 33 38	0 35 52	2 34 8	4 36 22	6 34 38	8 36 52	10 39 5	12 37 21	14 39 35	16 37 51	1
18 44 58	20 47 11	22 37 35	0 39 48	2 38 5	4 40 18	6 38 35	8 40 48	10 43 1	12 41 18	14 43 31	16 41 48	2
18 48 55	20 51 8	22 41 32	0 43 45	2 42 1	4 44 15	6 42 31	8 44 45	10 46 58	12 45 14	14 47 28	16 45 44	3
18 52 51	20 55 5	22 45 28	0 47 41	2 45 58	4 48 11	6 46 28	8 48 41	10 50 54	12 49 11	14 51 24	16 49 41	4
18 56 48	20 59 1	22 49 25	0 51 38	2 49 54	4 52 8	6 50 24	8 52 38	10 54 51	12 53 8	14 55 21	16 53 37	5
19 0 44	21 2 58	22 53 21	0 55 34	2 53 51	4 56 4	6 54 21	8 56 34	10 58 48	12 57 4	14 59 17	16 57 34	6
19 4 41	21 6 54	22 57 18	0 59 31	2 57 48	5 0 1	6 58 18	9 0 31	11 2 44	13 1 1	15 3 14	17 1 31	7
19 8 38	21 10 51	23 1 14	1 3 27	3 1 44	5 3 57	7 2 14	9 4 27	11 6 41	13 4 57	15 7 10	17 5 27	8
19 12 34	21 14 47	23 5 11	1 7 24	3 5 41	5 7 54	7 6 11	9 8 24	11 10 37	13 8 54	15 11 7	17 9 24	9
19 16 31	21 18 44	23 9 7	1 11 21	3 9 37	5 11 51	7 10 7	9 12 21	11 14 34	13 12 50	15 15 4	17 13 20	10
19 20 27	21 22 40	23 13 4	1 15 17	3 13 34	5 15 47	7 14 4	9 16 17	11 18 30	13 16 47	15 19 0	17 17 17	11
19 24 24	21 26 37	23 17 1	1 19 14	3 17 30	5 19 44	7 18 0	9 20 14	11 22 27	13 20 43	15 22 57	17 21 13	12
19 28 20	21 30 34	23 20 57	1 23 10	3 21 27	5 23 40	7 21 57	9 24 10	11 26 23	13 24 40	15 26 53	17 25 10	13
19 32 17	21 34 30	23 24 54	1 27 7	3 25 23	5 27 37	7 25 54	9 28 7	11 30 20	13 28 37	15 30 50	17 29 6	14
19 36 13	21 38 27	23 28 50	1 31 3	3 29 20	5 31 33	7 29 50	9 32 3	11 34 16	13 32 33	15 34 46	17 33 3	15
19 40 10	21 42 23	23 32 47	1 35 0	3 33 17	5 35 30	7 33 47	9 36 0	11 38 13	13 36 30	15 38 43	17 37 0	16
19 44 7	21 46 20	23 36 43	1 38 56	3 37 13	5 39 26	7 37 43	9 39 56	11 42 10	13 40 26	15 42 39	17 40 56	17
19 48 3	21 50 16	23 40 40	1 42 53	3 41 10	5 43 23	7 41 40	9 43 53	11 46 6	13 44 23	15 46 36	17 44 53	18
19 52 0	21 54 13	23 44 36	1 46 50	3 45 6	5 47 20	7 45 36	9 47 50	11 50 3	13 48 19	15 50 33	17 48 49	19
19 55 56	21 58 9	23 48 33	1 50 46	3 49 3	5 51 16	7 49 33	9 51 46	11 53 59	13 52 16	15 54 29	17 52 46	20
19 59 53	22 2 6	23 52 30	1 54 43	3 52 59	5 55 13	7 53 29	9 55 43	11 57 56	13 56 12	15 58 26	17 56 42	21
20 3 49	22 6 3	23 56 26	1 58 39	3 56 56	5 59 9	7 57 26	9 59 39	12 1 52	14 0 9	16 2 22	18 0 39	22
20 7 46	22 9 59	0 0 23	2 2 36	4 0 52	6 3 6	8 1 23	10 3 36	12 5 49	14 4 6	16 6 19	18 4 36	23
20 11 42	22 13 56	0 4 19	2 6 32	4 4 49	6 7 2	8 5 19	10 7 32	12 9 45	14 8 2	16 10 15	18 8 32	24
20 15 39	22 17 52	0 8 16	2 10 29	4 8 46	6 10 59	8 9 16	10 11 29	12 13 42	14 11 59	16 14 12	18 12 29	25
20 19 36	22 21 49	0 12 12	2 14 25	4 12 42	6 14 55	8 13 12	10 15 25	12 17 39	14 15 55	16 18 8	18 16 25	26
20 23 32	22 25 45	0 16 9	2 18 22	4 16 39	6 18 52	8 17 9	10 19 22	12 21 35	14 19 52	16 22 5	18 20 22	27
20 27 29	22 29 42	0 20 5	2 22 19	4 20 35	6 22 49	8 21 5	10 23 19	12 25 32	14 23 48	16 26 2	18 24 18	28
20 31 25		0 24 2	2 26 15	4 24 32	6 26 45	8 25 2	10 27 15	12 29 28	14 27 45	16 29 58	18 28 15	29
20 35 22		0 27 59	2 30 12	4 28 28	6 30 42	8 28 58	10 31 12	12 33 25	14 31 41	16 33 55	18 32 11	30
20 39 18		0 31 55		4 32 25		8 32 55	10 35 8		14 35 38		18 36 8	31

1911

	Jan.	Feb.	Mar.	April	May	June	July	Aug.	Sept.	Oct.	Nov.	Dec.
1	18 40 5	20 42 18	22 32 41	0 34 55	2 33 11	4 35 24	6 33 41	8 35 54	10 38 8	12 36 24	14 38 37	16 36 54
2	18 44 1	20 46 14	22 36 38	0 38 51	2 37 8	4 39 21	6 37 38	8 39 51	10 42 4	12 40 21	14 42 34	16 40 51
3	18 47 58	20 50 11	22 40 34	0 42 48	2 41 4	4 43 18	6 41 34	8 43 48	10 46 1	12 44 17	14 46 31	16 44 47
4	18 51 54	20 54 8	22 44 31	0 46 44	2 45 1	4 47 14	6 45 31	8 47 44	10 49 57	12 48 14	14 50 27	16 48 44
5	18 55 51	20 58 4	22 48 28	0 50 41	2 48 57	4 51 11	6 49 27	8 51 41	10 53 54	12 52 11	14 54 24	16 52 40
6	18 59 47	21 2 1	22 52 24	0 54 37	2 52 54	4 55 7	6 53 24	8 55 37	10 57 50	12 56 7	14 58 20	16 56 37
7	19 3 44	21 5 57	22 56 21	0 58 34	2 56 51	4 59 4	6 57 21	8 59 34	11 1 47	13 0 4	15 2 17	17 0 34
8	19 7 40	21 9 54	23 0 17	1 2 30	3 0 47	5 3 0	7 1 17	9 3 30	11 5 44	13 4 0	15 6 13	17 4 30
9	19 11 37	21 13 50	23 4 14	1 6 27	3 4 44	5 6 57	7 5 14	9 7 27	11 9 40	13 7 57	15 10 10	17 8 27
10	19 15 34	21 17 47	23 8 10	1 10 24	3 8 40	5 10 53	7 9 10	9 11 23	11 13 37	13 11 53	15 14 7	17 12 23
11	19 19 30	21 21 43	23 12 7	1 14 20	3 12 37	5 14 50	7 13 7	9 15 20	11 17 33	13 15 50	15 18 3	17 16 20
12	19 23 27	21 25 40	23 16 3	1 18 17	3 16 33	5 18 47	7 17 3	9 19 17	11 21 30	13 19 46	15 22 0	17 20 16
13	19 27 23	21 29 37	23 20 0	1 22 13	3 20 30	5 22 43	7 21 0	9 23 13	11 25 26	13 23 43	15 25 56	17 24 13
14	19 31 20	21 33 33	23 23 57	1 26 10	3 24 26	5 26 40	7 24 56	9 27 10	11 29 23	13 27 40	15 29 53	17 28 9
15	19 35 16	21 37 30	23 27 53	1 30 6	3 28 23	5 30 36	7 28 53	9 31 6	11 33 19	13 31 36	15 33 49	17 32 6
16	19 39 13	21 41 26	23 31 50	1 34 3	3 32 20	5 34 33	7 32 50	9 35 3	11 37 16	13 35 33	15 37 46	17 36 3
17	19 43 9	21 45 23	23 35 46	1 37 59	3 36 16	5 38 29	7 36 46	9 38 59	11 41 13	13 39 29	15 41 42	17 39 59
18	19 47 6	21 49 19	23 39 43	1 41 56	3 40 13	5 42 26	7 40 43	9 42 56	11 45 9	13 43 26	15 45 39	17 43 56
19	19 51 3	21 53 16	23 43 39	1 45 53	3 44 9	5 46 23	7 44 39	9 46 52	11 49 6	13 47 22	15 49 36	17 47 52
20	19 54 59	21 57 12	23 47 36	1 49 49	3 48 6	5 50 19	7 48 36	9 50 49	11 53 2	13 51 19	15 53 32	17 51 49
21	19 58 56	22 1 9	23 51 32	1 53 46	3 52 2	5 54 16	7 52 32	9 54 46	11 56 59	13 55 15	15 57 29	17 55 45
22	20 2 52	22 5 6	23 55 29	1 57 42	3 55 59	5 58 12	7 56 29	9 58 42	12 0 55	13 59 12	16 1 25	17 59 42
23	20 6 49	22 9 2	23 59 26	2 1 39	3 59 55	6 2 9	8 0 25	0 2 39	12 4 52	14 3 9	16 5 22	18 3 39
24	20 10 45	22 12 59	0 3 22	2 5 35	4 3 52	6 6 5	8 4 22	0 6 35	12 8 48	14 7 5	16 9 18	18 7 35
25	20 14 42	22 16 55	0 7 19	2 9 32	4 7 49	6 10 2	8 8 19	0 10 32	12 12 45	14 11 2	16 13 15	18 11 32
26	20 18 39	22 20 52	0 11 15	2 13 28	4 11 45	6 13 58	8 12 15	0 14 28	12 16 42	14 14 58	16 17 11	18 15 28
27	20 22 35	22 24 48	0 15 12	2 17 25	4 15 42	6 17 55	8 16 12	0 18 25	12 20 38	14 18 55	16 21 8	18 19 25
28	20 26 32	22 28 45	0 19 8	2 21 22	4 19 38	6 21 52	8 20 8	0 22 21	12 24 35	14 22 51	16 25 5	18 23 21
29	20 30 28		0 23 5	2 25 18	4 23 35	6 25 48	8 24 5	0 26 18	12 28 31	14 26 48	16 29 1	18 27 18
30	20 34 25		0 27 1	2 29 15	4 27 31	6 29 45	8 28 1	0 30 15	12 32 28	14 30 44	16 32 58	18 31 14
31	20 38 21		0 30 58		4 31 28		8 31 58	0 34 11		14 34 41		18 35 11

1912

	Jan.	Feb.	Mar.	April	May	June	July	Aug.	Sept.	Oct.	Nov.	Dec.
1	18 39 8	20 41 21	22 35 41	0 37 54	2 36 11	4 38 24	6 36 41	8 38 54	10 41 7	12 39 24	14 41 37	16 39 54
2	18 43 4	20 45 17	22 39 38	0 41 51	2 40 7	4 42 21	6 40 37	8 42 51	10 45 4	12 43 20	14 45 34	16 43 50
3	18 47 1	20 49 14	22 43 34	0 45 47	2 44 4	4 46 17	6 44 34	8 46 47	10 49 0	12 47 17	14 49 30	16 47 47
4	18 50 57	20 53 11	22 47 31	0 49 44	2 48 0	4 50 14	6 48 30	8 50 44	10 52 57	12 51 14	14 53 27	16 51 43
5	18 54 54	20 57 7	22 51 27	0 53 40	2 51 57	4 54 10	6 52 27	8 54 40	10 56 53	12 55 10	14 57 23	16 55 40
6	18 58 50	21 1 4	22 55 24	0 57 37	2 55 54	4 58 7	6 56 24	8 58 37	11 0 50	12 59 7	15 1 20	16 59 37
7	19 2 47	21 5 0	22 59 20	1 1 33	2 59 50	5 2 3	7 0 20	9 2 33	11 4 47	13 3 3	15 5 16	17 3 33
8	19 6 43	21 8 57	23 3 17	1 5 30	3 3 47	5 6 0	7 4 17	9 6 30	11 8 43	13 7 0	15 9 13	17 7 30
9	19 10 40	21 12 53	23 7 13	1 9 27	3 7 43	5 9 56	7 8 13	9 10 27	11 12 40	13 10 56	15 13 10	17 11 26
10	19 14 37	21 16 50	23 11 10	1 13 23	3 11 40	5 13 53	7 12 10	9 14 23	11 16 36	13 14 53	15 17 6	17 15 23
11	19 18 33	21 20 46	23 15 6	1 17 20	3 15 36	5 17 50	7 16 6	9 18 20	11 20 33	13 18 49	15 21 3	17 19 19
12	19 22 30	21 24 43	23 19 3	1 21 16	3 19 33	5 21 46	7 20 3	9 22 16	11 24 29	13 22 46	15 24 59	17 23 16
13	19 26 26	21 28 40	23 23 0	1 25 13	3 23 29	5 25 43	7 23 59	9 26 13	11 28 26	13 26 43	15 28 56	17 27 13
14	19 30 23	21 32 36	23 26 56	1 29 9	3 27 26	5 29 39	7 27 56	9 30 9	11 32 22	13 30 39	15 32 52	17 31 9
15	19 34 19	21 36 33	23 30 53	1 33 6	3 31 23	5 33 36	7 31 53	9 34 6	11 36 19	13 34 36	15 36 49	17 35 6
16	19 38 16	21 40 29	23 34 49	1 37 2	3 35 19	5 37 32	7 35 49	9 38 2	11 40 16	13 38 32	15 40 45	17 39 2
17	19 42 12	21 44 26	23 38 46	1 40 59	3 39 16	5 41 29	7 39 46	9 41 59	11 44 12	13 42 29	15 44 42	17 42 59
18	19 46 9	21 48 22	23 42 42	1 44 56	3 43 12	5 45 26	7 43 42	9 45 56	11 48 9	13 46 25	15 48 39	17 46 55
19	19 50 6	21 52 19	23 46 39	1 48 52	3 47 9	5 49 22	7 47 39	9 49 52	11 52 5	13 50 22	15 52 35	17 50 52
20	19 54 2	21 56 15	23 50 35	1 52 49	3 51 5	5 53 19	7 51 35	9 53 49	11 56 2	13 54 18	15 56 32	17 54 48
21	19 57 59	22 0 12	23 54 32	1 56 45	3 55 2	5 57 15	7 55 32	9 57 45	11 59 58	13 58 15	16 0 28	17 58 45
22	20 1 55	22 4 9	23 58 29	2 0 42	3 58 58	6 1 12	7 59 29	10 1 42	12 3 55	14 2 12	16 4 25	18 2 42
23	20 5 52	22 8 5	0 2 25	2 4 38	4 2 55	6 5 8	8 3 25	10 5 38	12 7 51	14 6 8	16 8 21	18 6 38
24	20 9 48	22 12 2	0 6 22	2 8 35	4 6 52	6 9 5	8 7 22	10 9 35	12 11 48	14 10 5	16 12 18	18 10 35
25	20 13 45	22 15 58	0 10 18	2 12 31	4 10 48	6 13 1	8 11 18	10 13 31	12 15 45	14 14 1	16 16 14	18 14 31
26	20 17 41	22 19 55	0 14 15	2 16 28	4 14 45	6 16 58	8 15 15	10 17 28	12 19 41	14 17 58	16 20 11	18 18 28
27	20 21 38	22 23 51	0 18 11	2 20 25	4 18 41	6 20 55	8 19 11	10 21 25	12 23 38	14 21 54	16 24 8	18 22 24
28	20 25 35	22 27 48	0 22 8	2 24 21	4 22 38	6 24 51	8 23 8	10 25 21	12 27 34	14 25 51	16 28 4	18 26 21
29	20 29 31	22 31 44	0 26 4	2 28 18	4 26 34	6 28 48	8 27 4	10 29 18	12 31 31	14 29 47	16 32 1	18 30 17
30	20 33 28		0 30 1	2 32 14	4 30 31	6 32 44	8 31 1	10 33 14	12 35 27	14 33 44	16 35 57	18 34 14
31	20 37 24		0 33 58		4 34 27		8 34 58	10 37 11		14 37 41		18 38 11

1913

	Jan.	Feb.	Mar.	April	May	June	July	Aug.	Sept.	Oct.	Nov.	Dec.
1	18 42 7	20 44 20	22 34 44	0 36 57	2 35 14	4 37 27	6 35 44	8 37 57	10 40 10	12 38 27	14 40 40	16 38 57
2	18 46 4	20 48 17	22 38 41	0 40 54	2 39 10	4 41 24	6 39 40	8 41 54	10 44 7	12 42 24	14 44 37	16 42 53
3	18 50 0	20 52 14	22 42 37	0 44 50	2 43 7	4 45 20	6 43 37	8 45 50	10 48 3	12 46 20	14 48 33	16 46 50
4	18 53 57	20 56 10	22 46 34	0 48 47	2 47 3	4 49 17	6 47 34	8 49 47	10 52 0	12 50 17	14 52 30	16 50 47
5	18 57 53	21 0 7	22 50 30	0 52 43	2 51 0	4 53 13	6 51 30	8 53 43	10 55 57	12 54 13	14 56 26	16 54 43
6	19 1 50	21 4 3	22 54 27	0 56 40	2 54 57	4 57 10	6 55 27	8 57 40	10 59 53	12 58 10	15 0 23	16 58 40
7	19 5 46	21 8 0	22 58 23	1 0 36	2 58 53	5 1 6	6 59 23	9 1 36	11 3 50	13 2 6	15 4 19	17 2 36
8	19 9 43	21 11 56	23 2 20	1 4 33	3 2 50	5 5 3	7 3 20	9 5 33	11 7 46	13 6 3	15 8 16	17 6 33
9	19 13 40	21 15 53	23 6 16	1 8 30	3 6 46	5 9 0	7 7 16	9 9 30	11 11 43	13 9 59	15 12 13	17 10 29
10	19 17 36	21 19 49	23 10 13	1 12 26	3 10 43	5 12 56	7 11 13	9 13 26	11 15 39	13 13 56	15 16 9	17 14 26
11	19 21 33	21 23 46	23 14 10	1 16 23	3 14 39	5 16 53	7 15 9	9 17 23	11 19 36	13 17 52	15 20 6	17 18 22
12	19 25 29	21 27 43	23 18 6	1 20 19	3 18 36	5 20 49	7 19 6	9 21 19	11 23 32	13 21 49	15 24 2	17 22 19
13	19 29 26	21 31 39	23 22 3	1 24 16	3 22 32	5 24 46	7 23 3	9 25 16	11 27 29	13 25 46	15 27 59	17 26 16
14	19 33 22	21 35 36	23 25 59	1 28 12	3 26 29	5 28 42	7 26 59	9 29 12	11 31 26	13 29 42	15 31 55	17 30 12
15	19 37 19	21 39 32	23 29 56	1 32 9	3 30 26	5 32 39	7 30 56	9 33 9	11 35 22	13 33 39	15 35 52	17 34 9
16	19 41 16	21 43 29	23 33 52	1 36 5	3 34 22	5 36 35	7 34 52	9 37 5	11 39 19	13 37 35	15 39 48	17 38 5
17	19 45 12	21 47 25	23 37 49	1 40 2	3 38 19	5 40 32	7 38 49	9 41 2	11 43 15	13 41 32	15 43 45	17 42 2
18	19 49 9	21 51 22	23 41 45	1 43 59	3 42 15	5 44 29	7 42 45	9 44 59	11 47 12	13 45 28	15 47 42	17 45 58
19	19 53 5	21 55 18	23 45 42	1 47 55	3 46 12	5 48 25	7 46 42	9 48 55	11 51 8	13 49 25	15 51 38	17 49 55
20	19 57 2	21 59 15	23 49 39	1 51 52	3 50 8	5 52 22	7 50 38	9 52 52	11 55 5	13 53 21	15 55 35	17 53 51
21	20 0 58	22 3 12	23 53 35	1 55 48	3 54 5	5 56 18	7 54 35	9 56 48	11 59 1	13 57 18	15 59 31	17 57 48
22	20 4 55	22 7 8	23 57 32	1 59 45	3 58 1	6 0 15	7 58 32	10 0 45	12 2 58	14 1 15	16 3 28	18 1 45
23	20 8 51	22 11 5	0 1 28	2 3 41	4 1 58	6 4 11	8 2 28	10 4 41	12 6 55	14 5 11	16 7 24	18 5 41
24	20 12 48	22 15 1	0 5 25	2 7 38	4 5 55	6 8 8	8 6 25	10 8 38	12 10 51	14 9 8	16 11 21	18 9 38
25	20 16 45	22 18 58	0 9 21	2 11 34	4 9 51	6 12 4	8 10 21	10 12 34	12 14 48	14 13 4	16 15 18	18 13 34
26	20 20 41	22 22 54	0 13 18	2 15 31	4 13 48	6 16 1	8 14 18	10 16 31	12 18 44	14 17 1	16 19 14	18 17 31
27	20 24 38	22 26 51	0 17 14	2 19 28	4 17 44	6 19 58	8 18 14	10 20 28	12 22 41	14 20 57	16 23 11	18 21 27
28	20 28 34	22 30 47	0 21 11	2 23 24	4 21 41	6 23 54	8 22 11	10 24 24	12 26 37	14 24 54	16 27 7	18 25 24
29	20 32 31		0 25 7	2 27 21	4 25 37	6 27 51	8 26 7	10 28 21	12 30 34	14 28 50	16 31 4	18 29 21
30	20 36 27		0 29 4	2 31 17	4 29 34	6 31 47	8 30 4	10 32 17	12 34 30	14 32 47	16 35 0	18 33 17
31	20 40 24		0 33 1		4 33 31		8 34 1	10 36 14		14 36 44		18 37 14

1914

Jan.	Feb.	Mar.	April	May	June	July	Aug.	Sept.	Oct.	Nov.	Dec.	
18 41 10	20 43 23	22 33 47	0 36 0	2 34 17	4 36 30	6 34 47	8 37 0	10 39 13	12 37 30	14 39 43	16 38 0	1
18 45 7	20 47 20	22 37 44	0 39 57	2 38 13	4 40 27	6 38 43	8 40 57	10 43 10	12 41 27	14 43 40	16 41 56	2
18 49 3	20 51 17	22 41 40	0 43 53	2 42 10	4 44 23	6 42 40	8 44 53	10 47 6	12 45 23	14 47 36	16 45 53	3
18 53 0	20 55 13	22 45 37	0 47 50	2 46 7	4 48 20	6 46 37	8 48 50	10 51 3	12 49 20	14 51 33	16 49 50	4
18 56 56	20 59 10	22 49 33	0 51 46	2 50 3	4 52 16	6 50 33	8 52 46	10 55 0	12 53 16	14 55 29	16 53 46	5
19 0 53	21 3 6	22 53 30	0 55 43	2 54 0	4 56 13	6 54 30	8 56 43	10 58 56	12 57 13	14 59 26	16 57 43	6
19 4 50	21 7 3	22 57 26	0 59 40	2 57 56	5 0 9	6 58 26	9 0 39	11 2 53	13 1 9	15 3 23	17 1 39	7
19 8 46	21 10 59	23 1 23	1 3 36	3 1 53	5 4 6	7 2 23	9 4 36	11 6 49	13 5 6	15 7 19	17 5 36	8
19 12 43	21 14 56	23 5 19	1 7 33	3 5 49	5 8 3	7 6 19	9 8 33	11 10 46	13 9 2	15 11 16	17 9 32	9
19 16 39	21 18 52	23 9 16	1 11 29	3 9 46	5 11 59	7 10 16	9 12 29	11 14 42	13 12 59	15 15 12	17 13 29	10
19 20 36	21 22 49	23 13 13	1 15 26	3 13 42	5 15 56	7 14 12	9 16 26	11 18 39	13 16 56	15 19 9	17 17 25	11
19 24 32	21 26 46	23 17 9	1 19 22	3 17 39	5 19 52	7 18 9	9 20 22	11 22 35	13 20 52	15 23 5	17 21 22	12
19 28 29	21 30 42	23 21 6	1 23 19	3 21 36	5 23 49	7 22 6	9 24 19	11 26 32	13 24 49	15 27 2	17 25 19	13
19 32 25	21 34 39	23 25 2	1 27 15	3 25 32	5 27 45	7 26 2	9 28 15	11 30 29	13 28 45	15 30 58	17 29 15	14
19 36 22	21 38 35	23 28 59	1 31 12	3 29 29	5 31 42	7 29 59	9 32 12	11 34 25	13 32 42	15 34 55	17 33 12	15
19 40 19	21 42 32	23 32 55	1 35 9	3 33 25	5 35 38	7 33 55	9 36 9	11 38 22	13 36 38	15 38 52	17 37 8	16
19 44 15	21 46 28	23 36 52	1 39 5	3 37 22	5 39 35	7 37 52	9 40 5	11 42 18	13 40 35	15 42 48	17 41 5	17
19 48 12	21 50 25	23 40 48	1 43 2	3 41 18	5 43 32	7 41 48	9 44 2	11 46 15	13 44 31	15 46 45	17 45 1	18
19 52 8	21 54 21	23 44 45	1 46 58	3 45 15	5 47 28	7 45 45	9 47 58	11 50 11	13 48 28	15 50 41	17 48 58	19
19 56 5	21 58 18	23 48 42	1 50 55	3 49 11	5 51 25	7 49 41	9 51 55	11 54 8	13 52 25	15 54 38	17 52 55	20
20 0 1	22 2 15	23 52 38	1 54 51	3 53 8	5 55 21	7 53 38	9 55 51	11 58 4	13 56 21	15 58 34	17 56 51	21
20 3 58	22 6 11	23 56 35	1 58 48	3 57 5	5 59 18	7 57 35	9 59 48	12 2 1	14 0 18	16 2 31	18 0 48	22
20 7 54	22 10 8	0 0 31	2 2 44	4 1 1	6 3 14	8 1 31	10 3 44	12 5 58	14 4 14	16 6 27	18 4 44	23
20 11 51	22 14 4	0 4 28	2 6 41	4 4 58	6 7 11	8 5 28	10 7 41	12 9 54	14 8 11	16 10 24	18 8 41	24
20 15 48	22 18 1	0 8 24	2 10 38	4 8 54	6 11 8	8 9 24	10 11 37	12 13 51	14 12 7	16 14 21	18 12 37	25
20 19 44	22 21 57	0 12 21	2 14 34	4 12 51	6 15 4	8 13 21	10 15 34	12 17 47	14 16 4	16 18 17	18 16 34	26
20 23 41	22 25 54	0 16 17	2 18 31	4 16 47	6 19 1	8 17 17	10 19 31	12 21 44	14 20 0	16 22 14	18 20 30	27
20 27 37	22 29 50	0 20 14	2 22 27	4 20 44	6 22 57	8 21 14	10 23 27	12 25 40	14 23 57	16 26 10	18 24 27	28
20 31 34		0 24 11	2 26 24	4 24 40	6 26 54	8 25 10	10 27 24	12 29 37	14 27 54	16 30 7	18 28 24	29
20 35 30		0 28 7	2 30 20	4 28 37	6 30 50	8 29 7	10 31 20	12 33 33	14 31 50	16 34 3	18 32 20	30
20 39 27		0 32 4		4 32 34		8 33 4	10 35 17		14 35 47		18 36 17	31

1915

Jan.	Feb.	Mar.	April	May	June	July	Aug.	Sept.	Oct.	Nov.	Dec.	
18 40 13	20 42 27	22 32 50	0 35 3	2 33 20	4 35 33	6 33 50	8 36 3	10 38 16	12 36 33	14 38 46	16 37 3	1
18 44 10	20 46 23	22 36 47	0 39 0	2 37 16	4 39 30	6 37 46	8 40 0	10 42 13	12 40 30	14 42 43	16 40 59	2
18 48 6	20 50 20	22 40 43	0 42 56	2 41 13	4 43 26	6 41 43	8 43 56	10 46 9	12 44 26	14 46 39	16 44 56	3
18 52 3	20 54 16	22 44 40	0 46 53	2 45 10	4 47 23	6 45 40	8 47 53	10 50 6	12 48 23	14 50 36	16 48 53	4
18 55 59	20 58 13	22 48 36	0 50 49	2 49 6	4 51 19	6 49 36	8 51 49	10 54 3	12 52 19	14 54 32	16 52 49	5
18 59 56	21 2 9	22 52 33	0 54 46	2 53 2	4 55 16	6 53 33	8 55 46	10 57 59	12 56 16	14 58 29	16 56 46	6
19 3 53	21 6 6	22 56 29	0 58 43	2 56 59	4 59 12	6 57 29	8 59 42	11 1 56	13 0 12	15 2 26	17 0 42	7
19 7 49	21 10 2	23 0 26	1 2 39	3 0 56	5 3 9	7 1 26	9 3 39	11 5 52	13 4 9	15 6 22	17 4 39	8
19 11 46	21 13 59	23 4 22	1 6 36	3 4 52	5 7 6	7 5 22	9 7 36	11 9 49	13 8 5	15 10 19	17 8 35	9
19 15 42	21 17 56	23 8 19	1 10 32	3 8 49	5 11 2	7 9 19	9 11 32	11 13 45	13 12 2	15 14 15	17 12 32	10
19 19 39	21 21 52	23 12 16	1 14 29	3 12 45	5 14 59	7 13 15	9 15 29	11 17 42	13 15 59	15 18 12	17 16 28	11
19 23 35	21 25 49	23 16 12	1 18 25	3 16 42	5 18 55	7 17 12	9 19 25	11 21 38	13 19 55	15 22 8	17 20 25	12
19 27 32	21 29 45	23 20 9	1 22 22	3 20 39	5 22 52	7 21 9	9 23 22	11 25 35	13 23 52	15 26 5	17 24 22	13
19 31 28	21 33 42	23 24 5	1 26 18	3 24 35	5 26 48	7 25 5	9 27 18	11 29 32	13 27 48	15 30 1	17 28 18	14
19 35 25	21 37 38	23 28 2	1 30 15	3 28 32	5 30 45	7 29 2	9 31 15	11 33 28	13 31 45	15 33 58	17 32 15	15
19 39 22	21 41 35	23 31 58	1 34 12	3 32 28	5 34 42	7 32 58	9 35 12	11 37 25	13 35 41	15 37 55	17 36 11	16
19 43 18	21 45 31	23 35 55	1 38 8	3 36 25	5 38 38	7 36 55	9 39 8	11 41 21	13 39 38	15 41 51	17 40 8	17
19 47 15	21 49 28	23 39 51	1 42 5	3 40 21	5 42 35	7 40 51	9 43 5	11 45 18	13 43 34	15 45 48	17 44 4	18
19 51 11	21 53 25	23 43 48	1 46 1	3 44 18	5 46 31	7 44 48	9 47 1	11 49 14	13 47 31	15 49 44	17 48 1	19
19 55 8	21 57 21	23 47 45	1 49 58	3 48 14	5 50 28	7 48 44	9 50 58	11 53 11	13 51 28	15 53 41	17 51 57	20
19 59 4	22 1 18	23 51 41	1 53 54	3 52 11	5 54 24	7 52 41	9 54 54	11 57 7	13 55 24	15 57 37	17 55 54	21
20 3 1	22 5 14	23 55 38	1 57 51	3 56 8	5 58 21	7 56 38	9 58 51	12 1 4	13 59 21	16 1 34	17 59 51	22
20 6 57	22 9 11	23 59 34	2 1 47	4 0 4	6 2 17	8 0 34	10 2 47	12 5 1	14 3 17	16 5 30	18 3 47	23
20 10 54	22 13 7	0 3 31	2 5 44	4 4 1	6 6 14	8 4 31	10 6 44	12 8 57	14 7 14	16 9 27	18 7 44	24
20 14 51	22 17 4	0 7 27	2 9 41	4 7 57	6 10 11	8 8 27	10 10 40	12 12 54	14 11 10	16 13 24	18 11 40	25
20 18 47	22 21 0	0 11 24	2 13 37	4 11 54	6 14 7	8 12 24	10 14 37	12 16 50	14 15 7	16 17 20	18 15 37	26
20 22 44	22 24 57	0 15 21	2 17 34	4 15 50	6 18 4	8 16 20	10 18 34	12 20 47	14 19 3	16 21 17	18 19 33	27
20 26 40	22 28 54	0 19 17	2 21 30	4 19 47	6 22 0	8 20 17	10 22 30	12 24 43	14 23 0	16 25 13	18 23 30	28
20 30 37		0 23 14	2 25 27	4 23 43	6 25 57	8 24 13	10 26 27	12 28 40	14 26 57	16 29 10	18 27 27	29
20 34 33		0 27 10	2 29 23	4 27 40	6 29 53	8 28 10	10 30 23	12 32 36	14 30 53	16 33 6	18 31 23	30
20 38 30		0 31 7		4 31 37		8 32 7	10 34 20		14 34 50		18 35 20	31

1916

Jan.	Feb.	Mar.	April	May	June	July	Aug.	Sept.	Oct.	Nov.	Dec.	
18 39 16	20 41 29	22 35 50	0 38 3	2 36 19	4 38 33	6 36 49	8 39 3	10 41 16	12 39 32	14 41 46	16 40 2	1
18 43 13	20 45 26	22 39 46	0 41 59	2 40 16	4 42 29	6 40 46	8 42 59	10 45 12	12 43 29	14 45 42	16 43 59	2
18 47 9	20 49 23	22 43 43	0 45 56	2 44 12	4 46 26	6 44 42	8 46 56	10 49 9	12 47 26	14 49 39	16 47 55	3
18 51 6	20 53 19	22 47 39	0 49 52	2 48 9	4 50 22	6 48 39	8 50 52	10 53 6	12 51 22	14 53 35	16 51 52	4
18 55 2	20 57 16	22 51 36	0 53 49	2 52 6	4 54 19	6 52 36	8 54 49	10 57 2	12 55 19	14 57 32	16 55 49	5
18 58 59	21 1 12	22 55 32	0 57 46	2 56 2	4 58 15	6 56 32	8 58 45	11 0 59	12 59 15	15 1 28	16 59 45	6
19 2 56	21 5 9	22 59 29	1 1 42	2 59 59	5 2 12	7 0 29	9 2 42	11 4 55	13 3 12	15 5 25	17 3 42	7
19 6 52	21 9 5	23 3 25	1 5 39	3 3 55	5 6 9	7 4 25	9 6 39	11 8 52	13 7 8	15 9 22	17 7 38	8
19 10 49	21 13 2	23 7 22	1 9 35	3 7 52	5 10 5	7 8 22	9 10 35	11 12 48	13 11 5	15 13 18	17 11 35	9
19 14 45	21 16 58	23 11 19	1 13 32	3 11 48	5 14 2	7 12 18	9 14 32	11 16 45	13 15 1	15 17 15	17 15 31	10
19 18 42	21 20 55	23 15 15	1 17 28	3 15 45	5 17 58	7 16 15	9 18 28	11 20 41	13 18 58	15 21 11	17 19 28	11
19 22 38	21 24 52	23 19 12	1 21 25	3 19 41	5 21 55	7 20 12	9 22 25	11 24 38	13 22 55	15 25 8	17 23 24	12
19 26 35	21 28 48	23 23 8	1 25 21	3 23 38	5 25 51	7 24 8	9 26 21	11 28 34	13 26 51	15 29 4	17 27 21	13
19 30 31	21 32 45	23 27 5	1 29 18	3 27 35	5 29 48	7 28 5	9 30 18	11 32 31	13 30 48	15 33 1	17 31 18	14
19 34 28	21 36 41	23 31 1	1 33 14	3 31 31	5 33 44	7 32 1	9 34 14	11 36 28	13 34 44	15 36 57	17 35 14	15
19 38 25	21 40 38	23 34 58	1 37 11	3 35 28	5 37 41	7 35 58	9 38 11	11 40 23	13 38 41	15 40 54	17 39 11	16
19 42 21	21 44 34	23 38 54	1 41 8	3 39 24	5 41 38	7 39 54	9 42 8	11 44 21	13 42 37	15 44 51	17 43 7	17
19 46 18	21 48 31	23 42 51	1 45 4	3 43 21	5 45 34	7 43 51	9 46 4	11 48 17	13 46 34	15 48 47	17 47 4	18
19 50 14	21 52 27	23 46 48	1 49 1	3 47 17	5 49 31	7 47 47	9 50 1	11 52 14	13 50 30	15 52 44	17 51 0	19
19 54 11	21 56 24	23 50 44	1 52 57	3 51 14	5 53 27	7 51 44	9 53 57	11 56 10	13 54 27	15 56 40	17 54 57	20
19 58 7	22 0 21	23 54 41	1 56 54	3 55 10	5 57 24	7 55 41	9 57 54	12 0 7	13 58 24	16 0 37	17 58 53	21
20 2 4	22 4 17	23 58 37	2 0 50	3 59 7	6 1 20	7 59 37	10 1 50	12 4 3	14 2 20	16 4 33	18 2 50	22
20 6 0	22 8 14	0 2 34	2 4 47	4 3 4	6 5 17	8 3 34	10 5 47	12 8 0	14 6 17	16 8 30	18 6 47	23
20 9 57	22 12 10	0 6 30	2 8 43	4 7 0	6 9 13	8 7 30	10 9 43	12 11 57	14 10 13	16 12 26	18 10 43	24
20 13 54	22 16 7	0 10 27	2 12 40	4 10 57	6 13 10	8 11 27	10 13 40	12 15 53	14 14 10	16 16 23	18 14 40	25
20 17 50	22 20 3	0 14 23	2 16 37	4 14 53	6 17 7	8 15 23	10 17 37	12 19 50	14 18 6	16 20 20	18 18 36	26
20 21 47	22 24 0	0 18 20	2 20 33	4 18 50	6 21 3	8 19 20	10 21 33	12 23 46	14 22 3	16 24 16	18 22 33	27
20 25 43	22 27 56	0 22 17	2 24 30	4 22 46	6 25 0	8 23 16	10 25 30	12 27 43	14 25 59	16 28 13	18 26 29	28
20 29 40	22 31 53	0 26 13	2 28 26	4 26 43	6 28 56	8 27 13	10 29 26	12 31 39	14 29 56	16 32 9	18 30 26	29
20 33 36		0 30 10	2 32 23	4 30 40	6 32 53	8 31 10	10 33 23	12 35 36	14 33 53	16 36 6	18 34 23	30
20 37 33		0 34 6		4 34 36		8 35 6	10 37 19		14 37 49		18 38 19	31

1917

	Jan.	Feb.	Mar.	April	May	June	July	Aug.	Sept.	Oct.	Nov.	Dec.
1	18 42 16	20 44 29	22 34 52	0 37 6	2 35 22	4 37 35	6 35 52	8 38 5	10 40 19	12 38 35	14 40 48	16 39 5
2	18 46 12	20 48 25	22 38 49	0 41 2	2 39 19	4 41 32	6 39 49	8 42 2	10 44 15	12 42 32	14 44 45	16 43 2
3	18 50 9	20 52 22	22 42 46	0 44 59	2 43 15	4 45 29	6 43 45	8 45 59	10 48 12	12 46 28	14 48 42	16 46 58
4	18 54 5	20 56 19	22 46 42	0 48 55	2 47 12	4 49 25	6 47 42	8 49 55	10 52 8	12 50 25	14 52 38	16 50 55
5	18 58 2	21 0 15	22 50 39	0 52 52	2 51 8	4 53 22	6 51 38	8 53 52	10 56 5	12 54 21	14 56 35	16 54 51
6	19 1 58	21 4 12	22 54 35	0 56 48	2 55 5	4 57 18	6 55 35	8 57 48	11 0 1	12 58 18	15 0 31	16 58 48
7	19 5 55	21 8 8	22 58 32	1 0 45	2 59 2	5 1 15	6 59 32	9 1 45	11 3 58	13 2 15	15 4 28	17 2 44
8	19 9 52	21 12 5	23 2 28	1 4 41	3 2 58	5 5 11	7 3 28	9 5 41	11 7 55	13 6 11	15 8 24	17 6 41
9	19 13 48	21 16 1	23 6 25	1 8 38	3 6 55	5 9 8	7 7 25	9 9 38	11 11 51	13 10 8	15 12 21	17 10 38
10	19 17 45	21 19 58	23 10 21	1 12 35	3 10 51	5 13 4	7 11 21	9 13 34	11 15 48	13 14 4	15 16 17	17 14 34
11	19 21 41	21 23 54	23 14 18	1 16 31	3 14 48	5 17 1	7 15 18	9 17 31	11 19 44	13 18 1	15 20 14	17 18 31
12	19 25 38	21 27 51	23 18 15	1 20 28	3 18 44	5 20 58	7 19 14	9 21 28	11 23 41	13 21 57	15 24 11	17 22 27
13	19 29 34	21 31 48	23 22 11	1 24 24	3 22 41	5 24 54	7 23 11	9 25 24	11 27 37	13 25 54	15 28 7	17 26 24
14	19 33 31	21 35 44	23 26 8	1 28 21	3 26 37	5 28 51	7 27 7	9 29 21	11 31 34	13 29 50	15 32 4	17 30 20
15	19 37 27	21 39 41	23 30 4	1 32 17	3 30 34	5 32 47	7 31 4	9 33 17	11 35 30	13 33 47	15 36 0	17 34 17
16	19 41 24	21 43 37	23 34 1	1 36 14	3 34 31	5 36 44	7 35 1	9 37 14	11 39 27	13 37 44	15 39 57	17 38 13
17	19 45 21	21 47 34	23 37 57	1 40 10	3 38 27	5 40 40	7 38 57	9 41 10	11 43 24	13 41 40	15 43 53	17 42 10
18	19 49 17	21 51 30	23 41 54	1 44 7	3 42 24	5 44 37	7 42 54	9 45 7	11 47 20	13 45 37	15 47 50	17 46 7
19	19 53 14	21 55 27	23 45 50	1 48 4	3 46 20	5 48 34	7 46 50	9 49 3	11 51 17	13 49 33	15 51 46	17 50 3
20	19 57 10	21 59 23	23 49 47	1 52 0	3 50 17	5 52 30	7 50 47	9 53 0	11 55 13	13 53 30	15 55 43	17 54 0
21	20 1 7	22 3 20	23 53 44	1 55 57	3 54 13	5 56 27	7 54 43	9 56 57	11 59 10	13 57 26	15 59 40	17 57 56
22	20 5 3	22 7 17	23 57 40	1 59 53	3 58 10	6 0 23	7 58 40	10 0 53	12 3 6	14 1 23	16 3 36	18 1 53
23	20 9 0	22 11 13	0 1 37	2 3 50	4 2 6	6 4 20	8 2 36	10 4 50	12 7 3	14 5 19	16 7 33	18 5 49
24	20 12 56	22 15 10	0 5 33	2 7 46	4 6 3	6 8 16	8 6 33	10 8 46	12 10 59	14 9 16	16 11 29	18 9 46
25	20 16 53	22 19 6	0 9 30	2 11 43	4 10 0	6 12 13	8 10 30	10 12 43	12 14 56	14 13 13	16 15 26	18 13 43
26	20 20 50	22 23 3	0 13 26	2 15 39	4 13 56	6 16 9	8 14 26	10 16 39	12 18 53	14 17 9	16 19 22	18 17 39
27	20 24 46	22 26 59	0 17 23	2 19 36	4 17 53	6 20 6	8 18 23	10 20 36	12 22 49	14 21 6	16 23 19	18 21 36
28	20 28 43	22 30 56	0 21 19	2 23 33	4 21 49	6 24 3	8 22 19	10 24 32	12 26 46	14 25 2	16 27 15	18 25 32
29	20 32 39		0 25 16	2 27 29	4 25 46	6 27 59	8 26 16	10 28 29	12 30 42	14 28 59	16 31 12	18 29 29
30	20 36 36		0 29 12	2 31 26	4 29 42	6 31 56	8 30 12	10 32 26	12 34 39	14 32 55	16 35 9	18 33 25
31	20 40 32		0 33 9		4 33 39		8 34 9	10 36 22		14 36 52		18 37 22

1918

	Jan.	Feb.	Mar.	April	May	June	July	Aug.	Sept.	Oct.	Nov.	Dec.
1	18 41 18	20 43 32	22 33 55	0 36 8	2 34 25	4 36 38	6 34 55	8 37 8	10 39 21	12 37 38	14 39 51	16 38 8
2	18 45 15	20 47 28	22 37 52	0 40 5	2 38 22	4 40 35	6 38 51	8 41 5	10 43 18	12 41 35	14 43 48	16 42 4
3	18 49 12	20 51 25	22 41 48	0 44 1	2 42 18	4 44 31	6 42 48	8 45 1	10 47 14	12 45 31	14 47 44	16 46 1
4	18 53 8	20 55 21	22 45 45	0 47 58	2 46 15	4 48 28	6 46 45	8 48 58	10 51 11	12 49 28	14 51 41	16 49 57
5	18 57 5	20 59 18	22 49 41	0 51 55	2 50 11	4 52 24	6 50 41	8 52 54	10 55 8	12 53 24	14 55 37	16 53 54
6	19 1 1	21 3 15	22 53 38	0 55 51	2 54 8	4 56 21	6 54 38	8 56 51	10 59 4	12 57 21	14 59 34	16 57 51
7	19 4 58	21 7 11	22 57 35	0 59 48	2 58 4	5 0 18	6 58 34	9 0 48	11 3 1	13 1 17	15 3 30	17 1 47
8	19 8 54	21 11 8	23 1 31	1 3 44	3 2 1	5 4 14	7 2 31	9 4 44	11 6 57	13 5 14	15 7 27	17 5 44
9	19 12 51	21 15 4	23 5 28	1 7 41	3 5 57	5 8 11	7 6 27	9 8 41	11 10 54	13 9 10	15 11 24	17 9 40
10	19 16 47	21 19 1	23 9 24	1 11 37	3 9 54	5 12 7	7 10 24	9 12 37	11 14 50	13 13 7	15 15 20	17 13 37
11	19 20 44	21 22 57	23 13 21	1 15 34	3 13 51	5 16 4	7 14 20	9 16 34	11 18 47	13 17 3	15 19 17	17 17 33
12	19 24 41	21 26 54	23 17 17	1 19 30	3 17 47	5 20 0	7 18 17	9 20 30	11 22 43	13 21 0	15 23 13	17 21 30
13	19 28 37	21 30 50	23 21 14	1 23 27	3 21 44	5 23 57	7 22 14	9 24 27	11 26 40	13 24 57	15 27 10	17 25 26
14	19 32 34	21 34 47	23 25 10	1 27 24	3 25 40	5 27 53	7 26 10	9 28 23	11 30 37	13 28 53	15 31 6	17 29 23
15	19 36 30	21 38 43	23 29 7	1 31 20	3 29 37	5 31 50	7 30 7	9 32 20	11 34 33	13 32 50	15 35 3	17 33 20
16	19 40 27	21 42 40	23 33 4	1 35 17	3 33 33	5 35 47	7 34 3	9 36 17	11 38 30	13 36 46	15 38 59	17 37 16
17	19 44 23	21 46 37	23 37 0	1 39 13	3 37 30	5 39 43	7 38 0	9 40 13	11 42 26	13 40 43	15 42 56	17 41 13
18	19 48 20	21 50 33	23 40 57	1 43 10	3 41 26	5 43 40	7 41 56	9 44 10	11 46 23	13 44 39	15 46 53	17 45 9
19	19 52 16	21 54 30	23 44 53	1 47 6	3 45 23	5 47 36	7 45 53	9 48 6	11 50 19	13 48 36	15 50 49	17 49 6
20	19 56 13	21 58 26	23 48 50	1 51 3	3 49 20	5 51 33	7 49 50	9 52 3	11 54 16	13 52 32	15 54 46	17 53 2
21	20 0 10	22 2 23	23 52 46	1 54 59	3 53 16	5 55 29	7 53 46	9 55 59	11 58 12	13 56 29	15 58 42	17 56 59
22	20 4 6	22 6 19	23 56 43	1 58 56	3 57 13	5 59 26	7 57 43	9 59 56	12 2 9	14 0 26	16 2 39	18 0 56
23	20 8 3	22 10 16	0 0 39	2 2 53	4 1 9	6 3 22	8 1 39	10 3 52	12 6 6	14 4 22	16 6 35	18 4 52
24	20 11 59	22 14 12	0 4 36	2 6 49	4 5 6	6 7 19	8 5 36	10 7 49	12 10 2	14 8 19	16 10 32	18 8 49
25	20 15 56	22 18 9	0 8 32	2 10 46	4 9 2	6 11 16	8 9 32	10 11 45	12 13 59	14 12 15	16 14 28	18 12 45
26	20 19 52	22 22 6	0 12 29	2 14 42	4 12 59	6 15 12	8 13 29	10 15 42	12 17 55	14 16 12	16 18 25	18 16 42
27	20 23 49	22 26 2	0 16 26	2 18 39	4 16 55	6 19 9	8 17 25	10 19 39	12 21 52	14 20 8	16 22 22	18 20 38
28	20 27 45	22 29 59	0 20 22	2 22 35	4 20 52	6 23 5	8 21 22	10 23 35	12 25 48	14 25 4	16 26 18	18 24 35
29	20 31 42		0 24 19	2 26 32	4 24 49	6 27 2	8 25 19	10 27 32	12 29 45	14 28 1	16 30 15	18 28 31
30	20 35 39		0 28 15	2 30 28	4 28 45	6 30 58	8 29 15	10 31 28	12 33 41	14 31 58	16 34 11	18 32 28
31	20 39 35		0 32 12		4 32 42		8 33 12	10 35 25		14 35 55		18 36 25

1919

	Jan.	Feb.	Mar.	April	May	June	July	Aug.	Sept.	Oct.	Nov.	Dec.
1	18 40 21	20 42 34	22 32 58	0 35 11	2 33 28	4 35 41	6 33 58	8 36 11	10 38 24	12 36 41	14 38 54	16 37 10
2	18 44 18	20 46 31	22 36 54	0 39 8	2 37 24	4 39 37	6 37 54	8 40 7	10 42 21	12 40 37	14 42 50	16 41 7
3	18 48 14	20 50 27	22 40 51	0 43 4	2 41 21	4 43 34	6 41 51	8 44 4	10 46 17	12 44 34	14 46 47	16 45 3
4	18 52 11	20 54 24	22 44 48	0 47 1	2 45 17	4 47 30	6 45 47	8 48 0	10 50 14	12 48 30	14 50 43	16 49 0
5	18 56 7	20 58 21	22 48 44	0 50 57	2 49 14	4 51 27	6 49 44	8 51 57	10 54 10	12 52 27	14 54 40	16 52 57
6	19 0 4	21 2 17	22 52 41	0 54 54	2 53 10	4 55 24	6 53 40	8 55 54	10 58 7	12 56 23	14 58 36	16 56 53
7	19 4 0	21 6 14	22 56 37	0 58 50	2 57 7	4 59 20	6 57 37	8 59 50	11 2 3	13 0 20	15 2 33	17 0 50
8	19 7 57	21 10 10	23 0 34	1 2 47	3 1 3	5 3 17	7 1 33	9 3 47	11 6 0	13 4 16	15 6 30	17 4 46
9	19 11 54	21 14 7	23 4 30	1 6 43	3 5 0	5 7 13	7 5 30	9 7 43	11 9 56	13 8 13	15 10 26	17 8 43
10	19 15 50	21 18 3	23 8 27	1 10 40	3 8 57	5 11 10	7 9 27	9 11 40	11 13 53	13 12 10	15 14 23	17 12 39
11	19 19 47	21 22 0	23 12 23	1 14 37	3 12 53	5 15 6	7 13 23	9 15 36	11 17 49	13 16 6	15 18 19	17 16 36
12	19 23 43	21 25 56	23 16 20	1 18 33	3 16 50	5 19 3	7 17 20	9 19 33	11 21 46	13 20 3	15 22 16	17 20 32
13	19 27 40	21 29 53	23 20 16	1 22 30	3 20 46	5 22 59	7 21 16	9 23 29	11 25 43	13 23 59	15 26 12	17 24 29
14	19 31 36	21 33 50	23 24 13	1 26 26	3 24 43	5 26 56	7 25 13	9 27 26	11 29 39	13 27 56	15 30 9	17 28 26
15	19 35 33	21 37 46	23 28 10	1 30 23	3 28 39	5 30 53	7 29 9	9 31 23	11 33 36	13 31 52	15 34 5	17 32 22
16	19 39 29	21 41 43	23 32 6	1 34 19	3 32 36	5 34 49	7 33 6	9 35 19	11 37 32	13 35 49	15 38 2	17 36 19
17	19 43 26	21 45 39	23 36 3	1 38 16	3 36 32	5 38 46	7 37 2	9 39 16	11 41 29	13 39 45	15 41 59	17 40 15
18	19 47 23	21 49 36	23 39 59	1 42 12	3 40 29	5 42 42	7 40 59	9 43 12	11 45 25	13 43 42	15 45 55	17 44 12
19	19 51 19	21 53 32	23 43 56	1 46 9	3 44 26	5 46 39	7 44 56	9 47 9	11 49 22	13 47 38	15 49 52	17 48 8
20	19 55 16	21 57 29	23 47 52	1 50 5	3 48 22	5 50 35	7 48 52	9 51 5	11 53 18	13 51 35	15 53 48	17 52 5
21	19 59 12	22 1 25	23 51 49	1 54 2	3 52 19	5 54 32	7 52 49	9 55 2	11 57 15	13 55 32	15 57 45	17 56 1
22	20 3 9	22 5 22	23 55 45	1 57 59	3 56 15	5 58 29	7 56 45	9 58 58	12 1 12	13 59 28	16 1 41	17 59 58
23	20 7 5	22 9 19	23 59 42	2 1 55	4 0 12	6 2 25	8 0 42	10 2 55	12 5 8	14 3 25	16 5 38	18 3 55
24	20 11 2	22 13 15	0 3 39	2 5 52	4 4 8	6 6 22	8 4 38	10 6 52	12 9 5	14 7 21	16 9 34	18 7 51
25	20 14 58	22 17 12	0 7 35	2 9 48	4 8 5	6 10 18	8 8 35	10 10 48	12 13 1	14 11 18	16 13 31	18 11 48
26	20 18 55	22 21 8	0 11 32	2 13 45	4 12 1	6 14 15	8 12 31	10 14 45	12 16 58	14 15 14	16 17 28	18 15 44
27	20 22 52	22 25 5	0 15 28	2 17 41	4 15 58	6 18 11	8 16 28	10 18 41	12 20 54	14 19 11	16 21 24	18 19 41
28	20 26 48	22 29 1	0 19 25	2 21 38	4 19 55	6 22 8	8 20 25	10 22 38	12 24 51	14 23 7	16 25 21	18 23 37
29	20 30 45		0 23 21	2 25 34	4 23 51	6 26 4	8 24 21	10 26 34	12 28 47	14 27 4	16 29 17	18 27 34
30	20 34 41		0 27 18	2 29 31	4 27 48	6 30 1	8 28 18	10 30 31	12 32 44	14 31 1	16 33 14	18 31 31
31	20 38 38		0 31 14		4 31 44		8 32 14	10 34 27		14 34 57		18 35 27

1920

Day	Jan.	Feb.	Mar.	April	May	June	July	Aug.	Sept.	Oct.	Nov.	Dec.
1	18 39 24	20 41 37	22 35 57	0 38 10	2 36 27	4 38 40	6 36 57	8 39 10	10 41 23	12 39 40	14 41 53	16 40 9
2	18 43 20	20 45 33	22 39 53	0 42 7	2 40 23	4 42 36	6 40 53	8 43 6	10 45 20	12 43 36	14 45 49	16 44 6
3	18 47 17	20 49 30	22 43 50	0 46 3	2 44 20	4 46 33	6 44 50	8 47 3	10 49 16	12 47 33	14 49 46	16 48 2
4	18 51 13	20 53 27	22 47 47	0 50 0	2 48 16	4 50 30	6 48 46	8 50 59	10 53 13	12 51 29	14 53 42	16 51 59
5	18 55 10	20 57 23	22 51 43	0 53 56	2 52 13	4 54 26	6 52 43	8 54 56	10 57 9	12 55 26	14 57 39	16 55 56
6	18 59 6	21 1 20	22 55 40	0 57 53	2 56 9	4 58 23	6 56 39	8 58 53	11 1 6	12 59 22	15 1 35	16 59 52
7	19 3 3	21 5 16	22 59 36	1 1 49	3 0 6	5 2 19	7 0 36	9 2 49	11 5 2	13 3 19	15 5 32	17 3 49
8	19 7 0	21 9 13	23 3 33	1 5 46	3 4 3	5 6 16	7 4 32	9 6 46	11 8 59	13 7 15	15 9 29	17 7 45
9	19 10 56	21 13 9	23 7 29	1 9 42	3 7 59	5 10 12	7 8 29	9 10 42	11 12 56	13 11 12	15 13 25	17 11 42
10	19 14 53	21 17 6	23 11 26	1 13 39	3 11 56	5 14 9	7 12 26	9 14 39	11 16 52	13 15 9	15 17 22	17 15 38
11	19 18 49	21 21 2	23 15 22	1 17 36	3 15 52	5 18 5	7 16 22	9 18 35	11 20 49	13 19 5	15 21 18	17 19 35
12	19 22 46	21 24 59	23 19 19	1 21 32	3 19 49	5 22 2	7 20 19	9 22 32	11 24 45	13 23 2	15 25 15	17 23 31
13	19 26 42	21 28 56	23 23 16	1 25 29	3 23 45	5 25 59	7 24 15	9 26 28	11 28 42	13 26 58	15 29 11	17 27 28
14	19 30 39	21 32 52	23 27 12	1 29 25	3 27 42	5 29 55	7 28 12	9 30 25	11 32 38	13 30 55	15 33 8	17 31 25
15	19 34 35	21 36 49	23 31 9	1 33 22	3 31 38	5 33 52	7 32 8	9 34 22	11 36 35	13 34 51	15 37 4	17 35 21
16	19 38 32	21 40 45	23 35 5	1 37 18	3 35 35	5 37 48	7 36 5	9 38 18	11 40 31	13 38 48	15 41 1	17 39 18
17	19 42 29	21 44 42	23 39 2	1 41 15	3 39 32	5 41 45	7 40 1	9 42 15	11 44 28	13 42 44	15 44 58	17 43 14
18	19 46 25	21 48 38	23 42 58	1 45 11	3 43 28	5 45 41	7 43 58	9 46 11	11 48 24	13 46 41	15 48 54	17 47 11
19	19 50 22	21 52 35	23 46 55	1 49 8	3 47 25	5 49 38	7 47 55	9 50 8	11 52 21	13 50 37	15 52 51	17 51 7
20	19 54 18	21 56 31	23 50 51	1 53 5	3 51 21	5 53 34	7 51 51	9 54 4	11 56 17	13 54 34	15 56 47	17 55 4
21	19 58 15	22 0 28	23 54 48	1 57 1	3 55 18	5 57 31	7 55 48	9 58 1	12 0 14	13 58 31	16 0 44	17 59 0
22	20 2 11	22 4 25	23 58 45	2 0 58	3 59 14	6 1 28	7 59 44	10 1 57	12 4 11	14 2 27	16 4 40	18 2 57
23	20 6 8	22 8 21	0 2 41	2 4 54	4 3 11	6 5 24	8 3 41	10 5 54	12 8 7	14 6 24	16 8 37	18 6 54
24	20 10 4	22 12 18	0 6 38	2 8 51	4 7 7	6 9 21	8 7 37	10 9 51	12 12 4	14 10 20	16 12 33	18 10 50
25	20 14 1	22 16 14	0 10 34	2 12 47	4 11 4	6 13 17	8 11 34	10 13 47	12 16 0	14 14 17	16 16 30	18 14 47
26	20 17 58	22 20 11	0 14 31	2 16 44	4 15 1	6 17 14	8 15 30	10 17 44	12 19 57	14 18 13	16 20 27	18 18 43
27	20 21 54	22 24 7	0 18 27	2 20 40	4 18 57	6 21 10	8 19 27	10 21 40	12 23 53	14 22 10	16 24 23	18 22 40
28	20 25 51	22 28 4	0 22 24	2 24 37	4 22 54	6 25 7	8 23 24	10 25 37	12 27 50	14 26 6	16 28 20	18 26 36
29	20 29 47	22 32 0	0 26 20	2 28 34	4 26 50	6 29 3	8 27 20	10 29 33	12 31 46	14 30 3	16 32 16	18 30 33
30	20 33 44		0 30 17	2 32 30	4 30 47	6 33 0	8 31 17	10 33 30	12 35 43	14 34 0	16 36 13	18 34 30
31	20 37 40		0 34 14		4 34 43		8 35 13	10 37 26		14 37 56		18 38 26

1921

Day	Jan.	Feb.	Mar.	April	May	June	July	Aug.	Sept.	Oct.	Nov.	Dec.
1	18 42 23	20 44 36	22 34 59	0 37 12	2 35 29	4 37 42	6 35 59	8 38 12	10 40 25	12 38 42	14 40 55	16 39 12
2	18 46 19	20 48 32	22 38 56	0 41 9	2 39 26	4 41 39	6 39 56	8 42 9	10 44 22	12 42 38	14 44 52	16 43 8
3	18 50 16	20 52 29	22 42 52	0 45 6	2 43 22	4 45 35	6 43 52	8 46 5	10 48 18	12 46 35	14 48 48	16 47 5
4	18 54 12	20 56 26	22 46 49	0 49 2	2 47 19	4 49 32	6 47 49	8 50 2	10 52 15	12 50 32	14 52 45	16 51 1
5	18 58 9	21 0 22	22 50 46	0 52 59	2 51 15	4 53 29	6 51 45	8 53 58	10 56 12	12 54 28	14 56 41	16 54 58
6	19 2 5	21 4 19	22 54 42	0 56 55	2 55 12	4 57 25	6 55 42	8 57 55	11 0 8	12 58 25	15 0 38	16 58 55
7	19 6 2	21 8 15	22 58 39	1 0 52	2 59 8	5 1 22	6 59 38	9 1 52	11 4 5	13 2 21	15 4 34	17 2 51
8	19 9 59	21 12 12	23 2 35	1 4 48	3 3 5	5 5 18	7 3 35	9 5 48	11 8 1	13 6 18	15 8 31	17 6 48
9	19 13 55	21 16 8	23 6 32	1 8 45	3 7 1	5 9 15	7 7 31	9 9 45	11 11 58	13 10 14	15 12 28	17 10 44
10	19 17 52	21 20 5	23 10 28	1 12 41	3 10 58	5 13 11	7 11 28	9 13 41	11 15 54	13 14 11	15 16 24	17 14 41
11	19 21 48	21 24 1	23 14 25	1 16 38	3 14 55	5 17 8	7 15 25	9 17 38	11 19 51	13 18 7	15 20 21	17 18 37
12	19 25 45	21 27 58	23 18 21	1 20 35	3 18 51	5 21 4	7 19 21	9 21 34	11 23 47	13 22 4	15 24 17	17 22 34
13	19 29 41	21 31 55	23 22 18	1 24 31	3 22 48	5 25 1	7 23 18	9 25 31	11 27 44	13 26 1	15 28 14	17 26 30
14	19 33 38	21 35 51	23 26 15	1 28 28	3 26 44	5 28 58	7 27 14	9 29 27	11 31 41	13 29 57	15 32 10	17 30 27
15	19 37 34	21 39 48	23 30 11	1 32 24	3 30 41	5 32 54	7 31 11	9 33 24	11 35 37	13 33 54	15 36 7	17 34 24
16	19 41 31	21 43 44	23 34 8	1 36 21	3 34 37	5 36 51	7 35 7	9 37 21	11 39 34	13 37 50	15 40 3	17 38 20
17	19 45 28	21 47 41	23 38 4	1 40 17	3 38 34	5 40 47	7 39 4	9 41 17	11 43 30	13 41 47	15 44 0	17 42 17
18	19 49 24	21 51 37	23 42 1	1 44 14	3 42 30	5 44 44	7 43 0	9 45 14	11 47 27	13 45 43	15 47 57	17 46 13
19	19 53 21	21 55 34	23 45 57	1 48 10	3 46 27	5 48 40	7 46 57	9 49 10	11 51 23	13 49 40	15 51 53	17 50 10
20	19 57 17	21 59 30	23 49 54	1 52 7	3 50 24	5 52 37	7 50 54	9 53 7	11 55 20	13 53 36	15 55 50	17 54 6
21	20 1 14	22 3 27	23 53 50	1 56 4	3 54 20	5 56 33	7 54 50	9 57 3	11 59 16	13 57 33	15 59 46	17 58 3
22	20 5 10	22 7 24	23 57 47	2 0 0	3 58 17	6 0 30	7 58 47	10 1 0	12 3 13	14 1 30	16 3 43	18 1 59
23	20 9 7	22 11 20	0 1 44	2 3 57	4 2 13	6 4 27	8 2 43	10 4 56	12 7 10	14 5 26	16 7 39	18 5 56
24	20 13 3	22 15 17	0 5 40	2 7 53	4 6 10	6 8 23	8 6 40	10 8 53	12 11 6	14 9 23	16 11 36	18 9 53
25	20 17 0	22 19 13	0 9 37	2 11 50	4 10 6	6 12 20	8 10 36	10 12 50	12 15 3	14 13 19	16 15 32	18 13 49
26	20 20 57	22 23 10	0 13 33	2 15 46	4 14 3	6 16 16	8 14 33	10 16 46	12 18 59	14 17 16	16 19 29	18 17 46
27	20 24 53	22 27 6	0 17 30	2 19 43	4 17 60	6 20 13	8 18 29	10 20 43	12 22 56	14 21 12	16 23 26	18 21 42
28	20 28 50	22 31 3	0 21 26	2 23 39	4 21 56	6 24 9	8 22 26	10 24 39	12 26 52	14 25 9	16 27 22	18 25 39
29	20 32 46		0 25 23	2 27 36	4 25 53	6 28 6	8 26 23	10 28 36	12 30 49	14 29 5	16 31 19	18 29 35
30	20 36 43		0 29 19	2 31 33	4 29 49	6 32 2	8 30 19	10 32 32	12 34 45	14 33 2	16 35 15	18 33 32
31	20 40 39		0 33 16		4 33 46		8 34 16	10 36 29		14 36 59		18 37 28

1922

Day	Jan.	Feb.	Mar.	April	May	June	July	Aug.	Sept.	Oct.	Nov.	Dec.
1	18 41 25	20 43 38	22 34 2	0 36 15	2 34 31	4 36 45	6 35 1	8 37 15	10 39 28	12 37 44	14 39 57	16 38 14
2	18 45 22	20 47 35	22 37 58	0 40 11	2 38 28	4 40 41	6 38 58	8 41 11	10 43 24	12 41 41	14 43 54	16 42 11
3	18 49 18	20 51 31	22 41 55	0 44 8	2 42 25	4 44 38	6 42 54	8 45 8	10 47 21	12 45 37	14 47 51	16 46 7
4	18 53 15	20 55 28	22 45 51	0 48 5	2 46 21	4 48 34	6 46 51	8 49 4	10 51 17	12 49 34	14 51 47	16 50 4
5	18 57 11	20 59 24	22 49 48	0 52 1	2 50 18	4 52 31	6 50 48	8 53 1	10 55 14	12 53 30	14 55 44	16 54 0
6	19 1 8	21 3 21	22 53 45	0 55 58	2 54 14	4 56 27	6 54 44	8 56 57	10 59 10	12 57 27	14 59 40	16 57 57
7	19 5 4	21 7 18	22 57 41	0 59 54	2 58 11	5 0 24	6 58 41	9 0 54	11 3 7	13 1 24	15 3 37	17 1 53
8	19 9 1	21 11 14	23 1 38	1 3 51	3 2 7	5 4 21	7 2 37	9 4 50	11 7 4	13 5 20	15 7 33	17 5 50
9	19 12 57	21 15 11	23 5 34	1 7 47	3 6 4	5 8 17	7 6 34	9 8 47	11 11 0	13 9 17	15 11 30	17 9 47
10	19 16 54	21 19 7	23 9 31	1 11 44	3 10 0	5 12 14	7 10 30	9 12 44	11 14 57	13 13 13	15 15 26	17 13 43
11	19 20 51	21 23 4	23 13 27	1 15 40	3 13 57	5 16 10	7 14 27	9 16 40	11 18 53	13 17 10	15 19 23	17 17 40
12	19 24 47	21 27 0	23 17 24	1 19 37	3 17 54	5 20 7	7 18 23	9 20 37	11 22 50	13 21 6	15 23 20	17 21 36
13	19 28 44	21 30 57	23 21 20	1 23 33	3 21 50	5 24 3	7 22 20	9 24 33	11 26 46	13 25 3	15 27 16	17 25 33
14	19 32 40	21 34 53	23 25 17	1 27 30	3 25 47	5 28 0	7 26 17	9 28 30	11 30 43	13 28 59	15 31 13	17 29 29
15	19 36 37	21 38 50	23 29 13	1 31 27	3 29 43	5 31 56	7 30 13	9 32 26	11 34 39	13 32 56	15 35 9	17 33 26
16	19 40 33	21 42 47	23 33 10	1 35 23	3 33 40	5 35 53	7 34 10	9 36 23	11 38 36	13 36 53	15 39 6	17 37 22
17	19 44 30	21 46 43	23 37 7	1 39 20	3 37 36	5 39 50	7 38 6	9 40 19	11 42 33	13 40 49	15 43 2	17 41 19
18	19 48 26	21 50 40	23 41 3	1 43 16	3 41 33	5 43 46	7 42 3	9 44 16	11 46 29	13 44 46	15 46 59	17 45 16
19	19 52 23	21 54 36	23 45 0	1 47 13	3 45 29	5 47 43	7 45 59	9 48 13	11 50 26	13 48 42	15 50 55	17 49 12
20	19 56 20	21 58 33	23 48 56	1 51 9	3 49 26	5 51 39	7 49 56	9 52 9	11 54 22	13 52 39	15 54 52	17 53 9
21	20 0 16	22 2 29	23 52 53	1 55 6	3 53 23	5 55 36	7 53 52	9 56 6	11 58 19	13 56 35	15 58 49	17 57 5
22	20 4 13	22 6 26	23 56 49	1 59 2	3 57 19	5 59 32	7 57 49	10 0 2	12 2 15	14 0 32	16 2 45	18 1 2
23	20 8 9	22 10 22	0 0 46	2 2 59	4 1 16	6 3 29	8 1 46	10 3 59	12 6 12	14 4 28	16 6 42	18 4 58
24	20 12 6	22 14 19	0 4 42	2 6 56	4 5 12	6 7 25	8 5 42	10 7 55	12 10 8	14 8 25	16 10 38	18 8 55
25	20 16 2	22 18 16	0 8 39	2 10 52	4 9 9	6 11 22	8 9 39	10 11 52	12 14 5	14 12 22	16 14 35	18 12 51
26	20 19 59	22 22 12	0 12 36	2 14 49	4 13 5	6 15 19	8 13 35	10 15 48	12 18 2	14 16 18	16 18 31	18 16 48
27	20 23 55	22 26 9	0 16 32	2 18 45	4 17 2	6 19 15	8 17 32	10 19 45	12 21 58	14 20 15	16 22 28	18 20 45
28	20 27 52	22 30 5	0 20 29	2 22 42	4 20 58	6 23 12	8 21 28	10 23 42	12 25 55	14 24 11	16 26 24	18 24 41
29	20 31 49		0 24 25	2 26 38	4 24 55	6 27 8	8 25 25	10 27 38	12 29 51	14 28 8	16 30 21	18 28 38
30	20 35 45		0 28 22	2 30 35	4 28 52	6 31 5	8 29 21	10 31 35	12 33 48	14 32 4	16 34 18	18 32 34
31	20 39 42		0 32 18		4 32 48		8 33 18	10 35 31		14 36 1		18 36 31

1923	Jan.	Feb.	Mar.	April	May	June	July	Aug.	Sept.	Oct.	Nov.	Dec.
1	18 40 27	20 42 41	22 33 4	0 35 17	2 33 34	4 35 47	6 34 4	8 36 17	10 38 30	12 36 47	14 39 0	16 37 16
2	18 44 24	20 46 37	22 37 1	0 39 14	2 37 30	4 39 44	6 38 0	8 40 13	10 42 27	12 40 43	14 42 56	16 41 13
3	18 48 20	20 50 34	22 40 57	0 43 10	2 41 27	4 43 40	6 41 57	8 44 10	10 46 23	12 44 40	14 46 53	16 45 10
4	18 52 17	20 54 30	22 44 54	0 47 7	2 45 23	4 47 37	6 45 53	8 48 7	10 50 20	12 48 36	14 50 49	16 49 6
5	18 56 14	20 58 27	22 48 50	0 51 3	2 49 20	4 51 33	6 49 50	8 52 3	10 54 16	12 52 33	14 54 46	16 53 3
6	19 0 10	21 2 23	22 52 47	0 55 0	2 53 17	4 55 30	6 53 46	8 56 0	10 58 13	12 56 29	12 58 43	16 56 59
7	19 4 7	21 6 20	22 56 43	0 58 57	2 57 13	4 59 26	6 57 43	8 59 56	11 2 9	13 0 26	15 2 39	17 0 56
8	19 8 3	21 10 16	23 0 40	1 2 53	3 1 10	5 3 23	7 1 40	9 3 53	11 6 6	13 4 23	15 6 36	17 4 52
9	19 12 0	21 14 13	23 4 37	1 6 50	3 5 6	5 7 19	7 5 36	9 7 49	11 10 3	13 8 19	15 10 32	17 8 49
10	19 15 56	21 18 10	23 8 33	1 10 46	3 9 3	5 11 16	7 9 33	9 11 46	11 13 59	13 12 16	15 14 29	17 12 45
11	19 19 53	21 22 6	23 12 30	1 14 43	3 12 59	5 15 13	7 13 29	9 15 42	11 17 56	13 16 12	15 18 25	17 16 42
12	19 23 49	21 26 3	23 16 26	1 18 39	3 16 56	5 19 9	7 17 26	9 19 39	11 21 52	13 20 9	15 22 22	17 20 39
13	19 27 46	21 29 59	23 20 23	1 22 36	3 20 52	5 23 6	7 21 22	9 23 36	11 25 49	13 24 5	15 26 18	17 24 35
14	19 31 43	21 33 56	23 24 19	1 26 32	3 24 49	5 27 2	7 25 19	9 27 32	11 29 45	13 28 2	15 30 15	17 28 32
15	19 35 39	21 37 52	23 28 16	1 30 29	3 28 46	5 30 59	7 29 15	9 31 29	11 33 42	13 31 58	15 34 12	17 32 28
16	19 39 36	21 41 49	23 32 12	1 34 25	3 32 42	5 34 55	7 33 12	9 35 25	11 37 38	13 35 55	15 38 8	17 36 25
17	19 43 32	21 45 45	23 36 9	1 38 22	3 36 39	5 38 52	7 37 9	9 39 22	11 41 35	13 39 51	15 42 5	17 40 21
18	19 47 29	21 49 42	23 40 5	1 42 19	3 40 35	5 42 48	7 41 5	9 43 18	11 45 31	13 43 48	15 46 1	17 44 18
19	19 51 25	21 53 39	23 44 2	1 46 15	3 44 32	5 46 45	7 45 2	9 47 15	11 49 28	13 47 45	15 49 58	17 48 14
20	19 55 22	21 57 35	23 47 59	1 50 12	3 48 28	5 50 42	7 48 58	9 51 11	11 53 25	13 51 41	15 53 54	17 52 11
21	19 59 18	22 1 32	23 51 55	1 54 8	3 52 25	5 54 38	7 52 55	9 55 8	11 57 21	13 55 38	15 57 51	17 56 8
22	20 3 15	22 5 28	23 55 52	1 58 5	3 56 21	5 58 35	7 56 51	9 59 5	12 1 18	13 59 34	16 1 47	18 0 4
23	20 7 12	22 9 25	23 59 48	2 2 1	4 0 18	6 2 31	8 0 48	10 3 1	12 5 14	14 3 31	16 5 44	18 4 1
24	20 11 8	22 13 21	0 3 45	2 5 58	4 4 15	6 6 28	8 4 44	10 6 58	12 9 11	14 7 27	16 9 41	18 7 57
25	20 15 5	22 17 18	0 7 41	2 9 54	4 8 11	6 10 24	8 8 41	10 10 54	12 13 7	14 11 24	16 13 37	18 11 54
26	20 19 1	22 21 14	0 11 38	2 13 51	4 12 8	6 14 21	8 12 38	10 14 51	12 17 4	14 15 20	16 17 34	18 15 50
27	20 22 58	22 25 11	0 15 34	2 17 48	4 16 4	6 18 17	8 16 34	10 18 47	12 21 0	14 19 17	16 21 30	18 19 47
28	20 26 54	22 29 8	0 19 31	2 21 44	4 20 1	6 22 14	8 20 31	10 22 44	12 24 57	14 23 14	16 25 27	18 23 43
29	20 30 51		0 23 28	2 25 41	4 23 57	6 26 11	8 24 27	10 26 40	12 28 54	14 27 10	16 29 23	18 27 40
30	20 34 47		0 27 24	2 29 37	4 27 54	6 30 7	8 28 24	10 30 37	12 32 50	14 31 7	16 33 20	18 31 37
31	20 38 44		0 31 21		4 31 50		8 32 20	10 34 34		14 35 3		18 35 33

1924	Jan.	Feb.	Mar.	April	May	June	July	Aug.	Sept.	Oct.	Nov.	Dec.
1	18 39 30	20 41 43	22 36 3	0 38 16	2 36 33	4 38 46	6 37 3	8 39 16	10 41 29	12 39 46	14 41 59	16 40 15
2	18 43 26	20 45 40	22 40 0	0 42 13	2 40 29	4 42 42	6 40 59	8 43 12	10 45 26	12 43 42	14 45 55	16 44 12
3	18 47 23	20 49 36	22 43 56	0 46 9	2 44 26	4 46 39	6 44 56	8 47 9	10 49 22	12 47 39	14 49 52	16 48 9
4	18 51 19	20 53 33	22 47 53	0 50 6	2 48 22	4 50 36	6 48 52	8 51 6	10 53 19	12 51 35	14 53 48	16 52 5
5	18 55 16	20 57 29	22 51 49	0 54 2	2 52 19	4 54 32	6 52 49	8 55 2	10 57 15	12 55 32	14 57 45	16 56 2
6	18 59 12	21 1 26	22 55 46	0 57 59	2 56 15	4 58 29	6 56 45	8 58 59	11 1 12	12 59 28	15 1 42	16 59 58
7	19 3 9	21 5 22	22 59 42	1 1 55	3 0 12	5 2 25	7 0 42	9 2 55	11 5 8	13 3 25	15 5 38	17 3 55
8	19 7 6	21 9 19	23 3 39	1 5 52	3 4 9	5 6 22	7 4 39	9 6 52	11 9 5	13 7 21	15 9 35	17 7 51
9	19 11 2	21 13 15	23 7 35	1 9 49	3 8 5	5 10 18	7 8 35	9 10 48	11 13 1	13 11 18	15 13 31	17 11 48
10	19 14 59	21 17 12	23 11 32	1 13 45	3 12 2	5 14 15	7 12 32	9 14 45	11 16 58	13 15 15	15 17 28	17 15 44
11	19 18 55	21 21 8	23 15 29	1 17 42	3 15 58	5 18 11	7 16 28	9 18 41	11 20 55	13 19 11	15 21 24	17 19 41
12	19 22 52	21 25 5	23 19 25	1 21 38	3 19 55	5 22 8	7 20 25	9 22 38	11 24 51	13 23 8	15 25 21	17 23 38
13	19 26 48	21 29 2	23 23 22	1 25 35	3 23 51	5 26 5	7 24 21	9 26 35	11 28 48	13 27 4	15 29 17	17 27 34
14	19 30 45	21 32 58	23 27 18	1 29 31	3 27 48	5 30 1	7 28 18	9 30 31	11 32 44	13 31 1	15 33 14	17 31 31
15	19 34 42	21 36 55	23 31 15	1 33 28	3 31 44	5 33 58	7 32 14	9 34 28	11 36 41	13 34 57	15 37 10	17 35 27
16	19 38 38	21 40 51	23 35 11	1 37 24	3 35 41	5 37 54	7 36 11	9 38 24	11 40 37	13 38 54	15 41 7	17 39 24
17	19 42 35	21 44 48	23 39 8	1 41 21	3 39 38	5 41 51	7 40 8	9 42 21	11 44 34	13 42 50	15 45 4	17 43 20
18	19 46 31	21 48 44	23 43 4	1 45 18	3 43 34	5 45 47	7 44 4	9 46 17	11 48 30	13 46 47	15 49 0	17 47 17
19	19 50 28	21 52 41	23 47 1	1 49 14	3 47 31	5 49 44	7 48 1	9 50 14	11 52 27	13 50 44	15 52 57	17 51 13
20	19 54 24	21 56 37	23 50 57	1 53 11	3 51 27	5 53 40	7 51 57	9 54 10	11 56 24	13 54 40	15 56 53	17 55 10
21	19 58 21	22 0 34	23 54 54	1 57 7	3 55 24	5 57 37	7 55 54	9 58 7	12 0 20	13 58 37	16 0 50	17 59 7
22	20 2 17	22 4 31	23 58 51	2 1 4	3 59 20	6 1 34	7 59 50	10 2 4	12 4 17	14 2 33	16 4 46	18 3 3
23	20 6 14	22 8 27	0 2 47	2 5 0	4 3 17	6 5 30	8 3 47	10 6 0	12 8 13	14 6 30	16 8 43	18 7 0
24	20 10 11	22 12 24	0 6 44	2 8 57	4 7 13	6 9 27	8 7 43	10 9 57	12 12 10	14 10 26	16 12 40	18 10 56
25	20 14 7	22 16 20	0 10 40	2 12 53	4 11 10	6 13 23	8 11 40	10 13 53	12 16 6	14 14 23	16 16 36	18 14 53
26	20 18 4	22 20 17	0 14 37	2 16 50	4 15 7	6 17 20	8 15 37	10 17 50	12 20 3	14 18 19	16 20 33	18 18 49
27	20 22 0	22 24 13	0 18 33	2 20 46	4 19 3	6 21 16	8 19 33	10 21 46	12 23 59	14 22 16	16 24 29	18 22 46
28	20 25 57	22 28 10	0 22 30	2 24 43	4 23 0	6 25 13	8 23 30	10 25 43	12 27 56	14 26 13	16 28 26	18 26 42
29	20 29 53	22 32 6	0 26 26	2 28 40	4 26 56	6 29 10	8 27 26	10 29 39	12 31 52	14 30 9	16 32 22	18 30 39
30	20 33 50		0 30 23	2 32 36	4 30 53	6 33 6	8 31 23	10 33 36	12 35 49	14 34 6	16 36 19	18 34 36
31	20 37 46		0 34 20		4 34 49		8 35 19	10 37 32		14 38 2		18 38 32

1925	Jan.	Feb.	Mar.	April	May	June	July	Aug.	Sept.	Oct.	Nov.	Dec.
1	18 42 29	20 44 42	22 35 5	0 37 19	2 35 35	4 37 48	6 36 5	8 38 18	10 40 31	12 38 48	14 41 1	16 39 18
2	18 46 25	20 48 38	22 39 2	0 41 15	2 39 32	4 41 45	6 40 2	8 42 15	10 44 28	12 42 45	14 44 58	16 43 14
3	18 50 22	20 52 35	22 42 59	0 45 12	2 43 28	4 45 41	6 43 58	8 46 11	10 48 25	12 46 41	14 48 54	16 47 11
4	18 54 18	20 56 32	22 46 55	0 49 8	2 47 25	4 49 38	6 47 55	8 50 8	10 52 21	12 50 38	14 52 51	16 51 8
5	18 58 15	21 0 28	22 50 52	0 53 5	2 51 22	4 53 35	6 51 51	8 54 5	10 56 18	12 54 34	14 56 47	16 55 4
6	19 2 11	21 4 25	22 54 48	0 57 1	2 55 18	4 57 31	6 55 48	8 58 1	11 0 14	12 58 31	15 0 44	16 59 1
7	19 6 8	21 8 21	22 58 45	1 0 58	2 59 14	5 1 28	6 59 44	9 1 58	11 4 11	13 2 27	15 4 41	17 2 57
8	19 10 5	21 12 18	23 2 41	1 4 54	3 3 11	5 5 24	7 3 41	9 5 54	11 8 7	13 6 24	15 8 37	17 6 54
9	19 14 1	21 16 14	23 6 38	1 8 51	3 7 8	5 9 21	7 7 38	9 9 51	11 12 4	13 10 20	15 12 34	17 10 50
10	19 17 58	21 20 11	23 10 34	1 12 48	3 11 4	5 13 17	7 11 34	9 13 47	11 16 0	13 14 17	15 16 30	17 14 47
11	19 21 54	21 24 7	23 14 31	1 16 44	3 15 1	5 17 14	7 15 31	9 17 44	11 19 57	13 18 14	15 20 27	17 18 43
12	19 25 51	21 28 4	23 18 28	1 20 41	3 18 57	5 21 10	7 19 27	9 21 40	11 23 54	13 22 10	15 24 23	17 22 40
13	19 29 47	21 32 1	23 22 24	1 24 37	3 22 54	5 25 7	7 23 24	9 25 37	11 27 50	13 26 7	15 28 20	17 26 37
14	19 33 44	21 35 57	23 26 21	1 28 34	3 26 50	5 29 4	7 27 20	9 29 34	11 31 47	13 30 3	15 32 16	17 30 33
15	19 37 40	21 39 54	23 30 17	1 32 30	3 30 47	5 33 0	7 31 17	9 33 30	11 35 43	13 34 0	15 36 13	17 34 30
16	19 41 37	21 43 50	23 34 14	1 36 27	3 34 43	5 36 57	7 35 13	9 37 27	11 39 40	13 37 56	15 40 10	17 38 26
17	19 45 34	21 47 47	23 38 10	1 40 23	3 38 40	5 40 53	7 39 10	9 41 23	11 43 36	13 41 53	15 44 6	17 42 23
18	19 49 30	21 51 43	23 42 7	1 44 20	3 42 37	5 44 50	7 43 7	9 45 20	11 47 33	13 45 49	15 48 3	17 46 19
19	19 53 27	21 55 40	23 46 3	1 48 16	3 46 33	5 48 46	7 47 3	9 49 16	11 51 29	13 49 46	15 51 59	17 50 16
20	19 57 23	21 59 36	23 50 0	1 52 13	3 50 30	5 52 43	7 51 0	9 53 13	11 55 26	13 53 43	15 55 56	17 54 12
21	20 1 20	22 3 33	23 53 56	1 56 10	3 54 26	5 56 40	7 54 56	9 57 9	11 59 23	13 57 39	15 59 52	17 58 9
22	20 5 16	22 7 30	23 57 53	2 0 6	3 58 23	6 0 36	7 58 53	10 1 6	12 3 19	14 1 36	16 3 49	18 2 6
23	20 9 13	22 11 26	0 1 50	2 4 3	4 2 19	6 4 33	8 2 49	10 5 3	12 7 16	14 5 32	16 7 45	18 6 2
24	20 13 9	22 15 23	0 5 46	2 7 59	4 6 16	6 8 29	8 6 46	10 8 59	12 11 12	14 9 29	16 11 42	18 9 59
25	20 17 6	22 19 19	0 9 43	2 11 56	4 10 12	6 12 26	8 10 42	10 12 56	12 15 9	14 13 25	16 15 39	18 13 55
26	20 21 3	22 23 16	0 13 39	2 15 52	4 14 9	6 16 22	8 14 39	10 16 52	12 19 5	14 17 22	16 19 35	18 17 52
27	20 24 59	22 27 12	0 17 36	2 19 49	4 18 6	6 20 19	8 18 36	10 20 49	12 23 2	14 21 18	16 23 32	18 21 48
28	20 28 56	22 31 9	0 21 32	2 23 45	4 22 2	6 24 15	8 22 32	10 24 45	12 26 58	14 25 15	16 27 28	18 25 45
29	20 32 52		0 25 29	2 27 42	4 25 59	6 28 12	8 26 29	10 28 42	12 30 55	14 29 12	16 31 25	18 29 42
30	20 36 49		0 29 25	2 31 39	4 29 55	6 32 9	8 30 25	10 32 38	12 34 52	14 33 8	16 35 21	18 33 38
31	20 40 45		0 33 22		4 33 52		8 34 22	10 36 35		14 37 5		18 37 35

1926

Jan.	Feb.	Mar.	April	May	June	July	Aug.	Sept.	Oct.	Nov.	Dec.	
18 41 31	20 43 44	22 34 8	0 36 21	2 34 38	4 36 51	6 35 8	8 37 21	10 39 34	12 37 51	14 40 4	16 38 20	1
18 45 28	20 47 41	22 38 5	0 40 18	2 38 34	4 40 47	6 39 4	8 41 17	10 43 31	12 41 47	14 44 0	16 42 17	2
18 49 24	20 51 38	22 42 1	0 44 14	2 42 31	4 44 44	6 43 1	8 45 14	10 47 27	12 45 44	14 47 57	16 46 14	3
18 53 21	30 55 34	22 45 58	0 48 11	2 46 27	4 48 41	6 46 57	8 49 11	10 51 24	12 49 40	14 51 53	16 50 10	4
18 57 17	20 59 31	22 49 54	0 52 7	2 50 24	4 52 37	6 50 54	8 53 7	10 55 20	12 53 37	14 55 50	16 54 7	5
19 1 14	21 3 27	22 53 51	0 56 4	2 54 20	4 56 34	6 54 50	8 57 4	10 59 17	12 57 33	14 59 47	16 58 3	6
19 5 11	21 7 24	22 57 47	1 0 0	2 58 17	5 0 30	6 58 47	9 1 0	11 3 13	13 1 30	15 3 43	17 2 0	7
19 9 7	21 11 20	23 1 44	1 3 57	3 2 14	5 4 27	7 2 44	9 4 57	11 7 10	13 5 27	15 7 40	17 5 56	8
19 13 4	21 15 17	23 5 40	1 7 53	3 6 10	5 8 23	7 6 40	9 8 53	11 11 6	13 9 23	15 11 36	17 9 53	9
19 17 0	21 19 13	23 9 37	1 11 50	3 10 7	5 12 20	7 10 37	9 12 50	11 15 3	13 13 20	15 15 33	17 13 50	10
19 20 57	21 23 10	23 13 33	1 15 47	3 14 3	5 16 16	7 14 33	9 16 46	11 19 0	13 17 16	15 19 29	17 17 46	11
19 24 53	21 27 7	23 17 30	1 19 43	3 18 0	5 20 13	7 18 30	9 20 43	11 22 56	13 21 13	15 23 26	17 21 43	12
19 28 50	21 31 3	23 21 27	1 23 40	3 21 56	5 24 10	7 22 26	9 24 40	11 26 53	13 25 9	15 27 22	17 25 39	13
19 32 46	21 35 0	23 25 23	1 27 36	3 25 53	5 28 6	7 26 23	9 28 36	11 30 49	13 29 6	15 31 19	17 29 36	14
19 36 43	21 38 56	23 29 20	1 31 33	3 29 49	5 32 3	7 30 19	9 32 33	11 34 46	13 33 2	15 35 16	17 33 32	15
19 40 40	21 42 53	23 33 16	1 35 29	3 33 46	5 35 59	7 34 16	9 36 29	11 38 42	13 36 59	15 39 12	17 37 29	16
19 44 36	21 46 49	23 37 13	1 39 26	3 37 43	5 39 56	7 38 13	9 40 26	11 42 39	13 40 56	15 43 9	17 41 25	17
19 48 33	21 50 46	23 41 9	1 43 22	3 41 39	5 43 52	7 42 9	9 44 22	11 46 35	13 44 52	15 47 5	17 45 22	18
19 52 29	21 54 42	23 45 6	1 47 19	3 45 36	5 47 49	7 46 6	9 48 19	11 50 32	13 48 49	15 51 2	17 49 19	19
19 56 26	21 58 39	23 49 2	1 51 16	3 49 32	5 51 46	7 50 2	9 52 15	11 54 29	13 52 45	15 54 58	17 53 15	20
20 0 22	22 2 36	23 52 59	1 55 12	3 53 29	5 55 42	7 53 59	9 56 12	11 58 25	13 56 42	15 58 55	17 57 12	21
20 4 19	22 6 32	23 56 56	1 59 9	3 57 25	5 59 39	7 57 55	10 0 9	12 2 22	14 0 38	16 2 51	18 1 8	22
20 8 15	22 10 29	0 0 52	2 3 5	4 1 22	6 3 35	8 1 52	10 4 5	12 6 18	14 4 35	16 6 48	18 5 5	23
20 12 12	22 14 25	0 4 49	2 7 2	4 5 18	6 7 32	8 5 48	10 8 2	12 10 15	14 8 31	16 10 45	18 9 1	24
20 16 9	22 18 22	0 8 45	2 10 58	4 9 15	6 11 28	8 9 45	10 11 58	12 14 11	14 12 28	16 14 41	18 12 58	25
20 20 5	22 22 18	0 12 42	2 14 55	4 13 12	6 15 25	8 13 42	10 15 55	12 18 8	14 16 24	16 18 38	18 16 54	26
20 24 2	22 26 15	0 16 38	2 18 51	4 17 8	6 19 21	8 17 38	10 19 51	12 22 4	14 20 21	16 22 34	18 20 51	27
20 27 58	22 30 11	0 20 35	2 22 48	4 21 5	6 23 18	8 21 35	10 23 48	12 26 1	14 24 18	16 26 31	18 24 48	28
20 31 55		0 24 31	2 26 45	4 25 1	6 27 15	8 25 31	10 27 44	12 29 58	14 28 14	16 30 27	18 28 44	29
20 35 51		0 28 28	2 30 41	4 28 58	6 31 11	8 29 28	10 31 41	12 33 54	14 32 11	16 34 24	18 32 41	30
20 39 48		0 32 25		4 32 54		8 33 24	10 35 38		14 36 7		18 36 37	31

1927

Jan.	Feb.	Mar.	April	May	June	July	Aug.	Sept.	Oct.	Nov.	Dec.	
18 40 34	20 42 47	22 33 11	0 35 24	2 33 40	4 35 54	6 34 10	8 36 24	10 38 37	12 36 53	14 39 7	16 37 23	1
18 44 30	20 46 44	22 37 7	0 39 20	2 37 37	4 39 50	6 38 7	8 40 20	10 42 33	12 40 50	14 43 3	16 41 20	2
18 48 27	20 50 40	22 41 4	0 43 17	2 41 33	4 43 47	6 42 3	8 44 17	10 46 30	12 44 46	14 47 0	16 45 16	3
18 52 23	20 54 37	22 45 0	0 47 13	2 45 30	4 47 43	6 46 0	8 48 13	10 50 26	12 48 43	14 50 56	16 49 13	4
18 56 20	20 58 33	22 48 57	0 51 10	2 49 27	4 51 40	6 49 57	8 52 10	10 54 23	12 52 40	14 54 53	16 53 9	5
19 0 17	21 2 30	22 52 53	0 55 6	2 53 23	4 55 36	6 53 53	8 56 6	10 58 20	12 56 36	14 58 49	16 57 6	6
19 4 13	21 6 26	22 56 50	0 59 3	2 57 20	4 59 33	6 57 50	9 0 3	11 2 16	13 0 33	15 2 46	17 1 3	7
19 8 10	21 10 23	23 0 46	1 3 0	3 1 16	5 3 29	7 1 46	9 3 59	11 6 13	13 4 29	15 6 42	17 4 59	8
19 12 6	21 14 20	23 4 43	1 6 56	3 5 13	5 7 26	7 5 43	9 7 56	11 10 9	13 8 26	15 10 39	17 8 56	9
19 16 3	21 18 16	23 8 40	1 10 53	3 9 9	5 11 23	7 9 39	9 11 53	11 14 6	13 12 22	15 14 36	17 12 52	10
19 19 59	21 22 13	23 12 36	1 14 49	3 13 6	5 15 19	7 13 36	9 15 49	11 18 2	13 16 19	15 18 32	17 16 49	11
19 23 56	21 26 9	23 16 33	1 18 46	3 17 2	5 19 16	7 17 32	9 19 46	11 21 59	13 20 15	15 22 29	17 20 45	12
19 27 52	21 30 6	23 20 29	1 22 42	3 20 59	5 23 12	7 21 29	9 23 42	11 25 55	13 24 12	15 26 25	17 24 42	13
19 31 49	21 34 2	23 24 26	1 26 39	3 24 56	5 27 9	7 25 26	9 27 39	11 29 52	13 28 9	15 30 22	17 28 38	14
19 35 46	21 37 59	23 28 22	1 30 35	3 28 52	5 31 5	7 29 22	9 31 35	11 33 49	13 32 5	15 34 18	17 32 35	15
19 39 42	21 41 55	23 32 19	1 34 32	3 32 49	5 35 2	7 33 19	9 35 32	11 37 45	13 36 2	15 38 15	17 36 32	16
19 43 39	21 45 52	23 36 15	1 38 29	3 36 45	5 38 58	7 37 15	9 39 28	11 41 42	13 39 58	15 42 11	17 40 28	17
19 47 35	21 49 48	23 40 12	1 42 25	3 40 42	5 42 55	7 41 12	9 43 25	11 45 38	13 43 55	15 46 8	17 44 25	18
19 51 32	21 53 45	23 44 9	1 46 22	3 44 38	5 46 52	7 45 8	9 47 22	11 49 35	13 47 51	15 50 5	17 48 21	19
19 55 28	21 57 42	23 48 5	1 50 18	3 48 35	5 50 48	7 49 5	9 51 18	11 53 31	13 51 48	15 54 1	17 52 18	20
19 59 25	22 1 38	23 52 2	1 54 15	3 52 31	5 54 45	7 53 1	9 55 15	11 57 28	13 55 44	15 57 58	17 56 14	21
20 3 21	22 5 35	23 55 58	1 58 11	3 56 28	5 58 41	7 56 58	9 59 11	12 1 24	13 59 41	16 1 54	18 0 11	22
20 7 18	22 9 31	23 59 55	2 2 8	4 0 25	6 2 38	8 0 55	10 3 8	12 5 21	14 3 38	16 5 51	18 4 7	23
20 11 15	22 13 28	0 3 51	2 6 4	4 4 21	6 6 34	8 4 51	10 7 4	12 9 17	14 7 34	16 9 47	18 8 4	24
20 15 11	22 17 24	0 7 48	2 10 1	4 8 18	6 10 31	8 8 48	10 11 1	12 13 14	14 11 31	16 13 44	18 12 1	25
20 19 8	22 21 21	0 11 44	2 13 58	4 12 14	6 14 28	8 12 44	10 14 57	12 17 11	14 15 27	16 17 40	18 15 57	26
20 23 4	22 25 17	0 15 41	2 17 54	4 16 11	6 18 24	8 16 41	10 18 54	12 21 7	14 19 24	16 21 37	18 19 54	27
20 27 1	22 29 14	0 19 38	2 21 51	4 20 7	6 22 21	8 20 37	10 22 51	12 25 4	14 23 20	16 25 34	18 23 50	28
20 30 57		0 23 34	2 25 47	4 24 4	6 26 17	8 24 34	10 26 47	12 29 0	14 27 17	16 29 30	18 27 47	29
20 34 54		0 27 31	2 29 44	4 28 0	6 30 14	8 28 30	10 30 44	12 32 57	14 31 13	16 33 27	18 31 43	30
20 38 51		0 31 27		4 31 57		8 32 27	10 34 40		14 35 10		18 35 40	31

1928

Jan.	Feb.	Mar.	April	May	June	July	Aug.	Sept.	Oct.	Nov.	Dec.	
18 39 37	20 41 50	22 36 10	0 38 23	2 36 40	4 38 53	6 37 10	8 39 23	10 41 36	12 39 53	14 42 6	16 40 23	1
18 43 33	20 45 46	22 40 6	0 42 20	2 40 36	4 42 49	6 41 6	8 43 19	10 45 33	12 43 49	14 46 2	16 44 19	2
18 47 30	20 49 43	22 44 3	0 46 16	2 44 33	4 46 46	6 45 3	8 47 16	10 49 29	12 47 46	14 49 59	16 48 16	3
18 51 26	20 53 39	22 48 0	0 50 13	2 48 29	4 50 43	6 48 59	8 51 13	10 53 26	12 51 42	14 53 56	16 52 12	4
18 55 23	20 57 36	22 51 56	0 54 9	2 52 26	4 54 39	6 52 56	8 55 9	10 57 22	12 55 39	14 57 52	16 56 9	5
18 59 19	21 1 33	22 55 53	0 58 6	2 56 22	4 58 36	6 56 52	8 59 6	11 1 19	12 59 35	15 1 49	17 0 5	6
19 3 16	21 5 29	22 59 49	1 2 2	3 0 19	5 2 32	7 0 49	9 3 2	11 5 15	13 3 32	15 5 45	17 4 2	7
19 7 12	21 9 26	23 3 46	1 5 59	3 4 16	5 6 29	7 4 46	9 6 59	11 9 12	13 7 29	15 9 42	17 7 59	8
19 11 9	21 13 22	23 7 42	1 9 55	3 8 12	5 10 25	7 8 42	9 10 55	11 13 9	13 11 25	15 13 38	17 11 55	9
19 15 6	21 17 19	23 11 39	1 13 52	3 12 9	5 14 22	7 12 39	9 14 52	11 17 5	13 15 22	15 17 35	17 15 52	10
19 19 2	21 21 15	23 15 35	1 17 49	3 16 5	5 18 18	7 16 35	9 18 48	11 21 2	13 19 18	15 21 31	17 19 48	11
19 22 59	21 25 12	23 19 32	1 21 45	3 20 2	5 22 15	7 20 32	9 22 45	11 24 58	13 23 15	15 25 28	17 23 45	12
19 26 55	21 29 8	23 23 29	1 25 42	3 23 58	5 26 12	7 24 28	9 26 42	11 28 55	13 27 11	15 29 25	17 27 41	13
19 30 52	21 33 5	23 27 25	1 29 38	3 27 55	5 30 8	7 28 25	9 30 38	11 32 51	13 31 8	15 33 21	17 31 38	14
19 34 48	21 37 2	23 31 22	1 33 35	3 31 51	5 34 5	7 32 21	9 34 35	11 36 48	13 35 4	15 37 18	17 35 34	15
19 38 45	21 40 58	23 35 18	1 37 31	3 35 48	5 38 1	7 36 18	9 38 31	11 40 44	13 39 1	15 41 14	17 39 31	16
19 42 41	21 44 55	23 39 15	1 41 28	3 39 45	5 41 58	7 40 15	9 42 28	11 44 41	13 42 58	15 45 11	17 43 28	17
19 46 38	21 48 51	23 43 11	1 45 24	3 43 41	5 45 54	7 44 11	9 46 24	11 48 38	13 46 54	15 49 7	17 47 24	18
19 50 35	21 52 48	23 47 8	1 49 21	3 47 38	5 49 51	7 48 8	9 50 21	11 52 34	13 50 51	15 53 4	17 51 21	19
19 54 31	21 56 44	23 51 4	1 53 18	3 51 34	5 53 48	7 52 4	9 54 17	11 56 31	13 54 47	15 57 0	17 55 17	20
19 58 28	22 0 41	23 55 1	1 57 14	3 55 31	5 57 44	7 56 1	9 58 14	12 0 27	13 58 44	16 0 57	17 59 14	21
20 2 24	22 4 37	23 58 58	2 1 11	3 59 27	6 1 41	7 59 57	10 2 11	12 4 24	14 2 40	16 4 54	18 3 10	22
20 6 21	22 8 34	0 2 54	2 5 7	4 3 24	6 5 37	8 3 54	10 6 7	12 8 20	14 6 37	16 8 50	18 7 7	23
20 10 17	22 12 31	0 6 51	2 9 4	4 7 20	6 9 34	8 7 50	10 10 4	12 12 17	14 10 33	16 12 47	18 11 3	24
20 14 14	22 16 27	0 10 47	2 13 0	4 11 17	6 13 30	8 11 47	10 14 0	12 16 13	14 14 30	16 16 43	18 15 0	25
20 18 10	22 20 24	0 14 44	2 16 57	4 15 14	6 17 27	8 15 44	10 17 57	12 20 10	14 18 27	16 20 40	18 18 57	26
20 22 7	22 24 20	0 18 40	2 20 53	4 19 10	6 21 23	8 19 40	10 21 53	12 24 7	14 22 23	16 24 36	18 22 53	27
20 26 4	22 28 17	0 22 37	2 24 50	4 23 7	6 25 20	8 23 37	10 25 50	12 28 3	14 26 20	16 28 33	18 26 50	28
20 30 0	22 32 13	0 26 33	2 28 47	4 27 3	6 29 17	8 27 33	10 29 46	12 32 0	14 30 16	16 32 29	18 30 46	29
20 33 57		0 30 30	2 32 43	4 31 0	6 33 13	8 31 30	10 33 43	12 35 56	14 34 13	16 36 26	18 34 43	30
20 37 53		0 34 26		4 34 56		8 35 26	10 37 40		14 38 9		18 38 39	31

1929

	Jan.	Feb.	Mar.	April	May	June	July	Aug.	Sept.	Oct.	Nov.	Dec.
1	18 42 36	20 44 49	22 35 13	0 37 26	2 35 43	4 37 56	6 36 13	8 38 26	10 40 39	12 38 56	14 41 9	16 39 26
2	18 46 32	20 48 46	22 39 9	0 41 22	2 39 39	4 41 52	6 40 9	8 42 22	10 44 36	12 42 52	14 45 5	16 43 22
3	18 50 29	20 52 42	22 43 6	0 45 19	2 43 36	4 45 49	6 44 6	8 46 19	10 48 32	12 46 49	14 49 2	16 47 19
4	18 54 26	20 56 39	22 47 2	0 49 16	2 47 32	4 49 45	6 48 2	8 50 15	10 52 29	12 50 45	14 52 59	16 51 15
5	18 58 22	21 0 35	22 50 59	0 53 12	2 51 29	4 53 42	6 51 59	8 54 12	10 56 25	12 54 42	14 56 55	16 55 12
6	19 2 19	21 4 32	22 54 56	0 57 9	2 55 25	4 57 39	6 55 55	8 58 9	11 0 22	12 58 38	15 0 52	16 59 8
7	19 6 15	21 8 29	22 58 52	1 1 5	2 59 22	5 1 35	6 59 52	9 2 5	11 4 18	13 2 35	15 4 48	17 3 5
8	19 10 12	21 12 25	23 2 49	1 5 2	3 3 18	5 5 32	7 3 48	9 6 2	11 8 15	13 6 32	15 8 45	17 7 1
9	19 14 8	21 16 22	23 6 45	1 8 58	3 7 15	5 9 28	7 7 45	9 9 58	11 12 11	13 10 28	15 12 41	17 10 58
10	19 18 5	21 20 18	23 10 42	1 12 55	3 11 12	5 13 25	7 11 42	9 13 55	11 16 8	13 14 25	15 16 38	17 14 55
11	19 22 2	21 24 15	23 14 38	1 16 51	3 15 8	5 17 21	7 15 38	9 17 51	11 20 5	13 18 21	15 20 34	17 18 51
12	19 25 58	21 28 11	23 18 35	1 20 48	3 19 5	5 21 18	7 19 35	9 21 48	11 24 1	13 22 18	15 24 31	17 22 48
13	19 29 55	21 32 8	23 22 31	1 24 45	3 23 1	5 25 14	7 23 31	9 25 44	11 27 58	13 26 14	15 28 28	17 26 44
14	19 33 51	21 36 4	23 26 28	1 28 41	3 26 58	5 29 11	7 27 28	9 29 41	11 31 54	13 30 11	15 32 24	17 30 41
15	19 37 48	21 40 1	23 30 24	1 32 38	3 30 54	5 33 8	7 31 24	9 33 38	11 35 51	13 34 7	15 36 21	17 34 37
16	19 41 44	21 43 58	23 34 21	1 36 34	3 34 51	5 37 4	7 35 21	9 37 34	11 39 47	13 38 4	15 40 17	17 38 34
17	19 45 41	21 47 54	23 38 18	1 40 31	3 38 47	5 41 1	7 39 17	9 41 31	11 43 44	13 42 1	15 44 14	17 42 30
18	19 49 37	21 51 51	23 42 14	1 44 27	3 42 44	5 44 57	7 43 14	9 45 27	11 47 40	13 45 57	15 48 10	17 46 27
19	19 53 34	21 55 47	23 46 11	1 48 24	3 46 41	5 48 54	7 47 11	9 49 24	11 51 37	13 49 54	15 52 7	17 50 24
20	19 57 31	21 59 44	23 50 7	1 52 20	3 50 37	5 52 50	7 51 7	9 53 20	11 55 34	13 53 50	15 56 3	17 54 20
21	20 1 27	22 3 40	23 54 4	1 56 17	3 54 34	5 56 47	7 55 4	9 57 17	11 59 30	13 57 47	16 0 0	17 58 17
22	20 5 24	22 7 37	23 58 0	2 0 14	3 58 30	6 0 44	7 59 0	10 1 13	12 3 27	14 1 43	16 3 57	18 2 13
23	20 9 20	22 11 33	0 1 57	2 4 10	4 2 27	6 4 40	8 2 57	10 5 10	12 7 23	14 5 40	16 7 53	18 6 10
24	20 13 17	22 15 30	0 5 53	2 8 7	4 6 23	6 8 37	8 6 53	10 9 7	12 11 20	14 9 36	16 11 50	18 10 6
25	20 17 13	22 19 27	0 9 50	2 12 3	4 10 20	6 12 33	8 10 50	10 13 3	12 15 16	14 13 33	16 15 46	18 14 3
26	20 21 10	22 23 23	0 13 47	2 16 0	4 14 16	6 16 30	8 14 46	10 17 0	12 19 13	14 17 30	16 19 43	18 18 0
27	20 25 6	22 27 20	0 17 43	2 19 56	4 18 13	6 20 26	8 18 43	10 20 56	12 23 9	14 21 26	16 23 39	18 21 56
28	20 29 3	22 31 16	0 21 40	2 23 53	4 22 10	6 24 23	8 22 40	10 24 53	12 27 6	14 25 23	16 27 36	18 25 53
29	20 33 0		0 25 36	2 27 49	4 26 6	6 28 19	8 26 36	10 28 49	12 31 3	14 29 19	16 31 32	18 29 49
30	20 36 56		0 29 33	2 31 46	4 30 3	6 32 16	8 30 33	10 32 46	12 34 59	14 33 16	16 35 29	18 33 46
31	20 40 53		0 33 29		4 33 59		8 34 29	10 36 42		14 37 12		18 37 42

1930

	Jan.	Feb.	Mar.	April	May	June	July	Aug.	Sept.	Oct.	Nov.	Dec.
1	18 41 39	20 43 52	22 34 16	0 36 29	2 34 46	4 36 59	6 35 16	8 37 29	10 39 42	12 37 59	14 40 12	16 38 29
2	18 45 35	20 47 49	22 38 12	0 40 25	2 38 42	4 40 55	6 39 12	8 41 25	10 43 39	12 41 55	14 44 8	16 42 25
3	18 49 32	20 51 45	22 42 9	0 44 22	2 42 39	4 44 52	6 43 9	8 45 22	10 47 35	12 45 52	14 48 5	16 46 22
4	18 53 29	20 55 42	22 46 5	0 48 19	2 46 35	4 48 48	6 47 5	8 49 18	10 51 32	12 49 48	14 52 2	16 50 18
5	18 57 25	20 59 38	22 50 2	0 52 15	2 50 32	4 52 45	6 51 2	8 53 15	10 55 28	12 53 45	14 55 58	16 54 15
6	19 1 22	21 3 35	22 53 58	0 56 12	2 54 28	4 56 42	6 54 58	8 57 12	10 59 25	12 57 41	14 59 55	16 58 11
7	19 5 18	21 7 31	22 57 55	1 0 8	2 58 25	5 0 38	6 58 55	9 1 8	11 3 21	13 1 38	15 3 51	17 2 8
8	19 9 15	21 11 28	23 1 52	1 4 5	3 2 22	5 4 35	7 2 51	9 5 5	11 7 18	13 5 35	15 7 48	17 6 4
9	19 13 11	21 15 25	23 5 48	1 8 1	3 6 18	5 8 31	7 6 48	9 9 1	11 11 14	13 9 31	15 11 44	17 10 1
10	19 17 8	21 19 21	23 9 45	1 11 58	3 10 15	5 12 28	7 10 45	9 12 58	11 15 11	13 13 28	15 15 41	17 13 58
11	19 21 4	21 23 18	23 13 41	1 15 54	3 14 11	5 16 24	7 14 41	9 16 54	11 19 8	13 17 24	15 19 37	17 17 54
12	19 25 1	21 27 14	23 17 38	1 19 51	3 18 8	5 20 21	7 18 38	9 20 51	11 23 4	13 21 21	15 23 34	17 21 51
13	19 28 58	21 31 11	23 21 34	1 23 48	3 22 4	5 24 17	7 22 34	9 24 47	11 27 1	13 25 17	15 27 31	17 25 47
14	19 32 54	21 35 7	23 25 31	1 27 44	3 26 1	5 28 14	7 26 31	9 28 44	11 30 57	13 29 14	15 31 27	17 29 44
15	19 36 51	21 39 4	23 29 27	1 31 41	3 29 57	5 32 11	7 30 27	9 32 41	11 34 54	13 33 10	15 35 24	17 33 40
16	19 40 47	21 43 0	23 33 24	1 35 37	3 33 54	5 36 7	7 34 24	9 36 37	11 38 50	13 37 7	15 39 20	17 37 37
17	19 44 44	21 46 57	23 37 21	1 39 34	3 37 50	5 40 4	7 38 20	9 40 34	11 42 47	13 41 4	15 43 17	17 41 33
18	19 48 40	21 50 54	23 41 17	1 43 30	3 41 47	5 44 0	7 42 17	9 44 30	11 46 43	13 45 0	15 47 13	17 45 30
19	19 52 37	21 54 50	23 45 14	1 47 27	3 45 44	5 47 57	7 46 14	9 48 27	11 50 40	13 48 57	15 51 10	17 49 27
20	19 56 33	21 58 47	23 49 10	1 51 23	3 49 40	5 51 53	7 50 10	9 52 23	11 54 37	13 52 53	15 55 6	17 53 23
21	20 0 30	22 2 43	23 53 7	1 55 20	3 53 37	5 55 50	7 54 7	9 56 20	11 58 33	13 56 50	15 59 3	17 57 20
22	20 4 27	22 6 40	23 57 3	1 59 17	3 57 33	5 59 47	7 58 3	10 0 16	12 2 30	14 0 46	16 3 0	18 1 16
23	20 8 23	22 10 36	0 1 0	2 3 13	4 1 30	6 3 43	8 2 0	10 4 13	12 6 26	14 4 43	16 6 56	18 5 13
24	20 12 20	22 14 33	0 4 56	2 7 10	4 5 26	6 7 40	8 5 56	10 8 10	12 10 23	14 8 39	16 10 53	18 9 9
25	20 16 16	22 18 29	0 8 53	2 11 6	4 9 23	6 11 36	8 9 53	10 12 6	12 14 19	14 12 36	16 14 49	18 13 6
26	20 20 13	22 22 26	0 12 50	2 15 3	4 13 19	6 15 33	8 13 49	10 16 3	12 18 16	14 16 33	16 18 46	18 17 3
27	20 24 9	22 26 23	0 16 46	2 18 59	4 17 16	6 19 29	8 17 46	10 19 59	12 22 12	14 20 29	16 22 42	18 20 59
28	20 28 6	22 30 19	0 20 43	2 22 56	4 21 13	6 23 26	8 21 43	10 23 56	12 26 9	14 24 26	16 26 39	18 24 56
29	20 32 2		0 24 39	2 26 52	4 25 9	6 27 22	8 25 39	10 27 52	12 30 6	14 28 22	16 30 35	18 28 52
30	20 35 59		0 28 36	2 30 49	4 29 6	6 31 19	8 29 36	10 31 49	12 34 2	14 32 19	16 34 32	18 32 49
31	20 39 56		0 32 32		4 33 2		8 33 32	10 35 45		14 36 15		18 36 45

1931

	Jan.	Feb.	Mar.	April	May	June	July	Aug.	Sept.	Oct.	Nov.	Dec.
1	18 40 42	20 42 55	22 33 19	0 35 32	2 33 48	4 36 2	6 34 18	8 36 32	10 38 45	12 37 1	14 39 15	16 37 31
2	18 44 38	20 46 51	22 37 15	0 39 28	2 37 45	4 39 58	6 38 15	8 40 28	10 42 41	13 40 58	14 43 11	16 41 28
3	18 48 35	20 50 48	22 41 12	0 43 25	2 41 41	4 43 55	6 42 11	8 44 25	10 46 38	12 44 55	14 47 8	16 45 24
4	18 52 31	20 54 45	22 45 8	0 47 21	2 45 38	4 47 51	6 46 8	8 48 21	10 50 34	12 48 51	14 51 4	16 49 21
5	18 56 28	20 58 41	22 49 5	0 51 18	2 49 34	4 51 48	6 50 4	8 52 18	10 54 31	12 52 48	14 55 1	16 53 18
6	19 0 24	21 2 38	22 53 1	0 55 14	2 53 31	4 55 44	6 54 1	8 56 14	10 58 28	12 56 44	14 58 57	16 57 14
7	19 4 21	21 6 35	22 56 58	0 59 11	2 57 28	4 59 41	6 57 58	9 0 11	11 2 24	13 0 41	15 2 54	17 1 11
8	19 8 18	21 10 31	23 0 54	1 3 7	3 1 24	5 3 37	7 1 54	9 4 7	11 6 21	13 4 37	15 6 50	17 5 7
9	19 12 14	21 14 27	23 4 51	1 7 4	3 5 21	5 7 34	7 5 51	9 8 4	11 10 17	13 8 34	15 10 47	17 9 4
10	19 16 11	21 18 24	23 8 47	1 11 1	3 9 17	5 11 31	7 9 47	9 12 1	11 14 14	13 12 30	15 14 44	17 13 0
11	19 20 7	21 22 20	23 12 44	1 14 57	3 13 14	5 15 27	7 13 44	9 15 57	11 18 10	13 16 27	15 18 40	17 16 57
12	19 24 4	21 26 17	23 16 40	1 18 54	3 17 10	5 19 24	7 17 40	9 19 54	11 22 7	13 20 24	15 22 37	17 20 53
13	19 28 0	21 30 14	23 20 37	1 22 50	3 21 7	5 23 20	7 21 37	9 23 50	11 26 3	13 24 20	15 26 33	17 24 50
14	19 31 57	21 34 10	23 24 34	1 26 47	3 25 3	5 27 17	7 25 34	9 27 47	11 30 0	13 28 17	15 30 30	17 28 47
15	19 35 53	21 38 7	23 28 30	1 30 43	3 29 0	5 31 13	7 29 30	9 31 43	11 33 57	13 32 13	15 34 26	17 32 43
16	19 39 50	21 42 3	23 32 27	1 34 40	3 32 57	5 35 10	7 33 27	9 35 40	11 37 53	13 36 10	15 38 23	17 36 40
17	19 43 47	21 46 0	23 36 23	1 38 36	3 36 53	5 39 6	7 37 23	9 39 37	11 41 50	13 40 6	15 42 20	17 40 36
18	19 47 43	21 49 56	23 40 20	1 42 33	3 40 50	5 43 3	7 41 20	9 43 33	11 45 46	13 44 3	15 46 16	17 44 33
19	19 51 40	21 53 53	23 44 16	1 46 30	3 44 46	5 47 0	7 45 16	9 47 30	11 49 43	13 47 59	15 50 13	17 48 29
20	19 55 36	21 57 49	23 48 13	1 50 26	3 48 43	5 50 56	7 49 13	9 51 26	11 53 39	13 51 56	15 54 9	17 52 26
21	19 59 33	22 1 46	23 52 10	1 54 23	3 52 39	5 54 53	7 53 9	9 55 23	11 57 36	13 55 52	15 58 6	17 56 22
22	20 3 29	22 5 43	23 56 6	1 58 19	3 56 36	5 58 49	7 57 6	9 59 19	12 1 32	13 59 49	16 2 8	18 0 19
23	20 7 26	22 9 39	0 0 3	2 2 16	4 0 33	6 2 46	8 1 3	10 3 16	12 5 29	14 3 46	16 5 59	18 4 16
24	20 11 22	22 13 36	0 3 59	2 6 12	4 4 29	6 6 42	8 4 59	10 7 12	12 9 26	14 7 42	16 9 55	18 8 12
25	20 15 19	22 17 32	0 7 55	2 10 9	4 8 26	6 10 39	8 8 56	10 11 9	12 13 22	14 11 39	16 13 52	18 12 9
26	20 19 16	22 21 29	0 11 53	2 14 5	4 12 22	6 14 36	8 12 52	10 15 5	12 17 19	14 15 35	16 17 49	18 16 5
27	20 23 12	22 25 25	0 15 49	2 18 2	4 16 19	6 18 32	8 16 49	10 19 2	12 21 15	14 19 32	16 21 45	18 20 2
28	20 27 9	22 29 22	0 19 45	2 21 59	4 20 15	6 22 29	8 20 45	10 22 59	12 25 12	14 23 28	16 25 42	18 23 58
29	20 31 5		0 23 42	2 25 55	4 24 12	6 26 25	8 24 42	10 26 55	12 29 8	14 27 25	16 29 38	18 27 55
30	20 35 2		0 27 39	2 29 52	4 28 8	6 30 22	8 28 38	10 30 52	12 33 5	14 31 21	16 33 35	18 31 52
31	20 38 58		0 31 35		4 32 5		8 32 35	10 34 48		14 35 18		18 35 48

1932

Jan.	Feb.	Mar.	April	May	June	July	Aug.	Sept.	Oct.	Nov.	Dec.	
18 39 45	20 41 58	22 36 18	0 38 31	2 36 48	4 39 1	6 37 18	8 39 31	10 41 44	12 40 1	14 42 14	16 40 31	1
18 43 41	20 45 55	22 40 15	0 42 28	2 40 44	4 42 58	6 41 14	8 43 28	10 45 41	12 43 58	14 46 11	16 44 27	2
18 47 38	20 49 51	22 44 11	0 46 24	2 44 41	4 46 54	6 45 11	8 47 24	10 49 38	12 47 54	14 50 7	16 48 24	3
18 51 34	20 53 44	22 48 8	0 50 21	2 48 37	4 50 51	6 49 8	8 51 21	10 53 34	12 51 51	14 54 4	16 52 21	4
18 55 31	20 57 44	22 52 4	0 54 17	2 52 34	4 54 47	6 53 4	8 55 17	10 57 31	12 55 47	14 58 0	16 56 17	5
18 59 27	21 1 41	22 56 1	0 58 14	2 56 31	4 58 44	6 57 1	8 59 14	11 1 27	12 59 44	15 1 57	17 0 14	6
19 3 24	21 5 37	22 59 57	1 2 10	3 0 27	5 2 40	7 0 57	9 3 10	11 5 24	13 3 40	15 5 54	17 4 10	7
19 7 21	21 9 34	23 3 54	1 6 7	3 4 24	5 6 37	7 4 54	9 7 7	11 9 20	13 7 37	15 9 50	17 8 7	8
19 11 17	21 13 30	23 7 50	1 10 4	3 8 20	5 10 34	7 8 50	9 11 4	11 13 17	13 11 33	15 13 47	17 12 3	9
19 15 14	21 17 27	23 11 47	1 14 0	3 12 17	5 14 30	7 12 47	9 15 0	11 17 13	13 15 30	15 17 43	17 16 0	10
19 19 10	21 21 24	23 15 44	1 17 57	3 16 13	5 18 27	7 16 43	9 18 57	11 21 10	13 19 27	15 21 40	17 19 57	11
19 23 7	21 25 20	23 19 40	1 21 53	3 20 10	5 22 23	7 20 40	9 22 53	11 25 6	13 23 23	15 25 36	17 23 53	12
19 27 3	21 29 17	23 23 37	1 25 50	3 24 7	5 26 20	7 24 37	9 26 50	11 29 3	13 27 20	15 29 33	17 27 49	13
19 31 0	21 33 13	23 27 33	1 29 46	3 28 3	5 30 16	7 28 33	9 30 46	11 33 0	13 31 16	15 33 29	17 31 46	14
19 34 56	21 37 10	23 31 30	1 33 43	3 32 0	5 34 13	7 32 30	9 34 43	11 36 56	13 35 13	15 37 26	17 35 43	15
19 38 53	21 41 6	23 35 26	1 37 40	3 35 56	5 38 10	7 36 26	9 38 40	11 40 53	13 39 9	15 41 23	17 39 39	16
19 42 50	21 45 3	23 39 23	1 41 36	3 39 53	5 42 6	7 40 23	9 42 36	11 44 49	13 43 6	15 45 19	17 43 36	17
19 46 46	21 48 59	23 43 19	1 45 33	3 43 49	5 46 3	7 44 19	9 46 33	11 48 46	13 47 2	15 49 16	17 47 32	18
19 50 43	21 52 56	23 47 16	1 49 29	3 47 46	5 49 59	7 48 16	9 50 29	11 52 42	13 50 59	15 53 12	17 51 29	19
19 54 39	21 56 53	23 51 13	1 53 26	3 51 42	5 53 56	7 52 12	9 54 26	11 56 39	13 54 56	15 57 9	17 55 26	20
19 58 36	22 0 49	23 55 9	1 57 22	3 53 39	5 57 52	7 56 9	9 58 22	12 0 35	13 58 52	16 1 5	17 59 22	21
20 2 32	22 4 46	23 59 6	2 1 19	3 59 36	6 1 49	8 0 6	10 2 19	12 4 32	14 2 49	16 5 2	18 3 19	22
20 6 29	22 8 42	0 3 2	2 5 15	4 3 32	6 5 45	8 4 2	10 6 15	12 8 29	14 6 45	16 8 58	18 7 15	23
20 10 25	22 12 39	0 6 59	2 9 12	4 7 29	6 9 42	8 7 59	10 10 12	12 12 25	14 10 42	16 12 55	18 11 12	24
20 14 22	22 16 35	0 10 55	2 13 9	4 11 25	6 13 39	8 11 55	10 14 9	12 16 22	14 14 38	16 16 52	18 15 8	25
20 18 19	22 20 32	0 14 52	2 17 5	4 15 22	6 17 35	8 15 52	10 18 5	12 20 18	14 18 35	16 20 48	18 19 5	26
20 22 15	22 24 28	0 18 48	2 21 2	4 19 18	6 21 32	8 19 48	10 22 2	12 24 15	14 22 31	16 24 45	18 23 1	27
20 26 12	22 28 25	0 22 45	2 24 58	4 23 15	6 25 28	8 23 45	10 25 58	12 28 11	14 26 28	16 28 41	18 26 58	28
20 30 8	22 32 22	0 26 42	2 28 55	4 27 11	6 29 25	8 27 42	10 29 55	12 32 8	14 30 25	16 32 38	18 30 55	29
20 34 5		0 30 38	2 32 51	4 31 8	6 33 21	8 31 38	10 33 51	12 36 4	14 34 21	16 36 34	18 34 51	30
20 38 1		0 34 35		4 35 5		8 35 35	10 37 48		14 38 18		18 38 47	31

1933

Jan.	Feb.	Mar.	April	May	June	July	Aug.	Sept.	Oct.	Nov.	Dec.	
18 42 44	20 44 58	22 35 21	0 37 34	2 35 51	4 38 4	6 36 21	8 38 34	10 40 47	12 39 4	14 41 17	16 39 34	1
18 46 41	20 48 54	22 39 18	0 41 31	2 39 47	4 42 1	6 40 17	8 42 31	10 44 44	12 43 1	14 45 14	16 43 30	2
18 50 37	20 52 51	22 43 14	0 45 27	2 43 44	4 45 57	6 44 14	8 46 27	10 48 41	12 46 57	14 49 10	16 47 27	3
18 54 34	20 56 47	22 47 11	0 49 24	2 47 41	4 49 54	6 48 11	8 50 24	10 52 37	12 50 54	14 53 7	16 51 24	4
18 58 30	21 0 44	22 51 7	0 53 20	2 51 37	4 53 50	6 52 7	8 54 20	10 56 34	12 54 50	14 57 3	16 55 20	5
19 2 27	21 4 40	22 55 4	0 57 17	2 55 34	4 57 47	6 56 4	8 58 17	11 0 30	12 58 47	15 1 0	16 59 17	6
19 6 24	21 8 37	22 59 0	1 1 14	2 59 30	5 1 44	7 0 0	9 2 14	11 4 27	13 2 43	15 4 57	17 3 13	7
19 10 20	21 12 33	23 2 57	1 5 10	3 3 27	5 5 40	7 3 57	9 6 10	11 8 23	13 6 40	15 8 53	17 7 10	8
19 14 17	21 16 30	23 6 54	1 9 7	3 7 23	5 9 37	7 7 53	9 10 7	11 12 20	13 10 36	15 12 50	17 11 6	9
19 18 13	21 20 27	23 10 50	1 13 3	3 11 20	5 13 33	7 11 50	9 14 3	11 16 16	13 14 33	15 16 46	17 15 3	10
19 22 10	21 24 23	23 14 47	1 17 0	3 15 16	5 17 30	7 15 47	9 18 0	11 20 13	13 18 30	15 20 43	17 19 0	11
19 26 6	21 28 20	23 18 43	1 20 56	3 19 13	5 21 26	7 19 43	9 21 56	11 24 10	13 22 26	15 24 39	17 22 56	12
19 30 3	21 32 16	23 22 40	1 24 53	3 23 10	5 25 23	7 23 40	9 25 53	11 28 6	13 26 23	15 28 36	17 26 53	13
19 34 0	21 36 13	23 26 36	1 28 49	3 27 6	5 29 19	7 27 36	9 29 49	11 32 3	13 30 19	15 32 32	17 30 49	14
19 37 56	21 40 9	23 30 33	1 32 46	3 31 3	5 33 16	7 31 33	9 33 46	11 35 59	13 34 16	15 36 29	17 34 46	15
19 41 53	21 44 6	23 34 29	1 36 43	3 34 59	5 37 13	7 35 29	9 37 43	11 39 56	13 38 12	15 40 26	17 38 42	16
19 45 49	21 48 2	23 38 26	1 40 39	3 38 56	5 41 9	7 39 26	9 41 39	11 43 52	13 42 9	15 44 22	17 42 39	17
19 49 45	21 51 59	23 42 23	1 44 36	3 42 52	5 45 6	7 43 22	9 45 36	11 47 49	13 46 5	15 48 19	17 46 35	18
19 53 42	21 55 56	23 46 19	1 48 32	3 46 49	5 49 2	7 47 19	9 49 32	11 51 45	13 50 2	15 52 15	17 50 32	19
19 57 39	21 59 52	23 50 16	1 52 29	3 50 45	5 52 59	7 51 16	9 53 29	11 55 42	13 53 59	15 56 12	17 54 29	20
20 1 35	22 3 49	23 54 12	1 56 25	3 54 42	5 56 55	7 55 12	9 57 25	11 59 38	13 57 55	16 0 8	17 58 25	21
20 5 32	22 7 45	23 58 9	2 0 22	3 58 39	6 0 52	7 59 9	10 1 22	12 3 35	14 1 52	16 4 5	18 2 22	22
20 9 29	22 11 42	0 2 5	2 4 18	4 2 35	6 4 48	8 3 5	10 5 18	12 7 32	14 5 48	16 8 1	18 6 18	23
20 13 25	22 15 38	0 6 2	2 8 15	4 6 32	6 8 45	8 7 2	10 9 15	12 11 28	14 9 45	16 11 58	18 10 15	24
20 17 22	22 19 35	0 9 58	2 12 12	4 10 28	6 12 42	8 10 58	10 13 12	12 15 25	14 13 41	16 15 55	18 14 11	25
20 21 18	22 23 31	0 13 55	2 16 8	4 14 25	6 16 38	8 14 55	10 17 8	12 19 21	14 17 38	16 19 51	18 18 8	26
20 25 15	22 27 28	0 17 51	2 20 5	4 18 21	6 20 35	8 18 51	10 21 5	12 23 18	14 21 34	16 23 48	18 22 4	27
20 29 11	22 31 25	0 21 48	2 24 1	4 22 18	6 24 31	8 22 48	10 25 1	12 27 14	14 25 31	16 27 44	18 26 1	28
20 33 8		0 25 45	2 27 58	4 26 15	6 28 28	8 26 45	10 28 58	12 31 11	14 29 28	16 31 41	18 29 58	29
20 37 4		0 29 41	2 31 54	4 30 11	6 32 24	8 30 41	10 32 54	12 35 8	14 33 24	16 35 37	18 33 54	30
20 41 1		0 33 38		4 34 8		8 34 38	10 36 51		14 37 21		18 37 51	31

1934

Jan.	Feb.	Mar.	April	May	June	July	Aug.	Sept.	Oct.	Nov.	Dec.	
18 41 47	20 44 1	22 34 24	0 36 37	2 34 54	4 37 7	6 35 24	8 37 37	10 39 50	12 38 7	14 40 20	16 38 37	1
18 45 44	20 47 57	22 38 21	0 40 34	2 38 50	4 41 4	6 39 20	8 41 34	10 43 47	12 42 4	14 44 17	16 42 33	2
18 49 40	20 51 54	22 42 17	0 44 30	2 42 47	4 45 0	6 43 17	8 45 30	10 47 44	12 46 0	14 48 13	16 46 30	3
18 53 37	20 55 50	22 46 14	0 48 27	2 46 44	4 48 57	6 47 14	8 49 27	10 51 40	12 49 57	14 52 10	16 50 27	4
18 57 33	20 59 47	22 50 10	0 52 23	2 50 40	4 52 53	6 51 10	8 53 23	10 55 37	12 53 53	14 56 6	16 54 23	5
19 1 30	21 3 43	22 54 7	0 56 20	2 54 37	4 56 50	6 55 7	8 57 20	10 59 33	12 57 50	15 0 3	16 58 20	6
19 5 27	21 7 40	22 58 3	1 0 17	2 58 33	5 0 47	6 59 3	9 1 17	11 3 30	13 1 46	15 4 0	17 2 16	7
19 9 23	21 11 36	23 2 0	1 4 13	3 2 30	5 4 43	7 3 0	9 5 13	11 7 26	13 5 43	15 7 56	17 6 13	8
19 13 20	21 15 33	23 5 57	1 8 10	3 6 26	5 8 40	7 6 56	9 9 10	11 11 23	13 9 39	15 11 53	17 10 9	9
19 17 16	21 19 30	23 9 53	1 12 6	3 10 23	5 12 36	7 10 53	9 13 6	11 15 19	13 13 36	15 15 49	17 14 6	10
19 21 13	21 23 26	23 13 50	1 16 3	3 14 19	5 16 33	7 14 49	9 17 3	11 19 16	13 17 33	15 19 46	17 18 2	11
19 25 9	21 27 23	23 17 46	1 19 59	3 18 16	5 20 29	7 18 46	9 20 59	11 23 12	13 21 29	15 23 42	17 21 59	12
19 29 6	21 31 19	23 21 43	1 23 56	3 22 13	5 24 26	7 22 43	9 24 56	11 27 9	13 25 26	15 27 39	17 25 56	13
19 33 3	21 35 16	23 25 39	1 27 52	3 26 9	5 28 22	7 26 39	9 28 52	11 31 6	13 29 22	15 31 35	17 29 52	14
19 36 59	21 39 12	23 29 36	1 31 49	3 30 6	5 32 19	7 30 36	9 32 49	11 35 2	13 33 19	15 35 32	17 33 49	15
19 40 56	21 43 9	23 33 32	1 35 46	3 34 2	5 36 16	7 34 32	9 36 46	11 38 59	13 37 15	15 39 29	17 37 45	16
19 44 52	21 47 5	23 37 29	1 39 42	3 37 59	5 40 12	7 38 29	9 40 42	11 42 55	13 41 12	15 43 25	17 41 42	17
19 48 49	21 51 2	23 41 26	1 43 39	3 41 55	5 44 9	7 42 25	9 44 39	11 46 52	13 45 8	15 47 22	17 45 38	18
19 52 45	21 54 59	23 45 22	1 47 35	3 45 52	5 48 5	7 46 22	9 48 35	11 50 48	13 49 5	15 51 18	17 49 35	19
19 56 42	21 58 55	23 49 19	1 51 32	3 49 48	5 52 2	7 50 18	9 52 32	11 54 45	13 53 2	15 55 15	17 53 31	20
20 0 38	22 2 52	23 53 15	1 55 28	3 53 45	5 55 58	7 54 15	9 56 28	11 58 41	13 56 58	15 59 11	17 57 28	21
20 4 35	22 6 48	23 57 12	1 59 25	3 57 42	5 59 55	7 58 12	10 0 25	12 2 38	14 0 55	16 3 8	18 1 25	22
20 8 32	22 10 45	0 1 8	2 3 21	4 1 38	6 3 51	8 2 8	10 4 21	12 6 35	14 4 51	16 7 4	18 5 21	23
20 12 28	22 14 41	0 5 5	2 7 18	4 5 35	6 7 48	8 6 5	10 8 18	12 10 31	14 8 48	16 11 1	18 9 18	24
20 16 25	22 18 38	0 9 1	2 11 15	4 9 31	6 11 45	8 10 1	10 12 15	12 14 28	14 12 44	16 14 58	18 13 14	25
20 20 21	22 22 34	0 12 58	2 15 11	4 13 28	6 15 41	8 13 58	10 16 11	12 18 24	14 16 41	16 18 54	18 17 11	26
20 24 18	22 26 31	0 16 55	2 19 8	4 17 24	6 19 38	8 17 54	10 20 8	12 22 21	14 20 37	16 22 51	18 21 7	27
20 28 14	22 30 28	0 20 51	2 23 4	4 21 21	6 23 34	8 21 51	10 24 4	12 26 17	14 24 34	16 26 47	18 25 4	28
20 32 11		0 24 48	2 27 1	4 25 17	6 27 31	8 25 48	10 28 1	12 30 14	14 28 31	16 30 44	18 29 1	29
20 36 7		0 28 44	2 30 57	4 29 14	6 31 27	8 29 44	10 31 57	12 34 10	14 32 27	16 34 40	18 32 57	30
20 40 4		0 32 41		4 33 11		8 33 41	10 35 54		14 36 24		18 36 54	31

1935	Jan.	Feb.	Mar.	April	May	June	July	Aug.	Sept.	Oct.	Nov.	Dec.
1	18 40 50	20 43 3	22 33 27	0 35 40	2 33 57	4 36 10	6 34 27	8 36 40	10 38 53	12 37 10	14 39 23	16 37 40
2	18 44 47	20 47 0	22 37 24	0 39 37	2 37 53	4 40 7	6 38 23	8 40 37	10 42 50	12 41 6	14 43 20	16 41 36
3	18 48 43	20 50 57	22 41 20	0 43 33	2 41 50	4 44 3	6 42 20	8 44 33	10 46 46	12 45 3	14 47 16	16 45 33
4	18 52 40	20 54 53	22 45 17	0 47 30	2 45 46	4 48 0	6 46 16	8 48 30	10 50 43	12 49 0	14 51 13	16 49 29
5	18 56 36	20 58 50	22 49 13	0 51 26	2 49 43	4 51 56	6 50 13	8 52 26	10 54 39	12 52 56	14 55 9	16 53 26
6	19 0 33	21 2 46	22 53 10	0 55 23	2 53 40	4 55 53	6 54 10	8 56 23	10 58 36	12 56 53	14 59 6	16 57 23
7	19 4 30	21 6 43	22 57 6	0 59 20	2 57 36	4 59 49	6 58 6	9 0 20	11 2 33	13 0 49	15 3 2	17 1 19
8	19 8 26	21 10 39	23 1 3	1 3 16	3 1 33	5 3 46	7 2 3	9 4 16	11 6 29	13 4 46	15 6 59	17 5 16
9	19 12 23	21 14 26	23 4 59	1 7 13	3 5 30	5 7 43	7 6 0	9 8 13	11 10 26	13 8 42	15 10 55	17 9 12
10	19 16 19	21 18 32	23 8 56	1 11 9	3 9 26	5 11 39	7 9 56	9 12 9	11 14 22	13 12 39	15 14 52	17 13 9
11	19 20 16	21 22 29	23 12 53	1 15 6	3 13 22	5 15 36	7 13 52	9 16 6	11 18 19	13 16 35	15 18 49	17 17 5
12	19 24 12	21 26 26	23 16 49	1 19 2	3 17 19	5 19 32	7 17 49	9 20 2	11 22 15	13 20 32	15 22 45	17 21 2
13	19 28 9	21 30 22	23 20 46	1 22 59	3 21 16	5 23 29	7 21 45	9 23 59	11 26 12	13 24 29	15 26 42	17 24 58
14	19 32 5	21 34 19	23 24 42	1 26 55	3 25 12	5 27 25	7 25 42	9 27 55	11 30 8	13 28 25	15 30 38	17 28 55
15	19 36 2	21 38 15	23 28 39	1 30 52	3 29 9	5 31 22	7 29 39	9 31 52	11 34 5	13 32 22	15 34 35	17 32 52
16	19 39 59	21 42 12	23 32 35	1 34 48	3 33 5	5 35 18	7 33 35	9 35 48	11 38 2	13 36 18	15 38 31	17 36 48
17	19 43 55	21 46 8	23 36 32	1 38 45	3 37 2	5 39 15	7 37 32	9 39 45	11 41 58	13 40 15	15 42 28	17 40 45
18	19 47 52	21 50 5	23 40 28	1 42 42	3 40 58	5 43 12	7 41 28	9 43 42	11 45 55	13 44 11	15 46 25	17 44 41
19	19 51 48	21 54 1	23 44 25	1 46 38	3 44 55	5 47 8	7 45 25	9 47 38	11 49 51	13 48 8	15 50 21	17 48 38
20	19 55 45	21 57 58	23 48 22	1 50 35	3 48 51	5 51 5	7 49 21	9 51 35	11 53 48	13 52 4	15 54 18	17 52 34
21	19 59 41	22 1 55	23 52 18	1 54 31	3 52 48	5 55 1	7 53 18	9 55 31	11 57 44	13 56 1	15 58 14	17 56 31
22	20 3 38	22 5 51	23 56 15	1 58 28	3 56 44	5 58 58	7 57 15	9 59 28	12 1 41	13 59 58	16 2 11	18 0 27
23	20 7 34	22 9 48	0 0 11	2 2 25	4 0 41	6 2 54	8 1 11	10 3 24	12 5 37	14 3 54	16 6 7	18 4 24
24	20 11 31	22 13 44	0 4 8	2 6 21	4 4 38	6 6 51	8 5 8	10 7 21	12 9 34	14 7 51	16 10 4	18 8 21
25	20 15 28	22 17 41	0 8 4	2 10 17	4 8 34	6 10 47	8 9 4	10 11 17	12 13 31	14 11 47	16 14 0	18 12 17
26	20 19 24	22 21 37	0 12 1	2 14 14	4 12 31	6 14 44	8 13 1	10 15 14	12 17 27	14 15 44	16 17 57	18 16 14
27	20 23 21	22 25 34	0 15 57	2 18 11	4 16 27	6 18 41	8 16 57	10 19 11	12 21 24	14 19 40	16 21 54	18 20 10
28	20 27 17	22 29 30	0 19 54	2 22 7	4 20 24	6 22 37	8 20 54	10 23 7	12 25 20	14 23 37	16 25 50	18 24 7
29	20 31 14		0 23 51	2 26 4	4 24 20	6 26 34	8 24 50	10 27 4	12 29 17	14 27 33	16 29 47	18 28 3
30	20 35 10		0 27 47	2 30 0	4 28 17	6 30 30	8 28 47	10 31 0	12 33 13	14 31 30	16 33 43	18 32 0
31	20 39 7		0 31 44		4 32 13		8 32 44	10 34 57		14 35 26		18 35 56

1936	Jan.	Feb.	Mar.	April	May	June	July	Aug.	Sept.	Oct.	Nov.	Dec.
1	18 39 53	20 42 6	22 36 26	0 38 40	2 36 56	4 39 9	6 37 26	8 39 39	10 41 53	12 40 9	14 42 22	16 40 39
2	18 43 50	20 46 3	22 40 23	0 42 36	2 40 53	4 43 6	6 41 23	8 43 36	10 45 49	12 44 6	14 46 19	16 44 36
3	18 47 46	20 49 59	22 44 20	0 46 33	2 44 49	4 47 3	6 45 19	8 47 32	10 49 46	12 48 2	14 50 15	16 48 32
4	18 51 43	20 53 56	22 48 16	0 50 29	2 48 46	4 50 59	6 49 16	8 51 29	10 53 42	12 51 59	14 54 12	16 52 29
5	18 55 39	20 57 53	22 52 13	0 54 26	2 52 42	4 54 56	6 53 12	8 55 26	10 57 39	12 55 55	14 58 9	16 56 25
6	18 59 36	21 1 49	22 56 9	0 58 22	2 56 39	4 58 52	6 57 9	8 59 22	11 1 35	12 59 52	15 2 5	17 0 22
7	19 3 32	21 5 46	23 0 6	1 2 19	3 0 35	5 2 49	7 1 6	9 3 19	11 5 32	13 3 49	15 6 2	17 4 18
8	19 7 29	21 9 42	23 4 2	1 6 15	3 4 32	5 6 45	7 5 2	9 7 15	11 9 28	13 7 45	15 9 58	17 8 15
9	19 11 26	21 13 39	23 7 59	1 10 12	3 8 29	5 10 42	7 8 59	9 11 12	11 13 25	13 11 42	15 13 55	17 12 12
10	19 15 22	21 17 35	23 11 55	1 14 9	3 12 25	5 14 39	7 12 55	9 15 8	11 17 22	13 15 38	15 17 51	17 16 8
11	19 19 19	21 21 32	23 15 52	1 18 5	3 16 22	5 18 35	7 16 52	9 19 5	11 21 18	13 19 35	15 21 48	17 20 5
12	19 23 15	21 25 28	23 19 48	1 22 2	3 20 18	5 22 32	7 20 48	9 23 2	11 25 15	13 23 31	15 25 44	17 24 1
13	19 27 12	21 29 25	23 23 45	1 25 58	3 24 15	5 26 28	7 24 45	9 26 58	11 29 11	13 27 28	15 29 41	17 27 58
14	19 31 8	21 33 22	23 27 42	1 29 55	3 28 11	5 30 25	7 28 41	9 30 55	11 33 8	13 31 24	15 33 38	17 31 54
15	19 35 5	21 37 18	23 31 38	1 33 51	3 32 8	5 34 21	7 32 38	9 34 51	11 37 4	13 35 21	15 37 34	17 35 51
16	19 39 1	21 41 15	23 35 35	1 37 48	3 36 5	5 38 18	7 36 35	9 38 48	11 41 1	13 39 17	15 41 31	17 39 47
17	19 42 58	21 45 11	23 39 31	1 41 44	3 40 1	5 42 14	7 40 31	9 42 44	11 44 57	13 43 14	15 45 27	17 43 44
18	19 46 55	21 49 8	23 43 28	1 45 41	3 43 58	5 46 11	7 44 28	9 46 41	11 48 54	13 47 11	15 49 24	17 47 41
19	19 50 50	21 53 4	23 47 24	1 49 38	3 47 54	5 50 7	7 48 24	9 50 37	11 52 51	13 51 7	15 53 20	17 51 37
20	19 54 48	21 57 0	23 51 21	1 53 34	3 51 51	5 54 4	7 52 21	9 54 34	11 56 47	13 55 4	15 57 17	17 55 34
21	19 58 44	22 0 57	23 55 17	1 57 31	3 55 47	5 58 1	7 56 17	9 58 31	12 0 44	13 59 0	16 1 13	17 59 30
22	20 2 41	22 4 54	23 59 14	2 1 27	3 59 44	6 1 57	8 0 14	10 2 27	12 4 40	14 2 57	16 5 10	18 3 27
23	20 6 38	22 8 51	0 3 11	2 5 24	4 3 40	6 5 54	8 4 10	10 6 24	12 8 37	14 6 53	16 9 7	18 7 23
24	20 10 34	22 12 47	0 7 7	2 9 20	4 7 37	6 9 50	8 8 7	10 10 20	12 12 33	14 10 50	16 13 3	18 11 20
25	20 14 30	22 16 44	0 11 4	2 13 17	4 11 34	6 13 47	8 12 4	10 14 17	12 16 30	14 14 46	16 17 0	18 15 16
26	20 18 27	22 20 40	0 15 0	2 17 13	4 15 30	6 17 43	8 16 0	10 18 13	12 20 26	14 18 43	16 20 56	18 19 13
27	20 22 24	22 24 37	0 18 57	2 21 10	4 19 27	6 21 40	8 19 57	10 22 10	12 24 23	14 22 40	16 24 53	18 23 10
28	20 26 20	22 28 33	0 22 53	2 25 7	4 23 23	6 25 36	8 23 53	10 26 6	12 28 20	14 26 36	16 28 49	18 27 6
29	20 30 17	22 32 31	0 26 50	2 29 3	4 27 20	6 29 33	8 27 50	10 30 3	12 32 16	14 30 33	16 32 46	18 31 3
30	20 34 13		0 30 46	2 33 0	4 31 16	6 33 30	8 31 46	10 34 0	12 36 13	14 34 29	16 36 42	18 34 59
31	20 38 10		0 34 43		4 35 13		8 35 43	10 37 56		14 38 26		18 38 56

1937	Jan.	Feb.	Mar.	April	May	June	July	Aug.	Sept.	Oct.	Nov.	Dec.
1	18 42 52	20 45 6	22 35 29	0 37 42	2 35 59	4 38 12	6 36 29	8 38 42	10 40 55	12 39 12	14 41 25	16 39 42
2	18 46 49	20 49 2	22 39 26	0 41 39	2 39 55	4 42 9	6 40 25	8 42 39	10 44 52	12 43 8	14 45 22	16 43 38
3	18 50 45	20 52 59	22 43 22	0 45 35	2 43 52	4 46 5	6 44 22	8 46 35	10 48 48	12 47 5	14 49 18	16 47 35
4	18 54 42	20 56 55	22 47 19	0 49 32	2 47 49	4 50 2	6 48 18	8 50 32	10 52 45	12 51 1	14 53 15	16 51 31
5	18 58 39	21 0 52	22 51 15	0 53 28	2 51 45	4 53 58	6 52 15	8 54 28	10 56 41	12 54 58	14 57 11	16 55 28
6	19 2 35	21 4 48	22 55 12	0 57 25	2 55 42	4 57 55	6 56 12	8 58 25	11 0 38	12 58 55	15 1 8	16 59 24
7	19 6 32	21 8 45	22 59 8	1 1 22	2 59 38	5 1 51	7 0 8	9 2 21	11 4 35	13 2 51	15 5 4	17 3 21
8	19 10 28	21 12 42	23 3 5	1 5 18	3 3 35	5 5 48	7 4 5	9 6 18	11 8 31	13 6 48	15 9 1	17 7 18
9	19 14 25	21 16 38	23 7 2	1 9 15	3 7 31	5 9 45	7 8 1	9 10 15	11 12 28	13 10 44	15 12 57	17 11 14
10	19 18 21	21 20 35	23 10 58	1 13 11	3 11 28	5 13 41	7 11 58	9 14 11	11 16 24	13 14 41	15 16 54	17 15 11
11	19 22 18	21 24 31	23 14 55	1 17 8	3 15 24	5 17 38	7 15 54	9 18 8	11 20 21	13 18 37	15 20 51	17 19 7
12	19 26 14	21 28 28	23 18 51	1 21 4	3 19 21	5 21 34	7 19 51	9 22 4	11 24 17	13 22 34	15 24 47	17 23 4
13	19 30 11	21 32 24	23 22 48	1 25 1	3 23 18	5 25 31	7 23 48	9 26 1	11 28 14	13 26 30	15 28 44	17 27 0
14	19 34 8	21 36 21	23 26 44	1 28 57	3 27 14	5 29 27	7 27 44	9 29 57	11 32 10	13 30 27	15 32 40	17 30 57
15	19 38 4	21 40 17	23 30 41	1 32 54	3 31 11	5 33 24	7 31 41	9 33 54	11 36 7	13 34 24	15 36 37	17 34 53
16	19 42 1	21 44 14	23 34 37	1 36 51	3 35 7	5 37 20	7 35 37	9 37 50	11 40 4	13 38 20	15 40 33	17 38 50
17	19 45 57	21 48 10	23 38 34	1 40 47	3 39 4	5 41 17	7 39 34	9 41 47	11 44 0	13 42 17	15 44 30	17 42 47
18	19 49 54	21 52 7	23 42 31	1 44 44	3 43 0	5 45 14	7 43 30	9 45 44	11 47 57	13 46 14	15 48 26	17 46 43
19	19 53 50	21 56 4	23 46 27	1 48 40	3 46 57	5 49 10	7 47 27	9 49 40	11 51 53	13 50 10	15 52 23	17 50 40
20	19 57 47	22 0 0	23 50 24	1 52 37	3 50 53	5 53 7	7 51 23	9 53 37	11 55 50	13 54 6	15 56 20	17 54 36
21	20 1 43	22 3 57	23 54 20	1 56 33	3 54 50	5 57 3	7 55 20	9 57 33	11 59 46	13 58 3	16 0 16	17 58 33
22	20 5 40	22 7 53	23 58 17	2 0 30	3 58 47	6 1 0	7 59 17	10 1 30	12 3 43	14 2 0	16 4 13	18 2 29
23	20 9 37	22 11 50	0 2 13	2 4 26	4 2 43	6 4 56	8 3 13	10 5 26	12 7 39	14 5 56	16 8 9	18 6 26
24	20 13 33	22 15 46	0 6 10	2 8 23	4 6 40	6 8 53	8 7 10	10 9 23	12 11 36	14 9 53	16 12 6	18 10 23
25	20 17 30	22 19 43	0 10 6	2 12 20	4 10 36	6 12 49	8 11 6	10 13 19	12 15 33	14 13 49	16 16 2	18 14 19
26	20 21 26	22 23 39	0 14 3	2 16 16	4 14 33	6 16 46	8 15 3	10 17 16	12 19 29	14 17 46	16 19 59	18 18 16
27	20 25 23	22 27 36	0 18 0	2 20 13	4 18 29	6 20 43	8 18 59	10 21 12	12 23 26	14 21 42	16 23 55	18 22 12
28	20 29 19	22 31 33	0 21 56	2 24 9	4 22 26	6 24 39	8 22 56	10 25 9	12 27 22	14 25 39	16 27 52	18 26 9
29	20 33 16		0 25 53	2 28 6	4 26 22	6 28 36	8 26 52	10 29 6	12 31 19	14 29 35	16 31 49	18 30 5
30	20 37 13		0 29 49	2 32 2	4 30 19	6 32 32	8 30 49	10 33 2	12 35 15	14 33 32	16 35 45	18 34 2
31	20 41 9		0 33 46		4 34 16		8 34 46	10 36 59		14 37 28		18 37 58

Jan.	Feb.	Mar.	April	May	June	July	Aug.	Sept.	Oct.	Nov.	Dec.	**1938**
18 41 55	20 44 8	22 34 32	0 36 45	2 35 1	4 37 15	6 35 32	8 37 45	10 39 58	12 38 14	14 40 28	16 38 44	1
18 45 52	20 48 5	22 38 28	0 40 41	2 38 58	4 41 11	6 39 28	8 41 41	10 43 54	12 42 11	14 44 24	16 42 41	2
18 49 48	20 52 1	22 42 25	0 44 38	2 42 55	4 45 8	6 43 25	8 45 38	10 47 51	12 46 7	14 48 21	16 46 37	3
18 53 45	20 55 58	22 46 22	0 48 35	2 46 51	4 49 4	6 47 21	8 49 34	10 51 47	12 50 4	14 52 17	16 50 34	4
18 57 41	20 59 54	22 50 18	0 52 31	2 50 48	4 53 1	6 51 18	8 53 31	10 55 44	12 54 1	14 56 14	16 54 30	5
19 1 38	21 3 51	22 54 14	0 56 28	2 54 44	4 56 57	6 55 14	8 57 27	10 59 41	12 57 57	15 0 10	16 58 27	6
19 5 34	21 7 48	22 58 11	1 0 24	2 58 41	5 0 54	6 59 11	9 1 24	11 3 37	13 1 54	15 4 7	17 2 24	7
19 9 31	21 11 44	23 2 8	1 4 21	3 2 37	5 4 51	7 3 7	9 5 21	11 7 34	13 5 50	15 8 3	17 6 20	8
19 13 27	21 15 41	23 6 4	1 8 17	3 6 34	5 8 47	7 7 4	9 9 17	11 11 30	13 9 47	15 12 0	17 10 17	9
19 17 24	21 19 37	23 10 1	1 12 14	3 10 30	5 12 44	7 11 0	9 13 14	11 15 27	13 13 43	15 15 57	17 14 13	10
19 21 21	21 23 34	23 13 57	1 16 10	3 14 27	5 16 40	7 14 57	9 17 10	11 19 23	13 17 40	15 19 53	17 18 10	11
19 25 17	21 27 31	23 17 54	1 20 7	3 18 24	5 20 37	7 18 54	9 21 7	11 23 20	13 21 36	15 23 50	17 22 6	12
19 29 14	21 31 27	23 21 50	1 24 3	3 22 20	5 24 33	7 22 50	9 25 3	11 27 16	13 25 33	15 27 46	17 26 3	13
19 33 10	21 35 23	23 25 47	1 28 0	3 26 17	5 28 30	7 26 47	9 29 0	11 31 13	13 29 30	15 31 43	17 29 59	14
19 37 7	21 39 20	23 29 43	1 31 57	3 30 13	5 32 26	7 30 43	9 32 56	11 35 10	13 33 26	15 35 39	17 33 56	15
19 41 3	21 43 17	23 33 40	1 35 53	3 34 10	5 36 23	7 34 40	9 36 52	11 39 6	13 37 22	15 39 36	17 37 53	16
19 45 0	21 47 13	23 37 37	1 39 50	3 38 6	5 40 20	7 38 36	9 40 49	11 43 3	13 41 19	15 43 32	17 41 49	17
19 48 56	21 51 10	23 41 33	1 43 46	3 42 3	5 44 16	7 42 33	9 44 46	11 46 59	13 45 16	15 47 29	17 45 46	18
19 52 53	21 55 6	23 45 30	1 47 43	3 45 59	5 48 13	7 46 29	9 48 43	11 50 56	13 49 12	15 51 26	17 49 42	19
19 56 50	21 59 3	23 49 26	1 51 39	3 49 56	5 52 9	7 50 26	9 52 39	11 54 52	13 53 9	15 55 22	17 53 39	20
20 0 46	22 3 0	23 53 23	1 55 36	3 53 53	5 56 6	7 54 23	9 56 36	11 58 49	13 57 5	15 59 19	17 57 35	21
20 4 43	22 6 56	23 57 19	1 59 32	3 57 49	6 0 2	7 58 19	10 0 32	12 2 46	14 1 2	16 3 15	18 1 32	22
20 8 39	22 10 52	0 1 16	2 3 29	4 1 46	6 3 59	8 2 16	10 4 29	12 6 42	14 4 59	16 7 12	18 5 28	23
20 12 36	22 14 49	0 5 12	2 7 26	4 5 42	6 7 55	8 6 12	10 8 25	12 10 39	14 8 55	16 11 8	18 9 25	24
20 16 32	22 18 46	0 9 9	2 11 22	4 9 39	6 11 52	8 10 9	10 12 22	12 14 35	14 12 52	16 15 5	18 13 22	25
20 20 29	22 22 42	0 13 6	2 15 19	4 13 35	6 15 49	8 14 5	10 16 19	12 18 32	14 16 48	16 19 1	18 17 18	26
20 24 25	22 26 39	0 17 2	2 19 15	4 17 32	6 19 45	8 18 2	10 20 15	12 22 28	14 20 45	16 22 58	18 21 15	27
20 28 22	22 30 35	0 20 59	2 23 12	4 21 28	6 23 42	8 21 58	10 24 12	12 26 25	14 24 41	16.26 55	18 25 11	28
20 32 19		0 24 55	2 27 8	4 25 25	6 27 38	8 25 55	10 28 8	12 30 22	14 28 38	16 30 51	18 29 8	29
20 36 15		0 28 52	2 31 5	4 29 22	6 31 35	8 29 52	10 32 5	12 34 18	14 32 34	16 34 48	18 33 4	30
20 40 12		0 32 48		4 33 18		8 33 48	10 36 1		14 36 31		18 37 1	31

Jan.	Feb.	Mar.	April	May	June	July	Aug.	Sept.	Oct.	Nov.	Dec.	**1939**
18 40 57	20 43 11	22 33 34	0 35 47	2 34 4	4 36 17	6 34 34	8 36 47	10 39 0	12 37 17	14 39 30	16 37 47	1
18 44 54	20 47 7	22 37 31	0 39 44	2 38 0	4 40 14	6 38 30	8 40 44	10 42 57	12 41 13	14 43 27	16 41 43	2
18 48 51	20 51 4	22 41 27	0 43 40	2 41 57	4 44 10	6 42 27	8 44 40	10 46 53	12 45 10	14 47 23	16 45 40	3
18 52 47	20 55 0	22 45 24	0 47 37	2 45 54	4 48 7	6 46 24	8 48 37	10 50 50	12 59 6	14 51 20	16 49 36	4
18 56 44	20 58 57	22 49 20	0 51 34	2 49 50	4 52 3	6 50 20	8 52 33	10 54 46	12 53 3	14 55 16	16 53 33	5
19 0 40	21 2 54	22 53 17	0 55 30	2 53 47	4 56 0	6 54 17	8 56 30	10 58 43	12 57 0	14 59 13	16 57 29	6
19 4 37	21 6 50	22 57 14	0 59 27	2 57 43	4 59 56	6 58 13	9 0 26	11 2 40	13 0 56	15 3 9	17 1 26	7
19 8 33	21 10 47	23 1 10	1 3 23	3 1 40	5 3 53	7 2 10	9 4 23	11 6 36	13 4 53	15 7 6	17 5 22	8
19 12 30	21 14 44	23 5 7	1 7 20	3 5 36	5 7 50	7 6 6	9 8 20	11 10 33	13 8 49	15 11 2	17 9 19	9
19 16 26	21 18 40	23 9 3	1 11 16	3 9 33	5 11 46	7 10 3	9 12 16	11 14 29	13 12 46	15 14 59	17 13 16	10
19 20 23	21 22 36	23 13 0	1 15 13	3 13 29	5 15 43	7 13 59	9 16 13	11 18 26	13 16 42	15 18 55	17 17 12	11
19 24 20	21 26 33	23 16 56	1 19 9	3 17 26	5 19 39	7 17 56	9 20 9	11 22 22	13 20 39	15 22 52	17 21 9	12
19 28 16	21 30 29	23 20 53	1 23 6	3 21 23	5 23 36	7 21 53	9 24 6	11 26 19	13 24 35	15 26 49	17 25 5	13
19 32 13	21 34 26	23 24 49	1 27 3	3 25 19	5 27 32	7 25 49	9 28 2	11 30 15	13 28 32	15 30 45	17 29 2	14
19 36 9	21 38 22	23 28 46	1 30 59	3 29 16	5 31 29	7 29 46	9 31 59	11 34 12	13 32 29	15 34 42	17 32 58	15
19 40 6	21 42 19	23 32 43	1 34 56	3 33 12	5 35 25	7 33 42	9 35 55	11 38 9	13 36 25	15 38 38	17 36 55	16
19 44 2	21 46 16	23 36 39	1 38 52	3 37 9	5 39 22	7 37 39	9 39 52	11 42 5	13 40 22	15 42 35	17 40 52	17
19 47 59	21 50 12	23 40 36	1 42 49	3 41 5	5 43 19	7 41 35	9 43 49	11 46 2	13 44 18	15 46 31	17 44 48	18
19 51 55	21 54 9	23 44 32	1 46 45	3 45 2	5 47 15	7 45 32	9 47 45	11 49 58	13 48 15	15 50 28	17 48 45	19
19 55 52	21 58 5	23 48 29	1 50 42	3 48 58	5 51 12	7 49 28	9 51 42	11 53 55	13 52 11	15 54 24	17 52 41	20
19 59 49	22 2 2	23 52 25	1 54 38	3 52 55	5 55 8	7 53 25	9 55 38	11 57 51	13 56 8	15 58 21	17 56 38	21
20 3 45	22 5 58	23 56 22	1 58 35	3 56 52	5 59 5	7 57 22	9 59 35	12 1 48	14 0 4	16 2 18	18 0 34	22
20 7 42	22 9 55	0 0 18	2 2 31	4 0 48	6 3 1	8 1 18	10 3 31	12 5 44	14 4 1	16 6 14	18 4 31	23
20 11 38	22 13 51	0 4 15	2 6 28	4 4 45	6 6 58	8 5 15	10 7 28	12 9 41	14 7 58	16 10 11	18 8 27	24
20 15 35	22 17 48	0 8 11	2 10 25	4 8 41	6 10 55	8 9 11	10 11 24	12 13 38	14 11 54	16 14 7	18 12 24	25
20 19 31	22 21 45	0 12 8	2 14 21	4 12 38	6 14 51	8 13 8	10 15 21	12 17 34	14 15 51	16 18 4	18 16 21	26
20 23 28	22 25 41	0 16 5	2 18 18	4 16 34	6 18 48	8 17 4	10 19 18	12 21 31	14 19 47	16 22 0	18 20 17	27
20 27 24	22 29 38	0 20 1	2 22 14	4 20 31	6 22 44	8 21 1	10 23 14	12 25 27	14 23 44	16 25 57	18 24 14	28
20 31 21		0 23 58	2 26 11	4 24 27	6 26 41	8 24 57	10 27 11	12 29 24	14 27 40	16 29 53	18 28 10	29
20 35 18		0 27 54	2 30 7	4 28 24	6 30 37	8 28 54	10 31 7	12 33 20	14 31 37	16 33 50	18 32 7	30
20 39 14		0 31 51		4 32 21		8 32 51	10 35 4		14 35 33		18 36 3	31

Jan.	Feb.	Mar.	April	May	June	July	Aug.	Sept.	Oct.	Nov.	Dec.	**1940**
18 40 0	20 42 13	22 36 33	0 38 46	2 37 3	4 39 16	6 37 33	8 39 46	10 41 59	12 40 16	14 42 29	16 40 46	1
18 43 56	20 46 10	22 40 30	0 42 43	2 40 59	4 43 13	6 41 29	8 43 43	10 45 56	12 44 12	14 46 25	16 44 42	2
18 47 53	20 50 6	22 44 26	0 46 39	2 44 56	4 47 9	6 45 26	8 47 39	10 49 52	12 48 9	14 50 22	16 48 39	3
18 51 50	20 54 3	22 48 23	0 50 36	2 48 53	4 51 6	6 49 22	8 51 36	10 53 49	12 52 5	14 54 19	16 52 35	4
18 55 46	20 57 59	22 52 19	0 54 33	2 52 49	4 55 2	6 53 19	8 55 32	10 57 45	12 56 2	14 58 15	16 56 32	5
18 59 43	21 1 56	22 56 16	0 58 29	2 56 46	4 58 59	6 57 16	8 59 29	11 1 42	12 59 58	15 2 12	17 0 28	6
19 3 39	21 5 52	23 0 13	1 2 26	3 0 42	5 2 55	7 1 12	9 3 25	11 5 38	13 3 55	15 6 8	17 4 25	7
19 7 36	21 9 49	23 4 9	1 6 22	3 4 39	4 6 52	7 5 9	9 7 22	11 9 35	13 7 52	15 10 5	17 8 21	8
19 11 32	21 13 46	23 8 6	1 10 19	3 8 35	5 10 49	7 9 5	9 11 18	11 13 32	13 11 48	15 14 1	17 12 18	9
19 15 29	21 17 42	23 12 2	1 14 15	3 12 32	5 14 45	7 13 2	9 15 15	11 17 28	13 15 45	15 17 58	17 16 15	10
19 19 25	21 21 39	23 15 59	1 18 12	3 16 28	5 18 42	7 16 58	9 19 12	11 21 25	13 19 41	15 21 54	17 20 11	11
19 23 22	21 25 35	23 19 55	1 22 8	3 20 25	5 22 38	7 20 55	9 23 8	11 25 21	13 23 38	15 25 51	17 24 8	12
19 27 19	21 29 32	23 23 52	1 26 5	3 24 22	5 26 35	7 24 51	9 27 5	11 29 18	13 27 34	15 29 48	17 28 4	13
19 31 15	21 33 28	23 27 48	1 30 1	3 28 18	5 30 31	7 28 48	9 31 1	11 33 14	13 31 31	15 33 44	17 32 1	14
19 35 12	21 37 25	23 31 45	1 33 58	3 32 15	5 34 28	7 32 45	9 34 58	11 37 11	13 35 27	15 37 41	17 35 57	15
19 39 8	21 41 21	23 35 41	1 37 55	3 36 11	5 38 24	7 36 41	9 38 54	11 41 7	13 39 24	15 41 37	17 39 54	16
19 43 5	21 45 18	23 39 38	1 41 51	3 40 8	5 42 21	7 40 38	9 42 51	11 45 4	13 43 21	15 45 34	17 43 50	17
19 47 1	21 49 15	23 43 35	1 45 48	3 44 4	5 46 18	7 44 34	9 46 47	11 49 1	13 47 17	15 49 30	17 47 47	18
19 50 58	21 53 11	23 47 31	1 49 44	3 48 1	5 50 14	7 48 31	9 50 44	11 52 57	13 51 14	15 53 27	17 51 44	19
19 54 54	21 57 8	23 51 28	1 53 41	3 51 57	5 54 11	7 52 27	9 54 41	11 56 54	13 55 10	15 57 23	17 55 40	20
19 58 51	22 1 4	23 55 24	1 57 37	3 55 54	5 58 7	7 56 24	9 58 37	12 0 50	13 59 7	16 1 20	17 59 37	21
20 2 48	22 5 1	23 59 21	2 1 34	3 59 51	6 2 4	8 0 20	10 2 34	12 4 47	14 3 3	16 5 17	18 3 33	22
20 6 44	22 8 57	0 3 17	2 5 30	4 3 47	6 6 0	8 4 17	10 6 30	12 8 43	14 7 0	16 9 13	18 7 30	23
20 10 41	22 12 54	0 7 14	2 9 27	4 7 44	6 9 57	8 8 14	10 10 27	12 12 40	14 10 56	16 13 10	18 11 26	24
20 14 37	22 16 50	0 11 10	2 13 24	4 11 40	6 13 53	8 12 10	10 14 23	12 16 36	14 14 53	16 17 6	18 15 23	25
20 18 34	22 20 47	0 15 7	2 17 20	4 15 37	6 17 50	8 16 7	10 18 20	12 20 33	14 18 50	16 21 3	18 19 19	26
20 22 30	22 24 44	0 19 4	2 21 17	4 19 33	6 21 47	8 20 3	10 22 16	12 24 30	14 22 46	16 24 59	18 23 16	27
20 26 27	22 28 40	0 23 0	2 25 13	4 23 30	6 25 43	8 24 0	10 26 13	12 28 26	14 26 43	16 28 56	18 27 13	28
20 30 23	22 32 37	0 26 57	2 29 10	4 27 26	6 29 40	8 27 56	10 30 10	12 32 23	14 30 39	16 32 52	18 31 9	29
20 34 20		0 30 53	2 33 6	4 31 23	6 33 36	8 31 53	10 34 6	12 36 19	14 34 36	16 36 49	18 35 6	30
20 38 17		0 34 50		4 35 20		8 35 49	10 38 3		14 38 32		18 39 2	31

1941

	Jan.	Feb.	Mar.	April	May	June	July	Aug.	Sept.	Oct.	Nov.	Dec.
1	18 42 59	20 45 12	22 35 36	0 37 49	2 36 5	4 38 18	6 36 35	8 38 48	10 41 2	12 39 18	14 41 31	16 39 48
2	18 46 55	20 49 9	22 39 32	0 41 45	2 40 2	4 42 15	6 40 32	8 42 45	10 44 58	12 43 15	14 45 28	16 43 44
3	18 50 52	20 53 5	22 43 29	0 45 42	2 43 58	4 46 12	6 44 28	8 46 41	10 48 55	12 47 11	14 49 24	16 47 41
4	18 54 48	20 57 2	22 47 25	0 49 38	2 47 55	4 50 8	6 48 25	8 50 38	10 52 51	12 51 8	14 53 21	16 51 38
5	18 58 45	21 0 58	22 51 22	0 53 35	2 51 51	4 54 5	6 52 21	8 54 35	10 56 48	12 55 4	14 57 17	16 55 34
6	19 2 42	21 4 55	22 55 18	0 57 31	2 55 48	4 58 1	6 56 18	8 58 31	11 0 44	12 59 1	15 1 14	16 59 31
7	19 6 38	21 8 51	22 59 15	1 1 28	2 59 45	5 1 58	7 0 14	9 2 28	11 4 41	13 2 57	15 5 11	17 3 27
8	19 10 35	21 12 48	23 3 11	1 5 25	3 3 41	5 5 54	7 4 11	9 6 24	11 8 37	13 6 54	15 9 7	17 7 24
9	19 14 31	21 16 44	23 7 8	1 9 21	3 7 38	5 9 51	7 8 8	9 10 21	11 12 34	13 10 50	15 13 4	17 11 20
10	19 18 28	21 20 41	23 11 5	1 13 18	3 11 34	5 13 47	7 12 4	9 14 17	11 16 30	13 14 47	15 17 0	17 15 17
11	19 22 24	21 24 38	23 15 1	1 17 14	3 15 31	5 17 44	7 16 1	9 18 14	11 20 27	13 18 44	15 20 57	17 19 13
12	19 26 21	21 28 34	23 18 58	1 21 11	3 19 27	5 21 41	7 19 57	9 22 10	11 24 24	13 22 40	15 24 53	17 23 10
13	19 30 17	21 32 31	23 22 54	1 25 7	3 23 24	5 25 37	7 23 54	9 26 7	11 28 20	13 26 37	15 28 50	17 27 7
14	19 34 14	21 36 27	23 26 51	1 29 4	3 27 20	5 29 34	7 27 50	9 30 4	11 32 17	13 30 33	15 32 46	17 31 3
15	19 38 11	21 40 24	23 30 47	1 33 0	3 31 17	5 33 30	7 31 47	9 34 0	11 36 13	13 34 30	15 36 43	17 35 0
16	19 42 7	21 44 20	23 34 44	1 36 57	3 35 14	5 37 27	7 35 43	9 37 57	11 40 10	13 38 26	15 40 40	17 38 56
17	19 46 4	21 48 17	23 38 40	1 40 53	3 39 10	5 41 23	7 39 40	9 41 53	11 44 6	13 42 23	15 44 36	17 42 53
18	19 50 0	21 52 13	23 42 37	1 44 50	3 43 7	5 45 20	7 43 37	9 45 50	11 48 3	13 46 19	15 48 33	17 46 49
19	19 53 57	21 56 10	23 46 33	1 48 47	3 47 3	5 49 16	7 47 33	9 49 46	11 51 59	13 50 16	15 52 29	17 50 46
20	19 57 54	22 0 7	23 50 30	1 52 43	3 51 0	5 53 13	7 51 30	9 53 43	11 55 56	13 54 13	15 56 26	17 54 42
21	20 1 50	22 4 3	23 54 27	1 56 40	3 54 56	5 57 10	7 55 26	9 57 39	11 59 53	13 58 9	16 0 22	17 58 39
22	20 5 47	22 8 0	23 58 23	2 0 36	3 58 53	6 1 6	7 59 23	10 1 36	12 3 49	14 2 6	16 4 19	18 2 36
23	20 9 43	22 11 56	0 2 20	2 4 33	4 2 49	6 5 3	8 3 19	10 5 33	12 7 46	14 6 2	16 8 15	18 6 32
24	20 13 40	22 15 53	0 6 16	2 8 29	4 6 46	6 8 59	8 7 16	10 9 29	12 11 42	14 9 59	16 12 12	18 10 29
25	20 17 36	22 19 49	0 10 13	2 12 26	4 10 43	6 12 56	8 11 12	10 13 26	12 15 39	14 13 55	16 16 9	18 14 25
26	20 21 33	22 23 46	0 14 9	2 16 22	4 14 39	6 16 52	8 15 9	10 17 22	12 19 35	14 17 52	16 20 5	18 18 22
27	20 25 29	22 27 42	0 18 6	2 20 19	4 18 36	6 20 49	8 19 6	10 21 19	12 23 32	14 21 48	16 24 2	18 22 18
28	20 29 26	22 31 39	0 22 2	2 24 16	4 22 32	6 24 45	8 23 2	10 25 15	12 27 28	14 25 45	16 27 58	18 26 15
29	20 33 22		0 25 59	2 28 12	4 26 29	6 28 42	8 26 59	10 29 12	12 31 25	14 29 42	16 31 55	18 30 11
30	20 37 19		0 29 56	2 32 9	4 30 25	6 32 39	8 30 55	10 33 8	12 35 22	14 33 38	16 35 51	18 34 8
31	20 41 15		0 33 52		4 34 22		8 34 52	10 37 5		14 37 35		18 38 5

1942

	Jan.	Feb.	Mar.	April	May	June	July	Aug.	Sept.	Oct.	Nov.	Dec.
1	18 42 1	20 44 14	22 34 38	0 36 51	2 35 8	4 37 21	6 35 38	8 37 51	10 40 4	12 38 20	14 40 34	16 38 50
2	18 45 58	20 48 11	22 38 34	0 40 48	2 39 4	4 41 17	6 39 34	8 41 47	10 44 0	12 42 17	14 44 30	16 42 47
3	18 49 54	20 52 8	22 42 31	0 44 44	2 43 1	4 45 14	6 43 31	8 45 44	10 47 57	12 46 14	14 48 27	16 46 43
4	18 53 51	20 56 4	22 56 28	0 48 41	2 46 57	4 49 10	6 47 27	8 49 40	10 51 54	12 50 10	14 52 23	16 50 40
5	18 57 47	21 0 1	22 50 24	0 52 37	2 50 54	4 53 7	6 51 24	8 53 37	10 55 50	12 54 7	14 56 20	16 54 36
6	19 1 44	21 3 57	22 54 21	0 56 34	2 54 50	4 57 4	6 55 20	8 57 33	10 59 47	13 58 3	15 0 16	16 58 33
7	19 5 40	21 7 54	22 58 17	1 0 30	2 58 47	5 1 0	6 59 17	9 1 30	11 3 43	13 2 0	15 4 13	17 2 30
8	19 9 37	21 11 50	23 2 14	1 4 27	3 2 43	5 4 57	7 3 13	9 5 27	11 7 40	13 5 56	15 8 9	17 6 26
9	19 13 34	21 15 47	23 6 10	1 8 23	3 6 40	5 8 53	7 7 10	9 9 23	11 11 36	13 9 53	15 12 6	17 10 23
10	19 17 30	21 19 43	23 10 7	1 12 20	3 10 37	5 12 50	7 11 6	9 13 20	11 15 33	13 13 49	15 16 3	17 14 19
11	19 21 27	21 23 40	23 14 3	1 16 17	3 14 33	5 16 46	7 15 3	9 17 16	11 19 29	13 17 46	15 19 59	17 18 16
12	91 25 23	21 27 36	23 18 0	1 20 13	3 18 30	5 20 43	7 19 0	9 21 13	11 23 26	13 21 43	15 23 56	17 22 12
13	19 29 20	21 31 33	23 21 57	1 24 10	3 22 26	5 24 39	7 22 56	9 25 9	11 27 23	13 25 39	15 27 52	17 26 9
14	19 33 16	21 35 30	23 25 53	1 28 6	3 26 23	5 28 36	7 26 53	9 29 6	11 31 19	13 29 36	15 31 49	17 30 5
15	19 37 13	21 39 26	23 29 50	1 32 3	3 30 19	5 32 33	7 30 49	9 33 2	11 35 16	13 33 32	15 35 45	17 34 2
16	19 41 9	21 43 23	23 33 46	1 35 59	3 34 16	5 36 29	7 34 46	9 36 59	11 39 12	13 37 29	15 39 42	17 37 59
17	19 45 6	21 47 19	23 37 43	1 39 56	3 38 12	5 40 26	7 38 42	9 40 56	11 43 9	13 41 25	15 43 38	17 41 55
18	19 49 3	21 51 16	23 41 39	1 43 52	3 42 9	5 44 22	7 42 39	9 44 52	11 47 5	13 45 22	15 47 35	17 45 52
19	19 52 59	21 55 12	23 45 36	1 47 49	3 46 6	5 48 19	7 46 36	9 48 49	11 51 2	13 49 18	15 51 32	17 49 48
20	19 56 56	21 59 9	23 49 32	1 51 45	3 50 2	5 52 15	7 50 32	9 52 45	11 54 58	13 53 15	15 55 28	17 53 45
21	20 0 52	22 3 5	23 53 29	1 55 42	3 53 59	5 56 12	7 54 29	9 56 42	11 58 55	13 57 12	15 59 25	17 57 41
22	20 4 49	22 7 2	23 57 25	1 59 39	3 57 55	6 0 8	7 58 25	10 0 38	12 2 51	14 1 8	16 3 21	18 1 38
23	20 8 45	22 10 59	0 1 22	2 3 35	4 1 52	6 4 5	8 2 22	10 4 35	12 6 48	14 5 5	16 7 18	18 5 35
24	20 12 42	22 14 55	0 5 19	2 7 32	4 5 48	6 8 2	8 6 18	10 8 31	12 10 45	14 9 1	16 11 14	18 9 31
25	20 16 38	22 18 52	0 9 15	2 11 28	4 9 45	6 11 58	8 10 15	10 12 28	12 14 41	14 12 58	16 15 11	18 13 28
26	20 20 35	22 22 48	0 13 12	2 15 25	4 13 41	6 15 55	8 14 11	10 16 25	12 18 38	14 16 54	16 19 7	18 17 24
27	20 24 32	22 26 45	0 17 8	2 19 21	4 17 38	6 19 51	8 18 8	10 20 21	12 22 34	14 20 51	16 23 4	18 21 21
28	20 28 28	22 30 41	0 21 5	2 23 18	4 21 35	6 23 48	8 22 5	10 24 18	12 26 31	14 24 47	16 27 1	18 25 17
29	20 32 25		0 25 1	2 27 14	4 25 31	6 27 44	8 26 1	10 28 14	12 30 27	14 28 44	16 30 57	18 29 14
30	20 36 21		0 28 58	2 31 11	4 29 28	6 31 41	8 29 58	10 32 11	12 34 24	14 32 40	16 34 54	18 33 10
31	20 40 18		0 32 54		4 33 24		8 33 54	10 36 7		14 36 37		18 37 7

1943

	Jan.	Feb.	Mar.	April	May	June	July	Aug.	Sept.	Oct.	Nov.	Dec.
1	18 41 4	20 43 17	22 33 40	0 35 53	2 34 10	4 36 23	6 34 40	8 36 53	10 39 6	12 37 23	14 39 36	16 37 53
2	18 45 0	20 47 13	22 37 37	0 39 50	2 38 7	4 40 20	6 38 36	8 40 50	10 43 3	12 41 19	14 43 33	16 41 49
3	18 48 57	20 51 10	22 41 33	0 43 46	2 42 3	4 44 16	6 42 33	8 44 46	10 46 59	12 45 16	14 47 29	16 45 46
4	18 52 53	20 55 6	22 45 30	0 47 43	2 46 0	4 48 13	6 46 30	8 48 43	10 50 56	12 49 13	14 51 26	16 49 42
5	18 56 50	20 59 3	22 49 26	0 51 40	2 49 56	4 52 9	6 50 26	8 52 39	10 54 53	12 53 9	14 55 22	16 53 39
6	19 0 46	21 3 0	22 53 23	0 55 36	2 53 53	4 56 6	6 54 23	8 56 36	10 58 49	12 57 6	14 59 19	16 57 35
7	19 4 43	21 6 56	22 57 20	0 59 33	2 57 49	5 0 3	6 58 19	9 0 32	11 2 46	13 1 2	15 3 15	17 1 33
8	19 8 39	21 10 53	23 1 16	1 3 29	3 1 46	5 3 59	7 2 16	9 4 29	11 6 42	13 4 59	15 7 12	17 5 29
9	19 12 36	21 14 49	23 5 13	1 7 26	3 5 42	5 7 56	7 6 12	9 8 26	11 10 39	13 8 55	15 11 8	17 9 25
10	19 16 33	21 18 46	23 9 9	1 11 22	3 9 39	5 11 52	7 10 9	9 12 22	11 14 36	13 12 52	15 15 5	17 13 22
11	19 20 29	21 22 42	23 13 6	1 15 19	3 13 36	5 15 49	7 14 5	9 16 19	11 18 32	13 16 48	15 19 2	17 17 18
12	19 24 26	21 26 39	23 17 2	1 19 15	3 17 32	5 19 45	7 18 2	9 20 15	11 22 28	13 20 45	15 22 58	17 21 15
13	19 28 22	21 30 35	23 20 59	1 23 12	3 21 29	5 23 42	7 21 59	9 24 12	11 26 25	13 24 41	15 26 55	17 25 11
14	19 32 19	21 34 32	23 24 55	1 27 9	3 25 25	5 27 38	7 25 55	9 28 8	11 30 21	13 28 38	15 30 51	17 29 8
15	19 36 15	21 38 29	23 28 52	1 31 5	3 29 22	5 31 35	7 29 52	9 32 5	11 34 18	13 32 35	15 34 48	17 33 4
16	19 40 12	21 42 25	23 32 49	1 35 2	3 33 18	5 35 32	7 33 48	9 36 1	11 38 15	13 36 31	15 38 44	17 37 1
17	19 44 8	21 46 22	23 36 45	1 38 58	3 37 15	5 39 28	7 37 45	9 39 58	11 42 11	13 40 28	15 42 41	17 40 58
18	19 48 5	21 50 18	23 40 42	1 42 55	3 41 11	5 43 25	7 41 41	9 43 55	11 46 8	13 44 24	15 46 37	17 44 55
19	19 52 2	21 54 15	23 44 38	1 46 51	3 45 8	5 47 21	7 45 38	9 47 51	11 50 4	13 48 21	15 50 34	17 48 51
20	19 55 58	21 58 11	23 48 35	1 50 48	3 49 4	5 51 18	7 49 34	9 51 48	11 54 1	13 52 17	15 54 31	17 52 47
21	19 59 55	22 2 8	23 52 31	1 54 44	3 53 1	5 55 14	7 53 31	9 55 44	11 57 57	13 56 14	15 58 27	17 56 44
22	20 3 51	22 6 4	23 56 28	1 58 41	3 56 58	5 59 11	7 57 28	9 59 41	12 1 54	14 0 10	16 2 24	18 0 40
23	20 7 48	22 10 1	0 0 24	2 2 38	4 0 54	6 3 7	8 1 24	10 3 37	12 5 50	14 4 7	16 6 20	18 4 37
24	20 11 44	22 13 57	0 4 21	2 6 34	4 4 51	6 7 4	8 5 21	10 7 34	12 9 47	14 8 4	16 10 17	18 8 33
25	20 15 41	22 17 54	0 8 18	2 10 31	4 8 47	6 11 1	8 9 17	10 11 30	12 13 44	14 12 0	16 14 13	18 12 30
26	20 19 37	22 21 51	0 12 14	2 14 27	4 12 44	6 14 57	8 13 14	10 15 27	12 17 40	14 15 57	16 18 10	18 16 27
27	20 23 34	22 25 47	0 16 11	2 18 24	4 16 40	6 18 54	8 17 10	10 19 24	12 21 37	14 19 53	16 22 6	18 20 24
28	20 27 31	22 29 44	0 20 7	2 22 20	4 20 37	6 22 50	8 21 7	10 23 20	12 25 33	14 23 50	16 26 3	18 24 20
29	20 31 27		0 24 4	2 26 17	4 24 34	6 26 47	8 25 3	10 27 17	12 29 30	14 27 46	16 30 0	18 28 16
30	20 35 24		0 28 0	2 30 13	4 28 30	6 30 43	8 29 0	10 31 14	12 33 26	14 31 43	16 33 56	18 32 13
31	20 39 20		0 31 57		4 32 27		8 32 57	10 35 10		14 35 39		18 36 9

1944

Jan.	Feb.	Mar.	April	May	June	July	Aug.	Sept.	Oct.	Nov.	Dec.	
18 40 6	20 42 20	22 36 39	0 38 52	2 37 9	4 39 22	6 37 39	8 39 52	10 42 5	12 40 22	14 42 35	16 40 52	1
18 44 3	20 46 13	22 40 36	0 42 49	2 41 6	4 43 19	6 41 35	8 43 49	10 46 2	12 44 18	14 46 32	16 44 48	2
18 47 59	20 50 12	22 44 32	0 46 46	2 45 2	4 47 15	6 45 32	8 47 45	10 49 58	12 48 15	14 50 28	16 48 45	3
18 51 56	20 54 9	22 48 29	0 50 42	2 48 59	4 51 12	6 49 29	8.51 42	10 53 55	12 52 12	14 54 25	16 52 41	4
18 55 52	20 58 5	22 52 25	0 54 39	2 52 55	4 55 8	6 53 25	8 55 38	10 57 52	12 56 8	14 58 21	16 56 38	5
18 59 49	21 2 2	22 56 22	0 58 35	2 56 52	4 59 5	6 57 22	8 59 35	11 1 48	13 0 5	15 2 18	17 0 35	6
19 3 45	21 5 59	23 0 19	1 2 32	3 0 48	5 3 2	7 1 18	9 3 32	11 5 45	13 4 1	15 6 14	17 4 31	7
19 7 42	21 9 55	23 4 16	1 6 28	3 4 45	5 6 58	7 5 15	9 7 28	11 9 41	13 7 58	15 10 11	17 8 28	8
19 11 38	21 13 52	23 8 12	1 10 25	3 8 41	5 10 55	7 9 11	9 11 25	11 13 38	13 11 54	15 14 8	17 12 24	9
19 15 35	21 17 48	23 12 8	1 14 21	3 12 38	5 14 51	7 13 8	9 15 21	11 17 34	13 15 51	15 18 4	17 16 21	10
19 19 32	21 21 45	23 16 5	1 18 18	3 16 35	5 18 48	7 17 5	9 19 18	11 21 31	13 19 47	15 22 1	17 20 17	11
19 23 28	21 25 41	23 20 1	1 22 14	3 20 31	5 22 44	7 21 1	9 23 14	11 25 27	13 23 44	15 25 57	17 24 14	12
19 27 25	21 29 38	23 23 58	1 26 11	3 24 28	5 26 41	7 24 58	9 27 11	11 29 24	13 27 41	15 29 54	17 28 10	13
19 31 21	21 33 34	23 27 54	1 30 8	3 28 24	5 30 37	7 28 54	9 31 7	11 33 21	13 31 37	15 33 50	17 32 7	14
19 35 18	21 37 31	23 31 51	1 34 4	3 32 21	5 34 34	7 32 51	9 35 4	11 37 17	13 35 34	15 37 47	17 36 4	15
19 39 14	21 41 28	23 35 48	1 38 1	3 36 17	5 38 31	7 36 47	9 39 1	11 41 14	13 39 30	15 41 43	17 40 0	16
19 43 11	21 45 24	23 39 44	1 41 57	3 40 14	5 42 27	7 40 44	9 42 57	11 45 10	13 43 27	15 45 40	17 43 57	17
19 47 7	21 49 21	23 43 41	1 45 54	3 44 10	5 46 24	7 44 40	9 46 54	11 49 7	13 47 23	15 49 37	17 47 53	18
19 51 4	21 53 18	23 47 37	1 49 50	3 48 7	5 50 20	7 48 37	9 50 50	11 53 3	13 51 20	15 53 33	17 51 50	19
19 55 0	21 57 14	23 51 34	1 53 47	3 52 4	5 54 17	7 52 34	9 54 47	11 57 0	13 55 16	15 57 30	17 55 46	20
19 58 57	22 1 10	23 55 30	1 57 43	3 56 0	5 58 13	7 56 30	9 58 43	12 0 56	13 59 13	16 1 26	17 59 43	21
20 2 51	22 5 7	23 59 27	2 1 40	3 59 57	5 2 10	8 0 27	10 2 40	12 4 53	14 3 10	16 5 23	18 3 39	22
20 6 50	22 9 3	0 3 23	2 5 37	4 3 53	6 6 6	8 4 23	10 6 36	12 8 50	14 7 6	16 9 19	18 7 36	23
20 10 47	22 13 0	0 7 20	2 9 33	4 7 50	6 10 3	8 8 20	10 10 33	12 12 46	14 11 3	16 13 16	18 11 33	24
20 14 43	22 16 57	0 11 17	2 13 30	4 11 46	6 14 0	8 12 16	10 14 29	12 16 43	14 14 59	16 17 12	18 15 29	25
20 18 40	22 20 53	0 15 13	2 17 26	4 15 43	6 17 56	8 16 13	10 18 26	12 20 39	14 18 56	16 21 9	18 19 26	26
20 22 36	22 24 50	0 19 10	2 21 23	4 19 39	6 21 53	8 20 9	10 22 23	12 24 36	14 22 52	16 25 6	18 23 22	27
20 26 33	22 28 46	0 23 6	2 25 19	4 23 36	6 25 49	8 24 6	10 26 19	12 28 32	14 26 49	16 29 2	18 27 19	28
20 30 30	22 32 43	0 27 3	2 29 16	4 27 33	6 29 46	8 28 3	10 30 16	12 32 29	14 30 45	16 32 59	18 31 15	29
20 34 26		0 30 59	2 33 12	4 31 29	6 33 42	8 31 59	10 34 12	12 36 25	14 34 42	16 36 55	18 35 12	30
20 38 23		0 34 56		4 35 26		8 35 56	10 38 9		14 38 39		18 39 9	31

1945

Jan.	Feb.	Mar.	April	May	June	July	Aug.	Sept.	Oct.	Nov.	Dec.	
18 43 5	20 45 18	22 35 42	0 37 55	2 36 12	4 38 25	6 36 42	8 38 55	10 41 8	12 39 25	14 41 38	16 39 54	1
18 47 2	20 49 15	22 39 38	0 41 52	2 40 8	4 42 21	6 40 38	8 42 51	10 45 5	12 43 21	14 45 34	16 43 51	2
18 50 58	20 53 11	22 43 35	0 45 48	2 44 5	4 46 18	6 44 35	8 46 48	10 49 1	12 47 18	14 49 31	16 47 48	3
18 54 55	20 57 8	22 47 31	0 49 45	2 48 1	4 50 14	6 48 31	8 50 44	10 52 58	12 51 14	14 53 27	16 51 44	4
18 58 51	21 1 5	22 51 28	0 53 41	2 51 58	4 54 11	6 52 28	8 54 41	10 56 54	12 55 11	14 57 24	16 55 41	5
19 2 48	21 5 1	22 55 25	0 57 38	2 55 54	4 58 8	6 56 24	8 58 38	11 0 51	12 59 7	15 1 20	16 59 38	6
19 6 44	21 8 58	22 59 21	1 1 34	2 59 51	5 2 4	7 0 21	9 2 34	11 4 47	13 3 4	15 5 17	17 3 34	7
19 10 41	21 12 54	23 3 18	1 5 31	3 3 47	5 6 1	7 4 17	9 6 31	11 8 44	13 7 0	15 9 14	17 7 30	8
19 14 38	21 16 51	23 7 14	1 9 27	3 7 44	5 9 57	7 8 14	9 10 27	11 12 40	13 10 57	15 13 10	17 11 27	9
19 18 34	21 20 47	23 11 11	1 13 24	3 11 40	5 13 54	7 12 11	9 14 24	11 16 37	13 14 54	15 17 7	17 15 23	10
19 22 31	21 24 44	23 15 7	1 17 21	3 15 37	5 17 50	7 16 7	9 18 20	11 20 34	13 18 50	15 21 3	17 19 20	11
19 26 28	21 28 40	23 19 4	1 21 17	3 19 33	5 21 47	7 20 4	9 22 17	11 24 30	13 22 47	15 25 0	17 23 17	12
19 30 24	21 32 37	23 23 0	1 25 14	3 23 30	5 25 44	7 24 0	9 26 13	11 28 27	13 26 44	15 28 56	17 27 13	13
19 34 20	21 36 34	23 26 57	1 29 10	3 27 27	5 29 40	7 27 57	9 30 10	11 32 24	13 30 40	15 32 53	17 31 10	14
19 38 17	21 40 30	23 30 54	1 33 7	3 31 23	5 33 37	7 31 53	9 34 7	11 36 20	13 34 36	15 36 50	17 35 6	15
19 42 13	21 44 27	23 34 50	1 37 3	3 35 20	5 37 33	7 35 50	9 38 3	11 40 16	13 38 33	15 40 46	17 39 3	16
19 46 10	21 48 24	23 38 47	1 41 0	3 39 16	5 41 30	7 39 47	9 42 0	11 44 13	13 42 29	15 44 43	17 42 59	17
19 50 7	21 52 20	23 42 43	1 44 56	3 43 13	5 45 26	7 43 43	9 45 56	11 48 9	13 46 26	15 48 40	17 46 56	18
19 54 3	21 56 16	23 46 40	1 48 53	3 47 10	5 49 23	7 47 40	9 49 53	11 52 6	13 50 23	15 52 36	17 50 52	19
19 58 0	22 0 13	23 50 36	1 52 49	3 51 6	5 53 19	7 51 36	9 53 49	11 56 2	13 54 19	15 56 32	17 54 49	20
20 1 56	22 4 9	23 54 33	1 56 46	3 55 3	5 57 16	7 55 33	9 57 46	11 59 59	13 58 16	16 0 29	17 58 46	21
20 5 53	22 8 6	23 58 29	2 0 43	3 58 59	6 1 13	7 59 29	10 1 42	12 3 56	14 2 12	16 4 25	18 2 42	22
20 9 49	22 12 3	0 2 26	2 4 39	4 2 56	6 5 9	8 3 26	10 5 39	12 7 52	14 6 9	16 8 22	18 6 39	23
20 13 46	22 15 59	0 6 23	2 8 36	4 6 52	6 9 6	8 7 22	10 9 36	12 11 49	14 10 5	16 12 19	18 10 35	24
20 17 42	22 19 56	0 10 19	2 12 32	4 10 49	6 13 2	8 11 19	10 13 32	12 15 45	14 14 2	16 16 15	18 14 32	25
20 21 39	22 23 52	0 14 16	2 16 29	4 14 45	6 16 59	8 15 15	10 17 29	12 19 42	14 17 58	16 20 12	18 18 28	26
20 25 36	22 27 49	0 18 12	2 20 25	4 18 42	6 20 55	8 19 12	10 21 25	12 23 38	14 21 55	16 24 8	18 22 25	27
20 29 32	22 31 45	0 22 9	2 24 22	4 22 39	6 24 52	8 23 9	10 25 22	12 27 35	14 25 52	16 28 5	18 26 21	28
20 33 29		0 26 5	2 28 18	4 26 35	6 28 48	8 27 5	10 29 18	12 31 31	14 29 48	16 32 1	18 30 18	29
20 37 25		0 30 2	2 32 15	4 30 22	6 32 45	8 31 2	10 33 15	12 35 28	14 33 45	16 35 58	18 34 15	30
20 41 22		0 33 58		4 34 28		8 34 58	10 37 11		14 37 42		18 38 11	31

1946

Jan.	Feb.	Mar.	April	May	June	July	Aug.	Sept.	Oct.	Nov.	Dec.	
18 42 8	20 44 21	22 34 45	0 36 58	2 35 14	4 37 28	6 35 44	8 37 58	10 40 11	12 38 27	14 40 40	16 38 57	1
18 46 4	20 48 18	22 38 41	0 40 54	2 39 11	4 41 24	6 39 41	8 41 54	10 44 7	12 42 24	14 44 37	16 42 54	2
18 50 1	20 52 14	22 42 38	0 44 51	2 43 7	4 45 21	6 43 37	8 45 51	10 48 4	12 46 20	14 48 34	16 46 50	3
18 53 57	20 56 11	22 46 34	0 48 47	2 47 4	4 49 17	6 47 34	8 49 47	10 52 0	12 50 17	14 52 30	16 50 47	4
18 57 54	21 0 7	22 50 31	0 52 44	2 51 0	4 53 14	6 51 30	8 53 44	10 55 57	12 54 14	14 56 27	16 54 43	5
19 1 51	21 4 4	22 54 27	0 56 40	2 54 57	4 57 10	6 55 27	8 57 40	10 59 53	12 58 10	15 0 23	16 58 40	6
19 5 47	21 8 0	22 58 24	1 0 37	2 58 54	5 1 7	6 59 24	9 1 37	11 3 50	13 2 7	15 4 20	17 2 37	7
19 9 44	21 11 57	23 2 20	1 4 34	3 2 50	5 5 3	7 3 20	9 5 33	11 7 47	13 6 3	15 8 16	17 6 33	8
19 13 40	21 15 53	23 6 17	1 8 30	3 6 47	5 9 0	7 7 17	8 9 30	11 11 43	13 10 0	15 12 13	17 10 30	9
19 17 37	21 19 50	23 10 13	1 12 27	3 10 43	5 12 57	7 11 13	9 13 27	11 15 40	13 13 56	15 16 9	17 14 26	10
19 21 33	21 23 47	23 14 10	1 16 23	3 14 40	5 16 53	7 15 10	9 17 23	11 19 36	13 17 53	15 20 6	17 18 23	11
19 25 30	21 27 43	23 18 7	1 20 20	3 18 36	5 20 50	7 19 6	9 21 20	11 23 33	13 21 49	15 24 3	17 22 19	12
19 29 26	21 31 40	23 22 3	1 24 16	3 22 33	5 24 46	7 23 3	9 25 16	11 27 29	13 25 46	15 27 59	17 26 16	13
19 33 23	21 35 36	23 26 0	1 28 13	3 26 29	5 28 43	7 27 0	9 29 13	11 31 26	13 29 42	15 31 56	17 30 12	14
19 37 20	21 39 33	23 29 56	1 32 9	3 30 26	5 32 39	7 30 56	9 33 9	11 35 22	13 33 39	15 35 52	17 34 9	15
19 41 16	21 43 29	23 33 53	1 36 6	3 34 23	5 36 36	7 34 53	9 37 6	11 39 19	13 37 36	15 39 49	17 38 6	16
19 45 13	21 47 26	23 37 49	1 40 3	3 38 19	5 40 32	7 38 49	9 41 2	11 43 16	13 41 32	15 43 45	17 42 2	17
19 49 9	21 51 22	23 41 46	1 43 59	3 42 16	5 44 29	7 42 46	9 44 59	11 47 12	13 45 29	15 47 42	17 45 59	18
19 43 6	21 55 19	23 45 42	1 47 56	3 46 12	5 48 26	7 46 42	9 48 56	11 51 9	13 49 25	15 51 39	17 49 55	19
19 57 2	21 59 16	23 49 39	1 51 52	3 50 9	5 52 22	7 50 39	9 52 52	11 55 5	13 53 22	15 55 35	17 53 52	20
20 0 59	22 3 12	23 53 36	1 55 49	3 54 5	5 56 19	7 54 35	9 56 49	11 59 2	13 57 18	15 59 32	17 57 49	21
20 4 55	22 7 9	23 57 32	1 59 45	3 58 2	6 0 15	7 58 32	10 0 45	12 2 58	14 1 15	16 3 28	18 1 45	22
20 8 52	22 11 5	0 1 29	1 3 42	4 1 59	6 4 12	8 2 29	10 4 42	12 6 55	14 5 12	16 7 25	18 5 42	23
20 12 48	22 15 2	0 5 25	1 7 38	4 5 55	6 8 8	8 6 25	10 8 38	12 10 51	14 9 8	16 11 21	18 9 38	24
20 16 45	22 18 58	0 9 22	1 11 35	4 9 52	6 12 5	8 10 22	10 12 35	12 14 48	14 13 5	16 15 18	18 13 35	25
20 20 42	22 22 55	0 13 18	1 15 32	4 13 48	6 16 1	8 14 18	10 16 31	12 18 45	14 17 1	16 19 14	18 17 31	26
20 24 38	22 26 51	0 17 15	1 19 28	4 17 45	6 19 58	8 18 15	10 20 28	12 22 41	14 20 58	16 23 11	18 21 28	27
20 28 35	22 30 48	0 21 11	1 23 25	4 21 41	6 23 55	8 22 11	10 24 25	12 26 38	14 24 54	16 27 8	18 25 24	28
20 32 31		0 25 8	1 27 21	4 25 38	6 27 51	8 26 8	10 28 21	12 30 35	14 28 51	16 31 4	18 29 21	29
20 36 28		0 29 5	1 31 18	4 29 34	6 31 48	8 30 5	10 32 18	12 34 31	14 32 47	16 35 1	18 33 17	30
20 40 24		0 33 1		4 33 31		8 34 1	10 36 14		14 36 44		18 37 14	31

1947

	Jan.	Feb.	Mar.	April	May	June	July	Aug.	Sept.	Oct.	Nov.	Dec.
1	18 41 10	20 43 24	22 33 47	0 36 0	2 34 17	4 36 30	6 34 47	8 37 0	10 39 14	12 37 30	14 39 43	16 38 0
2	18 45 7	20 47 20	22 37 44	0 39 57	2 38 14	4 40 27	6 38 44	8 40 57	10 43 10	12 41 27	14 43 40	16 41 57
3	18 49 4	20 51 17	22 41 40	0 43 54	2 42 10	4 44 23	6 42 40	8 44 53	10 47 7	12 45 24	14 47 38	16 45 53
4	18 53 0	20 55 13	22 45 37	0 47 50	2 46 7	4 48 20	6 46 37	8 48 50	10 51 3	12 49 20	14 51 33	16 49 50
5	18 56 57	20 59 10	22 49 34	0 51 47	2 50 3	4 52 17	6 50 33	8 52 47	10 55 0	12 53 16	14 55 30	16 53 46
6	19 0 53	21 3 7	22 53 30	0 55 43	2 54 0	4 56 13	6 54 30	8 56 43	10 58 56	12 57 13	14 59 26	16 57 43
7	19 4 50	21 7 3	22 57 27	0 59 40	2 57 56	5 0 10	6 58 26	9 0 40	11 2 53	13 1 10	15 3 23	17 1 39
8	19 8 46	21 11 0	23 1 23	1 3 36	3 1 53	5 4 6	7 2 23	9 4 36	11 6 49	13 5 6	15 7 19	17 5 36
9	19 12 43	21 14 56	23 5 20	1 7 33	3 5 50	5 8 3	7 6 20	9 8 33	11 10 46	13 9 3	15 11 16	17 9 33
10	19 16 40	21 18 53	23 9 16	1 11 29	3 9 46	5 11 59	7 10 16	9 12 30	11 14 43	13 12 59	15 15 12	17 13 29
11	19 20 36	21 22 49	23 13 13	1 15 26	3 13 43	5 15 56	7 14 13	9 16 26	11 18 39	13 16 56	15 19 9	17 17 26
12	19 24 33	21 26 46	23 17 9	1 19 23	3 17 39	5 19 52	7 18 9	9 20 22	11 22 36	13 20 52	15 23 5	17 21 22
13	19 28 29	21 30 42	23 21 6	1 23 19	3 21 36	5 23 49	7 22 6	9 24 19	11 26 32	13 24 49	15 27 2	17 25 19
14	19 32 26	21 34 39	23 25 3	1 27 16	3 25 32	5 27 46	7 26 2	9 28 16	11 30 29	13 28 45	15 30 59	17 29 15
15	19 36 22	21 38 36	23 28 59	1 31 12	3 29 29	5 31 42	7 29 59	9 32 12	11 34 25	13 32 42	15 34 55	17 33 12
16	19 40 19	21 42 32	23 32 56	1 35 9	3 33 25	5 35 39	7 33 55	9 36 9	11 38 22	13 36 38	15 38 52	17 37 8
17	19 44 15	21 46 29	23 36 52	1 39 5	3 37 22	5 39 35	7 37 52	9 40 5	11 42 18	13 40 35	15 42 48	17 41 5
18	19 48 12	21 50 25	23 40 49	1 43 2	3 41 19	5 43 32	7 41 49	9 44 2	11 46 15	13 44 32	15 46 45	17 45 2
19	19 52 9	21 54 22	23 44 45	1 46 59	3 45 15	5 47 28	7 45 45	9 47 59	11 50 12	13 48 28	15 50 41	17 48 58
20	19 56 5	21 58 18	23 48 42	1 50 55	3 49 12	5 51 25	7 49 42	9 51 55	11 54 8	13 52 25	15 54 38	17 52 55
21	20 0 2	22 2 15	23 52 38	1 54 52	3 53 8	5 55 22	7 53 38	9 55 51	11 58 5	13 56 21	15 58 34	17 56 51
22	20 3 58	22 6 11	23 56 35	1 58 48	3 57 5	5 59 18	7 57 35	9 59 48	12 2 1	14 0 18	16 2 31	18 0 48
23	20 7 55	22 10 8	0 0 31	2 2 45	4 1 1	6 3 15	8 1 31	10 3 45	12 5 58	14 4 14	16 6 28	18 4 44
24	20 11 51	22 14 5	0 4 28	2 6 41	4 4 58	6 7 11	8 5 28	10 7 41	12 9 54	14 8 11	16 10 24	18 8 41
25	20 15 48	22 18 1	0 8 25	2 10 38	4 8 54	6 11 8	8 9 24	10 11 38	12 13 51	14 12 7	16 14 21	18 12 37
26	20 19 44	22 21 58	0 12 21	2 14 34	4 12 51	6 15 4	8 13 21	10 15 34	12 17 47	14 16 4	16 18 17	18 16 34
27	20 23 41	22 25 54	0 16 18	2 18 31	4 16 48	6 19 1	8 17 18	10 19 31	12 21 44	14 20 1	16 22 14	18 20 31
28	20 27 38	22 29 51	0 20 14	2 22 27	4 20 44	6 22 57	8 21 14	10 23 27	12 25 41	14 23 57	16 26 10	18 24 27
29	20 31 34		0 24 11	2 26 24	4 24 41	6 26 54	8 25 11	10 27 24	12 29 37	14 27 54	16 30 7	18 28 24
30	20 35 31		0 28 7	2 30 21	4 28 37	6 30 51	8 29 7	10 31 20	12 33 34	14 31 51	16 34 3	18 32 20
31	20 39 27		0 32 4		4 32 34		8 33 4	10 35 17		14 35 47		18 36 17

1948

	Jan.	Feb.	Mar.	April	May	June	July	Aug.	Sept.	Oct.	Nov.	Dec.
1	18 40 13	20 42 27	22 36 47	0 39 0	2 37 17	4 39 30	6 37 47	8 40 0	10 42 13	12 40 30	14 42 43	16 41 0
2	18 44 10	20 46 23	22 40 43	0 42 56	2 41 13	4 43 26	6 41 43	8 43 56	10 46 10	12 44 26	14 46 39	16 44 56
3	18 48 7	20 50 20	22 44 40	0 46 53	2 45 10	4 47 23	6 45 40	8 47 53	10 50 6	12 48 23	14 50 36	16 48 53
4	18 52 3	20 54 16	22 48 36	0 50 50	2 49 6	4 51 19	6 49 36	8 51 50	10 54 3	12 52 19	14 54 33	16 52 49
5	18 56 0	20 58 13	22 52 33	0 54 46	2 53 3	4 55 16	6 53 33	8 55 46	10 57 59	12 56 16	14 58 29	16 56 46
6	18 59 56	21 2 9	22 56 30	0 58 43	2 56 59	4 59 13	6 57 29	8 59 43	11 1 56	13 0 12	15 2 26	17 0 42
7	19 3 53	21 6 6	23 0 26	1 2 39	3 0 56	5 3 9	7 1 26	9 3 39	11 5 52	13 4 9	15 6 22	17 4 39
8	19 7 49	21 10 3	23 4 23	1 6 36	3 4 52	5 7 6	7 5 22	9 7 36	11 9 49	13 8 6	15 10 19	17 8 36
9	19 11 46	21 13 59	23 8 19	1 10 32	3 8 49	5 11 2	7 9 19	9 11 32	11 13 46	13 12 2	15 14 15	17 12 32
10	19 15 42	21 17 56	23 12 16	1 14 29	3 12 46	5 14 59	7 13 16	9 15 29	11 17 42	13 15 59	15 18 12	17 16 29
11	19 19 39	21 21 53	23 16 12	1 18 25	3 16 42	5 18 55	7 17 12	9 19 26	11 21 39	13 19 55	15 22 8	17 20 25
12	19 23 36	21 25 49	23 20 9	1 22 22	3 20 39	5 22 52	7 21 9	9 23 22	11 25 35	13 23 52	15 26 5	17 24 22
13	19 27 32	21 29 46	23 24 5	1 26 19	3 24 35	5 26 49	7 25 5	9 27 19	11 29 32	13 27 48	15 30 2	17 28 18
14	19 31 29	21 33 42	23 28 2	1 30 15	3 28 32	5 30 45	7 29 2	9 31 15	11 33 28	13 31 45	15 33 58	17 32 15
15	19 35 25	21 37 38	23 31 59	1 34 12	3 32 28	5 34 42	7 32 59	9 35 12	11 37 25	13 35 41	15 37 55	17 36 11
16	19 39 22	21 41 35	23 35 55	1 38 8	3 36 25	5 38 38	7 36 55	9 39 8	11 41 21	13 39 38	15 41 51	17 40 8
17	19 43 18	21 45 32	23 39 52	1 42 5	3 40 21	5 42 35	7 40 52	9 43 5	11 45 18	13 43 35	15 45 48	17 44 5
18	19 47 15	21 49 28	23 43 48	1 46 1	3 44 18	5 46 32	7 44 48	9 47 1	11 49 14	13 47 31	15 49 44	17 48 1
19	19 51 11	21 53 25	23 47 45	1 49 58	3 48 15	5 50 28	7 48 45	9 50 58	11 53 11	13 51 28	15 53 41	17 51 58
20	19 55 8	21 57 21	23 51 41	1 53 54	3 52 11	5 54 24	7 52 41	9 54 54	11 57 8	13 55 24	15 57 37	17 55 54
21	19 59 5	22 1 18	23 55 38	1 57 51	3 56 8	5 58 21	7 56 38	9 58 51	12 1 4	13 59 21	16 1 34	17 59 51
22	20 3 1	22 5 14	23 59 34	2 1 48	4 0 4	6 2 18	8 0 34	10 2 48	12 5 1	14 3 17	16 5 31	18 3 47
23	20 6 58	22 9 11	0 3 31	2 5 44	4 4 1	6 6 14	8 4 31	10 6 44	12 8 57	14 7 14	16 9 27	18 7 44
24	20 10 54	22 13 7	0 7 28	2 9 41	4 7 58	6 10 11	8 8 27	10 10 41	12 12 54	14 11 10	16 13 24	18 11 40
25	20 14 51	22 17 4	0 11 24	2 13 37	4 11 54	6 14 7	8 12 24	10 14 37	12 16 50	14 15 7	16 17 20	18 15 37
26	20 18 47	22 21 1	0 15 21	2 17 34	4 15 50	6 18 4	8 16 21	10 18 34	12 20 47	14 19 4	16 21 17	18 19 34
27	20 22 44	22 24 57	0 19 17	2 21 30	4 19 47	6 22 0	8 20 17	10 22 30	12 24 43	14 23 0	16 25 13	18 23 30
28	20 26 40	22 28 54	0 23 14	2 25 27	4 23 44	6 25 57	8 24 14	10 26 27	12 28 40	14 26 57	16 29 10	18 27 27
29	20 30 37	22 32 50	0 27 10	2 29 23	4 27 40	6 29 53	8 28 10	10 30 23	12 32 37	14 30 53	16 33 6	18 31 23
30	20 34 34		0 31 7	2 33 20	4 31 37	6 33 50	8 32 7	10 34 20	12 36 33	14 34 50	16 37 3	18 35 20
31	20 38 30		0 35 3		4 35 33		8 36 3	10 38 17		14 38 46		18 39 16

1949

	Jan.	Feb.	Mar.	April	May	June	July	Aug.	Sept.	Oct.	Nov.	Dec.
1	18 43 13	20 45 26	22 35 50	0 38 3	2 36 20	4 38 33	6 36 50	8 39 3	10 41 16	12 39 33	14 41 46	16 40 3
2	18 47 9	20 49 23	22 39 46	0 41 9	2 40 16	4 42 29	6 40 46	8 42 59	10 45 13	12 43 29	14 45 42	16 43 59
3	18 51 6	20 53 19	22 43 43	0 45 56	2 44 13	4 46 26	6 44 43	8 46 56	10 49 9	12 47 26	14 49 39	16 47 56
4	18 55 3	20 57 16	22 47 39	0 49 53	2 48 9	4 50 23	6 48 39	8 50 53	10 53 6	12 51 22	14 53 36	16 51 52
5	18 58 59	21 1 12	22 51 36	0 53 49	2 52 6	4 54 19	6 52 36	8 54 49	10 57 2	12 55 19	14 57 32	16 55 49
6	19 2 56	21 5 9	22 55 33	0 57 46	2 56 2	4 58 16	6 56 32	8 58 46	11 0 59	12 59 15	15 1 29	16 59 45
7	19 6 52	21 9 6	22 59 29	1 1 42	2 59 59	5 2 12	7 0 29	9 2 42	11 4 55	13 3 12	15 5 25	17 3 42
8	19 10 49	21 13 2	23 3 26	1 5 39	3 3 55	5 6 9	7 4 25	9 6 39	11 8 52	13 7 9	15 9 22	17 7 39
9	19 14 45	21 16 59	23 7 22	1 9 35	3 7 52	5 10 5	7 8 22	9 10 35	11 12 49	13 11 5	15 13 18	17 11 35
10	19 18 42	21 20 55	23 11 19	1 13 32	3 11 49	5 14 2	7 12 19	9 14 32	11 16 45	13 15 2	15 17 15	17 15 32
11	19 22 38	21 24 52	23 15 15	1 17 28	3 15 45	5 17 58	7 16 15	9 18 28	11 20 42	13 18 58	15 21 11	17 19 28
12	19 26 35	21 28 48	23 19 12	1 21 25	3 19 42	5 21 55	7 20 12	9 22 25	11 24 38	13 22 55	15 25 8	17 23 25
13	19 30 32	21 32 45	23 23 8	1 25 22	3 23 38	5 25 52	7 24 8	9 26 22	11 28 35	13 26 51	15 29 5	17 27 21
14	19 34 28	21 36 41	23 27 5	1 29 18	3 27 35	5 29 48	7 28 5	9 30 18	11 32 31	13 30 48	15 33 1	17 31 18
15	19 38 25	21 40 38	23 31 2	1 33 15	3 31 31	5 33 45	7 32 1	9 34 15	11 36 28	13 34 44	15 36 58	17 35 14
16	19 42 21	21 44 35	23 34 58	1 37 11	3 35 28	5 37 41	7 35 58	9 38 11	11 40 24	13 38 41	15 40 54	17 39 11
17	19 46 18	21 48 31	23 38 55	1 41 8	3 39 24	5 41 38	7 39 55	9 42 8	11 44 21	13 42 38	15 44 51	17 43 8
18	19 50 14	21 52 28	23 42 51	1 45 4	3 43 21	5 45 34	7 43 51	9 46 4	11 48 18	13 46 34	15 48 47	17 47 4
19	19 54 11	21 56 24	23 46 48	1 49 1	3 47 18	5 49 31	7 47 48	9 50 1	11 52 14	13 50 31	15 52 44	17 51 1
20	19 58 8	22 0 21	23 50 44	1 52 57	3 51 14	5 53 27	7 51 44	9 53 57	11 56 11	13 54 27	15 56 40	17 54 57
21	20 2 4	22 4 17	23 54 41	1 56 54	3 55 11	5 57 24	7 55 41	9 57 54	12 0 7	13 58 24	16 0 37	17 58 54
22	20 6 1	22 8 14	23 58 37	2 0 51	3 59 7	6 1 21	7 59 37	10 1 51	12 4 4	14 2 20	16 4 34	18 2 50
23	20 9 57	22 12 10	0 2 34	2 4 47	4 3 4	6 5 17	8 3 34	10 5 47	12 8 0	14 6 17	16 8 30	18 6 47
24	20 13 54	22 16 7	0 6 31	2 8 44	4 7 0	6 9 14	8 7 30	10 9 44	12 11 57	14 10 13	16 12 27	18 10 43
25	20 17 50	22 20 4	0 10 27	2 12 40	4 10 57	6 13 10	8 11 27	10 13 40	12 15 53	14 14 10	16 16 23	18 14 40
26	20 21 47	22 24 0	0 14 24	2 16 37	4 14 53	6 17 7	8 15 24	10 17 37	12 19 50	14 18 7	16 20 20	18 18 37
27	20 25 43	22 27 57	0 18 20	2 20 33	4 18 50	6 21 3	8 19 20	10 21 33	12 23 46	14 22 3	16 24 16	18 22 33
28	20 29 40	22 31 53	0 22 17	2 24 30	4 22 47	6 25 0	8 23 17	10 25 30	12 27 43	14 26 0	16 28 13	18 26 30
29	20 33 37		0 26 13	2 28 26	4 26 43	6 28 56	8 27 13	10 29 26	12 31 40	14 29 56	16 32 10	18 30 26
30	20 37 33		0 30 10	2 32 23	4 30 40	6 32 53	8 31 10	10 33 23	12 35 36	14 33 53	16 36 6	18 34 23
31	20 41 30		0 34 6		4 34 36		8 35 6	10 37 20		14 37 49		18 38 19

1950

Jan.	Feb.	Mar.	April	May	June	July	Aug.	Sept.	Oct.	Nov.	Dec.	
18 42 16	20 44 29	22 34 53	0 37 6	2 35 23	4 37 36	6 35 53	8 38 6	10 40 19	12 38 36	14 40 49	16 39 6	1
18 46 12	20 48 26	22 38 49	0 41 3	2 39 19	4 41 32	6 39 49	8 42 2	10 44 16	12 42 32	14 44 46	16 43 2	2
18 50 9	20 52 22	22 42 46	0 44 59	2 43 16	4 45 29	6 43 46	8 45 59	10 48 12	12 46 29	14 48 42	16 46 59	3
18 54 6	20 56 19	22 46 42	0 48 56	2 47 12	4 49 26	6 47 42	8 49 56	10 52 9	12 50 25	14 52 39	16 50 55	4
18 58 2	21 0 15	22 50 39	0 52 52	2 51 9	4 53 22	6 51 39	8 53 52	10 56 5	12 54 22	14 56 35	16 54 52	5
19 1 59	21 4 12	22 54 36	0 56 49	2 55 5	4 57 19	6 55 35	8 57 49	11 0 2	12 58 19	15 0 32	16 58 48	6
19 5 55	21 8 9	22 58 32	1 0 45	2 59 2	5 1 15	6 59 32	9 1 45	11 3 58	13 2 15	15 4 28	17 2 45	7
19 9 52	21 12 5	23 2 29	1 4 42	3 2 59	5 5 12	7 3 29	9 5 42	11 7 55	13 6 12	15 8 25	17 6 42	8
19 13 48	21 16 2	23 6 25	1 8 38	3 6 55	5 9 8	7 7 25	9 9 38	11 11 52	13 10 8	15 12 21	17 10 38	9
19 17 45	21 19 58	23 10 22	1 12 35	3 10 52	5 13 5	7 11 22	9 13 35	11 15 48	13 14 5	15 16 18	17 14 35	10
19 21 42	21 23 55	23 14 18	1 16 32	3 14 48	5 17 1	7 15 18	9 17 31	11 19 45	13 18 1	15 20 14	17 18 31	11
19 25 38	21 27 51	23 18 15	1 20 28	3 18 45	5 20 58	7 19 15	9 21 28	11 23 41	13 21 58	15 24 11	17 22 28	12
19 29 35	21 31 48	23 22 11	1 24 25	3 22 41	5 24 55	7 23 11	9 25 25	11 27 38	13 25 54	15 28 8	17 26 24	13
19 33 31	21 35 44	23 26 8	1 28 21	3 26 38	5 28 51	7 27 8	9 29 21	11 31 34	13 29 51	15 32 4	17 30 21	14
19 37 28	21 39 41	23 30 5	1 32 18	3 30 34	5 32 48	7 31 4	9 33 18	11 35 31	13 33 48	15 36 1	17 34 18	15
19 41 24	21 43 38	23 34 1	1 36 14	3 34 31	5 36 44	7 35 1	9 37 14	11 39 27	13 37 44	15 39 57	17 38 14	16
19 45 21	21 47 34	23 37 58	1 40 11	3 38 27	5 40 41	7 38 58	9 41 11	11 43 24	13 41 41	15 43 54	17 42 11	17
19 49 17	21 51 31	23 41 54	1 44 7	3 42 24	5 44 37	7 42 54	9 45 7	11 47 21	13 45 37	15 47 50	17 46 7	18
19 53 14	21 55 27	23 45 51	1 48 4	3 46 21	5 48 34	7 46 51	9 49 4	11 51 17	13 49 34	15 51 47	17 50 4	19
19 57 11	21 59 24	23 49 47	1 52 0	3 50 17	5 52 30	7 50 47	9 53 0	11 55 14	13 53 30	15 55 44	17 54 0	20
20 1 7	22 3 20	23 53 44	1 55 57	3 54 14	5 56 27	7 54 44	9 56 57	11 59 10	13 57 27	15 59 40	17 57 57	21
20 5 4	22 7 17	23 57 40	1 59 54	3 58 10	6 0 24	7 58 40	10 0 54	12 3 7	14 1 23	16 3 37	18 1 53	22
20 9 0	22 11 13	0 1 37	2 3 50	4 2 7	6 4 20	8 2 37	10 4 50	12 7 3	14 5 20	16 7 33	18 5 50	23
20 12 57	22 15 10	0 5 34	2 7 47	4 6 3	6 8 17	8 6 33	10 8 47	12 11 0	14 9 17	16 11 30	18 9 47	24
20 16 53	22 19 7	0 9 30	2 11 43	4 10 0	6 12 13	8 10 30	10 12 43	12 14 56	14 13 13	16 15 26	18 13 43	25
20 20 50	22 23 3	0 13 27	2 15 40	4 13 57	6 16 10	8 14 27	10 16 40	12 18 53	14 17 10	16 19 23	18 17 40	26
20 24 46	22 27 0	0 17 23	2 19 36	4 17 53	6 20 6	8 18 23	10 20 36	12 22 50	14 21 6	16 23 19	18 21 36	27
20 28 43	22 30 56	0 21 20	2 23 33	4 21 50	6 24 3	8 22 20	10 24 33	12 26 46	14 25 3	16 27 16	18 25 33	28
20 32 40		0 25 16	2 27 29	4 25 46	6 28 0	8 26 16	10 28 29	12 30 43	14 28 59	16 31 13	18 29 29	29
20 36 36		0 29 13	2 31 26	4 29 43	6 31 56	8 30 13	10 32 26	12 34 39	14 32 56	16 35 9	18 33 26	30
20 40 33		0 33 9		4 33 39		8 34 9	20 36 23		14 36 52		18 37 22	31

1951

Jan.	Feb.	Mar.	April	May	June	July	Aug.	Sept.	Oct.	Nov.	Dec.	
18 41 19	20 43 32	22 33 56	0 36 9	2 34 26	4 36 39	6 34 56	8 37 9	10 39 22	12 37 39	14 39 52	16 38 9	1
18 45 16	20 47 29	22 37 52	0 40 6	2 38 22	4 40 35	6 38 52	8 41 6	10 43 19	12 41 35	14 43 49	16 42 5	2
18 49 12	20 51 25	22 41 49	0 44 2	2 42 19	4 44 32	6 42 49	8 45 2	10 47 15	12 45 32	14 47 45	16 46 2	3
18 53 9	20 55 22	22 45 46	0 47 59	2 46 15	4 48 29	6 46 45	8 48 59	10 51 12	12 49 28	14 51 42	16 49 58	4
18 57 5	20 59 19	22 49 42	0 51 55	2 50 12	4 52 25	6 50 42	8 52 55	10 55 8	12 53 25	14 55 38	16 53 55	5
19 1 2	21 3 15	22 53 39	0 55 52	2 54 8	4 56 22	6 54 38	8 56 52	10 59 5	12 57 22	14 59 35	16 57 52	6
19 4 58	21 7 12	22 57 35	0 59 49	2 58 5	5 0 18	6 58 35	9 0 48	11 3 1	13 1 18	15 3 31	17 1 48	7
19 8 55	21 11 8	23 1 32	1 3 45	3 2 2	5 4 15	7 2 32	9 4 45	11 6 58	13 5 15	15 7 28	17 5 45	8
19 12 51	21 15 5	23 5 28	1 7 41	3 5 58	5 8 11	7 6 28	9 8 41	11 10 55	13 9 11	15 11 24	17 9 41	9
19 16 48	21 19 1	23 9 25	1 11 38	3 9 55	5 12 8	7 10 25	9 12 38	11 14 51	13 13 8	15 15 21	17 13 38	10
19 20 45	21 22 58	23 13 21	1 15 35	3 13 51	5 16 5	7 14 21	9 16 35	11 18 48	13 17 4	15 19 18	17 17 34	11
19 24 41	21 26 54	23 17 18	1 19 31	3 17 48	5 20 1	7 18 18	9 20 31	11 22 44	13 21 1	15 23 14	17 21 31	12
19 28 38	21 30 51	23 21 14	1 23 28	3 21 44	5 23 58	7 22 14	9 24 28	11 26 41	13 24 57	15 27 11	17 25 27	13
19 32 34	21 34 48	23 25 11	1 27 24	3 25 41	5 27 54	7 26 11	9 28 24	11 30 37	13 28 54	15 31 7	17 29 24	14
19 36 31	21 38 44	23 29 8	1 31 21	3 29 37	5 31 51	7 30 7	9 32 21	11 34 34	13 32 51	15 35 4	17 33 21	15
19 40 27	21 42 41	23 33 4	1 35 17	3 33 34	5 35 47	7 31 4	9 36 17	11 38 31	13 36 47	15 39 0	17 37 17	16
19 44 24	21 46 37	23 37 1	1 39 14	3 37 31	5 39 44	7 38 1	9 40 14	11 42 27	13 40 44	15 42 57	17 41 14	17
19 48 20	21 50 34	23 40 57	1 43 10	3 41 27	5 43 40	7 41 57	9 44 10	11 46 24	13 44 40	15 46 53	17 45 10	18
19 52 17	21 54 30	23 44 54	1 47 7	3 45 24	5 47 37	7 45 54	9 48 7	11 50 20	13 48 37	15 50 50	17 49 7	19
19 56 14	21 58 27	23 48 50	1 51 4	3 49 20	5 51 34	7 49 50	9 52 4	11 54 17	13 52 33	15 54 47	17 53 3	20
20 0 10	22 2 23	23 52 47	1 55 0	3 53 17	5 55 30	7 53 47	9 56 0	11 58 13	13 56 30	15 58 43	17 57 0	21
20 4 7	22 6 20	23 56 43	1 58 57	3 57 13	5 59 27	7 57 43	9 59 57	12 2 10	14 0 26	16 2 40	18 0 56	22
20 8 3	22 10 17	0 0 40	2 2 53	4 1 10	6 3 23	8 1 40	10 3 53	12 6 6	14 4 23	16 6 36	18 4 53	23
20 12 0	12 14 13	0 4 37	2 6 50	4 5 6	6 7 20	8 5 37	10 7 50	12 10 3	14 8 20	16 10 33	18 8 50	24
20 15 56	12 18 10	0 8 33	2 10 46	4 9 3	6 11 16	8 9 33	10 11 46	12 13 59	14 12 16	16 14 29	18 12 46	25
20 19 53	22 22 6	0 12 30	2 14 43	4 13 0	6 15 13	8 13 30	10 15 43	12 17 56	14 16 13	16 18 26	18 16 43	26
20 23 50	22 26 3	0 16 26	2 18 39	4 16 56	6 19 9	8 17 26	10 19 39	12 21 53	14 20 9	16 22 22	18 20 39	27
20 27 46	22 29 59	0 20 23	2 22 36	4 20 53	6 23 6	8 21 23	10 23 36	12 25 49	14 24 6	16 26 19	18 24 36	28
20 31 43		0 24 19	2 26 33	4 24 49	6 27 3	8 25 19	10 27 33	12 29 46	14 28 2	16 30 16	18 28 32	29
20 35 39		0 28 16	2 30 29	4 28 46	6 30 59	8 29 16	10 31 29	12 33 42	14 31 59	16 34 12	18 32 29	30
20 39 36		0 32 12		4 32 42		8 33 12	10 35 26		14 35 55		18 36 25	31

1952

Jan.	Feb.	Mar.	April	May	June	July	Aug.	Sept.	Oct.	Nov.	Dec.	
18 40 22	20 42 35	22 36 57	0 39 9	2 37 25	4 39 39	6 37 55	8 40 9	10 42 22	12 40 38	14 42 52	16 41 8	1
18 44 19	20 46 32	22 40 52	0 43 5	2 41 22	4 43 35	6 41 52	8 44 5	10 46 18	12 44 35	14 46 48	16 45 5	2
18 48 15	20 50 28	22 44 49	0 47 2	2 45 18	4 47 32	6 45 48	8 48 2	10 50 15	12 48 31	14 50 45	16 49 1	3
18 52 12	20 54 25	22 48 45	0 50 58	2 49 15	4 51 28	6 49 45	8 51 58	10 54 11	12 52 28	14 54 41	16 52 58	4
18 56 8	20 58 22	22 52 42	0 54 55	2 53 11	4 55 25	6 53 41	8 55 55	10 58 8	12 56 25	14 58 38	16 56 55	5
19 0 5	21 2 18	22 56 38	0 58 51	2 57 8	4 59 21	6 57 38	8 59 51	11 2 5	13 0 21	15 2 34	17 0 51	6
19 4 1	21 6 15	23 0 35	1 2 48	3 1 5	5 3 18	7 1 35	9 3 48	11 6 1	13 4 18	15 6 31	17 4 48	7
19 7 58	21 10 11	23 4 31	1 6 44	3 5 1	5 7 14	7 5 31	9 7 44	11 9 58	13 8 14	15 10 27	17 8 44	8
19 11 54	21 14 8	23 8 28	1 10 41	3 8 58	5 11 11	7 9 28	9 11 41	11 13 54	13 12 11	15 14 24	17 12 41	9
19 15 51	21 18 4	23 12 24	1 14 38	3 12 54	5 15 8	7 13 24	9 15 38	11 17 51	13 16 7	15 18 21	17 16 37	10
19 19 48	21 22 1	23 16 21	1 18 34	3 16 51	5 19 4	7 17 21	9 19 34	11 21 47	13 20 4	15 22 17	17 20 34	11
19 23 44	21 25 57	23 20 18	1 22 31	3 20 47	5 23 1	7 21 17	9 23 31	11 25 44	13 24 0	15 26 14	17 24 30	12
19 27 41	21 29 54	23 24 14	1 26 27	3 24 44	5 26 57	7 25 14	9 27 27	11 29 40	13 27 57	15 30 10	17 28 27	13
19 31 37	21 33 51	23 28 11	1 30 24	3 28 40	5 30 54	7 29 11	9 31 24	11 33 37	13 31 54	15 34 7	17 32 24	14
19 35 34	21 37 47	23 32 7	1 34 20	3 32 37	5 34 50	7 33 7	9 35 20	11 37 34	13 35 50	15 38 3	17 36 20	15
19 39 30	21 41 44	23 36 4	1 38 17	3 36 34	5 38 47	7 37 4	9 39 17	11 41 30	13 39 47	15 42 0	17 40 17	16
19 43 27	21 45 40	23 40 0	1 42 13	3 40 30	5 42 43	7 41 0	9 43 13	11 45 27	13 43 43	15 45 56	17 44 13	17
19 47 24	21 49 37	23 43 57	1 46 10	3 44 27	5 46 40	7 44 57	9 47 10	11 49 23	13 47 40	15 49 53	17 48 10	18
19 51 20	21 53 33	23 47 53	1 50 7	3 48 23	5 50 37	7 48 53	9 51 7	11 53 20	13 51 36	15 53 50	17 52 6	19
19 55 17	21 57 30	23 51 50	1 54 3	3 52 20	5 54 33	7 52 50	9 55 3	11 57 16	13 55 33	15 57 46	17 56 3	20
19 59 13	22 1 26	23 55 47	1 58 0	3 56 16	5 58 30	7 56 46	9 59 0	12 1 13	13 59 29	16 1 43	17 59 59	21
20 3 10	22 5 23	23 59 43	2 1 56	4 0 13	6 2 26	8 0 43	10 2 56	12 5 9	14 3 26	16 5 39	18 3 56	22
20 7 6	22 9 20	0 3 40	2 5 53	4 4 9	6 6 23	8 4 40	10 6 53	12 9 6	14 7 23	16 9 36	18 7 53	23
20 11 3	22 13 16	0 7 36	2 9 49	4 8 6	6 10 19	8 8 36	10 10 49	12 13 2	14 11 19	16 13 32	18 11 49	24
20 14 59	22 17 13	0 11 33	2 13 46	4 12 3	6 14 16	8 12 33	10 14 46	12 16 59	14 15 16	16 17 29	18 15 46	25
20 18 56	22 21 9	0 15 29	2 17 42	4 15 59	6 18 12	8 16 29	10 18 42	12 20 56	14 19 12	16 21 25	18 19 42	26
20 22 53	22 25 6	0 19 26	2 21 39	4 19 56	6 22 9	8 20 26	10 22 39	12 24 52	14 23 9	16 25 22	18 23 39	27
20 26 49	22 29 2	0 23 22	2 25 36	4 23 52	6 26 6	8 24 22	10 26 36	12 28 49	14 27 5	16 29 19	18 27 35	28
20 30 46	22 32 59	0 27 19	2 29 32	4 27 49	6 30 2	8 28 19	10 30 32	12 32 45	14 31 2	16 33 15	18 31 32	29
20 34 42		0 31 15	2 33 29	4 31 45	6 33 59	8 32 15	10 34 29	12 36 42	14 34 58	16 37 12	18 35 28	30
20 38 39		0 35 12		4 35 42		8 36 12	10 38 25		14 38 55		18 39 25	31

1953

	Jan.	Feb.	Mar.	April	May	June	July	Aug.	Sept.	Oct.	Nov.	Dec.
1	18 43 22	20 45 35	22 35 58	0 38 12	2 36 28	4 38 41	6 36 58	8 39 11	10 41 25	12 39 41	14 41 55	16 40 11
2	18 47 18	20 49 31	22 39 55	0 42 8	2 40 25	4 42 38	6 40 55	8 43 8	10 45 21	12 43 38	14 45 51	16 44 8
3	18 51 15	20 53 28	22 43 52	0 46 5	2 44 21	4 46 35	6 44 51	8 47 5	10 49 18	12 47 34	14 49 48	16 48 4
4	18 55 11	20 57 25	22 47 48	0 50 1	2 48 18	4 50 31	6 48 48	8 51 1	10 53 14	12 51 31	14 53 44	16 52 1
5	18 59 8	21 1 21	22 51 45	0 53 58	2 52 14	4 54 28	6 52 44	8 54 58	10 57 11	12 55 28	14 57 41	16 55 57
6	19 3 4	21 5 18	22 55 41	0 57 54	2 56 11	4 58 24	6 56 41	8 58 54	11 1 7	12 59 24	15 1 37	16 59 54
7	19 7 1	21 9 14	22 59 38	1 1 51	3 0 8	5 2 21	7 0 38	9 2 51	11 5 4	13 3 21	15 5 34	17 3 51
8	19 10 57	21 13 11	23 3 34	1 5 47	3 4 4	5 6 17	7 4 34	9 6 47	11 9 1	13 7 17	15 9 30	17 7 47
9	19 14 54	21 17 7	23 7 31	1 9 44	3 8 1	5 10 14	7 8 31	9 10 44	11 12 57	13 11 14	15 13 27	17 11 44
10	19 18 51	21 21 4	23 11 27	1 13 41	3 11 57	5 14 10	7 12 27	9 14 41	11 16 54	13 15 10	15 17 23	17 15 40
11	19 22 47	21 25 0	23 15 24	1 17 37	3 15 54	5 18 7	7 16 24	9 18 37	11 20 50	13 19 7	15 21 20	17 19 37
12	19 26 44	21 28 57	23 19 21	1 21 34	3 19 50	5 22 4	7 20 20	9 22 34	11 24 47	13 23 3	15 25 17	17 23 33
13	19 30 40	21 32 54	23 23 17	1 25 30	3 23 47	5 26 0	7 24 17	9 26 30	11 28 43	13 27 0	15 29 13	17 27 30
14	19 34 37	21 36 50	23 27 14	1 29 27	3 27 43	5 29 57	7 28 13	9 30 27	11 32 40	13 30 56	15 33 10	17 31 26
15	19 38 33	21 40 47	23 31 10	1 33 23	3 31 40	5 33 53	7 32 10	9 34 23	11 36 36	13 34 53	15 37 6	17 35 23
16	19 42 30	21 44 43	23 35 7	1 37 20	3 35 37	5 37 50	7 36 7	9 38 20	11 40 33	13 38 50	15 41 3	17 39 20
17	19 46 27	21 48 40	23 39 3	1 41 16	3 39 33	5 41 46	7 40 3	9 42 16	11 44 30	13 42 46	15 44 59	17 43 16
18	19 50 23	21 52 36	23 43 0	1 45 13	3 43 30	5 45 43	7 44 0	9 46 13	11 48 26	13 46 43	15 48 56	17 47 13
19	19 54 20	21 56 33	23 46 56	1 49 10	3 47 26	5 49 40	7 47 56	9 50 9	11 52 23	13 50 39	15 52 52	17 51 9
20	19 58 16	22 0 29	23 50 53	1 53 6	3 51 23	5 53 36	7 51 53	9 54 6	11 56 19	13 54 36	15 56 49	17 55 6
21	20 2 13	22 4 26	23 54 49	1 57 3	3 55 19	5 57 33	7 55 49	9 58 3	12 0 16	13 58 32	16 0 46	17 59 2
22	20 6 9	22 8 23	23 58 46	2 0 59	3 59 16	6 1 29	7 59 46	10 1 59	12 4 12	14 2 29	16 4 42	18 2 59
23	20 10 6	22 12 19	0 2 43	2 4 56	4 3 12	6 5 26	8 3 43	10 5 56	12 8 9	14 6 25	16 8 39	18 6 55
24	20 14 2	22 16 16	0 6 39	2 8 52	4 7 9	6 9 22	8 7 39	10 9 52	12 12 5	14 10 22	16 12 35	18 10 52
25	20 17 59	22 20 12	0 10 36	2 12 49	4 11 6	6 13 19	8 11 36	10 13 49	12 16 2	14 14 19	16 16 32	18 14 49
26	20 21 56	22 24 9	0 14 32	2 16 45	4 15 2	6 17 15	8 15 32	10 17 45	12 19 59	14 18 15	16 20 28	18 18 45
27	20 25 52	22 28 5	0 18 29	2 20 42	4 18 59	6 21 12	8 19 29	10 21 42	12 23 55	14 22 12	16 24 25	18 22 42
28	20 29 49	22 32 2	0 22 25	2 24 39	4 22 55	6 25 9	8 23 25	10 25 38	12 27 52	14 26 8	16 28 22	18 26 38
29	20 33 45		0 26 22	2 28 35	4 26 52	6 29 5	8 27 22	10 29 35	12 31 48	14 30 5	16 32 18	18 30 35
30	20 37 42		0 30 18	2 32 32	4 30 48	6 33 2	8 31 18	10 33 32	12 35 45	14 34 1	16 36 15	18 34 31
31	20 41 38		0 34 15		4 34 45		8 35 15	10 37 28		14 37 58		18 38 28

1954

	Jan.	Feb.	Mar.	April	May	June	July	Aug.	Sept.	Oct.	Nov.	Dec.
1	18 42 24	20 44 38	22 35 1	0 37 14	2 35 31	4 37 44	6 36 1	8 38 14	10 40 28	12 38 44	14 40 57	16 39 14
2	18 46 21	20 48 34	22 38 58	0 41 11	2 39 28	4 41 41	6 39 58	8 42 11	10 44 24	12 42 41	14 44 54	16 43 11
3	18 50 18	20 52 31	22 42 54	0 45 8	2 43 24	4 45 37	6 43 54	8 46 7	10 48 21	12 46 37	14 48 50	16 47 7
4	18 54 14	20 56 27	22 46 51	0 49 4	2 47 21	4 49 34	6 47 51	8 50 4	10 52 17	12 50 34	14 52 47	16 51 4
5	18 58 11	21 0 24	22 50 48	0 53 1	2 51 17	4 53 31	6 51 47	8 54 1	10 56 14	12 54 30	14 56 44	16 55 0
6	19 2 7	21 4 21	22 54 44	0 56 57	2 55 14	4 57 27	6 55 44	8 57 57	11 0 10	12 58 27	15 0 40	16 58 57
7	19 6 4	21 8 17	22 58 41	1 0 54	2 59 10	5 1 24	6 59 40	9 1 54	11 4 7	13 2 23	15 4 37	17 2 53
8	19 10 0	21 12 14	23 2 37	1 4 50	3 3 7	5 5 20	7 3 37	9 5 50	11 8 3	13 6 20	15 8 33	17 6 50
9	19 13 57	21 16 10	23 6 34	1 8 47	3 7 4	5 9 17	7 7 34	9 9 47	11 12 0	13 10 17	15 12 30	17 10 46
10	19 17 54	21 20 7	23 10 30	1 12 43	3 11 0	5 13 13	7 11 30	9 13 43	11 15 57	13 14 13	15 16 26	17 14 43
11	19 21 50	21 24 3	23 14 27	1 16 40	3 14 57	5 17 10	7 15 27	9 17 40	11 19 53	13 18 10	15 20 23	17 18 40
12	19 25 47	21 28 0	23 18 23	1 20 37	3 18 53	5 21 6	7 19 23	9 21 36	11 23 50	13 22 6	15 24 19	17 22 36
13	19 29 43	21 31 56	23 22 20	1 24 33	3 22 50	5 25 3	7 23 20	9 25 33	11 27 46	13 26 3	15 28 16	17 26 33
14	19 33 40	21 35 53	23 26 17	1 28 30	3 26 46	5 29 0	7 27 16	9 29 30	11 31 43	13 29 59	15 32 13	17 30 29
15	19 37 36	21 39 50	23 30 13	1 32 26	3 30 43	5 32 56	7 31 13	9 33 26	11 35 39	13 33 56	15 36 9	17 34 26
16	19 41 33	21 43 46	23 34 10	1 36 23	3 34 39	5 36 53	7 35 9	9 37 23	11 39 36	13 37 52	15 40 6	17 38 22
17	10 45 29	21 47 43	23 38 6	1 40 19	3 38 36	5 40 49	7 39 6	9 41 19	11 43 32	13 41 49	15 44 2	17 42 19
18	19 49 26	21 51 39	23 42 3	1 44 16	3 42 33	5 44 46	7 43 3	9 45 16	11 47 29	13 45 46	15 47 59	17 46 15
19	19 53 23	21 55 36	23 45 59	1 48 12	3 46 29	5 48 42	7 46 59	9 49 12	11 51 26	13 49 42	15 51 55	17 50 12
20	19 57 19	21 59 32	23 49 56	1 52 9	3 50 26	5 52 39	7 50 56	9 53 9	11 55 22	13 53 39	15 55 52	17 54 9
21	20 1 16	22 3 29	23 53 52	1 56 6	3 54 22	5 56 35	7 54 52	9 57 5	11 59 19	13 57 35	15 59 48	17 58 5
22	20 5 12	22 7 25	23 57 49	2 0 2	3 58 19	6 0 32	7 58 49	10 1 2	12 3 15	14 1 32	16 3 45	18 2 2
23	20 9 9	22 11 22	0 1 45	2 3 59	4 2 15	6 4 29	8 2 45	10 4 59	12 7 12	14 5 28	16 7 42	18 5 58
24	20 13 5	22 15 19	0 5 42	2 7 55	4 6 12	6 8 25	8 6 42	10 8 55	12 11 8	14 9 25	16 11 38	18 9 55
25	20 17 2	22 19 15	0 9 39	2 11 52	4 10 8	6 12 22	8 10 38	10 12 52	12 15 5	14 13 21	16 15 35	18 13 51
26	20 20 58	22 23 12	0 13 35	2 15 48	4 14 5	6 16 18	8 14 35	10 16 48	12 19 1	14 17 18	16 19 31	18 17 48
27	20 24 55	22 27 8	0 17 32	2 19 45	4 18 2	6 20 15	8 18 32	10 20 45	12 22 58	14 21 15	16 23 28	18 21 45
28	20 28 52	22 31 5	0 21 28	2 23 41	4 21 58	6 24 11	8 22 28	10 24 41	12 26 54	14 25 11	16 27 24	18 25 41
29	20 32 48		0 25 25	2 27 38	4 25 55	6 28 8	8 26 25	10 28 38	12 30 51	14 29 8	16 31 21	18 29 38
30	20 36 45		0 29 21	2 31 35	4 29 51	6 32 5	8 30 21	10 32 34	12 34 48	14 33 4	16 35 17	18 33 34
31	20 40 41		0 33 18		4 33 48		8 34 18	10 36 31		14 37 1		18 37 31

1955

	Jan.	Feb.	Mar.	April	May	June	July	Aug.	Sept.	Oct.	Nov.	Dec.
1	18 41 27	20 43 41	22 34 4	0 36 17	2 34 34	4 36 47	6 35 4	8 37 17	10 39 30	12 37 47	14 40 0	16 38 17
2	18 45 24	20 47 37	22 38 1	0 40 14	2 38 30	4 40 44	6 39 0	8 41 14	10 43 27	12 41 43	14 43 57	16 42 13
3	18 49 20	20 51 34	22 41 57	0 44 10	2 42 27	4 44 40	6 42 57	8 45 10	10 47 23	12 45 40	14 47 53	16 46 10
4	18 53 17	20 55 30	22 45 54	0 48 7	2 46 24	4 48 37	6 46 53	8 49 7	10 51 20	12 49 36	14 51 50	16 50 6
5	18 57 14	20 59 27	22 49 50	0 52 3	2 50 20	4 52 33	6 50 50	8 53 3	10 55 16	12 53 33	14 55 46	16 54 3
6	19 1 10	21 3 23	22 53 47	0 56 0	2 54 17	4 56 30	6 54 47	8 57 0	10 59 13	12 57 30	14 59 43	16 57 59
7	19 5 7	21 7 20	22 57 43	0 59 57	2 58 13	5 0 26	6 58 43	9 0 56	11 3 10	13 1 26	15 3 39	17 1 56
8	19 9 3	21 11 16	23 1 40	1 3 53	3 2 10	5 4 23	7 2 40	9 4 53	11 7 6	13 5 23	15 7 36	17 5 53
9	19 13 0	21 15 13	23 5 37	1 7 50	3 6 6	5 8 20	7 6 36	9 8 50	11 11 3	13 9 19	15 11 32	17 9 49
10	19 16 56	21 19 10	23 9 33	1 11 46	3 10 3	5 12 16	7 10 33	9 12 46	11 14 59	13 13 16	15 15 29	17 13 46
11	19 20 53	21 23 6	23 13 30	1 15 43	3 13 59	5 16 13	7 14 29	9 16 43	11 18 56	13 17 12	15 19 26	17 17 42
12	19 24 49	21 27 3	23 17 26	1 19 39	3 17 56	5 20 9	7 18 26	9 20 39	11 22 52	13 21 9	15 23 22	17 21 39
13	19 28 46	21 30 59	23 21 23	1 23 36	3 21 53	5 24 6	7 22 22	9 24 36	11 26 49	13 25 5	15 27 19	17 25 35
14	19 32 43	21 34 56	23 25 19	1 27 32	3 25 49	5 28 2	7 26 19	9 28 32	11 30 45	13 29 2	15 31 15	17 29 32
15	19 36 39	21 38 52	23 29 16	1 31 29	3 29 46	5 31 59	7 30 16	9 32 29	11 34 42	13 32 59	15 35 12	17 33 29
16	19 40 36	21 42 49	23 33 12	1 35 26	3 33 42	5 35 55	7 34 12	9 36 25	11 38 39	13 36 55	15 39 8	17 37 25
17	19 44 32	21 46 45	23 37 9	1 39 22	3 37 39	5 39 52	7 38 9	9 40 22	11 42 35	13 40 52	15 43 5	17 41 22
18	19 48 29	21 50 42	23 41 6	1 43 19	3 41 35	5 43 49	7 42 5	9 44 19	11 46 32	13 44 48	15 47 1	17 45 18
19	19 52 25	21 54 39	23 45 2	1 47 15	3 45 32	5 47 45	7 46 2	9 48 15	11 50 28	13 48 45	15 50 58	17 49 15
20	19 56 22	21 58 35	23 48 59	1 51 12	3 49 28	5 51 42	7 49 58	9 52 12	11 54 25	13 52 41	15 54 55	17 53 11
21	20 0 18	22 2 32	23 52 55	1 55 8	3 53 25	5 55 38	7 53 55	9 56 8	11 58 21	13 56 38	15 58 51	17 57 8
22	20 4 15	22 6 28	23 56 52	1 59 5	3 57 22	5 59 35	7 57 52	10 0 5	12 2 18	14 0 34	16 2 48	18 1 4
23	20 8 12	22 10 25	0 0 48	2 3 1	4 1 18	6 3 31	8 1 48	10 4 1	12 6 14	14 4 31	16 6 44	18 5 1
24	20 12 8	22 14 21	0 4 45	2 6 58	4 5 15	6 7 28	8 5 45	10 7 58	12 10 11	14 8 28	16 10 41	18 8 58
25	20 16 5	22 18 18	0 8 41	2 10 55	4 9 11	6 11 24	8 9 41	10 11 54	12 14 8	14 12 24	16 14 37	18 12 54
26	20 20 1	22 22 14	0 12 38	2 14 51	4 13 8	6 15 21	8 13 38	10 15 51	12 18 4	14 16 21	16 18 34	18 16 51
27	20 23 58	22 26 11	0 16 34	2 18 48	4 17 4	6 19 18	8 17 34	10 19 48	12 22 1	14 20 17	16 22 30	18 20 47
28	20 27 54	22 30 8	0 20 31	2 22 44	4 21 1	6 23 14	8 21 31	10 23 44	12 25 57	14 24 14	16 26 27	18 24 44
29	20 31 51		0 24 28	2 26 41	4 24 57	6 27 11	8 25 27	10 27 41	12 29 54	14 28 10	16 30 24	18 28 40
30	20 35 47		0 28 24	2 30 37	4 28 54	6 31 7	8 29 24	10 31 37	12 33 50	14 32 7	16 34 20	18 32 37
31	20 39 44		0 32 21		4 32 51		8 33 21	10 35 34		41 36 3		18 36 33

1956

Jan.	Feb.	Mar.	April	May	June	July	Aug.	Sept.	Oct.	Nov.	Dec.	
18 40 30	20 42 43	22 37 3	0 39 16	2 37 33	4 39 46	6 38 3	8 40 16	10 42 29	12 40 46	14 42 59	16 41 16	1
18 44 27	20 46 40	22 41 0	0 43 13	2 41 30	4 43 43	6 42 0	8 44 13	10 46 26	12 44 43	14 46 56	16 45 12	2
18 48 23	20 50 36	22 44 56	0 47 10	2 45 26	4 47 39	6 45 56	8 48 9	10 50 23	12 48 39	14 50 52	16 49 9	3
18 52 20	20 54 33	22 48 53	0 51 6	2 49 23	4 51 36	6 49 53	8 52 6	10 54 19	12 52 36	14 54 49	16 53 6	4
18 56 16	20 58 29	22 52 50	0 55 3	2 53 19	4 55 33	6 53 49	8 56 2	10 58 16	12 56 32	14 58 45	16 57 2	5
19 0 13	21 2 26	22 56 46	0 58 59	2 57 16	4 59 29	6 57 46	8 59 59	11 2 12	13 0 29	15 2 42	17 0 59	6
19 4 9	21 6 23	23 0 43	1 2 56	3 1 12	5 3 26	7 1 42	9 3 56	11 6 9	13 4 25	15 6 38	17 4 55	7
19 8 6	21 10 19	23 4 39	1 6 52	3 5 9	5 7 22	7 5 39	9 7 52	11 10 5	13 8 22	15 10 35	17 8 52	8
19 12 2	21 14 16	23 8 36	1 10 49	3 9 5	5 11 19	7 9 35	9 11 49	11 14 2	13 12 18	15 14 32	17 12 48	9
19 15 59	21 18 12	23 12 32	1 14 45	3 13 2	5 15 15	7 13 32	9 15 45	11 17 58	13 16 15	15 18 28	17 16 45	10
19 19 56	21 22 9	23 16 29	1 18 42	3 16 59	5 19 12	7 17 29	9 19 42	11 21 55	13 20 12	15 22 25	17 20 41	11
19 23 52	21 26 5	23 20 25	1 22 39	3 20 55	5 23 8	7 21 25	9 23 38	11 25 52	13 24 8	15 26 21	17 24 38	12
19 27 49	21 30 2	23 24 22	1 26 35	3 24 52	5 27 5	7 25 22	9 27 35	11 29 48	13 28 5	15 30 18	17 28 35	13
19 31 45	21 33 58	23 28 19	1 30 32	3 28 48	5 31 2	7 29 18	9 31 31	11 33 45	13 32 1	15 34 14	17 32 31	14
19 35 42	21 37 55	23 32 15	1 34 28	3 32 45	5 34 58	7 33 15	9 35 28	11 37 41	13 35 58	15 38 11	17 36 28	15
19 39 38	21 41 52	23 36 12	1 38 25	3 36 41	5 38 55	7 37 11	9 39 25	11 41 38	13 39 54	15 42 7	17 40 24	16
19 43 35	21 45 48	23 40 8	1 42 21	3 40 38	5 42 51	7 41 8	9 43 21	11 45 34	13 43 51	15 46 4	17 44 21	17
19 47 31	21 49 45	23 44 5	1 46 18	3 44 35	5 46 48	7 45 4	9 47 18	11 49 31	13 47 47	15 50 1	17 48 17	18
19 51 28	21 53 41	23 48 1	1 50 14	3 48 31	5 50 44	7 49 1	9 51 14	11 53 27	13 51 44	15 53 57	17 52 14	19
19 55 25	21 57 38	23 51 58	1 54 11	3 52 28	5 54 41	7 52 58	9 55 11	11 57 24	13 55 40	15 57 54	17 56 10	20
19 59 21	22 1 34	23 55 54	1 58 8	3 56 24	5 58 37	7 56 54	9 59 7	12 1 20	13 59 37	16 1 50	18 0 7	21
20 3 18	22 5 31	23 59 51	2 2 4	4 0 21	6 2 34	8 0 51	10 3 4	12 5 17	14 3 34	16 5 47	18 4 4	22
20 7 14	22 9 27	0 3 47	2 6 1	4 4 17	6 6 31	8 4 47	10 7 0	12 9 14	14 7 30	16 9 43	18 8 0	23
20 11 11	22 13 24	0 7 44	2 9 57	4 8 14	6 10 27	8 8 44	10 10 57	12 13 10	14 11 27	16 13 40	18 11 57	24
20 15 7	22 17 21	0 11 41	2 13 54	4 12 10	6 14 24	8 12 40	10 14 54	12 17 7	14 15 23	16 17 36	18 15 53	25
20 19 4	22 21 17	0 15 37	2 17 50	4 16 7	6 18 20	8 16 37	10 18 50	12 21 3	14 19 20	16 21 33	18 19 50	26
20 23 0	22 25 14	0 19 34	2 21 47	4 20 4	6 22 17	8 20 33	10 22 47	12 25 0	14 23 16	16 25 30	18 23 46	27
20 26 57	22 29 10	0 23 30	2 25 43	4 24 0	6 26 13	8 24 30	10 26 43	12 28 56	14 27 13	16 29 26	18 27 43	28
20 30 54	22 33 7	0 27 27	2 29 40	4 27 57	6 30 10	8 28 27	10 30 40	12 32 53	14 31 10	16 33 23	18 31 39	29
20 34 50		0 31 23	2 33 37	4 31 53	6 34 6	8 32 23	10 34 36	12 36 49	14 35 6	16 37 19	18 35 36	30
20 38 47		0 35 20		4 35 50		8 36 20	10 38 33		14 39 3		18 39 33	31

1957

Jan.	Feb.	Mar.	April	May	June	July	Aug.	Sept.	Oct.	Nov.	Dec.	
18 43 29	20 45 42	22 36 6	0 38 19	2 36 36	4 38 49	6 37 6	8 39 19	10 41 32	12 39 49	14 42 2	16 40 18	1
18 47 26	20 49 39	22 40 2	0 42 16	2 40 32	4 42 45	6 41 2	8 43 15	10 45 28	12 43 45	14 45 58	16 44 15	2
18 51 22	20 53 35	22 43 59	0 46 12	2 44 29	4 46 42	6 44 59	8 47 12	10 49 25	12 47 42	14 49 55	16 48 11	3
18 55 19	20 57 32	22 47 56	0 50 9	2 48 25	4 50 38	6 48 55	8 51 8	10 53 22	12 51 38	14 53 51	16 52 8	4
18 59 15	21 1 29	22 51 52	0 54 5	2 52 22	4 54 35	6 52 52	8 55 5	10 57 18	12 55 35	14 57 48	16 56 5	5
19 3 12	21 5 25	22 55 49	0 58 2	2 56 18	4 58 32	6 56 48	8 59 2	11 1 15	12 59 31	15 1 44	17 0 1	6
19 7 8	21 9 22	22 59 45	1 1 58	3 0 15	5 2 28	7 0 45	9 2 58	11 5 11	13 3 28	15 5 41	17 3 58	7
19 11 5	21 13 18	23 3 42	1 5 55	3 4 11	5 6 25	7 4 41	9 6 55	11 9 8	13 7 24	15 9 38	17 7 54	8
19 15 2	21 17 15	23 7 38	1 9 51	3 8 8	5 10 21	7 8 38	9 10 51	11 13 4	13 11 21	15 13 34	17 11 51	9
19 18 58	21 21 11	23 11 35	1 13 48	3 12 5	5 14 18	7 12 35	9 14 48	11 17 1	13 15 17	15 17 31	17 15 47	10
19 22 55	21 25 8	23 15 31	1 17 45	3 16 1	5 18 14	7 16 31	9 18 44	11 20 57	13 19 14	15 21 27	17 19 44	11
19 26 51	21 29 4	23 19 28	1 21 41	3 19 58	5 22 11	7 20 28	9 22 41	11 24 54	13 23 11	15 25 24	17 23 40	12
19 30 48	21 33 1	23 23 25	1 25 38	3 23 54	5 26 8	7 24 24	9 26 37	11 28 51	13 27 7	15 29 20	17 27 37	13
19 34 44	21 36 58	23 27 21	1 29 34	3 27 51	5 30 4	7 28 21	9 30 34	11 32 47	13 31 4	15 33 17	17 31 34	14
19 38 41	21 40 54	23 31 18	1 33 31	3 31 47	5 34 1	7 32 17	9 34 31	11 36 44	13 35 0	15 37 13	17 35 30	15
19 42 37	21 44 51	23 35 14	1 37 27	3 35 44	5 37 57	7 36 14	9 38 27	11 40 40	13 38 57	15 41 10	17 39 27	16
19 46 34	21 48 47	23 39 11	1 41 24	3 39 40	5 41 54	7 40 10	9 42 24	11 44 37	13 42 53	15 45 7	17 43 23	17
19 50 31	21 52 44	23 43 7	1 45 20	3 43 37	5 45 50	7 44 7	9 46 20	11 48 33	13 46 50	15 49 3	17 47 20	18
19 54 27	21 56 40	23 47 4	1 49 17	3 47 34	5 49 47	7 48 4	9 50 17	11 52 30	13 50 46	15 53 0	17 51 16	19
19 58 24	22 0 37	23 51 0	1 53 14	3 51 30	5 53 43	7 52 0	9 54 13	11 56 26	13 54 43	15 56 56	17 55 13	20
20 2 20	22 4 33	23 54 57	1 57 10	3 55 27	5 57 40	7 55 57	9 58 10	12 0 23	13 58 40	16 0 53	17 59 9	21
20 6 17	22 8 30	23 58 53	2 1 7	3 59 23	6 1 36	7 59 53	10 2 6	12 4 20	14 2 36	16 4 49	18 3 6	22
20 10 13	22 12 27	0 2 50	2 5 3	4 3 20	6 5 33	8 3 50	10 6 3	12 8 16	14 6 33	16 8 46	18 7 3	23
20 14 10	22 16 23	0 6 47	2 9 0	4 7 16	6 9 30	8 7 46	10 10 0	12 12 13	14 10 29	16 12 42	18 10 59	24
20 18 6	22 20 20	0 10 43	2 12 56	4 11 13	6 13 26	8 11 43	10 13 56	12 16 9	14 14 26	16 16 39	18 14 56	25
20 22 3	22 24 16	0 14 40	2 16 53	4 15 9	6 17 23	8 15 39	10 17 53	12 20 6	14 18 22	16 20 36	18 18 52	26
20 26 0	22 28 13	0 18 36	2 20 49	4 19 6	6 21 19	8 19 36	10 21 49	12 24 2	14 22 19	16 24 32	18 22 49	27
20 29 56	22 32 9	0 22 33	2 24 46	4 23 3	6 25 16	8 23 33	10 25 46	12 27 59	14 26 15	16 28 29	18 26 45	28
20 33 53		0 26 29	2 28 42	4 26 59	6 29 12	8 27 29	10 29 42	12 31 55	14 30 12	16 32 25	18 30 42	29
20 37 49		0 30 26	2 32 39	4 30 56	6 33 9	8 31 26	10 33 39	12 35 52	14 34 9	16 36 22	18 34 38	30
20 41 46		0 34 22		4 34 52		8 35 22	10 37 35		14 38 5		18 38 35	31

1958

Jan.	Feb.	Mar.	April	May	June	July	Aug.	Sept.	Oct.	Nov.	Dec.	
18 42 32	20 44 45	22 35 8	0 37 21	2 35 38	4 37 51	6 36 8	8 38 21	10 40 34	12 38 51	14 41 4	16 39 21	1
18 46 28	20 48 41	22 39 5	0 41 18	2 39 35	4 41 48	6 40 5	8 42 18	10 44 31	12 42 48	14 45 1	16 43 17	2
18 50 25	20 52 38	22 43 1	0 45 15	2 43 31	4 45 44	6 44 1	8 46 14	10 48 27	12 46 44	14 48 57	16 47 14	3
18 54 21	20 56 35	22 46 58	0 49 11	2 47 28	4 49 41	6 47 58	8 50 11	10 52 24	12 50 41	14 52 54	16 51 10	4
18 58 18	21 0 31	22 50 55	0 53 8	2 51 24	4 53 37	6 51 54	8 54 7	10 56 21	12 54 37	14 56 50	16 55 7	5
19 2 14	21 4 28	22 54 51	0 57 4	2 55 21	4 57 34	6 55 51	8 58 4	11 0 17	12 58 34	15 0 47	16 59 3	6
19 6 11	21 8 24	22 58 48	1 1 1	2 59 17	5 1 31	6 59 47	9 2 1	11 4 14	13 2 30	15 4 43	17 3 0	7
19 10 7	21 12 21	23 2 44	1 4 57	3 3 14	5 5 27	7 3 44	9 5 57	11 8 10	13 6 27	15 8 40	17 6 57	8
19 14 4	21 16 17	23 6 41	1 8 54	3 7 10	5 9 24	7 7 40	9 9 54	11 12 7	13 10 24	15 12 36	17 10 53	9
19 18 1	21 20 14	23 10 37	1 12 50	3 11 7	5 13 20	7 11 37	9 13 50	11 16 3	13 14 20	15 16 33	17 14 50	10
19 21 57	21 24 10	23 14 34	1 16 47	3 15 4	5 17 17	7 15 34	9 17 47	11 20 0	13 18 16	15 20 30	17 18 46	11
19 25 54	21 28 7	23 18 30	1 20 44	3 19 0	5 21 13	7 19 30	9 21 43	11 23 56	13 22 13	15 24 26	17 22 43	12
19 29 50	21 32 3	23 22 27	1 24 40	3 22 57	5 25 10	7 23 27	9 25 40	11 27 53	13 26 10	15 28 23	17 26 39	13
19 33 47	21 36 0	23 26 24	1 28 37	3 26 53	5 29 6	7 27 23	9 29 36	11 31 50	13 30 6	15 32 19	17 30 36	14
19 37 43	21 39 57	23 30 20	1 32 33	3 30 50	5 33 3	7 31 20	9 33 33	11 35 46	13 34 3	15 36 16	17 34 33	15
19 41 40	21 43 53	23 34 17	1 36 30	3 34 46	5 37 0	7 35 16	9 37 30	11 39 43	13 37 59	15 40 12	17 38 29	16
19 45 36	21 47 50	23 38 13	1 40 26	3 38 43	5 40 56	7 39 13	9 41 26	11 43 39	13 41 56	15 44 9	17 42 26	17
19 49 33	21 51 46	23 42 10	1 44 23	3 42 39	5 44 53	7 43 9	9 45 23	11 47 36	13 45 52	15 48 5	17 46 22	18
19 53 30	21 55 43	23 46 6	1 48 19	3 46 36	5 48 49	7 47 6	9 49 19	11 51 32	13 49 49	15 52 2	17 50 19	19
19 57 26	21 59 39	23 50 3	1 52 16	3 50 33	5 52 46	7 51 3	9 53 16	11 55 29	13 53 45	15 55 59	17 54 15	20
20 1 23	22 3 36	23 53 59	1 56 12	3 54 29	5 56 42	7 54 59	9 57 12	11 59 25	13 57 42	15 59 55	17 58 12	21
20 5 19	22 7 32	23 57 56	2 0 9	3 58 26	6 0 39	7 58 56	10 1 9	12 3 22	14 1 39	16 3 52	18 2 8	22
20 9 16	22 11 29	0 1 53	2 4 6	4 2 23	6 4 35	8 2 52	10 5 5	12 7 19	14 5 35	16 7 48	18 6 5	23
20 13 12	22 15 26	0 5 49	2 8 2	4 6 19	6 8 32	8 6 49	10 9 2	12 11 15	14 9 32	16 11 45	18 10 2	24
20 17 9	22 19 22	0 9 46	2 11 59	4 10 15	6 12 29	8 10 45	10 12 59	12 15 12	14 13 28	16 15 42	18 13 58	25
20 21 5	22 23 19	0 13 42	2 15 55	4 14 12	6 16 25	8 14 42	10 16 55	12 19 8	14 17 25	16 19 38	18 17 55	26
20 25 2	22 27 15	0 17 39	2 19 52	4 18 8	6 20 22	8 18 38	10 20 52	12 23 5	14 21 22	16 23 34	18 21 51	27
20 28 59	22 31 12	0 21 35	2 23 48	4 22 5	6 24 18	8 22 35	10 24 48	12 27 1	14 25 18	16 27 31	18 25 48	28
20 32 55		0 25 32	2 27 45	4 26 2	6 28 15	8 26 32	10 28 45	12 30 58	14 29 14	16 31 28	18 29 44	29
20 36 52		0 29 28	2 31 41	4 29 58	6 32 11	8 30 28	10 32 41	12 34 54	14 33 11	16 35 24	18 33 41	30
20 40 48		0 33 25		4 33 55		8 34 25	10 36 38		14 37 7		18 37 37	31

1959

	Jan.	Feb.	Mar.	April	May	June	July	Aug.	Sept.	Oct.	Nov.	Dec.
1	18 41 34	20 43 47	22 34 11	0 36 24	2 34 40	4 36 54	6 35 10	8 37 24	10 39 37	12 37 53	14 40 6	16 38 23
2	18 45 31	20 47 44	22 38 7	0 40 20	2 38 37	4 40 50	6 39 7	8 41 20	10 43 33	12 41 50	14 44 3	16 42 20
3	18 49 27	20 51 40	22 42 4	0 44 17	2 42 34	4 44 47	6 43 3	8 45 17	10 47 30	12 45 46	14 47 59	16 46 16
4	18 53 24	20 55 37	22 46 0	0 48 13	2 46 30	4 48 43	6 47 0	8 49 13	10 51 26	12 49 43	14 51 56	16 50 13
5	18 57 20	20 59 33	22 49 57	0 52 10	2 50 27	4 52 40	6 50 57	8 53 10	10 55 23	12 53 39	14 55 53	16 54 9
6	19 1 17	21 3 30	22 53 53	0 56 7	2 54 23	4 56 36	6 54 53	8 57 6	10 59 19	12 57 36	14 59 49	16 58 6
7	19 5 13	21 7 27	22 57 50	1 0 3	2 58 20	5 0 33	6 58 50	9 1 3	11 3 16	13 1 33	15 3 46	17 2 2
8	19 9 10	21 11 23	23 1 47	1 4 0	3 2 16	5 4 30	7 2 46	9 4 59	11 7 13	13 5 29	15 7 42	17 5 59
9	19 13 6	21 15 20	23 5 43	1 7 56	3 6 13	5 8 26	7 6 43	9 8 56	11 11 9	13 9 26	15 11 39	17 9 56
10	19 17 3	21 19 16	23 9 40	1 11 53	3 10 9	5 12 23	7 10 39	9 12 53	11 15 6	13 13 22	15 15 35	17 13 52
11	19 21 0	21 23 13	23 13 36	1 15 49	3 14 6	5 16 19	7 14 36	9 16 49	11 19 2	13 17 19	15 19 32	17 17 49
12	19 24 56	21 27 9	23 17 33	1 19 46	3 18 2	5 20 16	7 18 32	9 20 46	11 22 59	13 21 15	15 23 28	17 21 45
13	19 28 53	21 31 6	23 21 29	1 23 42	3 21 59	5 24 12	7 22 29	9 24 42	11 26 55	13 25 12	15 27 25	17 25 42
14	19 32 49	21 35 2	23 25 26	1 27 39	3 25 56	5 28 9	7 26 26	9 28 39	11 30 52	13 29 8	15 31 22	17 29 38
15	19 36 46	21 38 59	23 29 22	1 31 36	3 29 52	5 32 5	7 30 22	9 32 35	11 34 48	13 33 5	15 35 18	17 33 35
16	19 40 42	21 42 56	23 33 19	1 35 32	3 33 49	5 36 2	7 34 19	9 36 32	11 38 45	13 37 2	15 39 15	17 37 31
17	19 44 39	21 46 52	23 37 16	1 39 29	3 37 45	5 39 59	7 38 15	9 40 28	11 42 42	13 40 58	15 43 11	17 41 28
18	19 48 35	21 50 49	23 41 12	1 43 25	3 41 42	5 43 55	7 42 12	9 44 25	11 46 38	13 44 55	15 47 8	17 45 25
19	19 52 32	21 54 45	23 45 9	1 47 22	3 45 38	5 47 52	7 46 8	9 48 22	11 50 35	13 48 51	15 51 4	17 49 21
20	19 56 29	21 58 42	23 49 5	1 51 18	3 49 35	5 51 48	7 50 5	9 52 18	11 54 31	13 52 48	15 55 1	17 53 18
21	20 0 25	22 2 38	23 53 2	1 55 15	3 52 31	5 55 45	7 54 1	9 56 15	11 58 28	13 56 44	15 58 57	17 57 14
22	20 4 22	22 6 35	23 56 58	1 59 11	3 57 28	5 59 41	7 57 58	10 0 11	12 2 24	14 0 41	16 2 54	18 1 11
23	20 8 18	22 10 31	0 0 55	2 3 8	4 1 25	6 3 38	8 1 55	10 4 8	12 6 21	14 4 37	16 6 51	18 5 7
24	20 12 15	22 14 28	0 4 51	2 7 5	4 5 21	6 7 34	8 5 51	10 8 4	12 10 17	14 8 34	16 10 47	18 9 4
25	20 16 11	22 18 25	0 8 48	2 11 1	4 9 18	6 11 31	8 9 48	10 12 1	12 14 14	14 12 31	16 14 44	18 13 0
26	20 20 8	22 22 21	0 12 45	2 14 58	4 13 14	6 15 28	8 13 44	10 15 57	12 18 11	14 16 27	16 18 40	18 16 57
27	20 24 4	22 26 18	0 16 41	2 18 54	4 17 11	6 19 24	8 17 41	10 19 54	12 22 7	14 20 24	16 22 37	18 20 54
28	20 28 1	22 30 14	0 20 38	2 22 51	4 21 7	6 23 21	8 21 37	10 23 50	12 26 4	14 24 20	16 26 33	18 24 50
29	20 31 58		0 24 34	2 26 47	4 25 4	6 27 17	8 25 34	10 27 47	12 30 0	14 28 17	16 30 30	18 28 47
30	20 35 54		0 28 31	2 30 44	4 29 1	6 31 14	8 29 30	10 31 44	12 33 57	14 32 13	16 34 26	18 32 43
31	20 39 51		0 32 27		4 32 57		8 33 27	10 35 40		14 36 10		18 36 40

1960

	Jan.	Feb.	Mar.	April	May	June	July	Aug.	Sept.	Oct.	Nov.	Dec.
1	18 40 36	20 42 50	22 37 10	0 39 23	2 37 39	4 39 53	6 38 9	8 40 22	10 42 36	12 40 52	14 43 5	16 41 22
2	18 44 33	20 46 46	22 41 6	0 43 19	2 41 36	4 43 49	6 42 6	8 44 19	10 46 32	12 44 49	14 47 2	16 45 19
3	18 48 29	20 50 43	22 45 3	0 47 16	2 45 32	4 47 46	6 46 2	8 48 16	10 50 29	12 48 45	14 50 58	16 49 15
4	18 52 26	20 54 39	22 48 59	0 51 12	2 49 29	4 51 42	6 49 59	8 52 12	10 54 25	12 52 42	14 54 55	16 53 12
5	18 56 23	20 58 36	22 52 56	0 55 9	2 53 26	4 55 39	6 53 55	8 56 9	10 58 22	12 56 38	14 58 52	16 57 8
6	19 0 19	21 2 32	22 56 52	0 59 5	2 57 22	4 59 35	6 57 52	9 0 5	11 2 18	13 0 35	15 2 48	17 1 5
7	19 4 16	21 6 29	23 0 49	1 3 2	3 1 19	5 3 32	7 1 49	9 4 2	11 6 15	13 4 31	15 6 45	17 5 1
8	19 8 12	21 10 25	23 4 45	1 6 59	3 5 15	5 7 28	7 5 45	9 7 58	11 10 11	13 8 28	15 10 41	17 8 58
9	19 12 9	21 14 22	23 8 42	1 10 55	3 9 12	5 11 25	7 9 42	9 11 55	11 14 8	13 12 25	15 14 38	17 12 54
10	19 16 5	21 18 19	23 12 39	1 14 52	3 13 8	5 15 22	7 13 38	9 15 51	11 18 5	13 16 21	15 18 34	17 16 51
11	19 20 2	21 22 15	23 16 35	1 18 48	3 17 5	5 19 18	7 17 35	9 19 48	11 22 1	13 20 18	15 22 31	17 20 48
12	19 23 58	21 26 12	23 20 32	1 22 45	3 21 1	5 23 15	7 21 31	9 23 45	11 25 58	13 24 14	15 26 27	17 24 44
13	19 27 55	21 30 8	23 24 28	1 26 41	3 24 58	5 27 11	7 25 28	9 27 41	11 29 54	13 28 11	15 30 24	17 28 41
14	19 31 52	21 34 5	23 28 25	1 30 38	3 28 55	5 31 8	7 29 24	9 31 38	11 33 51	13 32 7	15 34 21	17 32 37
15	19 35 48	21 38 1	23 32 21	1 34 34	3 32 51	5 35 4	7 33 21	9 35 34	11 37 47	13 36 4	15 38 17	17 36 34
16	19 39 45	21 41 58	23 36 18	1 38 31	3 36 48	5 39 1	7 37 18	9 39 31	11 41 44	13 40 0	15 42 14	17 40 30
17	19 43 41	21 45 54	23 40 14	1 42 28	3 40 44	5 42 57	7 41 14	9 43 27	11 45 40	13 43 57	15 46 10	17 44 27
18	19 47 38	21 49 51	23 44 11	1 46 24	3 44 41	5 46 54	7 45 11	9 47 24	11 49 37	13 47 54	15 50 7	17 48 23
19	19 51 34	21 53 48	23 48 8	1 50 21	3 48 37	5 50 51	7 49 8	9 51 20	11 53 34	13 51 50	15 54 3	17 52 20
20	19 55 31	21 57 44	23 52 4	1 54 17	3 52 34	5 54 47	7 53 4	9 55 17	11 57 30	13 55 47	15 58 0	17 56 17
21	19 59 27	22 1 41	23 56 1	1 58 14	3 56 30	5 58 44	7 57 0	9 59 14	12 1 27	13 59 43	16 1 56	18 0 13
22	20 3 24	22 5 37	23 59 57	2 2 10	4 0 27	6 2 40	8 0 57	10 3 10	12 5 23	14 3 40	16 5 53	18 4 10
23	20 7 21	22 9 34	0 3 54	2 6 7	4 4 24	6 6 37	8 4 53	10 7 7	12 9 20	14 7 36	16 9 50	18 8 6
24	20 11 17	22 13 30	0 7 50	2 10 3	4 8 20	6 10 33	8 8 50	10 11 3	12 13 16	14 11 33	16 13 46	18 12 3
25	20 15 14	22 17 27	0 11 47	2 14 0	4 12 17	6 14 30	8 12 47	10 15 0	12 17 13	14 15 29	16 17 43	18 15 59
26	20 19 10	22 21 23	0 15 43	2 17 57	4 16 13	6 18 26	8 16 43	10 18 56	12 21 9	14 19 26	16 21 39	18 19 56
27	20 23 7	22 25 20	0 19 40	2 21 53	4 20 10	6 22 23	8 20 40	10 22 53	12 25 6	14 23 23	16 25 36	18 23 52
28	20 27 3	22 29 17	0 23 37	2 25 50	4 24 6	6 26 20	8 24 36	10 26 49	12 29 3	14 27 19	16 29 32	18 27 49
29	20 31 0	22 33 13	0 27 33	2 29 47	4 28 3	6 30 16	8 28 33	10 30 46	12 32 59	14 31 16	16 33 29	18 31 46
30	20 34 56		0 31 30	2 33 43	4 31 59	6 34 13	8 32 29	10 34 42	12 36 56	14 35 12	16 37 25	18 35 42
31	20 38 53		0 35 26		4 35 56		8 36 26	10 38 39		14 39 9		18 39 39

1961

	Jan.	Feb.	Mar.	April	May	June	July	Aug.	Sept.	Oct.	Nov.	Dec.
1	18 43 35	20 45 48	22 36 12	0 38 25	2 36 42	4 38 55	6 37 12	8 39 25	10 41 38	12 39 55	14 42 8	16 40 24
2	18 47 32	20 49 45	22 40 9	0 42 22	2 40 38	4 42 51	6 41 8	8 43 21	10 45 35	12 43 51	14 46 4	16 44 21
3	18 51 28	20 53 42	22 44 5	0 46 18	2 44 35	4 46 48	6 45 5	8 47 18	10 49 31	12 47 48	14 50 1	16 48 17
4	18 55 25	20 57 38	22 48 2	0 50 15	2 48 31	4 50 45	6 49 1	8 51 14	10 53 28	12 51 44	14 53 57	16 52 14
5	18 59 21	21 1 35	22 51 58	0 54 11	2 52 28	4 54 41	6 52 58	8 55 11	10 57 24	12 55 41	14 57 54	16 56 11
6	19 3 18	21 5 31	22 55 55	0 58 8	2 56 24	4 58 38	6 56 54	8 59 8	11 1 21	12 59 37	15 1 50	17 0 7
7	19 7 15	21 9 28	22 59 51	1 2 4	3 0 21	5 2 34	7 0 51	9 3 4	11 5 17	13 3 34	15 5 47	17 4 4
8	19 11 11	21 13 24	23 3 48	1 6 1	3 4 18	5 6 31	7 4 47	9 7 1	11 9 14	13 7 30	15 9 44	17 8 0
9	19 15 8	21 17 21	23 7 44	1 9 58	3 8 14	5 10 27	7 8 44	9 10 57	11 13 10	13 11 27	15 13 40	17 11 57
10	19 19 4	21 21 17	23 11 41	1 13 54	3 12 11	5 14 24	7 12 41	9 14 54	11 17 7	13 15 24	15 17 37	17 15 53
11	19 23 1	21 25 14	23 15 37	1 17 51	3 16 7	5 18 20	7 16 37	9 18 50	11 21 4	13 19 20	15 21 33	17 19 50
12	19 26 57	21 29 11	23 19 34	1 21 47	3 20 4	5 22 17	7 20 34	9 22 47	11 25 0	13 23 17	15 25 30	17 23 46
13	19 30 54	21 33 7	23 23 31	1 25 44	3 24 0	5 26 14	7 24 30	9 26 43	11 28 57	13 27 13	15 29 26	17 27 43
14	19 34 50	21 37 4	23 27 27	1 29 40	3 27 57	5 30 10	7 28 27	9 30 40	11 32 53	13 31 10	15 33 23	17 31 40
15	19 38 47	21 41 0	23 31 24	1 33 37	3 31 53	5 34 7	7 32 23	9 34 37	11 36 50	13 35 6	15 37 19	17 35 36
16	19 42 44	21 44 57	23 35 20	1 37 33	3 35 50	5 38 3	7 36 20	9 38 33	11 40 45	13 39 3	15 41 16	17 39 33
17	19 46 40	21 48 53	23 39 17	1 41 30	3 39 47	5 42 0	7 40 16	9 42 30	11 44 43	13 42 59	15 45 13	17 43 29
18	19 50 37	21 52 50	23 43 13	1 45 26	3 43 43	5 45 56	7 44 13	9 46 26	11 48 39	13 46 56	15 49 9	17 47 26
19	19 54 33	21 56 46	23 47 10	1 49 23	3 47 40	5 49 53	7 48 10	9 50 23	11 52 36	13 50 52	15 53 6	17 51 22
20	19 58 30	22 0 43	23 51 6	1 53 20	3 51 36	5 53 49	7 52 6	9 54 19	11 56 32	13 54 49	15 57 2	17 55 19
21	20 2 26	22 4 40	23 55 3	1 57 16	3 55 33	5 57 46	7 56 3	9 58 16	12 0 29	13 58 46	16 0 59	17 59 15
22	20 6 23	22 8 36	23 59 0	2 1 13	3 59 29	6 1 43	7 59 59	10 2 12	12 4 26	14 2 42	16 4 55	18 3 12
23	20 10 19	22 12 33	0 2 56	2 5 9	4 3 26	6 5 39	8 3 56	10 6 9	12 8 22	14 6 39	16 8 52	18 7 9
24	20 14 16	22 16 29	0 6 53	2 9 6	4 7 22	6 9 36	8 7 52	10 10 6	12 12 19	14 10 35	16 12 48	18 11 5
25	20 18 13	22 20 26	0 10 49	2 13 2	4 11 19	6 13 32	8 11 49	10 14 2	12 16 15	14 14 32	16 16 45	18 15 2
26	20 22 9	22 24 22	0 14 46	2 16 59	4 15 16	6 17 29	8 15 45	10 17 59	12 20 12	14 18 28	16 20 42	18 18 58
27	20 26 6	22 28 19	0 18 42	2 20 55	4 19 12	6 21 25	8 19 42	10 21 55	12 24 8	14 22 25	16 24 38	18 22 55
28	20 30 2	22 32 15	0 22 39	2 24 52	4 23 9	6 25 22	8 23 39	10 25 52	12 28 5	14 26 21	16 28 35	18 26 51
29	20 33 59		0 26 35	2 28 49	4 27 5	6 29 18	8 27 35	10 29 48	12 32 1	14 30 18	16 32 31	18 30 48
30	20 37 55		0 30 32	2 32 45	4 31 2	6 33 15	8 31 32	10 33 45	12 35 58	14 34 15	16 36 28	18 34 45
31	20 41 52		0 34 29		4 34 58		8 35 28	10 37 41		14 38 11		18 38 41

1962

Day	Jan.	Feb.	Mar.	April	May	June	July	Aug.	Sept.	Oct.	Nov.	Dec.
1	18 42 38	20 44 51	22 35 14	0 37 28	2 35 44	4 37 57	6 36 14	8 38 27	10 40 40	12 38 57	14 41 10	16 39 27
2	18 46 34	20 48 47	22 39 11	0 41 24	2 39 41	4 41 54	6 40 11	8 42 24	10 44 37	12 42 54	14 45 7	16 43 23
3	18 50 31	20 52 44	22 43 7	0 45 21	2 43 37	4 45 50	6 44 7	8 46 20	10 48 34	12 46 50	14 49 3	16 47 20
4	18 54 27	20 56 41	22 47 4	0 49 17	2 47 34	4 49 47	6 48 4	8 50 17	10 52 30	12 50 47	14 53 0	16 51 16
5	18 58 24	21 0 37	22 51 1	0 53 14	2 51 30	4 53 44	6 52 0	8 54 13	10 56 27	12 54 43	14 56 56	16 55 13
6	19 2 20	21 4 34	22 54 57	0 57 10	2 55 27	4 57 40	6 55 57	8 58 10	11 0 23	12 58 40	15 0 53	16 59 10
7	19 6 17	21 8 30	22 58 54	1 1 7	2 59 23	5 1 37	6 59 53	9 2 7	11 4 20	13 2 36	15 4 49	17 3 6
8	19 10 14	21 12 27	23 2 50	1 5 3	3 3 20	5 5 33	7 3 50	9 6 3	11 8 16	13 6 33	15 8 46	17 7 3
9	19 14 10	21 16 23	23 6 47	1 9 0	3 7 17	5 9 30	7 7 46	9 10 0	11 12 13	13 10 29	15 12 43	17 10 59
10	19 18 7	21 20 20	23 10 43	1 12 56	3 11 13	5 13 26	7 11 43	9 13 56	11 16 9	13 14 26	15 16 39	17 14 56
11	19 22 3	21 24 16	23 14 40	1 16 53	3 15 10	5 17 23	7 15 40	9 17 53	11 20 6	13 18 23	15 20 36	17 18 52
12	19 26 0	21 28 13	23 18 36	1 20 50	3 19 6	5 21 19	7 19 36	9 21 49	11 24 3	13 22 19	15 24 32	17 22 49
13	19 29 56	21 32 10	23 22 33	1 24 46	3 23 3	5 25 16	7 23 33	9 25 46	11 27 59	13 26 16	15 28 29	17 26 46
14	19 33 53	21 36 6	23 26 30	1 28 43	3 26 59	5 29 13	7 27 29	9 29 42	11 31 56	13 30 12	15 32 25	17 30 42
15	19 37 49	21 40 3	23 30 26	1 32 39	3 30 56	5 33 9	7 31 26	9 33 39	11 35 52	13 34 9	15 36 22	17 34 39
16	19 41 46	21 43 59	23 34 23	1 36 36	3 34 52	5 37 6	7 35 22	9 37 36	11 39 49	13 38 5	15 40 18	17 38 35
17	19 45 43	21 47 56	23 38 19	1 40 32	3 38 49	5 41 2	7 39 19	9 41 32	11 43 45	13 42 2	15 44 15	17 42 32
18	19 49 39	21 51 52	23 42 16	1 44 29	3 42 46	5 44 59	7 43 15	9 45 29	11 47 42	13 45 58	15 48 12	17 46 28
19	19 53 36	21 55 49	23 46 12	1 48 25	3 46 42	5 48 55	7 47 12	9 49 25	11 51 38	13 49 55	15 52 8	17 50 25
20	19 57 32	21 59 45	23 50 9	1 52 22	3 50 39	5 52 52	7 51 9	9 53 22	11 55 35	13 53 52	15 56 5	17 54 21
21	20 1 29	22 3 42	23 54 5	1 56 19	3 54 35	5 56 48	7 55 5	9 57 18	11 59 31	13 57 48	16 0 1	17 58 18
22	20 5 25	22 7 39	23 58 2	2 0 15	3 58 32	6 0 45	7 59 2	10 1 15	12 3 28	14 1 45	16 3 58	18 2 15
23	20 9 22	22 11 35	0 1 59	2 4 12	4 2 28	6 4 42	8 2 58	10 5 11	12 7 25	14 5 41	16 7 54	18 6 11
24	20 13 18	22 15 32	0 5 55	2 8 8	4 6 25	6 8 38	8 6 55	10 9 8	12 11 21	14 9 38	16 11 51	18 10 8
25	20 17 15	22 19 28	0 9 52	2 12 5	4 10 21	6 12 35	8 10 51	10 13 5	12 15 18	14 13 34	16 15 47	18 14 4
26	20 21 12	22 23 25	0 13 48	2 16 1	4 14 18	6 16 31	8 14 48	10 17 1	12 19 14	14 17 31	16 19 44	18 18 1
27	20 25 8	22 27 21	0 17 45	2 19 58	4 18 15	6 20 28	8 18 44	10 20 58	12 23 11	14 21 27	16 23 41	18 21 57
28	29 29 5	22 31 18	0 21 41	2 23 54	4 22 11	6 24 24	8 22 41	10 24 54	12 27 7	14 25 24	16 27 37	18 25 54
29	20 33 1		0 25 38	2 27 51	4 26 8	6 28 21	8 26 38	10 28 51	12 31 4	14 29 20	16 31 34	18 29 50
30	20 36 58		0 29 34	2 31 48	4 30 4	6 32 17	8 30 34	10 32 47	12 35 0	14 33 17	16 35 30	18 33 47
31	20 40 54		0 33 31		4 34 1		8 34 31	10 36 44		14 37 14		18 37 44

1963

Day	Jan.	Feb.	Mar.	April	May	June	July	Aug.	Sept.	Oct.	Nov.	Dec.
1	18 41 40	20 43 53	22 34 17	0 36 30	2 34 47	4 37 0	6 35 17	8 37 30	10 39 43	12 38 0	14 40 13	16 38 29
2	18 45 37	20 47 50	22 38 13	0 40 27	2 38 43	4 40 56	6 39 13	8 41 26	10 43 40	12 41 56	14 44 9	16 42 26
3	18 49 33	20 51 46	22 42 10	0 44 23	2 42 40	4 44 53	6 43 10	8 45 23	10 47 36	12 45 53	14 48 6	16 46 23
4	18 53 30	20 55 43	22 46 7	0 48 20	2 46 36	4 48 49	6 47 6	8 49 19	10 51 33	12 49 49	14 52 2	16 50 19
5	18 57 26	20 59 40	22 50 3	0 52 16	2 50 33	4 52 46	6 51 3	8 53 16	10 55 29	12 53 46	14 55 59	16 54 16
6	19 1 23	21 3 36	22 54 0	0 56 13	2 54 29	4 56 43	6 54 59	8 57 13	10 59 26	12 57 42	14 59 55	16 58 12
7	19 5 19	21 7 33	22 57 56	1 0 9	2 58 26	5 0 39	6 58 56	9 1 9	11 3 22	13 1 39	15 3 52	17 2 9
8	19 9 16	21 11 29	23 1 53	1 4 6	3 2 22	5 4 36	7 2 52	9 5 6	11 7 19	13 5 35	15 7 49	17 6 5
9	19 13 13	21 15 26	23 5 49	1 8 2	3 6 19	5 8 32	7 6 49	9 9 2	11 11 15	13 9 32	15 11 45	17 10 2
10	19 17 9	21 19 22	23 9 46	1 11 59	3 10 16	5 12 29	7 10 46	9 12 59	11 15 12	13 13 29	15 15 42	17 13 58
11	19 21 6	21 23 19	23 13 42	1 15 56	3 14 12	5 16 25	7 14 42	9 16 55	11 19 9	13 17 25	15 19 38	17 17 55
12	19 25 2	21 27 15	23 17 39	1 19 52	3 18 9	5 20 22	7 18 39	9 20 52	11 23 5	13 21 22	15 23 35	17 21 52
13	19 28 59	21 31 12	23 21 35	1 23 49	3 22 5	5 24 19	7 22 35	9 24 48	11 27 2	13 25 18	15 27 31	17 25 48
14	19 32 55	21 35 9	23 25 32	1 27 45	3 26 2	5 28 15	7 26 32	9 28 45	11 30 58	13 29 15	15 31 28	17 29 45
15	19 36 52	21 39 5	23 29 29	1 31 42	3 29 58	5 32 12	7 30 28	9 32 42	11 34 55	13 33 11	15 35 24	17 33 41
16	19 40 48	21 43 2	23 33 25	1 35 38	3 33 55	5 36 8	7 34 25	9 36 38	11 38 51	13 37 8	15 39 21	17 37 38
17	19 44 45	21 46 58	23 37 22	1 39 35	3 37 51	5 40 5	7 38 21	9 40 35	11 42 48	13 41 4	15 43 18	17 41 34
18	19 48 42	21 50 55	23 41 18	1 43 31	3 41 48	5 44 1	7 42 18	9 44 31	11 46 44	13 45 1	15 47 14	17 45 31
19	19 52 38	21 54 51	23 45 15	1 47 28	3 45 45	5 47 58	7 46 15	9 48 28	11 50 41	13 48 58	15 51 11	17 49 27
20	19 56 35	21 58 48	23 49 11	1 51 25	3 49 41	5 51 54	7 50 11	9 52 24	11 54 37	13 52 54	15 55 7	17 53 24
21	20 0 31	22 2 44	23 53 8	1 55 21	3 53 38	5 55 51	7 54 8	9 56 21	11 58 34	13 56 51	15 59 4	17 57 21
22	20 4 28	22 6 41	23 57 4	1 59 18	3 57 34	5 59 48	7 58 4	10 0 17	12 2 31	14 0 47	16 3 0	18 1 17
23	20 8 24	22 10 38	0 1 1	2 3 14	4 1 31	6 3 44	8 2 1	10 4 14	12 6 27	14 4 44	16 6 57	18 5 14
24	20 12 21	22 14 34	0 4 58	2 7 11	4 5 27	6 7 41	8 5 57	10 8 11	12 10 24	14 8 40	16 10 54	18 9 10
25	20 16 17	22 18 31	0 8 54	2 11 7	4 9 24	6 11 37	8 9 54	10 12 7	12 14 20	14 12 37	16 14 50	18 13 7
26	20 20 14	22 22 27	0 12 51	2 15 4	4 13 20	6 15 34	8 13 50	10 16 4	12 18 17	14 16 33	16 18 47	18 17 3
27	20 24 11	22 26 24	0 16 47	2 19 0	4 17 17	6 19 30	8 17 47	10 20 0	12 22 13	14 20 30	16 22 43	18 21 0
28	20 28 7	22 30 20	0 20 44	2 22 57	4 21 14	6 23 27	8 21 44	10 23 57	12 26 10	14 24 27	16 26 40	18 24 56
29	20 32 4		0 24 40	2 26 54	4 25 10	6 27 23	8 25 40	10 27 53	12 30 6	14 28 23	16 30 36	18 28 53
30	20 36 0		0 28 37	2 30 50	4 29 7	6 31 20	8 29 37	10 31 50	12 34 3	14 32 20	16 34 33	18 32 50
31	20 39 57		0 32 33		4 33 3		8 33 33	10 35 46		14 36 16		18 36 46

1964

Day	Jan.	Feb.	Mar.	April	May	June	July	Aug.	Sept.	Oct.	Nov.	Dec.
1	18 40 43	20 42 56	22 37 16	0 39 29	2 37 46	4 39 59	6 38 16	8 40 19	10 42 42	12 40 59	14 43 12	16 41 29
2	18 44 39	20 46 53	22 41 13	0 43 26	2 41 42	4 43 56	6 42 12	8 44 26	10 46 39	12 44 55	14 47 9	16 45 25
3	18 48 36	20 50 49	22 45 9	0 47 22	2 45 39	4 47 52	6 46 9	8 48 22	10 50 35	12 48 52	14 51 5	16 49 22
4	18 52 32	20 54 46	22 49 6	0 51 19	2 49 36	4 51 49	6 50 5	8 52 19	10 54 32	12 52 48	14 55 2	16 53 18
5	18 56 29	20 58 42	22 53 2	0 55 15	2 53 32	4 55 45	6 54 2	8 56 15	10 58 28	12 56 45	14 58 58	16 57 15
6	19 0 26	21 2 39	22 56 59	0 59 12	2 57 29	4 59 42	6 57 59	9 0 12	11 2 25	13 0 42	15 2 55	17 1 11
7	19 4 22	21 6 35	23 0 55	1 3 8	3 1 25	5 3 38	7 1 55	9 4 8	11 6 22	13 4 38	15 6 51	17 5 8
8	19 8 19	21 10 32	23 4 52	1 7 5	3 5 22	5 7 35	7 5 52	9 8 5	11 10 18	13 8 35	15 10 48	17 9 5
9	19 12 15	21 14 28	23 8 48	1 11 2	3 9 18	5 11 31	7 9 48	9 12 1	11 14 15	13 12 31	15 14 44	17 13 1
10	19 16 12	21 18 25	23 12 45	1 14 58	3 13 15	5 15 28	7 13 45	9 15 58	11 18 11	13 16 28	15 18 41	17 16 58
11	19 20 8	21 22 22	23 16 42	1 18 55	3 17 11	5 19 25	7 17 42	9 19 55	11 22 8	13 20 24	15 22 38	17 20 54
12	19 24 5	21 26 18	23 20 38	1 22 51	3 21 8	5 23 21	7 21 38	9 23 51	11 26 4	13 24 21	15 26 34	17 24 51
13	19 28 1	21 30 15	23 24 35	1 26 48	3 25 4	5 27 18	7 25 35	9 27 48	11 30 1	13 28 17	15 30 31	17 28 47
14	19 31 58	21 34 11	23 28 31	1 30 44	3 29 1	5 31 14	7 29 31	9 31 44	11 33 57	13 32 14	15 34 27	17 32 44
15	19 35 55	21 38 8	23 32 28	1 34 41	3 32 58	5 35 11	7 33 28	9 35 41	11 37 54	13 36 11	15 38 24	17 36 40
16	19 39 51	21 42 4	23 36 24	1 38 37	3 36 54	5 39 7	7 37 24	9 39 37	11 41 51	13 40 7	15 42 20	17 40 37
17	19 43 48	21 46 1	23 40 21	1 42 34	3 40 51	5 43 4	7 41 21	9 43 34	11 45 47	13 44 4	15 46 17	17 44 34
18	19 47 44	21 49 57	23 44 17	1 46 31	3 44 47	5 47 1	7 45 17	9 47 30	11 49 44	13 48 0	15 50 13	17 48 30
19	19 51 41	21 53 54	23 48 14	1 50 27	3 48 44	5 50 57	7 49 14	9 51 27	11 53 40	13 51 57	15 54 10	17 52 27
20	19 55 37	21 57 50	23 52 11	1 54 24	3 52 40	5 54 54	7 53 10	9 55 24	11 57 37	13 55 53	15 58 7	17 56 23
21	19 59 34	22 1 47	23 56 7	1 58 20	3 56 37	5 58 50	7 57 7	9 59 20	12 1 33	13 59 50	16 2 3	18 0 20
22	20 3 30	22 5 44	0 0 4	2 2 17	4 0 33	6 2 47	8 1 3	10 3 17	12 5 30	14 3 46	16 6 0	18 4 16
23	20 7 27	22 9 40	0 4 0	2 6 13	4 4 30	6 6 43	8 5 0	10 7 13	12 9 27	14 7 43	16 9 56	18 8 13
24	20 11 23	22 13 37	0 7 57	2 10 10	4 8 27	6 10 40	8 8 57	10 11 10	12 13 23	14 11 40	16 13 53	18 12 10
25	20 15 20	22 17 33	0 11 53	2 14 6	4 12 23	6 14 36	8 12 53	10 15 6	12 17 19	14 15 36	16 17 49	18 16 6
26	20 19 17	22 21 30	0 15 50	2 18 3	4 16 20	6 18 33	8 16 50	10 19 3	12 21 16	14 19 33	16 21 46	18 20 3
27	20 23 13	22 25 26	0 19 46	2 22 0	4 20 16	6 22 30	8 20 46	10 22 59	12 25 13	14 23 29	16 25 42	18 23 59
28	20 27 10	22 29 23	0 23 43	2 25 56	4 24 13	6 26 26	8 24 43	10 26 56	12 29 9	14 27 26	16 29 39	18 27 56
29	20 31 6	22 33 19	0 27 40	2 29 53	4 28 9	6 30 23	8 28 40	10 30 53	12 33 6	14 31 22	16 33 36	18 31 52
30	20 35 3		0 31 36	2 33 49	4 32 6	6 34 19	8 32 36	10 34 49	12 37 2	14 35 19	16 37 32	18 35 49
31	20 38 59		0 35 33		4 36 2		8 36 32	10 38 46		14 39 15		18 39 45

Tables of houses

Since it is impossible here to give tables of houses for every degree of latitude, the following are examples of tables giving ascendants for anyone born at any time on or near the latitudes of London and New York. You look up in the S.T. column the figure nearest to your S.T. at birth, and find its corresponding ascendant in the next column.

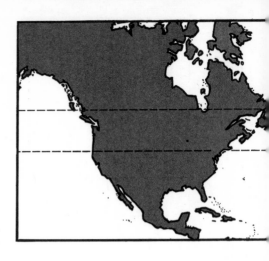

Table of Houses for London.   Latitude 51° 32′ N

Sidereal Time	Ascen	Sidereal Time	Ascen	Sidereal Time	Ascen	Sidereal Time	Ascen	Sidereal Time	Ascen	Sidereal Time	Ascen
H. M. S.	° ♋ ′	H. M. S.	° ♍ ′	H. M. S.	° ♎ ′	H. M. S.	° ♐ ′	H. M. S.	° ♑ ′	H. M. S.	° ♊ ′
0 0 0	26 36	3 51 15	7 21	8 8 45	22 40	12 0 0	3 23	15 51 15	27 15	20 8 45	2 45
0 3 40	27 17	3 55 25	8 5	8 12 54	23 24	12 3 40	4 4	15 55 25	28 42	20 12 54	4 9
0 7 20	27 56	3 59 36	8 49	8 17 3	24 7	12 7 20	4 45	15 59 36	0≈11	20 17 3	5 32
0 11 0	28 42	4 3 48	9 33	8 21 11	24 50	12 11 0	5 26	16 3 48	1 42	20 21 11	6 53
0 14 41	29 17	4 8 0	10 17	8 25 19	25 34	12 14 41	6 7	16 8 0	3 16	20 25 19	8 12
0 18 21	29 55	4 12 13	11 2	8 29 26	26 18	12 18 21	6 48	16 12 13	4 53	20 29 26	9 27
0 22 2	0♌34	4 16 26	11 46	8 33 31	27 1	12 22 2	7 29	16 16 26	6 32	20 33 31	10 43
0 25 42	1 14	4 20 40	12 30	8 37 37	27 44	12 25 42	8 10	16 20 40	8 13	20 37 37	11 58
0 29 23	1 55	4 24 55	13 15	8 41 41	28 26	12 29 23	8 51	16 24 55	9 57	20 41 41	13 9
0 33 4	2 33	4 29 10	14 0	8 45 45	29 8	12 33 4	9 33	16 29 10	11 44	20 45 45	14 18
0 36 45	3 14	4 33 26	14 45	8 49 48	29 50	12 36 45	10 15	16 33 26	13 34	20 49 48	15 25
0 40 26	3 54	4 37 42	15 30	8 53 51	0♏32	12 40 26	10 57	16 37 42	15 26	20 53 51	16 32
0 44 8	4 33	4 41 59	16 15	8 57 52	1 15	12 44 8	11 40	16 41 59	17 20	20 57 52	17 39
0 47 50	5 12	4 46 16	17 0	9 1 53	1 58	12 47 50	12 22	16 46 16	19 18	21 1 53	18 44
0 51 32	5 52	4 50 34	17 45	9 5 53	2 39	12 51 32	13 4	16 50 34	21 22	21 5 53	19 48
0 55 14	6 30	4 54 52	18 30	9 9 53	3 21	12 55 14	13 47	16 54 52	23 29	21 9 53	20 51
0 58 57	7 9	4 59 10	19 16	9 13 52	4 3	12 58 57	14 30	16 59 10	25 36	21 13 52	21 53
1 2 40	7 50	5 3 29	20 3	9 17 50	4 44	13 2 40	15 14	17 3 29	27 46	21 17 50	22 53
1 6 23	8 30	5 7 49	20 49	9 21 47	5 26	13 6 23	15 59	17 7 49	0✕0	21 21 47	23 52
1 10 7	9 9	5 12 9	21 35	9 25 44	6 7	13 10 7	16 44	17 12 9	2 19	21 25 44	24 51
1 13 51	9 48	5 16 29	22 20	9 29 40	6 48	13 13 51	17 29	17 16 29	4 40	21 29 40	25 48
1 17 35	10 28	5 20 49	23 6	9 33 35	7 29	13 17 35	18 14	17 20 49	7 2	21 33 35	26 44
1 21 20	11 8	5 25 9	23 51	9 37 29	8 9	13 21 20	19 0	17 25 9	9 26	21 37 29	27 40
1 25 6	11 48	5 29 30	24 37	9 41 23	8 50	13 25 6	19 45	17 29 30	11 54	21 41 23	28 34
1 28 52	12 28	5 33 51	25 23	9 45 16	9 31	13 28 52	20 31	17 33 51	14 24	21 45 16	29 29
1 32 38	13 8	5 38 12	26 9	9 49 9	10 11	13 32 38	21 18	17 38 12	17 0	21 49 9	0♋22
1 36 25	13 48	5 42 34	26 55	9 53 1	10 51	13 36 25	22 6	17 42 34	19 33	21 53 1	1 15
1 40 12	14 28	5 46 55	27 41	9 56 52	11 32	13 40 12	22 54	17 46 55	22 6	21 56 52	2 7
1 44 0	15 8	5 51 17	28 27	10 0 43	12 12	13 44 0	23 42	17 51 17	24 40	22 0 43	2 57
1 47 48	15 48	5 55 38	29 13	10 4 33	12 53	13 47 48	24 31	17 55 38	27 20	22 4 33	3 48
1 51 37	16 28	6 0 0	30 0	10 8 23	13 33	13 51 37	25 20	18 0 0	30 0	22 8 23	4 38
1 55 27	17 8	6 4 22	0♎47	10 12 12	14 13	13 55 27	26 10	18 4 22	2♈39	22 12 12	5 28
1 59 17	17 48	6 8 43	1 33	10 16 0	14 53	13 59 17	27 2	18 8 43	5 19	22 16 0	6 17
2 3 8	18 28	6 13 5	2 19	10 19 48	15 33	14 3 8	27 53	18 13 5	7 55	22 19 48	7 5
2 6 59	19 9	6 17 26	3 5	10 23 35	16 13	14 6 59	28 45	18 17 26	10 29	22 23 35	7 53
2 10 51	19 49	6 21 48	3 51	10 27 22	16 52	14 10 51	29 36	18 21 48	13 2	22 27 22	8 42
2 14 44	20 29	6 26 9	4 37	10 31 8	17 32	14 14 44	0♑29	18 26 9	15 36	22 31 8	9 29
2 18 37	21 10	6 30 30	5 23	10 34 54	18 13	14 18 37	1 23	18 30 30	18 6	22 34 54	10 16
2 22 31	21 51	6 34 51	6 9	10 38 40	18 52	14 22 31	2 18	18 34 51	20 34	22 38 40	11 2
2 26 25	22 32	6 39 11	6 55	10 42 25	19 31	14 26 25	3 14	18 39 11	22 59	22 42 25	11 47
2 30 20	23 14	6 43 31	7 40	10 46 9	20 11	14 30 20	4 11	18 43 31	25 22	22 46 9	12 31
2 34 16	23 55	6 47 51	8 26	10 49 53	20 50	14 34 16	5 9	18 47 51	27 42	22 49 53	13 16
2 38 13	24 36	6 52 11	9 12	10 53 37	21 30	14 38 13	6 7	18 52 11	29 58	22 53 37	14 1
2 42 10	25 17	6 56 31	9 58	10 57 20	22 9	14 42 10	7 6	18 56 31	2♉13	22 57 20	14 45
2 46 8	25 58	7 0 50	10 43	11 1 3	22 49	14 46 8	8 6	19 0 50	4 24	23 1 3	15 28
2 50 7	26 40	7 5 8	11 28	11 4 46	23 28	14 50 7	9 8	19 5 8	6 30	23 4 46	16 11
2 54 7	27 22	7 9 26	12 14	11 8 28	24 8	14 54 7	10 11	19 9 26	8 36	23 8 28	16 54
2 58 7	28 4	7 13 44	12 59	11 12 10	24 47	14 58 7	11 15	19 13 44	10 40	23 12 10	17 37
3 2 8	28 46	7 18 1	13 45	11 15 52	25 27	15 2 8	12 20	19 18 1	12 39	23 15 52	18 20
3 6 9	29 28	7 22 18	14 30	11 19 34	26 6	15 6 9	13 27	19 22 18	14 35	23 19 34	19 3
3 10 12	0♍12	7 26 34	15 15	11 23 15	26 45	15 10 12	14 35	19 26 34	16 28	23 23 15	19 45
3 14 15	0 54	7 30 50	16 0	11 26 56	27 25	15 14 15	15 43	19 30 50	18 17	23 26 56	20 26
3 18 19	1 36	7 35 5	16 45	11 30 37	28 5	15 18 19	16 52	19 35 5	20 3	23 30 37	21 8
3 22 23	2 20	7 39 20	17 30	11 34 18	28 44	15 22 23	18 3	19 39 20	21 48	23 34 18	21 50
3 26 29	3 2	7 43 34	18 15	11 37 58	29 24	15 26 29	19 16	19 43 34	23 29	23 37 58	22 31
3 30 35	3 45	7 47 47	18 59	11 41 39	0♐2	15 30 35	20 32	19 47 47	25 9	23 41 39	23 12
3 34 41	4 28	7 52 0	19 43	11 45 19	0 43	15 34 41	21 48	19 52 0	26 45	23 45 19	23 53
3 38 49	5 11	7 56 12	20 27	11 49 0	1 23	15 38 49	23 8	19 56 12	28 18	23 49 0	24 32
3 42 57	5 54	8 0 24	21 11	11 52 40	2 3	15 42 57	24 29	20 0 24	29 49	23 52 40	25 15
3 47 6	6 38	8 4 35	21 56	11 56 20	2 43	15 47 6	25 51	20 4 35	1♊19	23 56 20	25 56
3 51 15	7 21	8 8 45	22 40	12 0 0	3 23	15 51 15	27 15	20 8 45	2 45	24 0 0	26 36

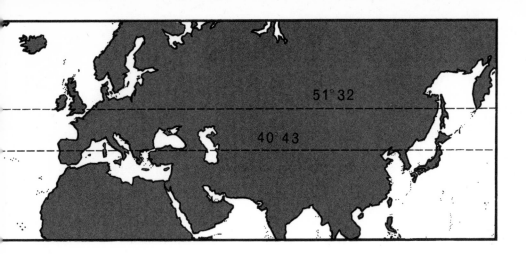

51° 32

40° 43

Table of Houses for New York. Latitude 40° 43′ N

Sidereal Time H. M. S.	Ascen ° ♋ ′	Sidereal Time H. M. S.	Ascen ° ♍ ′	Sidereal Time H. M. S.	Ascen ° ♎ ′	Sidereal Time H. M. S.	Ascen ° ♐ ′	Sidereal Time H. M. S.	Ascen ° ≈ ′	Sidereal Time H. M. S.	Ascen ° ♉ ′
0 0 0	18 53	3 51 15	4 32	8 8 45	25 28	12 0 0	11 7	15 51 15	9 8	20 8 45	20 52
0 3 40	19 38	3 55 25	5 22	8 12 54	26 17	12 3 40	11 52	15 55 25	10 31	20 12 54	22 14
0 7 20	20 23	3 59 36	6 10	8 17 3	27 5	12 7 20	12 37	15 59 36	11 56	20 17 3	23 35
0 11 0	21 12	4 3 48	7 0	8 21 11	27 54	12 11 0	13 19	16 3 48	13 23	20 21 11	24 55
0 14 41	21 55	4 8 0	7 49	8 25 19	28 43	12 14 41	14 7	16 7 0	14 50	20 25 19	26 14
0 18 21	22 40	4 12 13	8 40	8 29 26	29 31	12 18 21	14 52	16 12 13	16 19	20 29 26	27 32
0 22 2	23 24	4 16 26	9 30	8 33 31	0 ♏ 20	12 22 2	15 38	16 16 26	17 50	20 33 31	28 46
0 25 42	24 8	4 20 40	10 19	8 37 37	1 8	12 25 42	16 23	16 20 40	19 22	20 37 37	0 ♊ 3
0 29 23	24 54	4 24 55	11 10	8 41 41	1 56	12 29 23	17 11	16 24 55	20 56	20 41 41	1 17
0 33 4	25 37	4 29 10	12 0	8 45 45	2 43	12 33 4	17 58	16 29 10	22 30	20 45 45	2 29
0 36 45	26 22	4 33 26	12 51	8 49 48	3 31	12 36 45	18 45	16 33 26	24 7	20 49 48	3 41
0 40 26	27 5	4 37 42	13 41	8 53 51	4 18	12 40 26	19 32	16 37 42	25 44	20 53 51	4 51
0 44 8	27 50	4 41 59	14 32	8 57 52	5 6	12 44 8	20 20	16 41 59	27 23	20 57 52	6 1
0 47 50	28 33	4 46 16	15 23	9 1 53	5 53	12 47 50	21 8	16 46 16	29 4	21 1 53	7 9
0 51 32	29 18	4 50 34	16 14	9 5 53	6 40	12 51 32	21 57	16 50 34	0 ✕ 45	21 5 53	8 16
0 55 14	0 ♌ 3	4 54 52	17 5	9 9 53	7 27	12 55 14	22 43	16 54 52	2 27	21 9 53	9 23
0 58 57	0 46	4 59 10	17 56	9 13 52	8 13	12 58 57	23 33	16 59 10	4 11	21 13 52	10 30
1 2 40	1 31	5 3 29	18 47	9 17 50	9 0	13 2 40	24 22	17 3 29	5 56	21 17 50	11 33
1 6 23	2 14	5 7 49	19 39	9 21 47	9 46	13 6 23	25 11	17 7 49	7 43	21 21 47	12 37
1 10 7	2 58	5 12 9	20 30	9 25 44	10 33	13 10 7	26 1	17 12 9	9 30	21 25 44	13 41
1 13 51	3 43	5 16 29	21 22	9 29 40	11 19	13 13 51	26 51	17 16 29	11 18	21 29 40	14 43
1 17 35	4 27	5 20 49	22 13	9 33 35	12 4	13 17 35	27 40	17 20 49	13 8	21 33 35	15 44
1 21 20	5 12	5 25 9	23 5	9 37 29	12 50	13 21 20	28 32	17 25 9	14 57	21 37 29	16 45
1 25 6	5 56	5 29 30	23 57	9 41 23	13 36	13 25 6	29 23	17 29 30	16 48	21 41 23	17 45
1 28 52	6 40	5 33 51	24 49	9 45 16	14 21	13 28 52	0 ♑ 14	17 33 51	18 41	21 45 16	18 44
1 32 38	7 25	5 38 12	25 40	9 49 9	15 7	13 32 38	1 7	17 38 12	20 33	21 49 9	19 42
1 36 25	8 9	5 42 34	26 32	9 53 1	15 52	13 36 25	2 0	17 42 34	22 25	21 53 1	20 40
1 40 12	8 53	5 46 55	27 25	9 56 52	16 38	13 40 12	2 52	17 46 55	24 19	21 56 52	21 37
1 44 0	9 38	5 51 17	28 16	10 0 43	17 22	13 44 0	3 46	17 51 17	26 12	22 0 43	22 33
1 47 48	10 24	5 55 38	29 8	10 4 33	18 7	13 47 48	4 40	17 55 38	28 7	22 4 33	23 30
1 51 37	11 8	6 0 0	30 0	10 8 23	18 52	13 51 37	5 35	18 0 0	30 0	22 8 23	24 25
1 55 27	11 53	6 4 22	0 ♎ 52	10 12 12	19 36	13 55 27	6 30	18 4 22	1 ♈ 53	22 12 12	25 19
1 59 17	12 38	6 8 43	1 44	10 16 0	20 22	13 59 17	7 27	18 8 43	3 48	22 16 0	26 14
2 3 8	13 22	6 13 5	2 35	10 19 48	21 7	14 3 8	8 20	18 13 5	5 41	22 19 48	27 8
2 6 59	14 8	6 17 26	3 28	10 23 35	21 51	14 6 59	9 20	18 17 26	7 35	22 23 35	28 0
2 10 51	14 53	6 21 48	4 20	10 27 22	22 35	14 10 51	10 18	18 21 48	9 27	22 27 22	28 53
2 14 44	15 39	6 26 9	5 11	10 31 8	23 20	14 14 44	11 16	18 26 9	11 19	22 31 8	29 46
2 18 37	16 24	6 30 30	6 3	10 34 54	24 4	14 18 37	12 15	18 30 30	13 12	22 34 54	0 ♋ 37
2 22 31	17 10	6 34 51	6 55	10 38 40	24 48	14 22 31	13 15	18 34 51	15 3	22 38 40	1 28
2 26 25	17 56	6 39 11	7 47	10 42 25	25 33	14 26 25	14 16	18 39 11	16 52	22 42 25	2 20
2 30 20	18 41	6 43 31	8 38	10 46 9	26 17	14 30 20	15 17	18 43 31	18 42	22 46 9	3 9
2 34 16	19 27	6 47 51	9 30	10 49 53	27 2	14 34 16	16 19	18 47 51	20 30	22 49 53	3 59
2 38 13	20 14	6 52 11	10 21	10 53 37	27 46	14 38 13	17 23	18 52 11	22 17	22 53 37	4 49
2 42 10	21 0	6 56 31	11 13	10 57 20	28 29	14 42 10	18 27	18 56 31	24 4	22 57 20	5 38
2 46 8	21 47	7 0 50	12 4	11 1 3	29 14	14 46 8	19 30	19 0 50	25 49	23 1 3	6 27
2 50 7	22 33	7 5 8	12 55	11 4 45	29 58	14 50 7	20 37	19 5 8	27 33	23 4 45	7 17
2 54 7	23 20	7 9 26	13 46	11 8 28	0 ♐ 42	14 54 7	21 44	19 9 20	29 15	23 8 28	8 3
2 58 7	24 7	7 13 44	14 37	11 12 10	1 27	14 58 7	22 52	19 13 44	0 ♉ 56	23 12 10	8 52
3 2 8	24 54	7 18 1	15 28	11 15 52	2 10	15 2 8	23 59	19 18 1	2 37	23 15 52	9 40
3 6 9	25 42	7 22 18	16 19	11 19 34	2 55	15 6 9	25 9	19 22 18	4 16	23 19 34	10 28
3 10 12	26 29	7 26 34	17 9	11 23 15	3 38	15 10 12	26 19	19 26 34	5 53	23 23 15	11 15
3 14 15	27 17	7 30 50	18 0	11 26 56	4 23	15 14 15	27 31	19 30 50	7 30	23 26 56	12 2
3 18 19	28 4	7 35 5	18 50	11 30 37	5 6	15 18 19	28 43	19 35 5	9 4	23 30 37	12 49
3 22 23	28 52	7 39 20	19 41	11 34 18	5 52	15 22 23	29 57	19 39 20	10 38	23 34 18	13 37
3 26 29	29 40	7 43 34	20 30	11 37 58	6 36	15 26 29	1 ≈ 14	19 43 34	12 10	23 37 58	14 22
3 30 35	0 ♍ 29	7 47 47	21 20	11 41 39	7 20	15 30 35	2 28	19 47 47	13 41	23 41 39	15 8
3 34 41	1 17	7 52 0	22 11	11 45 19	8 5	15 34 41	3 46	19 52 0	15 10	23 45 19	15 53
3 38 49	2 6	7 56 12	23 0	11 49 0	8 51	15 38 49	5 5	19 56 12	16 37	23 49 0	16 41
3 42 57	2 55	8 0 24	23 50	11 52 40	9 37	15 42 57	6 25	20 0 24	18 4	23 52 40	17 23
3 47 6	3 43	8 4 35	24 38	11 56 20	10 22	15 47 6	7 46	20 4 35	19 29	23 56 20	18 8
3 51 15	4 32	8 8 45	25 28	12 0 0	11 7	15 51 15	9 8	20 8 45	20 52	24 0 0	18 53

A Southern Hemisphere horoscope

Horoscopes of natives born south of the equator are calculated by the same method as that used for northerners—with only two differences:

1. To compensate for the difference in sidereal time in southern latitudes, 12 hours must be added to the s.t. calculated for the time of birth.

2. Since no tables of houses are available for the Southern Hemisphere, the native's ascendant sign will be sign of the Zodiac directly *opposite* to that given in the tables compiled for the corresponding northern latitude. For example, 15° Scorpio would be reversed to 15° Taurus.

Steps for calculation

Date of birth	January 10, 1939
Place	Melbourne, Australia
Latitude	37° 58′ S.
Longitude	145° 0′ E.
Local time	7 A.M.
G.M.T.	5 P.M.

S.T. at Greenwich at noon on January 10	19	16	27
+ interval from noon	5		
+ acceleration on interval at the rate of 10 seconds per hour			50
	24	17	17
˙Longitude 145° x 4	9	40	
Local S.T. at birth	33	57	17
Add 12 hours for latitude 37° 58′ S.	12		
	45	57	17
Subtract 24 (to bring the figure within the 24-hour span of a sidereal day)	24		
	21	57	17

Look this figure up in the table of houses and find the ascendant, 22° Gemini; reverse sign to 22° Sagittarius

Appendix 4

Simplified ephemerides of the planets

After the ascendant and the Sun-sign, the most important astrological factors are the positions of the planets in relation to the Zodiac. For example, five planets in a sign give that sign great emphasis; or a planet occupying its "own" sign strengthens the sign's importance. By using the following simplified ephemerides, you can find the approximate positions on your birthday of most planets; the tables list the Zodiac signs occupied by each of seven planets during the different months of every year from 1901 to 1964. When a planet moved out of a sign during the month, the date of the change is given. For example, in January 1902, Mercury moved out of Capricorn into Aquarius on the 12th. (Sometimes planets appear to move backward through the Zodiac and are called *retrograde*.) The tables cannot take into consideration specific degrees of positions; nor, for reasons of space, do they list the positions of the Moon (which moves into a different sign every two or three days) or of Pluto, which moves very slowly and has little influence on individuals.

1901

Mercury ☿	Venus ♀	Mars ♂	Jupiter ♃	Saturn ♄	Uranus ♅	Neptune ♆
1 ♐ 2 ♑ 20 ♒	1 ♐ 16 ♑	1 ♍	1 ♐ 18 ♑	1 ♑	1 ♐	1 ♊
6 ♓ 16 ♈	20 ♒	♍	♑	♑	♐	♊
9 ♓	3 ♓ 29 ♈	♍	♑	♑	♐	♊
1 ♈	24 ♉	♍	♑	♑	♐	♊
4 ♉ 19 ♊	19 ♊	♍	♑	♑	♐	♊
2 ♋	11 ♋	♍	♑	♑	♐	♊
♋	3 ♌ 27 ♍	14 ♎	♑	♑	♐	20 ♋
9 ♌ 25 ♍	23 ♎	♎	♑	♑	♐	♋
11 ♎	19 ♏	14 ♏	♑	♑	♐	♋
3 ♏	15 ♐	17 ♐	♑	♑	♐	♋
♏	8 ♑	24 ♑	♑	♑	♐	♋
8 ♐ 26 ♑	3 ♒	30 ♒	♑	♑	♐	♋

1902

Mercury ☿	Venus ♀	Mars ♂	Jupiter ♃	Saturn ♄	Uranus ♅	Neptune ♆	
1 ♑ 12 ♒ 31 ♓	1 ♒ 8 ♓	1 ♒	1 ♑ 28 ♒	1 ♒	1 ♐	1 ♊	Jan.
19 ♒	7 ♒	5 ♓	♒	♒	♐	♊	Feb.
16 ♓	♒	18 ♈	♒	♒	♐	♊	March
9 ♈ 26 ♉	3 ♓	30 ♉	♒	♒	♐	♊	April
11 ♊ 29 ♋	7 ♈	♉	♒	♒	♐	♊	May
♋	5 ♉	10 ♊	♒	♒	♐	♊	June
♋	24 ♊ 26 ♋	20 ♋	♒	♒	♐	♊	July
12 ♌ 16 ♍	18 ♌	♋	♒	♒	♐	♊	Aug.
4 ♎	11 ♍	1 ♌	♒	♒	♐	♊	Sept.
3 ♏ 12 ♎	7 ♎	19 ♍	♒	♒	♐	♊	Oct.
11 ♏	2 ♏ 26 ♐	♍	♒	♒	♐	♊	Nov.
1 ♐ 19 ♑	18 ♑	17 ♎	♒	♒	♐	♊	Dec.

1903

	Mercury ☿	Venus ♀	Mars ♂	Jupiter ♃	Saturn ♄	Uranus ♅	Neptune ♆
Jan.	1 ♑ 5 ♒	1 ♑ 9 ♒	1 ♎	1 ♒	1 ♒	1 ♐	1 ♋
Feb.	♒	2 ♓ 29 ♈	♎	9 ♓	♒	♐	♋
March	13 ♓	26 ♉	♎	♓	♒	♐	♋
April	1 ♈ 18 ♉	20 ♊	24 ♍	♓	♒	♐	♋
May	4 ♊	14 ♋	29 ♎	♓	♒	♐	♋
June	♊	7 ♌	♎	♓	♒	♐	♋
July	10 ♋ 24 ♌	5 ♍	♎	♓	♒	♐	♋
Aug.	8 ♍ 30 ♎	♍	11 ♏	♓	♒	♐	♋
Sept.	♎	♍	26 ♐	♓	♒	♐	♋
Oct.	♎	♍	♐	♓	♒	♐	♋
Nov.	5 ♏ 24 ♐	8 ♎	3 ♑	♓	♒	♐	♋
Dec.	12 ♑ 31 ♒	11 ♏	9 ♒	♓	♒	♐	♋

1904

	Mercury ☿	Venus ♀	Mars ♂	Jupiter ♃	Saturn ♄	Uranus ♅	Neptune ♆
Jan.	1 ♒ 16 ♑	1 ♏ 6 ♐ 30 ♑	1 ♒ 16 ♓	1 ♓	1 ♒	1 ♐	1 ♋
Feb.	14 ♒	22 ♒	27 ♈	28 ♈	♒	♐	♋
March	5 ♓ 24 ♈	18 ♓	♈	♈	♒	♐	♋
April	9 ♉	12 ♈	10 ♉	♈	♒	♐	♋
May	♉	9 ♉	21 ♊	♈	♒	♐	♋
June	15 ♊	3 ♊ 25 ♋	30 ♋	♈	♒	♐	♋
July	2 ♋ 15 ♌ 31 ♍	18 ♌	♋	♈	♒	♐	♋
Aug.	♍	11 ♍	11 ♌	♈	♒	♐	♋
Sept.	♍	6 ♎	27 ♍	♈	♒	♐	♋
Oct.	8 ♎ 28 ♏	2 ♍ 27 ♐	♍	♈	♒	♐	♋
Nov.	16 ♐	19 ♑	19 ♎	♈	♒	♐	♋
Dec.	5 ♑	11 ♒	♎	♈	♒	19 ♑	♋

1905

	Mercury ☿	Venus ♀	Mars ♂	Jupiter ♃	Saturn ♄	Uranus ♅	Neptune ♆
Jan.	1 ♑	1 ♒ 5 ♓	1 ♎ 17 ♏	1 ♈	1 ♒	1 ♑	1 ♋
Feb.	8 ♒ 26 ♓	3 ♈	♏	♈	♒	♑	♋
March	16 ♈	11 ♉	♏	16 ♉	17 ♓	♑	♋
April	4 ♉ 25 ♈	♉	♏	♉	♓	♑	♋
May	17 ♉	2 ♈	♏	♉	♓	♑	♋
June	10 ♊ 23 ♋	1 ♉	♏	♉	♓	♑	♋
July	7 ♌ 25 ♍	10 ♊	♏	♉	♓	♑	♋
Aug.	♍	6 ♋ 31 ♌	26 ♐	1 ♊	♓	♑	♋
Sept.	♍	25 ♍	♐	♊	29 ♒	♑	♋
Oct.	1 ♎ 21 ♏	21 ♎	8 ♑	♊	♒	♑	♋
Nov.	9 ♐	16 ♏	15 ♒	22 ♉	♒	♑	♋
Dec.	2 ♑ 10 ♐	10 ♐	24 ♓	♉	3 ♓	♑	♋

1906

	Mercury ☿	Venus ♀	Mars ♂	Jupiter ♃	Saturn ♄	Uranus ♅	Neptune ♆
Jan.	1 ♐ 13 ♑	1 ♐ 2 ♑ 24 ♒	1 ♓	1 ♉	1 ♓	1 ♑	1 ♋
Feb.	1 ♒ 18 ♓	16 ♓	5 ♈	♉	♓	♑	♋
March	8 ♈	14 ♈	20 ♉	22 ♊	♓	♑	♋
April	♈	9 ♉	♉	♊	♓	♑	♋
May	16 ♉	4 ♊ 27 ♋	2 ♊	♊	♓	♑	♋
June	2 ♊ 15 ♋ 29 ♌	19 ♌	12 ♋	♊	♓	♑	♋
July	♌	14 ♍	24 ♌	30 ♋	♓	♑	♋
Aug.	♌	11 ♎	♌	♋	♓	♑	♋
Sept.	6 ♍ 24 ♎	10 ♏	8 ♍	♋	♓	♑	♋
Oct.	13 ♏	13 ♐	29 ♎	♋	♓	♑	♋
Nov.	4 ♐	♐	♎	♋	♓	♑	♋
Dec.	5 ♏ 15 ♐	10 ♏ 30 ♐	20 ♏	♋	♓	♑	♋

1907

	Mercury ☿	Venus ♀	Mars ♂	Jupiter ♃	Saturn ♄	Uranus ♅	Neptune ♆
Jan.	1 ♐ 7 ♑ 25 ♒	1 ♐	1 ♏	1 ♋	1 ♓	1 ♑	1 ♋
Feb.	11 ♓	7 ♑	9 ♐	♋	♓	♑	♋
March	5 ♈	5 ♒ 31 ♓	♐	♋	♓	♑	♋
April	♈	27 ♈	2 ♑	♋	♓	♑	♋
May	9 ♉ 24 ♊	24 ♉	♑	♋	♓	♑	♋
June	7 ♋ 25 ♌	18 ♊	♑	♋	♓	♑	♋
July	29 ♋	11 ♋	♑	♋	♓	♑	♋
Aug.	10 ♌ 30 ♍	3 ♌ 27 ♍	♑	8 ♌	♓	♑	♋
Sept.	16 ♎	22 ♎	♑	♌	♓	♑	♋
Oct.	7 ♏	18 ♏	9 ♒	♌	♓	♑	♋
Nov.	♏	11 ♐	♒	♌	♓	♑	♋
Dec.	12 ♐ 31 ♑	3 ♑ 25 ♒	♒	♌	♓	♑	♋

1908

	Mercury ☿	Venus ♀	Mars ♂	Jupiter ♃	Saturn ♄	Uranus ♅	Neptune ♆
Jan.	1 ♑ 17 ♒	1 ♒ 18 ♓	1 ♓ 11 ♈	1 ♌	1 ♓	1 ♑	1 ♋
Feb.	4 ♓	14 ♈	26 ♉	♌	♓	♑	♋
March	♓	12 ♉	♉	♌	11 ♈	♑	♋
April	12 ♈	8 ♊	10 ♊	♌	♈	♑	♋
May	1 ♉ 15 ♊ 30 ♋	6 ♋	22 ♋	♌	♈	♑	♋
June	♋	♋	♋	♌	♈	♑	♋
July	♋	♋	4 ♌	♌	♈	♑	♋
Aug.	6 ♌ 21 ♍	♋	20 ♍	31 ♍	♈	♑	♋
Sept.	8 ♎	7 ♌	♍	♍	♈	♑	♋
Oct.	1 ♏ 31 ♎	6 ♍	9 ♎	♍	♈	♑	♋
Nov.	13 ♏	3 ♎ 30 ♏	28 ♏	♍	♈	♑	♋
Dec.	5 ♐ 23 ♑	24 ♐	♏	♍	♈	♑	♋

1909

	Mercury ☿	Venus ♀	Mars ♂	Jupiter ♃	Saturn ♄	Uranus ♅	Neptune ♆
Jan.	1 ♑ 9 ♒	1 ♐ 16 ♑	1 ♏ 13 ♐	1 ♍	1 ♈	1 ♑	1 ♌
Feb.	♒	7 ♒	24 ♑	♍	♈	♑	♌
March	15 ♓	3 ♓ 29 ♈	♑	♍	♈	♑	♌
April	5 ♈ 22 ♉	24 ♉	6 ♒	♍	♈	♑	♌
May	7 ♊	18 ♊	21 ♓	♍	♈	♑	♌
June	♊	10 ♋	♓	♍	♈	♑	♌
July	13 ♋ 29 ♌	3 ♌ 27 ♍	16 ♈	♍	♈	♑	♌
Aug.	12 ♍	23 ♎	♈	♍	♈	♑	♌
Sept.	1 ♎	19 ♏	♈	♍	♈	♑	♌
Oct.	♎	14 ♐	4 ♓	9 ♎	♈	♑	♌
Nov.	9 ♏ 28 ♐	7 ♑	19 ♈	♎	♈	♑	♌
Dec.	16 ♑	3 ♒	♈	♎	♈	♑	♌

1910

	Mercury ☿	Venus ♀	Mars ♂	Jupiter ♃	Saturn ♄	Uranus ♅	Neptune ♆
Jan.	1 ♑ 2 ♒	1 ♒ 11 ♓ 30 ♒	1 ♈ 27 ♉	1 ♎	1 ♈	1 ♒	1 ♋
Feb.	2 ♑ 13 ♒	♒	♉	♎	♈	♒	♋
March	10 ♓ 29 ♈	♒	18 ♊	♎	♈	♒	♋
April	14 ♉	4 ♓	♊	♎	♈	♒	♋
May	3 ♊ 30 ♉	7 ♈	2 ♋	♎	28 ♉	♒	♋
June	15 ♊	5 ♉	15 ♌	♎	♉	♒	♋
July	6 ♋ 20 ♌	1 ♊ 25 ♋	♌	♎	♉	♒	♋
Aug.	6 ♍ 28 ♎	17 ♌	2 ♍	♎	♉	♒	♋
Sept.	28 ♍	11 ♍	21 ♎	♎	♉	♒	♋
Oct.	12 ♎	6 ♎	♎	♎	♉	♒	♋
Nov.	2 ♏ 21 ♐	1 ♏ 25 ♐	9 ♏	20 ♏	24 ♈	♒	♋
Dec.	9 ♑	18 ♑	23 ♐	♏	♈	♒	♋

1911

	Mercury ☿	Venus ♀	Mars ♂	Jupiter ♃	Saturn ♄	Uranus ♅	Neptune ♆
Jan.	1 ♑	1 ♑ 9 ♒	1 ♐	1 ♏	1 ♈	1 ♑	1 ♋
Feb.	11 ♒	1 ♓ 27 ♈	1 ♑	♏	12 ♉	♑	♋
March	3 ♓ ♈	26 ♉	11 ♒	♏	♉	4 ♒	♋
April	7 ♉	20 ♊	20 ♓	♏	♉	♒	♋
May	♉	13 ♋	♓	♏	♉	♒	♋
June	14 ♊ 29 ♋	6 ♌	2 ♈	♏	♉	♒	♋
July	12 ♌ 29 ♍	5 ♍	18 ♉	♏	♉	14 ♑	♋
Aug.	♍	♍	♉	♏	♉	♑	♋
Sept.	♍	♍	9 ♊	♏	♉	♑	♋
Oct.	6 ♎ 25 ♏	♍	♊	♏	♉	♑	♋
Nov.	14 ♐	9 ♎	24 ♉	♏	♉	♑	♋
Dec.	3 ♑ 28 ♐	10 ♏	♉	19 ♐	♉	25 ♒	♋

1912

	Mercury ☿	Venus ♀	Mars ♂	Jupiter ♃	Saturn ♄	Uranus ♅	Neptune ♆
Jan.	1 ♐ 15 ♑	1 ♏ 6 ♐ 30 ♑	1 ♉	1 ♐	1 ♉	1 ♒	1 ♋
Feb.	5 ♒ 24 ♓	22 ♒	7 ♊	♐	♉	♒	♋
March	12 ♈	17 ♓	♊	♐	♉	♒	♋
April	♈	12 ♈	5 ♋	♐	♉	♒	♋
May	18 ♉	8 ♉	24 ♌	♐	♉	♒	♋
June	6 ♊	2 ♊ 25 ♋	♌	♐	♉	♒	♋
July	3 ♌ 24 ♍	17 ♌	13 ♍	♐	24 ♊	♒	♋
Aug.	21 ♌	10 ♍	♍	♐	♊	♒	♋
Sept.	9 ♍ 28 ♎	6 ♎	2 ♎	♐	♊	♒	♋
Oct.	17 ♏	2 ♏ 26 ♐	21 ♏	♐	♊	♒	♋
Nov.	6 ♐	18 ♑	♏	♐	12 ♉	♒	♋
Dec.	♐	11 ♒	3 ♐	♐	♉	♒	♋

1913

	Mercury ☿	Venus ♀	Mars ♂	Jupiter ♃	Saturn ♄	Uranus ♅	Neptune ♆
Jan.	1 ♐ 10 ♑ 28 ♒	1 ♒ 5 ♓	1 ♐ 10 ♑	1 ♐ 2 ♑	1 ♉	1 ♒ ♒	1 ♋ ♋
Feb.	15 ♓	3 ♈	16 ♒	♑	♉	♒	♋
March	5 ♈	12 ♉	27 ♓	♑	♉	♒	♋
April	7 ♓ 12 ♈	25 ♈	♓	♑	12 ♊	♒	♋
May	13 ♉ 29 ♊	♈	7 ♈	♑	♊	♒	♋
June	11 ♋ 26 ♌	3 ♉	19 ♉	♑	♊	♒	♋
July	♌	10 ♊	♉	♑	♊	♒	♋
Aug.	♌	6 ♋ 31 ♌	1 ♊	♑	♊	♒	♋
Sept.	3 ♍ 20 ♎	25 ♍	16 ♋	♑	♊	♒	29 ♌
Oct.	10 ♏	21 ♎	♋	♑	♊	♒	♌
Nov.	2 ♐	16 ♏	♋	♑	♊	♒	♌
Dec.	♐	10 ♐	♋	♑	♊	♒	♌

1914

	Mercury ☿	Venus ♀	Mars ♂	Jupiter ♃	Saturn ♄	Uranus ♅	Neptune ♆
Jan.	1 ♐ 4 ♑ 21 ♒	1 ♑ 23 ♒	1 ♋	1 ♑ 12 ♒	1 ♊	1 ♒	1 ♋
Feb.	7 ♓	16 ♓	♋	♒	♊	♒	♋
March	♓	13 ♈	♋	♒	♊	♒	♋
April	16 ♈	9 ♉	26 ♌	♒	♊	♒	♋
May	6 ♉ 20 ♊	3 ♊ 26 ♋	♌	♒	♊	♒	♋
June	3 ♋ 28 ♌	18 ♌	21 ♍	♒	♊	♒	♋
July	7 ♋	13 ♍	♍	♒	♊	♒	19 ♌
Aug.	10 ♌ 26 ♍	11 ♎	14 ♎	♒	23 ♋	♒	♌
Sept.	12 ♎	10 ♏	♎	♒	♋	♒	♌
Oct.	4 ♏	14 ♐	2 ♏	♒	♋	♒	♌
Nov.	♏	♐	14 ♐	♒	♋	♒	♌
Dec.	9 ♐ 28 ♑	2 ♏	22 ♑	♒	9 ♊	♒	♌

1915

Mercury ☿	Venus ♀	Mars ♂	Jupiter ♃	Saturn ♄	Uranus ♅	Neptune ♆
1 ♑ 14 ♒	1 ♏ 2 ♐	1 ♑ 27 ♒	1 ♒ 24 ♓	1 ♊	1 ♒	1 ♌
1 ♓ 25 ♒	7 ♑	♒	♓	♊	♒	♌
17 ♓	5 ♒ 31 ♓	6 ♓	♓	♊	♒	12 ♋
10 ♈ 28 ♉	26 ♈	16 ♈	♓	♊	♒	♋
12 ♊ 29 ♋	23 ♉	28 ♉	♓	11 ♋	♒	10 ♌
♋	17 ♊	♉	♓	♋	♒	♌
♋	11 ♋	9 ♊	♓	♋	♒	♌
3 ♌ 18 ♍	2 ♌ 26 ♍	19 ♋	♓	♋	♒	♌
5 ♎	21 ♎	♋	♓	♋	♒	♌
2 ♏ 19 ♎	17 ♏	4 ♌	♓	♋	♒	♌
13 ♏	10 ♐	♌	♓	♋	♒	♌
3 ♐ 20 ♑	3 ♑ 25 ♒	9 ♍	♓	♋	♒	♌

1916

Mercury ☿	Venus ♀	Mars ♂	Jupiter ♃	Saturn ♄	Uranus ♅	Neptune ♆	
1 ♑ 6 ♒	1 ♒ 18 ♓	1 ♍ 25 ♌	1 ♓	1 ♋	1 ♒	1 ♌	Jan.
♒	13 ♈	♌	9 ♈	♋	♒	♌	Feb.
13 ♓	12 ♉	♌	♈	♋	♒	♌	March
2 ♈ 18 ♉	8 ♊	♌	♈	♋	♒	♌	April
4 ♊	6 ♋	23 ♍	♈	♋	♒	♌	May
♊	♋	♍	♈	♋	♒	♌	June
11 ♋ 25 ♌	♋	23 ♎	6 ♉	♋	♒	♌	July
9 ♍ 29 ♎	♋	♎	♉	♋	♒	♌	Aug.
♎	7 ♌	12 ♏	♉	16 ♌	♒	♌	Sept.
♎	6 ♍	25 ♐	16 ♈	♌	♒	♌	Oct.
5 ♏ 24 ♐	2 ♎ 29 ♏	♐	♈	♌	♒	♌	Nov.
12 ♑ 31 ♒	24 ♐	2 ♑	♈	♌	♒	♌	Dec.

1917

Mercury ☿	Venus ♀	Mars ♂	Jupiter ♃	Saturn ♄	Uranus ♅	Neptune ♆
1 ♒ 19 ♑	1 ♐ 15 ♑	1 ♑ 6 ♒	1 ♈	1 ♌ 10 ♋	1 ♒	1 ♌
13 ♒	7 ♒	13 ♓	23 ♉	♋	♒	♌
7 ♓ 25 ♈	2 ♓ 28 ♈	26 ♈	♉	♋	♒	♌
10 ♉	23 ♉	♈	♉	♋	♒	♌
♉	18 ♊	7 ♉	♉	♋	♒	♌
16 ♊	10 ♋	18 ♊	♉	4 ♌	♒	♌
3 ♋ 16 ♌	2 ♌ 26 ♍	28 ♋	9 ♊	♌	♒	♌
1 ♍ 29 ♎	22 ♎	♋	♊	♌	♒	♌
12 ♍	18 ♏	9 ♌	♊	♌	♒	♌
10 ♎ 29 ♏	14 ♐	28 ♍	♊	♌	♒	♌
17 ♐	7 ♑	♍	♊	♌	♒	♌
6 ♑	3 ♒	♍	♊	♌	♒	♌

1918

Mercury ☿	Venus ♀	Mars ♂	Jupiter ♃	Saturn ♄	Uranus ♅	Neptune ♆	
1 ♑	1 ♒	1 ♍ 6 ♎	1 ♊ 10 ♉	1 ♌	1 ♒	1 ♌	Jan.
9 ♒ 28 ♓	♒	♎	12 ♊	♌	♒	♌	Feb.
17 ♈	♒	3 ♍	♊	♌	♒	♌	March
5 ♉	4 ♓	♍	♊	♌	♒	♌	April
4 ♈ 14 ♉	6 ♈	♍	♊	♌	11 ♓	♌	May
11 ♊ 25 ♋	4 ♉	12 ♎	♊	♌	27 ♒	♌	June
8 ♌ 26 ♍	1 ♊ 25 ♋	♎	13 ♋	♌	♒	♌	July
♍	17 ♌	21 ♏	♋	♌	♒	♌	Aug.
♍	10 ♍	♏	♋	♌	♒	♌	Sept.
3 ♎ 22 ♏	6 ♎	4 ♐	♋	♌	♒	♌	Oct.
11 ♐	1 ♏ 25 ♐	11 ♑	♋	8 ♍	♒	♌	Nov.
2 ♑ 16 ♐	17 ♑	17 ♒	♋	♍	♒	♌	Dec.

1919

	Mercury ☿	Venus ♀	Mars ♂	Jupiter ♃	Saturn ♄	Uranus ♅	Neptune ♆
Jan.	1 ♐ 14 ♑	1 ♑ 8 ♒	1 ♒ 24 ♓	1 ♋	1 ♍ 11 ♌	1 ♒	1 ♌
Feb.	2 ♒ 20 ♓	1 ♓ 27 ♈	♓	♋	♌	14 ♓	♌
March	9 ♈	25 ♉	6 ♈	♋	♌	♓	♌
April	♈	19 ♊	18 ♉	♋	♌	♓	♌
May	17 ♉	13 ♋	29 ♊	♋	♌	♓	♌
June	3 ♊ 16 ♋	6 ♌	♊	♋	♌	♓	♌
July	1 ♌	5 ♍	9 ♋	23 ♌	20 ♍	♓	♌
Aug.	♌	♍	20 ♌	♌	♍	♓	♌
Sept.	7 ♍ 25 ♎	♍	♌	♌	♍	♓	♌
Oct.	15 ♏	♍	6 ♍	♌	♍	♓	♌
Nov.	5 ♐	9 ♎	29 ♎	♌	♍	♓	♌
Dec.	♐	10 ♏	♎	♌	♍	♓	♌

1920

	Mercury ☿	Venus ♀	Mars ♂	Jupiter ♃	Saturn ♄	Uranus ♅	Neptune ♆
Jan.	1 ♐ 8 ♑ 26 ♒	1 ♏ 6 ♐ 24 ♑	1 ♎	1 ♌	1 ♍	1 ♓	1 ♌
Feb.	12 ♓	21 ♒	4 ♏	♌	♍	♓	♌
March	3 ♈ 18 ♓	16 ♓	♏	♌	♍	♓	♌
April	17 ♈	11 ♈	20 ♎	♌	♍	♓	♌
May	11 ♉ 25 ♊	8 ♉	♎	♌	♍	♓	♌
June	7 ♋ 24 ♌	2 ♊ 24 ♋	♎	♌	♍	♓	♌
July	♌	17 ♌	17 ♏	♌	♍	♓	♌
Aug.	30 ♍	10 ♍	♏	15 ♍	♍	♓	♌
Sept.	16 ♎	5 ♎	8 ♐	♍	♍	♓	♌
Oct.	7 ♏	1 ♏ 26 ♐	18 ♑	♍	♍	♓	♌
Nov.	♏	18 ♑	24 ♒	♍	♍	♓	♌
Dec.	12 ♐ 31 ♑	10 ♒	♒	♍	♍	♓	♌

1921

	Mercury ☿	Venus ♀	Mars ♂	Jupiter ♃	Saturn ♄	Uranus ♅	Neptune ♆
Jan.	1 ♑ 18 ♒	1 ♒ 4 ♓	1 ♒ 2 ♓	1 ♍	1 ♍	1 ♓	1 ♌
Feb.	4 ♓	3 ♈	13 ♈	♍	♍	♓	♌
March	♓	13 ♉	28 ♉	♍	♍	♓	♌
April	13 ♈	18 ♈	♉	♍	♍	♓	♌
May	2 ♉ 16 ♊ 31 ♋	♈	9 ♊	♍	♍	♓	♌
June	♋	5 ♉	19 ♋	♍	♍	♓	♌
July	♋	10 ♊	31 ♌	♍	♍	♓	♌
Aug.	7 ♌ 22 ♍	6 ♋ 30 ♌	♌	♍	♍	♓	♌
Sept.	9 ♎	24 ♍	15 ♍	24 ♎	29 ♎	♓	♌
Oct.	2 ♏	20 ♎	♍	♎	♎	♓	♌
Nov.	6 ♎ 13 ♏	15 ♏	6 ♎	♎	♎	♓	♌
Dec.	6 ♐ 24 ♑	9 ♐	29 ♏	♎	♎	♓	♌

1922

	Mercury ☿	Venus ♀	Mars ♂	Jupiter ♃	Saturn ♄	Uranus ♅	Neptune ♆
Jan.	1 ♑ 10 ♒ 30 ♓	1 ♑ 23 ♒	1 ♏	1 ♎	1 ♎	1 ♓	1 ♌
Feb.	11 ♒	15 ♓	22 ♐	♎	♎	♓	♌
March	16 ♓	13 ♈	♐	♎	♎	♓	♌
April	7 ♈ 24 ♉	8 ♉	♐	♎	♎	♓	♌
May	9 ♊	3 ♊ 26 ♋	♐	♎	♎	♓	♌
June	1 ♋ 11 ♊	18 ♌	♐	♎	♎	♓	♌
July	14 ♋ 30 ♌	13 ♍	♐	♎	♎	♓	♌
Aug.	14 ♍	10 ♎	♐	♎	♎	♓	♌
Sept.	2 ♎	10 ♏	13 ♑	♎	♎	♓	♌
Oct.	♎	16 ♐	27 ♒	♎	♎	♓	♌
Nov.	10 ♏ 29 ♐	25 ♏	♒	3 ♏	♎	♓	♌
Dec.	17 ♑	♏	8 ♓	♏	♎	♓	♌

1923

	Mercury ☿	Venus ♀	Mars ♂	Jupiter ♃	Saturn ♄	Uranus ♅	Neptune ♆
Jan.	1 ♑ 3 ♒	1 ♏ 4 ♐	1 ♓ 21 ♈	1 ♏	1 ♎	1 ♓	1 ♌
Feb.	♒	6 ♑	♈	♏	♎	♓	♌
March	11 ♓ 30 ♈	5 ♒ 30 ♓	7 ♉	♏	♎	♓	♌
April	17 ♉	26 ♈	19 ♊	♏	♎	♓	♌
May	3 ♊	23 ♉	31 ♋	♏	♎	♓	♌
June	♊	17 ♊	♋	♏	♎	♓	♌
July	8 ♋ 22 ♌	10 ♋	12 ♌	♏	♎	♓	♌
Aug.	6 ♍ 28 ♎	2 ♌ 26 ♍	28 ♍	♏	♎	♓	♌
Sept.	♎	21 ♎	♍	♏	♎	♓	♌
Oct.	4 ♏ 11 ♎	17 ♏	17 ♎	♏	♎	♓	♌
Nov.	3 ♏ 22 ♐	10 ♐	♎	♏	♎	♓	♌
Dec.	10 ♑ 31 ♒	2 ♑ 24 ♒	7 ♏	3 ♐	♎	♓	♌

1924

	Mercury ☿	Venus ♀	Mars ♂	Jupiter ♃	Saturn ♄	Uranus ♅	Neptune ♆
Jan.	1 ♒ 7 ♑	1 ♒ 17 ♓	1 ♏ 23 ♐	1 ♐	1 ♎ 6 ♏	1 ♓	1 ♌
Feb.	12 ♒	13 ♈	♐	♐	♏	♓	♌
March	3 ♓ 21 ♈	12 ♉	7 ♑	♐	20 ♎	♓	♌
April	7 ♉	8 ♊	21 ♒	♐	♎	♓	♌
May	♉	6 ♋	♒	♐	♎	♓	♌
June	14 ♊ 30 ♋	♋	15 ♓	♐	♎	♓	♌
July	12 ♌ 29 ♍	♋	♓	♐	♎	♓	♌
Aug.	♍	♋	♓	♐	♎	♓	♌
Sept.	♍	7 ♌	♓	♐	25 ♏	♓	♌
Oct.	7 ♎ 26 ♏	6 ♍	♓	♐	♏	♓	♌
Nov.	14 ♐	2 ♎ 29 ♏	♓	♐	♏	♓	♌
Dec.	3 ♑	23 ♐	19 ♈	18 ♑	♏	♓	♌

1925

	Mercury ☿	Venus ♀	Mars ♂	Jupiter ♃	Saturn ♄	Uranus ♅	Neptune ♆
Jan.	1 ♐ 14 ♑	1 ♐ 15 ♑	1 ♈	1 ♑	1 ♏	1 ♓	1 ♌
Feb.	6 ♒ 24 ♓	6 ♒	2 ♉	♑	♏	♓	♌
March	13 ♈	2 ♓ 28 ♈	27 ♊	♑	♏	♓	♌
April	♈	23 ♉	♊	♑	♏	♓	♌
May	18 ♉	17 ♊	10 ♋	♑	♏	♓	♌
June	8 ♊	9 ♋	22 ♌	♑	♏	♓	♌
July	4 ♋ 25 ♍	2 ♌ 26 ♍	♌	♑	♏	♓	♌
Aug.	♍	22 ♎	9 ♍	♑	♏	♓	♌
Sept.	29 ♎	18 ♏	28 ♎	♑	♏	♓	♌
Oct.	18 ♏	14 ♐	♎	♑	♏	♓	♌
Nov.	7 ♐	7 ♑	16 ♏	♑	♏	♓	♌
Dec.	♐	3 ♒	31 ♐	27 ♒	♏	♓	♌

1926

	Mercury ☿	Venus ♀	Mars ♂	Jupiter ♃	Saturn ♄	Uranus ♅	Neptune ♆
Jan.	1 ♐ 11 ♑ 30 ♒	1 ♒	1 ♐	1 ♒	1 ♏	1 ♓	1 ♌
Feb.	16 ♓	♒	9 ♑	♒	♏	♓	♌
March	6 ♈	♒	20 ♒	♒	♏	♓	♌
April	♈	4 ♓	30 ♓	♒	♏	♓	♌
May	14 ♉ 30 ♊	6 ♈	♓	♒	♏	♓	♌
June	12 ♋ 28 ♌	4 ♉ 30 ♊	13 ♈	♒	♏	♓	♌
July	♌	24 ♋	♈	♒	♏	♓	♌
Aug.	♌	16 ♌	3 ♉	♒	♏	♓	♌
Sept.	4 ♍ 21 ♎	9 ♍	♉	♒	♏	♓	♌
Oct.	11 ♏	5 ♎ 31 ♏	♉	♒	♏	♓	♌
Nov.	3 ♐ 27 ♏	24 ♐	♉	♒	♏	♓	♌
Dec.	15 ♐	17 ♑	♉	♒	17 ♐	♓	♌

1927

	Mercury ☿	Venus ♀	Mars ♂	Jupiter ♃	Saturn ♄	Uranus ♅	Neptune ♆
Jan.	1 ♐ 5 ♑ 22 ♒	1 ♑ 8 ♒ 31 ♓	1 ♉	1 ♒ 6 ♓	1 ♐	1 ♓	1 ♌
Feb.	9 ♓	26 ♈	27 ♊	♓	♐	♓	♌
March	♓	25 ♉	♊	♓	♐	24 ♈	♌
April	17 ♈	19 ♊	17 ♋	♓	♐	♈	♌
May	7 ♉ 22 ♊	12 ♋	♋	♓	♐	♈	♌
June	5 ♋ 26 ♌	6 ♌	2 ♌	2 ♈	♐	♈	♌
July	16 ♋	5 ♍	21 ♍	♈	10 ♏	♈	♌
Aug.	10 ♌ 27 ♍	♍	♍	♈	♏	♈	♌
Sept.	14 ♎	♍	10 ♎	18 ♓	2 ♐	♈	12 ♍
Oct.	5 ♏	♍	29 ♏	♓	♐	♈	♍
Nov.	♏	9 ♎	♏	♓	♐	♈	♍
Dec.	11 ♐ 29 ♑	10 ♏	11 ♐	♓	♐	1 ♓ 21 ♈	♍

1928

	Mercury ☿	Venus ♀	Mars ♂	Jupiter ♃	Saturn ♄	Uranus ♅	Neptune ♆
Jan.	1 ♑ 15 ♒	1 ♏ 5 ♐ 29 ♑	1 ♐ 19 ♑	1 ♓ 19 ♈	1 ♐	1 ♈	1 ♍
Feb.	2 ♓	21 ♒	25 ♒	♈	♐	♈	29 ♌
March	2 ♒ 15 ♓	16 ♓	♒	♈	♐	♈	♌
April	10 ♈ 28 ♉	11 ♈	4 ♓	♈	♐	♈	♌
May	13 ♊ 29 ♋	7 ♉	16 ♈	♈	♐	♈	♌
June	♋	1 ♊ 24 ♋	28 ♉	12 ♉	♐	♈	♌
July	♋	16 ♌	♉	♉	♐	♈	13 ♍
Aug.	4 ♌ 18 ♍	9 ♍	12 ♊	♉	♐	♈	♍
Sept.	6 ♎	4 ♎	♊	♉	♐	♈	♍
Oct.	1 ♏ 23 ♎	1 ♏ 25 ♐	3 ♋	♉	♐	♈	♍
Nov.	12 ♏	17 ♑	♋	30 ♈	♐	♈	♍
Dec.	3 ♐ 21 ♑	10 ♒	21 ♊	♈	♐	♈	♍

1929

	Mercury ☿	Venus ♀	Mars ♂	Jupiter ♃	Saturn ♄	Uranus ♅	Neptune ♆
Jan.	1 ♑ 7 ♒	1 ♒ 4 ♓	1 ♊	1 ♈ 22 ♉	1 ♐	1 ♈	1 ♍
Feb.	♒	3 ♈	♊	♉	♐	♈	♍
March	14 ♓	15 ♉	11 ♋	♉	13 ♑	♈	♍
April	3 ♈ 20 ♉	12 ♈	♋	♉	♑	♈	♍
May	5 ♊	♈	8 ♌	♉	8 ♐	♈	♍
June	♊	5 ♉	30 ♌	21 ♊	♐	♈	♍
July	12 ♋ 26 ♌	9 ♊	♍	♊	♐	♈	♍
Aug.	10 ♍ 30 ♎	5 ♋ 30 ♌	21 ♎	♊	♐	♈	♍
Sept.	♎	24 ♍	♎	♊	♐	♈	♍
Oct.	♎	20 ♎	9 ♏	♊	♐	♈	♍
Nov.	7 ♏ 26 ♐	15 ♏	21 ♐	♊	29 ♑	♈	♍
Dec.	14 ♑	9 ♐ 31 ♑	29 ♑	♊	♑	♈	♍

1930

	Mercury ☿	Venus ♀	Mars ♂	Jupiter ♃	Saturn ♄	Uranus ♅	Neptune ♆
Jan.	1 ♒ 24 ♑	1 ♑ 22 ♒	1 ♑	1 ♊	1 ♑	1 ♈	1 ♍
Feb.	13 ♒	15 ♓	4 ♒	♊	♑	♈	♍
March	8 ♓ 27 ♈	12 ♈	14 ♓	♊	♑	♈	♍
April	12 ♉	8 ♉	24 ♈	♊	♑	♈	♍
May	♉	2 ♊ 25 ♋	♈	♊	♑	♈	♍
June	16 ♊	17 ♌	5 ♉	26 ♋	♑	♈	♍
July	5 ♋ 18 ♌	12 ♍	17 ♊	♋	♑	♈	♍
Aug.	2 ♍ 28 ♎	10 ♎	28 ♋	♋	♑	♈	♍
Sept.	19 ♍	10 ♏	♋	♋	♑	♈	♍
Oct.	11 ♎ 31 ♏	18 ♐	16 ♌	♋	♑	♈	♍
Nov.	19 ♐	17 ♏	♌	♋	♑	♈	♍
Dec.	7 ♑	♏	♌	♋	♑	♈	♍

1931

	Mercury ☿	Venus ♀	Mars ♂	Jupiter ♃	Saturn ♄	Uranus ♅	Neptune ♆
Jan.	1 ♑	1 ♏ 6 ♐	1 ♌	1 ♋	1 ♑	1 ♈	1 ♍
Feb.	10 ♒	7 ♑	♌	♋	♑	♈	♍
March	1 ♓ 19 ♈	5 ♒ 30 ♓	♌	♋	♑	♈	♍
April	6 ♉	26 ♈	♌	♋	♑	♈	♍
May	♉	23 ♉	♌	♋	♑	♈	♍
June	13 ♊ 27 ♋	17 ♊	6 ♍	♋	♑	♈	♍
July	10 ♌ 28 ♍	10 ♋	♍	7 ♌	♑	♈	♍
Aug.	♍	2 ♌ 26 ♍	2 ♎	♌	♑	♈	♍
Sept.	♍	21 ♎	21 ♏	♌	♑	♈	♍
Oct.	5 ♎ 24 ♏	17 ♏	♏	♌	♑	♈	♍
Nov.	12 ♐	10 ♐	3 ♐	♌	♑	♈	♍
Dec.	2 ♑ 21 ♐	2 ♑ 24 ♒	10 ♑	♌	♑	♈	♍

1932

	Mercury ☿	Venus ♀	Mars ♂	Jupiter ♃	Saturn ♄	Uranus ♅	Neptune ♆
Jan.	1 ♐ 15 ♑	1 ♒ 17 ♓	1 ♑ 15 ♒	1 ♌	1 ♑	1 ♈	1 ♍
Feb.	4 ♒ 22 ♓	13 ♈	22 ♓	♌	5 ♒	♈	♍
March	10 ♈	12 ♉	♓	♌	♒	♈	♍
April	♈	8 ♊	3 ♈	♌	♒	♈	♍
May	17 ♉	7 ♋	16 ♉	♌	♒	♈	♍
June	4 ♊ 17 ♋	♋	26 ♊	♌	♒	♈	♍
July	1 ♌ 26 ♍	14 ♊ 29 ♋	♊	30 ♍	♒	♈	♍
Aug.	12 ♌	♋	5 ♋	♍	♒	♈	♍
Sept.	8 ♍ 26 ♎	8 ♌	18 ♌	♍	♒	♈	♍
Oct.	16 ♏	6 ♍	♌	♍	♒	♈	♍
Nov.	5 ♐	2 ♎ 29 ♏	9 ♍	♍	♒	♈	♍
Dec.	♐	23 ♐	♍	♍	♒	♈	♍

1933

	Mercury ☿	Venus ♀	Mars ♂	Jupiter ♃	Saturn ♄	Uranus ♅	Neptune ♆
Jan.	1 ♐ 9 ♑ 27 ♒	1 ♐ 15 ♑	1 ♍	1 ♍	1 ♒	1 ♈	1 ♍
Feb.	12 ♓	6 ♒	♍	♍	♒	♈	♍
March	4 ♈ 25 ♓	2 ♓ 27 ♈	♍	♍	♒	♈	♍
April	17 ♈	23 ♉	♍	♍	♒	♈	♍
May	12 ♉ 27 ♊	17 ♊	♍	♍	♒	♈	♍
June	9 ♋ 26 ♌	9 ♋	♍	♍	♒	♈	♍
July	♌	2 ♌ 26 ♍	7 ♎	♍	♒	♈	♍
Aug.	♌	22 ♎	30 ♏	♍	♒	♈	♍
Sept.	1 ♍ 18 ♎	18 ♏	♏	8 ♎	♒	♈	♍
Oct.	9 ♏	14 ♐	13 ♐	♎	♒	♈	♍
Nov.	3 ♐ 14 ♏	7 ♑	20 ♑	♎	♒	♈	♍
Dec.	14 ♐	3 ♒	26 ♒	♎	♒	♈	♍

1934

	Mercury ☿	Venus ♀	Mars ♂	Jupiter ♃	Saturn ♄	Uranus ♅	Neptune ♆
Jan.	1 ♐ 2 ♑ 19 ♒	1 ♒	1 ♒	1 ♎	1 ♒	1 ♈	1 ♍
Feb.	6 ♓	♒	1 ♓	♎	♒	♈	♍
March	♓	♒	14 ♈	♎	♒	♈	♍
April	15 ♈	5 ♓	26 ♉	♎	♒	♈	♍
May	4 ♉ 18 ♊	6 ♈	♉	♎	6 ♓	♈	♍
June	2 ♋	4 ♉ 30 ♊	6 ♊	♎	♓	♈	♍
July	♋	24 ♋	16 ♋	♎	15 ♒	♈	♍
Aug.	9 ♌ 24 ♍	16 ♌	27 ♌	♎	♒	♈	♍
Sept.	11 ♎	9 ♍	♌	♎	♒	♈	♍
Oct.	3 ♏	5 ♎ 31 ♏	14 ♍	19 ♏	♒	♈	♍
Nov.	♏	24 ♐	♍	♏	♒	♈	♍
Dec.	8 ♐ 26 ♑	16 ♑	10 ♎	♏	♒	♈	♍

1935

	Mercury ☿	Venus ♀	Mars ♂	Jupiter ♃	Saturn ♄	Uranus ♅	Neptune ♆
Jan.	1 ♑ 12 ♒ 31 ♓	1 ♑ 7 ♒ 31 ♓	1 ♎	1 ♏	1 ♒ 22 ♓	1 ♈	1 ♍
Feb.	17 ♒	26 ♈	♎	♏	♓	♈	♍
March	17 ♓	25 ♉	♎	♏	♓	♈	♍
April	9 ♈ 26 ♉	19 ♊	♎	♏	♓	♈	♍
May	10 ♊ 30 ♋	12 ♋	♎	♏	1 ♓	1 ♉	♍
June	21 ♊	6 ♌	♎	♏	♓	♉	♍
July	14 ♋	5 ♍	♎	♏	♓	♉	♍
Aug.	1 ♌ 16 ♍	♍	4 ♏	♏	♓	♉	♍
Sept.	4 ♎	♍	20 ♐	♏	♓	♉	♍
Oct.	♎	♍	29 ♑	♏	♓	♉	♍
Nov.	11 ♏	10 ♎	♑	18 ♐	♓	♉	♍
Dec.	1 ♐ 19 ♑	10 ♏	4 ♒	♐	♓	15 ♈	♍

1936

	Mercury ☿	Venus ♀	Mars ♂	Jupiter ♃	Saturn ♄	Uranus ♅	Neptune ♆
Jan.	1 ♑ 5 ♒	1 ♏ 5 ♐ 29 ♑	1 ♒ 12 ♓	1 ♐	1 ♓	1 ♈	1 ♍
Feb.	♒	21 ♒	22 ♈	♐	♓	8 ♉	♍
March	12 ♓ 31 ♈	16 ♓	♈	♐	♓	♉	♍
April	17 ♉	11 ♈	5 ♉	♐	♓	♉	♍
May	3 ♊	7 ♉	17 ♊	♐	♓	♉	♍
June	♊	1 ♊ 24 ♋	26 ♋	♐	♓	♉	♍
July	9 ♋ 23 ♌	16 ♌	♋	♐	♓	♉	♍
Aug.	7 ♍ 29 ♎	9 ♍	7 ♌	♐	♓	♉	♍
Sept.	♎	4 ♎	23 ♍	♐	♓	♉	♍
Oct.	♎	1 ♏ 25 ♐	♍	♐	♓	♉	♍
Nov.	4 ♏ 23 ♐	17 ♑	14 ♎	♐	♓	♉	♍
Dec.	11 ♑ 30 ♒	10 ♒	♎	2 ♑	♓	♉	♍

1937

	Mercury ☿	Venus ♀	Mars ♂	Jupiter ♃	Saturn ♄	Uranus ♅	Neptune ♆
Jan.	1 ♒ 12 ♑	1 ♒ 4 ♓	1 ♎ 9 ♏	1 ♑	1 ♓	1 ♉	1 ♍
Feb.	13 ♒	3 ♈	♏	♑	♓	♉	♍
March	5 ♓ 23 ♈	19 ♉	20 ♐	♑	♓	♉	♍
April	9 ♉	4 ♈	♐	♑	17 ♈	♉	♍
May	♉	♈	9 ♏	♑	♈	♉	♍
June	15 ♊	6 ♉	♏	♑	♈	♉	♍
July	2 ♋ 14 ♌ 31 ♍	10 ♊	♏	♑	♈	♉	♍
Aug.	♍	5 ♋ 30 ♌	15 ♐	♑	♈	♉	♍
Sept.	♍	24 ♍	♐	♑	♈	♉	♍
Oct.	8 ♎ 28 ♏	20 ♎	1 ♑	♑	♈	♉	♍
Nov.	16 ♐	15 ♏	9 ♒	♑	11 ♓	♉	♍
Dec.	4 ♑	9 ♐ 31 ♑	19 ♓	10 ♒	26 ♈	♉	♍

1938

	Mercury ☿	Venus ♀	Mars ♂	Jupiter ♃	Saturn ♄	Uranus ♅	Neptune ♆
Jan.	1 ♑ 8 ♐ 13 ♑	1 ♑ 22 ♒	1 ♓ 31 ♈	1 ♒	1 ♈	1 ♉	1 ♍
Feb.	7 ♒ 26 ♓	15 ♓	♈	♒	♈	♉	♍
March	15 ♈	12 ♈	16 ♉	♒	♈	♉	♍
April	5 ♉ 20 ♈	8 ♉	27 ♊	26 ♓	♈	♉	♍
May	18 ♉	2 ♊ 25 ♋	♊	♓	♈	♉	♍
June	9 ♊ 23 ♋	17 ♌	7 ♋	♓	♈	♉	♍
July	6 ♌ 26 ♍	12 ♍	20 ♌	♓	♈	♉	♍
Aug.	♍	10 ♎	♌	22 ♒	♈	♉	♍
Sept.	♍	11 ♏	4 ♍	♒	♈	♉	♍
Oct.	1 ♎ 20 ♏	21 ♐	25 ♎	♒	♈	♉	♍
Nov.	9 ♐	10 ♏	♎	♒	♈	♉	♍
Dec.	♐	♏	15 ♏	15 ♓	♈	♉	♍

1939

Mercury ☿	Venus ♀	Mars ♂	Jupiter ♃	Saturn ♄	Uranus ♅	Neptune ♆
1 ♐ 13 ♑	1 ♏ 7 ♐	1 ♏	1 ♓	1 ♈	1 ♉	1 ♍
1 ♒ 18 ♓	7 ♑	2 ♐	♓	♈	♉	♍
8 ♈	4 ♒ 30 ♓	22 ♑	♓	♈	♉	♍
♈	25 ♈	♑	♓	♈	♉	♍
16 ♉	22 ♉	18 ♒	9 ♈	♈	♉	♍
2 ♊ 14 ♋	16 ♊	♒	♈	♈	♉	♍
29 ♌	10 ♋	♒	♈	♈	♉	♍
♌	1 ♌ 25 ♍	5 ♑	♈	1 ♉ 30 ♈	♉	♍
6 ♍ 23 ♎	20 ♎	15 ♒	♈	♈	♉	♍
13 ♏	16 ♏	♒	♈	♈	♉	♍
4 ♐	9 ♐	15 ♓	12 ♓	♈	♉	♍
2 ♏ 16 ♐	2 ♑ 24 ♒	♓	10 ♈	♈	♉	♍

1940

Mercury ☿	Venus ♀	Mars ♂	Jupiter ♃	Saturn ♄	Uranus ♅	Neptune ♆	
1 ♐ 7 ♑ 24 ♒	1 ♒ 17 ♓	1 ♓ 4 ♈	1 ♈	1 ♈	1 ♉	1 ♍	Jan.
10 ♓	12 ♈	21 ♉	♈	♈	♉	♍	Feb.
♓	11 ♉	♉	♈	31 ♉	♉	♍	March
17 ♈	8 ♊	6 ♊	♈	♉	♉	♍	April
8 ♉ 23 ♊	7 ♋	18 ♋	24 ♉	♉	♉	♍	May
5 ♋ 25 ♌	♋	30 ♌	♉	♉	♉	♍	June
23 ♋	6 ♊	♌	♉	♉	♉	♍	July
10 ♌ 28 ♍	1 ♋	16 ♍	♉	♉	♉	♍	Aug.
15 ♎	7 ♌	♍	♉	♉	♉	♍	Sept.
6 ♏	5 ♍	5 ♎	♉	♉	♉	♍	Oct.
♏	2 ♎ 28 ♏	24 ♏	♉	♉	♉	♍	Nov.
11 ♐ 30 ♑	23 ♐	♏	♉	♉	♉	♍	Dec.

1941

Mercury ☿	Venus ♀	Mars ♂	Jupiter ♃	Saturn ♄	Uranus ♅	Neptune ♆
1 ♑ 16 ♒	1 ♐ 14 ♑	1 ♏ 8 ♐	1 ♉	1 ♉	1 ♉	1 ♍
2 ♓	6 ♒	18 ♑	♉	♉	♉	♍
♓	1 ♓ 27 ♈	31 ♑	♉	♉	♉	♍
12 ♈ 30 ♉	22 ♉	♑	♉	♉	♉	♍
15 ♊ 30 ♋	17 ♊	12 ♓	♉	♉	♉	♍
♋	8 ♋	30 ♈	4 ♊	♉	♉	♍
♋	1 ♌ 25 ♍	♈	♊	♉	♉	♍
6 ♌ 20 ♍	21 ♎	♈	♊	♉	♉	♍
7 ♎	18 ♏	♈	♊	♉	♉	♍
2 ♏ 28 ♎	13 ♐	♈	♊	♉	♉	♍
14 ♏	7 ♑	♈	♊	♉	♉	23 ♎
5 ♐ 23 ♑	4 ♒	♈	♊	♉	♉	♎

1942

Mercury ☿	Venus ♀	Mars ♂	Jupiter ♃	Saturn ♄	Uranus ♅	Neptune ♆	
1 ♑ 9 ♒	1 ♒	1 ♈ 17 ♉	1 ♊	1 ♉	1 ♉	1 ♎	Jan.
♒	♒	♉	♊	♉	♉	12 ♍	Feb.
15 ♓	♒	12 ♊	♊	♉	♉	♍	March
5 ♈ 22 ♉	5 ♓	27 ♋	♊	♉	♉	♍	April
7 ♊	6 ♈	♋	♊	22 ♊	♉	♍	May
♊	2 ♉ 30 ♊	11 ♌	10 ♋	♊	20 ♊	♍	June
13 ♋ 29 ♌	24 ♋	29 ♍	♋	♊	♊	♍	July
12 ♍	16 ♌	♍	♋	♊	♊	♍	Aug.
1 ♎	9 ♍	17 ♎	♋	♊	♊	18 ♎	Sept.
♎	5 ♎ 31 ♏	♎	♋	♊	♊	♎	Oct.
8 ♏ 28 ♐	24 ♐	5 ♏	♋	♊	♊	♎	Nov.
15 ♑	16 ♑	19 ♐	♋	♊	8 ♉	♎	Dec.

1943

	Mercury ☿	Venus ♀	Mars ♂	Jupiter ♃	Saturn ♄	Uranus ♅	Neptune ♆
Jan.	1 ♑ 2 ♒ 30 ♑	1 ♑ 7 ♒ 31 ♓	1 ♐ 27 ♑	1 ♋	1 ♊	1 ♉	1 ♎
Feb.	14 ♒	26 ♈	♑	♋	♊	♉	♎
March	10 ♓ 29 ♈	24 ♉	6 ♒	♋	♊	♉	♎
April	14 ♉	18 ♊	14 ♓	♋	♊	9 ♊	♎
May	4 ♊ 24 ♉	12 ♋	27 ♈	♋	♊	♊	21 ♍
June	16 ♊	6 ♌	♈	20 ♌	♊	♊	♍
July	7 ♋ 20 ♌	6 ♍	10 ♉	♌	♊	♊	3 ♎
Aug.	4 ♍ 28 ♎	♍	27 ♊	♌	♊	♊	♎
Sept.	25 ♍	♍	♊	♌	♊	♊	♎
Oct.	12 ♎	♍	♊	♌	♊	♊	♎
Nov.	1 ♏ 20 ♐	10 ♎	♊	♌	♊	♊	♎
Dec.	8 ♑	10 ♏	♊	♌	♊	♊	♎

1944

	Mercury ☿	Venus ♀	Mars ♂	Jupiter ♃	Saturn ♄	Uranus ♅	Neptune ♆
Jan.	1 ♑	1 ♏ 5 ♐ 29 ♑	1 ♊	1 ♌	1 ♊	1 ♊	1 ♎
Feb.	11 ♒	20 ♒	♊	♌	♊	♊	♎
March	2 ♓ 20 ♈	16 ♓	29 ♋	♌	♊	♊	♎
April	6 ♉	10 ♈	♋	♌	♊	♊	♎
May	♉	7 ♉ 31 ♊	19 ♌	♌	♊	♊	♎
June	13 ♊ 28 ♋	23 ♋	♌	♌	20 ♋	♊	♎
July	11 ♌ 28 ♍	16 ♌	8 ♍	13 ♍	♋	♊	♎
Aug.	♍	9 ♍	29 ♎	♍	♋	♊	♎
Sept.	♍	4 ♎ 30 ♏	♎	♍	♋	♊	♎
Oct.	5 ♎ 24 ♏	25 ♐	17 ♏	♍	♋	♊	♎
Nov.	12 ♐	17 ♑	29 ♐	♍	♋	♊	♎
Dec.	2 ♑ 24 ♐	9 ♒	♐	♍	♋	♊	♎

1945

	Mercury ☿	Venus ♀	Mars ♂	Jupiter ♃	Saturn ♄	Uranus ♅	Neptune ♆
Jan.	1 ♐ 15 ♑	1 ♒ 4 ♓	1 ♐ 6 ♑	1 ♍	1 ♋	1 ♊	1 ♎
Feb.	4 ♒ 22 ♓	3 ♈	12 ♒	♍	♋	♊	♎
March	12 ♈	♈	22 ♓	♍	♋	♊	♎
April	♈	♈	♓	♍	♋	♊	♎
May	18 ♉	♈	3 ♈	♍	♋	♊	♎
June	6 ♊ 19 ♑	7 ♉	14 ♉	♍	♋	♊	♎
July	3 ♌ 25 ♍	9 ♊	27 ♊	♍	♋	♊	♎
Aug.	18 ♌	5 ♋ 29 ♌	♊	23 ♎	♋	♊	♎
Sept.	9 ♍ 28 ♎	23 ♍	8 ♋	♎	♋	♊	♎
Oct.	17 ♏	19 ♎	♋	♎	♋	♊	♎
Nov.	6 ♐	14 ♏	4 ♌	♎	♋	♊	♎
Dec.	♐	8 ♐ 30 ♑	♌	♎	♋	♊	♎

1946

	Mercury ☿	Venus ♀	Mars ♂	Jupiter ♃	Saturn ♄	Uranus ♅	Neptune ♆
Jan.	1 ♐ 10 ♑ 28 ♒	1 ♑ 22 ♒	1 ♌ 5 ♋	1 ♎	1 ♋	1 ♊	1 ♎
Feb.	15 ♓	14 ♓	♋	♎	♋	♊	♎
March	5 ♈	12 ♈	♋	♎	♋	♊	♎
April	1 ♓ 16 ♈	7 ♉	17 ♌	♎	♋	♊	♎
May	13 ♉ 29 ♊	2 ♊ 25 ♋	♌	♎	♋	♊	♎
June	11 ♋ 26 ♌	17 ♌	16 ♍	♎	♋	♊	♎
July	♌	12 ♍	♍	♎	17 ♌	♊	♎
Aug.	♌	10 ♎	9 ♎	♎	♌	♊	♎
Sept.	3 ♍ 20 ♎	11 ♏	28 ♏	♎	♌	♊	♎
Oct.	10 ♏	♏	♏	4 ♏	♌	♊	♎
Nov.	3 ♐ 20 ♏	♏	10 ♐	♏	♌	♊	♎
Dec.	15 ♐	♏	18 ♑	♏	♌	♊	♎

1947

Mercury ☿	Venus ♀	Mars ♂	Jupiter ♃	Saturn ♄	Uranus ♅	Neptune ♆	
1 ♐ 3 ♑ 21 ♒	1 ♏ 8 ♐	1 ♑ 23 ♒	1 ♏	1 ♌	1 ♊	1 ♎	Jan.
7 ♓	7 ♑	♒	♏	♌	♊	♎	Feb.
♓	4 ♒ 29 ♓	2 ♓	♏	♌	♊	♎	March
16 ♈	25 ♈	12 ♈	♏	♌	♊	♎	April
6 ♉ 20 ♊	22 ♉	24 ♉	♏	♌	♊	♎	May
3 ♋	16 ♊	♉	♏	♌	♊	♎	June
♋	9 ♋	4 ♊	♏	♌	♊	♎	July
10 ♌ 26 ♍	1 ♌ 25 ♍	14 ♋	♏	♌	♊	♎	Aug.
12 ♎	19 ♎	28 ♌	♏	♌	♊	♎	Sept.
4 ♏	16 ♏	♌	♏	♌	♊	♎	Oct.
♏	9 ♐	24 ♍	2 ♐	♌	♊	♎	Nov.
9 ♐ 27 ♑	1 ♑ 23 ♒	♍	♐	♌	♊	♎	Dec.

1948

Mercury ☿	Venus ♀	Mars ♂	Jupiter ♃	Saturn ♄	Uranus ♅	Neptune ♆	
1 ♑ 13 ♒	1 ♒ 16 ♓	1 ♍	1 ♐	1 ♌	1 ♊	1 ♎	Jan.
1 ♓ 22 ♒	12 ♈	23 ♌	♐	♌	♊	♎	Feb.
16 ♓	11 ♉	♌	♐	♌	♊	♎	March
9 ♈ 26 ♉	8 ♊	♌	♐	♌	♊	♎	April
11 ♊ 29 ♋	8 ♋	12 ♍	♐	♌	♊	♎	May
30 ♊	30 ♊	♍	♐	♌	♊	♎	June
12 ♋	♊	17 ♎	♐	♌	♊	♎	July
2 ♌ 16 ♍	3 ♋	♎	♐	28 ♍	28 ♋	♎	Aug.
4 ♎	7 ♌	7 ♏	♐	♍	♋	♎	Sept.
2 ♏ 14 ♎	5 ♍	21 ♐	♐	♍	♋	♎	Oct.
12 ♏	1 ♎ 28 ♏	27 ♑	15 ♑	♍	17 ♊	♎	Nov.
1 ♐ 19 ♑	22 ♐	♑	♑	♍	♊	♎	Dec.

1949

Mercury ☿	Venus ♀	Mars ♂	Jupiter ♃	Saturn ♄	Uranus ♅	Neptune ♆	
♑ 5 ♒	1 ♐ 14 ♑	1 ♑ 2 ♒	1 ♑	1 ♍	1 ♊	1 ♎	Jan.
♒	5 ♒	9 ♓	♑	♍	♊	♎	Feb.
13 ♓	1 ♓ 26 ♈	22 ♈	27 ♒	♍	♊	♎	March
2 ♈ 18 ♉	22 ♉	♈	♒	♍	♊	♎	April
4 ♊	16 ♊	3 ♉	♒	♍	♊	♎	May
♊	8 ♋ 30 ♌	13 ♊	♒	♍	9 ♋	♎	June
11 ♋ 25 ♌ 8 ♍	25 ♍	24 ♋	17 ♑	♍	♋	♎	July
29 ♎	21 ♎	♋	♑	♍	♋	♎	Aug.
♎	17 ♏	4 ♌	♑	♍	♋	♎	Sept.
♎	13 ♐	23 ♍	♑	♍	♋	♎	Oct.
5 ♏ 24 ♐	7 ♑	♍	18 ♒	♍	♋	♎	Nov.
12 ♑ 31 ♒	4 ♒	24 ♎	♒	♍	♋	♎	Dec.

1950

Mercury ☿	Venus ♀	Mars ♂	Jupiter ♃	Saturn ♄	Uranus ♅	Neptune ♆	
1 ♒ 17 ♑	1 ♒	1 ♎	1 ♒	1 ♍	1 ♋	1 ♎	Jan.
13 ♒	♒	♎	♒	♍	♋	♎	Feb.
7 ♓ 25 ♈	♒	♎	♒	♍	♋	♎	March
10 ♉	5 ♓	2 ♍	3 ♓	♍	♋	♎	April
♉	6 ♈	♍	♓	♍	♋	♎	May
16 ♊	3 ♉ 29 ♊	11 ♎	♓	♍	♋	♎	June
3 ♋ 16 ♌	23 ♋	♎	♓	♍	♋	♎	July
1 ♍ 31 ♎	15 ♌	15 ♏	♓	♍	♋	♎	Aug.
8 ♍	8 ♍	30 ♐	♓	♍	♋	♎	Sept.
9 ♎ 29 ♏	4 ♎ 30 ♏	♐	♓	♍	♋	♎	Oct.
17 ♐	23 ♐	7 ♑	♓	10 ♎	♋	♎	Nov
6 ♑	15 ♑	13 ♒	♓	♎	♋	♎	Dec.

1951

	Mercury ☿	Venus ♀	Mars ♂	Jupiter ♃	Saturn ♄	Uranus ♅	Neptune ♆
Jan.	1 ♑	1 ♑ 6 ♒ 30 ♓	1 ♒ 20 ♓	1 ♓	1 ♎	1 ♋	1 ♎
Feb.	9 ♒ 27 ♓	25 ♈	♓	♓	♎	♋	♎
March	17 ♈	24 ♉	2 ♈	♓	24 ♍	♋	♎
April	5 ♉ 29 ♈	18 ♊	14 ♉	19 ♈	♍	♋	♎
May	17 ♉	11 ♋	25 ♊	♈	♍	♋	♎
June	11 ♊ 25 ♋	5 ♌	♊	♈	♍	♋	♎
July	8 ♌ 26 ♍	6 ♍	4 ♋	♈	♍	♋	♎
Aug.	♍	♍	15 ♌	♈	3 ♎	♋	♎
Sept.	♍	♍	♌	♈	♎	♋	♎
Oct.	3 ♎ 22 ♏	♍	1 ♍	♈	♎	♋	♎
Nov.	10 ♐	10 ♎	23 ♎	♈	♎	♋	♎
Dec.	2 ♑ 13 ♐	10 ♏	♎	♈	♎	♋	♎

1952

	Mercury ☿	Venus ♀	Mars ♂	Jupiter ♃	Saturn ♄	Uranus ♅	Neptune ♆
Jan.	1 ♐ 14 ♑	1 ♏ 3 ♐ 28 ♑	1 ♎ 24 ♏	1 ♈	1 ♎	1 ♋	1 ♎
Feb.	2 ♒ 20 ♓	20 ♒	♏	♈	♎	♋	♎
March	8 ♈	15 ♓	♏	♈	♎	♋	♎
April	♈	11 ♈	♏	♈	♎	♋	♎
May	16 ♉	6 ♉ 31 ♊	28 ♎	6 ♉	♎	♋	♎
June	2 ♊ 15 ♋ 29 ♌	23 ♋	25 ♏	♉	♎	♋	♎
July	♌	15 ♌	♏	♉	♎	♋	♎
Aug.	♌	8 ♍	♏	♉	♎	♋	♎
Sept.	6 ♍ 24 ♎	3 ♎ 30 ♏	1 ♐	♉	♎	♋	♎
Oct.	13 ♏	24 ♐	13 ♑	♉	♎	♋	♎
Nov.	4 ♐	16 ♑	19 ♒ 28 ♓	♉	♎	♋	♎
Dec.	7 ♏ 14 ♐	9 ♒	♓	♉	♎	♋	♎

1953

	Mercury ☿	Venus ♀	Mars ♂	Jupiter ♃	Saturn ♄	Uranus ♅	Neptune ♆
Jan.	1 ♐ 7 ♑ 25 ♒	1 ♒ 4 ♓	1 ♓	1 ♉	1 ♎	1 ♋	1 ♎
Feb.	11 ♓	3 ♈	8 ♈	♉	♎	♋	♎
March	4 ♈ 14 ♓	♈	24 ♉	♉	♎	♋	♎
April	17 ♈	♈	♉	♉	♎	♋	♎
May	10 ♉ 25 ♊	♈	5 ♊	18 ♊	♎	♋	♎
June	7 ♋ 25 ♌	8 ♉	14 ♋	♊	♎	♋	♎
July	31 ♋	9 ♊	27 ♌	♊	♎	♋	♎
Aug.	9 ♌ 30 ♍	4 ♋ 29 ♌	♌	♊	♎	♋	♎
Sept.	16 ♎	23 ♍	11 ♍	♊	♎	♋	♎
Oct.	7 ♏	19 ♎	♍	♊	♎	♋	♎
Nov.	♏	13 ♏	1 ♎	♊	2 ♏	♋	♎
Dec.	12 ♐ 31 ♑	8 ♐ 30 ♑	24 ♏	♊	♏	♋	♎

1954

	Mercury ☿	Venus ♀	Mars ♂	Jupiter ♃	Saturn ♄	Uranus ♅	Neptune ♆
Jan.	1 ♑ 17 ♒	1 ♑ 21 ♒	1 ♏	1 ♊	1 ♏	1 ♋	1 ♎
Feb.	4 ♓	14 ♓	14 ♐	♊	♏	♋	♎
March	♓	11 ♈	♐	♊	♏	♋	♎
April	13 ♈	7 ♉	13 ♑	♊	♏	♋	♎
May	2 ♉ 16 ♊ 31 ♋	1 ♊ 24 ♋	♑	24 ♋	♏	♋	♎
June	♋	16 ♌	♑	♋	♏	♋	♎
July	♋	11 ♍	4 ♐	♋	♏	♋	♎
Aug.	7 ♌ 22 ♍	9 ♎	25 ♑	♋	♏	♋	♎
Sept.	9 ♎	11 ♏	♑	♋	♏	♋	♎
Oct.	2 ♏	♏	18 ♒	12 ♌	♏	♋	♎
Nov.	3 ♎ 14 ♏	♏	♒	♌	♏	♋	♎
Dec.	6 ♐ 24 ♑	♏	1 ♓	24 ♋	♏	♋	♎

1955

	Mercury ☿	Venus ♀	Mars ♂	Jupiter ♃	Saturn ♄	Uranus ♅	Neptune ♆
Jan.	1 ♑ 10 ♒ 31 ♓	1 ♏ 8 ♐	1 ♓ 15 ♈	1 ♋	1 ♏	1 ♋	1 ♎
Feb.	7 ♒	6 ♑	♈	♋	♏	♋	♎
March	16 ♓	4 ♒ 29 ♓	2 ♉	♋	♏	♋	♎
April	7 ♈ 24 ♉	25 ♈	15 ♊	♋	♏	♋	♎
May	8 ♊	21 ♉	26 ♋	♋	♏	♋	♎
June	♊	15 ♊	♋	1 ♌	♏	♋	♎
July	14 ♋ 30 ♌	8 ♋ 31 ♌	8 ♌	♌	♏	19 ♌	♎
Aug.	14 ♍	24 ♍	24 ♍	♌	♏	♌	♎
Sept.	2 ♎	19 ♎	♍	♌	♏	♌	♎
Oct.	♎	15 ♏	13 ♎	27 ♍	♏	♌	♎
Nov.	10 ♏ 29 ♐	8 ♐	♎	♍	♏	♌	♎
Dec.	17 ♑	1 ♑ 23 ♒	2 ♏	♍	♏	♌	♎

1956

	Mercury ☿	Venus ♀	Mars ♂	Jupiter ♃	Saturn ♄	Uranus ♅	Neptune ♆
Jan.	1 ♑ 3 ♒	1 ♒ 16 ♓	1 ♏ 17 ♐	1 ♍	1 ♏	1 ♌	1 ♎
Feb.	5 ♑ 13 ♒	11 ♈	29 ♑	10 ♌	4 ♐	♌	♎
March	10 ♓ 29 ♈	11 ♉	♑	♌	♐	♌	♎
April	14 ♉	7 ♊	12 ♒	♌	20 ♏	♌	♎
May	3 ♊	9 ♋	29 ♓	♌	♏	♌	♎
June	2 ♉ 13 ♊	24 ♊	♓	23 ♍	♏	♌	♎
July	7 ♋ 21 ♌	♊	♓	♍	♏	♌	♎
Aug.	5 ♍ 28 ♎	5 ♋	♓	♍	♏	♌	♎
Sept.	30 ♍	7 ♌	♓	♍	♏	♌	♎
Oct.	11 ♎	5 ♍	♓	♍	27 ♐	♌	♎
Nov.	2 ♏ 21 ♐	1 ♎ 27 ♏	♓	♍	♐	♌	♎
Dec.	9 ♑	22 ♐	6 ♈	8 ♎	♐	♌	3 ♏

1957

	Mercury ☿	Venus ♀	Mars ♂	Jupiter ♃	Saturn ♄	Uranus ♅	Neptune ♆
Jan.	1 ♑	1 ♐ 13 ♑	1 ♈	1 ♎	1 ♐	1 ♌	1 ♏
Feb.	11 ♒	5 ♒ 28 ♓	2 ♉	28 ♍	♐	♌	♏
March	3 ♓ 21 ♈	26 ♈	22 ♊	♍	♐	♌	♏
April	7 ♉	21 ♉	♊	♍	♐	♌	17 ♎
May	♉	16 ♊	5 ♋	♍	♐	♌	♎
June	14 ♊ 29 ♋	7 ♋ 30 ♌	18 ♌	♍	♐	♌	♎
July	12 ♌ 29 ♍	24 ♍	♌	♍	♐	♌	♎
Aug.	♍	20 ♎	4 ♍	4 ♎	♐	♌	♎
Sept.	♍	17 ♏	24 ♎	♎	♐	♌	♎
Oct.	6 ♎ 25 ♏	13 ♐	♎	♎	♐	♌	2 ♏
Nov.	14 ♐	6 ♑	12 ♏	♎	♐	♌	♏
Dec.	3 ♑ 29 ♐	4 ♒	26 ♐	♎	♐	♌	♏

1958

	Mercury ☿	Venus ♀	Mars ♂	Jupiter ♃	Saturn ♄	Uranus ♅	Neptune ♆
Jan.	1 ♐ 15 ♑	1 ♒	1 ♐	1 ♎	1 ♐	1 ♌	1 ♏
Feb.	6 ♒ 24 ♓	♒	4 ♑	8 ♏ 26 ♎	♐	♌	♏
March	13 ♈	♒	15 ♒	♎	♐	♌	♏
April	♈	5 ♓	24 ♓	♎	♐	♌	♏
May	18 ♉	5 ♈	♓	♎	♐	♌	♏
June	7 ♊ 21 ♋	3 ♉ 29 ♊	6 ♈	♎	♐	♌	♏
July	4 ♌ 25 ♍	23 ♋	24 ♉	♎	♐	♌	♏
Aug.	25 ♌	15 ♌	♉	♎	♐	♌	♏
Sept.	9 ♍ 29 ♎	8 ♍	30 ♊	17 ♏	♐	♌	♏
Oct.	18 ♏	4 ♎ 30 ♏	21 ♉	♏	♐	♌	♏
Nov.	7 ♐	23 ♐	♉	♏	♐	♌	♏
Dec.	♐	15 ♑	♉	♏	♐	♌	♏

1959

	Mercury ☿	Venus ♀	Mars ♂	Jupiter ♃	Saturn ♄	Uranus ♅	Neptune ♆
Jan.	1 ♐ 11 ♑ 30 ♒	1 ♑ 6 ♒ 30 ♓	1 ♉	1 ♏	1 ♐ 5 ♑	1 ♌	1 ♏
Feb.	16 ♓	24 ♈	16 ♊	♏	♑	♌	♏
March	6 ♈	23 ♉	♊	7 ♐	♑	♌	♏
April	♈	17 ♊	11 ♋	1 ♏	♑	♌	♏
May	14 ♉ 30 ♊	11 ♋	28 ♌	♏	♑	♌	♏
June	12 ♋ 27 ♌	5 ♌	♌	♏	♑	♌	♏
July	♌	6 ♍	17 ♍	♏	♑	♌	♏
Aug.	♌	♍	♍	♏	♑	♌	♏
Sept.	4 ♍ 21 ♎	18 ♌ 25 ♍	6 ♎	♏	♑	♌	♏
Oct.	11 ♏	♍	25 ♏	16 ♐	♑	♌	♏
Nov.	3 ♐ 25 ♏	10 ♎	♏	♐	♑	♌	♏
Dec.	16 ♐	9 ♏	7 ♐	♐	♑	♌	♏

1960

	Mercury ☿	Venus ♀	Mars ♂	Jupiter ♃	Saturn ♄	Uranus ♅	Neptune ♆
Jan.	1 ♐ 5 ♑ 22 ♒	1 ♏ 4 ♐ 28 ♑	1 ♐ 15 ♑	1 ♐	1 ♑	1 ♌	1 ♏
Feb.	8 ♓	19 ♒	21 ♒	♐	♑	♌	♏
March	♓	14 ♓	30 ♓	1 ♑	♑	♌	♏
April	16 ♈	9 ♈	♓	♑	♑	♌	♏
May	6 ♉ 21 ♊	6 ♉ 30 ♊	11 ♈	♑	♑	♌	♏
June	3 ♋ 26 ♌	22 ♋	23 ♉	12 ♐	♑	♌	♏
July	11 ♋	15 ♌	♉	♐	♑	♌	♏
Aug.	10 ♌ 26 ♍	8 ♍	5 ♊	♐	♑	♌	♏
Sept.	12 ♎	3 ♎ 29 ♏	21 ♋	♐	♑	♌	♏
Oct.	4 ♏	24 ♐	♋	26 ♑	♑	♌	♏
Nov.	♏	16 ♑	♋	♑	♑	♌	♏
Dec.	9 ♐ 28 ♑	9 ♒	♋	♑	♑	♌	♏

1961

	Mercury ☿	Venus ♀	Mars ♂	Jupiter ♃	Saturn ♄	Uranus ♅	Neptune ♆
Jan.	1 ♑ 14 ♒	1 ♒ 3 ♓	1 ♋	1 ♑	1 ♑	1 ♌	1 ♏
Feb.	1 ♓ 26 ♒	3 ♈	♋	♑	♑	♌	♏
March	16 ♓	♈	♋	4 ♒	21 ♒	♌	♏
April	10 ♈ 28 ♉	♈	♋	♒	♒	♌	♏
May	12 ♊ 29 ♋	♈	2 ♌	♒	♒	♌	♏
June	♋	8 ♉	25 ♍	♒	♒	♌	♏
July	♋	9 ♊	♍	♒	1 ♑	♌	♏
Aug.	3 ♌ 18 ♍	4 ♋ 28 ♌	17 ♎	♒	♑	♌	♏
Sept.	5 ♎	22 ♍	♎	7 ♑	♑	11 ♍	♏
Oct.	1 ♏ 20 ♎	18 ♎	6 ♏	11 ♒	♑	♍	♏
Nov.	12 ♏	13 ♏	17 ♐	♒	♑	♍	♏
Dec.	3 ♐ 20 ♑	7 ♐ 30 ♑	25 ♑	♒	15 ♒	♍	♏

1962

	Mercury ☿	Venus ♀	Mars ♂	Jupiter ♃	Saturn ♄	Uranus ♅	Neptune ♆
Jan.	1 ♑ 7 ♒	1 ♑ 20 ♒	1 ♑ 30 ♒	1 ♒	1 ♒	1 ♍	1 ♏
Feb.	♒	13 ♓	♒	♒	♒	♍	♏
March	14 ♓	11 ♈	9 ♓	15 ♓	♒	16 ♌	♏
April	3 ♈ 20 ♉	6 ♉	19 ♈	♓	♒	♌	♏
May	5 ♊	1 ♊ 24 ♋	♈	♓	♒	♌	♏
June	♊	16 ♌	1 ♉	♓	♒	23 ♍	♏
July	12 ♋ 26 ♌	11 ♍	12 ♊	♓	♒	♍	♏
Aug.	10 ♍ 30 ♎	9 ♎	23 ♋	♓	♒	♍	♏
Sept.	♎	11 ♏	♋	♓	♒	♍	♏
Oct.	♎	♏	8 ♌	♓	♒	♍	♏
Nov.	7 ♏ 26 ♐	♏	♌	♓	♒	♍	♏
Dec.	13 ♑	♏	♌	♓	♒	♍	♏

1963

	Mercury ☿	Venus ♀	Mars ♂	Jupiter ♃	Saturn ♄	Uranus ♅	Neptune ♆
Jan.	1 ♒ 22 ♑	1 ♏ 9 ♐	1 ♌	1 ♓	1 ♒	1 ♍	1 ♏
Feb.	14 ♒	6 ♑	♌	♓	♒	♍	♏
March	8 ♓ 26 ♈	3 ♒ 28 ♓	♌	♓	♒	♍	♏
April	12 ♉	24 ♈	♌	3 ♈	♒	♍	♏
May	♉	21 ♉	29 ♍	♈	♒	♍	♏
June	17 ♊	15 ♊	♍	♈	♒	♍	♏
July	5 ♋ 18 ♌	8 ♋ 31 ♌	27 ♎	♈	♒	♍	♏
Aug.	2 ♍ 29 ♎	23 ♍	♎	♈	♒	♍	♏
Sept.	15 ♍	18 ♎	16 ♏	♈	♒	♍	♏
Oct.	11 ♎ 30 ♏	15 ♏	29 ♐	♈	♒	♍	♏
Nov.	18 ♐	8 ♐ 30 ♑	♐	♈	♒	♍	♏
Dec.	7 ♑	22 ♒	6 ♑	♈	♒	♍	♏

1964

	Mercury ☿	Venus ♀	Mars ♂	Jupiter ♃	Saturn ♄	Uranus ♅	Neptune ♆
Jan.	1 ♑	1 ♒ 15 ♓	1 ♑ 11 ♒	1 ♈	1 ♒	1 ♍	1 ♏
Feb.	10 ♒ 29 ♓	11 ♈	17 ♓	♈	♒	♍	♏
March	17 ♈	10 ♉	24 ♈	♈	1 ♓	♍	♏
April	5 ♉	7 ♊	♈	20 ♉	♓	♍	♏
May	♉	10 ♋	11 ♉	♉	♓	♍	♏
June	11 ♊ 25 ♋	18 ♊	21 ♊	♉	♓	♍	♏
July	8 ♌ 26 ♍	♊	31 ♋	♉	♓	♍	♏
Aug.	♍	6 ♋	♋	♉	♓	♍	♏
Sept.	♍	7 ♌	12 ♌	♉	♓	♍	♏
Oct.	3 ♎ 22 ♏	4 ♍ 31 ♎	♌	♉	♓	♍	♏
Nov.	11 ♐	27 ♏	1 ♍	♉	♓	♍	♏
Dec.	1 ♑ 17 ♐	21 ♐	♍	♉	♓	♍	♏

1965

	Mercury ☿	Venus ♀	Mars ♂	Jupiter ♃	Saturn ♄	Uranus ♅	Neptune ♆
Jan.	1 ♐ 13 ♑	1 ♐ 12 ♑	1 ♍	1 ♉	1 ♓	1 ♍	1 ♏
Feb.	♑ 3 ♒ 21 ♓	♑ 5 ♒	♍	♉	♓	♍	♏
March	♓ 9 ♈	♓ 25 ♈	♍	♉	♓	♍	♏
April	♈	♈ 19 ♉	♍	♉ 23	♓	♍	♏
May	♈ 16 ♉	♉ 13 ♊	♍	♊	♓	♍	♏
June	♉ 2 ♌ 16 ♋	♊ 6 ♋	♍ 29 ♎	♊	♓	♍	♏
July	♋ 2 ♌ 31 ♍	♌ 26 ♍	♎	♊	♓	♍	♏
Aug.	♍ 3 ♌	♍ 20 ♎	♎ 20 ♏	♊	♓	♍	♏
Sept.	9 ♌ ♍ 25 ♎	♎ 14 ♏	♏	♊ 21 ♋	♓	♍	♏
Oct.	♎ 13 ♏	♏ 10 ♐	♏ 4	♋	♓	♍	♏
Nov.	♏ 2 ♐	♐ 6 ♑	♐ 14 ♑	♋ 17 ♊	♓	♍	♏
Dec.	♐	♑ 7 ♒	♑ 23 ♒	♊	♓	♍	♏

1966

	Mercury ☿	Venus ♀	Mars ♂	Jupiter ♃	Saturn ♄	Uranus ♅	Neptune ♆
Jan.	1 ♐ 8 ♑ 27 ♒	1 ♒	1 ♒ 30 ♓	1 ♊	1 ♓	1 ♍	1 ♏
Feb.	♒ 13 ♓	♒ 7 ♑ 25 ♒	♓	♊	♓	♍	♏
March	♓ 3 ♈ 22 ♓	♒	♓ 10 ♈	♊	♓	♍	♏
April	♓ 18 ♈	♒ 7 ♓	♈ 18 ♉	♊	♓	♍	♏
May	♈ 10 ♉ 25 ♊	♓ 5 ♈	♉ 29 ♊	♊ 6 ♋	♓	♍	♏
June	♊ 8 ♋ 27 ♌	1 ♉ 28 ♊	♊	♋	♓	♍	♏
July	♌	♊ 22 ♋	♊ 11 ♋	♋	♓	♍	♏
Aug.	♌	♋ 16 ♌	♋ 26 ♌	♋	♓	♍	♏
Sept.	♍ 17 ♎	♌ 9 ♍	♌	♋ 27 ♌	♓	♍	♏
Oct.	6 ♎ ♏ 30 ♐	♍ 3 ♎ 27 ♏	♌ 13 ♍	♌	♓	♍	♏
Nov.	♐ 21 ♏	♏ 22 ♐	♍	♌	♓	♍	♏
Dec.	♏ 12 ♐	♐ 14 ♑	♍ 4 ♎	♌	♓	♍	♏

Index

Acknowledgments

Key to picture positions : (T) top (C) center (B) bottom ; and combinations, e.g. (TL) top left

Aero Photo, Paris : 123 (B)
Alexandra Palace Race Track : 197(BR)
American Federation of Astrologers : 227, 233(BR)
Associated Press : 239(B)
Banque Nationale pour le Commerce et l'Industrie : 50
André Barbault *Défense et l'Illustration de l'Astrologie*, Éditions du Seuil : 47
Bayerische Staatsbibliothek, Munich : 127
Bettmann Archive : 43(T), 48(T)
Biblioteca Estense, Moderna : 149
Biblioteca Vaticana : 138
Bibliotèque Nationale : 15, 71, 82
A. and C. Black Ltd., photo : Gordon Anthony : 229
Bodleian Library photo : Oxford University Press : 136
British Museum (photographs reproduced by courtesy of the Trustees) : 159(B) ; photo John Freeman : 53, 72, 81, 174, 175, 180, 181(BL), 272, 275, 276, 279, 283(L) ; photo David Swann : 12(T and B), 20(L), 27, 33(L and R), 51, 61, 74, 75, 108, 109(T), 114, 118(TL), 119(TL), 120, 121, 122, 129(L), 141(T and B), 142(T), 147(T), 150, 152(T), 155(T), 157, 162, 163, 164(BL), 171, 177, 243
Photo : Mike Busselle : 203, 230. 233(BL), 268(B)
J. Calder Ltd., photo : Alan Daiches : 11 (B)
Culver Pictures Inc. : 199
Debeurme et Louvegnies, Paris : 237(B)
Doris Chase Doane *Astrology, 30 Years Research*, The Church of Light Inc. : 265
Ebertin Verlag : 221(B), 290
Éditions Rencontre : 173(CR)
Elle, Paris : 206(C)
Elliott and Fry Ltd. : 11(CL)
Eva, Milan : 206(T)
Hugh Evelyn Ltd. : 137
© W. Foulsham and Co. Ltd. : 248-9
Ernst L. Freud : 195
horoscopes cast by Arthur Gauntlett : 29(B), 78
Dr. Geuber : 45(T)
Giancolombo News, Milan : 18
René Groebli : 45(B)
Ara Guler : 111
© Philippe Halsman : 87(R)
Margaret Hone : 250
by courtesy of the Imperial War Museum : 56
Institut Belge d'Astrologie Scientifique : 233(T)
by permission of the International Publishing Co., Edinburgh, from one of the Leo textbooks : 324-5

Franz Jung : 222
Behram Kapadia : 109(B), 124, 189, 207
Elfriede Keiser : 219, 221 (T)
Keystone Press : 29(T), 59, 63, 69, 99, 185(C and B)
Keystone Press, Tokyo : 238, 239(T)
K. E. Krafft, *Astro-biology* : 24-5
Frau K. E. Krafft : 266
Sam Levin, Camera Press : 54(R)
Leykham A. G., Graz : 19(BL), 152(B)
Herbert List : 19(BR)
Joseph Norman Lockyer *Dawn of Civilization* Thames and Hudson Ltd. : 113
London Express News : 43(B), 65(BL), 241
Lowell Observatory : 184(BR)
Mansell Collection, photo Alinari : 115, 129(R)
horoscopes cast by Jeff Mayo : 249, 251, 263, 298-301
Middle East Archive, photo Alistair Duncan : 17
Mount Wilson and Palomar Observatories, California, U.S.A. : 9
Müller et Cie, Neuhausen am Rheinfall, Switzerland : 268-9
Musée du Louvre : 26(R), 118(B) ; photo Chuzeville, 54(L)
Museo Archaeologico, Florence : 119(TR)
Nationale Forschungs und Gedenkstätten der klassischen deutschen Literatur in Weimar : 225(B)
National Film Archives : 84(B), 101
National Gallery, London : 92
by courtesy of the Trustees of the National Maritime Museum, Greenwich : 184(TL)
Musée de la Tapisserie de la Reine Mathilde, Bayeux : 171(TR)
The Nautical Almanac, by permission of Controller of H.M.S.O.: 302-23. 327-43
The New York Sun Inc. : 173(BR)
Nixa Records Ltd. reproduced by permission of Pye Records Ltd. : 11(CR)
Odhams Press : 204
R. Oldenbourg, Munich : 153
by permission of Her Majesty's Postmaster General : 234(B)
Pictorial Press Ltd. : 19(T), 216
Planet News : 31, 200, 286
Paul Popper Ltd. : 67, 89
Radio Times Hulton Picture Library : 26(L), 79, 87(L), 94, 184(CL), 191, 205(L), 208, 283(L), 285, 343(B)
Rascher Verlag, Zurich : 224, 225
Real Cartuja Valldemosa, Mallorca : 102
Rolls Prestcold, photo David Swann : 236
Royal Astronomical Society, photo David Swann : 166(T)
Royal Shakespeare Company, photo Angus McBean : 161
Rudaux et Vaucouleurs *L'Astronomie*, Larousse Éditeurs : 65(T), 72-3 (drawn by John Messenger)

Sanforized Service, Manchester: 237(T)
by courtesy of the Director, Science Museum,
    London: 65(BR), 117, 154, 184(TR), 185;
    photo David Swann: 37
Staatliche Museen, Berlin: 119(B)·
Stevens Press: 206(B)
David Swann: 33(B), 145, 246, 259
Swiss National Tourist Office: 90
Theosophical Society: 188
© 1939 James Thurber: 97
Topix Picture Service: 240(T)
Twentieth Century Fox: 13, 14
Uffizi Gallery, Florence, photo G. B. Pineider:
    107, 135(T); photo Scala: 135(B)
Ullstein Verlag, Berlin: 213
Uni-Dia-Verlag, Stuttgart: 110
Universitätsbibliothek, Heidelberg, photo
    Lossen: 254-5
Joseph Wilpert *Die Römischen Mosaiken
    und Malereien der Kirchlichen Bauten*,
    Herder and Co. (1917): 131
John Wood: 57, 210
Mrs. W. B. Yeats, photo: Reading University:
    11(TL and TR)
Yerkes Observatory: 184(BL)
Dr. Adrian M. Ziegler: 240(B)
Acknowledgment is made for permission to
    reprint excerpts from the following works:
    The English Physician and Complete Herbal
    by Nicholas Culpeper, published by Arco
    Publications.
Old Moore's Monthly Messenger (1908),
    now incorporated in *Foulsham's Original
    Old Moore's Almanack*
Crome Yellow by Aldous Huxley, published by
    Chatto and Windus Ltd.; reprinted in U.S.A.
    by permission of Harper and Row Inc.
Nehru's Letters to his Sister, ed. Krishna
    Nehru Hutheesing, published by Faber and
    Faber Ltd.
Henry Miller: His World of Urania by Sydney
    Omarr, published by Villiers Publications Ltd.